THE FORMATION OF THE BIBLICAL CANON

VOLUME II

THE FORMATION OF THE BIBLICAL CANON

Volume II

The New Testament:
Its Authority and Canonicity

By
Lee Martin McDonald

Bloomsbury T&T Clark
An imprint of Bloomsbury Publishing Plc

B L O O M S B U R Y
LONDON · OXFORD · NEW YORK · NEW DELHI · SYDNEY

Bloomsbury T&T Clark

An imprint of Bloomsbury Publishing Plc

Imprint previously known as T&T Clark

50 Bedford Square	1385 Broadway
London	New York
WC1B 3DP	NY 10018
UK	USA

www.bloomsbury.com

BLOOMSBURY, T&T CLARK and the Diana logo are trademarks of Bloomsbury Publishing Plc

First published 2017
Reprinted 2017, 2018

British Library Cataloguing-in-Publication Data
A catalogue record for this book is available from the British Library.

ISBN:	HB:	978-0-5676-6884-4
	ePDF:	978-0-5676-6885-1
	ePub:	978-0-5676-6886-8

Library of Congress Cataloging-in-Publication Data
A catalog record for this book is available from the Library of Congress.

Cover image: The Letters of Saint Paul c. AD 180-200 CBL BP II, ff.15&90a © The Trustees of the
Chester Beatty Library, Dublin. Photographed by CSNTM

Typeset by Forthcoming Publications (www.forthpub.com)
Printed and bound in Great Britain

CONTENTS

Part 3
THE FORMATION OF THE NEW TESTAMENT CANON

PART 3

THE FORMATION
OF THE NEW TESTAMENT CANON

FROM STORY TO SCRIPTURE: THE EMERGENCE OF THE NEW TESTAMENT WRITINGS AS SCRIPTURE

I. WHEN AND WHERE THE NEW TESTAMENT BEGAN

The New Testament canon is a collection of writings that focus primarily on Jesus of Nazareth and the implications of his life and mission for those who followed him. The New Testament had its origin in Jesus whose early followers were significantly impacted by his life, teachings, and miracles and they believed that he was the one whom they had hoped would free their nation from the tyranny of Rome. They were surprised and filled with despair when Jesus was arrested and crucified. Their hopes were dashed, but soon after his death his earliest followers claimed that he was alive and had appeared to them. Their lives were transformed from despair to hope and they began to tell Jesus' story not only in the land where he lived, but also throughout the Greco-Roman world.

At first the story about Jesus was told orally to the emerging community of those who became new followers of Jesus, but subsequently it was also told in writing. Some of Jesus' story may have been written down *before* his death and subsequently included in the canonical Gospels. Dunn suggests the possibility that some of the stories about Jesus and his teachings circulating about him in Palestine both orally and in writing before his death and that some of these stories were included in the written stories about him after his death (the Gospels), especially and most likely the sayings now identified as Q material.[1] After the formation of a community of his followers, the significance of Jesus and the implications of his life ministry and fate for his followers were communicated in several literary genres including gospels (selective biographies), letters, sermons (Hebrews), and apocalyptic calls for faith and perseverance in difficult times (Revelation). Some fanciful stories about Jesus and alleged communications from his followers were eventually not included in the church's biblical canon.

---

[1] Dunn, *Jesus Remembered*, 173–254.

From the first third of the second century some early Christian texts began to be recognized as sacred Scripture on par with the church's first Scriptures. By the last quarter of the second century a collection of Christian writings had begun to be called "New Testament" scriptures and the church's first Scriptures began to be called "Old Testament" Scriptures. Together these two Testaments formed what later eventually was called the Christian Bible. By the third or fourth centuries, some followers of Jesus began to limit their sacred Scripture to a collection that roughly parallels what comprises the Christian Bibles today.

In their current form, the Gospels that focus largely on Jesus' pre-Easter teachings and activities were written from a post-Easter perspective. Indeed, those who wrote the Gospels as we now have them clearly knew the end of their story before they began telling it. For them, Jesus was the risen Lord and this belief was the essential presupposition for the eventual formation of the NT canon, but also the church itself. Scholars who seek to account for the origins of Christian faith in a so-called *historical* Jesus, that is, a Jesus devoid of the miracle stories about him including his resurrection from the dead and the later affirmations about him that were attributed to him by his followers, have considerable difficulty accounting for the origins of the Christian faith.[2] It was in the early church's belief in Jesus' resurrection and its acknowledgment of him as "Son of God" and Lord of the church (Rom 1:3–4; 10:9–10) that a New Testament collection of Christian Scriptures was born. This is the underlying assumption of the writings that became known as the New Testament.[3] The encounter with Jesus as the risen Lord is the presupposition for the continuing existence of a community of faith called the church.[4] This is true also for the emergence, organization, and structure of the church and production of its Scriptures that were eventually recognized as the NT, and also for the formation of the NT canon.

According to Sundberg, there were three stages in the history and formation of the NT canon: (1) the rise of the NT writings to the status of Scripture; (2) the conscious groupings of such literature into closed collections (e.g., the four Gospels and the Epistles of Paul); and (3) the later formation of a closed list of authoritative literature.[5] The transitions and processes that led to the recognition of Christian writings as Scripture, and eventually as canon, are the subjects of this and the following chapters. Because the early church left behind no record of how

---

[2]   I have discussed these attempts at length in *Story of Jesus in History and Faith.*

[3]   Lee M. McDonald and S. E. Porter, eds., *Early Christianity and Its Sacred Literature* (Peabody, MA: Hendrickson, 2000), 13–18, and 178–83.

[4]   For discussions on the presence, centrality, and value of religious experience in the NT, see L. T. Johnson, *Religious Experience in Earliest Christianity* (Minneapolis: Fortress, 1998); and K. Berger, *Identity and Experience in the New Testament*, trans. C. Muenchow (Minneapolis: Fortress, 2003).

[5]   Sundberg, "Making of the New Testament Canon," 1217. A careful description of the canonical process is in J. A. Sanders, *Canon and Community*, 21–45. Sanders's *From Sacred Story*, 127–47, 175–90, includes a discussion of the processes that led to a recognition of the authority and the stabilization of the OT biblical text, but what he says there is also applicable to the formation of the NT.

its biblical canon was both born or shaped, much of the information we possess is inferential and biblical scholars understandably often disagree on how and when the NT was formed.

As we have seen, the early churches did not begin with a firmly fixed canon of Old Testament Scriptures, but *most* of the Scriptures that they adopted from their Jewish siblings that were used in their preaching and teaching are those that later formed their OT Scriptures. The interpretation of their OT Scriptures was not so much rooted in a careful historical-critical interpretation of those Scriptures, but came as a result of their encounters with Jesus as risen Lord and their subsequent Christological and eschatological interpretations of those Scriptures. They believed that their first Scriptures pointed to the significance of the life and teachings of Jesus of Nazareth and also foretold his death and resurrection (1 Cor 15:3–4). The early Christian proclamation focused on Jesus their promised Messiah whom they believed called their community of faith into existence through his proclamation and teachings as well as in his death and resurrection.

The core of their OT Scriptures in the first century CE and following, as was also true for their Jewish siblings, was the Mosaic Law as well as a prophetic corpus that was eventually divided into the final two collections of the HB canon, namely the Prophets and Writings, designations that collectively identified the rest of the Jewish Scriptures in the second century CE. The Law, however, appeared at times to be at variance with the teachings of Jesus (e.g., Matt 5:21–22, 27–28, 31–32, 33–34, 38–39, 43–44), the teachings on salvation by grace by Paul (e.g., Gal 3–4; Rom 3–4), and among some of the Hellenistic Jewish Christians as in the case of the author of Hebrews (e.g., Heb 8:8–11). The early Christians' interpretation of their Scriptures is generally narrowly focused, despite multiple scriptural citations and quotations to support their teachings and proclamation. Their Christological and eschatological interpretation of Scripture and their most frequently cited OT texts in the NT came largely from the Law, Psalms, and Isaiah especially, but also other Latter Prophets as well.[6]

The problem of how to live free in Christ and yet be subject to the legal codes of the Law was a critical issue for early Gentile Christianity, and it dealt with it in several contrasting ways: (1) by ignoring vast portions of the Law and adopting something of a "canon within the canon" approach to the Scriptures; (2) by allegorizing legal portions of the OT in order to bring them into harmony with the teachings of Jesus; (3) by emphasizing the faith principle that preceded the Law

---

See also idem, "Text and Canon: Old Testament and New," in *Mélanges Dominique Barthélemy: Études bibliques*, ed. P. Casetti, O. Keel, and A. Schenker, Orbis biblicus et orientalis 38 (Göttingen: Vandenhoeck & Ruprecht, 1981), 373–94.

[6] According to Andrew E. Hill, *Baker's Handbook of Bible Lists* (Grand Rapids: Baker, 1981), 102–3, the Old Testament books most frequently cited (or quoted or alluded to) in the New Testament are the following (the number of references are in parentheses): Isaiah (419) Psalms (414) Exodus (240) Genesis (238) Deuteronomy (196) Ezekiel (141) Daniel (133) Jeremiah (125) Leviticus (107) Numbers (73).

(as Paul did in Gal 3–4 and Rom 3–4), which in effect created a "canon within the canon"; (4) by rejecting, like Marcion, the whole of the OT Scriptures; or (5) by redefining the meaning of the Law as Justin and others after him did in the second century churches. However the early Christians chose to deal with the issue, it did not appear possible to have complete loyalty to a literal understanding of the OT Scriptures and at the same time have loyalty to the essentials of the Christian faith and the Gentile mission of the church. Various hermeneutical steps were taken in order to continue the recognition and use of the church's OT Scriptures and enable them to be relevant to the needs of the churches and at one with the essentials of the Christian faith. This hermeneutical activity attests to the church's desire to have continuity and harmony in its two essential authorities, Jesus as their Lord and their sacred Scriptures.

The earliest *regula* (canon or authority) for the Christian community was, of course, Jesus himself (Matt 28:19; Rom 10:9; 1 Cor 7:10–12). His words, deeds, and fate were interpreted and accepted authoritatively in numerous sociological contexts where the early Christians lived. His words were accepted as and equated with sacred Scripture; for example, we see in 1 Tim 5:18 a reference to the words of Jesus that are introduced with "the scripture says" and then citations follow from Deut 25:4 and Matt 10:10//Luke 10:7. The prophetic voice, that many contemporary Jews believed had long before ceased in Israel, was now believed to be very much alive in the risen Christ and his church. The early followers of Jesus believed that the long absent but anticipated return of prophecy and the activity of the Spirit (Mal 4:5–6; cf. Joel 2:28–29; Ezek 36:27; 37:14; cf. 1 Macc 4:46; 9:27; 14:41) had returned in the life and fate of Jesus and was present among them. Not only was the Spirit alive and active in the mission of Jesus (Luke 4:1–19), but it was now also present in the church's preaching, teaching, and missional activity (John 14:26; 15:26; 16:12–13; 20:22; Acts 1:8; 2:8, 16–47). This power of God that was manifested in Jesus was now manifested in the church's witness to the risen Lord (Acts 1:8).[7]

The individual OT Scriptures that they cited most frequently in regard to the activity of Jesus, or the anticipated presence and activity of the Spirit among them, include the following (the number of times cited are in parentheses): Ps 110:1 (18); Dan 12:1 (13) Isa 6:1 and Ezek 1:26–28 (12); 2 Chr 18:18/Ps 47:8/1 Kgs 22:19 (11); Ps 2:7, Isa 53:7, Amos 3:13 and 4:13, and Lev 19:18 (10 each).

---

[7]   Although an interpretation of the book of Acts is plagued with difficulties because of historical and theological challenges, its depiction of the life and faith of the early church in its initial simplistic organization and theological affirmations appears reasonable, especially in its belief that the presence and power of the Spirit was among them. The presence of charismatic preachers called prophets in the early church (e.g., 1 Cor 12:28; Eph 2:20; 4:11) is further evidence of the widespread belief that the return of the presence of the Spirit and the age of fulfillment took place in Jesus and continued in the community that he founded.

II. FROM ORAL TRADITION TO WRITTEN DOCUMENTS

Jesus himself never wrote a book and neither did he tell any of his followers to write a book. The surviving NT writings were all produced in the last half of the first century CE, though it is possible that some other writings existed before that (Luke 1:1–3) and also possibly earlier editions of the books that now survive as in the case of Mark (sometimes referred to as UrMark). The Gospels appear to have played a significant role in the churches almost from the time they were produced. They were not initially called Scripture, but likely functioned that way since they told the story of Jesus, the Lord and final authority of the church. These writings were circulating in the churches in the first century and doubtless were read as authoritative texts for emerging Christianity. Although other NT writings also were welcomed in most churches, only the author of the book of Revelation appears to have claimed an inspired status for his writing (22:18–19). By implication this may possibly also be attributed to John 20:30–31.[8] Paul himself may have made a claim to inspiration for his letter to the Corinthians (1 Cor 7:40), or at least for advice that he gave to the church, but as we will see later, that does not mean that he thought that he was writing Scripture to them when he composed his letters to the Corinthian church. The early Christians believed that the Spirit had inspired their proclamation and activities. The Gospels that told the story and words of Jesus, the Lord and highest authority for the early church, were read in the churches and they were among the first Christian writings to be used *as Scripture* and acknowledged as such in the second century.[9]

From the church's beginning, the followers of Jesus proclaimed his life, teachings, miracles, death, and resurrection both orally and subsequently in writing. While *some* of this tradition was written quite early (ca. 50–65),[10] it continued to be transmitted orally. As late as the second century, for example, Papias[11]

---

[8]   This passage and also 1 John 1:4; 2:1, 7, 12–14, 26, and 5:13 point to the value of a written message for the readers, though the writer(s) does not say that he is writing Scripture.

[9]   See, e.g., 1 Cor 7:10, 17; 9:14; 11:23; John 2:22; 6:63; 12:48–50; and 2 Pet 3:2. Notice also that the role of the Paraclete in John 14:26 is to bring to mind what Jesus said. In Rev 3:8–11, the risen Christ praised the Christians in Philadelphia because they "have kept my word and have not denied my name."

[10]   Many scholars agree that prior to the writings of the NT, some early writings that are no longer extant were produced for the church, such as Q, and possibly an earlier form of Mark ("UrMark"). Luke 1:1–4 indicates that Luke was aware of others who had similarly "set down an orderly account" (written?) of the story of Jesus.

[11]   Von Campenhausen, *Formation of the Christian Bible*, 129–30, 133, believes that it is possible to date Papias as early as the end of the first century, but it is more likely that he wrote while he was the leader of the church in Hierapolis perhaps in the third or fourth decade of the second century. He suggests that Papias may not have known of more Gospels than Matthew and Mark. He may well have lived and served as bishop of Hierapolis as early as 100–110 CE, but there is considerable debate both about the time of his service and death as well as Eusebius' accuracy in the way that he portrayed him. See, for example, Wm. R. Schrodel, "Papias," *ABD* 5:140; Charles E. Hill, "Papias of

continued to prefer oral communications about Jesus to messages written in books. He writes: "For I did not suppose that information from books would help me so much as the word of a living and surviving voice" (Eusebius, *Hist. eccl.* 3.39.4, LCL).[12] Although he did not reject the written traditions about Jesus, and he knew of the Gospels of Mark and Matthew, he clearly preferred the oral traditions communicated by survivors from the apostolic period. According to F. C. Baur, Papias appears to have wanted "to keep the immediacy of the original revelation as a present reality by clinging to the living word, not to the dead, transient written text."[13] Whatever the case, it is difficult to believe that Papias recognized Mark and Matthew as sacred Scripture at that time and still preferred hearing the living voice of the elders (apostles). The statement does not suggest that he saw the Gospels as Scripture so much as the "sayings" or *logia* of Jesus as sacred. I agree with Shanks that *ta logia* in Papias' reference to Mark's the "making of the Lord's oracles" and Matthew's production of *ta logion* are in reference to the sayings of Jesus, though I doubt that this is also a reference to the "deeds" or activity of Jesus as well.[14] Eusebius' quote above from Papias saying that "information from books" was not as helpful "so much as the word of a living and surviving voice," if correct, does not sound like a recognition of the sacred scriptural status of those books (Mark and Matthew), so much as an accurate reflection of the sayings of "the Lord." Since Eusebius in the fourth century was well aware of the notion of Christian scriptures, it is strange that he did not draw attention to Papias' recognition of Mark and Matthew as Scripture, had Papias accepted the Gospels as such. In the reference to the early Christians encouraging Mark to write down his remembrances from Peter, Eusebius claims that this encouragement was the "cause of the Scripture called 'the Gospel according to Mark'" and he adds that "And they say that the apostle [Peter], …was pleased at their zeal, and ratified the scripture for study in the churches" (Eusebius, *Hist. eccl.* 2.15.2, LCL). While Eusebius' recognition of the scriptural status of Mark in the fourth century is obvious, it is not at all clear that Papias or others at the time of the writing of Mark in the first century acknowledged the writing as Scripture.

Hierapolis," *Expository Times* 117 (2006): 309–15; Michael W. Holmes, *Apostolic Fathers: Greek Texts and English Translations*, 3rd ed. (Grand Rapids: Baker Academic, 2007), 563–69; and Monte A. Shanks, *Papias and the New Testament* (Eugene, OR: Pickwick, 2013), 119–38.

[12] Papias' statement is evidence of the growing use and significance of the Gospels (at least Matthew and Mark) in the church, but his comment suggests that the written Gospels were not yet equal in status with the OT Scriptures given that he preferred oral proclamations of Jesus over the written texts about him. It is difficult to see *at that time* whether the Gospels were read liturgically or scripturally in the church.

[13] F. C. Baur, as quoted by von Campenhausen, *Formation of the Christian Bible*, 135. R. M. Grant, "New Testament Canon," in Ackroyd and Evans, eds., *The Cambridge History of the Bible*, Vol. 1, *From the Beginnings to Jerome*, 290, also suggests that the author of the *Didache* either used Matthew or shared a tradition common with Matthew, including the oral traditions circulating about Jesus at the end of the first century.

[14] Shanks, *Papias and the New Testament*, 125–31.

In light of Papias' preference for the oral traditions over the writings of Mark and Matthew, Barr makes the interesting observation that both Plato and the Pharisees (and Papias?) had a "cultural presupposition" that the act of writing down a profound truth was "an unworthy mode of transmission."[15] Plato, telling the words of Socrates to Phaedrus, shows his concern that the mere writing of something adversely affects the superior ability of the mind to memorize:

> For this invention [writing] will produce forgetfulness in the minds of those who learn to use it, because they will not practice their memory. Their trust in writing, produced by external characters which are no part of themselves, will discourage the use of their own memory within them...
>
> He who thinks, then, that he has left behind him any art in writing, and he who receives it in the belief that anything in writing will be clear and certain, would be an utterly simple person, and in truth ignorant of the prophecy of Ammon, if he thinks written words are of any use except to remind him who knows the matter about which they are written. (Plato, *Phaedrus* 275AC, LCL)

Some rabbis similarly argued that the "Oral Torah" should not be put into writing (*b. Gittin* 60b;[16] see also *b. Temura* 14b).[17] Because Jesus neither wrote nor commanded his disciples to write anything, Barr concludes that the "idea of a Christian faith governed by Christian written holy Scriptures was not an essential part of the foundation plan of Christianity."[18] The church passed on this "living witness" of Jesus the Christ first through the apostles and subsequently through prophets and teachers, who continued to have a significant role in the Christian community well into the second century. Even in the late second century, the Christians had a great deal of appreciation for the oral tradition of the church.[19] Barr, of course, does not deny that the written HB Scriptures were profoundly important to the early Christians. The preference for oral tradition over written traditions eventually gives way to the latter by the end of the second century CE, although several earlier references show a move in that direction by around 130 and following as we will see below.

Perkins observes the practice of orthodox and gnostic Christians of the second century who preserved their link with the past largely through oral tradition.[20]

---

[15] Barr, *Holy Scripture*, 12, and he also suggests that this perspective may lie behind 2 Cor 3:6. Barr follows B. Gerhardsson, *Memory and Manuscript* (Grand Rapids: Eerdmans, 1998), 157–59, who cites an ancient rabbinic saying that "the Torah is transmitted on the lips" and must be transmitted orally.

[16] The text reads in part: "and it is written, 'For according to the mouth of these words.' (11) What are we to make of this? – It means: The words which are written thou art not at liberty to say by heart, and the words transmitted orally thou art not at liberty to recite from writing."

[17] Gerhardsson, *Memory and Manuscript*, 159.

[18] Barr, *Holy Scripture*, 12.

[19] Grant, "New Testament Canon," 297.

[20] Perkins, *Gnostic Dialogue*, 196–201.

Following von Campenhausen's lead,[21] she claims that the only authoritative written texts for Christians (both orthodox and gnostic) in this period were the OT writings that were perceived as witnesses to the tradition embodied in the community at large. Irenaeus, though strongly committed to a fixed written tradition of four Gospels, believed that the Christian community would have preserved its message accurately even if there had been no written Gospels:[22]

> Since therefore we have such proofs [of the truth], which is easily obtained from the Church, it is not necessary to seek the truth among others [heretics]. [This is so] because, the apostles, like a rich man who [deposited his money] in a bank, placed in her [the Church's] hands most copiously an abundance of all things pertaining to the truth: so that every man, whosoever will, can draw from her the water of life. For she is the entrance to life and all others are thieves and robbers. Because of this we are obligated to avoid them [the heretics], and to choose of the things pertaining to the Church with the utmost diligence laying hold of the tradition of the truth. Now how do we decide the issue? Suppose there arose a dispute relative to some important question among us. Should we not be obliged to turn to the most ancient Churches with which the apostles had dialogue and learn from them what is certain and clear in regard to the present question? And what should we do if the apostles themselves had not left us writings? Would it not be necessary, [in that case,] to follow the course of the tradition that they handed down to those to whom they entrusted the leadership of the Churches? (*Haer.* 3.4.1, ANF)

More specifically, while it is most likely that the canonical Gospels and some of the letters of Paul were highly influential in the worship and ministry of later first- and second-century churches, they were not generally viewed as on par with the church's OT Scriptures. It was not until the middle to end of the second century that some, not all, of the NT writings were viewed as sacred Scripture, though as we will see later, some were identified as Scripture as early as 120–130 CE. These Christian writings were welcomed and read in churches in the first century, but were not yet called Scripture. The NT writings were read in churches before they were accepted as authoritative Scripture. That is always the case. The OT Scriptures were the only writings initially recognized as sacred Scripture in the churches. This began to change in the Apostolic Fathers as Christian texts were cited more frequently and subsequently they gained greater acceptance as authoritative texts in the churches. Hermeneutical reflections at that time were thus largely on OT writings and not on Christian texts. The second-century churches reflect a growing awareness of the value of Christian writings,[23] and by the time of Justin it appears that churches were transitioning from oral Christian traditions to written Christian traditions. By the time of Irenaeus (170–180), several

---

[21]   Von Campenhausen, *Formation of the Christian Bible*, 103–21.

[22]   Perkins, *Gnostic Dialogue*, 197.

[23]   The primary focus of the NT Gospels is the words and deeds of Jesus; and in the Apostolic Fathers, with the exception of *1 Clement*, NT texts are referred to more frequently than are OT texts (but most of these refer to the words of Jesus and not the location of the texts themselves). See Aland, *Problem of the New Testament Canon*, 3.

Christian writings were regularly acknowledged as Christian Scripture. We see in Justin and Irenaeus the center of authority begins to move from oral traditions to written texts.

Why was the literature of the NT written down at all in the first place since we know that the church's message existed for a considerable period of time in oral form? Why was the written tradition preserved and eventually given priority in the church? Many motives are possible, but the first reason is that they likely knew that over time memory fails. Poorly kept or poorly remembered oral traditions could easily result in flawed theology and polity.[24] Second, even though fairly reliable means of communicating significant amounts of information through Jewish oral traditions was also employed by the early Christians,[25] the deaths of some of the first witnesses to the Christ event (the apostles) and the delay of the *Parousia* (the second coming of Jesus) must have influenced to some degree the need for writing down and preserving those oral traditions. As we saw earlier in Carr's work, memory of oral transmission had limitations.

Third, apologetic motives likely stand behind the writing of several of the NT documents. For example, the Acts may have been written in part to emphasize certain catholicizing tendencies in both Jewish Christianity (represented by Peter) and Hellenistic Christianity (represented especially by Paul) to come together as one unified church (Acts 15) and also that the church posed no threat to the Roman Empire. Portions of the Pastoral Epistles may have been written *in the name of Paul* to address later practical and organizational needs of the church as well as the doctrinal needs of a post-Marcionite Christian community.[26] Scholarly debate over the authorship of the Pastoral Epistles continues, but most NT scholars do not believe that these letters, as they currently are formed, are from Paul. It is quite possible, however, that portions of those letters have their roots in Paul himself and reflect historical circumstances in the first century (e.g., 2 Tim 1:8–15 and 4:6–22; Titus 1:5–16).

---

[24] For examples from the early church fathers that illustrate the difficulty of certifying oral tradition, see R. M. Grant, "The Creation of the Christian Tradition: From Tradition to Scripture and Back," in *Perspectives on Scripture and Tradition*, ed. J. F. Kelly (Notre Dame: Fides, 1976), 14–15, who also argues that as Christianity spread into the big cities the only tradition that could have survived was preserved in books.

[25] See especially Gerhardsson, *Memory and Manuscript*, 324–35; and Cranfield, "Gospel of Mark," *IDB* 3:271. See also the discussion of this above in Chapter 2 §III and in Carr, *Formation of the Hebrew Bible*, especially 26–101. He offers many examples for his proposal; see also his earlier *Writing on the Tablet of the Heart*. His proposal is summarized there in 3–14.

[26] The teachings that the resurrection was already past or that it was a spiritual event (2 Tim 2:18), that persons should abstain from marriage (1 Tim 2:15; 4:3; 5:14) as well as from certain foods (1 Tim 4:3; 5:23; Titus 1:15), and references to myths and genealogies (1 Tim 1:4; Titus 3:9) may all suggest some form of gnosticizing tendencies in the church. Perhaps also the focus on the Law (1 Tim 1:7–11) including some form of a Jewish-flavored heresy may also have motivated these writings. More specifically and obviously, the need to clarify the function of various offices and ministries in the church (1 Tim 3–5) probably suggests a developed Christian community that was most likely post-apostolic or at least post-Pauline.

Fourth, although most of the literature of the NT was written prior to the end of the first century (2 Peter may be the leading exception and possibly the Pastoral Epistles), the value of these writings in community worship, instruction, and apologetic purposes became apparent to the second-century churches. To some extent the NT authors themselves saw considerable value in reading the NT writings (e.g., Rom 15:15; 1 Cor 5:9; 2 Cor 1:13–14; Col 4:16; John 20:30–31; 1 John 2:1, 7–8).

Finally, the NT Epistles especially, but possibly also the Gospels, were written in part as matters of policy for an expanding church when it became more difficult to communicate in person. Some of the NT letters indicate that they were sent in lieu of a visit or to prepare the community for Paul's visits (e.g., Rom 1:9–15; 15:24; 2 Cor 1:13–16; Col 4:15–16; 1 Thess 3:5; cf. 2 John 12 and 3 John 13).[27] The letters and the Gospels clarified to the people what the missionaries were not able to say in person because of the distance. The NT writings offered valuable information and counsel that was critical in the life of the emerging churches.

Perhaps these reasons, and others, encouraged NT writers to produce Christian literature; however, with the exception of the author of the book of Revelation, none consciously wrote to produce Christian Scriptures alongside their OT Scriptures. Later, as the NT writings were read and cited in the churches and as they began significantly to impact the churches' witness, life, and worship, they began to be used *like* scripture without actually being called scripture. Around the middle of the second century, the NT writings were read in worship alongside their OT Scriptures and occasionally instead of the OT Scriptures (Justin, *1 Apol.* 67). When that happened, NT writings were functioning as scripture even if they were not yet generally called scripture. By 170–180 that began to change, and several Christian writings *began* to be called "Scripture" (the four Gospels and some letters of Paul). Again, texts function as scripture *before* they are called scripture. This recognition took longer for some NT writings than for others. Two collections of NT writings gained widespread recognition and acceptance (canon 1) in many early churches by the end of the end of the second century, namely the Gospels and the Letters of Paul. Doubtless, both collections and others as well were highly valued soon after they were written, but not yet called Scripture until much later.

Kruger claims that the NT writers were consciously aware of writing scripture when they wrote. He places their sense of being led by the spirit when they wrote as an equivalent to being inspired to write sacred Scripture.[28] Porter, apparently

---

[27]   Brown in J. C. Turro and R. E. Brown, "Canonicity," in *The Jerome Biblical Commentary*, ed. R. E. Brown, J. A. Fitzmyer, and R. E. Murphy (Englewood Cliffs, NJ: Prentice-Hall, 1968), 2:525, maintains that the geographical distance separating the churches was overcome through the circulation of letters.

[28]   See his arguments in Kruger, *Question of Canon*, 119–54. See also his earlier *Canon Revisited*, 184–94, but also much of the rest of his book argues for an early dating of this recognition of Christian writings as Scripture based on an early recognition of apostolic authority in the churches.

following Kruger here, similarly claims "the canon was established intrinsically by what the church viewed as its own internal criteria as soon as the literature was written, and the canon was closed as soon as the last of the apostles died."[29] He does not supply evidence for this conclusion, but it is obviously an "a priori assumption" of his that he sometimes accuses others of making.[30] Kruger's view ignores an important distinction that was later made by the churches, namely that the sense of being led by the Spirit is *not* the same as writing Scripture, that is, distinguishing those led by the Spirit from those who wrote Scripture by the power of the Spirit. Nor is writing something down superior to speaking in person as we see in 3 John 13. (I will address this issue later in Chapter 17 §IV.) His equating them as equal is not present in the NT except in Revelation (22:18–19) when the text from Deut 4:2 is reproduced to affirm the sacredness and inspirational status of that writing. However, the Deut 4:2 text was most likely a widespread convention that reflects the common practice of scribes changing the texts of manuscripts that they copied, often reflecting their own perspectives and views of teachings that they wanted to make more clear than the texts they were copying did. This convention (Deut 4:2) was *used in several ancient texts that were not considered Scripture* as in the cases of Irenaeus who does not refer to his writings as "scripture" (*Haer.* 1.27.2).[31] It is interesting that the designation is also found in the Qumran writings that were clearly welcomed as sacred Scripture, especially the Law of Moses, but the scribes regularly changed its text! (See earlier discussion of this practice at Qumran in their rewritten scriptures in Chapter 7 §II.B.)

Other than the author of Revelation, no other NT writer comes close to making the claim of writing Scripture. Paul certainly believed that what he wrote was important to be shared with other churches in the region (Col 4:16) because he thought it was beneficial to them in dealing with similar challenges facing the other churches. He no doubt also thought that the Spirit led him when he gave his advice to the Corinthians (1 Cor 7:40), but *Paul never calls his own writings scripture*. Many *later* churches believed that what he wrote was sacred scripture, but Paul does not make this claim. No one in the first century, to our knowledge, called Paul's writings Scripture, but in the early to middle second century that begins to happen, as we see in a second-century text (2 Pet 3:15–16).

---

[29]   Stanley E. Porter and Andrew W. Pitts, *Fundamentals of New Testament Textual Criticism* (Grand Rapids: Eerdmans, 2015), 30. Porter lists Kruger's work in his bibliography on canon and his argumentation is similar to Kruger's.

[30]   Ibid., 22.

[31]   See also M. J. Kruger's "Early Christian Attitudes Toward the Reproduction of Texts," in *The Early Text of the New Testament*, ed. Charles E. Hill and Michael J. Kruger (Oxford: Oxford University Press, 2014), 63–80, in which he argues that the use of the designation in Deut 4:2 always refers to the sacredness of the text that is not to be changed. If this is so, why do others not included in the biblical canon also use this same designation for their writings, as in the case of Irenaeus noted above? Kruger does not say. Further, why do the rest of the NT writers not use this text (Deut 4:2) in reference to their written texts?

There are other passages in 1 Corinthians that do not appear to be written by one who was consciously aware of writing sacred Scripture. For example, while Paul was addressing the divisions in the Corinthian church, he appears frustrated with the church and says that he thanks God that he baptized none of them except Crispus and Gaius, but then adds later, as if in an after thought, that he also baptized the household of Stephanus (1 Cor 1:14–16). If he was led by the Spirit and writing sacred Scripture in v. 14, why did he have to correct himself in v. 16? Also, in 2 Cor 12:2–3 while describing his vision, he expresses that he does not know whether he was in the body or out of the body, but God knew. If he was consciously aware that he was being led by the Spirit of God in what he was saying, why does he not know what was happening and admit that only God knows? Further on, in vv. 11–13, Paul appears very humanly frustrated by the comparisons others make between him and the "super apostles" and acknowledges: "I have been a fool! You forced me to it." Again, this does not appear to be the words of one who is consciously aware that he is writing sacred Scripture, but of one who is very humanly and personally defending his ministry. This frustration is obvious in vv. 14–21 and in 13:1–10 Paul seems unsure of what he will find when he comes to visit the Corinthians. Again, this lack of certainty and assurance does not appear to come from one who is consciously aware of writing Scripture.

Perhaps we need to clarify what is meant by Scripture here and at what point the humanness of a passage gives way to Scripture. In the letter to the Galatians, which has essentially the same message as the one in Romans, Paul is personally upset and angered by the Judaizers who have led his new converts away from the Gospel he preached to them. He expresses his frustration with those who wanted to circumcise these Gentile believers and says: "I wish those who unsettle you would castrate themselves" (Gal 5:12). Again, this does not sound like a person consciously aware that he is writing Scripture for the whole church, but rather one who is angered by individuals who have threatened his ministry. The passage does not sound like one who is aware that he is writing sacred Scripture for the whole church, but only one who is angry and using words that are not on par with his more thoughtful discussion of his gospel in the letter to the Romans that was evidently edited (written or rewritten) by Tertius (16:22).

The above examples are only a few of the places *in Paul's letters* where his consciousness of a situation is uncertain or where in his frustration he speaks in less flattering ways. These are places where he does not speak with the certainty that he is speaking in the power of the Spirit or led by God in all that he says, nor do these and other examples reflect his awareness that he is consciously writing Scripture for the whole church and for all ages. There is no doubt that Paul thought that he was right in his defense of his Gospel and that the Gospel that he shared with the people orally was from God, but this is far different from saying that all of his expressions in 1 and 2 Corinthians and Galatians where he expresses his personal anger and frustration (or foolishness, cf. 2 Cor 12:11) in very human terms suggests that he is consciously aware of writing Scripture. Why do we not let Paul say with less certainty that he is not writing what God has led him to say, but only that he has an "opinion" that he offers as a trustworthy servant of Christ (1 Cor 7:25)? Did he think he was right? Yes, of course, but does he put his opinion on the same level with the command of the Lord (Christ), or call his writings Scripture? No.

If sensing the leading of the Spirit in what one says is equal to Scripture, then we have to say it for others besides Paul and the other NT writers. Clement of Rome and Ignatius also sensed – and said – that they were filled with the Spirit when they wrote, so should their writings also be acknowledged as Christian Scripture? As we saw above, when Jesus spoke his words were viewed as equivalent to Scripture (1 Tim 5:18). However, while both Matthew and Luke contained the words of Jesus cited in 1 Tim 5:18, neither Gospel was called "Scripture" until the second century. 1 Timothy, as suggested earlier, is likely from the late first century or possibly even as late as the middle of the second century. It is difficult to agree with Kruger's argument unless at the same time we acknowledge that a lot of other Christian Scriptures were omitted from the NT since others also believed that the Spirit led them when they wrote, e.g., Clement of Rome (*1 Clem.* 63.2), Ignatius (Ign. *Phld.* 7.1b–2). See other examples of this below where I list several others who believed that what they and others wrote, when true, was inspired by the Spirit (Chapter 22 §II.F), including subsequent canons constructed at church councils, such as at the Council at Ephesus in 431. The members of the councils regularly stated that they were led by the Spirit in their decisions (see discussion of this in Chapter 17 §§II and IV below). If Paul's claim about being led by the Spirit is to be taken as consciously writing Scripture, then it follows that others also were consciously writing Scripture, but all of that is highly unlikely and no one credits these later authors with writing Scripture. In none of those cases, nor in the examples from Paul, did any of these writers claim that they were writing sacred Scripture. Similarly, with the one exception (the author of Revelation), no other NT writer made such a claim about his (her?) writings.

On the other side of this argument, what about those writers in the NT who do not claim that they were led by the Spirit to write what they wrote, as in the cases of the Gospels and Acts, as well as the Pastoral Epistles, Hebrews, James, 1–2–3 John, and Jude – in fact, most of the NT writers! Is consciously being led by the Spirit the primary criterion for deciding whether an ancient writing is Scripture? If so, does that exclude authors who do not make that claim? Such arguments based on being led by the Spirit need some adjustment before a coherent conclusion can be drawn about an author's conscious awareness of writing Scripture.

III. THE CANONICAL GOSPELS:
THEIR USE AND AUTHORITY IN THE EARLY CHURCHES

A. Authority of the Gospels in the Early Churches

It is not surprising that the early Christians made frequent use of the canonical Gospels. Given that Jesus was the final authority for the church, it would be strange, indeed, if the early Christians had ignored the various witnesses to his life, ministry, death, and resurrection that were circulating in the churches. The Gospels focused on Jesus' words and deeds and were soon welcomed in the churches, probably shortly after their production, and were frequently cited by the church fathers.[32] The authority of the Jesus tradition in the canonical gospels, and perhaps in a few noncanonical gospels, such as the *Gospel of the Hebrews*,[33] was acknowledged in the churches. Although Mark and Luke were looked upon initially as secondary gospels because they were not written by apostles (Tertullian, as we will see below), they nonetheless were welcomed as sacred documents because it was believed that they were put together by those who had been in contact with the apostles.

The sources used to produce the canonical Gospels included both oral and written traditions about Jesus, some of which were likely written before his death, and together eventually edited, and incorporated in the canonical Gospels. These Gospels were utilized in the church's worship and catechetical instruction in defense of its proclamation in the pagan world, and in its response to the challenges it faced at the end of the first century and throughout the second century. Smith suggests that those who wrote the Gospels initially did so with the idea of producing for the churches an authoritative guide to the Christian faith with the idea of continuing the biblical story. He adds that the continuation of the biblical story is a further distinguishing feature of the NT writings in general and that they presuppose the biblical story of salvation history for the people of God as they interpret history.[34] Von Campenhausen essentially agrees and says the Evangelists intended from the beginning that what they wrote would be read in the churches.[35] This does not mean that the authors intended from the start that their productions would be called or welcomed as "scripture" in the churches. That

---

[32]   See Richard Bauckham, *Jesus and the Eyewitnesses: The Gospels as Eyewitness Testimony* (Grand Rapids: Eerdmans, 2006), who makes a strong case for the Gospels reflecting early eyewitness testimony and also the widespread welcome of the Gospels in the early churches.

[33]   James R. Edwards, *The Hebrew Gospel and the Development of the Synoptic Tradition* (Grand Rapids: Eerdmans, 2009), argues the case for the use and reliability of much of the elements of the *Gospel of Hebrews* in the Gospel of Luke, especially in the Special Luke portions of Luke. It was also known to several of the early church fathers.

[34]   D. M. Smith, "When Did the Gospels Become Scripture?," *JBL* 119 (2000): 8–9.

[35]   Von Campenhausen, *Formation of the Christian Bible*, 122–23.

eventually happened, but generally in the last half of the second century, despite being read and cited in the second-century church fathers with one exception, the early second century gnostic who cites three Gospels and four letters of Paul as Scripture. Hippolytus of Rome claims that the gnostic Basilides who taught in Alexandria (ca. 117–138) made several citations of NT writings using various scriptural formulae. Basilides cited Luke, Matthew, and John in a scriptural fashion (see Hippolytus, *Ref.* 7.22.4), and also four of Paul's letters (Romans, 1–2 Corinthians, and Ephesians; see *Ref.* 7.25.1–3 and 7.26.7) using the scriptural formula "as it is written," but the use of such formulae when citing Christian texts was more common after the middle of the second century.[36] Grant notes that while Basilides is probably the first to use these formulae in reference to NT writings, he was likely not alone and cites church fathers citing NT texts using similar but not the same precise wording, namely Polycarp, and the authors of the *Epistle of Barnabas* and *2 Clement*.[37] We will discuss their uses of NT writings below (Chapter 16 §III).

Scholars have long been aware that the way the Gospels were crafted displays the church's long use of these materials in their oral transmission prior to being written down and included in the NT Gospels. Christians were not devoid of teaching materials before the Gospels were produced in the churches.[38] The early Christians employed many of the skills developed first by their Jewish siblings to transmit and teach orally their story about Jesus and religious traditions, whether in short parabolic stories or carefully constructed confessions that were balanced with similar structural sequences, some of which may have been sung in the early churches (e.g., 1 Cor 15:3–8; Phil 2:6–11). Gerhardsson supports this view with several examples of how these traditions were passed on in the churches.[39] Some scholars suggest that the early followers of Jesus were not sophisticated enough to utilize such methods, or that they were simply unaware of them. Gerhardsson calls this into question and lists three common and faulty assumptions that scholars of Christian origins often hold: (1) that there was no positive relationship between Pharisaic teachers on the one side and Jesus and the early church on the other; (2) that Jesus, his disciples, and other leaders of the early church were and remained simple and unlearned; and (3) that the "spontaneous charismatic aspect of Jesus and early Christianity ruled out acceptance of traditional forms, conscious technique and reasoned behaviour."[40]

---

[36] I owe these sources to Grant, *Formation of the New Testament*, 121–24. Grant notes that Mark's Gospel was apparently ignored.

[37] Ibid., 122–23.

[38] Teaching was an important ingredient in the churches from the beginning (Acts 2:42; 6:2–4; 28:31; 1 Cor 12:28; Rom 12:7; Eph 4:11; etc.). One cannot imagine that the teaching avoided references to Jesus traditions circulating in the churches.

[39] Gerhardsson, *Memory and Manuscript*, 324–35.

[40] Ibid., 23.

This does not mean, of course, that the Gospels were understood as sacred Scripture either in their oral transmission or even initially when those traditions were put into written form. Because their subject matter focused on the words and deeds of Jesus, however, it was clear early on that the churches for which they were produced would take these writings seriously. The widespread appeal of traditions about Jesus in the churches, even in their oral stages of development, can be seen in the NT writings themselves.[41] There is considerable evidence for a widespread acceptance of this tradition in its oral transmission stages, e.g., Paul refers to these traditions that he received and passed on to others (1 Cor 11:2; 15:3; 2 Thess 2:15; 3:6).[42] This can also be seen in the church fathers' dependence on the traditions about Jesus in the Gospels.[43]

How and when did the church adopt the canonical Gospels *as Scripture*, and when did it say "these four and no more" and put them in the place of priority that they have in surviving manuscripts and catalogues of NT Scriptures? When and why were they (usually) placed in their current order in the NT? The whole church did not immediately have, nor unanimously accept, all of the canonical Gospels, but it appears that there was widespread acceptance of Matthew and John, Mark and Luke less so. Other Christian writings competed for acceptance among the churches in the second century and later, but the four canonical Gospels appear to have held sway in the majority of churches. Some Christians in the second to the fourth centuries continued to make use of Tatian's harmony of the four Gospels, his *Diatessaron*, but some second-century churches also accepted some of the noncanonical gospels as in the case of the *Infancy Gospel of James*. The Syrian churches initially gave priority to Tatian's harmonization of the canonical Gospels over the individual canonical Gospels. Tatian's use of the canonical Gospels to produce his harmony underscores the value that he attributed to them, but he nevertheless felt free to harmonize them into one gospel and the history of his *Diatessaron* shows that some churches in Syria and elsewhere chose his harmony over the four distinct Gospels.

---

[41]   For a discussion of the influence of the sayings of Jesus in their oral or prewritten stage of development in the writings of Paul, see the older but still helpful contribution by David Dungan, *The Sayings of Jesus in the Churches of Paul: The Use of the Synoptic Tradition in the Regulation of Early Church Life* (Philadelphia: Fortress, 1971).

[42]   See also Acts 2:42 that speaks of the church's commitment to the Apostles' teaching. There are also other references to the early traditions about Jesus, e.g. Jas 5:2–3, cf. Matt 6:19; 5:12, cf. Matt 5:34–37; 5:14, cf. Mark 6:13; 2 Pet 1:17–18, cf. Matt 17:1–5 // Mark 9:2–7 // Luke 9:28–35.

[43]   For examples of the early churches' use of the canonical Gospels and other Christian literature, see H. Koester, *Ancient Christian Gospels: Their History and Development* (Philadelphia: Trinity, 1990); idem, *Synoptische Überlieferung bei den apostolischen Vätern*, Texte und Untersuchungen 65 (Berlin: Akademie-Verlag, 1957); E. Massaux, *The Influence of the Gospel of Saint Matthew on Christian Literature Before Saint Irenaeus*, trans. N. J. Belval and S. Hecht, ed. A. J. Bellinzoni, New Gospel Studies 5/1–3 (Macon, GA: Mercer University Press, 1990–93); and Metzger, *Canon of the New Testament*.

The churches of the first and second centuries welcomed and utilized the tradi-tions that they had received in oral and written form, as well as other traditions that were circulating among them in the noncanonical gospels such as the *Gospel of the Hebrews*.[44] While the available sources are scanty, we can still trace some of the developing influence and acceptance of the Gospel tradition in the churches as Scripture by the early to middle second century. Initially those traditions were received as reliable oral reports of the sayings and deeds of Jesus carried on by memory. Eventually they were written down from the 60s to the 90s CE, but the early second-century references or allusions to the traditions about Jesus are not attributed directly to specific Gospels. Rather, they are simply to the sayings and deeds of Jesus that we now know were common in the canonical Gospels. In other words, the early church fathers did not initially refer to Matthew's Gospel, but rather to what Jesus said that is found in Matthew's Gospel, and they would simply say: "Jesus said…" and then cite his words. Later those sayings were largely acknowledged as from the canonical Gospels, especially Matthew.

There are few references to the individual Gospels until the time of Irenaeus with the exception of the Papias tradition. Eusebius (ca. 320–30) cites Papias' own comments that he (ca. 130–40) knew of the traditions of Jesus in Mark and Matthew (mentioned in that order) and adds that Papias also made use of 1 John, 1 Peter, and the *Gospel of Hebrews* (*Hist. eccl.* 3.39.14–17). The names of the writers of the Gospels were relatively unimportant to the early church fathers until the latter part of the second century when Irenaeus appealed to apostolic authority in his arguments against heresy. At that time the names of authors of the Gospels was more important than earlier and apostolic names were attached to them. In the fourth century when matters of canon formation were discussed in the various churches it was assumed that if an apostle wrote a document, then it would be accepted as Scripture. Gregory describes this state of affairs: "When anyone had the question as to the sacred character of a book to decide, he was very likely to ask whether it was from an apostle or not."[45]

From the time when the Gospels and even the letters of Paul were written until the middle of the second century, apostolic authorship had not yet become the significant feature in Christian religious texts that it later became.[46] The canonical Gospels were all produced anonymously, but in the middle to late second century the names of apostles (Matthew and John) and those who assisted them (Mark

---

[44]   This point is argued well in Edwards, *Hebrew Gospel*; cf. also his article in "The Hebrew Gospel in Early Christianity," in McDonald and Charlesworth, eds., *"Non-Canonical" Religious Texts*, 116–52.

[45]   Gregory, *Canon and Text of New Testament*, 293.

[46]   For example, Clement of Rome shows an awareness of the language of 1 Cor 15:23 and 12:21 (*1 Clem.* 37.3–4), but makes no mention of Paul as the author, even though he knew it (*1 Clem.* 47.1–3). Because Paul's name appears on all of his writings, his name is more frequently mentioned in the second century, but not always.

and Luke) began to be attached to the canonical Gospels, as well as to other NT writings, evidently to lend credibility to their reports. What led the church to add apostolic names to the NT literature (the Gospels, but perhaps also 1 John, Hebrews) is seldom clear, but it probably started when both the eyewitnesses and those who heard them had died and the issue of credibility was raised in the churches. The churches addressed these concerns by appealing to apostolic authority and those closest to the apostles (Mark and Luke). As the church grew in size it faced many theological challenges and, in dealing with heretical challenges, Irenaeus argued that writings closer in proximity to the apostolic period were more trustworthy than those written later. This can also be seen in the Muratorian Fragment that rejects Shepherd of Hermas because it was written later than the apostolic period. Its author writes: "But Hermas wrote the *Shepherd* very recently, in our times, in the city of Rome..." (MF, lines 73–74).

At roughly the same time that apostolic names became more significant in the transmission of the NT writings and in the early church fathers, pseudonymous writings in the names of those from the apostolic community began to appear in the second century. As in the case of the NT canonical writings, the name of an apostle was apparently intended to validate the reliability and antiquity of a pseudonymous writing.

The early dating and reliability of Mark and Luke have in part been supported precisely because their work was *not* attributed to an apostle, but to two less known non-apostolic figures. How could works by non-apostolic writers have survived antiquity had they been produced in the second century when apostolic names were commonly attached to pseudonymous writings? Evidently it was because their credibility had already long been established in the churches. The canonical Gospels are *not pseudonymous*, of course, since they were written *anonymously* and apostolic names were attached to them in the middle to late second century when the importance of relating them to the apostolic period was widespread in the churches. Arguments for their authorship are more impressive for Mark and Luke than for Matthew and John, but all four reflect early traditions about Jesus. Their authorship continues to be debated among biblical scholars, but most agree that they are first century documents and that they reflect authentic sayings of Jesus.[47] The widespread acceptance and use of the canonical Gospels, especially Matthew, reflect the churches' widespread circulation of the Synoptic tradition in the churches. After long use in the churches, the Gospels of Matthew and John were widely acknowledged by a majority of second- and third-century churches to be apostolic texts. The long list of references to these works in the Apostolic Fathers and later shows that the early focus of the citations was on the sayings of Jesus and not on the individual gospels themselves. The presumption

---

[47] I have discussed in considerable detail the date and authorship of the canonical Gospels in *Story of Jesus in History and Faith*, 77–125.

of the tradition of Jesus in the NT Gospels and in many of the Epistles appears to be important in the NT and Apostolic Fathers.[48]

The NT is not a collection of writings that deposits the revelation of God into loosely connected texts, but rather it sets forth a story in which the revelation of God unfolds in a historical context and is subsequently proclaimed and explained. While extra-canonical gospels produced by anonymous and even pseudonymous writers may contain *some* authentic sayings of Jesus (e.g., *Gospel of Thomas*, *Dialogue of the Saviour*, *Apocryphon of John*, and *Sophia of Jesus Christ*), they are generally without a context or narrative for understanding them, but that is not the case in the canonical Gospels.

By the end of the second century, the canonical Gospels were commonly acknowledged as or called *Scripture*, though they were read *like scripture* likely before they were identified as such. There are no surviving manuscripts that contain the canonical Gospels alongside of non-canonical gospels and this suggests the early priority of the canonical Gospels. In most of the surviving NT manuscripts, the Gospels have a place of priority and by the early third century they and the book of Acts circulated together in a single codex (P[45]).

B. Citations of the Gospel Tradition in the Early Churches

The authority initially attributed to the canonical Gospels in the early churches was doubtless because the Gospels told the story of Jesus, the Lord and final authority of the church. This is why the early church writings appealed to the sayings of Jesus in the Gospels rather than to those who produced the Gospels. The widespread and early reception of the canonical Gospels in the churches was because they reflected a long-held tradition about Jesus that had been circulating in these churches from their beginning. That tradition (both oral and written) lies behind the canonical Gospels and was widely received in the churches years before the actual production of these Gospels.

Dungan claims that Paul was significantly interested in the sayings and traditions about Jesus, even when Paul does not specifically refer to the words and deeds of Jesus. He contends that even then Paul assumes familiarity with those teachings among his readers (e.g., 1 Cor 7:1–7; 9:4–18). Dungan concludes: "the alleged contrast between Pauline Christianity and that branch of the early Church which preserved the Palestinian Jesus-tradition that finally ended up in the

---

[48]   D. M. Smith makes this point in his "When Did the Gospels Become Scripture?," 17–18. Along with the Gospels, several of Paul's Letters were also read publicly in various churches (Col 4:16), and this suggests that many churches welcomed his letters as theologically helpful and practical quite early. Paul himself claimed the importance of his writings in his churches. Notice, for example, 1 Cor 5:3–5; 6:1–6; 7:10–11, 17–20, 40; 11:23–34; Gal 5:1–4. The author of 2 Pet 3:15–16 (perhaps ca. 110 or as late as ca. 140) places Paul's writings on par with Scripture and this may be reflective of what later churches acknowledged by the end of the second century.

Synoptic Gospels is a figment of the imagination. In fact, they were one and the same branch."[49] I heartily agree. Interestingly, Dungan also asserts that there are no parallels in that tradition to support Paul's stand on the law: "The reason Paul did not appeal to any sayings of Jesus in support of his stand on the Torah was because there weren't any."[50] That matter notwithstanding, Dungan concludes that Paul "stands squarely within the tradition that led to the Synoptic Gospels, and is of one mind with the editors of those gospels, not only in the way he understands what Jesus (the Lord) was actually commanding in the sayings themselves, but also in the way he prefigures the Synoptic editors' use of them."[51]

Koester agrees with Dungan here adding that, even though Paul's references to sayings of Jesus are rare, he nonetheless makes several allusions to the Synoptic sayings of Jesus (cf. e.g., 1 Cor 7:10–11 and Mark 10:11–12; 1 Cor 9:14 and Luke 10:7 [Q]; see also 1 Cor 11:23–26 and contrast this with Mark 14:22–25; cf. also 1 Cor 7:25 where Paul reflects "no command of the Lord"). Other Pauline parallels to the Synoptic tradition fit a particular pattern related to church life and order and are concentrated in Rom 12–14; 1 Cor 7–14; and 1 Thess 5.[52] Koester concludes that the Synoptic parallels are either church-order materials from the Gospel of Mark or sayings from Luke's Sermon on the Plain (Luke 6:17–49). Only in the case of 1 Cor 9:14 is the Synoptic parallel from a different context.[53] Paul's familiarity with the oral tradition that was later preserved in the Synoptic Gospels indicates that this oral tradition was commonly circulating in the first-century churches and likely accounts for the broad acceptance of the Synoptic Gospels. The Synoptic tradition also has significant parallels in James and 1–2 Peter. These include the following:

> Jas 1:5 and Luke 11:9/Matt 7:7
> Jas 2:5 and Luke 6:20/Matt 5:3
> Jas 4:2–3 and Matt 7:7, 11
> Jas 4:9 and Luke 6:21/Matt 5:4
> Jas 4:10 and Luke 14:11/Matt 23:12
> Jas 5:1 and Luke 6:24–25
> Jas 5:2–3 and Matt 6:20/Luke 12:33
> Jas 5:12 and Matt 5:34–37
> 1 Pet 2:12 and Matt 5:16
> 1 Pet 2:19–20 and Luke 6:32–33
> 1 Pet 3:9, 16 and Luke 6:28

---

49   Dungan, *Sayings of Jesus in the Churches of Paul*, 150.
50   Ibid.
51   Ibid., 139.
52   Other Pauline–Synoptic parallels include the following: Rom 12:14 and Luke 6:27 (Q) Rom 12:17 and Luke 6:29 (Q), Rom 12:18 and Mark 9:50 (possibly), Rom 13:7 and Mark 12:13–17; Rom 14:10 and Luke 6:37 (Q), Rom 14:13 and Mark 9:42, Rom 14:14 and Mark 7:15, 1 Thess 5:2 and Luke 12:39 (Q), 1 Thess 5:13 and Mark 9:50, 1 Thess 5:15 and Luke 6:29 (Q).
53   Koester, *Ancient Christian Gospels*, 52–54.

1 Pet 3:14 and Matt 5:10
1 Pet 4:14 and Luke 6:22
2 Pet 1:16–18 and Mark 9:2–8/Matt 17:1–8/Luke 9:28–36[54]

Numerous Synoptic parallels and citations may also be found in the writings of the second-century church fathers. The sayings of Jesus, whether oral or written, were considered canonical (canon 1), that is, they were authoritative traditions in the early churches, even though their location in the written Gospels and authorship was of little consequence until around the middle of the second century and later. The available second-century evidence allows us to infer that dependence on the Synoptic Gospels is likely when the word selection and word order in the church fathers closely matches that found in the Synoptic traditions.[55] In other cases, however, the words are similar but not exact, which suggests that the writers were either borrowing loosely from the Synoptic tradition or perhaps that a common oral tradition about Jesus was circulating in the early churches known to both the Evangelists and the second-century church fathers. Matthew was by far the most popular gospel quoted in the second century, having more parallels in the second-century writings than those in Mark, Luke, and John combined.[56]

Clement of Rome (ca. 95), for example, cites mostly the OT Scriptures, but reflects familiarity with the Gospel of Matthew and several other NT writings, especially Paul's Letters. He generally does not cite them by name or author, except in one case where he clearly states that Paul is the author of 1 Corinthians and then calls that letter a "gospel": "Take up the epistle of the blessed Paul the Apostle. What did he first write to you at the beginning *of the gospel* [τοῦ εὐαγγελίου]? With true inspiration [ἐπ' ἀληθείας πνευματικῶς] he charged you concerning himself and Cephas and Apollos, because even then you had made yourselves partisans" (*1 Clem.* 47.1–3, adapted from LCL).[57] The Pseudo-Clementine letter (ca. 130–40)

---

54   These are listed in ibid., 64–65 and 71–73.
55   See Massaux, *Influence of the Gospel of Saint Matthew*, 1:166–72; 2:351–66; and 3:250–58, for useful lists of parallels and citations of the canonical Gospel literature. See also the *Oxford Society of Historical Theology, New Testament in the Apostolic Fathers* (Oxford: Clarendon, 1905), for a helpful guide to many of these references. Koester's *Synoptische Überlieferung* is still one of the best discussions of the significance of these references, though his work is limited to the Synoptic Gospels.
56   Second-century parallels with the Synoptic Gospels are too numerous to list here; for a full list, see Massaux, *Influence of the Gospel of Saint Matthew*, 1:166–72; 2:351–66; and 3:250–58 (see also the useful addenda in 1:58, 83, 121; 2:25, 52, 164, 242, 262, 293; 3.9, 102, 115, 119, 132, 143, 181); and Metzger, *Canon of the New Testament*, 39–73. Some of the more obvious Matthean parallels are the following: *1 Clem.* 16.17 and Matt 11:29; *1 Clem.* 24.5 and Matt 13:3–9; *1 Clem.* 46.8 and Matt 26:24; 18:6; *2 Clem.* 3.2 and Matt 10:32; *2 Clem.* 4.2 and Matt 7:21; *2 Clem.* 6.2 and Matt 16:26; Ign. *Phld.* 3.1 and Matt 15:13; Ign. *Smyrn.* 1.1 and Matt 3:15; Pol. *Phil.* 2.3 and Matt 5:3, 10; Pol. *Phil.* 12.3 and Matt 5:16, 44, 48.
57   It may seem odd that Clement appealed to Paul's writings more than to the Synoptic tradition—and even stranger that Paul is later ignored by Justin in favor of the Synoptic tradition. There are no clear references to Paul in Justin's writings, but Clement of Rome acknowledges the inspiration of

known as *2 Clement* was written three or four decades after *1 Clement* and shows varying degrees of dependence on the Synoptic Gospels.[58]

My point here is that Christian writers in the early part of the second century have many parallels with the Synoptic tradition, whether oral or written. See for example:

> *Mart. Pol.* 4 and Matt 10:23
> *Mart. Pol.* 6.2 and Matt 10:36; 27:5
> *Mart. Pol.* 7.1 and Matt 26:55; 6:10
> *Mart. Pol.* 8.1 and Matt 21:7
> *Mart. Pol.* 11.2 and Matt 25:46
> *Mart. Pol.* 14.2 and Matt 20:22–23
> *Barn.* 4.14 and Matt 22:14
> *Barn.* 5.8–9 and Matt 9:13
> *Barn.* 7.9 and Matt 27:28

The Synoptic tradition was clearly well known in the second-century churches. Even though the NT writers are generally not mentioned by name as writers during this time (except for Paul in *1 Clem.* 47 and the NT writers named by Papias in Eusebius, *Hist. eccl.* 3.39.14–17), the many allusions to and direct citations from the Synoptic Gospels in the second and third centuries testify to their widespread acceptance in the early churches. In sum, all of this detail indicates that the sources from which the church fathers obtained their traditions about Jesus' sayings were widely known, but perhaps the historical settings of those traditions were unimportant to them. The early church fathers cite the sayings of Jesus more accurately than they do the various narrative materials in the Gospels. This may suggest that initially the sayings of Jesus circulated among the churches without the narratives in which they are currently located, or that the second-century church fathers saw the sayings of Jesus as more valuable for the churches and handed them on more carefully than the narratives where they were found.

Paul's writings (*1 Clem.* 47.1–2). A possible reason for this change is that Marcion appealed almost exclusively to Paul to justify his rejection of the Jewish Scriptures and traditions. Marcion's contemporary, Justin, was conversely anxious to root Christian faith squarely within the tradition of Israel and its Scriptures. Since Paul was used by Marcion to support his anti-Jewish bias, it is not surprising that Justin ignored Paul and appealed instead to the tradition that Marcion apparently rejected.

[58] Close similarities between *2 Clement* and the Synoptic Gospels reflect the author's dependence on them. See the following: *2 Clem.* 13 and Matt 5:7; 6:14; 7:1–2; *2 Clem.* 46 and Matt 26:24; 18:6; Mark 14:21; 9:42; Luke 22:22; 17:1–2. Some parallels between these two writings are not as sharp: *2 Clem.* 2.4 and Matt 9:13; Mark 2:17; *2 Clem.* 3.2 and Matt 10:32; *2 Clem.* 6.1 and Matt 6:24; Luke 16:13; *2 Clem.* 6.2 and Matt 16:26; Mark 8:36. Finally, other texts are close in subject matter, but do not use parallel words: *2 Clem.* 2.7 and Luke 19:10; *2 Clem.* 4.2 and Matt 7:21; *2 Clem.* 8.5 and Luke 16:10–12; *2 Clem.* 9.11 and Matt 12:50; Mark 3:35; Luke 8:21; *2 Clem.* 13.4 and Luke 6:32, 35.

C. The Ascendency of Authorship: From Oral Tradition to Memoirs

Given the place of priority that the apostles had in the NT and in the early church fathers, it often seems strange to students that several important books of the NT were produced anonymously, namely, the Gospels, Acts, Hebrews, and 1 John. In the mid-second century after the eyewitnesses and all those who heard them were gone, apostolic authorship and authority became a more important matter for the church. At the same time, numerous pseudonymous gospels, acts, letters, and apocalypses were produced in an apostle's name.[59] Ehrman argues that several pseudonymous writings were included in the NT canon and adds that they were also included with the intent to deceive readers.[60] This literature, so he claims, was produced when the practice of attaching apostolic names to literature had grown in significance in the churches (ca. 130–50 CE) and apostolicity was deemed necessary for acceptance in the churches.

When the canonical Gospels were written, apostolic authorship had not yet emerged as a significant feature of Christian writings in the churches, and this probably accounts for the anonymity of several NT writings.[61] Paul, however, did appeal to his own apostleship regularly when addressing congregations and appealing to his own rights as an apostle (1 Cor 9:1), but his emphasis was on his apostolic position rather than on his writings alone. When the notion emerged that apostolic authorship added credibility to the various traditions that were circulating about Jesus in the churches, then the names of apostles, who remembered the words and deeds of Jesus, were commonly noted and appealed to for guidance in church life and its witness.[62] This development also lies behind, and gave rise to, Irenaeus' notion of apostolic succession (*Haer.* 3.3.3 cited below). His argument was that those closest to Jesus were more likely to tell a reliable story about who Jesus was, what he said and did, and what was done to him than in stories by those who were not eyewitnesses.

---

[59] For an introduction and translation of many of these pseudonymous writings, along with significant comment, see Schneemelcher, ed., *New Testament Apocrypha* and J. K. Elliott, *Apocryphal New Testament*.

[60] See his *Forged: Writing in the Name of God – Why the Bible's Authors Are Not Who We Think They Are* (New York: Harper One, 2011).

[61] When Papias speaks of the church's traditions in Eusebius, *Hist. eccl.* 3.39.15–16, he discusses Mark first and then Matthew, though he considered Matthew to be the author of "oracles" or sayings of Jesus, but not necessarily a gospel with a historical narrative. In neither instance, however, does he call these productions gospels. At that time apostolic authorship as reliable eyewitness testimony supporting the apostolic tradition was apparently not as significant as it later became. This issue also helps us understand Papias' earlier preference for the oral tradition. Within one generation that all changed.

[62] The authority of the apostles was clearly acknowledged in the church's earliest traditions (1 Cor 12:28; Gal 1:15–17; 2:9; Eph 4:11; Acts 2:42; 6:2, 6; 8:1), but attaching their names to the story of Jesus to show the reliability of the reports was a later development.

Luke emphasizes the importance of eyewitnesses at the beginning of his Gospel (Luke 1:1–3) and in the selection of a replacement for Judas Iscariot (Acts 1:21–26). Paul underscores the role of witnesses to Jesus' resurrection appearances in 1 Cor 15:5–8, and in the Gospels the eyewitnesses to the resurrected Christ are a prominent feature. Those eyewitnesses, it was assumed everywhere, were essential to the credibility of the church's proclamation about Jesus and they would more likely be passed on carefully in the church's sacred traditions and in the traditions passed on to its successors. While Irenaeus preferred the use of the apostolic writings in his argument, he also acknowledged the importance of the apostolic tradition handed on in the churches: "For how should it be if the apostles themselves had not left us writings? Would it not be necessary in that case to follow the course of the tradition that they handed down to those to whom they handed over the leadership of the churches?" (*Haer.* 3.4.1; adapted from ANF).

From the time of Justin to the time of Irenaeus, apostolic authority in the churches was generally focused on the apostles *as a group* and not on individual apostles who produced two of the Gospels. The emergence of the importance of apostolic authority was accompanied in the churches by references to the "memoirs" or "remembrances" *of the apostles* (Justin, *1 Apol.* 64–67). Justin, for instance, does not specifically clarify which Gospel or Gospels he had in mind in making his case and he also cites or alludes to more traditions than those in the canonical Gospels. However, in the middle of the second century priority began to be given to certain writings precisely because of their supposed apostolic origin. Evidence for the widespread approval of "apostolic" literature in the churches by the latter half of the second century can be seen in the use and citation not only of canonical literature, but also of extracanonical literature that was produced pseudonymously under apostolic names, for example: *The Gospel of Thomas*, *Infancy Gospel of James*, *Acts of Paul*, *Gospel of Peter*, *Acts of Andrew*, and many others.

The gnostic community regularly appealed to "remembered" knowledge from the apostles, and these remembrances were the sources of a secret knowledge that the gnostics claimed was passed on by the apostles to certain individuals in the churches. In turn, those individuals remembered the words and committed them to writing. The implication of this was, of course, that the writings that contained the remembered apostolic words became recognized as authoritative teachings in their churches. Koester shows that the word "remember" was an important term for identifying the trustworthiness of oral tradition and that it played an important role in establishing the credibility of other literature. For example, in the *Apocryphon of James* (ca. 130–150), the author claims that "the twelve disciples [were] all sitting together at the same time and remembering what the Savior had said to each one of them, whether in secret or openly, and [putting it] in books."[63] This emphasis on the apostles is also found in the gnostic *Letter of*

---

63 Koester, *Ancient Christian Gospels*, 34, quoting Nag Hammadi Codex I.2, 7–15.

Peter to Philip, where what the apostles said by way of instruction from Jesus is repeated frequently to clarify its significance for faith (e.g., §§133, 136, 138–40). "Remembering the words of the Lord Jesus" that were passed on by the apostles early on became the pivotal sacred authority for their churches (see Acts 20:35; cf. also the earlier reference to 1 Tim 5:18).

Justin, writing from Rome (ca. 160), refers to the apostolic tradition: "For the apostles in the memoirs composed by them, which are called Gospels, have thus delivered to us what was enjoined upon them; 'that Jesus took bread, and when He had given thanks,' said, 'This do you in remembrance of me, this is my body'; and, 'after the same manner...'" (*1 Apol.* 66.3, adapted from ANF). For Justin, the "memoirs" (ἀπομνημονεύατα) were writings of the apostles that were also known as Gospels. In other words, they were reliable written reports of the good news about Jesus, and by Justin's time written documents were considered more reliable than the oral traditions circulating in the churches. Justin states that the Gospels, which he calls "memoirs of the apostles" (ἀπομνημονεύατα τῶν ἀποστολῶν), were used to establish doctrine (*Dial.* 100.1) and to relate the story of Jesus' passion. For instance, when introducing quotations from Luke 22:42, 44, he writes, "For in the memoirs which I say were drawn up by His apostles and those who followed them, [it is recorded that] 'His sweat fell down like drops of blood'" (*Dial.* 103.8, ANF). He also appeals to the canonical Gospels (e.g., Mark 14:22–24, which is similar to 1 Cor 11:23–25) when explaining the apostolic testimony regarding the Eucharist: "The Apostles commanded them: that Jesus, taking bread and having given thanks, he said..." (*1 Apol.* 66.3).[64] In his account of a typical worship service in the Christian community, he describes the use of the Gospels as readings in Christian worship, either alongside of or used alternatively with the OT writings ("prophets"). He writes: "On the day called Sunday there is a meeting in one place of those who live in cities or the country, and the *memoirs of the apostles or the writings of the prophets* are read as long as time permits" (*1 Apol.* 67.3).[65]

Koester claims that Justin does not employ any previously established philosophical memorabilia to try to make the gospels more acceptable to others, but rather he uses ἀπομνημόνευω, a compound of the common verb "I remember," to say what was reliably remembered and passed on in the churches. This word and its cognates, Koester explains, were "often used in the quotation formulae for orally transmitted sayings of Jesus."[66] While Justin uses this term only twice in his *1 Apology*, he uses it thirteen times in his *Dialogue with Trypho*.[67] Apparently

---

[64] Richardson, *Early Christian Fathers*, 286.

[65] Richardson, *Early Christian Fathers*, 287, emphasis added.

[66] Koester, *Ancient Christian Gospels*, 33–34, 38–39. The Papias tradition in Eusebius, *Hist. eccl.* 3.39.3–16, uses the similar and even parallel word ἀπομνημονευῶ several times.

[67] See *Dial.* 100.4; 101.3; 102.5; 103.6, 8; 104.1; 105.1, 5, 6; 106.1, 3, 4; 107.1. Justin also refers to Papias' statement about Mark "remembering" Peter's words (*Dial.* 106.3); see also Eusebius, *Hist. eccl.* 3.39.3–4, 15) and calls them "Memoirs of Peter" when referring to Mark 3:16–17.

Justin made use of "memoirs" (ἀπομνημονεύατα) to lend credibility to the Gospels that also supported his arguments against Trypho.

All of this presupposes that Justin himself accepted the Gospels as reliable history, but did he accept them as sacred Scripture? While the memoirs were read in worship along with or instead of the Prophets (a reference to all of the church's sacred Scriptures) – a very short step from recognizing their scriptural status – Justin nevertheless does not call them Scripture nor explicitly place them on an equal footing with the Prophets. Nevertheless, reading the Gospels instead of the Prophets in worship was surely an implication of their scriptural status in those churches. As noted earlier, the NT writings *functioned as Scripture* before they were *called* "Scripture" and this is a prime example of that. The designation "Scripture" generally comes after considerable use of a text and an acknowledgment of its authority.

Koester maintains that even though Justin uses the formula "it is written" in reference to Gospel quotations, this does not mean "it is written in Holy Scripture," but rather that "it is recorded in a written document that Jesus said" (as in *Dial.* 100.1).[68] He supports this argument by showing that quotations from the Gospels are sometimes referred to as "acts" (ἀχτῶν) (*1 Apol.* 35.9; 48.3; cf. 38.7), in which the Gospels are referred to as reliable witnesses to what Jesus did or said. Justin valued the Gospels for their reliability and believed that they faithfully documented the historical fulfillment of prophecy and therefore also the truth of the Christian faith. He drew frequently on the Gospels of Matthew and Luke in his summary of the life of Jesus (e.g., *1 Apol.* 31.7). But again, he does not generally cite the Gospels by their authors' names. The acknowledgment of the names of the authors of the Gospels comes later with Irenaeus. It is also important to note that then it was the "Gospel according to" either Matthew or John or Mark or Luke. There was only *one Gospel* shared in four different ways.

From the time of Justin to Irenaeus, the focus on apostolic authorship and the apostles as a group who proclaimed the church's traditions grew, but from Irenaeus to the early third century this emphasis shifted to individual apostolic authors. This can be seen in Tertullian giving priority to John and Matthew over Luke and Mark (notice the order) because the latter were not written by apostles: "Of the apostles, therefore, John and Matthew first instil faith into us; whilst of apostolic men, Luke and Mark renew it afterward" (*Marc.* 4.2.2, ANF). He likewise criticized Marcion for using only the Gospel of Luke instead of *one* by an apostle: "Luke, however, was not an apostle, but only an apostolic man; not a master, but a disciple, and so inferior to a master – at least as far subsequent to him as the apostle whom he followed was subsequent to the others" (*Marc.* 4.2.5, ANF). Tertullian received both Luke and Mark but did not place them on the same level as Matthew and John. He held the apostolic witness to be more important in the church than non-apostolic writings. While modern Christians

---

68   Koester, *Ancient Christian Gospels*, 41.

generally equate all biblical texts as equal in authority, Tertullian and others in his generation apparently did not. In a short time, the acceptance of the reliability and authority of apostolic documents in telling the story of Jesus no doubt contributed to the churches acknowledging their scriptural status as well. By the end of the second century, if it was believed that an apostle wrote a particular text, that text was acknowledged as sacred Scripture. While this process of recognition began with the citation of Gospel literature and Pauline letters in churches, the acknowledgment of the scriptural status of NT writings was not immediate but only gradually acknowledged. It also appears that both Justin and Irenaeus were central figures in this process.

D. The Emergence of Authorship: From Memoirs to Gospels

For centuries the church has referred to, cited, and quoted NT writings that describe the ministry, passion, and resurrection of Jesus as Gospels. It is easy to forget, however, that these literary compositions were *not* designated as scripture nor gospels when they were first produced. Initially the term Gospel referred to the "good news" of the Christian proclamation, but in the second century it was also used of a literary genre.

The term gospel (εὐαγγέλιον) is not only found in the NT writings, but is also common in the Greek OT (LXX). In Luke 4:18–19, Jesus cites Isa 61:1–2 speaking of the "good news" that God will bring to his people through him. In Rom 10:15, Paul cites Isa 52:7 to tell of the blessings of those who bring the "good news" or "glad tidings" to others, which is also similar to how the term was used in the Greco-Roman world. A well-known inscription at Priene speaks of the birth of Roman Emperor Caesar Augustus (Octavian) saying:

> And since Caesar through his appearance has exceeded the hopes of all former good messages (εὐαγγέλια), surpassing not only the benefactors who came before him, but also leaving no hope that anyone in the future would surpass him, and since for the world the birthday of the god was the beginning of his good messages (εὐαγγέλιον) [may it therefore be decided that…][69]

Christians did not invent this term, but they applied it to the "good news" or "glad tidings" that they proclaimed about Jesus. When Paul proclaimed the gospel, he normally focused on the grace of God that comes to the believer through the activity of God in Jesus. For him, the "gospel" had first of all to do with the substance of the proclamation about God's saving work in Jesus Christ (e.g., Rom 1:1–4, 15–16; 1 Cor 15:1–5; 1 Thess 1:5–9; 2:8–10).

---

[69] Trans. Koester, *Ancient Christian Gospels*, 3–4). See also Gerhard Friedrich, "εὐαγγελίζομαι," *TDNT* 2:707–37.

In the Gospels and Acts, εὐαγγέλιον is used for the good news of the announced kingdom of God that takes place in the ministry, passion, and resurrection of Jesus. For example, in the early church proclamation summarized in Acts 10:34–43, Peter preaches the gospel by telling the story of Jesus: "You know the message he sent to the people of Israel, preaching (εὐαγγελιζόμενος) peace by Jesus Christ – he is Lord of all." This proclamation in Acts is generally accompanied by a call to faith and repentance (Acts 8:12, 25, 40; 10:36; 11:20; 13:32; 14:7, 15, 21; 15:7; 16:10; 17:18; 20:24; cf. 28:31; see also Mark 1:1).[70] The term is not found in John's Gospel, but the basic contours of what John had to say are certainly compatible with the Synoptic Gospels, even if his particular gospel shares only a few of the stories in common with the Synoptic Gospels (roughly eight percent).

Eventually, the term gospel came also to refer to a particular genre of literature that focused on the story and significance of Jesus at roughly the same time that the memoirs or remembrances of the apostles were circulating in the churches. A few vague references in the early part of the second century to *gospel* may well suggest a written document. In the *Didache*,[71] for instance, the writer admonishes his readers: "And reprove one another not in wrath but in peace as you find in the Gospel, and let none speak with any who has done a wrong to his neighbor, nor let him hear a word from you until he repents. But your prayers and alms and all your acts perform as you find in the Gospel of our Lord" (*Did.* 15.3–4, LCL). The pseudonymous *2 Clement* (ca. 140–150) introduces a saying of Jesus from Luke 16:10–12 with the words, "For the Lord says in the Gospel" (*2 Clem.* 8.5, LCL). Speaking of those who deny their faith under threat of persecution, the *Martyrdom of Polycarp* (ca. 160–170) apparently refers to a written document: "For this reason, therefore, brethren, we do not commend those who give themselves up,

---

[70] Surprisingly, Acts 20:35 passes on a saying of Jesus not found in the canonical Gospels. Koester, *Ancient Christian Gospels*, 58–59, also notes that Paul, using the formula "as it is written," quotes a text in 1 Cor 2:9 that only roughly approximates Isa 64:4. The *Gospel of Thomas* 17 cites the same saying but attributes it to Jesus!

[71] While it is impossible to date the *Didache* with precision, it was likely written between 70 and 120. It shows both early conflicts between local church leaders and wandering charismatic prophets in the churches (*Did.* 11–13) and an early structure and worship order (*Did.* 14–15). Some scholars believe that the *Didache* depends on the *Epistle of Barnabas* (ca. 140 CE) because of the considerable similarity in their use of the "two ways" tradition (*Did.* 1–6; *Barn.* 18–20), which, however, may simply be an appeal by both writers to a common oral or written tradition (the wording is not close enough to betray dependence). While it may be that it was written as late as the middle of the second century (so Massaux, *Influence of the Gospel of Saint Matthew*, 3:1), this seems unlikely given the status of church worship and order in it. I suggest 90 CE, but scholars have not yet agreed on this matter. For more on the date and provenance of the *Didache*, see H. van de Sandt and D. Flusser, *The Didache: Its Jewish Sources and Its Place in Early Judaism and Christianity*, Compendia rerum iudaicarum ad Novum Testamentum 3/5 (Minneapolis: Fortress, 2002); K. Niederwimmer, *The Didache: A Commentary*, trans. L. M. Maloney, ed. H. W. Attridge, Hermeneia (Minneapolis: Fortress, 1998); and A. Milavec, *The Didache: Faith, Hope, and Life of the Earliest Christian Communities, 50–70 C.E.* (New York: Newman, 2003).

since the Gospel does not give this teaching" (*Mart. Pol.* 4.1, LCL). But it is also possible that "Gospel" was the all-inclusive designation for the Christian proclamation, including the traditions associated with it.

As noted above, the notion of a *written* Gospel may be traced back to Mark's opening line: "The beginning of the good news [or 'gospel', ἀρχὴ τοῦ εὐαγγελίου] of Jesus Christ, the Son of God" (Mark 1:1).[72] With this opening, Mark proceeds to tell the story of Jesus' activities and teachings, beginning with his fulfillment of the Scriptures (Mark 1:2–3; cf. Mal 3:1; Isa 40:3), and continuing with his healing ministry, exorcisms, teachings, and finally death and resurrection.[73] While the initiation of this designation may have begun with a reading of Mark 1:1, its use as a reference to a literary genre became more common around the middle of the second century. While gospel, as a literary genre, *generally* focused on the life, ministry, and fate of Jesus, Luke did not restrict himself to this pattern. Luke continued the story about how God advanced the work to include the origin of the church and its involvement in the influence and spread of the gospel (the Christian proclamation) to the nonbelieving communities, beginning in Jerusalem and eventually arriving in Rome.[74] While all four canonical Gospels tell the story of Jesus and his significance for faith, only Mark begins his story of Jesus using the term *gospel*. The other canonical Gospels did not follow this example. As we saw, one of the earliest references to the canonical Gospels as "gospels" comes from Justin (*1 Apol.* 66–67, esp. 66).

Although there are some notable similarities between ancient biographies and the canonical Gospels, there are no exact parallels because ancient biographies were not produced anonymously and generally did not focus on one short moment in the person's life, as in the case of the Gospels that focus primarily on Jesus' ministry, passion, and resurrection. More importantly, unlike other ancient biographies, the gospel about Jesus circulated in an oral tradition for decades prior to being put in written form. Contrary to some scholarly opinion, Philostratus' *Life of Apollonius of Tyana*, Xenophon's *Memorabilia*, and Suetonius's *Lives of the Caesars* are not comparable parallels. Stanton agrees that these ancient sources "all contain a memorable beginning and ending with climactic moments, dramatic

---

[72] The words "the Son of God" are likely a later addition to this opening statement since they are not found in Codex Vaticanus (B), though they are in the later Codex Sinaiticus (ℵ), hence, they were probably a later addition to Mark's Gospel.

[73] G. N. Stanton, *Gospels and Jesus* (Oxford: Oxford University Press, 1989), 30–33, makes this point.

[74] Acts, the second part of a two-part work, does not fit neatly within the traditional gospel genre (or *Gattung*). No evidence is available on when the two volumes were separated, except that Acts was not a part of Marcion's collection of NT writings (ca. 140–50). Acts may not have served Marcion's purposes well, but it is not clear that he was even aware of its existence. Whether he separated Acts from Luke, or, whether the two volumes were already separated when he made use of the Gospel of Luke is not clear in the early churches.

scenes and vividly drawn characters," but the canonical Gospels still have no parallels elsewhere in antiquity.[75]

By roughly 120–130, the term gospel began to be used in the churches *also* in reference to the written stories about Jesus and his teaching, but without changing its earlier meaning as a reference to the content or substance of the message of God's salvation in Jesus the Christ. While this change may have its roots in early Christian preaching, in the Gospel of Mark (1:1), and also in the writing down of the early Christian proclamation (Acts 10:34–43), it is not yet clear who was responsible for this change in the greater church. Since Justin may be the earliest writer to make an explicit reference to Gospels as literary productions, he did not specifically use the word gospel to describe the kerygma of the church or show an awareness of the kerygmatic structure of the gospel writings. It is therefore not likely that this notion began with him.

Koester posits that Marcion understood the tradition of Paul's gospel (Rom 2:16; 16:25; 2 Cor 4:3; Gal 1:11; 1 Thess 1:5; 2 Thess 1:8; 2:14) to be the substance of the Gospel of Luke. As a result, he suggests that Marcion may have been the first to equate the two.[76] Justin wrote a treatise against Marcion called "Stigma Against All Heresies" (referred to in *1 Apol.* 26.8) and was therefore likely to know about Marcion's equating Paul's "gospel" with Luke's written Gospel.[77] Among the Gospels, Marcion accepted only the Gospel of Luke and excised what did not please him, namely, the Jewish element and Luke's use of the OT Scriptures. Marcion accepted the letters of Paul (without the Pastorals), but denied that other apostles faithfully told the story of Jesus. Consequently he rejected the traditions about Jesus passed on in the Evangelists' names. Marcion accepted Paul's thesis that Jesus the Christ was the end of the law and humanity's only means of salvation, but unlike Paul Marcion believed that this meant a rejection of the Scriptures of Israel.

The notion of Paul's gospel being conveyed in the Gospel of Luke appears for the first time in Irenaeus, who possibly shows two understandings of the word gospel: the proclamation of the early church. He writes:

> for the Lord of all gave to His apostles the power of the Gospel through whom also we have known the truth, that is, the doctrine of the Son of God. (*Haer.* Preface, ANF)

---

[75]   Stanton, *Gospels and Jesus*, 28, but also 15–33. Burridge challenges this conclusion in his *What Are the Gospels? A Comparison with Graeco-Roman Biography*, SNTSMS 70 (Cambridge: Cambridge University Press, 1992). For further discussion, see C. H. Talbert, *What Is a Gospel? The Genre of the Canonical Gospels* (Philadelphia: Fortress, 1977); P. L. Shuler, *A Genre for the Gospels: The Biographical Character of Matthew* (Philadelphia: Fortress, 1982); D. E. Aune, *The New Testament in Its Literary Environment* (Philadelphia: Westminster, 1987), 17–76; and P. Cox, *Biography in Late Antiquity: A Quest for the Holy Man* (Berkeley: University of California Press, 1983).

[76]   Koester, *Synoptische Überlieferung*, 6–8; idem, *Ancient Christian Gospels*, 35–36.

[77]   Koester, *Ancient Christian Gospels*, 35–36.

> We have learned from none others the plan of our salvation, than from those through whom the Gospel has come down to us. (*Haer.* 3.1, ANF)

> Luke also, the companion of Paul, recorded in a book the Gospel preached by him. (*Haer.* 3.1, ANF)

Eusebius likewise passes on this tradition and indicates that the gospel proclaimed by the early church was also put in writing:

> Luke...had careful conversation with the other Apostles [besides Paul], and in two books left us examples of the medicine for souls which he gained from them – the Gospel, which he testifies that he had planned according to the tradition...and the Acts of the Apostles which he composed no longer on the evidence of hearing but of his own eyes. And they say that Paul was actually accustomed to quote from Luke's Gospel since when writing of some Gospel as his own he used to say, "According to my Gospel." (*Hist. eccl.* 3.4.6–7, LCL)

Perhaps as a result of Marcion's misunderstanding, he produced a list of books to read in his churches that included not only a truncated Gospel of Luke but also a list of ten truncated letters of Paul.[78] While Marcion may have rejected all Christian literature except the Pauline corpus and Luke, his followers seem to have been more open to reading additional Christian writings in their churches.

Hahneman, interestingly, suggests that Marcion, contrary to popular scholarly opinion, may not have rejected the other canonical Gospels (Matthew, Mark, and John). For example, Ephraem Syrus (ca. 306–73) claims that the followers of Marcion did not reject Matt 23:8 (see Ephraem, *Song* 24.1), and Marcus, a Marcionite, directly quotes John 13:34 and 15:19 in Adamantius' *Dialogue* 2.16, 20. Rather, as Hahneman claims, it appears that the Marcionites did not reject other Christian writings so much as they edited them for use in their churches. Marcion's followers included a collection of psalms and even admit verses from the other canonical Gospels into their Scriptures.[79] As we will see again in Chapter 18 §II, after Marcion some of his followers apparently cited positively the Gospel of Matthew. Origen quotes a Marcionite interpretation of Matt 19:12 in his

---

[78] He omitted the Pastoral Epistles from his collection, but added the *Letter to the Laodiceans*, which may be the same as the Letter to the Ephesians in the canonical NT.

[79] See G. M. Hahneman, *The Muratorian Fragment and the Development of the Canon*, Oxford Theological Monographs (Oxford: Clarendon, 1992), 90–92, who cites as evidence Adamantius' *Dialogue* 2.18 and Tertullian's *Marc.* 4.5. It is likely that the later Marcionites accepted the reading of Tatian's *Diatessaron* in their churches. For support of this, see R. Casey, "The Armenian Marcionites and the Diatessaron," *JBL* 57 (1938): 185–92. This all suggests, of course, that the contours of Marcion's canon may not have been so firmly fixed as was once thought and he may not have produced the earliest fixed biblical canon, as von Campenhausen, *Formation of the Christian Bible*, 152–53, and others after him claim. For an explanation and examples of this, see the introduction and translation of Adamantius in Robert A. Pretty, *Adamantius: Dialogue on the True Faith in God: De Recta in Deum Fide*, ed. Garry W. Trompf (Leuven: Peeters, 1997). For further discussion of this, see also the focus on Marcion below in Chapter 18 §II.

Commentary on Matthew 15.3. It is not certain that Marcion approved this, but it is instructive that the community he left behind was aware of and cited Matthew's Gospel.

Until the middle of the second century, the Gospels were used in the churches primarily as reliable witnesses to the sayings of Jesus and were not generally called "Scripture" or made equal to the Prophets – even if they were placed alongside of them and read in the churches. By this act, however, the Gospels were well on their way to becoming the new Scriptures of the church.[80]

Justin (150–160) speaks of "the apostles in the memoirs which are called gospels" (*1 Apol.* 63.3) and cites rather freely or loosely from Matthew and Mark.[81] Since his celebrated student, Tatian, knew the Gospel of John and included it in his *Diatessaron*, it is quite possible that Justin also knew of it including all four canonical Gospels,[82] but Justin largely made use of the Synoptic Gospels. It is often unclear clear which writings Justin had in mind when he spoke of the "memoirs of the apostles" or the "gospels." For example, when he refers to Jesus being born in a cave he may have in view the *Protevangelium of James* 18–19. He may show some awareness of the Arabic *Gospel of the Infancy* and possibly also *Gospel of Thomas* 13 (which may have been a common oral tradition) in his *Dial.* 88–89; and cites the apocryphal *Acts of Pilate* 6–8 in *1 Apol.* 48. Although Justin used the term gospel to refer to written stories about Jesus, it is not clear that he had only the canonical Gospels in mind when he spoke of Gospels.

We will now turn to a discussion of Paul's Letters and their acceptance as Scripture as well as to other NT writings that began to be cited as sacred Scripture by several early church fathers.

---

[80] See J. Barton, *How the Bible Came to Be* (Louisville: Westminster John Knox, 1997), 53–72, for a useful summary of this process.

[81] Quotations of Matthew and Mark in *1 Apology* include the following: Matt 22:14 in *1 Apol.* 4; Matt 9:18 in *1 Apol.* 5; Matt 20:16 in *1 Apol.* 6; Matt 22:45 in *1 Apol.* 12; Mark 10:23–24 in *1 Apol.* 20.

[82] The most significant parallel is *1 Apol.* 61.4–5, which is an almost word-for-word quotation of John 3:3–5. Other parallels are close, but not exact (see Massaux, *Influence of the Gospel of Saint Matthew*, 3:46–47): *1 Apol.* 6.2 and John 4:24; *1 Apol.* 32.9–11 and John 1:13–14; *1 Apol.* 33.2 and John 14:29; *1 Apol.* 35.8 and John 19:23–24; *1 Apol.* 52.12 and John 19:37; *1 Apol.* 63.15 and John 1:1; *2 Apol.* 6.3 and John 1:3.

CHAPTER 15

NEW TESTAMENT WRITINGS AS SCRIPTURE

I. PAUL'S LETTERS

In addition to his prominence in the book of Acts, which reports his harrowing missionary journeys, Paul is also known as the author of several NT letters. These letters were non-literary communications mainly sent to churches that he either founded or was about to visit and a few to individuals. While there is some literary character and style in these letters, they were often sent as a substitute for a face-to-face visit and not as formal literary documents. Formal literary and non-literary letters are well known in the ancient world, some of which were published after the deaths of the writers (e.g., Cicero, Pliny, Seneca, Alciphron, Aelian, and Philostratus). Some readers complained to Seneca about his non-formal and non-literary style of writing, but he responded to them that this is the way he wanted his letters to be. He writes:

> You have been complaining that my letters to you are rather carelessly written. Now who talks carefully unless he also desires to talk affectedly? I prefer that my letters should be just what my conversation would be if you and I were sitting in one another's company or taking walks together – spontaneous and easy; for my letters have nothing strained or artificial about them. (*Epistles* 75.1–2, LCL)

The nonliterary aspect of such correspondence, even when written well, lent itself to their production in codices or tablets, rather than on the more literary scrolls or rolls. The value of Paul presenting his theology through informal letters allows it to be much more personal and direct. It also allows him to respond appropriately to specific situations facing his churches. In some cases, Paul intended that his letters would be shared with or read in other churches (Col 4:16), but sometimes the issues addressed were much more localized, as in the case of 1–2 Corinthians and in some churches in the Galatian region. In time, other church leaders saw great value in reading his letters to their congregations as well.

The widespread practice of sharing such letters in various churches probably took place near the end of the first century, though it no doubt began on a limited scale. Scholars generally conclude that several of Paul's letters were circulating together in churches no later than the end of the first century, at least in Asia Minor and probably elsewhere as well. Clement of Rome (ca. 95) is the first of the Apostolic Fathers to refer to Paul's writings, especially 1 Corinthians, Ephesians, and possibly also the letter to Titus.

Later, as we will see below, some of Paul's letters were used or cited in the *Letters of Ignatius* (ca. 115), and they were used or cited thereafter with growing frequency in the churches. Goodspeed posits that nine of Paul's writings were collected and circulated together near the end of the first century under the cover of the Letter to the Ephesians.[1] He suggests that perhaps Onesimus, the runaway slave who worked with Paul and later became bishop in Ephesus after the death of Paul, produced this collection. Since no extant or known biblical manuscript introduces Paul's writings with Ephesians, Goodspeed's theory has largely been rejected.

A recent suggestion, put forth by Trobisch, is that Paul himself was responsible for the initial collection of his writings and that Paul even edited four of them (Romans, 1 and 2 Corinthians, and Galatians) and circulated them in Ephesus.[2] According to this theory, Rom 16 served as an introduction to that collection, and Ephesians and other letters were added to Paul's collection after his death in three stages: the collection of letters sent to churches (Ephesians–2 Thessalonians), personal letters (1 Timothy–Philemon), and Hebrews. The occasion for the base set of letters, he claims, was the collection of money for the Jerusalem church, which was discussed significantly in one of the four letters (2 Cor 9–13) and in a limited way in the other three. One of Paul's purposes for collecting these funds, he claims, was his attempt to resolve his conflict with the Jerusalem church (Gal 2:11–14). He rightly concludes that the seriousness of this conflict gave little chance for immediate resolution, but he probably overestimates the role that the collection of funds played in Romans, 1 Corinthians, and Galatians. In any case, according to Trobisch, in the process of collecting and sending these letters to Ephesus and subsequently elsewhere, Paul unconsciously initiated the birth of the NT canon. The problem with this ingenious proposal is the lack of evidence to substantiate it. Trobisch ably informs readers of the processes by which the Letters of Paul were produced, ordered, and transmitted by the early church, and even shows how P[46] (the oldest known manuscript containing a collection of Paul's letters, ca. 200 CE) arranged the letters according to length though Hebrews was placed after Romans and before 1 Corinthians (which is slightly longer than Hebrews), in order to keep the Corinthian letters from being separated in the corpus.[3]

---

[1]   E. J. Goodspeed, *The Key to Ephesians* (Chicago: University of Chicago Press, 1956); idem, *The Meaning of Ephesians* (Chicago: University of Chicago Press, 1933); and idem, *An Introduction to the New Testament* (Chicago: University of Chicago Press, 1937), 191–211.

[2]   D. Trobisch, *Paul's Letter Collection: Tracing the Origins* (Philadelphia: Fortress, 1994), 50–54.

[3]   Ibid., 16–17.

He also rightly observes the absence of the Pastorals and Philemon from P[46], but apparently does not see the possible implications of this for the formation of the NT canon or for a Pauline canon. Since P[46] is the earliest surviving manuscript of Paul's Letters, the omission of the Pastorals and Philemon in this document suggests that they had not yet been added to a recognized collection of Paul's Letters by the end of the second century. This could be a factor in determining the date of the *Muratorian Fragment*, which does include the Pastorals (see a more complete discussion of this in Chapter 21 §IV). It is also interesting that Marcion and Codex Vaticanus (B) also do not include the Pastoral Epistles. While the fragmentary state of P[46] may suggest that this argument is from silence, the known number of pages in P[46] does not have sufficient space for the rest of Paul's letters to be included in it, even if written in very small letters.

Trobisch makes a good case that Paul's letters were arranged into three groups within the Pauline corpus, each of which began with the largest book in that group. This explains why Ephesians, which is some nine hundred characters longer than Galatians, strangely stands after Galatians: Galatians is the smallest letter in the first group, and Ephesians is the largest in the second. He also correctly observes that chronology was not the chief factor in the sequence of each group. Trobisch rejects the popular view that 1–2 Corinthians is made up of four earlier writings of Paul, but claims instead that they contain seven letters that Paul himself later edited and sent out in their current form. He discerns individual letters in (1) 1 Cor 1:10–4:21; (2) 1 Cor 5:1–6:11; (3) 1 Cor 6:12–16:24; (4) 2 Cor 1:3–2:11; (5) 2 Cor 2:14–7:3; (6) 2 Cor 7:4–9:15; and (7) 2 Cor 10:1–13:13. Most scholars agree that there are natural breaks between these sections, but Trobisch has not sufficiently demonstrated his case for seven separate letters. He makes a good case that Rom 16 was later added to Paul's letter to the Romans and that that chapter's original destination was not the church at Rome, but rather the church at Ephesus. His discussion of the redactional inserts that Paul himself added to his own correspondence is helpful and gives the reader a feeling that we are looking over Paul's shoulder as he composes the letters.[4]

However, despite Trobisch's many positive contributions, several of his arguments go against his primary thesis. First, it is widely acknowledged that the style of writing in Galatians is hurried, choppy, and with unfinished sentences. It was not presented in a manner that reflects careful editing, such as we see in the case of Romans. It reflects the anger Paul had against those whom he believed were distorting the gospel he had proclaimed to the Gentiles. The contrast between Romans and Galatians is difficult to explain if one assumes that Paul had taken the time to edit Galatians at a later time. In other words, if Trobisch is correct,

---

[4] Ibid., 72–73. See also Trobisch's discussion of Paul's editing and production of his collection of letters in his *The First Edition of the New Testament* (Oxford: Oxford University Press, 2000), in which he explains much of this thesis. But again, what could have been does not mean there is evidence that it was.

we should expect to see more uniformity in style and presentation in these letters since they both have many similar teachings. Second, after observing that Marcus Tullius Cicero (died ca. 44 BCE) and Cyprian (died 258 CE) produced, edited, and circulated their own letters, Trobisch concludes that Paul must have done the same. This kind of argument, however, falls short of demonstration and is an argument from silence. What may have happened is not evidence that it in fact did happen. Third, it is strange that 1 Thessalonians, one of the earliest of Paul's writings, receives little attention in Trobisch's work. In fact, he has no significant discussion of 1 Thessalonians, Philippians, or Philemon, all of which are undisputed letters of Paul. Although Trobisch claims to trace the origins of Paul's letter collection, these letters and their place in the Pauline corpus deserve more attention than what he has given to them. Fourth, no biblical manuscripts show that Romans through Galatians ever circulated as a collection by itself or that Rom 16 introduced any of them. Finally, Trobisch's discussion of personal names in Paul's Letters is not convincing.[5] He asserts that Paul did not mention specific individuals in later correspondence that he had named in his earlier correspondence, because these individuals had ceased being his friends in the intervening time. This is entirely speculative and does not contribute to his primary thesis.[6]

Little factual information is available on what was taking place with Paul's Letters from the time of his death until the end of the first century. Clement of Rome and Ignatius of Antioch both knew and referred to several of Paul's Letters, and so did Marcion, who circulated a collection of ten of Paul's Letters in his churches. However the earlier history of those letters still remains a mystery, although Basilides in the early third century cited four of those letters as Scripture. Ignatius later may have followed Paul's example of writing to seven churches[7] and the author of Revelation likewise addresses seven churches perhaps also following by then (90–94 CE) a well-established pattern that had its origins in Paul.

Ephesians was most likely intended as an encyclical letter to all the faithful in Asia Minor since nothing in it ties it to any one particular community: ἐν ἐφέσῳ ("in Ephesus") in Eph 1:1 has limited and questionable manuscript support, and Eph 4:20–22 (cf. also 1:15; 3:1–2) suggests that the writer had not yet met the recipients of the letter. Since Paul had already visited Ephesus, it is doubtful that the letter as it now stands was intended for this congregation. The letter may reflect a post-Pauline era and (per Goodspeed) it may have been attached as an introduction to the Letters of Paul, although no textual evidence substantiates

---

[5]   Ibid., 59–62.

[6]   For a more detailed discussion of the problems with Trobisch's conclusions, see S. E. Porter, "When and How Was the Pauline Canon Compiled? An Assessment of Theories," in *The Pauline Canon*, ed. S. E. Porter, Pauline Studies 1 (Leiden: Brill, 2004), 95–128, here 113–21.

[7]   Eusebius mentions only seven letters of Ignatius in *Hist. eccl.* 3.36, but there were other writings attributed to Ignatius that circulated well into the Middle Ages. The surviving Greek manuscripts, however, only include the seven letters.

this claim. It is also possible that several of Paul's Letters, whether or not in a collection introduced by Ephesians, may have circulated in Asia Minor and possibly even among a wider audience by the end of the first century.

The familiarity of several of Paul's letters in other late first or early second century texts may be reflected in the following citations.

Similarities between the Pauline corpus and the *Didache* include:

> *Did.* 5.1 and Rom 1:29–30
> *Did.* 5.2 and Rom 12:9
> *Did.* 10.6 and 1 Cor 16:22
> *Did.* 13.1 and 1 Cor 9:13–14; (cf. Matt 10:10//Luke 10:7)
> *Did.* 16.4 and 2 Thess 2:9
> *Did.* 16.6–7 and 1 Cor 15:22; 1 Thess 4:16

Clement of Rome provides the earliest reference to Paul's death (*1 Clem.* 5.5–7), but also several references to and citations of several of Paul's writings. This suggests that a collection of Paul's writings were known as far west as Rome at the end of the first century. These parallels include:

> *1 Clem.* 13.1 and 1 Cor 1:31; 2 Cor 10:17
> *1 Clem.* 24.1 and 1 Cor 15:20
> *1 Clem.* 24.5 and 1 Cor 15:36–41
> *1 Clem.* 32.2 and Rom 9:3
> *1 Clem.* 33.1 and Rom 6:1
> *1 Clem.* 34.8 and 1 Cor 2:9
> *1 Clem.* 35.5 and Rom 1:29–32
> *1 Clem.* 35.7 and Rom 1:32
> *1 Clem.* 37.5 and 1 Cor 12:21
> *1 Clem.* 46.6–7 and Eph 4:4–6
> *1 Clem.* 47.1–2 and 1 Cor 1:10–17
> *1 Clem.* 48.5 and 1 Cor 12:8–9
> *1 Clem.* 49.5 and 1 Cor 13:4–7
> *1 Clem.* 50.6 and Rom 4:7–9
> *1 Clem.* 59.3 and Eph 1:18

Finally Ignatius of Antioch and Polycarp have several parallels with a collection of Pauline Letters including:

> *Eph.* 8.2 and Rom 8:5, 8
> *Eph.* 10.1 and 1 Thess 5:17
> *Eph.* 10.2–3 and Col 1:23; Rom 4:20; 1 Cor 16:13
> *Eph.* 14.1–2 and 1 Tim 1:5 (or common source, but order of faith and love are reversed.)
> *Eph.* 15.3 and 1 Cor 3:16
> *Eph.* 16.1 and 1 Cor 6:9–10; Eph 5:5
> *Eph.* 18.1 and Gal 5:11 and 1 Cor 1:20
> *Eph.* 18.2 and Rom 1:3 and 2 Tim 2:8
> *Eph.* 19.3 and Rom 6:4

Eph. 20.2 and Rom 1:3
Magn. 10.2 and 1 Cor 5:7
Trall. 5.2 and Col 1:16
Trall. 9.2 and 1 Cor 15:12–19
Trall. 12.3 and 1 Cor 9:27
Rom. 2.1 and 1 Thess 2:4
Rom. 4.3 and 1 Cor 7:22
Rom. 6.1 and 1 Cor 9:15
Rom. 7.2–3 and Rom 1:3 and 2 Tim 2:3
Rom. 9.2 and 1 Cor 15:8–9
Rom. 10.3 and 2 Thess 3:5
Phld. 3.3 and 1 Cor 6:9–10
Phld. 4.1 and 1 Cor 10:16–17
Phld. 7.1 and 1 Cor 2:10
Smyrn. intro. and 1 Cor 1:7
Smyrn. 1.1 and Rom 1:3
Smyrn. 1.2 and Eph 2:16
Smyrn. 4.2 and Phil 4:13
Smyrn. 10.2 and 2 Tim 1:16
Smyrn. 11.3 and Phil 3:15
Pol. 1.2 and Eph 4:2
Pol. 4.3 and 1 Tim 6:2
Pol. 5.1 and Eph 5:25, 29
Pol. 6.2 and 2 Tim 2:4

These references all suggest that several of Paul's Letters were widely known and highly esteemed in the late first and early second centuries in several churches. None of these sources say that Paul wrote "Scripture," but they are indicative of the circulation of his letters and the significant value attributed to them in the late first and early second centuries.[8]

Justin Martyr does not refer to Paul's writings or his ministry, and this neglect, some scholars suggest, may have been a response to Marcion's sole use of Paul's Letters to the exclusion of other NT writings (save Luke), and also the church's response to the gnostics' frequent appeal to Paul.[9] Absence of citation, of course, does not indicate Justin's ignorance of Paul or his letters, which would hardly have been possible at that time, but despite his neglect Paul's writings were highly esteemed in most churches both before and after Justin, even though there is little direct appeal to Paul in the apologetic writings in Justin's time.

It is safe to say that several of Paul's writings were circulating in Asia Minor at the end of the first century. Marcion probably took over an existing collection of

---

[8]   While Michael J. Kruger has produced a careful examination of how Paul's letters were received, he has not proved either that Paul viewed them as Scripture or that they were initially recognized as sacred Scripture in the earliest churches that welcomed them. See his discussion in *Question of Canon*, 119–54. I will return to his arguments in more detail below.

[9]   H. Y. Gamble, *The New Testament Canon: Its Making and Meaning*, Guides to Biblical Scholarship (Philadelphia: Fortress, 1985), 43–46.

Paul's writings.[10] Clement of Rome refers to four of Paul's Letters, and the early editorial work on the Corinthian letters, Romans, and Philippians suggests early interest in Paul's writings. It is generally agreed that in the second century, collections of some seven to ten Pauline Letters circulated in various cities of the Roman Empire, especially in Rome, Ephesus, and Alexandria. Polycarp of Smyrna spoke of Paul's Letters and encouraged his readers at Philippi to examine them carefully:

> For neither am I, nor is any other like me, able to follow the wisdom of the blessed and glorious Paul, who when he was among you in the presence of the men of that time taught accurately and steadfastly the word of truth, and also *when he was absent wrote letters to you*, from the study of which you will be able to build yourselves up into the faith given you. (Pol. *Phil*. 3.2, LCL, emphasis added)

Polycarp assumes, of course, that those in Philippi were aware of Paul's Letters (plural) just as he was at Smyrna and he underscores their value for building others up in their faith. The above examples are sufficient to show that Paul's writings, along with the Gospels, significantly influenced a number of early churches and doubtless show why they are among the earliest Christian writings to be identified as Scripture.[11]

II. NEW TESTAMENT WRITINGS FUNCTIONING AS SCRIPTURE

The early use of and references to the Gospels and Paul's Letters does not mean that these writings were received initially as sacred Scripture on par with the writings of the OT, but rather that they were useful in the life and ministry of the early churches. This is the first step in a canonical process that moves from the recognition of the authority of Christian writings to their scriptural status and eventually to their placement in a fixed collection or catalogue of Christian Scriptures.

When the NT writings were placed alongside the OT Scriptures and appealed to authoritatively in the life and worship of the early church, they *functioned* as Scripture in the church even if they were not yet called Scripture. Metzger comments that when the apostolic writings began to be translated into Syriac, Latin, and Coptic in the second and third centuries, this was done for the purpose of using them in public worship. This, of course, is one of the primary functions of sacred Scripture.[12] As Christian writings began to be used in worship in the Christian communities, they also began to take on a Scripture-like status, even

---

[10]   Ibid., 41.

[11]   See A. G. Patzia, "Canon," in *Dictionary of Paul and his Letters*, ed. G. F. Hawthorne and R. P. Martin (Downers Grove, IL: InterVarsity, 1993), 87–89.

[12]   Metzger, *Canon of the New Testament*, 6–7.

if they were not yet so acknowledged until later in the second century by several church fathers. This function occurred, as one would expect, earlier than the time when the term Scripture was actually employed to identify the Christian writings. Do the numerous references, citations, quotations, and allusions to the NT writings in the Apostolic Fathers at the end of the first and in the first half of the second century mean that the NT writings were considered Scripture? More specifically, we can ask when the NT writings were actually called "Scripture" (ἡ γραφή) and introduced with the usual scriptural designations such as "the Scripture says" (ἡ γραφή λέγει), "it is written" (γέγραπται), "that which is written" (τό γεγράμμενον), or any comparable formulas regularly used in reference to the OT Scriptures.[13] Scholars of the second century CE do not agree on *when* such designations were applied to NT writings, but certainly the words of Jesus had a Scripture-like status from the very beginning of the church (e.g., 1 Cor 7:10, 12, 17, 25; 1 Thess 4:15; Matt 28:18). It is not overstating the case to say for the church that "if Jesus said it, that settled the matter." He was, after all, the Lord of the church, and his words from the beginning of the church would have had significant authority attached to them, indeed, a scripture-like authority as we have already seen.

Clement of Rome acknowledges the authority of the teaching of Jesus for the church as follows:

> And so we should be humble-minded, brothers, laying aside all arrogance, conceit, foolishness, and forms of anger; and we should act *in accordance with what is written. For the Holy Spirit says*, "The one who is wise should not boast about his wisdom, nor the one who is strong about his strength, nor the one who is wealthy about his wealth; instead, the one who boasts should boast about the Lord, seeking after him and doing what is just and right." *We should especially remember the words the Lord Jesus spoke* when teaching about gentleness and patience. For he said: "Show mercy, that you may be shown mercy; forgive, that it may be forgiven you. As you do, so it will be done to you; as you give, so it will be given to you; as you judge, so you will be judged; as you show kindness, so will kindness be shown to you; the amount you dispense will be the amount your receive." Let us strengthen one another in this commandment and these demands, so that we may forge ahead, obedient to his words (which are well-suited for holiness) and humble-minded. For the holy word says, "Upon whom will I look, but upon the one who is meek and mild and who trembles at my sayings." (*1 Clem.* 13.1–4, LCL, emphasis added)

---

[13] For a helpful listing and discussion of these formulas, see B. M. Metzger, "Formulas Introducing Quotations of Scripture in the New Testament and in the Mishnah," in *Historical and Literary Studies: Pagan, Jewish, and Christian*, ed. B. M. Metzger, NTTS 8 (Leiden: Brill, 1968), 52–63. See also a careful assessment of these designations in Kenneth M. Penner, "Citation Formulae as Indices to Canonicity in Early Jewish and Early Christian Literature," in McDonald and Charlesworth, eds., *Jewish and Christian Scriptures*, 62–84. However, the use of the citation formulae alone does not determine the scriptural status of all books that may have had that status, as we saw in the NT's use of OT writings without these designations. They do, however, point in the direction of the acceptance of some NT writings as sacred Scripture.

And again,

> Why do we divide and tear asunder the members of Christ, and raise up strife against our own body, and reach such a pitch of madness as to forget that we are members one of another? *Remember the words of the Lord Jesus*; for he said, "Woe unto that man: it were good for him if he had not been born, than that he should offend one of my elect." (*1 Clem.* 46.7–8, LCL, emphasis added)

Clement's appeals for order are based on the warning of Jesus, which he introduces with "remember[ing] the words of the Lord Jesus." Metzger notes, however, that these are the only two direct references to the words of Jesus in *1 Clement*, compared with over one hundred references to the OT Scriptures.[14] Clement was also aware of Paul's Epistles and Hebrews, and he refers to them throughout his letter, as we saw, but he does not call them Scripture.[15] Had Paul's letters been viewed as Scripture in the first century, as we saw earlier argued by Kruger,[16] it is remarkable that those who cite him in the late first and early second centuries do not call his writings Scripture.

In his well-known *Letter to Flora*, gnostic teacher Ptolemy (ca. 160) frequently referred to the "words of the Savior" (e.g., 3.5, 8; 4.1, 4; cf. 7.5, 10) as the authority for his instruction. Ptolemy's devotion to the teaching of Jesus may be seen in his explanation of the proper way to understand the Law of Moses and Ptolemy's reference to those who have misunderstood it:

> That is what happens to people who do not see what follows from the *words of the Saviour*. For a house or city divided against itself cannot stand, our Saviour declared. Furthermore the apostle says that the creation of the world was peculiar to Him and that all things were made through him, and apart from him nothing was made, refuting the flimsy wisdom of these liars; not the creation of a god who corrupts, but of a just God who hates evil. That is the opinion of heedless men who do not understand the cause of the providence of the Demiurge, who are blind not only in the eye of the soul but also in that of the body.
>
> How they have strayed from the truth is clear to you from what has been said. Two groups have gone astray each in their peculiar fashion, the one through ignorance of the God of justice, the other through ignorance of the Father of All, whom only he who alone knew him revealed at his coming. Now it remains for us who have been granted the knowledge of both of these, to explain the Law to you with accuracy, what its nature is and the one by whom it has been given, the Lawgiver, proving *our demonstrations from the words of our Saviour*, through which alone it is possible without error to travel toward the comprehension of reality.
>
> First one must learn that the whole Law which is contained in the Pentateuch of Moses has not been decreed by some one person, I mean by God alone; but there are also some commandments in it given by men; and that it is tripartite *the words of the Saviour teach us*. For one part is ascribed to God himself and his legislation; another is ascribed to Moses, not meaning that God

---

[14] Metzger, *Canon of the New Testament*, 41–42.

[15] Ibid.

[16] See Chapter 14 §II.

gave the law through him, but that Moses legislated starting from his own understanding; and the third is ascribed to the elders of the people, who are themselves found from the beginning introducing ordinances of their own. How this came about *you may learn from the words of the Saviour.* When the Saviour was talking somewhere to those arguing with him about divorce, which was allowed by the Law, he said to them, Moses because of the hardness of your hearts permitted a man to put away his wife; from the beginning it was not so. For God joined them together, and what God has joined, let not a man, he said, put asunder. Here he shows that the law of God is one thing – it forbids a woman to be divorced by her husband – and the law of Moses is another – it permits this bond to be sundered because of hardness of heart. So in this way Moses ordains a law contrary to God, for divorce is contrary to no divorce. (Stevenson, *New Eusebius*, 92–93, emphasis added)

For both Clement of Rome and Ptolemy, the words of Jesus undoubtedly functioned as sacred Scripture even though the specific scriptural formulas are not used in these passages.

In terms of the NT literature itself, citations of or allusions to the words of Jesus in the Gospels (mostly Matthew) and to a lesser extent the NT Epistles were common in the second century, but do these citations mean that the works in which the words of Jesus are found were also viewed as sacred Scripture? Some scholars draw that conclusion, but it is unlikely that it reflects the early stages of canon formation. The process I suggest reflects recognition – sometimes explicit, sometimes veiled – of the esteem and authority of this literature in the Christian community because they contained sayings of Jesus, though the Gospels did not themselves initially have a scriptural status. Von Campenhausen similarly adds an important qualification to this by drawing a distinction between the authoritative words or commands of Jesus and the Gospels that contain them: the words of Jesus were given prominence and recognition in the written and oral tradition and had a Scripture-like status in the church from the beginning, but this, he claims, did not extend to the whole Gospel itself.[17] Until the middle second century, generally speaking most churches gave no prominence either to specific authors of the Gospels or to the Gospels themselves *as written documents.*[18] Although the Gospels were likely intended at the outset to be used (or read) in the churches alongside the OT Scriptures, they did not claim exclusive authority, and as von Campenhausen concludes, "nor did they acquire it,"[19] at least not at first, as we see in the history of Gospel transmission.

---

[17] Von Campenhausen, *Formation of the Christian Bible*, 118–21.

[18] Ibid., 121. Papias' mention of Mark and Matthew is not an exception since he preferred the oral traditions circulating in the churches. While the Gospels, especially Matthew's Gospel, were widely used in conveying the Christian proclamation, they were not cited by author or by their specific writings until the middle to late second century.

[19] Ibid., 123.

III. SCRIPTURE-LIKE REFERENCES
TO NEW TESTAMENT WRITINGS

The following examples show the positive attitudes in second-century Christianity toward several NT writings. As we will see in these examples, progressively several NT writings are cited authoritatively in the second-century churches. By the end of that century there is little doubt that some NT writings are cited as sacred Christian Scripture.

1. *2 Clement* (ca. 120–140, but no later than 170). The pseudonymous and unknown author of *2 Clement*, referring to the "Scripture," concludes that "the books and the Apostles declare" the existence of the church. He writes:

> Now I imagine that you are not ignorant that the living "Church is the body of Christ." For the Scripture says, "God made man male and female"; the male is Christ, the female is the church. And moreover *the books and the Apostles declare* that the Church belongs not to the present, but has existed from the beginning; for she was spiritual, as was also our Jesus, but he was made manifest in the last days that he might save us. (*2 Clem.* 14.2, LCL, emphasis added)

It is most likely that the reference to the "the books" (τά βιβλία) is the Jewish Scriptures (cf. 2 Tim 4:13), and that "the Apostles" (οἱ ἀπόστολοι), according to von Campenhausen, is also likely a reference to the NT tradition common in the churches in both oral and written form.[20] It is possible that a parallel may well be found in one of the latest books included in the New Testament. The author of 2 Peter (ca. 135–150) writes: "…that you should remember the words spoken in the past by the holy prophets, and the commandment of the Lord and Savior spoken through your apostles" (3:2). If so, then this text in the second century is an indication that the NT tradition proclaimed by the apostles was placed in a parallel relationship to the church's First Scriptures since both are appealed to in an authoritative manner for support of the author's teaching about the preexistent church. The "apostles" appear at this early date to function as the "guarantors" of the NT tradition.[21]

---

[20] See Von Campenhausen, *Formation of the Christian Bible*, 62; W. R. Farmer and D. M. Farkasfalvy, *Formation of the New Testament Canon*, Introduction by A. C. Outler, ed. H. W. Attridge (New York: Paulist, 1983), 173 n. 97. It is possible but doubtful that *ta biblia* refers to the Gospels; see Koester, *Synoptische Überlieferung*, 76–78. While it may be possible, as some have suggested, that the Gospels are intended here in the reference to "the apostles," it is more likely a reference to the tradition in them or the tradition circulating in the churches. It is several decades later that we *begin* to see references to the Gospels themselves.

[21] So argues Koester, *Synoptische Überlieferung*, 68. He also suggests that "the Apostles" may be a reference to the "commandment of the Lord" handed down to the apostles (2 Pet 3:2).

The author of *2 Clement* quoting the words of Jesus in Mark 2:17 (or Matt 9:13) *as Scripture* writes: "And another Scripture [γραφή] also says, 'I came not to call righteous, but sinners'; He means that those who are perishing must be saved, for it is great and wonderful to give strength, not to the things which are standing, but to those which are falling" (*2 Clem.* 2.4–6, LCL). Here, as in 14.2, the words of Jesus, which had not yet found a universally acknowledged fixed form, were apparently recognized as on par with or possibly even superior to the authority of the OT Scriptures when supporting arguments for theological positions and moral behavior in the early church.[22] The tradition that was sacred was not so much the written Gospels in which the tradition was found, but rather the sacred tradition itself. Whatever Jesus said was equal to sacred Scripture from the beginning (see also 1 Tim 5:18). Before the end of the second century it was concluded that the words of Jesus *and the place* where they were located, viz. in the Gospels, were sacred Scripture.

2. *Epistle of Barnabas* (ca. 90–130). A theological treatise that Clement of Alexandria believed was written by the Apostle Barnabas, but was more likely produced by an Alexandrian Gentile Christian who was concerned about the death of Jesus as a sacrifice in the OT sense and clarifying what he thought were the true meanings of the Jewish Scriptures. The author introduces one of two Gospel quotations (Matt 22:14) in a scripture-like manner stating: "Let us take heed lest *as it is written* [ὡς γέγραπαι] we be found 'many called but few chosen'" (*Barn.* 4.14, LCL, emphasis added). This text suggests that the words of Jesus were equal in authority to the OT – that is, the words of Jesus, when written down, became Scripture. Kümmel goes a step further and says that this text is evidence that an individual Gospel writing – the whole *text* itself – was beginning to be valued as equal in authority to the OT Scriptures.[23] More proof from antiquity is necessary, however, before accepting such a claim, but this was a bold step by the author of this ancient writing and when such statements are made, the notion of sacred Scripture is either present or not far away.

3. Ignatius (ca. 110–115). In an often-quoted passage from his *Letter to the Philadelphians*, Ignatius showed his preference for the gospel, which is probably the kerygma or preaching about Jesus that was current in the oral traditions of the church. Remarkably, he appears to prefer its authority even over the authority of the OT Scriptures:

> But I urge you to do nothing in a contemptuous way, but in accordance with what you have learned in Christ. For I heard some saying "If I do not find it in the ancient records,[24] I do not

---

[22] Kümmel, *Introduction to the New Testament*, 340.
[23] Ibid.
[24] Ehrman translates the Greek ἐν τοῖς ἀρχείοις as "in the ancient records." An earlier edition of the LCL translated it "charters," and most scholars consider the term to be a reference to the Jewish

believe in the gospel." And when I said to them, "It is written," they replied to me, "That is just the question." But for me, Jesus Christ is the ancient records: the sacred ancient records are his cross and death, and his resurrection, and the faith that comes through him – by which things I long to be made righteous by your prayer. (Ign. *Phld.* 8.2, LCL)

The reference to "charters" or "ancient records" likely refer to the church's OT Scriptures, and in this text it is also clear that Ignatius gave priority to the Gospel traditions about Jesus' death and resurrection over the earlier Scriptures. The Gospel, for him, was not necessarily a book, though he was doubtless familiar with the Gospel of Matthew circulating in the churches at that time. He was not speaking specifically about a particular gospel text, but rather the tradition about Jesus circulating in the churches. Ignatius was also familiar with the Gospel of John and, as we saw above, several of Paul's letters,[25] and his threefold locus of authority included Jesus, the Apostles, and Prophets (OT Scriptures), and probably in the order of priority. The Apostles appears to be for him the proclaimed Gospel, not simply one of the canonical Gospels. Of the three – Jesus, the apostles, and the prophets – he clearly gave priority to Jesus. In another place he explains:

Brethren, I am overflowing with love to you, and exceedingly joyful in watching over your safety. Yet not I, but Jesus Christ, whose bonds I bear, but am the more fearful in that I am not yet perfected; but your prayer will make me perfect for God, that I may attain the lot wherein I found mercy, making the Gospel *my refuge as the flesh of Jesus*, and *the Apostles as the presbytery of the Church*. And *the prophets also do we love, because they also have announced the Gospel*, and are hoping in him and waiting for him, by faith in whom they also obtain salvation, being united with Jesus Christ, for they are worthy of love and saints worthy of admiration, approved by Jesus Christ, and numbered together in the Gospel of the common hope. (Ign. *Phld.* 5.1–2, LCL, emphasis added)

4. Polycarp (ca. 140–155). In his *Letter to the Philippians*, Polycarp cites Ps 4:4 and Eph 4:26 and calls them both Scripture:[26]

For I am confident that you are well versed *in the sacred Scriptures [in sacris literis]*, and that nothing is hidden from you; but to me this has not been granted. Only, as it is said *in these Scriptures [modo, ut his scripturis dictum est]*, "*Be ye angry and do not sin, and do not let the sun go down on your anger.*" How fortunate is the one who remembers this; and I believe this to be the case among you. (Pol. *Phil.* 12.1, LCL, emphasis added)

Scriptures, namely the church's OT Scriptures. Metzger, *Canon of the New Testament*, 48, translates this term "archives."

[25] See Metzger, *Canon of the New Testament*, 43–49, for a helpful summary of Ignatius's familiarity with some of the NT literature, which includes probably the Gospels of Matthew and John and several letters of Paul. Although Ignatius did not call this literature Scripture, the obvious parallels noted by Metzger (and listed above) show Ignatius' knowledge and acceptance of them as documents that express for him the proper Christian attitudes and conduct and also reflect his appeal to them in a Scripture-like fashion.

[26] Since the original Greek text for this passage is missing and is supplied in Latin, an argument could be made for a late dating of this reference, though that is generally considered unlikely.

Polycarp consciously appears to have placed an OT Scripture and a Christian writing (Eph 4:26; cf. Ps 4:4 LXX) on an equal authoritative footing and in the same sentence. This is, of course, similar to 1 Tim 5:18 that does the same. The least one could say about this conjunction is that an authoritative appeal to these texts promises that persons following their advice will be blessed – and this is certainly equivalent to or a close description of inspired Scripture. Polycarp also recognizes the authority of Jesus' teaching in the Sermon on the Mount and admonishes his hearers to obey and imitate Jesus' examples. For example:

> Now "he who raised him" from the dead "will also raise us up" [2 Cor 4:14] if we do his will, and walk in his commandments and love the things which he loved, refraining from all unrighteousness, covetousness, love of money, evil speaking, false witness, "rendering not evil for evil, or railing for railing," or blow for blow [1 Pet 3:9], or curse for curse, but *remembering what the Lord taught* when he said, "Judge not that ye be not judged, forgive and it shall be forgiven unto you, be merciful that ye may obtain mercy, with what measure ye mete, it shall be measured to you again," [Matt 7:1–2] and, "Blessed are the poor, and they who are persecuted for righteousness' sake, for theirs is the Kingdom of God [Luke 6:20; Matt 5:20]." (Pol. *Phil.* 2.2–3, LCL, emphasis added)

It appears that the words of Jesus, the words of John, and Paul all had a scripture-like authority in the early Christian communities where Polycarp was ministering:

> For everyone who does not confess that Jesus Christ has come in the flesh is an anti-Christ [1 John 4:2]; and whosoever does not confess the testimony of the Cross is of the devil: and whosoever perverts the oracles of the Lord for his own lusts, and says that there is neither resurrection nor judgment – this man is the first-born of Satan. Wherefore, leaving the foolishness of the crowd, and their false teaching, let us turn back to the word which was delivered to us in the beginning, "watching unto prayer" and persevering in fasting, beseeching the all-seeing God in our supplications "to lead us not into temptation," even as the Lord said, "The spirit is willing, but the flesh is weak." (Pol. *Phil.* 7.1–2, LCL)

For Polycarp, Jesus serves as the rule or guide for the Christian community. He explains: "Let us then be imitators of his endurance, and if we suffer for his name's sake let us glorify him. For this is the example which he gave us in himself, and this is what we have believed [cf. 1 Pet 2:21]" (Pol. *Phil.* 8.2, LCL).

Like Ignatius, Polycarp gives evidence of a threefold locus of authority in the church: "So then 'let us serve him with fear and all reverence,' *as he himself commanded us*, and *as did the Apostles*, who brought us the Gospel, and the *Prophets who foretold the coming of our Lord*" (Pol. *Phil.* 6.3, LCL, emphasis added). What is abundantly clear from these examples is that Jesus himself was the authoritative canon of the church for Polycarp. The words of Jesus, when written down, take on the function of Scripture, even if they were not specifically called Scripture. But Polycarp also emphasized the Apostles and the Prophets. The "Apostles" here is not a reference to specific writings so much as the tradition about Jesus handed down from the apostolic community. The "Prophets" are clearly the church's First Scriptures, what they later called their OT Scriptures.

This tripartite locus of authority (Jesus, the Apostles, and the Prophets – notice the order) is characteristic of authority in churches in second-century Christianity.

5. 2 Peter (ca. 110 at the earliest and possibly as late as 140–150). The pseudon-ymous author of 2 Peter writing in Peter's name[27] refers in his concluding comments to Paul's writings being twisted by "ignorant and unstable" people "as they do *the other Scriptures*" (*hōs kai tas loipas graphas*) (3:15–16). This author apparently places Paul's letters on an equal footing with the OT Scriptures at that time. He is also aware of the heretical use of Paul's Letters that is possibly a veiled reference to Marcion or the gnostics.

6. Ptolemy (ca. 160). In his *Letter to Flora*, Ptolemy, a well-known gnostic writer, seeks to define the integrity of the Jewish Scriptures (3.6) and establish their correct interpretation. The author appeals throughout to the words of the Savior (3.5, 8; 4.1, 4; 5.10), including the teachings of Jesus (7.9), as his primary authority. He also cites John 1:3 with the words "the apostle says" (3:6) much as one would quote Scripture. Along with the properly interpreted Jewish Scriptures (OT), Ptolemy completes his threefold authority with the words of the Savior and the Apostles (at least John and probably Matthew), but, as we saw above, giving priority to the words of the Savior. The following is a portion of the text cited above:

> First one must learn that the whole Law which is contained in the Pentateuch of Moses has not been decreed by some one person, I mean by God alone; but there are also some command-ments in it given by men; and that it is tripartite *the words of the Saviour teach us*. For one part is ascribed to God himself and his legislation; another is ascribed to Moses, not meaning that God gave the law through him, but that Moses legislated starting from his own understanding;

---

[27]   The dating of 2 Peter is problematic. It is common for scholars to date all NT writings to the end of the first century if they cannot otherwise link them to the lives of the persons in whose names they were published. Most standard NT introductions date the book somewhere in the second century. 2 Peter likely condemns the gnostic interpretation of the Scriptures (2:4–10). I have revised my earlier view that 2 Peter could have been written as late as 180, and now agree with many others that it likely dates to approximately 135–150 at the latest. Since the author of *Apocalypse of Peter* (ca. 135–150) made use of 2 Peter for telling its story of the Transfiguration, it is likely that 2 Peter should have an earlier date than the one I proposed earlier based on what I considered early citations of the book. It is also possible, as we will see below, that the author of 2 Peter made use of the *Apocalypse of Peter* instead of the other way around. For a discussion of possible dates of *Apoc. Pet.* that cites 2 Peter, see Elliott, ed., *Apocryphal New Testament*, 593–95. Since 2 Peter is quite different in style and content from 1 Peter and depends heavily on Jude, it is not likely from the same author of 1 Peter, nor is it a first-century document. Athanasius (367) concluded that the Apostle Peter wrote it and subsequently included it in his NT canon, and it appears in several NT catalogues thereafter, but was in doubtful places or rejected in several other catalogues (see Appendix C). For a discussion of the dating of 2 Peter, see also Pearson, "James, 1–2 Peter, Jude," in *The New Testament and Its Modern Interpreters*, ed. E. J. Epp and G. W. MacRae, SBL: The Bible and Its Modern Interpreters 3 (Philadelphia: Fortress; Atlanta: Scholars Press, 1989), 382–85; and Koester, *Introduction to the New Testament*, 2:298–300.

and the third is ascribed to the elders of the people, who are themselves found from the beginning introducing ordinances of their own. How this came about you may learn *from the words of the Saviour*. (Stevenson, *New Eusebius*, 92, emphasis added)

Although Jesus is clearly his primary authority, Ptolemy also cites the apostle Paul as one would cite Scripture:

The *disciples of the Savior and the apostle Paul* showed that this theory is true, speaking of the part dealing with images, as we have already said, in mentioning "the Passover for us" and the "unleavened bread"; of the law interwoven with injustice when he says that "the law of commandments in ordinances was destroyed" [Eph 2:15]; and of that not mixed with anything inferior when he says that "the law is holy, and the commandment is holy and just and good" [Rom 7:12]. (Barnstone, *Other Bible*, 624, emphasis added)

These references are especially meaningful since Ptolemy comes from outside the mainstream of early proto-orthodox Christianity.

7. Martyrs of Lyons and Vienne in Gaul, now France (ca. 175–177). Eusebius mentions a letter that contains references, allusions, and quotations from both the NT and noncanonical literature (*Hist. eccl.* 5.1). In the *Acts of Martyrs* compiled by Eusebius, he shares letters telling the story of the church's martyrs. After telling the heroic story of Blandina's martyrdom and the cruelty of those who tortured her at the direction of Marcus Aurelius (ca. 177 CE) carried out by a local governor's hatred and cruelty toward Christians, the relevant part of the letter reads:

…and the governor and the people showed the like unrighteous hatred against us *that the Scripture* (ἡ γραφὴ) *might be fulfilled*, "Let him that is unlawful be unlawful still, and he that is righteous be righteous still." For those who had been strangled in the jail they threw to the dogs… (*Hist. eccl.* 5.1.58, LCL, emphasis added)

This text cites Rev 22:11 *as Scripture* and shows not only the high regard for the book of Revelation in the Western churches, but it is one of the earliest known references to the book as "Scripture." It is possible that this reference to "Scripture" was provided by Eusebius himself to clarify what he thought was intended by the writing he was quoting, which appears to be a common practice of Eusebius. As it stands, if the quote is authentic, it is the earliest reference to a text from Revelation acknowledged as Scripture.

8. Tatian (ca. 160–170). Tatian obviously did not consider the four canonical Gospels as inviolable Scripture, though he clearly saw their great value for the church, and likely even considered them Scripture since, as he knew from his mentor Justin that they were read in the churches in their worship services (*1 Apol.* 64–67). His harmony of the four Gospels made possible a text that eliminated the many differences between them and identified what he thought was

the one true Gospel. Tatian made many changes in the Gospel texts to produce his harmonization that functioned as Scripture in the Syrian churches up through the fifth century and in some other churches for much longer. His creation of the church's first known harmony of the four Evangelists – perhaps including other gospel traditions as well – into one account was known as the *Diatessaron* (= "Through Four," also known as the "*Gospel of the Mixed*"). According to Eusebius:

> Their former leader Tatian composed in some way a combination and collection of the gospels, and gave this the name of *The Diatessaron*, and this is still extant in some places. And they say that *he ventured to paraphrase some words of the apostles, as though correcting their style*. He has left a great number of writings, of which the most famous, quoted by many, is his discourse *Against the Greeks*. In it he deals with primitive history, and shows that Moses and the prophets of the Hebrews preceded all those who are celebrated among the Greeks. This seems to be the best and most helpful of all his writings. Such are the facts of this period. (*Hist. eccl.* 4.29.6–7, LCL, emphasis added)

Tatian's willingness to change or correct the four canonical Gospels is important to us in many regards, not the least of which is his perception about their sacred status. Although he valued them sufficiently that they served as his primary sources for compiling his *Diatessaron*, he was willing to change them, often significantly, in order to produce a unified or harmonized text. Eusebius indicates that Tatian also "ventured to paraphrase some words of the apostle," which is probably a reference to the Apostle Paul. While Tatian attributed high and perhaps scriptural value to the Gospels, he apparently did not view their texts as *inviolable* Scripture (Deut 4:2; Rev 22:18–19).

9. Athenagoras (ca. 180). Athenagoras, the late second-century church teacher, made considerable use of Paul's writings alongside the Gospels in a manner that shows that he had accepted them as normative Christian Scripture for the church. One example of his use of Paul illustrates this point. Citing 1 Cor 15:54, he says:

> The result of all of this is very plain to everyone – namely, that, in the language of the apostle [*kata ton apostolon*], "This corruptible (and dissoluble) must put on incorruption, in order that those who were dead…may, in accordance with justice, receive what he has done by the body, whether it be good or bad." (*Resurrection of the Dead* 18, ANF)

10. Theophilus of Antioch (ca. 190–200). This late second-century proto-orthodox teacher reflects dependence upon the writings of Paul and cites Rom 2:7–9 and 1 Cor 2:9 (cf. Isa 64:4) as "prophetic Scriptures." By his time there is little question about the scriptural status of several of Paul's writings in the church at Antioch and probably in many churches in other parts of the Roman Empire. Theophilus writes:

> But you also, please give reverential attention to *the prophetic Scriptures*, for they will make it plain to you how to escape the eternal punishments and obtain the eternal prizes of God. For He who gave the mouth for speech, and formed the ear to hear and made the eye to see will examine all things and will judge [with] righteous judgment. [He will also] render merited awards for those who seek immortality, and He will give life everlasting, joy, peace, rest, and abundance of good things, which *neither has the eye seen nor ear heard nor has it entered into the heart of man to conceive*. But to the unbelieving and despisers, who do not obey the truth but are obedient to adulteries and fornications, and filthiness, and covetousness, and unlawful idolatries, there shall be anger and wrath, tribulation and anguish, and at the last an everlasting fire shall possess them. (*Autol.* 1.14, adapted from ANF, emphasis added)

11. Summary. The significance of these selected references is that they show a growing tendency on the part of the second-century church fathers or teachers to transfer the recognized authority of the teaching of Jesus found in the Gospels to the documents themselves, including a scriptural authority, and also recognizing such authority in the Letters of Paul. This move toward the recognition of the authority of the church's written texts is seen most clearly in the writings of Justin who places the Gospels alongside of the "prophets," and after him with increasing frequency and clarity in the writings of Irenaeus, Theophilus of Antioch, and Athenagoras. While we cannot conclude from all of these references that they reflect the views of the whole church at that time, they are indicative of the growing appreciation of Christian writings as sacred Scripture. Initially, it appears that words of Jesus that are in the written Gospels are cited in a scriptural manner, but the Gospels themselves are not in view so much as the authority of Jesus. That begins to transfer to the written texts themselves by around 150–160.

By 200, an imprecise collection of Christian writings, which had as its core one or more canonical Gospels and several of the writings of Paul, had achieved for *some* Christians the status of Scripture. Subsequently other writings were added to this list as recognized Scriptures, but the churches were not in broad agreement on which books functioned as sacred Scripture until the end of the third to the middle of the fourth century. Recognizing Christian Scriptures was not a universal practice at the end of the second century, but as the churches were dealing with second century "heresies" (Marcion, gnostics, and Montanists), several church fathers such as Irenaeus, Athenagoras, Hippolytus, Tertullian, and others often referred to the writings produced by those in the apostolic community as aids for dealing with those issues. As we saw in Justin, some of those writings were also read in church worship services.

There was by no means a closed canon of NT writings at that time, though for Irenaeus the four canonical Gospels, and those gospels alone, had obtained scriptural status in the churches and no more gospel writings could be added to that collection. He was aware that other Christians not only read the four canonical Gospels in their churches, but other writings as well, including, for example, the *Gospel of Truth*. He refers to them with biting criticism (*Haer.* 3.11.9). The authority of Jesus was nevertheless the most important authority in the church from its beginning, but a growing recognition of the value and authority of several NT writings took place throughout the late first and second century. By the end of the second century it was not uncommon to refer to several NT writings as Scripture. Even though Jesus' surviving teachings were located almost exclusively in the written canonical Gospels, with a few notable exceptions such as in quotes circulating among the church fathers and in some manuscripts of the NT writings (the *agrapha* discussed below in §IV), until the middle of the second century the references were to the words of Jesus, not where they were found. The authoritative Scriptures for the church at that time were a collection of Jewish Scriptures that were now being called the church's OT Scriptures and the first listing of those Scriptures comes from Melito (ca. 170) mentioned earlier. Generally, the churches' primary authorities were the words of Jesus, the apostolic traditions about him, and the OT Scriptures. A case could be made that by the end of the second century, many, if not most, of the churches had begun to recognize as Scripture the canonical Gospels, most of the writings attributed to Paul, Acts, and also 1 Peter and 1 John. Other NT writings were circulating in the churches and gaining appreciation in various churches. For some churches, especially in the west, the book of Revelation was also gaining considerable recognition as a scriptural book.

Several important questions arise from the foregoing study, especially why literature that had not possessed a scriptural status in the first century had taken on that distinction in the churches by the end of the second century. Interestingly, several NT writings were generally cited more frequently in the second century than the church's OT Scriptures. This should not be surprising since the words of Jesus and his model appear to have taken highest priority in the church over other authorities and most of Jesus' words and actions cited were from the canonical Gospels.

This is somewhat parallel to the growth of the OT canon in Judaism. During the reforms of Josiah, the law (Deuteronomy most likely) had a scriptural-like importance for the Jews, though other writings such as the Royal Psalms and some of the prophetic literature (Former Prophets and Amos and Hosea) had some influence in Israel earlier, but they are not referred to as often as the Law. After the time of Ezra, the Law of Moses (Pentateuch) had the highest priority among the Jews and was cited far more frequently than all other prophetic texts. Although the Former Prophets and some of the Latter Prophets had some authority among the post-exilic Jews, that recognition was not comparable to the attention given to the Law (Torah). When many of the religious leaders believed that the prophetic presence had ceased in Israel, there was a tendency to "inscripturate" the writings from an earlier time when the prophetic presence of the Lord was believed to have resided in Israel. By no later than 200 BCE, several of the Former and Latter Prophets also obtained an important scriptural position among the Jews, though never more important than the Law.

This is somewhat paralleled in early Christianity. In the second century, the Gospels were increasingly valued and frequently cited by the church fathers because of their witness to the story of Jesus. The letters of Paul were also highly prized because of their theological and also practical value for the churches. By the middle of the second century there was a growing distinction between writings from the apostolic period and those that were not. After that, priority was given to Christian writings from the apostolic community and writings from that era were moving toward scriptural status. At the same time, pseudonymous writings in the names of apostolic figures were produced that aimed at acquiring the status of writings from the apostolic period.

In the second century there are examples of a time when churches apparently ceased recognizing the gift of prophecy, perhaps because of abuses of wandering charismatics who had abused their roles in the churches.[28] Although never clearly stated, it appears that in practice the age of prophecy largely, but not completely ceased in churches, and the offices of bishop and teacher had taken on increased authority in the churches with consequent diminishing roles for prophets. This absence appears to have given rise to the Montanist movement with its emphasis on the role of the Spirit and new prophecies. As we will see below (Chapter 18 §IV), this movement had a short life, but was quite influential in the last third of the second century and it even attracted the notable North African teacher, Tertullian. At any rate, probably because of the abuse of prophetic activity in the churches, prominence was given to the teachers in the churches and to the more stable bishop and presbyter offices, and also to the earlier Christian scriptures.

Chronological distance from the primary events that called the church into existence no doubt played some role in the recognition of the value of the written testimony of the apostolic community that inevitably took priority over the oral-memory transmission of the Christian proclamation. As the earliest voices and those who heard them were no longer around, it was logical that written texts would take priority in the churches providing important checks on the ever-expanding oral traditions. In this case, the Gospels took priority in the early churches, followed by the letters of Paul and subsequently other Christian writings. The further removed the church was from the eyewitnesses of the primary events in the church's confession of faith, it appears that the early Christian writings from that period became more venerated in the churches. It is likely that the Gospels had a widespread reception in churches almost from the time of their production, but the inclusion of apostolic names on them by the latter part of the second century illustrates the importance the churches were placing on writings from the apostolic period.

---

[28] Lucian, the well-known second-century satirist, wrote a scathing reflection of these Christian prophetic figures in his *The Passing of Peregrinus* who were known for taking money from Christians and for their luxurious and fanciful living.

The second-century sources listed above reflect the transition in the churches toward the recognition of NT writings as their sacred Scripture, but this calls for three important cautions. First, acknowledgment of the authority and scriptural status of one part of the NT at this time does not imply that all parts of it were so recognized. Second, although the NT writings (especially the Gospels and Paul) are frequently used in worship and catechetical teaching throughout the second century, they are not *generally* called Scripture until the latter part of that century and even later for other NT writings. The early examples listed above are exceptional and not the model found in all second-century churches. They do, however, provide early examples of the recognition of Christian writings and their use in a scriptural manner beginning in the middle of the second century. Third, even if some of the NT writings were recognized as having the status of Scripture in the second century, this is not the same as a closed biblical canon of NT Scriptures. The *Epistle of Barnabas* and *Shepherd of Hermas* were quite popular not only in the second century but also well into the fourth century and were occasionally cited as Scripture, but eventually that recognition ceased. What is clear is that with the recognition of the authority of certain Christian writings as Scripture in some churches, the canonical processes were well under way in the second century.

IV. AFTER THE SECOND CENTURY, WHAT THEN?

As we saw, in the second century, several church fathers made regular use of the canonical Gospels in worship, teaching, and in apologetic writings, but mostly they cited the words of Jesus that were in the Gospels, not the Gospels themselves. In addition they often cited several other sources, including some of the noncanonical gospels written in apostolic names that were later excluded from the churches' sacred collections. Long ago, Gould noted that the second-century church fathers cited extra-canonical sources "freely and without apology."[29] As we will see, this was especially true of Clement of Alexandria, and other church fathers as well. We have already observed the widespread acceptance of *1 Enoch* as Scripture, but also the *Epistle of Barnabas* and the *Shepherd of Hermas* as late as the fourth century (Codex Sinaiticus). See also Chapter 9 §V above for a discussion of noncanonical writings in the early church fathers.

Regardless of this, the image of Jesus in the majority of churches was not significantly changed despite the more sensational apocryphal gospels circulating mostly in the second and third centuries. Gould concluded from this: "the historicity [of the story of Jesus] is more triumphantly established by the corroborative

---

[29]   E. P. Gould, *A Critical and Exegetical Commentary on the Gospel According to St. Mark*, ICC (Edinburgh: T. &. T. Clark, 1896), xxxiii–xxxiv, who cites multiple examples of the use of the noncanonical sources in the early church fathers (xxxiv–xl).

testimony than by the absence of other witnesses."[30] Nevertheless, the first and second centuries were foundational for the acceptance of the canonical Gospels and writings of Paul as authoritative writings that became the early Christian Scriptures in the church. These writings reached the status of Scripture for many Christians in the latter half of the second century and eventually became the bedrock scriptural authority in most churches in the third and fourth centuries. Even so, as we have already seen, some early churches also received in a Scripture-like manner other writings that were eventually excluded from the NT canon.[31]

Even in the fourth century, when the four canonical Gospels were widely acknowledged in the majority of churches, we cannot say that in the second century only the four canonical Gospels and no others had received this recognition and acceptance in the churches. Numerous pseudonymous noncanonical gospels, acts, and letters continued to be read in several churches. As we will see below, the *Gospel of Peter* was read in some churches a generation after Irenaeus had declared that only the four canonical Gospels could be read in the churches. Also, the *Protoevangelium of James* had considerable influence in the fourth and fifth centuries and significantly affected the results of the Council of Ephesus in 431, which found support in this apocryphal gospel for its conclusion that Mary was the "mother of God," the *Theotokos* ("God-bearer"). Following this, the *Infancy Gospel of James* exerted considerable influence on Christian art and piety, and, as Mary was venerated, groups within the churches turned to it for inspiration and guidance.[32]

Other noncanonical gospels filled various voids in the NT texts, such as details about Jesus' birth, childhood, and family members, and even additional information about his resurrection and ascension. In other genres, the pseudonymous *Letter to the Laodiceans* was produced under Paul's name (see Col 4:16). The *Acts of Paul and Thecla* describes Paul's appearance and ministry in Iconium, although its focus is on a young woman named Thecla who converted to Christianity and became a remarkable witness for her faith. The early church seemed anxious to leave nothing to the imagination, and in the second and third centuries Christians produced many pseudonymous or apocryphal writings to fill the voids in the NT writings or to add their own spin on earlier Christian traditions circulating in the churches. Attaching an apostle's name to that literature helped it gain acceptance in some churches and the attribution of apostolic authorship added credibility to the churches' emerging collection of Christian writings.

As noted above, many sayings of Jesus circulating in the early churches were not included in any of the canonical Gospels. The so-called *agrapha*, that is, sayings

---

[30] Ibid., xxxiv–xl.

[31] Ibid., xxxiv–xlii.

[32] See R. F. Hock, "The Favored One: How Mary Became the Mother of God," *Bible Review* 17, no. 3 (2001): 13–25; and V. Limberis, "The Battle Over Mary," *Bible Review* 17, no. 3 (2001): 22–23.

of Jesus not found in the canonical Gospels, functioned in an authoritative manner in the churches that received them and passed them on to other Christians. These sayings, as noted earlier, are found in noncanonical literature (such as the *Gospel of Thomas* and *Gospel of Peter*), in writings of the early church fathers, and in several NT manuscripts. This collection now includes some 266 sayings of Jesus, but more may be tucked away in new discoveries of Christian manuscripts that are yet to be catalogued in libraries and museums in Europe.[33] Jeremias believes that only eighteen of these Jesus sayings are authentic, while Hofius claims that only nine of the *agrapha* need to be taken seriously, and of these only four are probably authentic to Jesus.[34] Here is the list of Hofius' nine probable sayings (the four most likely authentic *agrapha* are marked by an asterisk):

1. "As you are found, so will you be led away [to judgment]." (*Syriac Liber Graduum*, Sermon 3.3; 15.4)
2. "Ask for the great things, and God will add to you what is small." (Clement of Alexandria, *Strom.* 1.24.158)
3. "Be competent [approved] money-changers!" (*Pseudo-Clementine Homilies* 2.51.1; 3.50.2; 18.20.4)
*4. "On the same day he [Jesus] saw a man working on the sabbath. He said to him: 'Man, if you know what you are doing, you are blessed; but if you do not know, you are accursed and a transgressor of the law'" (Luke 6:5 Codex Bezae [D])
*5. "He who is near me is near the fire; he who is far from me is far from the kingdom." (*Gospel of Thomas* 82; Origen, *Homilies on Jeremiah* [Latin] 3.3; Didymus, *Commentary on Psalms* 88.8)
*6. "(He who today) stands far off will tomorrow be (near to you)." (Papyrus Oxyrhynchus 1224)
*7. "And only then shall you be glad, when you look on your brother with love." (*Gospel of the Hebrews* 5, preserved in Jerome, *Commentary on Ephesians* 5.4 [on Eph 5:4])
8. "The kingdom is like a wise fisherman who cast his net into the sea; he drew it up from the sea full of small fish; among them he found a large (and) good fish; that wise fisherman threw all the small fish down into the sea; he chose the large fish without regret." (*Gospel of Thomas* 8)

---

[33] For details, see Stroker, *Extracanonical Sayings of Jesus*; O. Hofius, "Unknown Sayings of Jesus," in *The Gospel and the Gospels*, ed. P. Stuhlmacher (Grand Rapids: Eerdmans, 1991), 336–60; idem, "Isolated Sayings of Jesus"; Theron, *Evidence of Tradition*, 96–99; Charlesworth and Evans, "Jesus in the Agrapha and Apocryphal Gospels"; W. Morrice, *Hidden Sayings of Jesus: Words Attributed to Jesus Outside the Four Gospels* (Peabody, MA: Hendrickson, 1997); and Jeremias, *Unknown Sayings of Jesus*.

[34] Jeremias, *Unknown Sayings of Jesus*, 42–43; Hofius, "Unknown Sayings of Jesus."

9. "How is it then with you? For you are here in the temple. Are you then clean?... Woe to you blind who see not! You have washed yourself in water that is poured forth, in which dogs and swine lie night and day, and washed and scoured your outer skin, which harlots and flute girls also anoint, bathe, scour, and beautify to arouse desire in men, but inwardly they are filled with scorpions and with [all manner of ev]il. But I and [my disciples], of whom you say that we have not [bathed, have bath]ed ourselves in the liv[ing and clean] water, which comes down from [the father in heaven]." (P.Oxy. 840.2)

These extracanonical sayings of Jesus no doubt functioned as canon 1, that is, as a sacred authority, in the communities in which they were discovered and received, though they never became a part of the fixed canonical collections (canon 2) in the developing Christian communities.

The question today is not so much whether authentic sayings of Jesus may be found here or there in noncanonical sources, but rather what to do with them. More specifically, if any of them are authentic, should they be added to the canonical Scriptures of the Christian community if it can be reasonably demonstrated that they are authentic sayings of Jesus? Should they inform the theology of the church or be read in churches today, as was likely true of them in ancient times? Should they form a part of the authoritative base for constructing the church's teachings or the identity of Jesus? Do they provide an independent tradition or source for scholars to reconstruct the life and teaching of Jesus? There is no agreement among scholars on these questions, but they do acknowledge that some authentic sayings of Jesus likely exist in the noncanonical sources. They do not agree on which *agrapha* are authentic, but a growing number of scholars agree that they should be included among the resources for historical-Jesus research. This also raises important questions relevant for understanding the formation of the biblical canon.

V. CONCLUSION

The above comments bring us back to our starting point, namely, that all writings of the NT and early Christianity derive their authority from the church's one true authority, Jesus the Christ and Lord of the church. All early Christian writings, which were believed to convey faithfully the story of Jesus and his significance for faith, were believed to be a derived authority from Jesus himself and were welcomed in the early church and utilized in its life and mission. Many of them were eventually included in the church's second collection of Scriptures, the New Testament. We have observed that the early Christians cited the NT writings differently after the middle of the second century than before. It was about that same time when these writings began to be called Scripture in its traditional sense.[35] When there was doubt about whether a writing faithfully told the story and significance of Jesus the Christ, various criteria were employed to discern the matter. The first criterion employed by the early churches was the coherence of the writing with what was already commonly received in the churches, that is the church's sacred traditions that had been handed on in the churches from their beginning and formed the core of what later was called "orthodoxy." Soon after that, apostolic authorship (e.g., Paul, John, etc.) or writings from the early apostolic community (Mark and Luke) became standards for determining the credibility and authority of a written document. By the fourth century, other criteria (e.g., antiquity and use or catholicity) were also employed by the church to decide the question of inclusion in the church's recognized Scriptures (see Chapter 22). In the transition of Christian writings from acknowledged authorities to sacred Scriptures, Justin, Irenaeus, Origen, Eusebius, and later key church leaders (Epiphanius, Rufinus, Jerome) filled pivotal roles. In the next chapter, we will examine some of these pivotal church fathers involved in the church's canonization processes.

---

[35]   Larry Hurtado makes a similar claim in his "The New Testament in the Second Century: Texts, Collections, and Canon," in *Transmission and Reception: New Testament Text-Critical and Exegetical Studies*, ed. J. W. Childers and D. C. Parker (Piscataway, NJ: Gorgias, 2006), 3–17, here 27.

CHAPTER 16

FROM SCRIPTURE TO CANON: TRACING THE ORIGINS

The corridors of canon research are dimly lit and the kind of evidence that one would hope to find is strangely missing, namely, a credible ancient document that tells what led the church to acknowledge a NT canon of Scriptures. More specifically, why were the NT scriptures included in that sacred collection and other books that appear to have been well received initially and reflected early orthodox traditions as well as some NT canon books eventually excluded (e.g., *1 Clement* and *Didache*)? Several key individuals played important roles in the initial processes of recognizing some Christian writings as Scripture and others were involved in the end of the canonization processes. They have left some important signposts that add clarity to the process.

I. JUSTIN AND THE ROOTS OF CHRISTIAN SCRIPTURE

Justin (writing ca. 150–160) offers two strands of evidence for the recognition of the scriptural status of the canonical Gospels. He first refers to Jesus' words in Matt 11:27 with the following scriptural designation: "In the Gospel *it is written* [γέγραπται] that He said: 'All things are delivered unto me by My Father'; and, 'no man knows the Father but the Son; nor the Son but the Father, and they to whom the Son will reveal Him'" (*Dial*. 100.1–2; cf. 101.3, ANF, emphasis added).[1] Justin's defense of the Christian proclamation appealed directly to Jesus' sayings in a scriptural fashion without identifying specifically by name the individual Gospels in which those teachings were found. Some of the sayings of Jesus may have been circulating in the oral traditions of the church in the mid-second century rather than in written texts.

---

[1]   Perhaps also he was unimpressed with Paul's focus on the cross, atonement, and Spirit or his lack of interest in philosophy and his apparent attacks on it (1 Cor 1:18–31; Col 2:8). Irenaeus overcame Justin's hesitation to use Paul and introduced Paul's Epistles as an important part of his NT.

Second, as we saw earlier, Justin made use of the Gospels, which he called the "memoirs of the apostles" (ἀπομνημονεύατα τῶν ἀποστολῶν), to establish Christian doctrine (*Dial.* 100.1) and to relate the story of Jesus' passion, and they were read in Christian worship sometimes alongside of the Prophets (a designation for all of the OT Scriptures) or instead of the Prophets (*1 Apol.* 67). For instance, as was noted earlier,[2] the Gospels were referred to as "memoirs of the apostles" and how they were read in early Christian worship services (see the above references to the significance of the death of Jesus or his traditions about breaking bread together). We observed that the Gospels were sometimes read alongside of or instead of the prophets (that is, the church's first Scriptures).[3] For Justin, the Synoptic Gospels[4] *functioned* authoritatively in the churches and were equal to the OT Scriptures.

Strangely, however, Justin makes no clear reference to Paul's writings that were surely known in Rome well before Justin's time. He does not refer to Paul or Paul's writings and placed little emphasis on the major themes of Paul's theology. He was likely aware of these letters, due to their popularity in the early church, but he may have wished to avoid Marcion's primary sources. Perhaps also he was unimpressed with Paul's focus on the cross, atonement, and Spirit or his lack of interest in philosophy and his apparent attacks on it (1 Cor 1:18–31; Col 2:8). Irenaeus overcame Justin's hesitation to use Paul and introduced Paul's Epistles as an important part of his NT, but without listing the individual letters he believed were written by Paul. On the other hand, Justin does refer to the book of Revelation favorably (*Dial.* 81.4), giving one of the earliest expositions of a text from that book that was welcomed in the Western churches and also in some churches in the East up to the end of the fourth century. He calls Revelation one of "our writings" (ἡμέτερα συγγράμματα) (*1 Apol.* 28.1).[5]

The mid-second century years were mixed and troubled for the emerging orthodox churches as a result of the impact of Marcion's challenge that rejected the churches' OT Scriptures (see Chapter 18 §II). Justin appears to have given implicit scriptural status to Christian writings, but also recognized that the church's First/OT Scriptures were also part of the Christian Scripture collection. In his defense of the OT, Justin became the first orthodox writer to set forth a doctrine of Holy Scripture. He specifically answered the question of how Christians could reject the normative status of the Law (a common practice by that time) and yet still accept the OT as Scripture. This problem was first addressed by Paul in Gal 3:15–22, who showed that historically faith preceded the Law and that the Law had only

---

[2]   See p. 27, above.
[3]   Translation from Richardson, *Early Christian Fathers*, 287.
[4]   Some scholars question whether Justin knew John's Gospel or ignored it.
[5]   See Schneemelcher, "General Introduction," 31–32.

a temporary purpose in the economy of God.[6] Although some scholars suggest that "law" in Paul was basically *halakah* (the legal prescriptive laws and regulations), Sanders stresses that it was also *haggadah* ("story" or *mythos*). *Haggadah* essentially answers who we are, and *halakah* answers what we are to do. Sanders posits that Paul maintained a high regard for the Torah as *haggadah*, but that the legal regulations of the Torah did not apply. For Paul, Jesus had become the "new Torah" and superseded the Torah era, but he did not eradicate the Torah, which was "caught up in Christ in a new age."[7]

Later, and in more detail, Justin tries to rescue the OT as a Christian book in two important ways. First, he appeals to a historical scheme of prophecy and fulfillment, namely, that the truthfulness of all Scripture is proved by the OT prophecies that were fulfilled in Jesus. His unwillingness to subject the OT to careful assessment and his appeal to its infallibility, even when he could not respond adequately to critical questions related to it, are well known. For example:

> If you spoke these words, Trypho, and then kept silence in simplicity and with no ill intent, neither repeating what goes before nor adding what comes after, you must be forgiven; but if you have done so because you imagined that you could throw doubt on the passage, in order that I might say the Scriptures contradicted one another, you have erred. But I shall not venture to suppose or to say such a thing, and if a Scripture that appears to be of such a kind be brought forward, and if there be a pretext for saying that it is contrary to some other, since I am entirely convinced that no Scripture contradicts another, I shall admit rather that I do not understand what is recorded, and shall strive to persuade those who imagine that the Scriptures are contradictory to be rather of the same opinion as myself. (*Dial.* 65.2, ANF)

More important in defending Justin's view of Christian use of the OT, he made little use of the readily available allegorical or typological exegesis of the law, which at any rate would have been understandable only to Christians and would not have satisfied the Marcionite Christians who rejected this kind of exegesis.[8]

Second, Justin uniquely interprets the legalistic aspects of the law as divine ordinances given by God because of Israelite disobedience. He argues that the various prescriptions and proscriptions of the law were intended solely for the Jews as punishment for their sins. Although Justin acknowledged that circumcision preceded Moses' giving of the law, he adds that the other ordinances came as a result of Israel's failure. Trypho apparently agrees with some of his argument:

---

[6]   J. A. Sanders' *From Sacred Story*, 115–23, offers suggested solutions to the problem of understanding Paul's view of the law. For a detailed discussion of the problem that the OT posed for Christian faith and Paul's solution to the problem – reading the Scriptures correctly through faith in Jesus Christ – see von Campenhausen's discussion in *Formation of the Christian Bible*, 21–61.

[7]   J. A. Sanders, *From Sacred Story*, 120.

[8]   Von Campenhausen, *Formation of the Christian Bible*, 93–94.

> Then I answered, "you [Trypho] perceive that God by Moses laid all such ordinances upon you on account of the hardness of your people's hearts, so that, by the large number of them, you might obey God continually in every action, before your eyes and never begin to act unjustly or impiously." (*Dial.* 46.5, ANF; see also 27.2–4)[9]

Even the Sabbath, circumcision, temple sacrifices, dietary laws, and ritual washings, Justin claims, were God's punishments for a disobedient people. In a clear reference to the recent edict of Roman Emperor Hadrian (135 CE) to expel the Jews from Jerusalem (renamed Aelia Capitolina), Justin argues that God gave circumcision to the Jews as a sign of identification so they could be punished:

> For the circumcision according to the flesh, which is from Abraham, was given for a sign; that you may be separated from other nations, and from us; and that you alone may suffer and your land be made desolate and your cities burned with fire, and so that strangers may eat your fruit in your presence, and not one of you may go up to Jerusalem. (*Dial.* 16.2, ANF 202)[10]

Justin concludes that the OT laws were not in themselves harmful and that it would not be wrong to keep them, even though they would not be beneficial to those who do (see *Dial.* 27.2–4 and 46.5). His attempt to rescue the OT as Christian Scripture in this way appears to have been both successful and influential since the same argument was picked up later by both Irenaeus (*Haer.* 4.15; 16.3, 5; 2.1, 28) and Tertullian (*Marc.* 2.18–22). Justin does not specifically call for a new collection of Christian Scriptures, even though he unquestionably recognizes the authority of the "memoirs of the apostles" for Christian faith and claims that they were used in Rome in liturgical readings along with the OT Scriptures (*1 Apol.* 66–67).[11] The "memoirs" were an authoritative guide to the teaching of Jesus on church matters, for example, on the Eucharist (*1 Apol.* 67), and they appear to have been restricted to the Synoptic Gospels.[12]

---

[9] Most scholars reject the reliability of most of the ancient dialogue with the Jews, which became a genre for promoting Christian propaganda at the expense of the Jews. In most cases the Jew in the dialogues is a "fall guy" who succumbs to the superior wisdom of the Christian and eventually becomes a Christian. These dialogues may reflect the great desire of the church to see the Jewish people respond favorably to the Christian gospel as well as the Christians' frustration because they did not. In this case, however, Trypho not only does not become a Christian, something highly unusual in this genre, but he also asks some probing questions that are not easy for Justin to answer. For these reasons, the *Dialogue with Trypho* is given more credibility than other dialogues in this genre.

[10] For further examples of this kind of meaning given to the OT laws, see *Dial.* 19.2, 5–6; 20.1, 4; 21.1; 22.1, 11; 23.5; 92.3. Von Campenhausen, *Formation of the Christian Bible*, 93–95, has a helpful discussion of this issue.

[11] Metzger, *Canon of the New Testament*, 145–46, cites several examples from Justin that show conclusively that the memoirists were the Gospel writers. See also Patterson, "Irenaeus and the Valentinians," 8–11; and Metzger, "Canon of the New Testament," 124. These memoirs are elsewhere described as "memoirs of all things concerning our Savior Jesus Christ" (*1 Apol.* 33, 66; Richardson, *Early Christian Fathers*, 263, 286).

[12] On Justin's usual neglect of John, see R. F. Collins, *Introduction to the New Testament*, 20–21. See also Metzger, *Canon of the New Testament*, 145–46, for another perspective.

In the earliest known description of a Christian worship service, Justin indicates that these memoirs were read along with the "prophets" (a designation for the whole of their OT Scriptures) or instead of the "prophets" and even had priority over them because they were read first:

> After these [services] we constantly remind each other of these things. Those who have more come to the aid of those who lack, and we are constantly together. Over all that we receive we bless the Maker of all things through his Son Jesus Christ and through the Holy Spirit. And on the day called Sunday there is a meeting in one place of those who live in cities or the country, and *the memoirs of the apostles or the writings of the prophets are read* as long as time permits. When the reader has finished, the president in a discourse urges and invites [us] to the imitation of these noble things. Then we all stand up together and offer prayers. And, as said before, when we have finished the prayer, bread is brought, and wine and water, and the president similarly sends up prayers and thanksgivings to the best of his ability, and the congregation assents, saying the Amen; the distribution, and reception of the consecrated [elements] by each one, takes place and they are sent to the absent by the deacons. Those who prosper, and who so wish, contribute, each one as much as he chooses to. What is collected is deposited with the president, and he takes care of orphans and widows, and those who are in bonds, and the strangers who are sojourners among [us], and, briefly, he is the protector of all those in need. We all hold this common gathering on Sunday, since it is the first day, on which God transforming darkness and matter made the universe, and Jesus Christ our Savior rose from the dead on the same day. For they crucified him on the day before Saturday, and on the day after Saturday, he appeared to his apostles and disciples and taught them these things which I have passed on to you also for your serious consideration. (*1 Apol.* 67, Richardson, *Early Christian Fathers*, 287–88, emphasis added)

"Imitation of these noble things" is a call for recognition of their value in the life of the Christian community. This practice of reading the Gospels and Prophets, likely followed or duplicated in other churches as well, eventually included reading all four Gospels as Scripture and other NT writings. Because the Gospels served the cultic and catechetical needs of the churches and were functioning as normative writings, it was not long after Justin that Irenaeus specifically called the Gospels and several other Christian writings Scripture. Justin's practice, and that of the church he attended in Rome, of placing Christian literature alongside the OT scriptures for reading during Christian worship services helped pave the way for Irenaeus' recognition of Christian writings as Scripture and his designation of two bodies of sacred literature as the "Old Testament" and the "New Testament." As we saw earlier, at about the same time Irenaeus argued for the four canonical Gospels as Christian Scripture, he and Melito in Sardis had already begun using the terms "Old Testament" and "New Testament" for their two-part Scriptures. Those designations may not have begun with them, but they are the earliest known church fathers who used them.

II. IRENAEUS AND THE PRINCIPLE OF SCRIPTURE

A. The Principle of Scripture

Irenaeus of Lyons (writing ca. 170–180) is the first known church father to promote a four-gospel Scripture canon, and he signals an important transition in the church when he specifically refers to NT writings as Scriptures. While Irenaeus was not the first to call Christian writings Scripture or use them in ways that function as Scripture, he is the first to introduce a closed four-Gospel canon and list specific groupings of Christian writings as Scripture. What Irenaeus included in his collection of Christian Scriptures is not clear from his extant writings, though Eusebius later supplies (creates?) a list.[13]

When the term canon came to mean a fairly precise collection of sacred writings in the latter part of the fourth century CE, the canonical Gospels were already in the place of priority in all such collections and they were frequently, though not always (see Appendix C), placed in the same order that they are found in the Bible today. It is difficult to establish precisely when the NT writings were recognized as sacred scripture, but there was a growing tendency in that direction even before Irenaeus, as we saw in the previous chapter, and that process began likely even before Justin. It is difficult to pinpoint precisely when this occurs, but the earliest writings to receive this designation were predominantly the canonical Gospels and some of the letters of Paul.

Irenaeus argued that the four canonical Gospels, an imprecise collection of other Christian writings, and an unspecified collection of OT writings were the normative Scriptures for the churches in his region. He unambiguously identified these writings as "Scripture" (see *Haer*. 1.9.4; 2.26.1–2; 3.1.1). Irenaeus promoted the necessity and authority of *only* the four canonical Evangelists, but he also argued for something else that no one before him or in his generation claimed: the Christian message was somehow incomplete if less than four Gospels were used to articulate the Christian faith or if more were used. Irenaeus is the first to limit any portion of Christian scriptures to a specific collection, a "fixed canon" if you please. He obviously knew of other writings circulating as "gospels" in the churches, e.g., he identifies and rejects the *Gospel of Judas* (*Haer*. 1.31.1),[14] but he rejected all but four of them.

---

[13]   In the fourth century, Eusebius (*Hist. eccl.* 5.8.2–8) analyzed Irenaeus' writings and claimed that he accepted in his NT Scriptures Matthew, Mark, Luke, John, Revelation, 1 John, 1 Peter, *Shepherd of Hermas*, and Wisdom of Solomon. It is not certain how Eusebius obtained this list or if he constructed it based on the texts that Irenaeus cited. Paul is listed, but his specific writings are not individually identified. See Appendix C for that list. The placing of Wisdom in a NT list is only found in fourth-century writings, namely in Eusebius here and Epiphanius who also adds Wisdom and Sirach in his NT list. See Appendix C.

[14]   The text in which he identifies and condemns this so-called gospel reads in part: "They [Cainites] produce a fictitious history of this kind, which they style the Gospel of Judas" (ANF).

As most New Testament scholars acknowledge, Luke made use of Mark and appears to have had other "accounts" before him ("Q" and "L" *at least*), but he tried to improve them, at least in the case of Mark, apparently wanting to correct his sources with a "[more] orderly account" (Luke 1:1–4).[15] Luke, Matthew, and even John must surely have known of Mark, even if John has a different focus in his story of Jesus' life, message, death, and resurrection. John does not suggest that his Gospel needs the other Gospels to support his claims or even that he supplements them.[16] Although Irenaeus may have seen the need for four "pillars" (i.e., Gospels) for the church, it is difficult to establish that the Evangelists themselves or anyone before Irenaeus saw that same need. Indeed, ample evidence shows that, even after Irenaeus, other gospels were circulating in some churches at the end of the second century, for example, the *Gospel of Peter* that Serapion allowed to be read for a brief time in his churches (see discussion below).

In defense of his view that the church should only use the four canonical Gospels, Irenaeus employs arguments that by today's standards are considered strange, and even in the ancient world his reasoning for limiting the Gospels to four was unlikely a convincing line of argument. He writes:

> It is not possible that the Gospels can be either more or fewer in number than they are. For, since there are four zones of the world in which we live, and four principal winds, while the Church is scattered throughout all the world and while the "pillar and ground" of the Church is the Gospel and the spirit of life, it is fitting, therefore, that she [the Church] should have four pillars, breathing out immortality on every side, and vivifying men afresh. From this fact, it is evident that the Word, the Artificer of all, who sits upon the cherubim and who contains all things and was manifested to men, has given us the Gospel under four aspects, but bound together by one Spirit... But that these [four canonical] Gospels alone are true and reliable and admit neither an increase nor diminution of the aforesaid number, I have proved by so many such arguments. (*Haer.* 3.11.8–9, ANF; cf. 3.1.1)

We should not conclude from this, however, that all four canonical Gospels – and only those Gospels – were widely received as Scriptures everywhere in the last part of the second century. The available evidence simply does not support this common assumption. For example, Clement of Alexandria (ca. 180) cites other noncanonical gospel sources in his *Stromata*, such as the *Gospel of the Egyptians* (eight times), the *Gospel of the Hebrews* (three times), and the *Traditions of Matthias* (three times). He introduces a reference to the *Gospel of the Hebrews*

---

[15] Gamble, *New Testament Canon*, 24–25, makes this argument and adds that Matthew and Luke must not have had a very high view of their sources (especially Mark), since they took liberties in adding to and altering the sources they used. I have discussed this at length in McDonald, *Story of Jesus in History and Faith*, 49–125.

[16] This is not the intent of his concluding remarks in John 20:30, though the hyperbole in the later Johannine appendix in 21:25 may warrant this speculation.

with the formula, "It is written" (*gegraptai*).[17] During a debate with a gnostic Christian, Clement quotes from the *Gospel according to the Egyptians*: "When Salome inquired how long death should have power, the Lord (not meaning that life is evil, and the creation bad) said: 'As long as you women give birth to children'" (*Strom.* 3.6.45). He even concedes: "We do not have this saying [of Jesus to Salome] in the four traditional Gospels, but in the *Gospel according to the Egyptians*."[18] He accepts the *Epistle of Barnabas* as apostolic and quotes *Barn.* 1.5 and 2.3 in an authoritative manner (*Strom.* 2.6 and 2.15.67). Clement also cites *1 Clement, Shepherd of Hermas*, Sirach, Tatian's *Against the Greeks, Preaching of Peter, Apocalypse of Peter*, and even the *Sibylline Oracles*. The point here is, of course, that Irenaeus' view of "these four and no more" was not universally accepted in his day. In fact, there is no other known source *in his day* that made this same unqualified claim.

Another example of other gospels circulating during and after the time of Irenaeus can be seen in the contemporary use of the *Gospel of Peter*. Around the year 200, when Bishop Serapion of Antioch was asked by the Christians in Rhossus for permission to read the *Gospel of Peter* in the church, he at first agreed. Would he reasonably have done so had he already accepted Irenaeus' notion of a closed four-Gospel canon? It was only later after reading that gospel for himself that Serapion concluded that it denied the humanity of Jesus, and he reversed his earlier decision to allow it to be read in the churches. He did so, not on the basis of a widely accepted closed four-Gospel canon, but on the basis of a *canon of truth* that. Serapion only subsequently concluded that the *Gospel of Peter* was contrary to the traditions about Jesus that were handed on the churches. Eusebius preserves Serapion's letter of reversal as follows:

> For our part, brethren, we receive both Peter and the other apostles as Christ, but the writings which falsely bear their names we reject, as men of experience, knowing that such were not handed down to us. For I myself, when I came among you, imagined that all of you clung to the true faith; and, without going through the Gospel put forward by them in the name of Peter, I said, "If this is the only thing that seemingly causes captious feelings among you, let it be read." But since I have now learned, from what has been told me, that their mind was lurking in some hole of heresy, I shall give diligence to come again to you; wherefore, brethren, expect me quickly. But we, brethren, gathering [an understanding] to what kind of heresy Marcianus [not likely Marcion] belonged (who used to contradict himself, not knowing what he was saying, as you will learn from what has been written to you), were enabled [to understand] by others who studied this very Gospel, that is by the successors of those who began it, whom we call Docetae [Docetics] (for most of the ideas belong to their teaching) – using [the material supplied] by them, [we] were enabled to go through it and discover that [the *Gospel of Peter* for] the most part indeed was in accordance with the true teaching of the Saviour, but that some things were added, which also we place below for your benefit. (*Hist. eccl.* 6.12.3–6, adapted from LCL)

---

[17] For a careful examination of the origin and use of this gospel in early Christianity, see J. R. Edwards, "Hebrew Gospel in Early Christianity"; as noted above, see also his earlier *Hebrew Gospel*.
[18] Ancient references to these sources are supplied by Metzger, *Canon of the New Testament*, 132, and 171.

This widespread concern for the truth – that is, the correct understanding of the tradition about Jesus in the churches – was significant in the Serapion's decision about what literature to read in church worship. What did not conform *to this tradition* was eventually considered heresy and rejected, but he did not make his decision based on a limited four-Gospel canon as did Irenaeus some thirty years before him.[19]

Finally, Justin's pupil, Tatian, compiled a harmony of the Gospels – his famous *Diatessaron* (see Chapter 16 §II.A) – using the four canonical Gospels and possibly also traditions from noncanonical gospels.[20] Originally known as "The Gospel of the Mixed" according to Ephraem Syrus, the *Diatessaron* was likely composed around 173–175 and probably in Syria, but possibly at Rome.[21] Tatian not only smoothed out some differences between the canonical Gospels, he also eliminated the genealogies of Jesus and Luke's ascension story.[22] The only extant piece of Tatian's *Diatessaron* is the following small, badly damaged fragment that nevertheless shows the nature and extent of Tatian's harmonizing work:[23]

---

[19]   A heretical group roughly contemporary with Irenaeus, the so-called Alogi in Asia Minor opposed the use of the Gospel of John, Acts, Hebrews, Revelation, and probably 1 John in their churches (see Epiphanius, *Pan.* 51; Irenaeus, *Haer.* 3.11.12). Likewise, the Ebionite Christians "use the Gospel according to Matthew only, and repudiate the Apostle Paul, maintaining that he was an apostate from the Law" (Irenaeus, *Haer.* 1.26.2, ANF). Eusebius' report that the Ebionites used the *Gospel of the Hebrews* (*Hist. eccl.* 3.27.4) seems to be confirmed by Epiphanius (*Pan.* 30), who claims that the Ebionites received the Gospel of Matthew, but called it the *Gospel of the Hebrews*.

[20]   Because Tatian founded a rigorous ascetic movement that rejected marriage and the use of wine, it is not surprising that he may have incorporated other writings into the *Diatessaron* to support those views. In his commentary on the *Diatessaron*, Ephraem Syrus (died ca. 373) claims that Tatian used noncanonical gospels. W. L. Petersen, "Tatian's Diatessaron," in Koester, *Ancient Christian Gospels*, 430, suggests that Tatian's other sources included the Jewish-Christian *Gospel of the Hebrews* and possibly also the *Gospel of the Egyptians*. Metzger, *Canon of the New Testament*, 115, concludes that Tatian regarded the four canonical Gospels as authoritative, "otherwise it is unlikely that Tatian would have dared to combine them into one gospel account." There is no evidence, however, that Tatian regarded only the four canonical Gospels as authoritative. His views, of course, were not like those of the later churches regarding the changing, eliminating, or adding Gospel texts that later were rejected.

[21]   Justin's harmony of the Gospels, which focused mostly on Matthew and Luke with some parallels to Mark and fewer still, if any, to the Gospel of John, may have influenced Tatian. See Koester, *Ancient Christian Gospels*, 365–402.

[22]   If the four canonical Gospels had been considered by Tatian and his community to be inviolable Scripture, why did he exclude some sections and change others? Petersen ("Tatian's Diatessaron," 430) cites important early witnesses (e.g., Theodoret of Cyrrhus, *History of Heresies* 1.20) to document that some pericopes were not included in the *Diatessaron*.

[23]   Although the original is lost (except for the small fragment reproduced above), scholars have been able to piece together the *Diatessaron* from various translations and writings from antiquity. A reconstructed text is available online at http://www.earlychristianwritings.com/text/diatessaron.html.

...the mother of the sons of Zebed]ee (Matt. xxvii.56) and Salome (Mark xv.40) and the wives [of those who] had followed him from [Galile]e to see the crucified (Luke xxiii.49b–c). And [the da]y was Preparation; the sabbath was daw[ning] (Luke xxiii.54). And when it was evening (Matt. xxvii.57), on the Prep[aration], that is, the day before the sabbath (Mark xv.42), [there came] up a man (Matt. xxvii.57), [from?] a c[i]ty of [Jude]a (Luke xxiii.51b), by name Jo[seph] (Matt. xxvii.57), be[ing] a member of the council (Luke xxiii.50), from Arimathea (Matt. xxvii.57), g[o]od and ri[ghteous] (Luke xxiii.50), being a disciple of Jesus, but se[cret]ly, for fear of the [Jew]s (John xix.38). And he (Matt. xxvii.57) was looking for [the] k[ingdom] of God (Luke xxiii.51c). This man [had] not [con]sented to [their] p[urpose] (Luke xxiii.51a).[24]

Tatian's *Diatessaron* was known as far east as China and as far west as England and was cited authoritatively as recently as the fourteenth century! Although probably originally produced in Syriac in Syria, the same location where Ephraem wrote a commentary on it, the *Diatessaron* was translated into Greek, Latin, Old High German, Georgian, Armenian, and others, and its influence was widely felt. Eusebius speaks of the continuing use of the *Diatessaron* in the fourth century in the West (*Hist. eccl.* 4.29.6), and it was widely used in the Syrian churches well into the sixth century. It continued to influence churches long after this, but eventually yielded ground to the later Syriac Peshitta translation of the NT, which included all four canonical Gospels. Roman Catholic and Eastern Orthodox churches eventually suppressed the *Diatessaron* because its author was viewed as a heretic. This document continues to be a valuable resource for textual criticism because it is one of the earliest witnesses to the text of the Gospels.[25]

The point here, of course, is that in Irenaeus' time few Christians limited the number of Gospels to be read in their churches to the same four that he did. It is also highly unlikely that all churches even possessed a copy of all four Gospels at that time. In fact, Irenaeus is the only known witness in his generation who acknowledges *only* the four canonical Gospels in his NT Scripture collection. Unlike Tertullian who followed him, Irenaeus did not distinguish between Matthew and John as apostolic authors and Luke and Mark who were not. At the end of the second century, it appears that a canonical Gospel could also be read alongside one or more noncanonical gospels. Although some scholars argue that Irenaeus' position on a fixed four-Gospel canon reflected the status of opinion on the matter in a majority of churches in his day, this does not square with the surviving evidence from that time.

Widespread acceptance of the four canonical Gospels took time, but limiting the Gospels to those four took even longer. It may be that Irenaeus' primary aim in his defense of the four was to defend the use of John's Gospel that was under attack in his time. It is noteworthy that the Muratorian Fragment, a likely late

---

[24] This translation comes from Metzger, *Canon of the New Testament*, 115, who supplies the bracketed words and the Scripture references.

[25] For an extended discussion of the *Diatessaron*, see Petersen: "Tatian's Diatessaron" and his "Diatessaron of Tatian."

fourth-century document, simply lists the four canonical Gospels with no defense like Irenaeus' defense of the four and this points to a later date than Irenaeus (see Chapter 21 §IV). In the fourth century, Eusebius listed the four canonical Gospels as a closed unit, giving them priority in a "recognized" (ὁμολογουμένα = *homolegoumena*) sacred collection. He describes them collectively as "the holy tetrad of the Gospels" (*Hist. eccl.* 3.25.1, LCL), but the four Gospels had not yet achieved this prominence at the end of the second century, which is likely why Irenaeus defended them so vigorously.

B. Irenaeus and the Notion of Canon

Irenaeus succinctly expresses the triptych of authority in the early church, that is, the threefold source of authority in the church. He writes: "The Lord doth testify, as the apostles confess, and as the prophets [OT] announce" (*Haer.* 3.17.4, ANF). His ordering of these three, with the prophets last, is still very much like that found elsewhere in second-century writers (e.g., Ign. *Phld.* 5.1–2).

According to von Campenhausen, Irenaeus marked "the transition from the earlier period of belief in tradition [primitive Christianity] to the new age of deliberate canonical standardization."[26] Unlike Justin, he did not defend the OT Scriptures alone, but explicitly named and defended the scriptural authority of Christian writings, especially the four Gospels as we saw. His point, however, was not so much to establish a biblical canon, or a closed collection of sacred writings, as it was to defend the *canon of truth*, the Christian message.[27] Apart from the four canonical Gospels, he does not list his own fixed list of Christian Scriptures, but as we saw, in the fourth century Eusebius may have simply tallied the references he found in Irenaeus and made such a list (see Appendix C). In fact, the "canon" of Irenaeus was not so much a list of inspired books, but rather a statement of the faith of and about Jesus the Christ that he believed had been passed on in the church by the apostles – that is, the apostolic tradition (*Haer.* 3.2.2). Irenaeus' summary of the faith on which the church depended for its life and witness is set forth in a major text that merits close attention since the tenets of faith expressed in this passage became the later foundation pillars of orthodoxy in the church and were a major part of most significant ancient creedal formulations. This canon, or *regula fidei* (lit. "rule of faith"), was also a distinguishing feature in later canonical decisions that incorporated or excluded certain Christian writings from the biblical canon. Writings that did not support this "canon of truth" were rejected. Irenaeus writes:

---

[26]   Von Campenhausen, *Formation of the Christian Bible*, 182.

[27]   See also Goodspeed, *A History of Early Christian Literature* (Chicago: University of Chicago Press, 1983), 120; and Patterson, "Irenaeus and the Valentinians: The Emergence of the Christian Scriptures," in *Studia Patristica* 18.3, ed. E. A. Livingstone (Leuven: Peeters, 1989), 189–220.

The Church, though dispersed throughout the whole world, even to the ends of the earth, has received from the apostles and their disciples this faith: It believes in one God, the Father Almighty, Maker of heaven, and earth and the sea and all things that are in them and in one Christ Jesus, the Son of God, who became incarnate for our salvation and in the Holy Spirit, who proclaimed through the prophets the dispensations of God, the advents, the birth from a virgin, the passion, the resurrection from the dead, and the ascension into heaven in the flesh of the beloved Christ Jesus, our Lord. He also proclaimed through the prophets his future manifestation from heaven in the glory of the Father "to gather all things in one," and to raise up anew all flesh of the whole human race. [This will take place] in order that to Christ Jesus, our Lord, God, Saviour, and King, according to the will of the invisible Father, "every knee should bow, of things in heaven, and things in earth, and things under the earth, and that every tongue should confess" him. And he will execute just judgment towards all sending into everlasting fire "spiritual wickednesses," and the angels who transgressed and became apostates, together with the ungodly, and unrighteous, and wicked, and profane among men. But he will, in the exercise of his grace, confer immortality on the righteous and holy, and those who have kept his commandments, and have persevered in his love, some from the beginning of their Christian course, and others from the time of their repentance. He will surround them with everlasting glory. (*Haer*. 1.10.1, ANF; cf. 3.4.2)

Irenaeus used the OT Scriptures, some non-canonical writings, and selected Christian Scriptures as a basis for demonstrating the authenticity of Christian teaching. He may have been the first, so far as our present knowledge shows, to use the terms Old Testament and New Testament,[28] and he accepted both Testaments as Scripture, that is, authoritative books for identifying Christian faith and conduct. For example, Irenaeus introduces a premise for his line of argument with these words: "Inasmuch, then, as in both testaments there is the same right-eousness of God [displayed]…" (*Haer*. 4.28.1, ANF). Elsewhere he illustrates his view of authority in the church this way:

The preaching of the apostles, the authoritative teaching of the Lord, the announcements of the prophets, the dictated utterances of the apostles, and the ministration of the law – all of which praise one and the same Being, the God and Father of all, and not many diverse beings…are all in harmony with our statements. (*Haer*. 2.35.4, ANF)

If, therefore, even in the New Testament the apostles are found granting certain precepts in consideration of human infirmity, …it ought not to be wondered at, if also in the Old Testament the same God permitted similar indulgences for the benefit of His people…so that they might obtain the gift of salvation through them. (*Haer*. 4.15.2 ANF)

Von Campenhausen, referring to Irenaeus' larger list of authoritative writings, explains that he was "the first catholic theologian who dared to adopt the Marcionite principle of a new 'Scripture' in order to use it in his turn against Marcion and all heretics."[29] Establishing a closed canon of inspired Scriptures, however, was not

---

[28] This does not necessarily mean that he coined the terms, but he is the first known writer to use them. Melito also used them at roughly the same time, as we saw above.

[29] Von Campenhausen, *Formation of the Christian Bible*, 186.

Irenaeus' primary concern, but rather a defense of the Christian message with all
the tools at his disposal. He sought to root his teaching in the apostolic teaching
and tradition that, he argued, was passed on in the church through the succession
of bishops as well as by the authority of both the OT and NT Scriptures.

Irenaeus' strongest argument was that the rule of faith, or the tradition that he
proclaimed, was rooted in an "apostolic succession." He regularly emphasized
this, but nowhere more clearly than in the following well-known text:

> The blessed apostles, then, having founded and built up the Church, committed into the hands
> of Linus the office of episcopate. Paul makes mention of this Linus in the Epistles to Timothy.
> Anacletus succeeded him, and Clement was allotted the bishopric. Clement, since he had seen
> the blessed apostles and had been conversant with them, might be said to have the preaching of
> the apostles still echoing in his ears, and their traditions before his eyes... Evaristus succeeded
> Clement, and he was succeeded by Sixtus, the sixth from the apostles. After him came
> Telephorus, who was gloriously martyred, then Hyginus, after him Pius, and then after him
> Anicetus was appointed. Anicetus was succeeded by Soter and Eleutherius, who is the twelfth
> from the apostles and now holds the inheritance of the episcopate. *In this order, and by this
> succession, the ecclesiastical tradition from the apostles and the preaching of the truth have
> come down to us.* And this is the most abundant proof that there is one and the same vivifying
> faith, which has been preserved in the Church from the apostles until now, and handed down in
> truth. (*Haer*. 3.3.3, adapted from ANF, emphasis added)[30]

If questions were not clearly dealt with in this "apostolic deposit," or if no
deposit had been left, where would one turn for the answer? For Irenaeus, the
obvious answer lies with those to whom the apostolic deposit was given: the
bishops of the churches: "For how should it be if the apostles themselves had not
left us writings? Would it not be necessary in that case to follow the course of the
tradition that they handed down to those to whom they handed over the leadership
of the churches?" (*Haer*. 3.4.1, adapted from ANF). The effect of Irenaeus'
concern to preserve the truth of the gospel was that the church began to recognize
a collection of authoritative NT writings (at first the Gospels especially, but also
Paul), which, as Koester notes, was later followed – though not uniformly – by
the churches in Asia Minor, Greece, Antioch, Carthage, and Rome.[31] The complete
collection of Christian Scriptures was not yet closed in Irenaeus' day, even though
he acknowledged only the four canonical Gospels.

With Irenaeus, the boundaries of the Christian faith became more precise than
before, relative to the catholic dimensions of the church. For him the church
was broader in scope than Marcion would allow, though not yet broad enough
to include Marcion or the gnostic Christians. The move toward a recognition
of the normative status of Christian writings as Scripture was emerging during

---

[30]   For Irenaeus, the apostolic witness was the primary determining principle for the recognition of
the authority of NT Scriptures (*Haer*. 3.2.2). He did not limit the succession of the apostolic witness,
however, to the bishops at Rome alone (*Haer*. 3.3.2).

[31]   Koester, *Introduction to the New Testament*, 2:11.

a period when the definition of what it meant to be a Christian was still being framed and challenged by so-called heretical elements in the church. What grew out of Irenaeus' and later Hippolytus' polemic against heresy was a church that was seeking to clarify its identity and its Scriptures within a broad and sometimes conflicting tradition that was still partially oral in form. Irenaeus' primary concern was to defend the Christian proclamation. That was his "canon," or *regula fidei*. He limited this message to the apostolic tradition resident in the churches, which in turn was reflected in the primary Christian literature of the first century, especially the four NT Gospels and an imprecise collection of Paul's Letters and other NT writings, but, as we saw above, also some so-called noncanonical writings.

C. Irenaeus' Influence

Irenaeus claims that his canon of faith (*regula fidei*) did not originate with him, but that he received it through a succession of the churches' bishops who received it from the apostles. Although some scholars question whether Irenaeus' canon of faith originated with the apostles, most agree that it reflects beliefs of long standing in the church. This canon is sometimes identified as "proto-orthodoxy," the antecedent of the later fourth-century Christian orthodoxy. Not only were there earlier creedal formulations, some of which are quite well known from the first century (1 Cor 15:3–4; Phil 2:5–11; Rom 10:9–10; 1 Tim 3:16),[32] there was also a high regard for the canonical Gospels (especially Matthew in Syria and in the West, John in Asia Minor), Paul's letters,[33] and other religious texts as well. Such precedents were not new in the time of Irenaeus, but the recognition and actual referral of such literature as sacred Scripture was more recent, even though it appears that the church had been moving in that direction for some time.

The Christian writings that became normative in second-century churches no doubt included what was also most relevant to the emerging churches' needs. That literature included certainly the canonical Gospels and several unspecified letters of Paul, as well as 1 Peter, 1 John, and Acts, but also other Christian documents that were not later included in the NT, also as we have seen. Most Christian churches at the end of the second century appear to have been in basic agreement with the core of Irenaeus' collection of NT Scriptures, namely the canonical Gospels and some of Paul's Letters, but some of them accepted other writings as well. No precise limitations were imposed on the collection of Christian writings at that time except that most probably welcomed the canonical Gospels, but not Irenaeus' self-imposed four-Gospel canon. What becomes apparent is that this widespread, but not exclusive, agreement emerged from the local churches themselves.

---

[32] Kelly, *Early Christian Doctrines*, 82–83, lists two other comparable creeds roughly contemporary with the last half of the second century.

[33] Clement of Rome speaks of Paul as inspired (*1 Clem.* 47.3) and refers or alludes to his letters several times (e.g., 13.1; 24.1; 33.1; 34.8, 37.3, 5; and especially 46.1–3).

At that time there was no church council deliberating which Christian writings were acceptable as Christian Scriptures. As we will see below (Chapter 21 §IX), there were, in fact, no council decisions regarding the scope of the NT Scriptures before the end of the fourth century.

What this suggests, of course, is considerable popularity of several creedal beliefs similar to those advanced by Irenaeus and some acknowledgment of the books that Irenaeus appealed to the most (the canonical Gospels and Paul). However, various churches continued for several centuries to appeal to several writings not later included in the Christian Bibles. In this sense, the literature that found wide acceptance in churches, for the most part, was also in basic agreement with the canon of faith circulating in churches. Objections against the gnostic heresies were not based on some new or developing notion of what was true, but on what had earlier roots within the church itself and was rooted in first-century churches and their leaders.

Among all of the diversity that existed in the early church, the broad parameters of the Christian proclamation were not in serious doubt. For example, though Christians debated the identity of Jesus, his humanity, and his relationship with God in the second century, there was still a core of teachings that had long been received in the churches. Most agreed by the end of the second century that Jesus was tempted, he tired, was hungry, ate, slept, and experienced suffering when he died – that is, he was human, but that he also was the Christ who died for sins and was raised from the dead and ascended into heaven. On the other hand, some churches continued to debate whether Jesus should be identified as a spirit, the Spirit, an angel, or as a divinely empowered human being. The range of perspectives on this topic in the second and third centuries appears to have been quite broad. The identity of Jesus, however, continued to be debated much longer, even past the later Trinitarian formulations in the fourth century.[34]

Nevertheless, by the end of the first century the true humanity of Jesus was widely accepted in most churches, but not unanimously, and one of the significant debates at the end of the first century had to do with whether Jesus only *appeared* to be human, that is the docetic controversy (1 John 4:1–3) that began in the late first century and continued well into the second century. Eschatological perspectives also varied in Christian literature, but theologies had a hope in the future

---

[34]   Athenagoras, of course, is an exception, but his conclusions are not representative of most Christologies in the second century. His Trinitarian-type of formulation is, however, anticipatory of the fourth century when the identity of Jesus and the relationship between God and Jesus the Christ are described in Greek philosophical categories, especially Platonic categories. Athenagoras comes close to the later position of the church when he says: "We speak of God, of his Son, his Word, and of the Holy Spirit; and we say that the Father, the Son, and the Spirit are united in power. For the Son is the intelligence, reason, and wisdom of the Father, and the Spirit is an effluence, as light from fire" (Athenagoras, *A Plea for the Christians*, 24; Richardson, *Early Christian Fathers*, 326). It is debatable whether Athenagoras' view of the Spirit was representative of the majority of views among the Ante-Nicene fathers.

blessing of God for those who put their faith in Jesus the Christ, the Savior and Son of God. Within this diversity, longstanding elements of Christian faith played an important role in the churches' decisions as to what literature was useful in their life, faith, and worship. It is difficult to imagine the church agreeing on the scope of its biblical canon before it came to some broad agreement on its core theological beliefs. In this sense, a fixed canon formation was not possible before there was a council of Nicea that focused on the identity of Jesus. How could there be a final agreement in the churches without broad agreement on the identity of Jesus?

The early proto-Orthodox and the Western Roman churches' opposition to Marcion's limited collection of Christian writings and his rejection of the OT came from local churches and was based on their belief in what was for them an historic tradition about the Christian faith circulating in the churches that was also normative for all churches. In other words, opposition to the so-called heresies of the second centuries did not come from organized church councils, but from local church leaders who appealed to the witness of the church and its OT Scriptures and the early Christian writings that developed from its traditions and continued to define them.

Early creedal statements, just like all subsequent creedal formulations, were forged in particular social and historical contexts and these often included controversial settings (e.g., the author of 1 John 4:1–3, 6, 13–16 opposed the Docetic heresy circulating in the late first century). The result was that the theology of the ancient Christian churches developed in different directions, being influenced by diverse social and theological contexts.[35] This, in part, is why ancient Christian theology was neither monolithic nor arrived at the same time, even if most churches finally agreed on its substance. Although there were common agreements on some foundational traditions and beliefs in the churches, there were still varieties of expressions of those beliefs among them. It appears that there was greater tolerance for diversity in the early churches than what took place after the second century.

At the end of the second century, when the Christian community was interacting with what some considered to be extreme diversity (i.e., heresy) in the church, there was a growing sense of the need for uniformity in the Christian community, especially in the churches of the West at much the same time when the Romans themselves were calling for uniformity in social and religious matters. For example, in January 250, the emperor Decius (died June 251) began the *first empire-wide* persecution of Christians with the execution of Bishop Fabian of

---

[35]   Understanding the social context in which early Christianity emerged and how it affected the early churches are quite helpful. The canonization of Scripture did not take place in a vacuum, but rather within the broader Greco-Roman culture. See Rutgers et al., eds., *The Use of Sacred Books in the Ancient World*, CBET 22 (Leuven: Peeters, 1998), for the published results of an international conference on the social context that gave rise to the Christian understanding of sacred literature.

Rome. In large measure this came as a result of the Romans' demand for unity and uniformity in the Empire and their fear of nonconformity. The short-lived Decian persecution had the unintended consequence of influencing and advancing orthodoxy by bringing to the fore the issue of the Christians' lack of uniformity with regard to their sacred writings and teachings.[36]

Whatever his original source or motivation, Irenaeus' influence on his and subsequent generations regarding the recognition of Christian Scriptures was significant – but not strong enough to solidify which Christian writings were recognized as Scripture. Von Campenhausen argues that Irenaeus' influence spread rapidly and that the move toward the recognition of new Scriptures in this era could not be checked.[37] Although there was broad agreement on accepting the canonical Gospels and Paul and perhaps 1 Peter and 1 John – even among some of the heretical groups – the collection of sacred Christian writings was not thereby closed, as von Campenhausen explains:

> Attempts were made to secure as comprehensive and solid a collection as possible; and in the process people from various churches naturally liked to adopt such books as confirmed their own points of view. There was thus a concern that recent works would find their way into the canon, as, for example, 2 Peter or the *Shepherd of Hermas*.[38]

D. Irenaeus' List of Scriptures

Except for the four canonical Gospels, Irenaeus did not make a complete list of the texts that he considered authoritative Christian scriptures. He listed the four canonical Gospels and often referred to many NT passages and other noncanonical books for support of his positions against heresy. This practice was not presented as something new, but was for him a reflection of a longstanding tradition in the church (see, e.g., *Haer*. 3.3.3; 3.11.8; 3.12.15; 3.14.1–15.1; 3.21.3–4). Irenaeus considered the NT Scriptures as equal to the OT Scriptures, even though he did not clearly define the parameters of either collection.[39] If his few references to and citations of Hebrews are any indication of what Irenaeus considered authoritative

---

[36] In the fourth century, another Roman emperor, Constantine, also tried to achieve harmony in Roman society. Using a vastly different methodology, he continually involved himself in church councils with the clear intention of bringing about harmony in the churches – not simply as a means of purifying Christian doctrine (see §VIII below).

[37] Von Campenhausen, *Formation of the Christian Bible*, 210.

[38] Ibid., 211. It is interesting that the *Shepherd of Hermas* appears in a ninth-century manuscript as an "ecclesiastical" document that was evidently alright for reading, likely in private, not the church (Paris, BNFm lat. 11553). This is mentioned in Pierre-Maurice Bogaert, "The Latin Bible c. 600–900," in *The New Cambridge History of The Bible: From 600–1450*, ed. Richard Marsden and E. Ann Matter (Cambridge: Cambridge University Press, 2012), 69–92, here 90. He observes that this book is mentioned in the Colophon of Esther among non-canonical "ecclesiastical" books. Bogart suggests that this may go back to a fifth-century antecedent.

[39] Goodspeed, "Canon of the New Testament," 64–65.

and inspired of God, he may not have considered this book equal in authority to the other NT writings. Also, and interestingly, he does not mention James, Jude, or 2 Peter. On the other hand, he appears to have acknowledged the authority of the *Shepherd of Hermas* and *1 Clement*. This may prove to be nothing of significance, but since he was writing to address specific issues (heresy), he would naturally utilize the writings that best suited his apologetic.

The Scriptures, for Irenaeus, were evidently made up of the still fluid collection of OT writings circulating in the churches and at least the four Gospels and several if not most of Paul's writings, but we cannot demonstrate this from his extant writings. In an overly optimistic statement about the interpretation of Scripture, he enthuses: "the entire Scriptures, the prophets and the Gospels, can be clearly, unambiguously understood by all" (*Haer*. 2.27.2, ANF). Later, however, he seems to reverse himself and says that if we fail to understand some parts of Scriptures we should leave these matters to God because the Scriptures "are indeed perfect since they were spoken by the Word of God and His Spirit" (2.28.2, ANF).

Failure to mention an ancient source does not necessarily mean that this source was either unknown or not viewed as authoritative by Irenaeus. The *ad hoc* nature of his writings must surely have had an affect on the literature that he cited to support his positions. For example, *Against Heresies* was sent to the churches and it argued especially against Marcionites and the gnostics. The sources that Irenaeus would have found helpful in his apologetic defense of orthodoxy do not necessarily include all of the sources that he thought were scriptural and authoritative in the churches. Even though he makes fewer references to the OT literature than to the NT literature, we cannot draw from this that he did not accept books that he did not cite. Therefore, contrary to the arguments of some scholars, we are unable to find in Irenaeus a canon of NT Scriptures. The description, or canon list, in Eusebius (*Hist. eccl.* 5.8.2–8) may well be an invention by Eusebius based on Irenaeus' citations rather than a list that Irenaeus himself composed. He recognized the "apostles" as a collection of Christian Scriptures, but he nowhere clarifies what other writings were in this group (see *Haer*. 1.3.6). Apart from his four-gospel canon, then, nothing in his writings suggests that he carried out any canonizing procedure on the rest of the NT literature. This became the task of later Christian writers, who now had in hand the principle of recognizing a new set of Christian writings.

III. CLEMENT OF ALEXANDRIA
AND A BROAD SCRIPTURE COLLECTION

Titus Flavius Clemens (ca. 150–215), more commonly known as Clement of Alexandria, was probably born in Athens of pagan parents. He converted to the Christian faith and came eventually to Alexandria to study under Pantaenus, the director of the catechetical school in Alexandria, the first known school of its kind in the church. He succeeded Pantaenus as director of the school (ca. 190–200) and expanded the original catechetical aim of the school (to educate new converts) to make it a training center "for the cultivation of theologians."[40] During the persecutions of Septimus Severus (emperor 193–211), Clement fled Egypt and finally settled in Cappadocia.[41]

Like others before him, Clement refers to or cites as Scripture many of the writings of the NT: the four canonical Gospels, Acts, fourteen Letters of Paul (the Pastorals and Hebrews were attributed to Paul), 1–2 John, 1 Peter, Jude, and Revelation. He makes no mention of James, 2 Peter, or 3 John. However, he also quotes from the *Epistle of Barnabas, 1 Clement, Shepherd of Hermas, Preaching of Peter, Sibylline Oracles,* and the *Didache* for support of his ideas. Eusebius describes the writings that informed Clement's theology as follows:

> Now in the *Stromateis* he [Clement] has composed a patchwork, not only of the divine Scripture, but of the writings of the Greeks as well, if he thought that they also had said anything useful, and he mentions opinions from many sources, explaining Greek and barbarian alike, and moreover sifts the false opinions of the heresiarchs; and unfolding much history he gives us a work of great erudition. With all these he mingles also the opinions of philosophers, and so he has suitably made the title of the *Stromateis* to correspond to the work itself. And in them *he has also made use of testimonies from the disputed writings, the book known as the Wisdom of Solomon, and the Wisdom of Jesus the Son of Sirach, and the Epistle to the Hebrews, and those of Barnabas, and Clement, and Jude; and he mentions Tatian's book Against the Greeks*, and Cassian, since he also had composed a chronography, and moreover Philo and Aristobulus and Josephus and Demetrius and Eupolemus, Jewish writers, in that they would show, all of them, in writing, that Moses and the Jewish race went back further in their origins than the Greeks. *And the books of Clement*, of which we are speaking, are full of much other useful learning. In the first of these he shows with reference to himself that he came very near to the successors of the Apostles; and he promises in them also to write a commentary on Genesis...
>
> And in the *Hypotyposeis*, to speak briefly, he has given concise explanations of all the Canonical [*endiathēkē*; lit. "testamented" or "encovenanted"] Scriptures, *not passing over even the disputed writings, I mean the Epistle of Jude and the remaining Catholic Epistles, and the Epistle of Barnabas, and the Apocalypse known as Peter's.* And as for the *Epistle to the Hebrews*, he says indeed that it is Paul's, but that it was written for Hebrews in the Hebrew tongue, and that Luke, having carefully translated it, published it for the Greeks; hence, as a result of this translation, the same complexion of style is found in this Epistle and in the Acts: but that the [words] "Paul an apostle" were naturally not prefixed. For, says he, "in writing to Hebrews who had conceived a prejudice against him and were suspicious of him, he very wisely did not repel them at the beginning by putting his name."...
>
> And again in the same books Clement has inserted a tradition of the primitive elders with regard to the order of the Gospels, as follows. He said that those Gospels were first written which include the genealogies, but that the Gospel according to Mark came into being in this manner: When Peter had publicly preached the word at Rome, and by the Spirit had proclaimed

---

[40]   J. H. Ellens, "The Ancient Library of Alexandria and Early Christian Theological Development," *Occasional Papers of the Institute for Antiquity and Christianity* 27 (1993): 33, 39.

[41]   See J. D. Crossan, *Four Other Gospels* (Minneapolis: Winston, 1985), 94–98, for an informative summary of Clement's life.

the Gospel, that those present, who were many, exhorted Mark, as one who had followed him for a long time and remembered what had been spoken, to make a record of what was said; and that he did this, and distributed the Gospel among those that asked him. And that when the matter came to Peter's knowledge he neither strongly forbade it nor urged it forward. But that John, last of all, conscious that the outward facts had been set forth in the Gospels, was urged on by his disciples, and, divinely moved by the Spirit, composed a spiritual Gospel. This is Clement's account. (*Hist. eccl.* 6.13.4–8; 6.14.1–3, 5–7; LCL)

Clement's scope of sacred Scriptures appears to have been much broader than that of Irenaeus. Metzger appropriately observes that Clement "delighted to welcome truth in unexpected places!"[42] Clement also knew of the *Gospel of the Hebrews*, *Gospel of the Egyptians*, and *Tradition of Matthias* and did not condemn them as heretical documents, though to our knowledge, he apparently did not acknowledge them as Scripture either.[43] What is most surprising about Clement is his high regard for Greek philosophy as a means of preparing one to receive the Christian message:

Even if Greek philosophy does not comprehend the truth in its entirety and, in addition, lacks the strength to fulfill the Lord's command, yet at least it prepares the way for the teaching which is royal in the highest sense of the word, by making a man self-controlled, by molding his character, and by making him ready to receive the truth. (*Strom.* 7.20, ANF)[44]

If Clement of Alexandria had a closed biblical canon, it is nowhere apparent or obvious. In his pursuit of the knowledge of God, he was informed by a broad spectrum and selection of literature.

IV. TERTULLIAN AND LEVELS OF SCRIPTURAL AUTHORITY

A well-educated native of Carthage in Africa and often called the "father of Latin theology" in the church, Tertullian (ca. 160–225), like Irenaeus before him, acknowledged all four canonical Gospels, but distinguished between those written by apostles and those "whose masters were apostles." He spoke thusly about them: "Of the apostles, therefore, John and Matthew first instill faith into us; whilst of apostolic men, Luke and Mark renew it afterwards. These all start with the same principles of faith" (Tertullian, *Marc.* 4.2.2, ANF). Both here and

---

[42] Metzger, "Canon of the New Testament," 124. See also Goodspeed, "Canon of the New Testament," 65.

[43] Metzger, "Canon of the New Testament," 124.

[44] J. E. L. Oulton and H. Chadwick, eds., *Alexandrian Christianity: Selected Translations of Clement and Origen*, Library of Christian Classics 2 (Philadelphia: Westminster, 1954), 21, note the parallel here with what Paul says about the Law of Moses being a *paidagōgos* (Gal 3:24) to bring one to Christ.

elsewhere Tertullian acknowledges that Mark and Luke were not apostles, and he places them in a lower category than Matthew and John. As noted earlier, he even criticizes Marcion for selecting Luke instead of an "apostolic" gospel:

> Now of the authors whom we possess, Marcion seems to have singled out Luke for his mutilating process. Luke, however, was not an apostle, but only an apostolic man; not a master, but a disciple, and so inferior to a master – at least as far subsequent to him as the apostle whom he followed…was subsequent to the others. (*Marc.* 4.2.5, ANF, emphasis added)

For Tertullian, apostolicity was the chief criterion for recognizing the authority of the Gospels. For him, this same apostolic authority, which was passed on by them through the succession of bishops, guaranteed the truthfulness of the gospel. The apostolic writings formed for him the NT:

> If I fail in resolving this article (of our faith) by passages which may admit of dispute out of the Old Testament, I will take out of the New Testament a confirmation of our view, that you may not straightway attribute to the Father every possible (relation and condition) which I ascribe to the Son. Behold, then, I find both in the Gospels and in the (writings of the) apostles [i.e., the epistles] a visible and an invisible God (revealed to us), under a manifest and personal distinction in the condition of both. (*Prax.* 15, ANF)

Tertullian cites or quotes the four canonical Gospels, thirteen Letters of Paul (not Hebrews), Acts, 1 John, 1 Peter, Jude, and Revelation; however, he did not produce a closed or fixed list of NT Scriptures, even though he regularly cited these and other writings in an authoritative manner. On one occasion he referred to these Scriptures as an "entire volume" (*Praescr.* 32). He adds that Rome "mingles the Law and the prophets in one volume" (*Praescr.* 36). Beare notes that before Tertullian became a Montanist he included in his collection of Scriptures the *Shepherd of Hermas*, but later dismissed it with scorn. Surprisingly, Tertullian also treats Hebrews as marginal because he believes that Barnabas wrote it.[45] Like other scholars, however, Beare overstates the case that Tertullian had a closed canon of Old and NT Scriptures. He cites as support the *Prax.* 15 text quoted above.[46] Nowhere in his extant writings, however, do we find any specific listing or identification of precisely what was in Tertullian's OT or NT. None of the NT books that Tertullian appears to have accepted as authoritative was later rejected by the church at large, but he also accepted as scripture *1 Enoch* because, he said, Jude did the same.[47] After his Montanist conversion, he also accepted the Montanist prophecies as sacred writings (for more discussion of this see Chapter 18 §IV).

---

[45] G. W. Beare, "Canon of the NT," *IDB* 1:528–29.

[46] Ibid., 528.

[47] See Tertullian's references to I Enoch in *Apol.* 22 (cf. *1 En.* 15:8, 9); *De cultu feminarum* 1.3.1 (*1 En.* 8:1, 3); 2.10 (*1 En.* 8:1); *De Idolatria* 4, 15 (*1 En.* 19:1; 99:6–7); 9 (*1 En.* 6; 14:5), 15; *De Virg. Veland.* 7 (*1 En.* 6; 14:5; see also *De Anima* 50).

V. ORIGEN AND THE USE OF WRITTEN TRADITIONS

Sundberg concludes that the transition from the authority of oral tradition to the authority of written traditions began with Irenaeus, but was completed with Origen (ca. 184–254).[48] Like Clement of Alexandria, Origen drew from the four canonical Gospels, Acts, fourteen Letters of Paul (including Hebrews), James, Jude" (see Appendix C.1), 1 John, *possibly* 2 Peter, 2–3 John, and Revelation. As in the case of Clement of Alexandria, once again Eusebius is a primary witness to what Origen considered to be scriptural.

In the first of his [Commentaries] on the Gospel according to Matthew, defending the canon [*kanona*] of the Church, he [Origen] gives his testimony that he knows only four Gospels, writing somewhat as follows:

> …having learnt by tradition concerning the four Gospels, which alone are unquestionable in the Church of God under heaven, that first was written that according to Matthew, who was once a tax-collector but afterwards an apostle of Jesus Christ, who published it for those who from Judaism came to believe, composed as it was in the Hebrew language. Secondly, that according to Mark, who wrote it in accordance with Peter's instructions, whom also Peter acknowledged as his son in the catholic epistle, speaking in these terms: "She that is in Babylon, elect together with you, saluteth you; and so doth Mark my son" [1 Peter 5:13]. And thirdly, that according to Luke, who wrote, for those who from the Gentiles [came to believe], the Gospel that was praised by Paul. After them all, that according to John.

And in the fifth of his *Expositions on the Gospel according to John*, Origen says in regard to the epistles of the apostles:

> But he who was made sufficient to become a minister of the new covenant, not of the letter but of the spirit, even Paul, who fully preached the Gospel from Jerusalem and round about even unto Illyricum, did not so much as write to all the churches that he taught; and even to those to which he wrote he sent but a few lines [*oligous stichous*]. And Peter, on whom the Church of Christ is built, against which the gates of Hades shall not prevail, has left one acknowledged epistle [*mian epistolēn homologoumenēn*], and, *it may be [estō], a second* also; for it is doubted. Why need I speak of him who leaned back on Jesus' breast, John, who has left behind one Gospel, confessing that he could write so many [books about Jesus] that even the world itself could not contain them; and *wrote also the Apocalypse*, being ordered to keep silence and not to write the voices of seven thunders? He has *left also an epistle* of a very few lines, and, *it may be, a second and a third*; for not all say that these are genuine. Only, the two of them together are not a hundred lines long.

Furthermore, he thus discusses the Epistle to the Hebrews, in his Homilies upon it:

> That the character of the diction of the epistle entitled To the Hebrews has not the apostle's [Paul's] rudeness in speech, who confessed himself rude in speech [2 Cor 11:6], that is, in style, but the epistle is better Greek in the framing of its diction, will be admitted by everyone who is

---

48 Sundberg, "Making of the New Testament Canon," 1222–23.

able to discern differences of style. But again, on the other hand, that the thoughts of the epistle are admirable, and not inferior to the acknowledged writings [*homologoumenōn grammatōn*] of the apostle, to this also everyone will consent as true who has given attention to reading the apostle.

Further on, he adds the following remarks:

But as for myself, if I were to state my own opinion, I should say that the thoughts are the apostle's, but that the style and composition belong to one who called to mind the apostle's teachings and, as it were, made short notes of what his master said. If any church, therefore, holds this epistle as Paul's, let it be commended for this also. For not without reason have the men of old time handed it down as Paul's. But who wrote the epistle, in truth God knows. Yet the account which has reached us [is twofold], some saying that Clement, who was bishop of the Romans, wrote the epistle, others, that it was Luke, he who wrote the Gospel and the Acts. (Eusebius, *Hist. eccl.* 6.25.3–14, LCL)[49]

Origen's NT canonical list has for some time been considered a likely creation of Eusebius and Rufinus in the fourth century, a hundred years and more after the death of Origen,[50] though it is quite possible that Eusebius is reporting what he knew to be a canonical list of the writings of the NT, and if so, this is possibly the first such collection of a fixed list of NT books. Rufinus' translations of Origen's works are clearly inferior and unreliable (e.g., whenever he found difficult passages in Origen, he simply left them out of his translation, believing that they were interpolations by heretics). Rufinus' inferior translations have led some to conclude that this practice calls into question the NT canon that Rufinus attributes to Origen. However, Rufinus is probably reliable here and his listing of Origen's NT canon goes as follows:[51]

But when our Lord Jesus Christ comes, whose arrival that prior son of Nun designated, he sends priests, his apostles, bearing "trumpets hammered thin," the magnificent and heavenly instruction of proclamation. Matthew first sounded the priestly trumpet in his gospel; Mark also; Luke and John each played their own priestly trumpets. Even Peter cries out with trumpets

---

[49] B. J. Bruce, *Origen: Homilies on Joshua*, Fathers of the Church: A New Translation 105 (Washington, DC: Catholic University of America Press, 2002), 75 n. 5, notes that Origen credits Peter with a second epistle and attributes Hebrews to Paul (*Homilies on Leviticus* 4.4; 9.9), which contradicts Eusebius's opposing claims (*Hist. eccl.* 6.25.8, 13).

[50] Kalin, "Re-examining New Testament Canon History," 277–79, argues that Origen's classification system was an invention of Eusebius and that Origen had neither a NT list of books nor any notion of a NT canon. See also Albert Sundberg, "Canon Muratori: A Fourth-Century List," *HTR* 66 (1973): 36–37; and Schneemelcher, "History of the New Testament Canon," 31.

[51] Kalin, "Re-examining New Testament Canon History," 281, claims that Rufinus' Latin translation of Origen's *Homilies on Joshua* 7.1 is inaccurate, and he doubts seriously whether the list in its present form is a reflection of Origen or Rufinus' own views more than a century later. Kalin cites numerous problems in the translation by Rufinus and concludes that he "does not believe that *Homilies on Joshua* 7.1 presents us with Origen's NT canon any more than Eusebius' *Hist. eccl.* 6.25 does."

in two of his epistles; also James[52] and Jude. In addition, John also sounds the trumpet through his epistles, and Luke, as he describes the Acts of the Apostles. And now that last one comes, the one who said, "I think God displays us apostles last," and in fourteen of his epistles, thundering with trumpets, he casts down the walls of Jericho and all the devices of idolatry and dogmas of philosophers, all the way to the foundations. (*Homilies on Joshua* 7.1, B. J. Bruce, *Origen*, 74–75)

In addition to writings "recognized" (*homologoumena*) as Scripture and a few doubtful writings (e.g., Hebrews, 2 Peter, 2–3 John, James, and Jude), Origen also refers to the *Epistle of Barnabas*, *Shepherd of Hermas*, and *Didache*, possibly or apparently acknowledging them as Scripture. Kalin observes that in his *Cels.* 1.63, Origen introduces the *Epistle of Barnabas* with the words, "*It is written* in the *catholic epistle* of Barnabas" (emphasis added). Likewise, in his *First Principles* 2.1.5, Origen establishes his argument on the basis of Scripture texts, among which he cites the *Shepherd of Hermas*.[53] If one claims that Origen acknowledged James and Jude as canon because he made use of them, then the same could also be said for *Epistle of Barnabas*, *Shepherd of Hermas*, and the *Didache*. Metzger, evidently seeking to support the notion of Origen's acceptance of the NT literature alone as his NT canon, observes that Origen never wrote a commentary on a book not found in the later NT.[54] Metzger does not point out, however, that so far as our present information goes, Origen did not write a commentary on every book of the NT. And if we carry Metzger's argument further, Origen's canon would be rather limited to the books that he both cited and on which he prepared commentaries! That would exclude several NT books!

However, Origen is likely to have produced a biblical canon of NT books in his *Homily on Joshua* 7.1. The lists of canonical books presented in both Rufinus and Eusebius probably reflect Origen's intent even if they may have "touched up" his list, but not necessarily the books in it.[55] The evidence from Origen is not strong enough to conclude that he accepted all of the writings that currently make up our NT canon – especially 2 Peter, 2 and 3 John, and Revelation. It is also not clear whether he accepted *Barnabas* and the *Shepherd of Hermas* or excluded them from his collection of sacred writings. Initially, he also seems to have accepted *1 Enoch* as scripture (*Cels.* 5.52, 54–55; *De Principiis* 1.3.3; 4.4.8; 4.35; cf. *1 En.* 21:1), but later changed his mind about the book and after Origen, the book's

---

[52] Beare, "Canon of the NT," 529, observes that Origen is the first writer to refer to James.

[53] Ibid., 281. M. J. Kruger, "Origen's List of New Testament Books in Homiliae in Josuam 7.1: A Fresh Look," in *Mark, Manuscripts, and Monotheism: Essays in Honor of Larry W. Hurtado*, ed. Chris Keith and Dieter T. Roth, LNTS 528 (London: Bloomsbury, 2014), 110 n. 69, has observed that Origen cites *Barnabas* 6 times (4 explicitly) and *Shepherd of Hermas* some 19 times (11 explicitly).

[54] Metzger, "Canon of the New Testament," 125.

[55] This is an important change from my earlier position on the authenticity of Origen's NT canon list in his *Hom. Jos.* 7.1. I will show below in Chapter 21 §I.A the arguments set forth recently by Kruger, "Origen's List of New Testament Books." I find many of his arguments convincing.

scriptural status was widely but not completely rejected.[56] Some scholars suggest that Origen never had a closed canon of NT Scriptures, but, as noted above, he may well have produced a list of Christian Scriptures since it is quite likely that he produced a list of Old Testament Scriptures (see discussions of Origen in Chapter 9 §V above).[57]

VI. EUSEBIUS AND THE EMERGENCE OF A FIXED BIBLICAL CANON

Bishop Eusebius of Caesarea (writing around 320–342), following Origen, set forth the second clearly identifiable listing or catalogue of NT Scriptures. This so-called canon is not, however, as precise as many subsequent theologians would have hoped, and what remains in Eusebius' and others' canon lists reflect a lack of unanimity on the scope of the church's Scriptures at the initial stages the emergence of biblical canon catalogues. Eusebius shares some of this uncertainty in the following:

> At this point it seems reasonable to summarize the writings of the New Testament which have been quoted. In the first place should be put the holy tetrad of the Gospels. To them follows the writing of the Acts of the Apostles. After this should be reckoned the Epistles of Paul. Following them the Epistle of John called the first, and in the same way should be recognized the Epistle of Peter. In addition to these should be put, if it seem desirable, the Revelation of John, the arguments concerning which we will expound at the proper time. These belong to the Recognized Books [ὁμολογουμένοις]. Of the Disputed Books [τῶν δ' ἀντιλεγομένων] which are nevertheless known to most are the Epistle called of James, that of Jude, the second Epistle of Peter, and the so-called second and third Epistles of John which may be the work of the evangelist or of some other with the same name. Among the books which are not genuine [ἐν τοῖς νόθοις] must be reckoned the Acts of Paul, the work entitled the Shepherd, the Apocalypse of Peter, and in addition to them the letter called of Barnabas and the so-called Teachings of the Apostles [*Didache*]. And in addition, as I said, the Revelation of John, if this view prevail. For, as I said, some reject it, but others count it among the Recognized Books. Some have also counted the Gospel according to the Hebrews in which those of the Hebrews who have accepted Christ take a special pleasure. These would all belong to the disputed books, but we have nevertheless been obliged to make a list of them, distinguishing between those writings which, according to the tradition of the Church [lit., ecclesiastical tradition], are true, genuine, and recognized [scriptures] [ἀληθεῖς καὶ ἀπλάστους καὶ ἀνωμολογημένας γραφὰς], and those which differ from them in that they are not canonical [οὐκ ἐνδιαθήκους] but disputed, yet nevertheless are known to most of the writers of the Church, in order that we might know them and the writings which are put forward by heretics under the name of the apostles containing gospels such as those of Peter, and Thomas, and Matthias, and some others besides, or Acts such as

---

[56] For a list of examples of early church acceptance of *1 Enoch* as scripture and later as rejected literature, see McDonald, "Parables of Enoch in Early Christianity," especially the summary lists on 357–62.

[57] In addition to the works by Kalin and Sundberg cited in the previous notes, see also Hahneman, *Muratorian Fragment*, 133, 136.

those of Andrew and John and the other apostles. To none of these has any who belonged to the succession of the orthodox ever thought it right to refer in his writings. Moreover, the type of phraseology differs from apostolic style, and the opinion and tendency of their contents is widely dissonant from true orthodoxy and clearly shows that they are the forgeries of heretics. They ought, therefore, to be reckoned not even among spurious [ἐν νόθοις] books but shunned as altogether wicked and impious. (*Hist. eccl.* 3.25.1–7, LCL)

Eusebius' list reflects the uncertainty and lack of unanimity in the churches about which writings were authoritative Scriptures. His threefold classification is similar to that in Origen in *Hist. eccl.* 6.24–25 and may well depend on him:[58]

1. Books recognized (ὁμολογουμένα) as authoritative Scripture:[59] the four Gospels, Acts, fourteen epistles of Paul,[60] 1 John, 1 Peter, and possibly Revelation.
2. Disputed books (ἀντιλεγομένος) known to most churches: James, Jude, 2 Peter,[61] 2 John, and 3 John, and the *Gospel of the Hebrews*.
3. Spurious books (νόθος) that are not genuine: *Acts of Paul*, *Shepherd of Hermas*, *Apocalypse of Peter*, *Barnabas*, *Didache*, and possibly Revelation.

One cannot argue with certainty that Eusebius himself accepted as canonical any more than the twenty books that he lists as widely "recognized" Scriptures (i.e., the books in the first category except for Hebrews and Revelation).[62] He had doubts about several others and had strong negative feelings about the final category. From this Metzger concludes that Eusebius saw that "it is not always possible to give a definite affirmative or negative answer to the question whether a book should be in the Canon."[63] Eusebius' view regarding the doubtful books did

---

[58] For an extended discussion of Eusebius' dependence on Origen for his understanding of canon formation, see Gallagher, *Hebrew Scripture*.

[59] Eusebius uses various terminology for this type of writing: ἐνδιάθηκον ("canonical" or "encovenanted") and ὁμολογουμένον ("recognized") (*Hist. eccl.* 3.3.3; 3.25.3), ἀνωμολόγηται ("admitted") (3.3.1; 3.25.6), ἐνδιάθηκον and ἐνδιαθήκους ("testamented" or "encovenanted") (3.3.1; 3.25.6), ἀναμφιλέκτω ("undisputed" or "unquestioned") (3.3.1), παραδόσεις γραφῇ ("handed down scripture" or "canonical scripture") (5.8.1).

[60] Elsewhere Eusebius attributes Hebrews to Paul, but like Origen not without question (*Hist. eccl.* 3.3.5; cf. also 6.25.11–14).

[61] Elsewhere Eusebius lists 2 Peter among the noncanonical writings: "Of Peter, one epistle, that which is called his first, is admitted, and the ancient presbyters used this in their own writings as unquestioned, but the so-called second Epistle we have not received as canonical [οὐκ ἐνδιάθηκον], but nevertheless it has appeared useful to many, and has been studied with other Scriptures" (*Hist. eccl.* 3.3.1, LCL).

[62] On two occasions Eusebius calls *1 Clement* "recognized": "There is one recognized [ὁμολογουμένη] epistle of Clement" (*Hist. eccl.* 3.16.1); "the recognized writing [ὁμολογουμένη γραφῇ] of Clement is well known" (*Hist. eccl.* 3.39.1). He does not, however, call it ἐνδιαθήκος ("testamented" or "encovenanted"), his favored word for Scripture.

[63] Metzger, "Canon of the New Testament," 125.

not prevail and all of the doubtful books except the *Gospel of the Hebrews* were eventually accepted in the churches, including Revelation that took longer in the Eastern churches. The church preferred certainty to ambiguity, though historically it took longer to agree on whether some books should receive the normative status of Scripture.

Up to this point we can detect in the greater church in the early fourth century widespread agreement on the canonical status (canon 2) of most of our NT writings, and, with the exception of Revelation, there was broad agreement on all of the books in the NT without church council decisions. However, by the end of the fourth century church councils began to discuss the parameters of the church's biblical canon (Hippo in 393, Carthage in 397 and 416). Eusebius' collection of twenty NT writings was widely recognized in the churches ("catholicity"), but the church hierarchy debated the remaining seven books of the New Testament and others as well in its subsequent councils well into the late fourth century and fifth centuries. As we see in the Appendix C, some doubts lingered among several church fathers over some of the NT books, but eventually all twenty-seven books now in all major Christian church Bibles were officially welcomed, but that does not mean that all doubt fell away as we see in the Reformation era when Luther expressed considerable doubts about James, Hebrews, Jude, and Revelation. The broad support for and use of the NT writings is undoubtedly one of the primary reasons that later church councils eventually recognized the authenticity and canonicity of the twenty-seven books that comprise the NT canon.

This does not mean that all churches excluded all other Christian writings, as we see in the various lists and catalogues published after Eusebius (see Chapter 21 and Appendix C). On the other hand, up to and including the time of Eusebius, no hierarchical council had been involved in any decisions regarding the status of Christian writings. Before Eusebius very few lists of NT Scriptures were produced. After Eusebius, numerous lists of authoritative NT writings began circulating in the churches, and it is probable that Eusebius was the leader who followed Origen in a move toward the stabilization of the biblical canon in the churches. This may have come as a result of his being asked by Constantine to produce fifty copies of the church's Scriptures, which involved the consequent need to identify precisely what those Scriptures were (see §§VIII and IX below).

In regard to the emergence of a fixed NT biblical canon in the fourth century, Eusebius was undoubtedly the most important person who influenced the church at large to come to grips with the scope of its scriptures. He provided a catalogue of books that included books approved, not approved but disputed, and rejected. Eventually, the church accepted the books in Eusebius' disputed list and rejected those in his spurious category, and this validates his decision to suspend judgment until the books in question proved themselves to be valuable to the churches. By classifying books in these three primary categories, Eusebius thereby provided a basis for genuine dialogue within churches about the sacredness of these books – a necessary step in the process of fixing or stabilizing the canon of NT Scriptures (canon 2). Kalin claims that Eusebius is pivotal in our understanding of the canonization process that began in the first century and was largely, though not completely, finished by the end of the fourth century.[64] Although discussions of a final canonical *text* of the church's Scriptures had not begun in the fourth century, a matter seldom discussed in antiquity, this does not take away from Eusebius' pivotal role in the canonization processes that focused on the *books* that formed the NT canon.

VII. THE BURNING OF SACRED BOOKS

On February 23, 303, Emperor Diocletian launched the last empire-wide persecution of Christians. His acts of hostility against the Christians are well known and were the last of the empire-wide persecutions against Christians. Problems of loyalty to the emperor through emperor worship and perceived threats of the disintegration of unity in the empire loomed large in the empire, especially in Britain, Persia, and North Africa. Diocletian, in an almost paranoid state of mind, significantly increased the size of the military and initiated many large rebuilding programs, hoping to return the empire to its former glory. Diocletian's edict (ca. 295) *Concerning Marriages* (*De nuptiis*) focused on the theme of a need to return to religious uniformity.[65]

For the Christians, however, Diocletian's actions aimed at restoring Roman virtues, including religious roots that lay in earlier acts of devotion to the Roman deities, had serious implications for them.

Diocletian insisted that no blood be shed, but demanded that all Christian churches be destroyed and that their sacred Scriptures be burned. Christians in public office were removed, and those in the upper classes had their privileges taken away. Finally, he declared that Christian slaves could no longer be freed. Unlike the earlier empire-wide Decian persecution (250–251) that required Christians to sacrifice to the emperor, the Diocletian persecution sought to destroy the organization and life of the church by eliminating Christian books, buildings, and offices held by Christians. Contrary to Diocletian's original plan, however, many Christians died when they refused to turn over their sacred Scriptures, and some Christians were forced under threat of death to offer pagan sacrifices as well.[66]

---

[64] E. R. Kalin, "New Testament Canon of Eusebius," in McDonald and Sanders, eds., *The Canon Debate*, 386–404.

[65] W. H. C. Frend, *The Rise of Christianity* (Philadelphia: Fortress, 1984), 452–61, has a helpful discussion of this matter.

[66] Ibid., 457–58.

In May 303, the Roman authorities attempted to destroy the Christian Scriptures in Alexandria, Egypt. The following report of this action reflects the seriousness with which the Emperor's edict was taken:

> In the eighth and seventh consulships of Diocletian and Maximian, 19th May, from the records of Munatius Felix, high priest of the province for life, mayor of the colony of Cirta, arrived at the house where the Christians used to meet, the mayor said to Paul the bishop: "Bring out the writings of the law and anything else you have here, according to the order, so that you may obey the command."
>
> The Bishop: "The readers have the scriptures, but we will give what we have here."
>
> The Mayor: "Point out the readers or send for them."
>
> The Bishop: "You all know them."
>
> The Mayor: "We do not know them."
>
> The Bishop: "The municipal office knows them, that is, the clerks Edusius and Junius."
>
> The Mayor: "Leaving over the matter of the readers, whom the office will point out, produce what you have."

Then follows an inventory of the church plate and other property, including large stores of male and female clothes and shoes, produced in the presence of the clergy, who include three priests, two deacons, and four subdeacons, all named, and a number of "diggers."

> The Mayor: "Bring out what you have."
>
> Silvanus and Carosus (two of the subdeacons): "We have thrown out everything that was here."
>
> The Mayor: "Your answer is entered on the record."

After some empty cupboards have been found in the library, Silvanus then produced a silver box and a silver lamp, which he said he had found behind a barrel.

> Victor (the mayor's clerk): "You would have been a dead man if you hadn't found them."
>
> The Mayor: "Look more carefully, in case there is anything left here."
>
> Silvanus: "There is nothing left. We have thrown everything out."
>
> And when the dining-room was opened, there were found there four bins and six barrels.
>
> The Mayor: "Bring out the scriptures that you have so that we can obey the orders and command of the emperors."
>
> Catullinus (another subdeacon) produced one very large volume.

The Mayor: "Why have you given one volume only? Produce the scriptures that you have."

Marcuclius and Catullinus (two subdeacons): "We haven't any more, because we are subdeacons; the readers have the books."

The Mayor: "Show me the readers."

Marcuclius and Catullinus: "We don't know where they live."

The Mayor: "If you don't know where they live, tell me their names."

Marcuclius and Catullinus: "We are not traitors: here we are, order us to be killed."

The Mayor: "Put them under arrest."

They apparently weakened so far as to reveal one reader, for the Mayor now moved on to the house of Eugenius, who produced four books.

The Mayor now turned on the other two subdeacons, Silvanus and Carosus:

The Mayor: "Show me the other readers."

Silvanus and Carosus: "The bishop has already said that Edusius and Junius the clerks know them all: they will show you the way to their houses."

Edusius and Junius: "We will show them, sir."

The Mayor went on to visit the six remaining readers. Four produced their books without demur. One declared he had none, and the Mayor was content with entering his statement of the record. The last was out, but his wife produced his books; the Mayor had the house searched by the public slave to make sure that none had been overlooked. This task over, he addressed the subdeacons: "If there has been any omission, the responsibility is yours." (*Gesta apud Zenophilum*, Stevenson, *New Eusebius*, 287–89)

Eusebius describes this persecution in significant detail, emphasizing especially the martyrs at Nicomedia (*Hist. eccl.* 8.5–6). His introduction to the Diocletian persecution specifically mentions the burning of the sacred Scriptures:

All things in truth were fulfilled in our day, when we saw with our very eyes the houses of prayer cast down to their foundations from top to bottom, and the inspired and sacred Scriptures committed to the flames in the midst of the market-places, and the pastors of the churches, some shamefully hiding themselves here and there, while others were ignominiously captured and made a mockery by their enemies; when also, according to another prophetic word, He poureth contempt upon princes, and causeth them to wander in the waste, where there is no way...

It was the nineteenth year of the reign of Diocletian, and the month Dystrus, or March, as the Romans would call it, in which, as the festival of the Saviour's Passion was coming on, an imperial letter was everywhere promulgated, ordering the razing of the churches to the ground and the destruction by fire of the Scriptures, and proclaiming that those who held high positions would lose all civil rights, while those in households, if they persisted in their profession of Christianity, would be deprived of their liberty. Such was the first document against us. But not

long afterwards we were further visited with other letters, and in them the order was given that
the presidents of the churches should all, in every place, be first committed to prison, and then
afterwards compelled by every kind of device to sacrifice [to the emperor]. (*Hist. eccl.* 8.2.1,
4–5, LCL)

During this persecution, Christians who yielded and handed over their Scriptures
to the Roman authorities were called *traditores* ("traitors"). Christians, especially
the Donatists, despised these traitors and they were not forgiving of those who
had betrayed their sacred Scriptures. These Donatists condemned all *traditor*
clergy as those who had committed a sacrilegious act worthy of damnation in
an everlasting fire because they sought "to destroy the testaments and divine
commands of Almighty God and our Lord Jesus Christ" (*Acta Saturnini* 18.701).[67]
Christians who did not give into the persecutions and tortures and survived were
called "confessors" (ὁμολογηταί), and those who suffered abuse and died were
called "martyrs" (μάρτυρες) or "witnesses." A problem emerged in the fourth-
century church about how to deal with the *traditores* or *lapsi*, and the controversy
eventually involved Constantine himself to settle the issue.[68] At any rate, the matter
of knowing which books could be handed over to the authorities without receiving
the charge of *traditor* became an important issue and was evidently settled in
individual churches, but not yet in regional or empire-wide church councils.

The handing over of Christian sacred writings to Roman authorities presupposes knowledge on the part of Christians at the local levels about what books
were considered sacred Scripture, though complete agreement on such matters
in all churches was not present then or for centuries later. Local churches likely
knew which books constituted their sacred scriptures. Even though there was
wide agreement on the majority of the NT Scriptures at that time, later on in the
fourth and fifth centuries church councils met to deliberate the matter of which
books would serve the church as its Scriptures. For the most part, the deliberations were over the "fringe" books in the NT canon, but not on the standards
(*homolegoumena*) that Eusebius catalogued in his three-part identification of
religious texts.

VIII. CONSTANTINE AND THE CALL TO UNIFORMITY

Diocletian's actions against the church to force loyalty to the emperor through
emperor worship, sacrifices to the emperor, and religious unity that included
conformity to pagan Roman worship were all in keeping with a characteristic
trait of Roman society that sought peace through conformity (*Pax Romana*).
Remarkably, this same tendency toward unity and conformity during the reign of
Constantine (306–337) had several important consequences for the church and this

---

67   Cited by Frend, *Rise of Christianity*, 462.
68   Kelly, *Early Christian Doctrines*, 410–12.

may have played a role in the churches' establishment of a biblical canon subsequently. During and after Constantine, many moves toward canon conformity or stabilization were initiated, and it is not likely by accident that various catalogues of authoritative Christian Scriptures emerge during this period of the church's history.

It is indisputable that the reign of Constantine marked the most significant transition of the church from a community persecuted by a pagan government to a community favored by the state. At first, it was an especially beneficial relationship for the church because the severe hostilities toward it ceased and reparations of lost properties and offices once held began. Later this union made even more profound and lasting changes in the makeup and mission of the church that were not as positive as the earlier ones that brought a cessation of hostilities toward Christians.

The so-called conversion of Constantine came as a result of his most famous vision of the cross reported by Eusebius (*Life of Constantine* 1.27–30; 3.2–3) and his conversion led to many significant benefits for the church, the most important of which was, of course, freedom for Christians to worship without fear of persecution (2.24). This began with Constantine's Edict of Milan in 313 that gave religious freedom to all Roman subjects, not just for the Christians, even though the Christians were clearly favored by the emperor and the edict was especially beneficial for them. These benefits increased later when Constantine ordered, at Rome's expense, the repair or replacement of church buildings that had been damaged or destroyed during the severe ten years of persecutions begun in 303. He also ordered at Rome's expense the bestowal of extravagant gifts upon the church (2.46; 3.1) and its leaders (3.16). Interestingly, he also requested that Eusebius produce fifty copies of the church's "inspired records" that had been destroyed (3.1). Those copies functioned in the New Rome, Constantinople, as the church's scriptures.[69] Finally, he "took vengeance" upon those who had persecuted the Christians (3.1).

Constantine's decisions had a significant impact on all churches that survived the persecutions. Indeed, as we can see in the euphoric manner in which Eusebius describes these events, he and the whole church were understandably delighted to see the end of the hostilities against them and rejoiced in the new honors and blessings bestowed upon them. They only had praise for Constantine, including such references to him as "like a powerful herald of God" (2.61), "pious emperor" (2.73), "divinely favored emperor" (3.1), and one who "thus made it his constant aim to glorify his Saviour God" (3.54).

Although Eusebius never mentioned any fault or weakness in Constantine, subsequent authors were not as favorable in their assessments.[70] It appears that

---

[69] I will return to this matter below and its possible implications for canon formation.

[70] R. MacMullen, *Christianizing the Roman Empire (A.D. 100–400)* (New Haven: Yale University Press, 1984), 43–58, raises valid questions about the extent of Constantine's conversion by highlighting his brutality toward non-Christians and his coercion of the church.

Constantine was initially only favorable toward Christianity but later became more accepting of its teachings. He was not baptized until shortly before his death. Following his conversion, he continued to revere the god of his father and tended toward a syncretistic Christianity in which he identified the Christian God with the sun. He made the first day of the week (the Lord's Day) a holiday and called it "the venerable day of the sun" (Sunday) which is still used today. Eusebius seems to have ignored many of Constantine's faults, even passing over his breaking of his pledge not to murder Caesar Licinius, his wife, and his son.

The above questions notwithstanding, the impact of Constantine's conversion on the church was highly significant and brought the church into an altogether new epoch in which church and state were at times indistinguishable. Eusebius proudly claims that with Constantine, "a new and fresh era of existence had begun to appear, and a light heretofore unknown suddenly [brought the church] to the dawn from the midst of darkness on the human race" (3.1).

Constantine's post-conversion involvement in the affairs of the church was extensive. Although he was initially invited *by the Christians* to become involved in settling church controversies, almost from the beginning he saw it as his duty to become involved in the decisions of the church. This involved his calling (in effect, ordering) bishops and other church leaders to come together and attend various church councils (3.6; 4.41–43), especially the first church ecumenical council, the Council of Nicea in 325. Constantine's goal was to resolve theological disputes in the churches (e.g., concerning Arius; 2.61), where to send bishops (e.g., Eusebius to Antioch; 3.59–61), settling the time for the celebration of Easter that had been a major dispute since the end of the second century (3.6–18), whether and how to punish heretics (3.20, 64–65), and when, where, and how to build churches (3.29–43).

Constantine not only arbitrated in such matters, but also reconvened a council when its decision went contrary to his own wishes, as in the case of the Donatist controversy in North Africa. Constantine threatened bishops under penalty of banishment if they did not obey his orders to convene at Tyre (4.41–42), and he even sent his representative of "consular rank" (Dionysus) to insure order at the church council and to remind the bishops of their duty (4.42). Finally, he ordered the same church leaders to come to Jerusalem to help him celebrate the dedication of the new church building there!

It is ironic that on one occasion he wrote that, while the bishops were overseers of the internal affairs of the church, he himself was a "bishop, ordained by God to overlook whatever is external to the church" (4.24). One is hard pressed, however, to find an internal issue in which he did not involve himself! No one would deny Constantine's interest in all matters related to the church, but it is clear from Eusebius that he would tolerate no threats to the rule of peace and harmony either in his empire or in the churches. Although he was not as cruel as his predecessors toward the church, he nonetheless demanded harmony (uniformity). Those whose doctrines were not in keeping with the orthodoxy of the day were banished into exile, their writings burned, and their meeting places confiscated (3.66).

Unity and peace were more important to Constantine than what he called the "trifling" matter of the dispute over the person of Christ. In his letter to Alexander, the Bishop of Alexandria, and to Arius the Presbyter, he states clearly his purpose for writing:

Victor Constantinus, Maximus Augustus, to Alexander and Arius.

"I call that God to witness, as well I may, who is the helper of my endeavors, and the Preserver of all men, that I had a twofold reason for undertaking that duty which I have now performed.

"My design then was, first, to bring the diverse judgments formed by all nations respecting the Deity to a condition, as it were, *of settled uniformity*; and, secondly, to restore to health the system of the world, then suffering under the malignant power of a grievous distemper. Keeping these objects in view, I sought to accomplish the one by the secret eye of thought, while the other I tried to rectify by the power of military authority. For I was aware that, if *I should succeed in establishing, according to my hopes, a common harmony of sentiment among all the servants of God*, the general course of affairs would also experience a change correspondent to the pious desires of them all.

"And yet, having made a careful enquiry into the origin and foundation of these differences, *I find the cause to be of a truly insignificant character, and quite unworthy of such fierce contention*. Feeling myself, therefore, compelled to address you in this letter, and to appeal at the same time to your unanimity and sagacity, I call on Divine Providence to assist me in the task, while I interrupt your dissension in the character of a minister of peace. And with reason: for if I might expect, with the help of a higher Power, to be able without difficulty, by a judicious appeal to the pious feelings of those who heard me, to recall them to a better spirit, even though the occasion of the disagreement were a greater one, how can I refrain from promising myself a far easier and more speedy adjustment of this difference, *when the cause which hinders general harmony of sentiment is intrinsically trifling and of little moment*?" (*Life of Constantine*, 2.64–65, 68, NPNF, emphasis added)

One may reasonably conclude from this that peace and harmony in the empire and among Christians were chief among Constantine's major doctrines. The majority of churches affirmed the doctrines he favored, and he expected all others to conform to them.

At times Constantine was gracious, generous, and even humble, but he did not easily or long tolerate differences of opinion or challenges to his authority in church matters (4.42). His understanding of harmony was not so much peaceful coexistence, as it was peace through uniformity in thinking – that is, he wanted to bring about a consensus among the people. On the one hand he destroyed several pagan temples and banned the practices of sacrificing and idol worship (2.44; 3.54–58), and on the other he intimidated the dissident bishops into conformity to his wishes or with those of the majority of the bishops (3.13).

As with earlier emperors, Constantine seems to have concluded that anything out of step with unity in the Empire was a threat that had to be dealt with and even severely if necessary. Several previous Roman rulers considered any opposition to or rejection of Roman deities as a threat to the empire. Constantine, at times, seems to have changed only the favored deity and religion, not the example of his predecessors. At times it appears that his overriding concern was not the moral and inner transformation of the Christian faith so much as peace and unity in the churches' outward social manifestations of it. Following Constantine's suppression of heresy, Eusebius wrote with pleasure. "Thus the members of the entire body became united, and compacted in one harmonious whole…while no heretical or schismatic body anywhere continued to exist" (3.66, NPNF).

That appears to be an over-statement of the facts since debates over the identity of Jesus the Christ continued long in the Arian controversies in the churches. The evidence of continuing divisions in churches, of course, does not support Eusebius' description, but the unity he describes likely reflects a widespread fear of the consequences for dissent in the churches at that time. Constantine's pressure to unify the church under the all-powerful state with the right to convene councils of bishops and to discipline dissident church members appears to have established the authoritative pattern for later popes to follow in dealing with ecclesiastical activities, heresy, and with the appointment of bishops in the church. One of Constantine's inherited titles, Pontifex Maximus ("chief priest") was kept throughout Constantine's rule and perhaps influenced his decision to become actively involved in church decisions. Beginning with Augustus (31 BCE–12 CE), this title was used by all subsequent Roman emperors. The title is also reflective of the kind of power that was later vested in the churches' popes. Constantine's power over the bishop's council, and even over decisions of local magistrates (3.20), is similar to practices followed later by some popes. Constantine's actions and decrees doubtless helped also to politicize the clergy.

The major consequence of Constantine's conversion for the church was the Christianizing of the Roman Empire, which not only included the cessation of the persecution of the Christians, but also guaranteed the triumph of orthodoxy (primarily Western orthodoxy) over the whole church. Major dissidents within the church were all but silenced during this time. The theological stance earlier and later identified with orthodoxy became the leading position of the church. Consequently, in terms of the formation of the Christian biblical canon, the theological positions adopted by the churches – or imposed on them – may well have played an important role in the process of identifying the Christian Scriptures that received priority and gained canonicity in the churches. Again, however, the majority of the books that obtained canonicity in the churches were already in place before the time of Constantine or any fourth-century decisions, but in the case of the disputed works, later church councils appear to have played an important role. In this sense, Constantine's actions toward the church surely must have had an important, if not easily measurable, impact on the formation of the Christian biblical canon.

However, this is not the same as saying that Constantine himself determined the scope of the Christian Bible, an argument that has been made by several scholars.[71] Much of what we have in the Christian Bible and the New Testament

---

[71]   This is a significant flaw in the otherwise fine contribution by David L. Dungan's *Constantine's Bible: Politics and the Making of the New Testament* (Minneapolis: Fortress, 2007). I was asked by

in particular was already widely recognized as the church's scriptures long before Constantine. It may be possible that Constantine's well-known preference for the book of Revelation was what eventually led to its acceptance, but that cannot be demonstrated. The notion of Johannine authorship of the book was likely more influential. While the church was obviously significantly better off after Constantine's conversion, the new epoch that began with a unity of church and state came at a high price for the church to pay for its new freedom and peace.

IX. PRODUCTION OF FIFTY SACRED BOOKS

When Constantine relocated the capital of his empire from Rome to Byzantium and named it "New Rome" (later "Constantinople" that is, the "City of Constantine," and subsequently Istanbul which means the same), he requested that Eusebius produce fifty copies of the church's Scriptures for the churches in the New Rome. Eusebius prepared them in accordance with the best literary productions of his day. Constantine's call for the careful, and indeed exquisite, production of these copies of the Christian Scriptures shows that at least Eusebius, who was charged with the duty of making them, was aware or soon became aware of the parameters of this collection of those Scriptures. His own choices in this matter no doubt are reflected in the fifty copies he produced. It is unlikely, as some have suggested, that Codices Vaticanus and Sinaiticus, both fourth-century productions, are examples of these fifty copies, but their exquisite style and professional format may suggest that they are copies of one or more of those initial fifty copies. Vaticanus (ca. 350) and Sinaiticus (ca. 360–375) were likely produced decades later than the copies Eusebius produced.

---

editors of Fortress Press to critique that volume before its publication and, unfortunately, none of the recommendations that I submitted were followed or even passed on to Dungan. Thinking that those changes would be made, I wrote a positive jacket blurb for the volume that was placed at the beginning of the volume. Later David Dungan told me that he had not received any of my suggested changes from his publisher. Dungan has a good analysis of Eusebius' twenty book canon, but jumps to the acceptance of a twenty-seven book canon and that the churches accepted the books in the current NT canon as a result of Constantine's pressure. That, of course, cannot be demonstrated and later church councils (Hippo in 393, Carthage in 397 and 416) only deliberated on the fringes of the NT canon. Dungan points to Constantine's ability to intimidate church councils as his primary evidence that he determined the contours of the church's Bible. He does not take into consideration that the variations in the NT manuscripts after Constantine (d. 337) reflect the circulation of other books in the churches' NT long after Constantine. Dungan also follows von Campenhausen and Metzger on the role of heresy leading the church to identify its scriptures, rather than the churches' *regula fidei*. Again, this is a good book, but weak on the points noted above. Dungan has a useful timeline of events related to the formation of the Bible on pp. 155–57. Also, his first four chapters are worth the price of the book! We disagree, however, on the extent of Constantine's influence on the whole of the church's biblical canon.

Not all Christians in the fourth century agreed on the scope of their NT canon, as we will see in Chapters 20 and 21 below. In fact, the differences of opinion on what constitutes the churches' sacred Scriptures have never been completely resolved or silenced in churches, in spite of the decisions of the later church councils. However, the decisions reached in this period with, the assistance of Constantine's request for fifty copies, were likely influential in decisions made by churches in subsequent generations.

The role of Constantine in the delimiting process of the Christian biblical canon may have been considerable if we acknowledge his role in the selection process and copying of the fifty copies, but nothing at present suggests that he was involved in the selection of the books that were included in those copies. While Eusebius himself did not acknowledge the scriptural status of the book of Revelation (*Hist. eccl.* 3.25.4), perhaps, as I noted above, because of Constantine's preference for the book, it was added. We do not know for sure why Revelation was included in the later carefully and professionally produced copies of the church's scriptures that we see in Vaticanus and Sinaiticus. Remarkably, Revelation was included in several fourth-century lists and manuscripts from the Eastern region of the empire, where its reception was often cold or even negative! If the matter of which books belonged in the Christian Bible was not finalized before Eusebius (ca. 325–330), as one surmises from his comments (*Hist. eccl.* 3.25.1–7), then it probably was settled at least *for Eusebius* by the time he produced the fifty copies of the Christian Scriptures. In Eusebius's own words, the production of these fifty copies of sacred Scriptures went as follows:

> Ever careful for the welfare of the churches of God, the emperor addressed me personally in a letter on the means of providing copies of the inspired oracles...
>
> "Victor Constantinus, Maximus Augustus, to Eusebius.
>
> "It happens, through the favoring providence of God our Saviour, that great numbers have united themselves to the most holy church in the city which is called by my name [Constantinople]. It seems, therefore, highly requisite, since that city is rapidly advancing in prosperity in all other respects, that the number of churches should also be increased. Will you, therefore, receive with all readiness my determination on this behalf? I have thought it expedient to instruct your Prudence to order fifty copies of the sacred Scriptures, the provision and use of which you know to be most needful for the instruction of the Church, *to be written on prepared parchment in a legible manner, and in a convenient, portable form [codex], by professional transcribers thoroughly practiced in their art.* The catholicus of the diocese has also received instructions *by letter from our Clemency to be careful to furnish all things necessary for the preparation of such copies; and it will be for you to take special care that they are completed with as little delay as possible.* You have authority also, in virtue of this letter, to use two of the public carriages for their conveyance, by which arrangement the copies when fairly written will most easily be forwarded for my personal inspection; and one of the deacons of your church may be entrusted with this service, who, on his arrival here, shall experience my liberality. God preserve you, beloved brother!"

Such were the emperor's commands, which were followed by the immediate execution of the work itself, which *we sent him in magnificent and elaborately bound volumes of a threefold and fourfold form (trissa kai tetrassa).*[72] This fact is attested by another letter, which the emperor wrote in acknowledgment, in which, having heard that the city Constantia in our country, the inhabitants of which had been more than commonly devoted to superstition, had been impelled by a sense of religion to abandon their past idolatry, he testified his joy, and approval of their conduct. (*Life of Constantine* 4.34, 36–37, NPNF, emphasis added)

By the time of Constantine's request of Eusebius (perhaps as late as ca. 334–336), one can presume that there was a fairly well-defined collection of both OT and NT Scriptures and that the fifty copies had a considerable impact not only on the churches in Constantinople, but on other churches in that vicinity as well. Several books of the NT, however, were still disputed (e.g., Hebrews and Revelation) and some books used earlier did not eventually make it into the NT canon (*Shepherd, Ep. Barnabas*) but were welcomed in some churches. The fact that the later Codex Sinaiticus (ca. 375) includes *Epistle of Barnabas* and *Shepherd of Hermas* suggests that the full parameters of the NT canon were not yet settled for all churches at that time. Eusebius' copies of the church's Scriptures may well have become the standard for subsequent expertly copied codices of the fourth and fifth centuries and later. While some scholars have posited that Codex Vaticanus, or Codex Sinaiticus, or Codex Washingtonianus may be among the fifty copies produced by Eusebius, the evidence is not conclusive. It has been suggested that Codex Vaticanus (B, ca. perhaps 350) may be a defective copy rejected by Eusebius, or a descendent of one of the fifty copies, but again, there is no evidence that demonstrates this outside of the obvious professional character of the text and format.[73] More likely, the kind of text employed in the fifty copies was a forerunner of the Byzantine (majority) text.[74]

If Constantine's fifty copies included the current twenty-seven books of the NT,[75] this in itself would no doubt have had a powerful impact on the eventual acceptance of a twenty-seven-book NT canon at least in the region of the new capital, Constantinople.[76] Whatever the case, Eusebius' account is significant in the ongoing history of the formation of the Christian biblical canon, and Constantine himself may have had some indefinable influence on the current form of our NT

---

[72] The words *trissa kai tetrassa* are perplexing. They may refer to making three or four copies at a time or to three or four columns per page. For discussion, see G. A. Robbins, "'Fifty Copies of Sacred Writings' (Vigiliae christianae 4.36): Entire Bibles or Gospel Books?" *Studia patristica* 19 (1989): 93–94.

[73] K. Lake, "The Sinaitic and Vatican Manuscripts and the Copies Sent by Eusebius to Constantine," *HTR* 11 (1918): 32–35; and T. C. Skeat, "The Use of Dictation in Ancient Book-Production," *Proceedings of the British Academy* 42 (1956): 195–97.

[74] F. F. Bruce, *Canon of Scripture*, 204.

[75] Robbins, "Fifty Copies of Sacred Writings," 97–98, argues that only the Gospels – not the entire Bible – were copied.

[76] F. F. Bruce, *Canon of Scripture*, 205.

canon,[77] or at least the format of subsequent copies of the church's Scriptures. Whatever was produced in the fifty copies probably had a wide influence, but it was not determinative for subsequent generations as we see in later deliberations on the contents of the biblical canon, the variations in the canon catalogues in the fourth century and following, and the continued use of noncanonical writings for centuries longer in the churches.

X. SUMMARY

The following brief summary of the historical development of the Christian canon up to this point is in order before looking at various authorities that influenced the churches following Constantine's declaration that granted churches the freedom to gather and worship in their accustomed manner. I will make seven points here and more in the following chapters:

1. The primary authority of the earliest Christian community was Jesus himself. Not only was the early church's faith linked to his death and resurrection, but it was also focused on the sayings or words of Jesus. The call to "remember the words of Jesus" reflects his unequalled authority in the early churches. Jesus' sayings were at first, and for some time, passed on in oral form in the churches, but many of them were written down quite early, perhaps even before the death of Jesus (Q?), and circulated among the Christians, even though the books in which they were found (the Gospels) were not initially viewed as Scripture. The Scriptures of the first-century Christians included the OT Scriptures, which were not yet well defined either by Christians or Jews before the separation of Christians from their Jewish siblings.

2. In the second century, Christian writings, especially the Gospels, began to be referred to with greater frequency in the life of the church. At first, the words of Jesus, when proclaimed orally or written down, functioned as Scripture, but the church's focus was not on books or their authors/editors where those sayings were found, but rather on the words, deeds, and fate of Jesus. In the second century, many (but not all) of the churches used the canonical Gospels, especially Matthew, and several of the Letters of Paul in their worship and teaching. Some of those were even acknowledged as Scripture by the middle to late second century and were used in admonitions to Christians and catechetical instruction. All Christian religious texts

---

[77] W. R. Farmer, *Jesus and the Gospel: Tradition, Scripture and Canon* (Philadelphia: Fortress, 1982), 273–75, argues that Constantine's call for fifty copies of the Scriptures influenced the form and status of the NT.

functioned *as Scripture* for some churches before they were actually called Scripture. The many allusions to the Pauline literature in the Apostolic Fathers shows a deep respect for Paul and a willingness to hear his advice on church matters (*1 Clem.* 47). By the end of the first century CE, limited collections of Paul's writings circulated freely among many churches, along with one or more of the canonical Gospels.

3. Justin defended the OT as Christian Scripture and also indicated that the church regularly read the Gospels ("memoirs of the apostles") in its worship alongside (*or instead of*) the OT Scriptures ("prophets").

4. With Irenaeus came the clearest initial designation of Christian writings as Scripture and the first NT collection of Scriptures separate from the OT Scriptures. Others before him made use of some Christian texts in a scriptural fashion, but Irenaeus clearly recognized their scriptural status and accepted only a closed four-Gospel canon identified by the names of the Evangelists who it was believed produced them. He was not precise on the boundaries of the rest of the Christian Scriptures and left no list behind indicating all of the Christian texts or other religious texts that he considered sacred scripture. This can only be partially surmised based on the texts that he cites in his ad hoc arguments against heresies. So far as can be determined from his writings, apart from the four canonical Gospels, he did not clarify what else was NT Scripture and what was not, though he obviously accepted several of Paul's writings as Christian Scripture and likely also the *Shepherd* and *1 Enoch.*

5. Diocletian's edict to force the Christians to hand over their sacred Scriptures for burning must have influenced many churches to come to grips with the question of which of their books were sacred Scripture and could not be turned over. Many Christians were willing to hand over some non-scriptural religious writings in an attempt to satisfy the authorities, and this act, of course, presumes a knowledge at the local level of what was and what was not considered Scripture.

6. Eusebius was instrumental in setting forth an early catalogue or list of sacred scripture collections in the churches and may be the first or second church father to produce canon catalogues or lists of the church's sacred Scriptures. If not him, then perhaps Origen before him since Eusebius seemed to be in lock step with Origen, especially in terms of Origen's primary criterion for acceptance, namely catholicity or widespread use in churches. This is the same as Eusebius' *homologoumena* argument noted above. He may have modeled his list after Origen's, but that is not clear. Eusebius' focus on the stabilization of the Scriptures of the church eventually became a dominant concern of many church leaders in the fourth century when "canon" came to mean a fairly precise collection of sacred writings.

7. Constantine played an important role in the churches' agreements on the broad outlines of the biblical canon through his many actions promoting unity and uniformity in the churches and asking Eusebius to produce fifty copies of those Scriptures. Whatever Eusebius produced doubtless had some impact on the churches in the region of New Rome, if not throughout various parts of the empire, even though there was as yet no consensus on the matter among the churches in the fourth century. We will see that in the variety of canon lists that reflect a post-Constantine era that there was broad, but not complete agreement on the scope of the NT. The final stabilization of the NT canon did not happen with Constantine, but perhaps because of his call to unity in the churches, the process of canonization was realized for most churches in the later fourth and fifth centuries. As we will see, however, that process was not complete for several more centuries.

We are not well served by those who insist on focusing on the inclusion and exclusion stages of canon development, as if the church was initially open to everything and then by the fourth century it began excluding books it no longer wanted. Inclusion and exclusion in the canonical processes were in a constant dynamic relationship almost from the beginning. Some Christians in the second century were just as opposed to some of the Christian writings as were some in the fourth century. Opposition to writings that did not conform to the *regula fidei* was also present earlier as it was later in the church, as we saw in Irenaeus' rejection and condemnation of the *Gospel of Judas* and various gnostic writings.[78] Several of the current NT writings were *functioning* as Scripture by the end of the first century for some church leaders and for others in the early to middle second century. By that time some of the Christian texts began to be called Scripture and by the end of the second century several others had that distinction, but not all of the NT Scriptures were so designated even then. For some NT books, the process of recognition and acceptance took much longer. Fixing the precise boundaries of the church's Scripture collection(s) was a later decision (ca. 350–450) for the majority of churches. The boundaries of the Christian biblical canon were in a state of flux for a considerable time in the church at large. Indeed, what was fixed in one church might still be in doubt or under debate in another – and that continued centuries longer as we will see below. The church never agreed fully on the scope of its Bible, though most eventually agreed on the scope of the NT canon.

We will now focus on the primary authorities in the early churches and subsequently on the role of heresies in prompting the churches to focus on the scope of its sacred Scriptures.

---

[78] Barton, *Holy Writings, Sacred Text*, 35–36, makes this point and underscores both the flux and stability in early Christianity.

CHAPTER 17

AUTHORITIES IN EARLY CHRISTIANITY: TRADITION, SCRIPTURE, AND THE SPIRIT

I. AUTHORITIES IN EARLY CHRISTIANITY

Early Christianity appealed to a number of authorities in their early years and the most important was, of course, Jesus. His followers acknowledged him as the Christ who had a special relationship with God, namely he was believed to be the unique Son of God and Lord of the church. They believed that he came to bring reconciliation between God and humanity including forgiveness of sins, and hope for the future. They also appealed frequently to other authorities, especially their OT Scriptures, creeds that summarized the core of their faith (1 Cor 15:3–8; Phil 2:6–11; 1 Tim 3:16, etc.), and subsequently their newly acquired Christian Scriptures, an emerging powerful episcopate comprised of church leadership, and finally their ecclesiastical canons or church council decisions. All of these authorities had their antecedents in the early church's tradition about Jesus and the implications of those traditions for faith, daily living, and Christian mission. These other authorities often overlapped in function and substance and together they formed the foundation from which early Christianity grew and developed into the church that it became. These authorities will be the focus of this chapter.

A. The Primary Authorities in Early Christianity and the Role of the Spirit

Jesus' life, ministry, and teachings were welcomed as guides and models for living by his followers. Their beliefs about his death and resurrection were the foundational elements that his followers acknowledged for establishing his identity as Son of God and Lord of the church (Matt 28:19; Rom 1:3–4; 10:9).

That primary authority was also coupled with early Christian interpretations of their First Scriptures that they had inherited (took over) from their Jewish siblings and later called their OT Scriptures. Those two authorities were soon joined with others, namely the oral and later written traditions about Jesus, many of which were eventually put in writings now called Gospels. Before long, several Christian writings that told the story of Jesus were circulating in churches and some of those apparently antedate the production of the canonical Gospels (Luke 1:1–3).

The earliest *canonical* Gospels were written around thirty or more years after the death of Jesus, but the early churches were not left in the meantime without a proclamation or foundation for their mission. From the church's beginning, the apostolic teachings about Jesus and the implications of that for Christian living and mission were at the heart of Christian gatherings. The brief summary of life in the early church (Acts 2:42) likely reflects practices that took place in their gatherings, namely they had a commitment to apostolic teaching, along with fellowship (which included practical caring for one another), breaking bread together, and prayers. The apostolic teaching about Jesus no doubt formed the core tradition at the center of those teachings and that tradition was circulating in churches from its very beginning. Paul, for instance, indicates that he passed on to the Corinthians *what he had also received* (1 Cor 15:3) and we know that he claims that what he received was from the Lord (Gal 1:1, 15–16). He also states that he had contact with the leaders of the church in Jerusalem (Gal 1:18–19; 2:1–2) but contended that his understanding was the same as theirs about who Jesus was, what he had done, and the implications of that for faith (1 Cor 15:3–11, 12–20).

Along with these traditions, several creeds that summarized those traditions also began circulating in churches (e.g., Rom 10:9; 1 Cor 15:3–8; Phil 2:6–11; 1 Tim 3:16). They identified and summarized the core teaching and proclamation of the early churches. These creeds were eventually expanded in various other creeds. We have already seen in Chapter 16 an early second-century form of a creed in Irenaeus (*Haer.* 1.10.1; cf. 3.4.2), but there were others such as the *Apostles' Creed*, *Nicene Creed*, and similar subsequent creedal formulations. Creeds have been prominent in churches almost from their beginning and they reflect an awareness of several beliefs and events and affirmations in biblical writings, including the NT creedal formulations. Some of the early creeds and hymns noted above expressed the core beliefs of Christian faith and were incorporated into some of the early as well as later Christian writings, some of which were eventually included in the church's NT canon. Early creedal formulations and hymns summarized the heart of Christian beliefs (such as the *Odes of Solomon*, ca. 100–125 CE) and they focused on God's activity in Jesus.

From its beginning and throughout the emergence of the early church, the words of Jesus had the highest priority in the churches. As we saw, Jesus himself contrasted his teaching with the Jewish scriptures and their oral traditions as in: "you have heard it said, but I say unto you…" (Matt 5:21, 27, 31, 33, 38, 43; cf. 28:19; cf. Mark 7:1–13). Jesus' *remembered* teachings had a scriptural authority attached to them as we saw in 1 Tim 5:18. Jesus' sayings or commands were, without question, the highest authority in the churches, as we see in Paul's contrast of his own words of advice and opinion with the commands of Jesus (1 Cor 7:10–12, 25; cf. also 1 Cor 11:23–26). I find Michael J. Kruger's position that Paul did not place the sayings of Jesus higher than his own in 1 Cor 7:10–12 unconvincing.[1] He suggests that Paul put his writing on par with that of Jesus' commands and did not place Jesus' words on a higher level than his own. He appears to start with a theological belief that the whole church recognized Paul's writings as sacred inviolable scripture – and that Scripture is Scripture no matter who says it. This, of course, is a much later belief that Kruger inserts into a context in which the priority of Jesus' teachings is obvious. Paul does not put his words on the same level as Jesus' command, but nonetheless believes his advice correct and even led by the Spirit. As we see in 7:25, Paul offers his own opinion in which he later says that he "thinks he has the Spirit of God" on the matter (δοκῶ δὲ κἀγὼ πνεῦμα θεοῦ ἔχειν, 1 Cor 7:40). If Kruger is right,[2] then other orthodox writers who believed that the Spirit led them in what they said or wrote (Clement of Rome, Ignatius, and most others who thought that they were teaching the truth and led by the Spirit) must have also been consciously writing Scripture. If that is the case, then many other "scriptures" are missing from the NT! More importantly, had Paul been actually conscious of writing Scripture, we might think that he would say so at least once in a while, but he never does and his writings were not called Scripture by anyone before the second century.

With the exception of 2 Pet 3:16 (ca. 130–150) that equates Paul's writings with the "other Scriptures," no other NT texts call Paul's writings Scripture until second-century church fathers begin using Paul's writings as Scripture and begin calling them such (ca. 130–170). Kruger, citing 1 Cor 14:37–38 as proof that Paul believed that what he was saying was a command of God, contends that this demonstrates that Paul believed he was writing "scripture." In this passage (14:37–38) Kruger seems to confuse the verb "I am writing" (γράφω) or the act of writing with γραφὴ ("scripture" or "writing"). He equates the act of writing with what is written (γραφὴ) and jumps to the conclusion that Paul is consciously writing Scripture.[3] While the text, like 1 Cor 7:10, claims to be a command of the Lord, and Paul distinguished what he says from what the Lord says, Kruger contends that in 7:10 he was passing on a command of the Lord. What followed was what Kruger thought was not simply Paul's opinion (7:25), but that it was also led by the Spirit and was therefore Scripture.

In 14:37–38, Paul shares with the Corinthians that what he is telling them comes directly from the Lord. Again, Paul is not speaking on his own authority, but the authority of the Lord (the risen Lord). At no place does Paul equate what he is

---

[1]   See Kruger, *The Question of Canon*, 127 n. 36.
[2]   Ibid., 187–88.
[3]   Ibid.

saying as on par with what Jesus the Lord has said or taught. This is Kruger's misunderstanding of Paul. Paul's message is that the spiritual utterances of the prophets are subject to control (14:26–33a) and they must not lead to confusion or chaos among those who meet in the name of the Lord. That is what Paul believes is a command of the Lord. In other words, he did not come to this on his own. If Paul was trying to say that whatever he wrote was sacred scripture on par with the Lord, one would think that he might have said so in 7:10–12 or elsewhere, but he does not. In 14:37–38, Paul has in mind his opponents who thought that they were "prophets" and "Spirit people" (4:18; 9:3),[4] and the command Paul has for his opponents, he believes, is from the Lord who is against what leads to confusion among his followers. Paul believed that he had a prophetic gift and was led by the Spirit to say what he said. No one disputes that; however, Paul's understanding of that prophetic gift never led him to say that those who prophesied in the churches were speaking or writing Scripture. The gift of prophecy to Paul was not equivalent to Scripture. There are, of course, no parallels in the canonical Gospels to Paul's statement in this passage, and some scholars have suggested that Paul has an *agraphon* in view in 14:37–38, a noncanonical saying of Jesus that was circulating in the churches. We already know that we do not have everything that Jesus said in the Gospels (John 20:30; 21:25) and there may have been a parallel saying of Jesus "out there" circulating in the churches, but that is not necessary here. Paul was not speaking on his own, but is sure that he has a command *from the Lord* on the matter at hand.

Kruger should see his inconsistency by an obvious interpretation of 1 Cor 7:10 that contrasts what the Lord commanded with what Paul said in 7:12 and 25, but he tries to equate the two saying that Paul was not distinguishing what he said from "the Lord" (Jesus) as if what the Lord said was more important than what he said. This is special pleading and does not get to the point Paul is making in both texts. When Paul is sure that he has a command from the Lord, he does not put what he has to say on the same level with Jesus. See also 1 Cor 11:17–22 in which Paul speaks against how the Corinthians observe the sacred meal, but then he goes on to say that how it is to be conducted is something that he got from the Lord Jesus and he spells it out (11:23–25). Why bring the Lord into the picture if Paul's word alone was of equal authority and sufficient for the occasion?

Another problem with Kruger's thesis is that it seems to ignore the fact that Paul never calls his own writings Scripture and Kruger has to infer in odd ways what the best commentators do not draw from the passage. Paul simply did not say that he was writing Scripture and later Clement of Rome, who cites or quotes Paul's writings some fifteen times, never once calls them Scripture, as we saw earlier in Chapter 15. Clement did believe that Paul was inspired, as we saw earlier, but

---

[4]   See Gordon D. Fee, *The First Epistle to the Corinthians*, NICNT (Grand Rapids: Eerdmans, 1987), 711–12.

Clement also thought that he himself was inspired! Ignatius has some thirty-five citations and references to and parallels with Paul's writings, but never calls any of Paul's writings "Scripture."[5] (See further discussion of Kruger's position and the place of inspiration in Chapter 22 §II.F.)

The authority of Jesus and the early apostolic teaching about him, including appeals to the OT Scriptures about him, all functioned as the primary major authorities that helped form the foundational identity of Jesus for early Christians and for the church itself. By the middle to end of the second century, *several* first-century Christian writings were beginning to be acknowledged as sacred scripture, though they doubtless had *functioned* that way earlier. Scriptural citation formulae, such as "as it is written" or "as the scripture says," are regularly, but not consistently used in the NT when citing the OT scriptures. Although the OT Scriptures are regularly introduced by those formulae in the NT and by the early church fathers, this was not uniform and those designations were not always used in reference to either the OT or NT writings. As we noted earlier, Mark indicates that Jesus cited Dan 7:13 (Mark 14:62) and he does so without any scriptural formulae. Few scholars suggest that Jesus was not quoting Scripture. Likewise, the author of Hebrews who cites OT texts proportionately more than any other NT author regularly does so without any of the usual citation formulae and with only one exception (Heb 10:7 citing Ps 40:6–8 LXX) and that is *in the quote itself.* No one would deny, however, the author's multiple citations and quotes were what he thought were scriptural references. This includes his citation of Wis 7:25 in Heb 1:3. The citation formulae were not always or consistently used either by the writers of the NT or by the early church fathers when they used or cited the NT writings. The authority of many NT writings was acknowledged earlier, but the citation of the NT writings as sacred Scripture was largely a later initiative.

Kruger has written a well-informed focus on the canonization of the NT books that many in the evangelical community have adopted. He has examined carefully most of the relevant biblical and extra-biblical sources that canon scholars regularly cite in their examinations of the canonization processes and generally does a good job of explaining them. The places where we disagree has especially to do with how he defines Scripture and canon and whether the NT writers were consciously aware that they were writing sacred Scripture when they wrote. Taking as a starting point the original notion or meaning of canon as a rule or authority and erasing the distinction between scripture and canon, he argues that if a NT writer, say Paul for instance, believed that he was led by the Spirit to say what he said (1 Cor 7:40), then he also believed that he was consciously

---

[5]   Kruger, *The Question of Canon,* 185–88, lists seven references that he claims support his thesis besides the two listed above (Mark 1:1; John 21:24; 1 Thess 2:13; 1 John 1:1–5; and Rev 1:1–3), but the only passage that fits appropriately is Rev 1:1–3; cf. 22:18–19, which I have already noted as the only NT author who claims to have written the equivalent of Scripture.

writing Scripture. Since, for him, the common distinctions between scripture and canon are invalid,[6] he argues for a much earlier date for the canonization of the NT than most scholars have advanced in recent years. This leads to his focus on the notion of canon solely as rule or authority and to conclude that if Paul believed that he was writing in an authoritative Spirit-led capacity that he was in fact writing Scripture and was consciously aware of doing so.[7]

A part of the problem with Kruger's proposal has to do with the difficulty of distinguishing between rule, or ecclesiastical authority attributed to those in the apostolic community, and the notion of inspiration in the early churches. Such distinctions are certainly difficult since, as we saw above, they are not always clear in early Christian writings.[8] This raises the problem of knowing when inspiration of the Spirit was operative and when it was not. Since no one said in antiquity that inspiration stopped after the NT writings were composed, what about the other texts that were also recognized as inspired by the same Holy Spirit? Are they also Scripture? As we will see, others after Paul also appealed to the same Holy Spirit that inspired Paul in regard to their own work (I have listed several examples of this in Chapter 22 §II.F).

If Kruger is correct in asserting that when Paul was led by the Spirit to write that he was consciously aware of writing Scripture, then there is no measurable difference between that notion of inspiration present in the writing of Scripture and any other writing that the early church writers believed was inspired by the same Holy Spirit. He writes: "if Apostolic authority allows one, by the Holy Spirit, to write (or speak) the very word of God, then how is this qualitatively different from Scripture?"[9] The difference is that Paul did not say that he was writing either "Scripture" to the Corinthians or even the "very word of God." That is an assumption not born out in an investigation of Paul. Paul specifically indicates that he is giving *his own opinion* in the passage in question (7:25) that he believes is from the Spirit (7:40), but he does not call his writings sacred Scripture. If Kruger is correct in what he says about Paul and his awareness of being led by the Spirit, then churches will certainly have much more scripture from antiquity to include in their Bibles than what is there now. If awareness of inspiration or leading by the Spirit were an adequate criterion for inclusion of a text in the NT, then many other texts would have been included. For example, was Paul also inspired to write Scripture when he wrote his lost *first* letter to the Corinthians (1 Cor 5:9) or the one that he wrote to the Laodiceans (Col 4:16)? If so, then we have lost some of the sacred Scriptures. Also, as we saw above and will see again (Chapter 22 §II.F), many others besides the writers of the NT believed that they too were writing by the power and inspiration of the Spirit when they wrote their works, but those were

---

6   Ibid., 27–46.
7   Ibid., 119–54.
8   Ibid., 121–30.
9   Ibid., 121–22.

not included in the NT. Did the church make a major mistake? I will note later that many church councils made the same claim to inspiration and should those be added to the Scripture collections that we now have?

Prior to the time of Jesus, the notion of the cessation of prophecy (see Chapter 5 §§V–VII above) was present among many Jews of late second Temple Judaism and Judaism of Late Antiquity. By approximately 160 BCE, some Hasmonean Jews claimed that the presence and power of the Holy Spirit and prophetic activity had ceased in the Jewish nation (see 1 Macc 4:45–46, 9:27 and 14:41). It came to be argued that with the last of the Hebrew prophets, Zechariah and Malachi, the prophetic role in Israel came to an end and that the day of prophetic activity would return when the Spirit came back in full measure. Exactly when and how this view emerged is difficult to pinpoint, but, as we saw earlier, it has been suggested by D. M. Carr that this notion emerged in a political context in which the affirmation of the authority of priestly activity in the absence of prophetic activity increased among the Jewish people following the recapture and cleansing of the Temple from the Selucids in 165 BCE.[10] The early church believed that in the activity, fate, and resurrection of Jesus the presence and power of the Spirit had returned (John 14–16; Acts 1:8; 2:1–17) and Paul claimed that he spoke in the power of the Spirit (1 Cor 14:37–38). He claims that he was speaking (writing) by the power of the Spirit or "has" the Spirit of God's leading in the matters he discusses with his churches (see also 1 Cor 7:40). However, and again, does this suggest that everyone who wrote in the power of the Spirit was also writing Scripture? As already observed, after the NT era several other writers believed that they too were writing in the power of the Spirit. Perhaps Kruger is trying to distinguish when someone is inspired by the Spirit from someone filled by the same Spirit or led by the Spirit. Another problem with such lines of reasonings is that in the early churches well into the fifth century it is difficult to tell who is speaking by the power of the Spirit and who is not. Indeed, about the only ones who are not are those whom others thought were writing heresy.[11] While being led by the Spirit was true of writers of the church's Scriptures, it was also true of others whose writings and proclamation were not placed in the church's Scriptures. In other words, the early churches did not always equate the leading of the Spirit with writing Scripture.

Again, when Paul said that he had not baptized anyone of the Corinthians except Crispus and Gaius (1 Cor 1:14), but then reversed himself in 1:16, acknowledging that he did baptize the household of Stephanus, *did he not know* if he

---

[10] Carr, *The Formation of the Hebrew Bible*, 153–79. See also Lim, *Formation of the Jewish Canon*, 6–9.

[11] Everett R. Kalin makes this point in his doctoral dissertation, "Argument from Inspiration in the Canonization of the New Testament" (ThD diss., Harvard University, 1967); and subsequently in his "The Inspired Community: A Glance at Canon History," *Concordia Theological Monthly* 42 (1971): 541–49.

baptized any others? Did he think that he was writing Scripture when he forgot and then corrected himself? Writing in anger often leads one to speak without much forethought as was the case in 1 Cor 1 when Paul was writing to address the divisions in the Corinthian church. In Paul's letter to the Galatians, which was written in anger against the Judaisers who were trying to impose circumcision on Gentile Christians, was Paul conscious of writing Scripture when in anger he used poor grammar, wrote unfinished sentences, and gave an outburst against those troubling his converts over circumcision and keeping the Law saying that he wished that "those who unsettle you would castrate themselves" (Gal 5:12)? One can, of course, suggest that the humanity of Scripture does not deny its inspiration, but does it really seem that Paul is consciously aware of writing Scripture in such moments? The letter to the Romans is much more deliberate and well written than Galatians, but tells essentially the same message. I would posit that such comments as we see in Galatians might give one pause about drawing conclusions about the leading of the Spirit in this instance, let alone being consciously aware of writing of sacred Scripture unless, as in 1 Cor 1:14–16, we are to conclude that Paul was led by the Spirit initially incorrectly in his first statement about who he baptized.

The point of the context in 1 Cor 1:10–17 shows that Paul was frustrated with members in the Corinthian church who were threatening its unity and perhaps its existence by inappropriate behavior and he expressed his disappointment in sharp terms, namely, "I thank God that I baptized none of you except…" and then subsequently, "oh yes, I also baptized…" This does not suggest that Paul was mindful that he was inspired by the Spirit to say what he had just said. One would think that he would once in a while say specifically that he was writing sacred Scripture if that were the case. The only text in the NT that specifically makes such a claim about Paul writing Scripture is in 2 Pet 3:15, which likely dates around 130–150. While Kruger contends that the writers of the New Testament were all consciously aware of writing Scripture, it is important to observe that only one writer of the New Testament comes close to saying that (Rev 22:18–19) and no one else makes that claim, nor do other NT or early church writers.

As was always the case, writings were used in an authoritative manner in churches before they are actually called Scripture. Did the early churches recognize the authority of NT writings before they called them Scripture? Yes, but that recognition did not transfer initially to the notion of scripture. Authority was reckoned to the Apostles by virtue of the office or positions they held in the churches because they had been with Jesus and were witnesses to his life, teaching, fate, and resurrection appearances.

The Gospels in particular functioned as Scripture in churches *before* they were called Scripture, because they told the story of Jesus' actions and teachings that functioned as authoritative models and teachings in the early churches. As we see in the oldest confessional creed in the New Testament (Rom 10:9), from the earliest stages of the early church, Jesus was accepted as Lord. Paul declared that the Gospel *he preached* was in fact "the very word of God" (1 Thess 2:13).

Paul is saying that the message the Thessalonians "heard" from him was the "word of God" and he is not speaking about the letter he wrote to them. If that is a reference to Paul's conscious awareness of writing Scripture, then we must admit that many others besides Paul also proclaimed the "Word of the Lord," but evidently their proclamations were not called "Scripture." The tradition about Jesus, however, was at the heart of the message that the early church proclaimed. If what Paul wrote in 1 Thess 2:13 were the only criterion, there is no basis for saying that the writing of Scripture ever ceased in the church, a point I have made elsewhere.

Kruger seems to conflate all inspired proclamation with Scripture, but appears to want to close its presence in the church with the final writing of the NT books. He does the same when he conflates scripture with canon as well.[12] The difficulty in this is that there is a challenge finding anything in the first five centuries that was believed to be true that was not also believed to be inspired by the same Holy Spirit. Kruger's position here fails to consider why the early church did not distinguish the inspiration and leading of the Spirit attributed to Paul from the same inspiration attributed to Clement of Rome, Ignatius, and Irenaeus. They also claimed to be inspired by God in their writings. The notion that persons could write in the power of the Spirit or be led to write Christian texts by the power of the Spirit continued well into the time of Basil the Great and is stated as the assumption for the church's decisions at ecclesiastical councils (see this point in Chapter 21 §IX.A–C below). There was a time when the writings of the NT were gradually recognized and identified as sacred scripture – and no others were considered – but there was no notion of a cessation of the inspiration of the Spirit at that time or later. When later documents were recognized as having been produced by the leading or inspiration of the Holy Spirit, they were not afforded scriptural or canonical status. The criterion here for rejecting such later additions to the church's Scriptures appears to be the historical criterion (antiquity) and the canon of truth (orthodoxy) and not whether one was led by the Spirit. I will return to this subject in Chapter 22 §II.F.

B. Major Challenges Facing the Early Christians

By the end of the first century, Christians were facing several significant challenges. The Apostles, who were the important eyewitnesses of the life, death, and resurrection of Jesus and earliest proclaimers of the Christian traditions, had all died. This vacuum of authority appears to have been filled initially in the churches by several post-apostolic figures who remembered hearing about Jesus directly from the Apostles or their students (e.g., Polycarp). Before the first and second generations of Christians had passed away, the churches appointed other individuals

---

[12] See Kruger's arguments in *Question of Canon*, 119–54.

to fill the leadership roles in the churches and these new leaders continued the earlier leadership roles in the churches (bishops or elders and deacons), but those who were taught directly by Jesus were all gone. By the end of the first century and for several decades of the second century, Christians were also facing several other significant challenges both internal and external. Among them was a disappointment in the churches that Jesus had not yet returned as they had expected. The author of 2 Pet 3:3–4, 8–10, for example, reflects this sentiment and the disappointment present in the early church.

The churches had new leadership and new challenges also emerged in their time, such as divisions in the churches and the emergence of various "heresies." An example of divisions in the churches over this can be seen in Clement of Rome's appeal to the Corinthians following the death of Peter and Paul when strife among the Corinthians had evidently returned (*1 Clem.* 1.1; 3.1–4; 5.1–7.5). His hope was to bring unity and peace to the church in Corinth. Theological differences seemed to grow considerably after the deaths of the apostolic community, especially in the emerging docetic heresy, as we see in Ignatius (*Magn.* 10.2–3; *Trall.* 10.1; cf. 1 John 4:2–3).

The separation of Jews and Christians, beginning in 62 CE to 135 following the Bar Kochba rebellion (132–135), which was also a messianic movement among the Jews, was largely finished when Christians did not support the second Jewish revolt against Rome because by participating they would have denied their own faith in Jesus as Messiah. With their separation from Judaism, they lost their recognition as a Jewish sect that afforded them the status of a licensed religion (*religio licita*) and freedom from persecution. Nero (ruled 38–68), the first Roman emperor to institute a local persecution of Christians in Rome,[13] was known for his exceptional cruelty against Christians. Later, Domitian (ruled 81–96) also severely persecuted the Christians with considerable cruelty (Suetonius, *Dom.* 12.2; more clearly in Pliny, *Ep.* 10.96.1 and Eusebius, *Hist. eccl.* 3.18.4). The murder of Domitian brought both jubilation among Roman senators (Suetonius, *Dom.* 23.1–2) and a brief cessation of hostilities against the Christians. After the Neronian and Domitian persecutions, some persecutions of Christians continued but generally only in isolated local areas. Universal persecutions did not take place in the empire until the middle of the third century with Decius (250–251). Because of increased *local* persecutions throughout the empire, various early Christians faced significant hardships including loss of property and occasionally even life (*1 Clem.* 5.1–7; 6.1–2; Rev 2:9–10; 3:9–10; Heb 10:32; Acts 16:16–40; the *Martyrdom of Polycarp*, passim). As a small religious minority at the turn of the first century numbering perhaps around only around 100,000 to 120,000 at most in the whole of the Roman Empire, Christians faced additional challenges

---

[13]   See for instance, Pliny, *Ep.* 10.96–97; Tacitus, *Ann.* 15.44; Tertullian, *Ad Nat.* 1.7.8–9; *Apol.* 5.3–4; and Eusebius, *Hist. eccl.* 4.26.9.

that often came to religious minorities in those days.[14] The general population in the Mediterranean world was roughly sixty to seventy million and the Jewish population was roughly six to seven million. By contrast, Christians were a small minority well into the seventh century in terms of their overall numbers.[15] Their numbers grew considerably after the conversion of Constantine, but they did not outnumber the Jews until well into the seventh and eighth centuries.

In the third and early fourth centuries, two major emperors led persecutions against Christians. Decius (249–251), noted above, forced all empire residents to offer sacrifices to him and obtain certificates of their obedience. As we saw, those who refused were tortured or executed and this led to the deaths of numerous Christians. Those persecutions ended when Decius was murdered in June of 251, but not before a heavy toll was taken against the church. In 303, Diocletian, seeking unity in the empire, sought to destroy the church and gave orders to destroy its buildings and sacred books. His reign initiated what was later called the "Era of the Martyrs." He abdicated his reign in 305, but the persecutions continued by Galerius and others until Constantine defeated Diocletian's successors in 313. During this persecution, Christians had to decide which books to turn over to the authorities. It is likely that some criteria developed then to distinguish the churches' most cherished books from other religious texts. They often turned over less important writings, but regularly tried to protect the most sacred books, sometimes with their lives. The decisions that churches had to make about which books were *most* valued and should not be turned over to the authorities likely took place no later than this time and in this sense individual sacred collections were present in most churches (see a discussion of this above in Chapter 16 §VII). This does not mean that all churches recognized and tried to save the same books in their collections.

Again, the disappointment over Jesus' failure to return as the early Christians had hoped, the death of the Apostles from whom they had learned so much about him, emerging heresies that were growing in the churches, and increasing incidences of persecution of Christians in various places without an end in sight presented the most significant challenges facing a new generation of Christians. They had a reputation of being ignorant, poor, and without status in the Empire. So how did these post-apostolic Christians respond to these challenges? As we will see, they came up with an effective three-fold response.

---

[14] Philip Schaff, *History of the Christian Church*, Vol. 2: *Ante-Nicene Christianity A.D. 100–325* (Grand Rapids: Eerdmans, repr. from Charles Scribner's Sons, 1910, 1980), 2:35–38.
[15] These numbers come from L. T. Johnson, "The New Testament's Anti-Jewish Slander and Conventions of Ancient Polemic," *JBL* 108 (1989): 419–41, especially 423. For a discussion of the early persecutions against the Christians in which Jewish participation was also involved, see also McDonald, "Anti-Judaism in the Early Church Fathers," 215–52.

C. The Church's Responses

Several important responses were made by the ancient churches to address the various crises they were facing and these had a major impact on the history of Christianity. These included especially an expanded role for bishops and church order, clarification of their faith in early creeds, and the *recognition of Christian scriptures* that had circulated in the churches from its beginning. Eventually, as a result of several of the factors listed in the previous two chapters, the church recognized a fixed collection of books that formed a Christian biblical canon. For a brief period several Christian apologists addressed criticisms of the Christians, but that did not continue for long. The following is a brief look at several of these responses that sustained the churches in difficult times and continued to affect the history of the church thereafter.

1. *The Episcopate and Church Order*. One highly significant response to the crises threatening unity in the churches and even their very existence was the empowering of the office of the bishop. This is first seen in the letters of Ignatius whose interest focused mostly on dealing with heresy and unity in the churches. He concluded that peace, unity, and purity in the churches were more likely if there was a strong bishop in charge of the churches (*Eph.* 2.2; 4.1; *Magn.* 6.1–2; 7.1–2; 13.2; *Trall.* 2.1; 3.1; 13.2; *Phld.* 2.1–2; 7.1–2; *Smyrn.* 8.1). Scholars are aware that the NT reflects several forms of church governance (Acts 6:3–5; 13:1–3; 15:6–30; 1 Cor 5:1–6; 6:1–6; Phil 1:1; 1 Tim 3:1–13; 2 Tim 2:2, 14), but all were quite simple and, while no particular forms of governance were commanded by Jesus, a variety of patterns of organization and governance emerged. The NT writers acknowledge the necessity of some form of leadership in the churches (Acts 15:1–6, 22–23; 1 Cor 6:1–7; Rom 16:1–3; Phil 1:1; 1 Pet 5:1–5; Matt 18:15–20), but the precise structures of those forms of organization are unclear, or at least they were different in various churches. Initially the apostles were in the first leadership roles, but soon other roles were found for church leadership, namely prophets, teachers, deacons, elders, and bishops serving in a variety of capacities in the churches' life and ministries.[16] Most NT letters were sent to churches without reference to specific leadership or structure (Gal 1:2; 1 Pet 1:1–2), though there were exceptions when special attention was given to the leadership of the churches following a general address to the congregation (Phil 1:1). Von Campenhausen aptly comments that the vitality of the church was not seen in its order or governance, but in its "fundamental principle of the Gospel" noting further that "order, like good works, always

---

[16]　While the notion of a priesthood is clearly present in the NT, the followers of Jesus did not at first use the title of "priest" for leaders in the churches except in the sense that all of the followers of Jesus formed a "priesthood" of believers (1 Pet 2:5, 9), that is, all were called to intercede on behalf of others and minster to them.

come in the second place, and can be rightly achieved only when what is first, the unique thing…is asserted and willed above all else."[17] He adds that initially "the primitive Church started…with, in almost every sphere of life, a multiplicity of forms and arrangements, to an extent embarrassing to Catholics, and indeed, astonishing even to us [Protestants]."[18]

Eventually many changes took place in ecclesiastical leadership roles, but by the early second century (Ignatius) the role of the bishop in particular was especially reinforced and was redefined to levels not found in the NT literature. The new and powerful role of the bishop emerged as a dominant feature in the churches from the second century onward. It did not emerge in a vacuum, but in the context of dealing with heresy, conflict in churches, and persecution. Irenaeus later emphasized the role of the bishop in faithfully delivering the sacred traditions or *regula fidei* to the churches, and, like Ignatius earlier and Cyprian later, he advocated for a strong bishop and episcopate as Christians continued to face threats of heresy and persecution.[19] Hans von Campenhausen observes that the increased power of bishops not only dealt with the problems of unity, heresy, and persecution, but also with changes in church structure and mission.[20]

Organizational structure and authority issues were not completely settled in the second or even third centuries, despite a significantly empowered episcopate from the early second century with Ignatius. Because of other pressing issues that affected their survivability, Christians did not have the luxury of focusing considerable attention on issues of structure and governance until some time later. Von Campenhausen suggests that since the early churches did not at first focus on structures and governance, there was a considerable variety in such matters in the early churches. But, again, since Jesus gave no clear command on how his followers should organize, the church's major focus was on its mission and not its organization. With the empowerment of the bishop, that began to change. Von Campenhausen concludes: questions of Church order emerged "only gradually, as the occasion demanded, and in a quite secondary manner," and he added that later it received considerable attention, adding that because of varied circumstances facing the early churches, their responses to issues such as structure, divorce, and various grievances also varied. He argues that initially there was "no uniform constitution, no agreed canon, no one formula of

---

[17] Hans von Campenhausen, *Tradition and Life in the Church: Essays and Lectures in Church History*, trans. A. V. Littledale (London: Collins, 1968), 126.

[18] Ibid., 131.

[19] O. M. Bakke, "The Episcopal Ministry and Unity of the Church from the Apostolic Fathers to Cyprian," in *The Formation of the Early Church*, ed. Jostein Ådna, WUNT 183 (Tübingen: Mohr Siebeck, 2005), 379–408.

[20] Hans von Campenhausen, *Ecclesiastical Authority and Spiritual Power in the Church of the First Three Centuries*, trans. J. A. Baker (London: A. & C. Black, 1969), 238–64.

confession."[21] This variability can also be seen in fourth-century editions of the *Apostles' Creed* and the *Nicene Creed*.[22]

The relationship between episcopal authority, church doctrine, and ecclesiastical and biblical canons became clearer later with Irenaeus' notion of apostolic succession.[23] Philip Schaff concluded that: "Tradition is thus intimately connected with the primitive episcopate. The latter was the vehicle of the former and both were looked upon as bulwarks against heresy." He added: "in the substance of its doctrine this apostolic tradition agrees with the holy scriptures, and though derived, as to its form, from the oral preaching of the apostles, is really, as to its contents, one and the same with those apostolic writings."[24] For him, the traditions, episcopate, rules, creeds, and scriptures of the church are not contrary to one another, but rather compliment and interpret one another.

2. *Tradition and the Scriptures.* Among the important responses to threats facing churches there was a renewed emphasis on the traditions of and about Jesus. While, as we saw above, several summaries of these traditions can be seen in the NT (1 Cor 15:3–8; Phil 2:6–11; 1 Tim 3:16), they were significantly expanded in the second century (as we saw in Irenaeus, *Haer.* 1.10.1). Contrary to the Marcionites and *some* of the gnostics who largely rejected the Jewish Scriptures, the early churches welcomed them as their First Scriptures and began calling them their "Old Testament" (ca. 170–180). In antiquity what was older had greater credibility than recent traditions and "Old" did not mean devoid of value and useless. The continuity of Christian faith with its inherited Jewish scriptures was highly significant for the early Christians, but so also were the apostolic traditions that focused on the teachings of Jesus and their implications for Christian behavior and church order.

As we saw in Chapter 15 §I–II, those traditions were eventually put in writing and sent to churches in lieu of a visit. Many of the remembered traditions about Jesus circulated at first orally even after the Gospels were written. Some oral traditions continued well into the second century, though many of them had been written down much earlier. By the last half of the first century many of the stories about Jesus had been included in "select" biographies that eventually were called "The Gospel" *according to* various individuals (see Mark 1:1). There was never more than *one* Gospel and it was presented in several literary expressions, as in "the Gospel *according to* Matthew," "the Gospel *according to* Mark," and so on. While there are four such expressions of the Gospel in the NT, there was never

---

[21] Von Campenhausen, *Tradition and Life in the Church*, 124.

[22] Schaff, *History of the Christian Church*, 2:534–37.

[23] R. W. Jenson, *Canon and Creed*, Interpretation (Louisville, KY: Westminster John Knox, 2010), 71–76. See also Frend, *The Early Church*, 66–68.

[24] Schaff, *History of the Christian Church*, 2:525, 528.

more than one Gospel and it included more than the four Gospels, namely it was the traditions about Jesus circulating in the early churches that was passed on from one generation to the next. After the NT letters were written, they too were immediately circulating in the churches and Paul, and probably others, intended them to be read in other churches (Col 4:16). Various NT writings were shared with and read in churches in the first century along with oral traditions about Jesus, some of which were put in writing. I mentioned that several Jesus sayings were not included in the canonical Gospels (John 20:30–31), but circulated in various ancient manuscripts, church fathers, and non-canonical writings in the early churches (see discussion of these "*agrapha*" in Chapter 15 §III and IV).

At the end of the second century, the Gospels and most of the letters attributed to Paul had already received considerable recognition as Christian Scripture. This was accompanied by an increased focus on theological creeds and guidelines for Christian behavior. There was no *universal* agreement on the "rules" of faith and regulations for church life, as the perspectives in many noncanonical writings in apostolic names in the second and third centuries attest, but by the middle of the third century, many churches were establishing guidelines for dealing with discipline related to apostates who abandoned their faith during the Decian persecution (249–250). Some Christian responses, such as those of the Novatians from the middle of the third to the fourth century, were very strict and less forgiving of those who had denied their faith while facing persecution, but the majority of churches found a way to offer mercy and forgiveness to the genuinely penitent following the persecutions.

As observed earlier, in the first century the canonical gospels were likely used *as* scripture, that is, religiously authoritative writings, but the focus was not on the Gospels themselves, but rather the stories about Jesus and his teachings in them. By the middle to late third century some church teachers, Origen likely and possibly Victorinus of Pettau (Slovenia), *began* constructing lists of Christian Scriptures. While Irenaeus identified and listed the four canonical Gospels as scripture, Bokedal observes that no other list of Gospels after him ever included other gospels combined *with* the canonical Gospels.[25] This likely reflects a broad though not universal acceptance of the four canonical Gospels from the third century forward.

The early church fathers appealed not only to the church's scriptures, but according to Irenaeus, also to its oral traditions handed down from the Apostles through the church's bishops to the churches (Irenaeus, *Haer.* 3.3.3). Citing Irenaeus (*Haer.* 3.4.1–2), Schaff contends that Irenaeus (ca. 180) "might conceive of a Christianity without scripture, but he could not imagine a Christianity without living tradition; and for this opinion he refers to barbarian tribes, who have the gospel *'sine charta et atramento'* [= without paper and ink], written in

---

[25]   Bokedal, *Formation and Significance*, 132–42.

their hearts."[26] In 1 Cor 11:2, the Apostle Paul commended Corinthian Christians for remembering the "traditions" (*tas paradoseis*) that he handed on to them (*paredoka*, see also 1 Cor 15:3; 2 Thess 2:15, and 3:6). The gospel he proclaimed to the Galatians appears to be that same tradition (Gal 1:6–9). This tradition was shared in Christian worship and catechetical instruction orally and eventually after these traditions were placed in written form, they were read in the churches. Since most ancient churches did not possess the same or even most of the NT books, they passed on the oral traditions available to them that were also reflected in the church's early creeds. All had received authoritative traditions whether orally or in writing. By the end of the second century, the four canonical Gospels and most of the letters attributed to Paul were circulating, either partially or completely in single codices in some churches as in the cases of P^{45} and P^{46} (for a discussion of these texts see Chapter 20 §III below).

Christian books were regularly read in ancient churches soon after their production. In the middle of the second century, Justin, in his description of a Christian worship service, says the "memoirs of the Apostles [Gospels] or the writings of the prophets [Jewish scriptures] are read as time permits" (*1 Apol.* 67). One of the primary advantages of acknowledging the Christian writings as Scripture was that they would subsequently be read in the churches. A restriction appears to have come toward the end of the second century beginning likely with Irenaeus who restricted what Gospels could be read in churches. Letters and Gospels were read in churches in the first century before they were designated Scripture, but that changed in the second century. Before then, the primary criterion appears to have been whether the writings were considered true and in accord with the church's early traditions. If so, they were read in churches as inspired sacred texts. Later it appears that they had to be approved, often by widespread recognition and after suitable examination of the theological positions taken in them.

Along with NT writings, several other Jewish and Christian religious texts were also read in some churches, such as *1 Enoch*, *Shepherd of Hermas*, *Didache*, *Epistle of Barnabas*, *1 Clement*, and the *Gospel of the Hebrews*. Eventually the majority of churches ceased reading most of these writings in their churches, though some writings that were rejected by the majority of churches, continued to be read in private. The debate over their authorship, date, and content continued for centuries. Shortly after the middle of the fourth century, several lists of sacred books began to be produced to identify for the churches which Christian writings could be read in churches. Among those who constructed such lists was the highly influential Athanasius of Alexandria (367), but even later Pseudo-Athanasius (ca. 500–550) and the *Stichometry of Nicephoris* (ca. 850) and others also made lists of sacred writings that could be read in churches (see Chapter 21 §I.A and Appendices A and C), and often lists of works such as the pseudepigraphal and

---

[26]   Schaff, *History of the Christian Church*, 2:256.

apocryphal writings that could not be read in churches. Some of those texts not to be read in churches were dubbed as "spoken against" (*antilegomena*) writings that continued to be read in some churches long *after* their official rejection. There is no other reason for listing them in disputed or rejected categories centuries after being rejected by the majority of churches than that some churches were still reading them.

As we saw earlier, Irenaeus argued that the apostolic traditions had been faithfully handed down in the churches through the succession of bishops. He appealed to traditions passed on in churches through the bishops to combat heresies, especially the Marcionites and gnostics (*Haer.* 1.100.9, 10; 3.3.1–2; 3.4.2; 3.33.7). Tertullian (*Praescr.* 100.13, 14, 17–19, 21, 35, 36, 40, 41; *De virgin. veland.* 100.1; *Prax.* 100.2) and later Cyprian (ca. 240–50) agreed. Cyprian added that: "custom without truth was only time-honored error" (*Ep.* 74; Cyprian, *De Unitate Eccl.* 100.9), underscoring that the truth in the traditions was essential, not simply that which has always been done or said before.

3. *Traditions and the Rule of Faith.* Before there was a *written* NT scripture, as we have seen, churches had a tradition (1 Cor 15:3–8) that functioned as a "rule of faith" and circulated in the church from its beginning, and that "rule" summarized the core Christian beliefs and practices. The apostolic traditions, initially oral and later written, identified core Christian faith. Near the end of the second century, Irenaeus and later Tertullian identified core beliefs as the "rule of faith" or "rule of truth" (Latin *regula fidei, regula veritatis,* or Greek, κανών τῆς πίστεως, κανών τῆς ἀληθείας) (*Haer.* 1.10.1–2; 3.3.2; 3.24.1.1; cf. 5.20.1). As we saw, the notion of "canon" eventually came to refer to a fixed collection of the church's scriptures, but initially it was the authoritative core beliefs or traditions that were circulating in the churches and formed the church's "rule of faith."[27] Cyprian used "rule of faith" along with *symbolum* (Σύμβολον) in his descriptions of theological issues. He applied *symbolum* especially to creedal baptismal confessions by which Christians distinguished themselves from Jews, heretics, and non-Christians. For him, the "church was never without a creed" (*Ecclesia sine symbolis nulla*) (*Ep.* 76, cf. 69).

In the second century, there was no discussion of a *fixed* collection of Christian scriptures, but only a "rule of faith" that had been passed on in the churches and defended by their newly recognized Christian Scriptures. In the third century, Origen is the most likely to have established something like a collection of NT writings, but that is uncertain as we saw earlier. There was a broad agreement (see below for a discussion of the importance of the *regula fidei* in dealing with heresy in the churches in Chapter 18), however, on this *regula fidei* in the proto-orthodox second-century church traditions, but not complete agreement as we

---

[27] Beyer, "κανών," *TDOT*, 3:596–602. See also Metzger, *Canon of the New Testament*, 289–93.

see in Chapter 18. There was no widespread notion of a fixed canon of Christian scriptures until the fourth century, though as we saw earlier, it is likely that Origen did construct such a list.[28] This rule of faith, however, was *normative in concept,* but its specific content often varied among the early church fathers. At first, the creeds of the early churches were delivered orally, but soon some of them were written down as we see in the structurally balanced form of the creed in 1 Cor 15:3–8, and it was later included in extended written summaries (Irenaeus, *Haer.* 1.10.1). The NT writings heavily influenced all subsequent church tradition and proved useful for apologetic, catechetical, and missional purposes. By the third and fourth centuries, many Christian scriptures began to be listed or catalogued (Grk. χατάλογος) (Eusebius, *Hist. eccl.* 6.25.1) as collections of the churches scriptures. Athanasius introduced the first and most famous twenty-seven-book NT canon in his 39th *Festal Letter* (367), as well as an Old Testament collection.

As Christianity developed and grew in size it faced new challenges related to the church's beliefs and guidelines for behavior. The emerging notions of faith and behavioral standards had their roots in the church's earliest oral traditions as well as its Scriptures. In Paul's writings, for instance, correct theology and ethical behavior were always connected (Rom 10:9 and Rom 12–14; cf. 1 Thess 1:3, but see later Ign. *Trall.* 9). Early church tradition influenced emerging creeds and conduct that developed in the second and later centuries. In the Reformation era, Protestants occasionally viewed church ecclesiastic canons or regulations as contrary to their Scriptures. Part Two of the *Augsburg Confession* (1530), for example, challenges ecclesiastical canons established by bishops because, it was argued, they were contrary to Scripture. However, before agreement could be found on the scope or canon of their Scriptures, Christian traditions and rules of faith proved significant in helping to shape the core of the church's scriptures.

The apostolic traditions entrusted to the bishops were the basis not only for rejecting heresy, but also the books that were not in harmony with those traditions (Irenaeus, *Haer.* 3.15.2–3; 3.20.1–5). Early church traditions, including the NT writings that were later recognized as Scripture, formed the rule of faith (*regula fidei*) that identified Christian faith. Conversely, the rule of faith that developed from tradition also helped shape the later NT canon. How could it be otherwise since those traditions and theological affirmations were the guidelines for what was acceptable as Christian Scripture and read in churches? An appeal to the church's traditions and scriptures often aimed at producing unity in churches. The church's earliest traditions and early creedal affirmations regularly summarized both core Christian beliefs and ecclesiastical practices and the scriptures that were to be read in the churches.

---

[28] For a discussion of this, see Gallagher, *Hebrew Scripture*, 214.

In early Christianity, traditions, creeds, and Christian scriptures were never viewed as contradictory or in competition, but rather complimentary and all were deemed sacred and inspired documents. Bokedal rightly concludes that scripture and the rule of faith were "two sides of the same norm."[29] The oral traditions circulating in the churches were eventually put in writing and continued to be normative for Christians. They helped form later church biblical and ecclesiastical canons.[30] At the core of the early traditions, there were creedal formulations in NT books (Rom 10:9–10; 1 Cor 15:3–8; Phil 2:6–11; 1 Tim 3:16), as well as the guidelines for church order and Christian behavior (e.g., Gal 5:15–26; Rom 12:3–15:13; Heb 13:1–17).

In the *Didache* (ca. 90–130?), an early collection of such regulations and guidelines are set forth regarding baptism, fasting, the Eucharist, worship order, how to recognize true and false prophets, and the selection of leadership. Later confessions of faith or doctrine affirmed in confessions prior to baptism, and expanded in church creeds also included ecclesiastical rules of conduct (Irenaeus, *Haer.* 1.10.1). In the *Apostolic Tradition*, sometimes attributed to Hippolytus of Rome (170–236), the regulations focused especially on ordination, baptism and Eucharistic prayers. The *regula fidei* was often a forerunner of the baptismal confessions, but it was flexible in terms of the regulations and specific questions in it.[31] The regulations for church life expanded considerably from the late second to the fourth century. While there were regular appeals to earlier apostolic traditions circulating in churches, the expansion of older regulations and the addition of new ones were commonplace. In doctrinal matters, later church councils also made considerable changes in liturgy, discipline, organization, and the like.[32]

4. *Oral and Written Sacred Traditions*. We saw earlier that Plato famously argued that written texts were unworthy instruments of communication because they discouraged the use of memory and could be changed by later copiers (Plato, *Phaedrus* 275AC). Some Pharisees similarly argued that the "Oral Torah" (the Jewish religious traditions that were codified in the Mishnah) should *not* be put into writing (*b. Gittin* 60b; *b. Temura* 14b). The sacredness of the Jewish Scriptures was always maintained as distinct from Jewish oral traditions, but the oral traditions, which some rabbis called the "Oral Torah," were gathered together and organized by Rabbi Judah the Prince and put in writing (ca. 200–220). Those traditions were called the Mishnah. The parallels with the church's written traditions (OT and NT) and various regulations for organization, behavior, and church practice are apparent, but without clear dependence.

---

[29] Bokedal, *Formation and Significance*, 281–84.
[30] Ibid., 281–308.
[31] Everett Ferguson, "Creeds, Councils, and Canons," in Harvey and Hunter, eds., *Oxford Handbook of Early Christian Studies*, 427–45, here 430–32.
[32] Ibid.

It is not clear that the notion of *Christian* scripture was an essential part of the foundation plan of Christianity,[33] which may account for the church's slow development in its selection of its own *Christian* Scriptures and finally a NT canon. This may be because Jesus gave no command to his disciples to write anything and it may also explain why some early Christians had a preference for oral traditions over written as we saw in the case of Papias, bishop of Hierapolis in Asia Minor, who famously preferred oral traditions over the written saying: "For I did not suppose that information from books would help me so much as the word of a living and surviving voice" (*Hist. eccl.* 3.39.4). As witnesses died out and memory began to fail, however, *written* traditions and NT books understandably took priority in the churches over fading oral traditions. Eventually, any reference to Christianity without sacred texts was unthinkable. Mitchell correctly claims that the early Christians could well imagine "a heaven without a temple (Rev. 21:22), but not one without a book."[34]

Many early traditions were later "codified" into creeds, NT scriptures, and ecclesiastical regulations on behavior and church governance. All were welcomed and functioned as Spirit-inspired traditions. The eventual triumph of Christian orthodoxy in the Roman Empire no doubt also had a significant impact on the books that were included the church's scriptures, but likely also for the disappearance of many so-called non-canonical books. Books not supportive of the orthodox traditions that were believed to be rooted in the church's creeds and traditions generally ceased being read or copied in churches and most of then disappeared altogether.

All early church guidelines for faith and conduct were rooted in sayings of Jesus, interpretations of the OT scriptures, and apostolic teaching circulating in the churches. As churches faced new challenges, however, some of those earlier traditions were later expanded and reinterpreted. The emerging written creeds and church canons (rules) reflected stronger dependence on an episcopate, expanded creeds, christological interpretations of their OT, and the recognition of Christian scriptures.

In the Reformation era, Protestant churches, after their separation from the Roman Catholic Church in 1517, established their canons of faith in 1530 in the Augsburg Confession. The use of "confession" stems from the church's use of creed, from *credo*, "I believe." It responds to Jesus' question of his disciples, "Who do you say that I am?" (Matt 16:15). Peter's *confessional* response (16:16) eventually became a baptismal confession, "I believe, therefore I confess" (*Credo, ergo confiteor*). Confessions, symbols, and creeds all had to do with church doctrine. In the Protestant tradition, the *regula fidei* or rule of faith was the

---

[33]   Grant suggests this in his "New Testament Canon," 297; so also Barr, *Holy Scripture*, 12.

[34]   Margaret M. Mitchell, "The Emergence of the Written Record," in *The Cambridge History of Christianity*: Vol. 1, *Origins to Constantine*, ed. M. Mitchell and F. M Young (Cambridge: Cambridge University Press, 2006), 177–94, here 177–82 and 194.

churches' scriptures and its "confession" was its rule of doctrine based on those scriptures. The ecclesiastical canons that governed church structure, worship, discipline, and practices appropriate for Christian living were all rooted in scripture. In early Christianity there was considerable overlap in the authority of scriptures, creeds, and ecclesiastical canons. In the eastern churches, ecclesiastical canons (regulations) began to be put in chronological order in the fourth century and organized in systematic collections in the sixth century.[35]

II. CREEDS, ECCLESIASTICAL TRADITION, AND BIBLICAL CANONS

Despite considerable overlap in the inspiration and authority of creeds and ecclesiastical and scriptural canons, there were also distinctions. The creeds were developed to give guidelines for understanding the parameters of Christian faith, and rules or canons of conduct were established summaries to identify the practical implications of true Christian belief. This is rooted in the NT, of course, where correct belief is regularly connected to correct behavior, especially in the letters of Paul. The creeds, ecclesiastical canons, and the biblical canons formed the boundaries of what constituted the essence of Christian faith and they functioned as the totality of regulations for church doctrine, conduct, and mission and often overlapped. The most famous creeds of the ancient churches include the *Nicene Creed* and the *Apostles' Creed*, and the best-known ecclesiastical canons in the ancient churches are the *Canons of Hippolytus* and the *Apostolic Constitutions*. When church councils began deliberating the scope of the Christian scriptures in 360, 393, 397, and 416, various canons of faith and conduct were also already present.[36] The first of these had an additional canon or rule added to it at a later time that was not a part of the original Laodicean canon, but it reflects a later perspective of the church's biblical canon (see discussion of canon 60 both earlier and below).

While creeds typically focused on doctrine and council deliberations on regulations related to behavior, structure, discipline, and ordination, church councils often discussed and debated both theological as well as practical issues facing churches such as re-baptizing errant members or excommunication. The Council of Nicea, the first ecumenical council, included between 258 and 318 bishops who dealt mostly with theological/christological controversy, but also several ecclesiastical canons were expanded in subsequent ecumenical councils.

---

[35] Ch. Munier, "Canonical Collections," in *Encyclopedia of the Early Church* (ed. Angelo Di Berardino; New York: Oxford University Press, 1992), 1:141–43, here 142.
[36] Ferguson, "Creeds, Councils, and Canons," 427–43; and also Schaff, *Creeds of Christendom* 2:529–30, and 534–37.

In the fourth century, Canon Law was expressed at ecumenical and local church councils, and in the fifth century earlier canons were often revised, expanded, or replaced and all began to be systematized and placed in various ecclesiastical canon lists not unlike when biblical books earlier began appearing in canon lists.

Biblical canons developed *after* and in light of church creeds. Churches could hardly determine the scope of their scriptures before they had broad agreement on the identity of Jesus and major Christian doctrine. Origen did not regularly use the term κανών, but rather the equivalent ἐνδιάθηκος ("encovenanted") to refer to a collection of sacred scriptural books. In his commentary on the *Song of Solomon*, later translated into Latin, Origen agreed with the Jews that there were only three books of Solomon "in the *canon* among the Hebrews" (*In Cant. prol.*). While he did not clearly or regularly employ κανών for a collection of books, he used ἐνδιάθηκος, and may have initiated the notion of a biblical canon as a collection of sacred books.[37]

Later, Eusebius also used ἐνδιάθηκος to identify a list of authoritative scriptures for the church (cf. 6.25.1). Athanasius is the first to employ κανών for a *fixed* list of Christian scriptures in his 39th *Festal Letter* (367). At the Council of Laodicea in 360, canon 59 restricted the reading of noncanonical books in worship. It stated: "Let no private psalms nor any uncanonical books be read in the church, but only the canonical ones of the New and Old Testament." Canon 60 was inserted later into the deliberations of the Council of Laodicea following canon 59 and is similar to the list provided by Cyril of Jerusalem (see Appendix C) that lists all of the NT books except Revelation. Canon 60 reads:

> It is proper to recognize as many books as these: of the Old Testament, 1. the Genesis of the world; 2. the Exodus from Egypt; 3. Leviticus; 4. Numbers; 5. Deuteronomy; 6. Joshua the son of Nun; 7. Judges and Ruth; 8. Esther; 9. First and Second Kings [i.e. First and Second Samuel]; 10. Third and Fourth Kings [i.e. First and Second Kings]; 11. First and Second Chronicles; 12. First and Second Ezra [i.e. Ezra and Nehemiah]; 13. the book of one hundred and fifty Psalms; 14. the Proverbs of Solomon; 15. Ecclesiastes; 16. Song of Songs; 17. Job; 18. the Twelve [minor] Prophets; 19. Isaiah; 20. Jeremiah and Baruch, Lamentations and the Epistle [of Jeremiah]; 21. Ezekiel; 22. Daniel. And the books of the New Testament: 4 Gospels, according to Matthew, Mark, Luke, and John; the Acts of the Apostles; seven catholic epistles, namely, 1 of James, 2 of Peter, 3 of John, 1 of Jude; fourteen epistles of Paul, 1 to the Romans, 2 to the Corinthians, 1 to the Galatians, 1 to the Ephesians, 1 to the Philippians, 1 to the Colossians, 2 to the Thessalonians, 1 to the Hebrews, 2 to Timothy, 1 to Titus, and 1 to Philemon. [Notice: Revelation is missing.]

If canon 60 was original to the Council of Laodicea, it would be the earliest *council* decision on the scope of the biblical canon, but, again, that is unlikely and it is difficult to determine the exact dating of canon 60. It is closer to the canon of Cyril of Jerusalem both in contents and order of books, so it may have been attached after canon 59 at a later time or someone else came to the same

---

[37] Gallagher, *Hebrew Scripture*, 38–39.

conclusions and attached it to canon 59 as canon 60. However, canon 59 is widely accepted as original to the document and gives guidelines on what books could or could not be read in churches.

Among those who helped form the later ecclesiastical canons, Hippolytus of Rome, in his *The Apostolic Tradition* (ca. 215), listed an influential collection of Church Orders providing various guidelines for church life. He wrote extensively against various heresies in the church, but also on church order and baptism.[38] Following him, Cyprian also had an important impact on the development of Canon Law in his rules dealing with those who had denied their faith during the Decian persecutions. His influence in this and other matters can be seen in the inclusion of his writings in a tenth-century manuscript that also includes in Latin the earlier Cheltenham canon (also known as the Mommsen Catalogue, ca. 350–360), a list of canonical books that were authorized to be read in the churches. This demonstrates his high esteem in the churches.[39] Cyprian argued that salvation was only in the church and whoever separates himself from the church also "separates himself from the promises of the Church" (*De unit*. 6). Later popes – a term variously used for bishops in the fourth century and later, but subsequently reserved for the bishop of Rome – and bishops of the church frequently cited Cyprian's writings.[40] *Nomocanons* (or canon law), a combination of the Greek *nomos* ("law") and *kanon* ("rule"), was first set forth by John Scholasticus (ca. 600 CE) to identify ecclesiastical and occasionally imperial laws. It became a designation mostly for what comprises *ecclesiastical* canons for the church.

Although scriptural priority is quite clear in the NT and in early church history, it is sometimes difficult to distinguish it later from the authority of creeds and ecclesiastical canons since all three made some claim to divine inspiration. See, for example, the introduction to one of Irenaeus' creeds in which he poses the question: "If the Apostles had not left to us the Scriptures, would it not be necessary to follow the order of tradition, which those to whom they committed the churches handed down?" (*Haer*. 3.4.1–2).[41] The ancient churches did not draw a fine distinction between church tradition and their Christian scriptures and both were considered inspired by God. For example, during the gathering of the "first church council," James and the elders met together and made decisions about whether Gentiles could be welcomed into the church apart from keeping the regulations of the Law. Their decision was introduced with "it seemed good to the Holy Spirit and to us…" (Acts 15:28). Later presbyters and bishops followed that precedent. At the Council of Trent, for example, the beginning of the Third

---

[38] J. Quasten, *Patrology, The Ante-Nicene Literature After Irenaeus* (Utrecht-Antwerp: Spectrum, 1950, 1975), 2:163–207.

[39] Metzger, *The Canon of the New Testament*, 222.

[40] Quasten, *Patrology*, 2:273–82.

[41] Schaff, *Creeds*, 2:15.

and Fourth Articles states: "The sacred and holy, ecumenical, and general Synod of Trent, – *lawfully assembled in the Holy Ghost*, the same three legates of the Apostolic See presiding…"[42] Later ecumenical councils were regularly treated as divine, saintly, and holy because the divine will (= the guidance of the Holy Spirit) was exercised through the leadership of the bishops.[43] In the Synod of Jerusalem and the Confession of Dositheus (March, 1672, Art. XI) states: "The Catholic Church is taught by the Holy Ghost through prophets [OT], apostles [NT], holy fathers, and synods, and therefore cannot err, or be delivered, or choose a lie for the truth."[44]

As is clear in the above summary, the relationships between creeds, Scripture, and canon law overlap considerably, but eventually canon law appears not to have been as closely connected to the ancient creeds and biblical canon of the church and questions began to be raised about this in some churches that led to the Reformation. Since the Reformation, Protestants have based their doctrines and rules for Christian conduct squarely on biblical interpretation, hence *sola scriptura* that preeminently reflects their preference for scripture as the sole self-revelation of God.[45]

Historically churches have claimed divine inspiration for their scriptures, but, as we saw above, some churches have also made such a claim for their council deliberations. For centuries little or no distinction was made between the inspiration of the church's Scriptures and the ecclesiastical canons of churches. In the fourth century, most Christians had recognized a higher status for the churches' Scriptures, but still there was considerable overlap in the authority of both scriptural and ecclesiastical canons (traditions) and they were often viewed as two sides of the same normative coin. Regularly NT scriptures are reflected in ancient creeds and ecclesiastical canons. Bokedal correctly acknowledges that the distinctions between canon law and Scripture are sometimes blurred in antiquity.[46] As we saw, Canon Law, in its formal sense, appears to have originated in third-century deliberations over the discipline and restoration of lapsed members following the Decian persecutions in 249–251.[47] When describing the early traditions and the Scriptures of the church, it sometimes appears that we are often talking about the same thing. The creeds, scriptures, and regulations for behavior and life in the churches were all viewed as inspired by God and authoritative. This all changed in the Reformation for the Protestants and the Scriptures alone were

---

[42]   Ibid., 2:77, 79, emphasis added.
[43]   A. Schminck, "Canon Law," in *Oxford Dictionary of Byzantium*, ed. P. Kazhdan (New York: Oxford University Press, 1991), 1:372–74, here 374.
[44]   Schaff, *Creeds*, 1:64.
[45]   A. I. C. Heron, "Doctrine of the Canon," in *The Encyclopedia of Christianity*, ed. E. Fahlbusch et al. (Grand Rapids: Eerdmans; Leiden: Brill, 1999), 1:344–45.
[46]   Bokedal, *Formation and Significance*, 281–84.
[47]   Henry Chadwick, "The Early Christian Community," in *The Oxford Illustrated History of Christianity*, ed. J. McManners (Oxford: Oxford University Press, 1990), 21–61, here 44–46.

given highest priority, but such distinctions were not always as clear earlier. It is difficult, however, to distinguish the Spirit's role in the origin of Scripture from the church's tradition and its role in councils and creeds of the church.

At the end of the second century there was no *formal* fixed biblical canon either in the east or west and the early creeds do not suggest a fixed collection of scriptures at that time and often do not mention them, though their affirmations are clearly rooted in the church's Scriptures. There is little doubt, however, that many of the books that eventually formed the NT canon had already gained wide recognition as scripture at that time. Verheyden correctly concludes "that one cannot speak of a concerted effort all through the second century to establish a formal canon of authoritative books, let alone a firm concern to create one canon for the whole of Christianity," but he goes on to say "quite paradoxically, that by the end of that century much of the canon is already in place…"[48] In terms of the books that were eventually included in the church's canon, he is certainly correct, though as we saw, the final recognition of a fixed biblical canon took much longer. The final selection of the books that functioned as the church's scriptures was a long, imprecise, and seldom universally acknowledged process. The "decanonized" books that had earlier received temporary recognition and authority in some churches accompanied the process and that too took much longer. How is it possible to tell a congregation that had revered some texts as sacred and read them in worship that this was no longer possible? While "top down" decisions determined what books were excluded from being read in churches, as we will see in the sacred collections in Chapter 21 and in the catalogues in Appendix C, such decisions were not uniformly welcomed in all churches and for centuries. Although the eastern churches at first rejected the book of Revelation, they eventually welcomed it, but it is still not read in their worship services and is never included in the Eastern Orthodox lectionaries. The apocryphal letter, *3 Corinthians*, is a pseudonymous correspondence attributed to Paul, and while the majority of churches excluded it, it remained in several church Scripture collections for centuries. It circulated in P^{72} (ca. 300), in some church manuscripts, and it continued in the Armenian scriptures along with *The Repose of the Evangelist John* (or *The Rest of the Blessed John*), and the *Petition of Euthalius* until the 1800s.[49]

It appears that there was widespread agreement on most of the church's Scriptures by the middle to late fourth century, though some churches still questioned the status of the book of Revelation, 2 and 3 John, 2 Peter, Jude, James, and Hebrews. Few early churches possessed the same collection of books, nor did most possess all of the books that they recognized as their NT, but most scripture

---

[48]   Joseph Verheyden, "The New Testament Canon," in Paget and Schaper, eds., *New Cambridge History of the Bible: Vol. 1, From the Beginnings to 600*, 389–411, here 399.

[49]   Metzger, *Canon of the New Testament*, 223; Schneemelcher, ed., *New Testament Apocrypha*, 2:217–31.

collections included one or more Gospels and at least several letters attributed to Paul and 1 Peter and 1 John and Acts. The Syriac Peshitta, one of the earliest translations of NT writings, for instance, contained only 22 of the 27 books of the NT. It omitted 2 Peter, 2–3 John, Jude and Revelation. Regular citations of these books, for the most part, only began in the fourth and fifth centuries, although the translation of Tatian's harmony of the four Gospels, the *Diatessaron*, into Syriac took place possibly near the end of the second century and was quite popular in some churches as late as the 1400s.[50]

The impetus for a listing of NT scriptures may have started with Origen, but that practice is more at home in the mid-fourth century and later. Armstrong, for instance, has suggested that Victorinus of Petau *may* have constructed a well-known list of Christian scriptures, now known as the Muratorian Fragment (or *Canon Muratori*), possibly following Origen in the third century,[51] contrary to popular notions of a late second-century date for the document or a late fourth-century dating. As we saw earlier, the first clearly established NT canon lists are from Origen (ca. 240) and Eusebius (ca. 311–317). After 360, *fixed* collections of the church scriptures (biblical canons) were quite common, but they were not all the same. The possibility of unity in the churches was strengthened through the development of their creeds, ecclesiastical laws, and biblical canons (for a list and discussion of some of these collections see Chapter 21 below).

III. A MIXTURE OF AUTHORITY

The early church's oral and written traditions about Jesus, creeds, their OT scriptures, and biblical and ecclesiastical canons all clarified for Christians the essence of their faith, appropriate behavior, and discipline, mission, and church structure. These authorities formed the sacred foundation of the ancient emerging churches. As we noted above, in the Reformation, Protestants determined that the church's creeds and ecclesiastical canons were subservient to the church's canon of scriptures. In 1537, Martin Luther argued that faith and conduct depend on the Scriptures alone and not on church tradition from the church fathers. He wrote: "For it will not do to frame articles of faith from the works or words of the holy Fathers; otherwise their kind of fare, of garments, of house, etc., would have to become an article of faith, as was done with relics. [We have, however, another rule, namely] The rule is: The Word of God shall establish articles of faith, and no one else, not even an angel" (*Smalcald Articles*, 2.2.15, Schaff trans.).

---

[50]   Peter J. Williams, "The Syriac Versions of the Bible," in Paget and Schaper, eds., *New Cambridge History of the Bible: Vol. 1, From the Beginnings to 600*, 527–35, here 528–30.

[51]   As noted earlier, J. J. Armstrong, "Victorinus of Pettau as the Author of the Canon Muratori," *VC* 62 (2008): 1–35, makes a case for Victorinus in the third century as the author of the Muratorian Fragment, but few scholars are convinced by his arguments. See a brief discussion of this article in Chapter 21 §I.D.

Historically, however, it is difficult to find in the early churches clear distinctions in these authorities or in the way that they were viewed and applied in early Christianity. There are times when it is obviously difficult to distinguish between church tradition, Scripture, creeds, and the decisions of church councils. However, there is no question that when the NT writings were acknowledged as Scripture, they formed a core authority in the early churches. What was not clear for several centuries, however, was the parameters or scope of that collection of Christian Scriptures.

It is also true that the church could not establish a canon of NT Scriptures without first establishing its core teachings and that it took some time for the churches to agree – largely – on those orthodox teachings. After that, it was easier to agree on what books of the NT cohered with the teachings that were foundational for early and subsequent Christianity. The question of the authority of Jesus as Lord of the church never wavered in antiquity, but who Jesus was (a divinely empowered human being, an angel, a divine being, etc.) and his relationship to God were less certain for a period of time in some churches. After such issues were clarified at Nicea, the matter of canon formation, that is, determining which books best cohered with the church's accepted traditions and teachings about Jesus, were then more clear to the majority of church leaders. After Nicea (325), lists or catalogues of Christian Scriptures began to appear. This matter will be examined in more detail in Chapters 21 and 22 when the focus is on the criteria for selection of books for the NT. The churches welcomed both OT and NT biblical canons, but the status of some of the books continued to vary long after the principle of a biblical canon and a fixed collection of Scriptures had been set in place. Some canonical books were questioned for centuries longer. It is nevertheless difficult to examine the formation of the church's Scriptures without also acknowledging the role of other canons of the church, namely its core traditions, creeds, and ecclesiastical canons that brought clarity to the scope of the church's NT canon.

IV. EARLY CHRISTIANITY, THE HOLY SPIRIT, AND SCRIPTURE

Von Campenhausen observes that early Christianity was not essentially a "religion of the Book," but rather "the religion of the Spirit and the living Christ."[52] The New Testament did not begin with a careful and detailed interpretation of the Hebrew Scriptures with their leading interpreters concluding that Jesus was the expected messianic figure for whom many Jews had hoped. Rather, as we saw earlier, it was their encounter with Jesus, whom they acknowledged as the Christ and through whom they experienced the presence and power of God in their lives.

---

[52] Von Campenhausen, *Formation of the Christian Bible*, 62–66. A similar stance could be argued for the ancient Jewish community of faith, as James Barr shows in his *Holy Scripture*, 2–7.

That encounter led them to search their Scriptures in order to establish a scriptural witness to substantiate and interpret the moment that they had experienced with Jesus.[53] Their prior recognition of the authority of the Jewish Scriptures was a critically important factor for them to understand their encounter with Jesus and so they investigated those Scriptures to understand and account for what they had experienced. For the early followers of Jesus, a new day had dawned in Jesus and in him they saw the presence and power of the Holy Spirit unleashed, a power that had been promised in their scriptures (Joel 2:28; cf. Ezek 36:26) and was now a present reality for them.

A. The Holy Spirit in the New Testament

Like their Jewish siblings, the followers of Jesus clearly believed that the Scriptures had their origin in God and that the scriptural authors were empowered by the Holy Spirit to write.[54] Some NT authors appear to have distinguished the earlier writing prophets from the more recent prophetic expressions (Matt 11:13; Mark 6:15; John 8:52; Heb 1:1–2). The book of Acts, for instance, reflects that some Jews in that era were unaware of the Holy Spirit's presence (Acts 19:2). This was not the case for the early Christians who believed that the blessings of the Spirit and the Lord had been transferred from their Jewish siblings to them (Gal 6:16). The Spirit descending on Jesus at his baptism (Mark 1:10; Luke 3:21–22; Matt 3:16–17) and the outpouring of the Spirit at Pentecost (Acts 1:8; 2:1–4; cf. John 14:26; 15:26; 20:22) both reflect this notion.

In the early churches the gift of prophecy was believed to be manifest among all believers (Acts 2:17–18 [citing Joel 2:28–32]; 13:1–2; 21:10) and was among the spiritual gifts for the church (Rom 12:6; 1 Cor 12:10, 28). The early followers of Jesus recognized that an important role of the Spirit was to empower them to proclaim and teach the message about their Christ (Acts 1:8; 1 Cor 14:31). Evidence of the presence of the Spirit's activity during the time of Jesus can be seen in Luke when it is said that Simeon, a righteous and devout man on whom "the Holy Spirit rested," also had a revelation from the Spirit about the "Lord's Messiah" (Luke 2:25–26). Subsequently, Anna, whom Luke calls a "prophet" (προφῆτις), served in the Temple in Jerusalem and praised God, and spoke of the child Jesus (Luke 2:36–38). John the Baptist was also acclaimed as a "prophet," that is, a Spirit-empowered person who was able to relate God's revelation (Mark 6:15; Matt 11:13–15; Luke 7:24–28). Some who witnessed the ministry of Jesus thought that he was one of the prophets (Mark 8:28; Matt 16:14; cf. Luke 9:19) – "one of the

---

[53] Leaney, "Theophany, Resurrection, and History," correctly observes that the early Christians were more concerned to find a Scripture "to fit a fact, and were far from inventing a fact to fit the Scripture," or finding a person to fit their interpretation of the Scriptures.

[54] An informed and detailed discussion of this is in Anthony C. Thiselton, *The Holy Spirit – In Biblical Teaching, Through the Centuries and Today* (Grand Rapids: Eerdmans, 2013), 33–162.

ancient prophets *arisen*" – perhaps suggesting the former age of prophecy had returned. It does not appear that there was a universal Jewish belief in the time of Jesus that the Spirit and prophetic activity were absent. We saw that earlier in our focus on the Dead Sea Scrolls, especially in the *Commentary on Habakkuk*.

From the church's beginning, Christians believed that they were living in the age of the Holy Spirit who was available to all who placed their trust in Jesus the Lord and Messiah (John 14:25; 15:26; 16:12–15; Acts 1:8; 2:17–18, 37–38; Rom 8:9–11; 10:9; 1 Cor 12:13, passim). The early Christians regularly acknowledged the presence, authority, and inspiration of the Holy Spirit for their own oral and written traditions (Acts 2:1–4, 17–22, 37–38; 1 Cor 11:2; Gal 1:6–8) and they incorporated some of them in their NT books, their creeds (Rom 10:9; 1 Cor 15:3–8; Phil 2:6–11; 1 Tim 3:16), and ecclesiastical regulations (e.g., Matt 5–11; Gal 5:16–26; 1 Cor 14:26–33, 37–40; 2 Cor 13:1–12; Rom 12–14; Jas 5:7–12). The church's Scriptures, creeds, ecclesiastical decisions, and regulations were all accepted as divinely inspired.

The early Christians' decision to recognize some of their own writings as sacred scripture may be rooted in, or at least connected to, the church's belief that the Spirit was present and active among them. While, as we will see in Chapter 22 §II. F, inspiration was not a criterion for canonicity, it was certainly assumed for those writings that the early churches believed were a true reflection of the sacred traditions handed down from the Apostles to them through Christian leaders, especially the church's bishops. They believed that their Jewish Scriptures were inspired by God (Gk. θεόπνευστος, "God-breathed") as we see in 2 Tim 3:16; but also by transfer, when the NT writings were acknowledged as sacred Scripture, the same affirmation was applicable to them. The early Christians believed that the Spirit was involved in their Christian traditions and writings as we see in 2 Pet 1:17–21 (citing Matt 17:1–5; Mark 9:2–7; Luke 9:28–35), which places the story of the transfiguration on par with other prophecy and scripture that came from the impulse of the Holy Spirit.

The emerging early churches received first an oral tradition about Jesus from those in the apostolic community, much of which was later included in the canonical Gospels. As noted earlier, Dunn makes a convincing argument that much of the material in the Gospels about Jesus' teaching and activity was remembered by his early followers from *before* his death and resurrection. This may account for the lack of reference to his death and resurrection in those texts that are sometimes referred to as Q material.[55] The implications of faith in Jesus as Messiah was also taught and proclaimed in the early churches as we see in the New Testament letters.

---

[55] Dunn, *Jesus Remembered*, 881–84, 147–49, 173–254. See also McDonald, *Story of Jesus in History*, 65–71.

There is little doubt that the earliest proclamations about Jesus after his resurrection were believed to be generated by the power of the Holy Spirit (Acts 1:8; 2:17–36). Those who received that message reported that something transformative occurred in them that they attributed to the work of the Holy Spirit. Belief in the Spirit's present activity is also clear in the Pauline letters (1 Cor 7:40; 12:34–37; 14:37–38; Gal 3:2–5; Rom 8:9–11, 14, 26–27). The early Christians believed that the Spirit was the source of their ability to proclaim the risen Christ as Lord (Acts 1:8; 4:31; 6:4–5). Indeed, when the early Christians proclaimed or taught the message of and about Jesus, they believed that they did so in the power of the Spirit (1 Cor 7:40).

What makes any discussion of the Holy Spirit challenging in relation to the writing of scripture and canon formation is the overlap in and often confusion among Christians over the meaning of the filling of the Spirit, inspiration, the act of writing of scripture, and the forming of a biblical canon. The early Christians did not distinguish between the Spirit's empowerment to preach and the Spirit's empowerment to write what was later called "Scripture." There appears to have been a connection in the thinking of the early Christians between the Holy Spirit, gifts of prophecy, and the notion of Scripture.[56] There is nothing in the NT that suggests an absence of the empowerment of the Spirit in proclaiming the Gospel or in teaching or writing or living the Christian Gospel. On the contrary, the early Christians believed that the Spirit was involved in all of these activities. The age of inspiration and the Spirit was also not considered over when the last Apostle died. As we will see below, the Montanists and their best-known convert, Tertullian, believed that the Spirit was still alive in the church and able to move others also to speak or write.

As the early churches *eventually* began to recognize Christian writings as sacred Scripture, it was reasonable for them to think that those who wrote them were filled with the Spirit and that they transmitted faithfully the Christian message in writing (1 Cor 7:40; Rev 22:18–19). Subsequently, many Christians believed that the authors of their sacred texts had written Scripture under the inspiration of the Holy Spirit. John in the book of Revelation[57] clearly assumed that his message came from the risen Lord through the power of the Holy Spirit and that it could not be changed, a signal of the book's sacredness and its being on par with the church's Scriptures (Rev 1:1–3, 10–11; 2:7, 11, 17, 29; 3:6, 13, 22). We see that the John who composed the book of Revelation was "in the spirit" and was told in a loud voice to "write in a book what you see…" (1:10). The warning at the end

---

[56]   Kalin, "Inspired Community."

[57]   While it is clear that John wrote the book of Revelation, it is not clear which John (Rev 1:1–9). According to Eusebius, Dionysius the Great of Alexandria (ca. 260–64) after his critical analysis of the book concluded that John, but not John the Apostle, wrote Revelation (*Hist. eccl.* 7.24–25). Eusebius placed Revelation among the doubtful books in his own collection of Christian writings (*Hist. eccl.* 3.24.18; 3.25.4), and later Cyril of Jerusalem rejected the book altogether and forbade its use in public or private readings (*Catechetical Lectures* 4.36).

of Revelation is that the words of "this book" are words of prophecy and cannot be changed (Rev 22:18–19; cf. Deut 4:2). This appears to be the clearest and only passage in the NT where the author perceived that he was writing "Scripture." For him, the words that came from the Lord through the Spirit cannot be altered. It is interesting that the NT book that most clearly affirmed the status of Scripture is also one of the most contested books that was finally included in the NT and still has its objectors to this day! Although it is included in the Eastern Orthodox New Testaments it is not read in those churches. Similarly, among churches that use lectionaries in their worship services, it is rare to find texts from the book of Revelation.

Again, both Jews and Christians believed that all Scripture came from God through the inspiration of the Holy Spirit (2 Tim 3:16), and those who wrote it were prophetic individuals filled or inspired by the Holy Spirit. The problem, however, is that it was and is seldom easy to identify or articulate this spiritual-prophetic activity. This is understandable since the Spirit's activity was understood to have no boundaries or human control. Some writings that were earlier believed to be inspired by the Spirit, and were also called Scripture with the presumption of inspiration, eventually were not included in the church's sacred Scripture collections (e.g., *Shepherd of Hermas*, *Epistle of Barnabas*, *Didache*). Because, like the wind, the Spirit blows where it chooses (John 3:5–8), it is difficult to grasp its role in all of its manifestations.[58] The church continues to attempt a coherent understanding of the Spirit's activity that garners approval in all churches, but that is a significant and challenging and as yet unfulfilled task.

Kalin has shown that there is no evidence that the early churches limited the activity of the Spirit to the writing of Scripture. Rather, they concluded that whatever was true, whether proclaimed orally or in writing, was also inspired by the Holy Spirit.[59] They claimed that the Spirit was involved in the production of their sacred Scriptures. Holladay correctly concludes that "no writing could have been included in the New Testament canon had it not been regarded as inspired."[60] The problem, however, is that historically divine inspiration is not easily identified. Kalin contends that almost everything that the early Christians believed to be true in the first five centuries was also believed by them to be

---

[58]   There are two helpful and well-written volumes that address the multiple dimensions of the Spirit's activity in antiquity and today that are worthy of an examination. The first is Thiselton, *Holy Spirit*, noted above; and Johnson T. K. Lim, ed., *The Holy Spirit: Unfinished Agenda* (Singapore: Genesis Books – Word N Works, 2014). This volume includes many scholars from around the globe who contribute on various aspects of biblical, theological, and historical understandings of the Spirit's activity.

[59]   Kalin, "Inspired Community," 541–49.

[60]   Carl R. Holladay, *A Critical Introduction to the New Testament: Interpreting the Message and Meaning of Jesus Christ* (Nashville: Abingdon, 2005), 586. Holladay is well aware that other writings that were not included in the New Testament were also recognized initially as "inspired" writings. His summary of canon formation is carefully constructed and well informed, especially in the CD attached to his volume that includes an updated treatment of NT canon formation.

"inspired by God."[61] It is certainly the case, as Holladay argues, that all Christian writings included in the biblical canon were believed to be inspired by the Holy Spirit. However, it appears that the only way they had for discerning the role of the Spirit in their sacred writings was through their understanding of the criteria of truth (orthodoxy) and tradition. If something was thought to be true and agreed with the tradition handed on in the churches, then, it appears, that it was also believed to be divinely inspired.

Kalin has shown that there was little distinction between the status of the writings that now comprise the NT canon and other such "inspired" writings that were also welcomed in the churches. For example, *Didache, 1 Clement, Epistle of Barnabas*, and *Shepherd of Hermas* are all found in surviving Christian manuscripts and all candidates for scriptural status among some early Christians in the second and third centuries.[62] Kelly concludes that it goes without saying that all of the church's scriptures were recognized by the church fathers as divinely inspired. They received their notion of inspiration from their earlier Jewish siblings who acknowledged all prophetic literature as divinely inspired.[63]

Eventually a distinction was made on the basis of other criteria besides truth (orthodoxy) alone. The other criteria were, as we will see, apostolicity, use or catholicity, antiquity, and adaptability. The more recent distinction between being filled with the Spirit and the notion of inspiration, with the latter reserved for sacred scripture alone, was not among earliest Christian teaching, but rather it came in the post-Reformation period. This confusion leads some to the conclusion that everything that was believed to be inspired was also sacred Scripture. Recognizing the difficulty of arguing the case of canonicity on the basis of inspiration, F. F. Bruce rightly concludes that "inspiration is no longer a criterion of canonicity: it is a corollary of canonicity."[64] (Additional discussion and examples of inspiration and its relation to canonicity can be seen below in Chapter 22 §II.F.)

As we saw in Chapter 5, many Jews believed that with the death of the final three prophets (Haggai, Zechariah, and Malachi) the Holy Spirit and prophetic activity had ceased among them (1 Macc 4:45b–46; 9:27; 14:41; 1QS 9:10–11; Josephus, *Ag. Apion* 1:39–40; *t. Sotah* 13:2–3; *b. Baba Batra* 14a–b and 15a; *b. Yoma* 21b; *b. Sanhedrin* 65b). Although there were disputes over the exact timing of this withdrawal, the belief itself appears to have been widespread in the Land of Israel and later in Babylon as well. This absence of the Spirit *may* be suggested or inferred from Jesus' promise to his disciples to send the Holy Spirit (John 14:26; 15:26; 16:13; cf. also John 7:39 and Acts 1:8).

While affirmation of the inspiration of ecclesiastical activities was not uncommon in antiquity, in the Protestant Reformation sharp distinctions were made between

---

61   Kalin, "Argument from Inspiration."
62   Ibid. See also his "Inspired Community"; and "Re-examining New Testament Canon History," 1.
63   Kelly, *Early Christian Doctrines*, 60–61.
64   F. F. Bruce, *Canon of Scripture*, 268.

ecclesiastical actions or deliberations and the church's Scriptures. Schaff observes that Protestants did not reject ecclesiastical canons, but they insisted that those canons always had to be dependent on church Scriptures. In Article 3 of the Augsburg Confession (1530), for example, Luther objected to the use of the Mass as a means of taking away sins and argued: "Our preachers have admonished concerning these opinions that they do depart from the holy Scriptures, and diminish the glory of the passion of Christ."[65]

B. The Early Church Fathers and the Holy Spirit

Christians are regularly challenged to find a rationale for limiting the formation of a biblical canon to a fixed collection of books or to a special form of the Spirit's activity in the early churches alone. In 172, Montanus from Phrygia and his two associates, Prisca and Maximilla, maintained that the Spirit's activity continued in the churches and the Spirit enabled them to produce what they considered to be inspired (Spirit-filled) literature. Tertullian agreed that the Spirit's activity was not limited to the earliest generations of the church and he joined the Montanus community. He argued that it was "mere prejudice to heed and value only past demonstrations of power and grace," concluding that "those people who condemn the one power of the one Holy Spirit in accordance with chronological era should beware" ("Introduction" to *Passio perpetuae* 1.1).

Although the early churches never claimed that the Spirit and prophetic activity had ceased, there came a time when in practice the historical argument became a widespread assumption in churches and there arose the notion that divine inspiration of the Christian Scriptures was limited to authors in close proximity to Jesus. That notion put chronological limits on what could legitimately be called Spirit-inspired Christian Scripture and the theological positions that were possible within the acceptable parameters of the church's canons of faith. While there was still considerable diversity in the majority of churches, there were also limits to that diversity. The writings of the Marcionites, gnostics, and Montanists and many others after them were all excluded. By the fourth century the Arians were excluded because of their understanding of Jesus' identity and their denial of the doctrine of the Trinity.

As we saw in Gal 6:16, some early Christians and even later early church fathers believed that the Spirit had been taken away from the Jews and given to the followers of Jesus who became the new "Israel of God." Justin Martyr argued that prophecy had been taken away from the Jews at the death of Jesus Christ (*Dial.* 53.3–4, also 82.1). Origen himself claimed that the Holy Spirit had "forsaken" the Jews because "they acted impiously against God and against the one prophesied by the prophets among them. But signs of the Holy Spirit were manifested at the beginning when Jesus was teaching…" (*Cels.* 7.8). Athanasius asked, "When did

---

[65]   Schaff, *Creeds*, 3:36–37.

prophecy and vision cease from Israel? Was it not when Christ came, the Holy One of holies? It is, in fact, a sign and notable proof of the coming of the Word that Jerusalem no longer stands, neither is prophet raised up nor vision revealed among them" (*Inc.* 39–40). Augustine observed that even the Jews were aware of the absence of prophets among them (*Civ.* 17.24).[66] On the other hand, the Apostolic Fathers, Apologists, and later Patristic Fathers all affirmed the continuing activity of the Spirit in the church and affirmed the Spirit's inspiration of their Scriptures. Thiselton offers many examples of this from Clement of Rome, Ignatius, Irenaeus, Tertullian, Origen, Basil, and others.[67]

C. The Holy Spirit and Canon Formation

The role of the Spirit in the formation of the church's biblical canon is a complex subject. That in part is because there is no specific reference to the role of the Spirit in shaping a fixed biblical canon. Tertullian's claim that the Spirit continues to be present and active in the church is difficult to deny or challenge with Scripture. He found no biblical, theological, or even historical arguments for concluding that the Spirit has stopped speaking in and through the followers of Jesus. In this sense, it is difficult to argue from Scripture that there is a closed biblical canon. The argument can be made historically, but it is more challenging to argue it biblically or theologically.

By the mid-third century CE, there was widespread but not complete agreement on most of the books that eventually comprised the Christian Scriptures. At that time the notion of a *fixed* collection of Scriptures had begun to emerge in many churches, though the recognition of their inspired status came earlier. The following overview will focus on the relationship between the Holy Spirit, inspiration, Scripture, and biblical canons.

D. Stating the Obvious

We have seen in this brief survey that sacred Scripture was always believed to have its origin in God and that it was inspired by the Holy Spirit. Although no biblical text says that the biblical books *alone* are inspired by the Holy Spirit, it is clear that all of the books that formed the church's Bible were accepted as divinely inspired writings. In the minds of the early church fathers, the Scriptures were inextricably bound to the activity and power of the Holy Spirit, but the specific details of how that worked is vague. Nevertheless, it was universally presumed and accepted.

---

[66]   For a useful discussion of this understanding of prophecy among Jews and Christians in antiquity, see L. S. Cook, *On the Question of the "Cessation of Prophecy" in Ancient Judaism*, 5–9 and 47–177.

[67]   Thiselton, *Holy Spirit*, 163–92.

Considerable confusion persists in this matter because the language that distinguishes inspired literature, the notion of scripture, and a fixed biblical canon is often imprecise in the ancient sources. This confusion, however, is consistent with what we might expect from a community that experienced what it believed was the power and presence of God, but did not yet have an informed or consistent vocabulary sufficient to articulate it.[68] The ancient sources share a consistent belief in the involvement of the Spirit in the origin of the churches' Scriptures, but initially there is nothing about a fixed or closed biblical canon.

V. THE HOLY SPIRIT AND CANON FORMATION: A SUMMARY

The role of the Spirit in the formation of the church's biblical canon is complex. Tertullian's claim that the Spirit continues to be present and active in the church is difficult to challenge on a scriptural basis. He found no biblical, theological, or even historical argument for concluding that the Spirit has stopped speaking in and through followers of Jesus. The ancient churches also affirmed a "historical" argument or criterion that affirms only those writings that were written in close historical proximity to Jesus and the Apostolic community. This is discussed in Chapter 22 §II.C below.

It is common today, especially since the Reformation, to conclude that only the writers of the New Testament were "inspired." Those who speak or write are regularly distinguished from those who wrote Scripture, and that distinction has a parallel in rabbinic Judaism that recognized that prophetic activity ceased in ancient Israel despite the continuing production of religious literature, but the early churches never argued that the Spirit had stopped functioning among them. While that is true in theory, in practice there came a time when Christians began to say that the Spirit was no longer leading prophetic individuals to write sacred Scripture. After that, a belief emerged that along with the Spirit's activity in the production, teaching, and preaching of the church's Scriptures, the Spirit continued to speak through the church's traditions, creeds, and ecclesiastical council decisions. The Scriptures were regularly a part of what was cited in such decisions about the prophetic activity, but there came a time when the church concluded that the writing of Scripture had ceased.

The early Christians believed that when Jesus spoke what he said was not only authoritative but even superior to their inherited Scriptures. They understood that the Spirit was upon him at his baptism and as he began his ministry (Luke 3:21–22; 4:1, 14). His words had the highest authority attached to them (1 Cor 7:10; 11:23–25), but from the beginning of the church the early Christians also

---

[68] Lim, *Formation of the Jewish Canon*, 3–6, acknowledges this uncertainty and the imprecise language in the early stages of the church's canon formation.

believed that the empowerment of the Holy Spirit was also given to them to carry out their mission as a witness of Jesus (Acts 1:8; John 20:21–23). Among the various functions of the Holy Spirit in the Bible, the empowerment of the Spirit is often connected to the notion of a Word coming from God to a prophet who spoke that Word in the name of God (Isa 6:6–8; Jer 1:4; 2:1–3; Ezek 6:1, passim). As we saw in Chapter 2, the very notion of Scripture stems from a belief that a word came from God that was delivered through prophetic (spirit-led) individuals empowered to speak or write that divine message.

VI. ARGUMENTS FOR EARLY NEW TESTAMENT CANONIZATION

There are several biblical scholars such as Michael Kruger, Charles Hill, and Stanley Porter who argue for an early first-century recognition of the scriptural status of the NT writings by the end of the second century. I have addressed several of their arguments already and will add to this in Chapters 20 and 22, but here I will briefly address some of Porter's arguments because they summarize clearly the perspectives and rationale of those who hold that position. Because Porter has recently summarized the most common arguments for an early formation of the NT canon, including arguments against a later formation of the NT canon, I have decided to respond briefly to a number of those arguments by responding not to his summation of my arguments, since you already have them, but rather how he employs four well-known NT texts to advance his view that the NT writers were consciously aware of writing Scripture when they composed their texts.[69] These include the following:

Romans 16:25–27. His selection of this text is surprising since Porter is surely aware of the mixed textual tradition of this text and several significant commentators reject its authenticity but claim that it was added to a Pauline collection in the second century – for example, J. Fitzmyer, who also concludes that the author is speaking of the "Jewish apocalyptic writings that bear on this 'ministry'," and adds that the ideas in this passage are found in Romans and that Paul elsewhere contends that Jesus came in accordance with those Scriptures.[70] Others also argue that Paul's reference to "prophetic writings" is to the Jewish Scriptures, Both Fitzmyer and others are also aware of the uncertainty over this text/doxology. Dunn, like Fitzmyer, agrees that the text was not written by Paul, but was perhaps added to Paul's letter to the Romans 150 years later and both are aware of the mixed textual support for this text and its place in some manuscripts (Latin) at the end of Rom 14. Dunn claims that the reference to "prophetic writings"

---

[69]   See Porter and Pitts, *Fundamentals of New Testament Criticism*, 9–32.
[70]   Joseph Fitzmyer, *Romans*, AB 33 (New York: Doubleday, 1993), 753–54.

is to the Jewish Scriptures (OT) in 16:26.[71] Käsemann also calls this passage an "Inauthentic Concluding Doxology" and questions the extent to which "the revelation of the eschatological mystery" took place in the OT prophecy and this suggests that perhaps in the later churches the apostolic witness was associated with the revelation in question in the passage.

The text here emphasizes the role of revelation along with the "prophetic writings," which makes it is unlikely that the text is referring to the letters of Paul by that designation.[72] While the doxology reflects several of the themes in Romans, it does not appear to be Paul's language. For Paul, the message of the revelation of Christ is in accord with the message of the Jewish Scriptures. His regular references to the OT Scriptures in chs. 9–11 suggest that these are the prophetical scriptures referred to in 16:26. In either case, the textual support for this passage is not impressive and it likely, if attributed to Paul, was a reference to the OT scriptures rather than to Paul's letters.

Colossians 4:16. Porter claims that Paul's admonition to the Colossian Christians to have his letter to them also read to the Laodicean Christians is evidence that he wanted his letters to be read to a wider audience than those addressed in the letter. He implies by this that Paul wanted all of his letters read in all of the churches, but there is no evidence for that. Porter appears to forget also that those two churches were not more than ten miles apart and likely were facing some of the same problems in the first century. There is nothing here to suggest that Paul was suggesting that his letters were scriptural. I have not found any commentators who suggest this view either. It is more likely that the problems in Colossae were also faced by some of the Christians at Laodicea.

1 Thessalonians 2:13. Porter lists this text in support of his position that Paul was aware that he was writing Scripture, namely by saying that what he proclaimed was the word of God and that the Thessalonians received it as not as a human word, but as it "really is, God's word." This text has nothing to do with the written text, namely a reference to Paul's letter or letters, but the message Paul proclaimed and they *heard*. It is not unusual for those who proclaimed the Christian Gospel to contend that they were proclaiming the word of God and this is what is found here. Even today, many preachers proclaim what they believe is the very word of God and not a human word and that was also the case in early Christianity. There is no

---

[71]   James D. G. Dunn, *Romans 9–16*, WBC 38B (Dallas: Word, 1988), 913–17. Douglas Moo, who is aware of the mixed textual support for this doxology, nevertheless concludes that Paul wrote this doxology, but also agrees that the reference is to the OT writings, not Paul's letters. See his *Romans*, NICNT (Grand Rapids: Eerdmans, 1996), 937–40.

[72]   See also the discussions of Brendan Byrne, *Romans*, Sacra Pagina 6 (Collegeville: Liturgical Press, 1996), who also calls this doxology an "(Inauthentic) Concluding Doxology" high lighting its weak textual support, 461–63, but adds that its late date could infer that the focus is also on NT texts, namely Paul's texts as scripture as we see in the second century 2 Pet 3:15–16.

inference here that what Paul was *writing* to the Thessalonians was sacred Scripture either in Paul's thinking or in those who heard him (Jews and Gentiles), but that was later (second century) perceived in the churches. Again, I know of no commentators or exegetes of this text who make Porter's argument in this text. In this text Paul is speaking of the Gospel that he preached to the Thessalonian Christians and praises them for not simply welcoming it as a human word, but as it was, the word of God. This passage says nothing about accepting a written text as Scripture.

1 Corinthians 14:37. Porter suggests that Paul is here claiming that his prophesying is a revelation from God and it is the same as scripture, but Paul encourages others in the Corinthian community to prophesy and not forbid others to speak in tongues. Does this suggest, following Porter's logic here, that others in the community who are also prophesying were also writing or producing Scripture? Is the ability to speak by the Spirit and prophesy equal to writing scripture? If so, as I have stated above, there would be many more claims to the production of Scripture than what we find in the NT. Again, it is difficult to find any commentators who conclude from this passage that Paul is claiming to write Scripture or that the gift of prophecy is the same as the gift of writing Scripture. As we see in 14:39, how is Paul distinguishing his prophecy in the Spirit from others exercising the same gift of prophecy in the early church? If the gift of prophecy is synonymous with the production of Scripture, then we are missing a lot of scripture if the revelations that other's prophesied in the first century were also Scripture. It is true that later Christians acknowledged that what Paul was writing was sacred scripture, but Paul himself does not make that claim for himself. Porter acknowledges that Paul "temporarily steps aside from his apostolic authority" in 1 Cor 7:25, but he evidently resumes his role of writing Scripture thereafter. That is a strange position to take because it indicates that 1 Corinthians was acknowledged as Scripture, but not those words when Paul offers his opinion. It is far better to say that Paul was mindful of being led by the Spirit when he taught and proclaimed the revelation about Jesus the Christ, but was unaware at that same time he was also writing sacred Scripture. The church leaders later perceived the sacredness of Paul's writings and included them in their biblical canon.

Again, it is difficult to find support for Porter's position among the commentators on this passage, but Porter's position here raises the question of whether the gift of prophecy automatically confers a scriptural status. If that were the case, the gift of prophecy would have initiated far more scriptural texts than what we have in our NT. Further, Porter's conclusion that "the canon was established *intrinsically by what the church* viewed as *its own internal criteria* as soon *as the literature was written*"[73] is confusing since Paul never calls his writings

---

[73]   Porter and Pitts, *Fundamentals of New Testament Criticism*, 30 (with emphasis added because these words are difficult to understand, and also because there is no evidence that the NT writings were received as Scripture as soon as they were written). What these "internal criteria" are is unclear.

"scripture" or "scriptures" (γραφή or γραφαί) and the first known writer to call NT writings (three Gospels and four letters of Paul) "scripture," as we saw earlier, was the gnostic teacher Basilides (ca. 130). If the NT canon were closed after the last apostle died, as Porter claims, one would think that someone at least would have said so. It is much more likely that after the NT writers wrote, others after them perceived their value both in their ecclesiastical teaching and in advancing the church's mission. As we saw earlier (Col 4:16), even in the first century some of the NT writings were being read in churches and eventually liturgically as sacred Scripture. After that they begin to be called Scripture. If the scriptural status of the writings produced by Paul or other NT writers was perceived by those who received those writings and the matter was settled when the final apostle died, as Porter contends,[74] one would think that the early canon lists and the contents of the surviving majuscule manuscripts of the NT would all have the same books, but they do not. There is considerable overlap, but seldom are the writings in these manuscript and catalog collections uniformly the same.

VII. CONCLUSION

No biblical text says that the biblical books *alone* are inspired by the Holy Spirit, only that all Scripture is inspired by God (2 Tim 3:16), and it is clear that all of the books that formed the church's Bible were accepted as inspired by the Holy Spirit. In the minds of the early church fathers, the Scriptures were inextricably bound to the activity and power of the Holy Spirit, but how that works is not uniform or specific in the surviving ancient sources. Nevertheless, this universal presumption was widely accepted in the churches.

Considerable confusion persists over the relation between Scripture and inspiration, or between those who wrote sacred Scripture and those who were led by the Spirit. The language available for clarifying what distinguishes inspired literature, the notion of scripture, and a fixed biblical canon is often elusive, but such language is also imprecise in the ancient church traditions. This appears to be true of Kruger's work noted above. He equates being led by the Spirit with the writing of Scripture and the notion of Scripture with canon. He assumes what was true at the end of the processes of canonization was there at the beginning, rather than a step in the direction toward canonization.[75] This leads us to the question of whether *all* of the writings that were initially believed to have been written under the influence and empowerment of the Holy Spirit were also believed to be sacred Scripture? Obviously the early churches said no. As we saw earlier, several writers claimed to write under inspiration (Clement of Rome, Ignatius, Irenaeus, and Tertullian), but if so, why were their writings not accepted into the biblical

---

[74] Ibid.
[75] Kruger, *Question of Canon*, 119–210.

canon? And what about the many creeds and council decisions that occurred much later whose writers claimed that what was written or decided was by the leading or inspiration of the Spirit? Should such writings also be given consideration for something like a scriptural status? I do not think so, and neither does Kruger, but the logic of his position leads in that direction. Without adequate explanation, he restricts such notions of being filled with the Spirit or inspired by the Spirit to the biblical literature. I do not think Kruger is clear on this point, but if he is right, then perhaps we need to revisit what goes into our biblical canon and include whatever the early churches believed was written or said by the power of the Spirit.

Confusion in clarifying the role of the Spirit in early Christianity is consistent with what we might expect from a community that experienced what it believed was the power and presence of God in the proclamation of and about Jesus, but as we observed above, they did not yet have a vocabulary adequate to articulate it.[76] The Spirit's involvement in the selection and listing of specific scriptures that formed a fixed collection of Scriptures is not altogether clear in the surviving sources of the church, but clearly the Scriptures that comprise the church's biblical canon were consistently viewed as inspired by the Holy Spirit.

---

[76]   So suggests Lim, *Formation of the Jewish Canon*, 3–6.

CHAPTER 18

THE INFLUENCE OF HERESY ON THE FORMATION OF THE BIBLE

I. INTRODUCTION: SOME CURRENT CONFUSION

While "heresy" and "heretic" are common designations today for those whose beliefs are different from the majority, their meaning is far from clear in antiquity. Normally the terms refers to individuals or groups *within* the Christian tradition who stray from orthodoxy, or the church's earliest foundational traditions, especially in reference to the nature of God or Jesus.[1] The difficulty in defining heresy in antiquity is that normative Christianity (orthodoxy) had not yet been fully defined or *universally* acknowledged in early Christianity until there was a major move in that direction such as the "proto-orthodoxy" promoted in the second- and third-century church fathers (Irenaeus, Hippolytus, Athenagoras, Tertullian, Origen, and Cyprian). These church leaders did not make their decisions about heresy based on an already formed Christian Bible, but based on what they believed were the earliest traditions and creeds passed on in the churches. For added support for their teachings, they regularly appealed to first-century Christian writings that were later included in the NT canon. From the middle to end of the first century, it appears that many divergent theological issues were circulating in the early churches (1 Cor 15:12–19; Col 2:8, 20–23; 2 Thess 2:1–3; 1 John 4:1–3; and Rev 2:14–15, 20–24). It is clear that the early Christian traditions and teachings circulating in many churches that were also expressed also in several Christian writings were regularly challenged in the first and second centuries.

---

[1]   In churches today the term heresy usually refers to those who make a conscious or willful rejection of beliefs that are considered normative by a church, a group of churches, or theologians within the greater church or to an introduction of new teachings that are contrary to established church traditions. Roman Catholics, for instance, define a heretic as a member of the church who denies the truth of any revealed teaching of the church. Protestants usually define a heretic as one who rejects any truth taught in the Bible. The term is not usually used of non-Christian groups, such as Buddhists or Hindus, but of those who claim to be Christian but reject *major* teachings in Christian Scriptures. Of course "major" is a debatable issue.

The so-called heretical groups were by no means insignificant in number, and indeed, if combined, they may for a time in the second century have outnumbered those in the so-called orthodox churches.[2] In response, the second- and third-century church teachers mentioned above sought to anchor their beliefs and practices in what they believed were the *earliest* traditions and creeds of the church supported by the *earliest* known Christian writings (hence, the criteria of apostolicity and antiquity). They believed that these sources supported their orthodox traditions and provided a more firm foundation for Christian beliefs than the other sects of Christianity that they considered outside of the boundaries of the earliest Christian teachings handed on in the churches.

For our purposes, the question here is whether the second-century heresies and those who espoused them had a significant influence on the selection of literature that was included in the Christian Bible. Several scholars (Harnack, von Campenhausen, Metzger, and others following them) contend that in response to three major second-century heretical groups, the churches came to the writings that make up the church's NT biblical canon. These second-century heresies included those of Marcion, the gnostics, and finally the Montanists.

By the mid-second century CE, church leaders had already recognized the value and usefulness of early Christian literature in their worship, instruction, and apologetic, but also in dealing with the heresies mentioned above. By the mid-to-late second century, the words Gospel and Apostle (sometimes Lord and Apostle), representing the words of and traditions about Jesus (Gospels) and the other writings attributed to the apostles, began to be placed alongside the Prophets (i.e., OT Scriptures) and all served as primary authorities in the second-century church fathers. As we will see, this triptych of authority is paralleled by the three major so-called heretical groups in the church. We will now examine the most prominent "heresies" in second-century Christianity and their influence, if any, on the formation of the NT canon.

II. MARCION AND MARCIONITES

Marcion (active ca. 140–160) was a wealthy ship owner and native of Sinope in Pontus and, like many of his contemporaries, recognized the importance of a collection of authoritative Christian writings for worship and teaching in his churches.[3] He even recognized the familiar gospel-apostle tradition that was

---

[2]   Bauer, *Orthodoxy and Heresy in Earliest Christianity* and J. M. Robinson and H. Koester, *Trajectories Through Early Christianity* (Philadelphia: Fortress, 1971), argue this view.

[3]   For a useful summary of Marcion's career and accomplishments, see J. J. Clabeaux, "Marcion," *ABD* 4:5144–16; idem, "Marcionite Prologues to Paul," *ABD* 4:520–21; and idem, *A Lost Edition of the Letters of Paul: A Reassessment of the Text of the Pauline Corpus Attested by Marcion*, Catholic

circulating in the churches,[4] but Marcion is best known for three important positions related to the Scriptures and God: (1) he rejected the Jewish Scriptures claiming that they could be made relevant to the church only by allegorizing them, an interpretive methodology that he rejected; (2) he did not believe that the God of the Jews was the same as the loving and unknown God of Jesus; and (3) he apparently[5] limited his collection of Christian Scriptures to an edited version of the Gospel of Luke and ten letters of Paul.[6]

One of Marcion's primary aims was the separation of the Christian tradition from its Jewish heritage and all references to its origin in Judaism. We have no indication from Marcion that he called the writings of Paul and Luke sacred "scripture," but they appear to have functioned that way in the communities he founded. He freely deleted from his truncated collection all references to the Jewish Scriptures (e.g., Marcion's edition of Luke's Gospel lacked the story of Jesus' birth and began with Luke 4:1).[7] Bishop Epiphanius of Salamis (315–403) identifies the specific books in Marcion's collection:

> Such is Marcion's spurious composition, which contains the text and wording of Luke's gospel and the incomplete writings of the apostle Paul, meaning not all of his letters, but only Romans, Colossians, Laodiceans,[8] Galatians, First and Second Corinthians, First and Second Thessalonians, Philemon, and Philippians. But he includes none of First and Second Timothy, Titus, and Hebrews [and even?] those he includes [are mutilated?], so that they are not complete, but are as though corrupted. (*Pan.* 11.9–11)[9]

Biblical Quarterly Monograph Series 21 (Washington, DC: Catholic University of America Press, 1989); and also John Barton, "Marcion Revisited," in McDonald and Sanders, eds., *The Canon Debate*, 341–54.

4   Interestingly, Von Campenhausen, *Formation of the Christian Bible*, 153, suggests that Marcion created the gospel-apostle form that was later followed by the church, but this conclusion is neither required nor even likely. However, this order more likely grew out of the church's recognition of its threefold canon of authority – law, gospel (Jesus), and apostle – well attested before the time of Marcion.

5   As we will see, Marcion's followers did not follow this collection only but also cited the Gospel of Matthew and other Christian writings besides.

6   Marcion may have been one of the first persons to call one of the canonical Gospels a "gospel." R. Collins, *Introduction to the New Testament*, 22, suggests this possibility since Marcion apparently assumed that when Paul spoke of "his gospel" he was referring to the Gospel of Luke. Collins claims that Marcion evidently presumed that Paul had in mind a written source, so he set out to restore it by cutting out the Jewish elements in it that were offensive to him.

7   His is the only known version of Luke's Gospel without the birth narrative and one that starts in 4:1.

8   Some scholars are convinced that "Laodiceans" is a reference to what we now know as Paul's letter to the Ephesians. Scholars are aware that the designation ἐν Ἐφέσῳ in Eph 1:1 is missing from the earliest manuscripts of that letter and it is unlikely that it was sent to Ephesus since Paul had been there and knew the people, but the text, as we saw earlier, does not reflect Paul's knowledge of them. He had only heard of them.

9   Quoted from A. J. Hultgren and S. A. Haggmark, eds., *The Earliest Christian Heretics: Readings from Their Opponents* (Minneapolis: Fortress, 1996), 115.

Many consider it strange that Marcion did not include the Pastoral Epistles or Hebrews, but perhaps he simply did not know about the Pastoral letters or like others rejected them as non-Pauline. We observed earlier that the Pastorals are also missing from P[46], the earliest manuscript collection of Paul's letters, and they are also missing in Codex Vaticanus and not generally cited before the late second and third centuries. The absence of the Pastorals may be because they did not exist in their current form when Marcion wrote, or that their contents did not meet his criteria for inclusion. Tertullian implies that Marcion specifically rejected them.[10] It may also be that since Hebrews includes numerous references to and citations of the Jewish scriptures, he dismissed it. This is guesswork, of course. Whether he was aware of any other letters attributed to Paul or the other canonical Gospels is debated, though, given their popularity in the second century, he was likely at least familiar with the Gospel of Matthew. His later followers certainly knew this Gospel and quoted it, as we will see below.

Marcion acknowledged that the Jewish Scriptures accurately reflected the creation of the world, but he also taught that *a god* (or a Demiurge[11]), who was both vengeful and evil, created the world. He encouraged his followers to read the Jewish Scriptures so they would know their incompatibility with Christian teaching. Unlike widespread Christian practice in the second century, he rejected the spiritualizing or allegorizing of the Jewish Scriptures to make them relevant and compatible to the Christian community. He rejected all Jewish influences on the early Christian proclamation, though he acknowledged that Jesus and Paul were Jews. Marcion's rejection of Jewish teachings may have stemmed from the current anti-Jewish sentiment that was widespread in the Roman Empire following the second Jewish revolt against Rome in Palestine (132–135 CE).

According to Harnack, Marcion established "the first biblical canon" and church leaders subsequently responded to his challenge first by excommunicating Marcion and then by establishing a larger collection of Christian scriptures and reemphasizing their acceptance of the Jewish Scriptures.[12] This view was popular in academic circles throughout most of the last century and it still has adherents to this day, but several scholars now acknowledge that Marcion's purpose was not so much an insight into the value of a limited number of NT writings or even

---

[10]   Tertullian suggests that Marcion rejected writings to one person and therefore excluded 1 and 2 Timothy and Titus "which all treat of ecclesiastical discipline. His aim was, I suppose, to carry out his interpolating process even to the number of (St. Paul's) letters" (*Marc*. 3.473–75).

[11]   "Demiurge" or "craftsman" (Gk. δημιουργός) is Plato's term for the creator of the universe. In the second and third centuries CE, the creator-god was also referred to by some gnostics as "Ialdabaoth," a nonspiritual being (Layton, *Gnostic Scriptures*, 12–16). Ptolemy, head of the Valentinian gnostic school in the second century, claimed that the Demiurge was an angel, the parent of all animate things, who was the God of Israel and ordinary Christians (ibid., 279).

[12]   See A. von Harnack, *Marcion: Das Evangelium vom fremden Gott*, 2nd ed. (Leipzig: Hinrichs, 1924); and idem, *The Origin of the New Testament and the Most Important Consequences of the New Creation*, trans. J. R. Wilkinson (New York: Macmillan, 1925).

to establish a biblical canon.[13] Rather, Marcion believed that the Christian gospel was absolute love and completely contrary to the legalistic and oppressive law of the Jewish Scriptures that was taught by the early church's leaders in Jerusalem, especially Peter and James.

Marcion wrote a collection of *Antitheses* that supported his rejection of the OT and his restriction of the NT to Luke and ten letters of Paul.[14] The book, *Antitheses*, was essentially Marcion's doctrinal handbook arguing for the incompatibility of law and gospel and an understanding of Marcion's gospel. Marcion believed that Judaism heavily influenced Peter and James and that only Paul adequately separated himself from it.[15]

Again, along with his rejection of the Jewish influences in early Christianity, Marcion also rejected the typological and allegorical hermeneutical approaches to the OT that Christian writers of his day commonly employed to make it relevant for Christian faith. In the ancient world, allegorizing ancient texts was a signal of recognizing their sacredness in a religious community. Indeed, as Barton observes, allegorizing a text was "the characteristic mark of a holy text in the ancient world."[16] This rejection of the Jewish Scriptures, which the churches welcomed as their First scriptures, supported Marcion's belief that Christianity was something completely new. He stressed that the God of the law was a Demiurge, a creator-god similar to the creator-god discussed in Gnosticism.[17] He argued that the God of the OT was not the same as the unknown God of the gospel and of Jesus; therefore, he turned his efforts toward a separation of Christianity from its Jewish roots and influences.

Earlier scholars accused Marcion of being a gnostic Christian, or at least that he was heavily influenced by them, and it appears that he borrowed the name of the evil god of creation from the gnostic community, but he himself was not likely a gnostic. Irenaeus, however, identifies Marcion as a gnostic, claiming that the gnostic Cerdo took his system of philosophy from the followers of Simon Magus (Acts 8:9–24) and that "Marcion of Pontus succeeded him [Cerdo], and developed his doctrine" (*Haer*. 1.27.1). Unlike several of the gnostics, however, Marcion rejected *all* of the Jewish Scriptures and the allegorical interpretations of these Scriptures. He avoided any focus on secret knowledge and had little sympathy

---

[13] Barton, *Holy Writings, Sacred Text*, 34–62; and idem, "Marcion Revisited."

[14] The *Antitheses* is now lost but it is discussed in ancient orthodox writings and, as a result, has been partially reconstructed.

[15] Jason D. BeDuhn offers valuable information about Marcion's collection of Christian writings and some of the implications from that collection in his *First New Testament*, 11–62 and 203–59.

[16] Barton, *Holy Writings, Sacred Text*, 61. He notes that Origen, in his defense of the church's apparent lack of sophistication, once spoke of "intelligent people who readily interpret allegorically" (*Cels*. 1.23; cf. also Barton, "Marcion Revisited," 349).

[17] For a summary of the major tenets of Gnosticism, see "Gnosticism," in *Oxford Dictionary of the Christian Church*, ed. F. L. Cross and E. Livingstone (Oxford: Oxford University Press, 2005), 687–88.

for the mythological speculations that were characteristic of the gnostic Christian movement. He apparently was also something of an ascetic and taught sexual abstinence: "The so-called Encratites proceeding from Saturninus and Marcion preached against marriage, annulling the original creation of God, and tacitly condemning him who made male and female" (Eusebius, *Hist. eccl.* 4.29.1–2, LCL).

Some scholars have speculated that Marcion's churches outnumbered, or at least equaled, those of the orthodox Christians in the mid-second century. Whether true or not, his influence can be seen in the large number of important church teachers at the end of the second century and up to the fifth century who attacked his views: Justin, Irenaeus, Hippolytus of Rome, Clement of Alexandria, Tertullian, Origen, Eusebius, Epiphanius, and Cyril of Jerusalem. Since all of Marcion's works have been lost (or destroyed), we are completely dependent on the early church fathers to reconstruct his views and activities. Fortunately, they appear to be consistent with each other in describing many important details about him and his followers, but, as in all anti-heretical literature of ancient times, they also tended to make *ad hominem* attacks against Marcion.

Tertullian's criticisms of Marcion included five lengthy books against him called *The Five Books against Marcion* (ca. 190–200). These books show not only the difficulty that the church had in answering Marcion's teachings, but they also show his significant influence in the greater churches for a considerable period of time. What led to Marcion's excommunication from the churches in Rome and elsewhere resulted in the strong criticisms against him by great teachers of the church long after his death. Commenting on Marcion's two best-known teachings, Tertullian writes, in a difficult passage to translate, the following:

> Marcion's special and principal work is the separation of the law and the gospel; and his disciples will not deny that in this point they have their very best pretext for initiating and confirming themselves in his heresy. These are Marcion's *Antitheses*, or contradictory propositions, which aim at distinguishing the gospel from the law in order that from the diversity of the two documents[18] that contains them, they may contend for a diversity of gods also. Since, therefore, it is this very contrast between the law and the gospel that has suggested [to the Marcionites] that the God of the gospel is different from the God of the law [at that time, law referred to all of the Jewish Scriptures], it is clear that, before the said separation [i.e., before the gospel came], that God [of the Christians] could not have been known who became known from the argument of the separation itself. He therefore could not have been revealed by Christ, who came before the separation, but must have been devised by Marcion who is the author of the breach of peace between the gospel and the law. Now this peace, which had remained unhurt and unshaken from Christ's appearance to the time of Marcion's audacious doctrine, was no doubt maintained by that way of thinking which firmly held that the God of both law and gospel was none other than the Creator, against whom after so long a time a separation has been introduced by the heretic of Pontus [i.e., Marcion]. (*Marc.* 1.19, adapted from ANF).

---

[18]   He does not specifically identify the "two documents," but perhaps they are a reference to the Gospel tradition that Marcion espoused and the Jewish Scriptures or Judaism itself.

In the fifth century, Cyril of Jerusalem warned his parishioners to avoid Marcionite churches,[19] and he attacked Marcion as "that mouthpiece of ungodliness" and the "second inventor of more mischief," Simon Magus of Acts 8 being the first. He writes:

> Being confuted by the testimonies from the Old Testament which are quoted in the New, he was the first who dared to cut those testimonies out, and leave the preaching of the word of faith without witness, thus effacing the true God: and sought to undermine the Church's faith, as if there were no heralds of it. (*Catechetical Lectures* 6.16, NPNF)

Marcion recognized perhaps more clearly than others of his day the difficulty of a literal interpretation of the OT for the early church. Paul himself spoke of the inability of the legal aspects of the law to bring persons into a right relationship with God and he denied works righteousness as a means of attaining salvation (Gal 3–4; Rom 4:5). This stands behind Marcion's rejection of the law. He also argued that the God of the OT was quite harsh, even cruel at times, and especially vengeful and changeable. The moral standard of an "eye for an eye" was hard for him to reconcile with Jesus' call to "turn the other cheek" and to love one's enemies (Matt 5:38–48). Marcion found it impossible to ascribe normative value to the Jewish Scriptures that he said were no longer binding on Christians. This was especially true of the legal and moral codes and traditions associated with keeping the law. Taking his cue from Paul, he argued that Christians are free from the law and, therefore, have no reason to give allegiance to that which has been rendered obsolete by faith in Jesus Christ.

Barton concludes that Marcion was important for two reasons: he rejected the OT, viewing it as the document of an alien religion, and he saw the role of Jesus as one who would deliver those in bondage from the evil creator-god of the OT.[20] Marcion concluded that only by arbitrary means of interpreting (i.e., allegory or typology or sometimes *pesher* exegesis) could the OT have the slightest camouflaged meaning at all.[21] Marcion's rejection of the OT writings, together with his use of a literal hermeneutical approach for interpreting it, stripped the church not only of its first Scriptures, but also of its prized claim to the heritage of Israel's antiquity and to being the religion of historical and scriptural fulfillment.[22]

Like Harnack before him, von Campenhausen concluded that Marcion was the originator of a collection of Christian Scriptures and also the first Christian biblical canon. After surveying the literature of the second century, he added confidently, "From every side we converge on the same result: the idea and reality of a Christian Bible were the work of Marcion, and the Church which rejected his

---

[19]   Clabeaux, "Marcion," 515.

[20]   Barton, "Marcion Revisited," 354.

[21]   Von Campenhausen, *Formation of the Christian Bible*, 148–74.

[22]   Ibid., 151.

point of view simply followed his example."[23] This is an overstatement, however, and flies in the face of several realities, namely, that other writers before Marcion appealed to the gospel-apostle model and that we do not have anything that survives directly from Marcion to show how he understood the word Scripture, let alone the notion of a biblical canon. If he had produced a fixed biblical canon, it is odd that his own followers apparently never followed it.

Because others had made use of a limited collection of Christian writings (Luke and Paul and others), Marcion thought that he was doing nothing unlike what other Christians before him had done, namely, adopting a particular gospel, such as Matthew alone, and in this instance the Gospel of Luke and welcoming besides several letters from Paul. It is unlikely that any first-century church had more than one gospel, and most had only a few of the letters of Paul and perhaps one or more of the Catholic Epistles (possibly 1 Peter and 1 John). Marcion evidently acknowledged the value of the gospel and apostle traditions in the church, but that is not why he was criticized.[24]

His primary uniqueness, a rejection of the Jewish Scriptures and their allegorical interpretation, is what led to his excommunication. Barton concludes that Marcion's aim was the exclusion of books that had a Jewish bias that were in use in the churches, not to produce a select collection and put them into a fixed tradition, let alone a biblical canon. He explains: "Marcion was not responsible for Christians' adopting a New Testament; he was responsible 'for their retaining the Old Testament.'" Barton concludes that "Marcion was not a major influence on the formation of the New Testament; he was simply a Marcionite."[25] Marcion's apparent rejection of some of the NT writings and all of the Jewish Scriptures suggests that some of those writings were already functioning authoritatively in some churches (canon 1), so the notion that he invented Christian Scriptures is not a careful reflection on Marcion's contributions or activities in antiquity.

Remarkably, *none of his many second-century critics accused him of seeking to establish a fixed biblical canon or of inventing the notion of Christian Scriptures.* Although Marcion restricted the use of some Christian writings in his churches, that is not the same as inventing the notion of Christian Scriptures or establishing a biblical canon. Had he intended the latter, it is amazing that not even his followers followed his example since they cited and interpreted Christian literature from other than Luke's Gospel and the Letters of Paul. For example, Hahneman has shown that later Marcionites welcomed verses from the other Gospels: Ephraem Syrus claimed that Marcionites had not rejected Matt 23:8; Adamantius said that Marcionites quoted John 13:34 and 15:19 and corrupted Matt 5:17.

---

[23] Ibid., 148. While I disagree with BeDuhn that Marcion created a biblical canon, his recent discussion of Marcion's background and activities are quite helpful. See his *First New Testament*.

[24] See F. Bovon, "Canonical Structure of Gospel and Apostle," in McDonald and Sanders, eds., *The Canon Debate*, 516–27, for evidence of the prevalence of this structure in the early church.

[25] Barton, "Marcion Revisited," 350, 354.

Origen even quotes a Marcionite interpretation of Matt 19:12.[26] Hahneman adds further that the Armenian Marcionites appear also to have received Tatian's *Diatessaron*. He concludes that since we have no direct evidence from Marcion or his followers that they intended to form a fixed Scripture canon, it is inappropriate to argue that he or they created one.[27]

Tertullian observes that "Marcion expressly and openly used the knife, not the pen, since he made such an excision of the Scriptures as suited his own subject matter" (*Praescr.* 38.7, ANF). More specifically, Tertullian mentions Marcion's process of excising the Jewish elements from Luke: "Now, of the authors whom we possess, Marcion seems to have singled out Luke for his mutilating process" (*Marc.* 4.2, ANF). Tertullian also comments on Marcion's editorial work on Paul's Epistles: "As our heretic is so fond of his pruning knife, I do not wonder when syllables are expunged by his hand, seeing that entire pages are usually the matter on which he practices his effacing process" (*Marc.* 5.18.1, ANF). Tertullian offers five examples of this "effacing process" in Ephesians (Laodiceans), which Tertullian (and evidently Marcion) believed was written by Paul (*Marc.* 5.16–18). It is difficult to conclude that later notions of inviolable Scripture were present when Marcion was active. His rejecting the OT Scriptures and cutting what he did not like from Luke's and Paul's writings are incompatible with later more developed notions of Scripture or canon. Marcion apparently added nothing new to these documents except perhaps his introductions, or prologues.[28] Had he accepted Luke and Paul's letters as Scripture in the sense that it was understood in the first- and second-century churches, however, it is hard to reconcile his mutilation of that literature with any known notions of scripture at that time.

We cannot be certain that Marcion had knowledge of all four canonical Gospels. For example, Papias, a contemporary of Marcion, refers only to Matthew and Mark. It is probable that he was at least aware of the Gospel of Matthew since his followers made use of it. Matthew was highly popular among Christians during the time of Marcion and so also was the Gospel of John which was especially popular in Asia Minor in the second century where Marcion lived.

It is doubtful that Marcion's collection of letters of Paul was the first collection of Pauline Epistles, as some have suggested. In fact, it makes more sense to assume that his collection was possible only because churches before him had

---

[26]   More details are given in Hahneman, *Muratorian Fragment*, 91.

[27]   Ibid., 92–93. See also Casey, "Armenian Marcionites."

[28]   The Marcionite prologues are listed in Theron, *Evidence of Tradition*, 78–83, and discussed in Clabeaux, "Marcionite Prologues to Paul." See also N. A. Dahl, "The Origin of the Earliest Prologues to the Pauline Letters," *Semeia* 12 (1978): 233–77. Whether Marcion produced these prologues is debated, but they were friendly to his positions and probably came from the second or third century. The church responded to these prologues by later producing their own "Anti-Marcionite prologues" to Christian writings; for a brief summary, see McDonald, "Anti-Marcionite (Gospel) Prologues," *ABD* 1:262–63; and Grant, "Oldest Gospel Prologues." Perhaps influenced by Marcion's prologues, Jerome produced his own Gospel prologues (see them in Theron, *Evidence of Tradition*, 51–55).

made use of Paul's writings and had circulated them to other churches (Col 4:16 should not be considered an isolated case). Dahl contends that a ten-letter Pauline corpus was available before the time of Marcion and that he simply made use of it and edited it.[29]

Marcion's rejection of Judaism can be seen in his (or his followers') prologues to the Epistles of Paul, which survive only in Medieval Latin Vulgate manuscripts. It is not clear how they managed to be included in the Scriptures of the orthodox community, but they are indicative of what is known of Marcion's or his followers' feelings toward those with Judaizing tendencies in the church. The following prologues to Paul's letters to Romans, 1 Corinthians, and Titus are not all of the prologues, but are representative of this line of thought.

> The Romans "live" in the regions of Italy. False apostles had reached them beforehand, and under the name of our Lord Jesus Christ they were misled into the Law and the Prophets. The Apostle [Paul], writing to them from Corinth, calls them back to the true evangelical faith.

> The Corinthians are Achaeans. And they similarly heard the word of truth from the Apostles, but they were subverted in many ways by false apostles – some were misled by verbose eloquence of philosophy, others by a sect of the Jewish law. [Paul], writing to them from Ephesus by Timothy, calls them back to the truth and evangelical wisdom.

> He [Paul] reminds and instructs Titus concerning the constitution of a presbytery and concerning spiritual walk and heretics who believe in Jewish books, and who must be avoided.[30]

In regard to canonical studies, Marcion undoubtedly was an important catalyst that led the second-century churches to respond strongly to his rejection of the church's Jewish first scriptures and many of the other Christian writings circulating among churches in the first third of the second century. Marcion may have spurred the greater church into coming to grips with the question of which literature best conveyed its true identity, but it is not certain whether that extended much past the church's reaffirmation of its OT Scriptures. He may also have contributed to the church's affirmation of more NT writings than Marcion was willing to accept, but this does not mean that anyone in the second century had in mind a biblical canon. The evidence for that is slim and only inferential and without any second-century comments on a limited collection. There was never a time in the second or third centuries when the Gospel of Luke was read or cited more than the Gospel of Matthew. Sanders argues that the church, in opposition to Marcion, insisted upon multiple voices from the church's First Testament as well as from other Christian literature rather than limiting its voice to Paul and Luke.[31] If so, Marcion may have

---

[29]   Dahl, "Origin of the Earliest Prologues."
[30]   Quoted from Theron, *Evidence of Tradition*, 79–83 (emphasis added), who translated them from Erwin Preuschen, *Analecta*.
[31]   J. A. Sanders, *Canon and Community*, 37.

been responsible for spurring the church into making more clear that it prized both its inherited Jewish Scriptures as well as its Christian writings, but, again, it is not clear that this was Marcion's intention. The available evidence is neither clear nor compelling in this matter and no second-century church father suggests that Marcion influenced the scope of the church's Scriptures. Churches responded to Marcion with a canon of faith, that is, a reiteration of the traditions of faith that had been passed on to it, but they did not respond to Marcion with a biblical canon. Heretics, it seems, tend to have had a positive effect upon the church by making it rethink important issues! The church's reaction to Marcion is clear and indicates both a prior commitment to the Jewish Scriptures that the church welcomed as their Scriptures from their inception and that included a reaffirmation of the faith that had been handed down to them. What Marcion was saying to the second-century churches was new to them and unacceptable.

Irenaeus (*Haer*. 4.29–34) and Tertullian (*Marc*. 4.2) especially reacted against Marcion's rejection of the OT and the other Gospel literature, but not by creating a NT canon. Rather they responded with a *regula fidei* or *canon of faith*, the church's longstanding traditions. It is with Marcion that we find the first clear references to Luke and to a specific collection of ten of Paul's letters, but neither Marcion nor the greater church that responded to him focused on a canon of Christian scriptures in the sense of a fixed list. As we saw above, even Marcion's followers who cited other NT writings did not seem to conclude that their founder had established a biblical canon. More complete collections of NT writings began to appear only later in the time of Irenaeus, whose four-gospel canon *may* have come in part as a response to the teachings of Marcion,[32] but that is not certain, and it is also possible that his four-gospel canon was his attempt to support the inclusion of the Gospel of John that had been rejected by the Alogists. Irenaeus does not credit Marcion for his defense of a four-gospel collection. Marcion's rejection of all Jewish influences on the Christian faith, and his exclusive opting for an edited Luke, has an interesting counterpart in the Ebionites, who, according to Irenaeus, welcomed only Matthew and rejected Paul: "Those who are called Ebionites…use the Gospel according to Matthew only, and repudiate the Apostle Paul, maintaining that he was an apostate from the Law" (*Haer*. 1.26.2, ANF).

It is far too strong and without any evidence to claim, as did Harnack and von Campenhausen, that Marcion was the "creator of the Christian holy Scripture,"[33] since, as we saw above, there were tendencies or moves toward recognizing multiple Christian writings as Scripture before Marcion. It is highly unlikely that a reaction to Marcion caused any churches to rethink the scope of their sacred texts. Justin, as we saw earlier, specifically refers to "gospels" (*1 Apol*. 64–67) that were read in the churches showing that churches in his region welcomed

---

[32] Von Campenhausen, *Formation of the Christian Bible*, 171, makes this suggestion.
[33] Ibid., 163.

more than one Gospel. The only question that scholars have is whether or not Justin also included the Gospel of John in that collection. However, it is generally acknowledged that Marcion constructed the first *known* clearly identified list of Christian writings (they were not yet universally called "Scripture" at this point). Despite Marcion's aim of separating Christianity from all influences of Judaism,[34] churches rejected his attempts and affirmed their acceptance of the Jewish Scriptures that soon would be called their Old Testament.

Clarifying their acceptance of the Jewish Scriptures and welcoming a broader collection of Christian writings in the churches is not the same as setting forth anything like a closed biblical canon in the second century. There is no surviving evidence that either Marcion or the church teachers who responded to him had anything like a biblical canon in view. Again, later Marcionite communities did not limit themselves to Marcion's collection of Christian writings, so it is not clear whether Marcion himself was even familiar with all or even many of the other early Christian writings that were eventually included in the NT canon. Those who followed Marcion felt free both to edit his work and apparently welcome into their collection of sacred texts verses from the canonical Gospels, especially Matthew and John, as we saw above. If the Marcionites added verses from other sources to their collection, they could also have added other sources that are not familiar to us as well. Obviously Marcion's collection of Luke and Paul was not for his followers an inviolable fixed catalogue of Scriptures to which nothing could be added or taken away.[35] Since the followers of Marcion also used a collection of psalms that was later rejected by the author of the Muratorian Fragment, it seems clear that in Marcion we are not yet talking about a closed biblical canon or even a biblical canon, but rather we are talking about a bias against Judaism. Marcion's collection of Luke's Gospel and letters of Paul may well have *functioned* as Scripture in his communities (canon 1), which as we have shown earlier they also did in other churches, but there was no discussion of a closed NT canon at that time. Apart from Tertullian's ridicule of Marcion for selecting Luke instead of an apostolic Gospel (Matthew or John), there is no explicit second-century condemnation of Marcion because of the books he selected, but precisely because of his rejection of the OT and the God of the OT.

Even though the church fathers eventually recognized the need for a canon of Christian Scriptures, they did so without the aid of Marcion.[36] He may have been one of the influences that caused the church to consider more carefully the scope of its authoritative literature, but this has yet to be demonstrated. There is no discussion of a fixed NT canon in the second century. The notion of canonicity – that is, a clearly defined and fixed catalogue of Scriptures – is not found in

---

[34]   Frend, *Rise of Christianity*, 212–17, calls this an "acute Hellenization of the Church."

[35]   Hahneman, *Muratorian Fragment*, 92.

[36]   For arguments in support of this position, see E. C. Blackman, *Marcion and His Influence* (London: SPCK, 1948), 32.

what we know about Marcion and his followers or in any second-century church fathers. It cannot be shown that establishing a biblical canon was either Marcion's intention or the greater church's intention when they responded to him.

Finally, the available historical sources for this period are quite limited and do not allow for firm conclusions in regard to Marcion, but his anti-Judaistic sentiments are well known. Could it be that he saw as a part of his mission the need to radicalize what he believed was the logical implications of Paul's message for his day, namely, the salvation of humanity apart from the works of the law? The Marcionite prologues – if Marcion in fact wrote them – *suggest* a scriptural function in the Marcionite churches, but the surviving evidence does allow for speculation beyond that.

III. GNOSTICS AND GNOSTICISM

One of the most influential heresies of the second century is commonly known as Gnostic Christianity. What the adherents of this group (or groups) of Christians taught or espoused is usually identified as "Gnosticism." The term gnostic comes from the Greek word γνωστικός that has ancient roots stemming from the word γνῶσις ("knowledge") suggesting something like "capable of attaining knowledge," but this notion of γνωστικός was rare among the Greeks. The designation came to refer to disciplines of study that suggested something along the lines of that which "leads to knowledge." The Greeks themselves did not speak of gnostics as those who pursued a particular form of knowledge for religious purposes. The term *gnostic* appears to have become a later designation attached to gnostic adherents by their opponents and appears as interchangeable with the word heresy.

Although the term gnostic eventually became associated with some ancient and highly diverse systems of thought in second-century Christianity, we do not know the precise origin or date of origin of such views, or even the circumstances that gave rise to it. In antiquity it was common to conclude that Simon Magus (Acts 8:9–24) was the founder of this community, but this is more ancient lore than factually based information. In the fifth century, for example, Cyril of Jerusalem states that "the inventor of all heresy was Simon Magus: that Simon, who in the Acts of the Apostles, thought to purchase with money the unsalable grace of the Spirit" (*Catechetical Lectures* 6.14, NPNF). Those drawn to this group were generally better educated than most, had little hope for the world improving (much like the Jewish apocalyptic writers), and produced a considerable amount of esoteric literature that generally denigrated the created world and focused on self-awareness.[37]

---

[37] Layton, *Gnostic Scriptures*, 5–9.

Although there is much that is not known about the community that was identified as gnostic Christians, there are some things about them that are known both from their opponents and from their own writings. We can say for certain that in the second century, a significant community of gnostic Christians emerged with a system (or several systems) of thought that challenged the basic underlying beliefs of traditional Christianity. Adherents of this new philosophy were labeled "gnostics" in subsequent generations (especially in the modern era), and what they taught or believed is now called "Gnosticism." They apparently flourished throughout the second and third centuries and continued to have adherents much longer than that in some areas (e.g., the Mandeans in the East).[38] They produced a vast amount of literature, and apparently were not interested in any fixed collection of Christian Scriptures. Much of their literature is their allegorical or spiritual interpretations of the OT and NT Scriptures, including pseudonymous writings attributed to biblical figures. *It may be* that they drew selectively from various Jewish and Christian writings, and their own writings were viewed as supplements to these for the sake of dialogue and clarification of the meaning of the former texts.

With the discovery of nearly fifty gnostic documents at Nag Hammadi, Egypt, in 1945, for the first time scholars were able to see direct information about the gnostic community in their own writings and expressing their perspectives.[39] Before then, scholarship was solely dependent upon the opponents of Gnosticism – namely, proto-orthodox and orthodox Christians – for its understanding of Gnosticism. The orthodox Christians always defined gnostics in a polemical context as heretics, especially Irenaeus, who levels severe attacks against them in book 1 of his *Against Heresies*. Remarkably, Irenaeus' identification of the views of and the charges against the gnostics are fairly consistent with what is found in gnostic Christian literature. With the discovery of the Nag Hammadi gnostic documents, which originally came from outside of Egypt and were later translated into Coptic, it is now possible to view gnostic Christianity from the gnostic perspective from around the mid-fourth century and before.

It is difficult to date the origins of gnostic belief and even more difficult to define or identify its adherents with a scheme of beliefs and practices. It is also a challenge to identify all of the characteristics attributed to them from an examination of their writings. There were apparently a variety of views and practices among the gnostic sects. Irenaeus, for example, criticizes the heretical teachings of Marcion, Tatian, Saturninus, and Valentinus because, he claims, they formed "one set of doctrines out of totally different systems of opinions, and then again

---

[38]   See E. Lupieri, *The Mandaeans: The Last Gnostics*, trans. C. Hindley (Grand Rapids: Eerdmans, 2002).
[39]   See J. M. Robinson, ed., *The Nag Hammadi Library in English*, 3rd ed. (San Francisco: Harper, 1988); and Layton, *Gnostic Scriptures*, for English translations.

others from others, they insist upon teaching something new, declaring themselves the inventors of any sort of opinion which they may have been able to call into existence" (*Haer*. 1.28.1, ANF). After criticizing these individuals, he goes on to say that "besides those, however, among these heretics who are Simonians [supposed followers of Simon Magus], and of whom we have already spoken, *a multitude of Gnostics have sprung up, and have been manifested like mushrooms growing out of the ground*" (*Haer*. 1.29.1, ANF, emphasis added).

Gnostic Christians apparently included in their systems of thought an amalgamation of several theological and philosophical perspectives in antiquity, including those of Iranian Zoroastrian theology, Jewish apocalypticism, Platonism, Hellenistic philosophy, and various elements of early Christianity, especially the notion of Jesus as redeemer. They saw themselves as Christians, that is, members of the greater church, but they tended to have an elitist perspective of themselves believing that while other Christians had a place in the family of God, they themselves had a higher standing because of their greater knowledge. They rejected all political and religious institutions, including their values, authorities, and most moral codes. Some gnostic Christians became ascetics, and others antinomian. Some rejected marriage and the pursuit of physical pleasure, while others entertained numerous spouses and sexual partners and embraced physical pleasures. Their adherents stretched from western Persia (now Iraq) in the east, to Lyon, France, in the west, and from Egypt in the south to Ancyra (now Ankara, Turkey) and Satala (in Asia Minor) in the north. Although we now have a valuable collection of their literature, it is not a complete collection and we are not yet certain about its date or provenance. The scholarly suggested dates range between roughly 10 BCE to the death of Plotinus the Neoplatonist in 270 CE.

Wink suggests that the key to understanding the diversity within this large gnostic community is their understanding of the "powers," that is, "the social structures of reality, political systems, [and] human institutions such as the family or religion."[40] Gnostics demonized all of these powers or institutions, believing that none of them will be saved from final destruction. Wink also observes that in gnostic thought salvation is not deliverance from personal sin, since that is based on imposed moral codes that the gnostics rejected, but rather on deliverance from the powers of the social and religious institutions that enslave. A "waking up" is needed (cf. 1 Thess 5:5–7) to find deliverance from such evils. The gnostic *Gospel of Philip*, for instance, appeals to its readers to recognize the root of evil (i.e., the powers), so they can be destroyed and have no power over them:

> Let each of us dig down after the root of evil that is within us, and let us pluck it out of our hearts from the root. It will be plucked out if we recognize it. But if we are ignorant of it, it takes root in us and produces its fruit in our heart. It masters us. We are its slaves. It takes us captive,

---

[40] W. Wink, *Cracking the Gnostic Code: The Powers in Gnosticism*, Society of Biblical Literature Monograph Series 46 (Atlanta: Scholars Press, 1993), vii, 17.

to make us do what we do not want; and what we do want we do not do. It is powerful because we have not recognized it. While it exists it is active. (*Gospel of Philip* 83.18–30, adapted from Wink, *Cracking the Gnostic Code*, 37)

Wink shows how the gnostic enterprise is both similar and contrary to what the NT teaches. Gnosticism, he explains, "taught escape from a world imprisoned under tyranny of evil powers. The New Testament teaches liberation from the tyranny of evil powers in order to recover a lost unity with the created world. This world is not only the sphere of alienated existence, but also the object of God's redemptive love. Therefore we are not to flee the world, but to recall it to its Source."[41]

Gnostic Christians generally believed that there was a divine spark (Spirit) from God in humanity and that it was their goal through special knowledge to be restored to God through the work of a redeemer, Jesus, who removed ignorance and restored self-knowledge to those who were spiritual.[42] Despite this common belief, scholars of this ancient phenomenon are generally agreed that they have yet to find a satisfactory definition that fits all traces of this community in antiquity – or even find a convenient term for this literature.[43] Although there is little agreement on a meaningful and accurate definition of Gnosticism, scholars continue to use the designation since there is little else to put in its place.

By way of summary, generally speaking, (1) gnostic Christians denied that the *Christian* God, the God of Jesus, was also the creator of the world. For them, matter was evil and was created by a Demiurge, an evil and distant emanation from the *plērōma* ("fullness") of the divine. In this they were similar to the Marcionites. (2) They often rejected the Jewish (HB/LXX) Scriptures, but not uniformly, unlike Marcion. They often allegorized them to find meaning for Christian faith, for example as in Ptolemy's *Letter to Flora*. (3) They distinguished the heavenly Savior/Redeemer from the human Jesus of Nazareth, a teaching not unlike various early Docetic (from the Greek δοκέω, "I seem" or "I appear") teachings that claimed that Jesus only "seemed" or "appeared" to be human, but in

---

[41]   Ibid., 52.

[42]   Grant, *Gnosticism*, 16.

[43]   Karen King, one of the leading scholars in the study of ancient Gnosticism, has helped in my understanding of Gnosticism and I am especially indebted to her for taking the time to share with me areas that I had earlier overlooked and where I could strengthen my understanding. She provides a careful and informed evaluation of this religious movement in her *The Gospel of Mary* (Santa Rosa, CA: Polebridge, 2003), her *Revelation of the Unknowable God with Text, Translation, and Notes to NHC IX,3 Allogenes* (Santa Rosa, CA: Polebridge, 1995), and her more recent work, *What Is Gnosticism?* (Cambridge, MA: Harvard University Press, 2003), 5–19. See also Rudolph, "'Gnosis' and 'Gnosticism'—The Problems of Their Definition and Their Relation to the Writings of the New Testament," in *The New Testament and Gnosis: Essays in Honour of Robert McL. Wilson*, ed. A. H. B. Logan and A. J. M. Wedderburn (Edinburgh: T. & T. Clark, 1983), 21–37; R. M. Grant, *Gnosticism: A Source Book of Heretical Writings from the Early Christian Period* (New York: Harper, 1961), 13–18; Layton, *Gnostic Scriptures*, 8–9; and Perkins, "Gnosticism and the Christian Bible," in McDonald and Sanders, eds., *The Canon Debate*, 355.

reality he was not. This teaching is what stands behind the condemnation in 1 John 4:2 and it is condemned especially more frequently in the *Letters* of Ignatius (e.g., Ign. *Eph.* 7.1–2; *Trall.* 10.1; *Smyrn.* 2.1). There are several similarities between the Docetics and the later gnostics. (4) They believed that *full* salvation was only for the pneumatics or spiritually elite (i.e., themselves), but that a lesser degree of salvation could be obtained by those who have only faith without this special *gnōsis*. Those completely involved in the world, however, had no hope of salvation. (5) They also claimed that they had received secret gospels from the apostles themselves.[44]

The esoteric writings of the gnostics, along with their claims to secret revelations from the apostles, were rejected by Irenaeus, who argued instead for the legitimacy of the Christian truth and its tradition, or rule of faith (*regula fidei*). He contends that this tradition was passed on in the church by apostolic succession through its bishops. He explains: "For if the apostles had known hidden mysteries, which they were in the habit of imparting to 'the perfect' apart and privately from the rest, they would have delivered them especially to those to whom they were also committing the leadership of the churches themselves" (*Haer.* 3.3.1, adapted from ANF). One can scarcely deny Irenaeus' logic here.

The question for us here is whether such writings prompted the Christians to distinguish the church's earliest Christian writings from the Gnostic writings and call the former a NT canon and the latter heresy. In their confrontation with the gnostic Christians, did they decide that the best way to deal with them was to decide which Christian writings were sacred and which were not? Did the gnostics consider what they wrote as sacred Scripture and binding upon their readers? We have no evidence that they did. Perkins concludes that the gnostics "never set up individuals as heroes of the divine" and did not observe the ecclesiastical structures that began to develop in the second and third centuries of the church.[45] Irenaeus accused the gnostic Christians of saying that the Scriptures were incorrect, that

---

[44] Because gnostic belief is highly complex, the student is advised to consult the following works: H. Jonas, *The Gnostic Religion* (Boston: Beacon, 1963); K. Rudolph, *Gnosis: The Nature and History of Gnosticism*, trans. and ed. R. M. Wilson (San Francisco: Harper & Row, 1987); Layton, *Gnostic Scriptures*, xv–xxvii, 5–22; T. P. van Baaren, "Towards a Definition of Gnosticism," in *Le origini dello gnosticismo*, ed. U. Bianchi, Studies in the History of Religions 12 (Leiden: Brill, 1967), 174–80; MacRae, "Why the Church Rejected Gnosticism," in *Jewish and Christian Self-Definition*, Vol. 1: *The Shaping of Christianity in the Second and Third Centuries*, ed. E. P. Sanders (Philadelphia: Fortress, 1980), 126–33, 236–38; G. Filoramo, *A History of Gnosticism*, trans. A. Alcock (Oxford: Blackwell, 1990); B. A. Pearson, *Gnosticism, Judaism, and Egyptian Christianity* (Minneapolis: Fortress, 1990); P. Perkins, *Gnosticism and the New Testament* (Minneapolis: Fortress, 1993); King, *What Is Gnosticism?*; B. Walker, *Gnosticism: Its History and Influence* (Wellingborough, England: Aquarian, 1989); J. E. Goehring et al., eds., *Gnosticism and the Early Christian World* (Sonoma, CA: Polebridge, 1990); Hedrick and Hodgson, eds., *Nag Hammadi, Gnosticism, and Early Christianity*; Logan, *Gnostic Truth and Christian Heresy: A Study in the History of Gnosticism* (Peabody, MA: Hendrickson, 1996).

[45] Perkins, *Gnostic Dialogue*, 192–96.

they were not authoritative, that they were ambiguous, and that the truth cannot be discovered by someone who is ignorant of their truth (*Haer*. 3.2.1).[46]

Perkins further challenges the tendency among scholars to assume that the gnostic Christians simply "followed the orthodox canon with one of their own." She concludes: "It should be apparent by now that nothing could be farther from the truth. These Gnostic writings reflect the liturgy, teaching, preaching and polemic of their respective communities. But they never claim to do more than to embody true tradition." Perkins concludes that the gnostics did not have a normative text that gave them the limits of their theological reflection,[47] and that "gnostic exegetes were only interested in elaborating their mythic and theological speculations concerning the origins of the universe, not in appropriating a received canonical tradition," and finally that "hermeneutics, not canon formation, is the central point at issue between Irenaeus and his Valentinian opponents."[48] I agree with her assessment.

More specifically, did the gnostics' production of esoteric literature force the Christians to come to grips with the scope of their own Scriptures? Since gnostics did not claim that they had produced sacred inspired Scripture that was binding on all, arguments against them were not based on establishing Christian Scriptures that were binding on all. They may well have been the first to acknowledge some NT writings as Scripture. As we will also see below (Chapter 21 §I) and as observed earlier, the gnostic Basilides of Alexandria may well have been among the first to recognize some of the NT writings as Christian Scripture. Irenaeus and others who argued against the gnostics in the second and third centuries did not combat heresy with a canon of Scripture, but rather with a canon of faith (*regula fidei*) that had been passed on by the apostles to their successors in the churches.

IV. MONTANISTS

Montanus, possibly a priest of Cybele,[49] and two women named Priscilla and Maximilla, came to Phrygia in Asia Minor around 170 CE claiming to be inspired by the Paraclete (Holy Spirit) and having an announcement of the Parousia (the

---

[46] Ibid., 199–200. See also her "Gnosticism and the Christian Bible." She challenges a common notion that Gnostic Christians and orthodox Christians had dueling scripture canons. She surveys the major texts that reflect the primary notions of Gnosticism that promulgate gnostic views and how they interpret several familiar OT texts. She also provides three helpful tables showing references in the Nag Hammadi library to Old Testament texts, Pauline Epistles, and the canonical Gospels. Genesis appears to be the most frequently cited OT book, but also Second Isaiah. Most references to the NT literature come from Matthew and John (see 368–69). Generally, however, she concludes that although these works were cited, there was "little engagement" with them.

[47] Perkins, *Gnostic Dialogue*, 201–2.

[48] Perkins, "Gnosticism and the Christian Bible," 371.

[49] Frend, *Rise of Christianity*, 253, makes this suggestion.

second coming of the Lord). The three of them had a major impact upon the people of Phrygia and were received with enthusiasm by many Christians throughout the Greco-Roman world. The Montanists were by far the most popular charismatic segment of Christianity in the second and third centuries. Their message had an apocalyptic focus and they strongly advocated their interpretation of the message of the book of Revelation. They emphasized prophecy, rigid asceticism, martyrdom, and the presence and power of the Holy Spirit. Frend points to the long history of prophetic movements in this region and observes that orthodox Christians were unprepared to deal with these people.[50] Unlike in many other religious groups at this time, both men and women could become prophets in Montanism.[51] By 200 they had expanded their influence to Rome and North Africa and their primary influence was among rural communities.[52]

What is most surprising about the Montanists, however, is that the best-known teacher and apologist for the Christian faith in the late second and early third centuries, Tertullian, became their convert. Numerous suggestions have been presented to explain this, but perhaps the Montanists' strong emphasis on a rigorous ascetic lifestyle enticed Tertullian who was already a highly disciplined man with little toleration for weak and undisciplined Christians. His hesitation to baptize converts or children too early, for example, is well known and illustrates his call for careful and consistent behavior:

> According to circumstance and disposition and even age of the individual person, it may be better to delay baptism; and especially so in the case of little children. Why, indeed, is it necessary – if it be not a case of necessity – that the sponsors too be thrust into danger, when they themselves may fail to fulfill their promises by reason of death, or when they may be disappointed by growth of an evil disposition?...
>
> For no less cause should the unmarried also be deferred, in whom there is an aptness to temptation – in virgins on account of their ripeness as also in the widowed on account of their freedom – until either they are married or are better strengthened for continence. Anyone who understands the seriousness of Baptism will fear its reception more than its deferral. Sound faith is secure of salvation! (Tertullian, *Baptism* 18.4, Jurgens, *Faith of the Early Fathers*, 128–29)

Tertullian may also have been impressed with the charismatic focus of the Montanists, which was acknowledged in the greater church as a legitimate and authentic expression of Christian faith, but which had declined significantly in the second-century churches perhaps as a result of the abuse of wandering charismatics who claimed a prophetic gift.

The most vigorous opponents of the Montanists in Asia Minor were the so-called *Alogi*, a heretical group that looked askance at both the Gospel of John and the book of Revelation because of their supposed gnostic origins. The Alogi

---

[50] Ibid., 254–55.

[51] In his discussion of Montanism, which he calls the "Cataphrygian heresy," Eusebius mentions several times that women were a significant part of that movement (*Hist. eccl.* 5.14–19).

[52] Frend, *Rise of Christianity*, 256.

even called the book of Hebrews into question because of its view of the hopeless condition of the apostate Christian, which coincided with the Montanists' harsh penitential practice.[53] The response of the church at large to the Montanists was a rejection of their movement and a reserve toward the Gospel of John because of its focus on the Paraclete and a similar reserve toward the book of Revelation (especially in the Eastern churches in the second and third centuries) because of its apocalyptic emphasis.

Von Campenhausen concludes that the emergence of Montanism was a significant factor in prompting orthodox Christians to determine the scope of the Christian Scriptures. His view is based on an observation from Hippolytus of Rome that the Montanists produced "innumerable books" (*Elenchus* 8.19.1). Von Campenhausen concludes from this that the church was forced to make a decision about the scope of its canon because of the ever-growing number of Montanist books. He explains:

> It is obvious that such an attitude can no longer be content with recognizing a rough list of sacred writings and with rejecting others as heretical forgeries; it now has to be clearly decided which books are to belong to the "New Testament" and which are not. At this point the final stage of the formation of the Canon has begun. It did not at once reach its goal; but the necessity of a "closed" canon had been grasped in principle.[54]

In other words, according to von Campenhausen, the Montanists generated numerous books that they believed were divinely inspired, and the greater church therefore saw the need to identify more precisely what literature was inspired by God and therefore could be read in the churches.[55] Hippolytus' well-known criticism of the Montanists and their books has bearing on this debate:

> But there are others who themselves are even more heretical in nature [than the foregoing], and are Phrygians by birth. These have been rendered victims of error from being previously captivated by [two] wretched women, called a certain Priscilla and Maximilla, whom they supposed [to be] prophetesses. And they assert that into these the Paraclete Spirit had departed; and antecedently to them, they in like manner consider Montanus as a prophet. And *being in possession of an infinite number of their books*, [the Phrygians] are overrun with delusion; and they do not judge whatever statements are made by them, according to [the criterion of] reason; nor do they give heed unto those who are competent to decide; but they are heedlessly swept onward, by the reliance which they place on these [imposters]. And they allege that they have learned something more through these, than from law, and prophets, and the Gospels. (*Ref.* 8.12, ANF, emphasis added)

Schneemelcher, however,[56] challenges this claim and questions whether the Montanists actually produced any literature. Tertullian, on the other hand,

---

[53]   So argue R. Collins, *Introduction to the New Testament*, 26; and von Campenhausen, *Formation of the Christian Bible*, 232.

[54]   Ibid., 231–32.

[55]   Ibid., 227–32.

[56]   Schneemelcher, *New Testament Apocrypha*, 685 n. 2.

acknowledges that the Montanists wrote newly inspired books and he defends the appropriateness of this recent revelation. Von Campenhausen, citing Tertullian's edits of the *Passio Perpetuae* that included the Introduction and Conclusion, says that Tertullian defended the production of new books that the Montanists believed were inspired by God and, as noted earlier, that it was mere prejudice "to heed and value only past demonstrations of power and grace." Further, Tertullian argued that: "those people who condemn the one power of the one Holy Spirit in accordance with chronological eras should beware." Von Campenhausen continues his understanding of Tertullian who says that, "It is the recent instances to which far higher respect ought to be paid; for they already belong to the time of the End, and are to be prized as a superabundant increase of grace," and von Campenhausen concludes with a final quote from Tertullian who said that these prophecies coming from the End times are from "God, in accordance with the testimony of scripture, [who] has destined for precisely this period of time."[57]

According to von Campenhausen, the mainstream churches rejected the Montanist prophecies essentially on the grounds that their prophecies were contrary to the earlier Christian writings (now called NT Scriptures).[58] Eusebius relates the testimony of a certain Apolinarius who challenged the practice of the Montanists' adding what he called "false prophecy" to the Christian writings circulating in the churches. He evidently did not reject writings that were in accord with what had already been received and circulated in the churches, but rather new so-called prophecies.

> For a long and protracted time, my dear Abercius Marcellus, I have been urged by you to compose a treatise against the sect of those called after Miltiades, but until now I was somewhat reluctant, not from any lack of ability to refute the lie and testify to the truth, but from timidity and scruples lest I might seem to some to be *adding to the writings or injunctions of the word of the new covenant of the gospel, to which no one who has chosen to live according to the gospel itself can add and from which he cannot take away.* But when I had just come to Ancyra in Galatia and perceived that the church in that place was torn in two by this new movement [the Montanists] which is not, as they call it, prophecy but much rather, as will be shown, false prophecy, I disputed concerning these people themselves and their propositions so far as I could, with the Lord's help, for many days continuously in the church. Thus the church rejoiced and was strengthened in the truth, but our opponents were crushed for the moment and our adversaries were distressed. (*Hist. eccl.* 5.16.3–4, LCL, emphasis added)

Von Campenhausen attempts an explanation of this passage concluding that what was intended was that "the composition of new authoritative writings was now thought of as outrageous presumption."[59]

---

[57] Von Campenhausen, *Formation of the Christian Bible*, 229, citing the "Introduction" to *Passio perpetuae* 1.1–2.

[58] Ibid., 231.

[59] Ibid., 230. This passage is difficult to understand since it appears from Eusebius' quote that Apolinarius was fearful that he himself would, by addressing the Montanist concern, be adding new books to a closed collection to which nothing else could be added. It is difficult to know precisely

From this and other criticisms against the Montanists, von Campenhausen argues that the church could no longer have a roughly defined canon of Scriptures and could no longer be content with rejecting heretical forgeries as they appeared. He concludes that the Montanists with their production of new so-called inspired books was the primary factor that led the churches to define more precisely which books belonged in their NT and which books did not.[60] It was at this point that von Campenhausen claims the last phase of the canonical process began.[61] Metzger, also draws this same conclusion, adding that with Marcion the church saw the need to expand its written corpus of authoritative writings and with the Montanists it saw the need to limit the corpus. This process of limitation, he claims, was "the first step [taken by the church] toward the adoption of a closed canon of Scripture."[62]

However, it is clear that this phase was by no means completed as a result of the polemic against the Montanists. Von Campenhausen and Metzger's conclusion is not drawn from the evidence of that period (late second or early third century), but from supposed actions of the church that are not in evidence. If the church at large was interested in closing the NT canon at this time, one might expect to find numerous lists of canonical literature in this period as well as some statement to the effect that the church was concerned about closing its collection of Christian Scriptures, but neither scholar offers such evidence. The church fathers in the proto-Orthodox communities argued against the Montanists with their *regula fidei* that was rooted in the church's traditions and the apostolic writings from the first century, but not with a new canon of Scriptures, or even a more precisely defined New Testament canon. They addressed the heretical issues with the church's traditions, creeds, and use of their Christian writings that were increasingly becoming recognized as Christian Scriptures.

Schneemelcher questions how much the Montanist movement was influenced by apocalyptic thoughts, or whether that sort of thinking was even in the forefront of the authentic sayings of Montanus and the prophetesses. He adds that since the cutting edge of the movement was its focus on ethical renewal, on the whole Montanism was a prophetic – not an apocalyptic – movement. He concludes that the sayings of Montanus and his prophetesses were collected and passed on in their churches as authoritative inspired teachings, and even used and defended as such by Tertullian. However, it is not clear that those writings became a canon of scriptures in those communities, and certainly not a *fixed* canon since, as we saw in Tertullian, the Montanists believed that the Spirit could still speak in

---

what Apolinarius had in mind. Surely he would not have fear about responding to what he believed to be heresy since that already had precedence in the churches by others and without attempting to add new texts to the Scriptures.

[60]   Ibid., 231.

[61]   Ibid., 232. See 232–42, discusses the rather troubled history in the church of the literature that the Montanists appealed to most, namely the various apocalypses, the Gospel of John, and Hebrews.

[62]   Metzger, *Canon of the New Testament*, 106.

divinely inspired writings. It is difficult to argue against Tertullian here since the church at that time never made a statement that the Spirit had ceased speaking in the churches or that newly written inspired writings could no longer emerge. It appears that what the church did not like was *what* the Montanists wrote, but not the notion that Spirit had ceased speaking in the churches.[63] Schneemelcher calls von Campenhausen's view that the Montanists influenced the church to establish its own biblical canon a hypothesis that must be distinguished from "demonstrable facts" and appropriately concludes that the available evidence does lead to such conclusions.[64]

IV. SUMMARY AND CONCLUSIONS

There is no convincing evidence that Marcion, the Gnostics, or the Montanists, the three leading "heresies" of the second century, were interested in producing a biblical canon or that the early churches responded to their threats and challenges by establishing a biblical canon of Christian Scriptures. Rather the response of the second-century churches to these divergences from the acknowledged apostolic traditions in the churches was to argue against these challenges with the church's *canon of faith* (*regula fidei*), that is, the sacred traditions and proclamations of the church that had been handed down in the churches by their bishops from the beginning both orally and in Christian writings. There is no record that the second-century churches were interested in producing a fixed or even fluid biblical canon of Christian writings. The churches met the challenges they faced with their sacred traditions that were summarized in the proto-orthodox creeds of the second and third centuries and reflected in the first-century Christian writings that had already begun to be called "scripture" from the middle to the end of the second century.

Marcion, whose primary concern was to eliminate from the churches all Judaistic influences, selected a limited collection of writings that he edited *significantly* in order to define more clearly his gospel and eliminate the influences of Judaism and its scriptures from his churches. It is not clear that Marcion called these writings (Luke and ten letters of Paul) "Scripture," though those writings no doubt functioned that way for him and his followers. The church did not respond to Marcion with a longer biblical canon, but rather with its rule or canon of faith that had its roots in the traditions passed on in the churches by those who were closest to Jesus. Likewise, the challenge that came from the emergence of multiple writings from the gnostic Christians and the Montanists did not lead the church to define the scope of its own scriptural traditions. The major sections of the NT Scriptures – especially the Gospels and some Letters of Paul – had already been welcomed in many churches in the second century doubtless because those

---

[63]   Schneemelcher, ed., *New Testament Apocrypha*, 686–89.
[64]   Schneemelcher, "General Introduction," 24.

writings cohered with the traditions already accepted perhaps by a majority of churches at that time. Those Christian writings were beginning to function as Scripture (canon 1) in the second century and the churches used them in worship, catechetical instruction, and in their apologetic. The traditions handed down to them in the churches and reflected in their emerging NT Scriptures were summarized in their creeds and with that arsenal they addressed the challenges of heresy in the churches. Eventually their defense eventually won the day well before orthodoxy in the fourth century had the power and wealth to impose itself on the churches as some scholars have advanced.

EXCURSUS:
THE NEW TESTAMENT APOCRYPHA

In addition to the books that were later included in the NT canon, a number of other Christian writings were produced that also battled for the heart and loyalties and reception of the ancient churches.[65] In the fourth century, Eusebius identified and challenged literature that was falsely produced under the name of an apostle that was circulating in a number of churches. It is obvious from Eusebius that by that time some church leaders distinguished genuine writings from those produced pseudonymously in apostolic names and the latter were rejected.

> Among the books which are not genuine must be reckoned the Acts of Paul, the work entitled the Shepherd, the Apocalypse of Peter, and in addition to them the letter called of Barnabas and the so-called Teachings of the Apostles [i.e., the *Didache*]. And in addition, as I said, the Revelation of John, if this view prevail. For as I said, some reject it, but others count it among the Recognized Books. Some have also counted the Gospel according to the Hebrews in which those of the Hebrews who have accepted Christ take a special pleasure. *These would all belong to the disputed books, but we have nevertheless been obliged to make a list of them, distinguishing between those writings which, according to the tradition of the Church, are true, genuine, and recognized, and those which differ from them in that they are not canonical but disputed,* yet nevertheless are known to most of the writers of the Church, in order that we might know them and *the writings that are put forward by heretics under the name of the apostles containing gospels such as those of Peter, and Thomas, and Matthias, and some others besides, or Acts such as those of Andrew and John and the other apostles.* To none of these has any who belonged to the succession of the orthodox ever thought it right to refer in his writings… They ought, therefore, to be reckoned not even among spurious books but shunned as altogether wicked and impious. (*Hist. eccl.* 3.25.4–7, LCL, emphasis added)

---

[65] Many of these are identified in B. D. Ehrman's *Lost Christianities: The Battles for Scripture and the Faiths We Never Knew* (New York: Oxford University Press, 2003) and also his *Lost Scriptures*. See also Thomas J. Tobias, Michael J. Kruger, and Tobias Nicklas, eds., *Gospel Fragments: The 'Unknown Gospel' on Papyrus Egerton 2, Papyrus Oxyrhynchus 840, and Other Gospel Fragments*, Oxford Early Christian Gospel Texts (Oxford: Oxford University Press, 2009).

The many ancient Christian apocryphal or pseudepigraphal writings, many of which are now lost, include gospels, acts, epistles, and apocalypses. This literature is generally sectarian and is commonly set forth in an apostolic name in order to find acceptance in various segments of the Christian community. The following writings, some of which currently exist only in fragments, are representative of this body of literature but it is not a complete list:[66]

1. Gospels[67]
   Protevangelium of James,
   Infancy Gospel of Thomas
   Gospel of Peter
   Gospel of Nicodemus
   Gospel of the Nazoreans
   Gospel of the Ebionites
   Gospel of the Hebrews
   Gospel of the Egyptians
   Gospel of Thomas
   Gospel of Philip
   Gospel of Mary
2. Acts[68]
   Acts of John
   Acts of Peter
   Acts of Paul
   Acts of Andrew
   Acts of Thomas
   Acts of Andrew and Matthias
   Acts of Philip
   Acts of Thaddaeus
   Acts of Peter and Paul
   Acts of Peter and Andrew
   Martyrdom of Matthew
   Slavonic Act of Peter
   Acts of Peter and the Twelve Apostles
3. Epistles[69]
   Third Corinthians
   Epistle to the Laodiceans
   Letters of Paul and Seneca
   Letters of Jesus and Abgar
   Letter of Lentulus
   Epistle of Titus

---

[66] Adapted from D. R. MacDonald, "Apocryphal New Testament," in Achtemeier et al., eds., *Harper's Bible Dictionary*, 38–39.

[67] For a careful discussion of apocryphal gospels, see Koester, *Ancient Christian Gospels*.

[68] The first five works are called the "Leucian Acts" and they often were circulated together. A useful source on these and other apocryphal acts is F. Bovon, A. G. Brock, and C. R. Matthews, *Apocryphal Acts of the Apostles* (Cambridge, MA: Harvard University Press, 1999).

[69] Some scholars include the canonical Pastoral Epistles and 2 Peter as pseudonymous writings in this category. Others add also Ephesians, Colossians, and 2 Thessalonians. The authorship of these letters are all debated in current New Testament Introductions.

4.   Apocalypses[70]
      Apocalypse of Peter
      Coptic Apocalypse of Paul
      Apocalypse of Paul
      First Apocalypse of James
      Second Apocalypse of James
      Apocryphon of John
      Sophia of Jesus Christ
      Letter of Peter to Philip
      Apocalypse of Mary

There are numerous other examples of pseudepigrapha, or pseudonymous writings, from antiquity besides those that were produced within Judaism and early Christianity. For example, well-known classical writers like Plato, Pythagoras, Socrates, Xenophon, Apollonius, and Galen all had writings attributed to them or falsely purported to be written by them by their students or others who came after them.[71]

A pseudonym is generally understood as a fictitious or assumed name used by authors who, for whatever reasons, wanted to conceal their identity. The practice of writing under an assumed name was common during the intertestamental period, when writers frequently made use of well-known names from the OT (Solomon, Enoch, Moses, etc.).[72] This practice may have begun when individuals believed that they had a prophetic word to say, but there was a widespread belief that the age of prophecy had ceased with the previously accepted prophets before the time of Ezra and Nehemiah. Consequently, those who thought that they had a prophetic word to say often said it in the name of a well-known biblical personality.

---

[70]   The term "apocalypse" is a transliteration of the Greek *apokalypsis* ("revelation, disclosure"). Aune, *Prophecy in Early Christianity*, 108, defines this literary genre as a form of revelatory literature in which the author narrates both the visions the writer has purportedly experienced and their meaning, usually elicited through a dialogue between the seer and an interpreting angel. The substance of these revelatory visions is the imminent intervention of God into human affairs to bring the present evil world system to an end and to replace it with an ideal one. This transformation is accompanied by the punishment of the wicked and the reward of the righteous. In this sense, such literature is often dualistic. A popular apocalypse in early Christianity that is not pseudonymous is the *Shepherd of Hermas*. There were more copies of this apocalypse recovered from antiquity than all of the books of the NT except the Gospels of Matthew and John. Likely because it was not viewed as pseudonymous, it continued in use in some churches well into the fourth century and was even attached, along with the *Epistle of Barnabas*, to Codex Sinaiticus near the end of the fourth century.
[71]   Charlesworth, "Pseudepigraphy," in *Encyclopedia of Early Christianity*, ed. E. Ferguson (New York: Garland, 1990), 776. See also Ehrman, *Lost Scriptures*.
[72]   For a brief discussion of this phenomenon in early Christianity, see Lee Martin McDonald, "Pseudonymous Writings and the New Testament," in Green and McDonald, eds., *The World of the New Testament: Cultural, Social, and Historical Contexts* (Grand Rapids: Baker Academic, 2013), 367–78.

The ethics of producing pseudonymous literature in the ancient Jewish and Christian communities is debated among scholars. As yet there is no agreement on why it emerged, though there is growing awareness that distinctions should be made in the kinds of literature that fall into this category. For some Christians, however, the main issue has to do with how forged documents can or ever could serve as inspired sacred literature for the church. There is no consensus among scholars over whether all of the writings identified in this category were intended to deceive though some scholars are convinced that all pseudonymous writings were so intended,[73] but not all scholars draw this conclusion (see discussion above in Chapter 4 §III).

Aune suggests three explanations for the practice of writing pseudonymous literature: (1) it arose at a time when the biblical canon was already closed and well-known names were used to secure acceptance, (2) it was used to protect the identity of the writer who might be in danger if his or her true identity were known, and (3) apocalyptic visionaries may have had visions from the figures to whom they attributed their work.[74] Aune believes that the first of these options is the more likely, but not without several qualifications. As a legitimating device intended to accord to the writing in question the esteem and prestige given to the earlier well-known figures, "pseudonymity is functional only if readers accept the false attribution."[75] It is probably best not to conclude that *all* writers of pseudepigrapha wrote for purposes of deception. Aune notes seven categories of pseudonymous writings in early Christian literature, including some in the biblical canon:

> (1) works not by an author but probably containing some of his own thoughts (Ephesians and Colossians); (2) documents by someone who was influenced by another person to whom the work is ascribed (1 Peter and maybe James); (3) compositions influenced by earlier works of an author to whom they are assigned (1 Timothy, 2 Timothy, Titus); (4) Gospels (eventually) attributed to an apostle but deriving from later circles or schools of learned individuals (Matthew and John); (5) Christian writings attributed by their authors to an Old Testament personality (Testament of Adam, Odes of Solomon, Apocalypse of Elijah, Ascension of Isaiah); (6) once-anonymous works now correctly (perhaps Mark, Luke, and Acts) or incorrectly credited to someone (some manuscripts attribute Hebrews to Paul); (7) compositions that intentionally try to deceive the reader into thinking that the author is someone famous (2 Peter).[76]

Some pseudonymous literature doubtless was produced with a view toward deception, but it is also quite possible that some books were written in the sincere belief that the writing represented that for which an earlier hero – often a prophetic figure or an apostle – was known. Many biblical scholars agree that pseudonymous

---

[73]   Ehrman, *Forged*. He claims that most of the NT writings are "forged" or pseudonymous writings intended to deceive readers.

[74]   Aune, *Prophecy in Early Christianity*, 109.

[75]   Ibid., 110.

[76]   Ibid.

writings are found in the biblical canon. For example, most scholars hold that the OT book of Daniel is pseudonymous, but a few argue that the earliest form of the book derives from the Hebrew prophet and that only its latest or final form stems from the mid-second century BCE. Some scholars question whether the Gospels of Matthew and John were written by these apostles, and many also dismiss Markan and Lukan authorship of the Gospels that have their names attached. In the strictest sense of the term, the canonical Gospels are not pseudepigraphal since the original Gospels did not originally have apostolic names attached to them. They should be more appropriately designated "anonymous" literature. One non-canonical gospel attributed to an apostle is the *Gospel of Thomas* (ca. 90 to 170 CE) that is difficult to date precisely, but is generally acknowledged as an anonymous document.[77] Further, most NT scholars agree that Paul did not write all of the literature that was later attributed to him, especially the Pastoral Epistles in their current form (1–2 Timothy and Titus), Hebrews, and possibly even Ephesians, Colossians, and 2 Thessalonians. Also, most agree that 2 Peter was not written by Peter, but rather in the second century.

Many other writings not in our NT canon are also generally acknowledged as pseudonymous works: *Didache, 2 Clement, Apostolic Constitutions, Gospel of Thomas, Barnabas,* and others. The practice of writing under an assumed name or category of office, as in the case of the *Didache* attributed to the Twelve Apostles, was quite common in the early church well into the second and third centuries. Some of that literature was called into question even in the second century (*Gospel of Judas*). Serapion of Antioch, noted earlier, questioned the *Gospel of Peter* in this account by Eusebius:

> [Serapion] has written refuting the false statements in it [Gospel of Peter], because of certain in the community of Rhossus, who on the ground of the said writing turned aside into heterodox teachings (*heterodoxous didaskalias*). It will not be unreasonable to quote a short passage from this work [Serapion's refutation], in which he puts forward the view he held about the book, writing as follows: "For our part, brethren, we receive both Peter and the other apostles as Christ, *but the writings which falsely bear their names* [*ta de onomati autōn pseudepigrapha*] we reject, as men of experience, knowing that such were not handed down to us." (*Hist. eccl.* 6.12.2–3, LCL, emphasis added)

Interestingly, the *Apostolic Constitutions* (ca. 350–400), which is a pseude-pigraphal work, warns Christians against reading pseudepigraphal literature! After first claiming to be apostles, the author(s) of this work go(es) on to warn about other pseudonymous writings:

> On whose account also we, who are now assembled in one place – Peter and Andrew; James and John, sons of Zebedee; Philip and Bartholomew; Thomas and Matthew; James the son of Alphaeus; and Lebbaeus who is surnamed Thaddaeus; and Simon the Canaanite, and Matthias, who instead of Judas was numbered with us; and James the brother of the Lord and bishop of

---

77   See Perrin, *Thomas and Tatian*, 1–47.

Jerusalem, and Paul the teacher of the Gentiles, the chosen vessel, having all met together, have written to you this Catholic doctrine for the confirmation of you, to whom the oversight of the universal church is committed...

We have sent all things. to you, that you may know our opinion, what it is; and that *you may not receive those books which obtain in our name*, but are written by the ungodly. For you are not to attend to the names of the apostles, but to the nature of the things, and their settled opinions. *For we know that Simon and Cleobius, and their followers, have compiled poisonous books under the name of Christ and of His disciples, and do carry them about in order to deceive you who love Christ, and us his servants.* And among the ancients also *some have written apocryphal books of Moses, and Enoch, and Adam, and Isaiah, and David, and Elijah, and of the three patriarchs, pernicious and repugnant to the truth.* The same things even now have the wicked heretics done, reproaching the creation, marriage, providence, the begetting of children, the law, and the prophets; inscribing certain barbarous names, and as they think, of angels, but to speak the truth of demons, which suggest things to them; whose doctrine eschew that you may not be partakers of the punishment due to those that write such things for the seduction and perdition of the faithful and unblameable disciples of the Lord Jesus. (*Apostolic Constitutions* 6.14, 16, ANF, emphasis added and text adapted)

This implies, of course, that, along with authorship, the standard applied to pseudepigraphy was orthodoxy. If a particular writing fit theologically with what was acceptable to a particular Christian community, then the writing itself was apparently acceptable, even though someone other than the author listed may have written it.[78] Generally speaking, however, by the fourth century, all *known* pseudonymous writings were rejected.

Koch observes that particular names were able to attract entire genres of literature. For example, all divine law came from Moses, wisdom from Solomon, and church regulations from apostles, as in the case of the *Didache* and the *Apostolic Constitutions*.[79] Pseudonymous writings thus imply on the part of the writer a consciousness that "association with a tradition confers legitimacy." Koch explains: "In many cases the authors to whom the writings are ascribed are considered as alive in heaven and therefore still effective in the present. To this extent attribution of authorship to men of God is the same as ascribing it to God, Jesus, or angels. Since what is involved is not the conscious use of an inaccurate name, the designation 'pseudonymous' should be used only with reservations."[80] Charlesworth agrees and warns against calling all such literature forgeries. Not all pseudepigraphal writings intended to deceive the original readers, he claims, but rather, the authors considered it acceptable to attribute writings to those who had inspired them.[81]

---

[78] For further discussion, see P. Jenkins, *Hidden Gospels: How the Search for Jesus Lost Its Way* (Oxford: Oxford University Press, 2001).
[79] K. Koch, "Pseudonymous Writing," *IDBSup*, 712–14.
[80] Ibid., 713.
[81] Charlesworth, "Pseudepigraphy," 766.

Disbelief and disappointment are the almost universal responses of Christians who hear for the first time that the ascribed author of one of the biblical books may not have actually written the work to which the supposed author's name is attached. This is understandable given the modern concern that comes from our living in an age when both plagiarism and writing in another person's name are looked upon as unethical. It is therefore easy to assume unethical motivations on the part of those who produced such literature in the ancient religious communities. Although deception may be the motive in some cases, in others the writings may have been written in honor of a particular hero in the prophetic or apostolic tradition.

Whether the author of the Pastoral Epistles in their current condition simply wanted apostolic sanction for his views on church organization and discipline and therefore attached Paul's name to his own writings is not easily determined, especially since some apparently authentic Pauline traditions are included in this collection. For example, I suggest the following, namely, the rejection of Paul in Asia Minor (2 Tim 1:15); the manner of the apostle's death (2 Tim 4:6–9), many of Paul's closing comments to colleagues in 2 Tim 4:9–22; and probably also the admonition to Titus (1:5–16) and the final words and encouragement to Titus (3:12–15), but possibly also more. The Pastorals do not focus on what are generally accepted as the major Pauline emphases in his widely acknowledged letters, especially justification by faith, reconciliation, the Holy Spirit, eschatology, and a more simple church organizational structure. A satisfactory explanation for the presence of authentic traditions within otherwise pseudonymous writings has not yet received widespread scholarly approval. The tendency among scholars is either to accept or reject writings in their totality as the work of an unknown author or to reject completely their authenticity. Partial authentic traditions in a pseudonymous work may be correct, such as in the description of Paul in the *Acts of Paul and Thecla*. Since it appears that all pseudonymous literature in the ancient world was not cut from the same cloth, care should be taken in each instance to determine not only authorship (whenever possible), but also the motive and procedure employed in producing the writing.

Again, a troubling question often comes from the more conservative students of Scripture, namely, how can a writing be maintained in our biblical canon if the work was not written by the one to whom it was ascribed? In other words, how can its inspiration be legitimate if it is a forgery? Along the same line, we may ask whether divine inspiration depends on knowing and identifying the correct authors? Is the writing inspired because a particular writer wrote it or because the writing inherently has a recognized message that addressed the needs and circumstances of the church or person(s) to whom it was addressed and continued to have relevance for churches in subsequent generations? Nothing in antiquity suggests that *only* those from the apostolic period were inspired and that all other voices were not. On the contrary, the earliest churches did not argue that the role of inspiration was limited to the apostles or their contemporaries or even to writings per se, but rather that inspiration was given to the whole church in perpetuity.

Acts 2:14–21 clearly shows that the early followers of Jesus believed they were in the "last days" when the presence of and empowerment by the Holy Spirit had been unleashed upon the church, and there is no definite time when this age was perceived to have stopped. They also believed that the role of inspiration was not restricted to writing, but that it included the ministry of proclamation (orally). The reason Hebrews, anonymously written, was retained in the biblical canon, despite the fact that many early church fathers doubted that it was written by Paul, was because it contained a valued message for Christians facing uncertain futures. Although some church fathers accepted Hebrews because they thought Paul wrote it, still many others had serious questions about its authorship and placed it in their canons *at the end* of their list of Paul's Letters, *generally* after the smallest of Paul's Letters, Philemon, and not before 2 Corinthians. According to its size, it would have been placed between 1 and 2 Corinthians or just after Romans to avoid splitting the two Corinthian letters. In other words, its place in our current biblical canon reflects the early church's uncertainty over its authorship, but not whether it had a message that was relevant for churches facing challenging circumstances and uncertain futures.

But again, what about questioning the canonical status of writings without apostolic authorship? If a writing made it into the biblical canon *only* because some believed that an earlier prophetic person or an apostle wrote it, should that disqualify it from being in the biblical canon? What do we do today when we can reasonably argue that an apostle did not write a book in the NT canon? It would be reasonable to withdraw the book if apostolic authorship alone were the sole criterion for canonicity or if inspiration and authentic authorship were inseparable. When the Gospels were first read in the churches, apostolicity and authorship were not significant matters. It is probably better to understand how or whether a document continued to address the continuing needs and mission of the church. All of the NT writings fit within the broad range of the earliest Christian traditions and beliefs, but do they continue to impact the church the same way today? Was a text's inspiration based on authorship or its faithfulness to the authentic witness of Jesus preserved in early Christian literature? I suspect that it was more the latter than the former, but in the fourth century the two were not generally separated and authentic authorship was more important.

It is important to remember here that even our present NT biblical canon is consciously not limited to apostolic authorship alone (e.g., Mark and Luke–Acts), but the church found these writings particularly helpful for use in worship, catechetical instruction, and mission. Can a similar case be made for continuing to include literature that was earlier attributed to an apostle, such as Hebrews, Revelation, the Pastorals, or even 2 Peter in their current condition,[82] but subsequently found not to the be case?[83]

The value of pseudonymous literature for the study of early Christianity should not be underestimated. Along with the canonical literature, the apocryphal and pseudepigraphal literature presents at times what Barnstone calls "a lucid picture of the life and ideals of early Christendom."[84] Without it we have an incomplete and sometimes vague understanding of the emergence and growth of early Christianity. That literature often helps clarify many questions about the context and interpretation of the NT literature itself. This literature also reflects the great diversity in the formative years of the Christian community, something that was not tolerated as much later on. This body of literature is invaluable in bringing some clarity to our understanding of many commonly used terms and ideas in the NT literature, for example, Son of Man, angels, eschatology, kingdom, messianic expectations, and the NT's use of the OT, but also the context of early Christianity. Most interpreters of Scripture today see the immense value of this literature for informing our understanding of the historical context of early Christianity and aiding our understanding of the theology of the NT literature. For our purposes, I add that not infrequently, it also aids in our understanding of the origins, growth, and stabilization of the Bible. In its wisdom, the ancient churches included the books that now comprise the NT and I would be hesitant to eliminate any of those books. On the other hand, most scholars today, whether conservative, moderate, or liberal in their thinking find a great deal of value in the study of the literature that was excluded. One need not expand or shrink the size of the NT canon to be informed by writings not included in it. We should be reminded that some early churches were informed by it and occasionally there are valuable lessons to be learned from a careful analysis of literature that was not included in the biblical canon.

---

[82]   For a helpful discussion of Pauline pseudonymous writings, see the collection of scholarly contributions in Stanley E. Porter and Gregory P. Fewster, eds., *Paul and Pseudepigraphy*, PAST 8 (Leiden: Brill, 2013). Especially significant in the volume, and for our purposes, is Porter's article, "Pauline Chronology and the Question of Pseudonymity of the Pastoral Epistles," 65–88, who presents the arguments fairly for both sides of the issues. He is more convinced than I am about Pauline authorship of 1 Timothy, but the arguments for Pauline authorship in whole or in part of 2 Timothy and perhaps Titus are worthy of more consideration than some scholars have thought. He and I have disagreed on this matter, but his volume and his contribution to it is more informed and more balanced than arguments presented by many other scholars.

[83]   For further study of this topic, see B. M. Metzger, "Literary Forgeries and Canonical Pseudepigrapha," *JBL* 91 (1972): 3–24, and D. G. Meade, *Pseudonymity and Canon: An Investigation into the Relationship of Authorship and Authority in Jewish and Earliest Christian Tradition* (Grand Rapids: Eerdmans, 1986).

[84]   Barnstone, *Other Bible*, xix.

CHAPTER 19

THE LITERARY ARTIFACTS OF ANTIQUITY AND CANONIZATION

Biblical scholars regularly investigate the physical and literary aspects of the ancient manuscripts and their texts in order to retrieve, analyze, and reconstruct the biblical texts. They regularly observe whether and how much care was taken in the copying and transmission of the biblical writings. Their investigations often show not only whether there was careful transmission of those ancient texts, but also what other books, if any, were in those manuscripts. Further, they seek to account for the numerous variants transmitted in those manuscripts, that is, whether they were accidental and easily corrected or intentional and need clarification on the context of intentional changes. Even when ancient scribes were aware that they were preserving *sacred* texts, there are often significant variations in the quality or care of the manuscripts they produced, including in the text itself. Text-critical scholars are aware that many of the accidental or intentional changes made in the transmission of the NT texts were multiplied in subsequent copies.

Some of the initial manuscripts may have lasted with regular careful use sometimes up to two hundred years. It has long been argued that biblical manuscripts or any ancient manuscripts seldom last longer than twenty to thirty years, but in a recent article Evans shares his investigations of the use of ancient manuscripts and how long they may have functioned in antiquity. He challenges earlier views that they only lasted around one generation at best and concludes that some of them may have lasted much longer and perhaps well over 200 years. After his survey of the length of time that ancient manuscripts were used in the Greco-Roman world, he concludes the following: "given that there is no evidence that early Christian scribal practices differed from pagan practices, we may rightly ask if early Christian writings, such as the autographs and first copies of the books that eventually would be recognized as canonical Scripture, also remained in use for one hundred years or more."[1] If correct, Evans' findings could be quite significant since it would be possible that some of the oldest surviving copies of NT writings that date from the second or third century may depend on original

---

[1]   This statement comes from personal correspondence with Professor Evans, who sent to me not only this brief summary, but also a copy of his paper, later published as C. A. Evans, "How Long Were Late Antique Books in Use?"

documents well into the third century. While this is possible, there is no way currently to demonstrate whether any of the earliest known surviving manuscripts of NT writings came from an original biblical manuscript. The time of use of any ancient manuscript depends on how often a manuscript was used and what care was given in its preservation. These factors varied and while it is possible that the earliest manuscripts known today may have derived from an "original" text, that is nearly impossible to demonstrate.

At some point, the autographs (original manuscripts) of the NT writings were lost, destroyed in persecutions, worn out, or stored in undisclosed locations. Because the autographs over time were no longer usable or available, and because their value in the life of the church was recognized, churches requested that literate individuals in their congregations (some more careful than others) make copies of these valuable texts so they could continue to be circulated in the churches. The question here, of course, is how faithful to the originals were the subsequent manuscripts that were often copied by literate amateurs. Because significant numbers of the NT texts have survived antiquity, somewhere in the vicinity of 5,740 portions of or complete copies of the NT texts, it is possible for textual critics in many instances to compare these manuscripts and arrive at a reasonable estimate of the original text of the NT writings. Those who copied the NT manuscripts not only reproduced unintentional errors in transmission, but occasionally and less often, made intentional changes in the NT texts either in order to make the biblical text more clear for a particular audience or to introduce later theological positions into those texts (e.g., 1 John 5:7–8). In what follows, I will focus on these and other related issues involved in the transmission of the NT writings that the early churches eventually affirmed as the second part of their sacred Scriptures.

I. INTRODUCTION:
THE IMPORTANCE OF ANCIENT ARTIFACTS

Until recently, the surviving ancient artifacts that have relevance for under-standing canon formation have largely been ignored, but that is changing and there is now a growing recognition of their importance for understanding not only the transmission of the biblical books and texts, but now also their canonization.[2] The surviving biblical manuscripts tell us broadly what sacred writings actually informed the life of various early Christian churches. Because much has been lost, there doubtless will remain a number of gaps in our understanding, but what does remain in the surviving artifacts often reveals important information regarding

---

[2]   A helpful and carefully written example of the recent interest in this matter can be seen in Stanley E. Porter's recent volume *How We Got the New Testament: Text, Transmission, Translation*, ASBT (Grand Rapids: Baker Academic, 2013), but there are many others, as we will see below.

which books and texts of those books informed the faith of the early Christians and were welcomed among the church's Scriptures. The writings contained in those manuscripts are not always the same as those that appear in canonical lists. Also, it is rare to find any ancient church in possession of copies of all of the books that comprise the present biblical canon until around the tenth century. Long after biblical canons were being formed, that is, when catalogues of the books that comprise the churches' Scriptures were constructed, some churches continued to reproduce and read in their services books that had not been recognized or authorized earlier by the majority of churches or church councils. There is little evidence that all churches agreed with council decisions about the scope of their Christian Scriptures. In fact, in several cases additional (noncanonical) books were included in some surviving biblical manuscripts and this continued for centuries after council decisions were made. Also, long after the majority of churches had agreed on the scope of their NT Scriptures, there is little evidence to suggest that all churches or even most of them had a copy of all of those sacred Scriptures. As we will see, the high cost of the materials to produce a copy of all of the church's Scriptures was beyond the ability of most of the smaller churches and so they were quite selective in what they could afford. That being the case in most instances, what resources most informed the faith of the ancient Christian churches?

The surviving manuscripts let us also see the sometimes misspelled words, omitted lines, duplication of lines or words, and other accidental variants in them. Further, the ancient translations not only inform us of the quality (sometimes quite poor) of the texts used for the translations, but also the quality of the translations that came from them. Also what books and what text were included in them? The earliest translations do not include all of the NT books and they sometimes include writings that were not later included in Christian Bibles. The ancient translations also show which books are more commonly found in the church that used those translations and which are not. Generally speaking, most of the translations include one or more of the Gospels and several Pauline letters, but they also show the limitations in the early translations. As we will see, in the first five centuries there are almost no translations that include all of the books of the NT, and several translations include other books that were not included in the NT. One is always tempted here to ask whether the theology of the early churches would have been significantly different if they had access to all of the books that are in the Bibles today and no other books!

Finally, we can add to this the question of whether the initial limitations on the size of the codex for transmitting the Scriptures influenced which books were included. In other words, since initially and until the fourth century the codex or book format was not capable of including all of the NT books let alone all of the books in the current Bible, did concerns over available space in a manuscript or codex have any bearing on what books were included in it? For example, the oldest collection of Paul's letters are in codex P[46], the number of pages in it is known despite its fragmentary condition, but there was insufficient space in the manuscript to include all of the letters later attributed to Paul and which are in our current NT Scriptures. The precise number of pages available in that manuscript had been determined and there was not sufficient room for the Pastoral Epistles, even if the size of the letters in the text had been considerably reduced in size. Had limited space *not* been a concern, would the ancient Christian manuscripts have included more books? That cannot be answered here, but the question is not insignificant. None of the earliest papyrus codices contain all of the books of the NT and some also include writings not included in the later biblical canons of the churches, for example P[72], which will be discussed below.[3] Because of limited space in the earlier papyrus codices in the first three centuries, what criteria were employed in determining which books to include in them?

By the fourth century CE, following considerable advances in the technology of producing codices and the production of majuscule or uncial manuscripts on parchment, there was sufficient capacity to include all of the books of the Christian OT and NT in one codex or volume. When discussions of the biblical canon took place in antiquity, they centered on the *books* that comprised the sacred collection and not on the particular text or translation of the Scriptures or even the space available to include them in such collections.

None of the earliest scrolls (rolls) or codices employed in transmitting the books of the NT had sufficient capacity to include all of the NT writings, though by the early third century the four Gospels and Acts could be included in one codex of roughly 200–220 pages, as we see in P[45]. Initially (i.e., for the first hundred years or so), only a few books at most could reasonably fit in a codex or scroll. Of the current 128 NT papyrus manuscripts[4] that comprise the earliest collection of NT manuscripts, only 14 of them include more than one book and some have no more than two documents. With advances in the size of the codex by the fourth century, one codex volume could then accommodate all of the church's OT and NT Scriptures in roughly 1600 pages. The question remains, however, whether the initial capacity of the codices had any effect on the contours or shape of the Bible?

It was quite common in the second and third centuries for biblical manuscripts to contain limited portions of our current NT canon such as one or more gospels and a few epistles at best and with a few notable exceptions. Further, of the earliest manuscripts that have survived none have *exactly* the same text in them despite considerable overlap. For canon formation purposes, the fourth century and later uncial and majuscule manuscripts are of particular interest for canon studies because they had a greater capacity and allowed for the inclusion of all of the

---

[3]   Besides Jude, and 1 and 2 Peter, this codex also includes the *Nativity of Mary*, correspondence of Paul with the Corinthians and *3 Corinthians*, *Ode* 11 from the *Odes of Solomon*, then Jude, followed by Melito's *Homily on the Passover*, a hymn fragment, the *Apology of Phileas*; and Pss 33 and 34. I will discuss this manuscript more in Chapter 20.

[4]   That number will doubtless increase to around 140 since other texts have been found and after assessment and cataloguing they will be added to the collection.

church's scriptures. These issues – books, text, transmission, and translation – and others related to ancient literary artifacts have a direct bearing on issues related to the authority and biblical canon of churches today. We will look more closely now at some of those manuscripts.

II. THE BIBLICAL MANUSCRIPTS

Until recently, NT manuscripts were regularly classified in four categories or families of clusters of manuscripts, namely the *Alexandrian*, *Western*, and *Byzantine* text families, and the so-called *Caesarean* (or "Neutral") text.[5] Text-critical scholars used to believe that each of the four text families was different from each other and could be identified by certain characteristics. The Alexandrian family was generally viewed as the most reliable text family and Western texts were considered the least reliable. Those categories or text families that earlier dominated the field of textual criticism of the NT for much of the last 100 years, have recently been revised and replaced by current text-critical scholars with better explanations for understanding the surviving texts of the NT. Several of these families were not so distinct as once thought and it is now common to hear that various NT manuscripts from these so-called textual families overlap in several instances (Codex Sinaiticus, ca. 375 CE, for instance). Our focus here will not be on these text families, but on recent research by several leading text-critical scholars who are rethinking the past perspectives and discussing emerging challenges in the textual-critical discipline.[6] I will say more about these text types below in §III, but first, I will focus on writing and the writing materials used to produce the NT books.

---

[5] These text families are described in Metzger, *Textual Commentary*, 4*–7*, and in B. M. Metzger and B. D. Ehrman, *The Text of the New Testament: Its Transmission, Corruption, and Restoration.* 3rd ed. (New York: Oxford University Press, 1992), 276–80 and 306–13.

[6] For example, see Eldon Epp, "Issues in New Testament Textual Criticism," in *Rethinking New Testament Textual Criticism*, ed. D. A. Black (Grand Rapids: Baker, 2002), 17–76. Thomas C. Geer Jr., rev. Jean-François, "Analyzing and Categorizing New Testament Greek Manuscripts," 497–518; E. J. Epp, "Textual Clusters: Their Past and Future in New Testament Textual Criticism," 519–79; and Daniel B. Wallace, "The Majority Text Theory: History, Methods, and Critique," 711–44, in *The Text of the New Testament in Contemporary Research: Essays on the Status Quaestionis*, ed. M. W. Holmes and B. D. Ehrman, 2nd ed. (Leiden: Brill, 2014). See also, Eldon J. Epp, *Perspectives on New Testament Criticism: Collected Essays, 1962–2004*, SNT 116 (Leiden: Brill, 2005), and his "In the Beginning Was the New Testament Text, but Which Text? A Consideration of 'Ausgangstext' and 'Initial Text," in *Texts and Traditions: Essays in Honour of J. Keith Elliott*, ed. Peter Doble and Jeffrey Kloha, NTTSD 47 (Leiden: Brill, 2014), 35–70; and Bart D. Ehrman, *Studies in the Textual Criticism of the New Testament*, NTTS 33 (Leiden: Brill, 2005), a collection of his previously published articles relevant to this discussion.

A. The Art of Writing

In the ancient world, the act of writing something down often carried with it the implication of something important and occasionally something with considerable authority, and sometimes even divine authority. Because writing materials were quite expensive in antiquity and often inaccessible to many, most of what was written was considered quite significant. Important communications were sometimes etched in stone or on ostraca (broken potsherds) or in other more permanent media (inscriptions on stone) and put on public display.

At first, ancient writings were inscribed on walls or on stone, wood, beaten metal, and eventually on clay tablets (ca. 3100 BCE and following). Some important writings were etched in stone (Exod 31:18) or painted on walls (Dan 5:5–9), or even placed on flattened metal (chiefly copper, such as the Copper Scroll among the Dead Sea Scrolls) or silver (sheets hammered to a smooth surface), and potsherds. Around the turn of the Common Era, flat wooden blocks were bound together with leather strings to make tablets (codices) with wax inside and a stylus that allowed a writer to make several notes and subsequently erase them and use the same wax in the codex again. Sometimes codices included several papyrus pages sewn together and used often for nonliterary documents such as bills of sale and personal correspondence, while more important writings were placed in a more literary format such as scrolls of papyrus sheets or animal skins sewn together and circulated in rolls. By far, however, papyrus (plural papyri; cf. from which the word "paper" derives) and animal skins were the most common writing materials employed during the time of Jesus and later. In the last decade of the first century, the author of Revelation spoke of a scroll with seven seals that were unsealed to reveal its contents (Rev 5:1–8:5). Scrolls occasionally were written on both sides (possibly the meaning of 5:1).

Papyrus manuscripts were cheaper to produce and among the most common writing material in antiquity. The papyrus plant grew in abundance along the banks of the Nile River in Egypt and was harvested and made into writing material. The material was often called *byblos* because large quantities of this material were shipped out of the Syrian harbor city of Byblos. Our word Bible comes from the plural of the Greek word *biblion* ("book"). Papyrus sheets were often pasted together end to end to form a lengthy roll or scroll. With the development of the codex, papyrus sheets were often combined with other sheets, folded and sewn at the middle edge to hold the pages together. The number of sheets that were combined to make a quire varied, but generally it included eight-folded sheets that produced sixteen pages on which one could write on both the front and back of each page. Over time multiple quires were sewn together, allowing for longer or multiple documents to be included in one codex.

By the fourth century scrolls and codices made of animal skins became the standard writing vehicles in churches for transmitting their Scriptures, but initially the majority of the Christian Scriptures were written on papyrus sheets folded and sewn together to form a codex (cf. 2 Tim 4:13) and sometimes a roll (perhaps about thirty percent of the time). Until the fourth century, these codices contained one or more Gospels along with Acts (P^{45}) or a collection of letters of Paul (P^{46}) or other combinations of Christian texts (P^{72}). The use of parchment manuscripts (both rolls or scrolls and also codices) first developed in ancient Pergamum, but soon the technology spread from there to the whole empire. The value of using parchment was that it was easier to write on and easier to erase when mistakes were made or when a writer wanted to reuse the same writing material for a different purpose. Because of the considerable expense of writing materials, it was not uncommon to erase parchment documents entirely and use them again for other purposes. Some biblical manuscripts are on reused parchment manuscripts and some earlier biblical manuscripts were erased and used for other purposes.

Before the collection and transmission of the books of the Bible began, other ancient peoples of the Middle East had already produced several important literary documents.[7] Long before the existence of the Jewish people, writing was a part of life in the ancient world. Mesopotamia and Egypt had distinctive scripts from around 3000 BCE, and these states had professional secretaries or scribes who, in special cases, functioned something like a secretary of state: they kept records, produced official state documents, and participated in recording many other literary and legal functions. Scribes often wore distinctive clothing to set them apart from others, and the custom of wearing a white tunic and carrying a bag containing writing equipment – ink, pens, brushes, writing material, and a cloth or rag for washing off errors – led to the scribal profession being identified as the "white kilt" profession (see, for example, Ezek 9:2–3, 11). Priestly scribal schools also existed in Israel following the Babylonian exile (ca. 530–500 BCE), but there is not much information about them before then. (For more discussion of the scribes and writings in antiquity, see Chapter 2 §IV.)

When the NT writings began to appear, the roll was used for almost all literary documents, but informal writings were sometimes put in notebooks (tablets) or handbooks (codices) and those writings often had more informality and abbreviations in them. Until the fifth or sixth century CE, as noted earlier, the Jews regularly used scrolls when copying their sacred Scriptures. At first single books, and then major sections of the HB, were placed on one scroll. But even when technology improved sufficiently so that the whole of the HB could be placed on a single scroll (fourth century CE), the Jews continued to separate the Torah

---

[7]   On the art and practice of writing in ancient Israel, see Demsky, "Writing in Ancient Israel and Early Judaism," in Mulder, ed., *Mikra*, 2–20; and Bar-Ilan, "Writing in Ancient Israel and Early Judaism."

or Pentateuch from the rest of the Jewish Scriptures and placed it on its own scroll that was some thirty or more feet in length. This practice meant that each of the three groupings of the HB writings were eventually transmitted together on separate scrolls devoted to Law, Prophets, or Writings. By the fourth century, Christians began putting all of their sacred writings, both OT and NT, in one book (or codex), and examples from that period include Codex Vaticanus and Codex Sinaiticus.[8]

The early copies of the NT Scriptures were normally produced on papyrus manuscripts in rolls or scrolls, and mostly in codices in capital letters (uncial or majuscule) without spaces between the words, possibly in order to conserve space on expensive writing materials. Generally non-professional materials, the codex for instance, were used in the early stages of transmitting Christian writings and that may reflect an earlier non-scriptural view of the materials such as Paul's letters (cf. 2 Tim 4:13) that were *ad hoc* addresses to local congregations. By the middle to late fourth century, Christian professional scribes began producing manuscripts on parchment and of higher quality using professional scribes, yet still, perhaps because of cost or custom, those manuscripts also had no spaces between words for several centuries more.

By the eighth century, scribes began to insert spaces between words and write in lowercase letters (*minuscule* manuscripts). These manuscripts are commonly called "cursive" (from Latin, *cursivus*, "to run") because of the practice of writing all of the letters of a word without lifting the pen from the page (i.e., a running hand), but with spaces between the words. Until Gutenberg invented moveable type and the printing press (1454) and published the whole Bible (1456), all biblical texts were produced by hand. After the seventh or eighth centuries they were produced in lowercase lettering often with colorful imagery (i.e., decorative letters and illustrations) especially at the beginning of books and chapters.[9]

---

[8]   For a helpful discussion with diagrams and illustrations of ancient writing and a useful bibliography on this subject, see E. Randolph Richards, "Reading, Writing, and Manuscripts," in Green and McDonald, eds., *The World of the New Testament*, 345–66.

[9]   For more information on the practice of writing and the materials used for writings in the ancient world, see Wegner, *Journey from Texts to Translations*; and for our purposes, see especially Hurtado, *Earliest Christian Artifacts*, 43–93; Stephen Emmel, "The Christian Book in Egypt: Innovation and the Coptic Tradition," in Sharpe and Van Kampen, eds., *The Bible as Book*, 35–43, and in the same volume T. S. Pattie, "The Creation of the Great Codices," 61–72; Thomas J. Kraus, *Ad Fontes: Original Manuscripts and Their Significance for Studying Early Christianity: Selected Essays*, TENT 3 (Leiden: Brill, 2007); Thomas J. Kraus and Tobias Nicklas, "The World of New Testament Manuscripts," in T. J. Kraus and T. Nicklas, *New Testament Manuscripts: Their Texts and Their World*, TENT 2 (Leiden: Brill, 2006), 1–11; and Porter, *How We Got the New Testament*, 77–146.

B. The Manuscripts and the Biblical Canon

One of the peculiarities of the early Christian community is its preference for the codex by no later than 100 CE. The codex undoubtedly appealed to Christians because of its portability and convenience (see discussion of this in Chapter 20 §II.A). Later improvements in the production of the codex allowed multiple books to be included in a single codex, and still later all of the church's sacred books in a single volume. This converged at roughly the same time as the emergence of a fixed biblical canon in the church. The technology of producing books and the capacity possible to contain all of the NT books, as noted above, may thus have played a role in the selection of which books were included or excluded from the Christian canon.

If it is true that the biblical manuscripts reflect what the early churches accepted as sacred Scripture – and not what later church councils dictated – then it follows that various lists or catalogues of sacred books may not be as important as the books in the surviving manuscripts for letting us know what the real situation was in the churches. In other words, what do the surviving biblical manuscripts tell us about which books were read as sacred Scripture in the churches?

The Greek New Testaments in use today list which manuscripts contain one or more books from each of several categories in the New Testament. For example, in the Nestle/Aland 28th Edition, a papyrus manuscript containing one or more Gospels is listed as "e," the book of Acts as "a" or "act," Paul's letters as "p," the General or Catholic letters as "c" or "cath" and Revelation as "r" and each is followed by a Roman numeral indicating the century in which the manuscript was produced. The uncial or majuscule manuscripts in this edition have the combined letters e a p r and the "a" stands for *Apostolos*, i.e. Acts and the Catholic Letters. This can be misleading since the novice may assume that if a manuscript is followed by an "e" that it contained all four Gospels, but that is seldom the case until much later in church history. Often a manuscript in question may only contain one of the Gospels and the contents of the text is still identified by "e." The same can be said about each of the letters used except in the case of "r" for Revelation.

Also, the charts in these Greek texts do not indicate what other non-canonical books were in a manuscript in question, as in the case of P⁷² noted earlier that receives a "cath" for the Catholic Epistles, but besides Jude and 1 and 2 Peter (that order), the manuscript also contains other non-canonical books as well. Later, Codex Sinaiticus (ℵ 01) is followed by e a p r, but that manuscript also includes the *Epistle of Barnabas* and *Shepherd of Hermas*. In other words, besides the NT books in question and not specifically which ones, some manuscripts also contain other books not later included in the NT. In the case of P72, again, the "cath" or "c" includes Jude, 1 and 2 Peter, but not other Catholic Letters nor the other noncanonical texts in it. The other books in this codex are not identified in any of the modern Greek NT manuscripts, but those additional books and their date, of course, have considerable relevance for understanding canon formation. While listing all of the books in each category is not the primary purpose of those who produce the modern Greek Texts and the cards or lists of books in the manuscripts, it seems odd that the Nestle/Aland and United Bible Society Greek New Testaments do not include all additional books in those listed or at least something like a "nc" for "noncanonical" along with the other letters. No critical edition of the Greek NT indicates that noncanonical writings were also occasionally included in the same manuscripts with the NT writings, but in the major uncial manuscript of the fourth and fifth centuries, namely Codices Vaticanus, Sinaiticus, and Alexandrinus, such noncanonical (by modern standards) books are also included.

It is rare also to find all of the Gospels or all of the letters of Paul in a single papyrus manuscript until the early third century. There are only a few places to turn to in order to discover the actual contents of the ancient biblical manuscripts, namely what books or fragments thereof are actually in the manuscripts.

Whatever else the ancient canonical lists show (see Appendices A and C), the manuscripts occasionally include noncanonical writings among the scripture collections of some ancient churches and they sometimes omit some NT books as well. An example of this is in Codex Vaticanus that omits the Pastoral Letters. Nothing in the standard Greek New Testaments indicates that the Pastoral Epistles are absent from it. The foldout cards in the Nestle-Aland Greek NT[28] and the UBS simply indicate that the major uncial manuscripts contain the Gospels, Acts combined with the Catholic Letters, and Paul's Letters, and Revelation (e a p r). The UBS[5] includes the "c" following "a" for Acts, as in "eacp" reflecting the sequence of Gospels, Acts followed by the Catholic Epistles, and Pauline Epistles, but e a c p r does not indicate what is included or missing. Unfortunately, much of the significant information about the full contents of the manuscripts must be found elsewhere. While it was obviously only the intent of the editors of the N/A[28] and UBS[5] to focus on the types of NT writings in the manuscripts, one wonders why it would not be possible to include more exact information that we discover in the manuscripts themselves. While it may be that there is little interest in such matters for most readers of the Greek New Testament, it would nevertheless be helpful to have this information available for those who read the NT carefully and critically. I will return to a few more comments about this in the next chapter.

Daryl Schmidt and Eldon Epp provide a valuable service for canon inquiry by reminding us of the many omissions in the available biblical apparatuses and by asking what all of this means for canon formation.[10] They rightly see that the manuscripts themselves served in a scriptural fashion in the communities where

---

[10]   D. D. Schmidt, "Greek New Testament as a Codex"; and Epp, "Issues in the Interrelation," in McDonald and Sanders, eds., *The Canon Debate*, 485–515; see also idem, "The Multivalence of the Term 'Original Text' in New Testament Textual Criticism," *HTR* 92 (1999): 245–81; and idem, "Textual Criticism in the Exegesis of the New Testament," in *Handbook to Exegesis of the New Testament*, ed. S. E. Porter, NTTS 25 (Leiden: Brill, 1997), 73–91.

they were found (or that produced them), and they contain not only biblical books, but also noncanonical books and they also note that the text of these books often varies from other manuscripts. As we have already observed, many unintentional errors and intentional changes entered into the copies of manuscripts, and these manuscripts with their variants served in a canonical manner in the churches that welcomed and read them. Epp correctly, in my opinion, concludes:

> Most if not all such competing variants were held to be canonical, wittingly or not, at various times and places in real-life Christian contexts, requiring the disquieting conclusion that canonicity of readings has virtually the same degree of multiformity as do the meaningful competing variants in a variation unit. That is, in many, many instances the term "canonical" can no longer be applied only to one variant reading; hence, no longer only to a single form of a New Testament writing.[11]

James Sanders, speaking about textual variations in the book of Psalms, agrees substantially with Epp and writes: "There were probably as many canons as there were communities." He explains that the problem of fluidity of these texts in the various communities brings "attention to the question of literature considered authoritative – that is, functionally canonical – by one Jewish or Christian community but not by another."[12] This is an important feature of canon inquiry that is seldom understood or focused on by contemporary canon scholars.

Schmidt notes that manuscripts containing all of the books of the NT – and only these books – are relatively late in the history of the church and few in number. While he correctly observes that some earlier manuscripts contain all of the writings of the NT, the oldest uncial manuscripts contain writings of both Testaments and also writings not found in Christian Bibles.[13]

Many students have assumed that in 367, when Athanasius sent out his *Thirty-Ninth Festal Letter* advising churches of the date when Easter should be celebrated, and in which he also listed the books in both the Old and New Testaments, the biblical canon had reached its final stabilization. In terms of the later canon lists circulating in churches and those derived from church councils, those decisions do not always reflect what actually was in the biblical manuscripts. After systematically going through many of the surviving manuscripts, both uncial and minuscule, Schmidt finds no exact parallels to Athanasius' specific book lists and their order until 1116 in a minuscule manuscript discovered in a monastery at Mount Athos in Greece.[14]

---

[11]   Epp, "Issues in the Interrelation," 515.
[12]   J. A. Sanders, "Scripture as Canon for Post-Modern Times," 58.
[13]   D. D. Schmidt, "Greek New Testament as Codex," 469.
[14]   Ibid., 476–77.

Epp shows that whatever else the lists from the fourth and fifth centuries may indicate, what in fact represents the various canons of the Christian communities up to and beyond that time is in the manuscripts that were actually used in the various churches. They reflect more accurately the actual situations in the churches. Moreover, there is less uniformity in them than one might expect given the listing of books in the church fathers and church councils.[15] Epp makes this point by noting that textual and biblical scholars tend only to discuss the *biblical* manuscripts found at Oxyrhynchus and not the noncanonical religious books also discovered there.[16] For example, the Egyptian Oxyrhynchus manuscript finds include the following noncanonical works:

> seven copies of the *Shepherd of Hermas*
> three copies of the *Gospel of Thomas*
> two copies of the *Gospel of Mary*
> one copy of the *Acts of Peter*
> one copy of the *Acts of John*
> one copy of the *Acts of Paul*
> one copy of the *Didache*
> one copy of the *Sophia of Jesus Christ*
> two copies of the *Gospel of Peter*
> single copies of three unknown gospels/sayings of Jesus
> one copy of the *Acts of Paul and Thecla*
> one copy of the *Protevangelium of James*
> one copy of the *Letter of Abgar to Jesus*

While many early NT manuscripts were found at Oxyrhynchus, we must not overlook the fact that the apocryphal books and the unknown gospel-like writings were also found there.[17]

We cannot repeat all of Epp's and Schmidt's arguments here, but their conclusions are well supported, and they raise important questions about which books of the NT, including those that are not in the NT, functioned as scripture for some of the early churches. It is likely that all of the biblical and noncanonical writings discovered in the ancient world functioned as Scripture and canon for some Christians in various communities where those books were found. A careful examination of the contents of the ancient biblical manuscripts is always in order and such studies have considerable importance for our understanding of the formation of the Christian Bibles.

---

[15]   Epp, "Issues in the Interrelation," 495–96. For example, the Pastoral Epistles are not in P[46] or Vaticanus, although at least one scholar holds that the Pastorals were originally in P[46]; see Duff, "P[46] and the Pastorals."

[16]   E. J. Epp, "The Oxyrhynchus New Testament Papyri: 'Not without Honor Except in Their Hometown'?," *JBL* 123 (2004): 14–17.

[17]   Ibid., 18. Epp further notes (18–20) the discovery at Oxyrhynchus of one Old Latin and twenty-three Greek manuscripts of the LXX that included portions of Wisdom of Solomon, Tobit, *Apocalypse of Baruch*, and *1 Enoch*.

III. THE ORIGIN AND FUNCTION
OF TEXTUAL CRITICISM

Textual criticism is sometimes referred to as "lower criticism," not because it is of lesser value, but because it is the foundational work on which all biblical inquiry is based. Unless there is some agreement on the wording of a biblical passage, it is difficult if not impossible to establish its original intent and its value for establishing the church's doctrine and mission. This is not to suggest that careful evaluation of the various biblical texts that survived antiquity will in the end yield exact information for every passage of the Bible. The original text of several passages is still unclear to textual critics and biblical scholars alike, even after long and difficult work has been spent on examining a variety of witnesses to ancient biblical texts. This process of evaluating textual variants is known as textual criticism. This discipline has often been overlooked or misunderstood in terms of its strategic importance not just for determining the most reliable text of the NT, but also for understanding the books and textual aspects involved in the processes of canonization.

The first responsibility of any interpreter of the Bible is to determine as precisely as possible what the author of a biblical text wrote. In this sense, the primary goal of textual criticism is to establish the most original or best wording of a text insofar as it can be recovered. Since none of the initial autographs have survived antiquity, text-critical scholars sift through and evaluate a myriad of ancient manuscripts that are at times remarkably different from each other, in order to determine the most plausible reading of a text in question. This goal, however, cannot always be achieved with final certainty, as recent textual critics readily acknowledge. Indeed, Epp has observed that scholars are finding the original text to be more and more elusive as new manuscripts are discovered and other factors such as deliberate or intentional changes are acknowledged and factored into the equation.[18]

When we understand the freedom with which some earlier copiers altered the texts of the NT, we begin to see the difficulty in trying to recover the original text. Most NT scholars today teach that Matthew and Luke made use of Mark's Gospel but they also acknowledge parallels between Matthew and Luke that are not found in Mark and these are generally referred to as Q (German: *Quelle* or "source"). The Q material sometimes has differences in the wording and sequence that Matthew and Luke have in common. For example, the Sermon on the Mount (Matt 5–7) is in large measure the Sermon on the Plain in Luke 6, but some of Matthew's Sermon on the Mount is not found in Luke 6, but rather scattered throughout Luke's Gospel.

---

[18] Epp, "Issues in New Testament Textual Criticism," 71–72.

Textual criticism is also useful in showing, for instance, that Mark 16:9–20 (a source for many sermons on missions) was not the original ending of that Gospel. Modern translators typically put these verses in a footnote or in brackets with explanations in footnotes indicating that those verses lack textual support. John 21 (also a source of many sermons on two NT words for love: *agapē* and *philia*) is well attested in Gospel manuscripts, but it was added to John's Gospel likely prior to the end of the second century when the textual history of that Gospel became more settled. Consequently, its authenticity is determined not so much by textual evidence, as by the context and internal evidence of the book itself.[19]

Which text and translation of Scripture, then, should be read in the pulpits or church Bible classes? Is it the text that was used in translating the *King James Version*, or the *New Revised Standard Version*, *New International Version*, and *New Jerusalem Bible*, or some other? While all of these translations are reasonably good and a great deal of work went into producing them, they do not translate the same biblical manuscripts or interpret the biblical texts in their original languages and texts exactly the same way. This is not just because of the variety of ways to translate Greek or Hebrew words or sentences, but because of the variety of differences in the text of manuscripts used in the translations. All translators carry their own preferences with them to their tasks. Frequently translators disagree in their preferences of one set of manuscripts over another to support a particular reading of a biblical text.

An important question naturally arises when discussing textual variants, namely, did many of the textual variants in the surviving manuscripts arise because early copiers of the church's Scriptures often had little hesitation about changing the texts they copied? Sometimes differences occur because copiers used different texts of the biblical books that were circulating in Christian churches. Sometimes the copiers made deliberate changes in the texts they were using as exemplars. Those variants of the biblical texts continued to be copied in subsequent transmissions of the biblical texts often along with the next copier's own changes included in the new copies. It is not clear that Matthew and Luke have had the same version of Mark or even Q before them.

---

[19]   For example, in John 20, Jesus appeared to the disciples, imparted the Holy Spirit to them, and commissioned them for ministry and then the book appears to close (20:30–31). In John 21, the disciples are back in Galilee fishing but not ministering and do not recognize him when he comes to them. Jesus' interaction with Peter about his love for him clearly seems designed to reverse Peter's threefold denial of Jesus rather than focusing on the differences in the two words for love in the passage. The oldest translations of this passage (Syriac Peshitta and Old Latin) do not have two different words for love here, but one. Be that as it may, John 21:24 clearly reflects other hands involved in this chapter (see "we know that his testimony is true"). Stanley Porter's contribution to my festschrift on this matter (in Craig A. Evans, ed., *From Biblical Faith to Biblical Criticism: Essays in Honor of Lee Martin McDonald* [Macon, GA: Mercer University Press, 2007]) contends that ch. 21 is an original part of John's Gospel but while this is not convincing to me, he carefully reflects on how scholars often can disagree on such matters.

Aland and Aland acknowledge that some variants in the biblical text may not be due to scribal error but due to "its [the biblical text's] character as a 'living text'."[20] This means that the copies Matthew and Luke used may already have included changes that earlier copiers thought important in the multiple churches that were using them. While the vast majority of textual changes are admittedly due to scribal error, intentional changes were often made on the basis of the copier's theological perspective, or simply the copiers' intent on clarifying the texts for their churches.

Bart D. Ehrman contends, that because the books of the emerging Christian Scriptures were circulating in manuscript form in the fourth century and were copied by hand, we should expect both intentional and unintentional changes. He concludes that the biblical texts were never inviolable and claims that while the vast majority of the changes were "the result of scribal ineptitude, carelessness, or fatigue, others were intentional, and reflect the controversial milieu within which they were produced." He points to examples where the current christological focus of the church led many copiers to make changes to bring out the clarity of their particular christological views as they were copying and transmitting the church's Scriptures. He claims that the scribes "occasionally altered the words of the text by putting them 'in other words.' To this extent, they were textual interpreters. At the same time, by *physically* altering the words, they did something quite different from other exegetes, and this difference is by no means to be minimized." Although other scholars challenge several of Ehrman's conclusions, he is probably correct that the fluidity of the text of the NT manuscripts continued well into the third and fourth centuries and beyond.[21] Aland and Aland challenge such conclusions and speak of "the tenacity of the New Testament textual tradition" concluding "some 10 to 20 percent of the Greek manuscripts have preserved faithfully the different text types of their various exemplars, even in the latest period when the dominance of the Byzantine Imperial text became so thoroughly pervasive. This is what makes it possible to retrace the original text of the New Testament through a broad range of witnesses."[22]

Initially, it appears that the NT writings were not treated as sacred and inviolable Scripture and many transcribers freely made changes to their texts for both practical (to clarify) and theological reasons. This, of course, complicates the task of textual criticism to recover the earliest and most reliable biblical text. Epp clarifies the problem when he asks, "If it is plausible that the Gospel of Mark used by Matthew differed from the Mark used by Luke, then which is the original Mark? And if it is plausible that our present Mark differed from Matthew's Mark,

---

[20] K. Aland and B. Aland, *The Text of the New Testament: An Introduction to the Critical Editions and to the Theory and Practice of Modern Textual Criticism*, rev. and enlarged ed., trans. E. R. Rhodes (Grand Rapids: Eerdmans, 1989), 69.

[21] For example, in his *Orthodox Corruption of Scripture*, 274–80.

[22] Aland and Aland, *Text of the New Testament*, 69–70.

and Luke's Mark, then do we not have three possible originals?"[23] Changes in the text occurred early on and the frequency of such changes creates a challenge for interpreters who want to establish the earliest text of Mark or other ancient NT texts. This leads us to a discussion of earlier notions of text types in the surviving manuscripts.

How can one decide among the various manuscripts that have survived antiquity? For almost a hundred years textual scholars focused on textual traditions that appeared to be related to several text types in the surviving manuscripts. These included the Alexandrian text believed to be the most reliable, and the Western text that had more variants and whose copiers freely made changes in the texts they copied and sometimes copied them poorly. The third major text type was called the Byzantine text. As I noted earlier, textual critics have recently reconsidered how distinct these textual families are, but for now we can say a few things about each of these manuscript collections.

(1) The Alexandrian text family began in Egypt probably in the early to middle second century and is generally known for its better preservation of the earliest texts of the NT with a more careful and accurate transmission of the biblical text. There are instances when the Western text appears to preserve a more reliable reading than the Alexandrian text,[24] but that is not the usual case and text critical scholars generally prefer readings from the Alexandrian text family. The chief witnesses to the Alexandrian text include P^{66}, P^{77}, Codex Vaticanus (B), and Codex Sinaiticus (א).[25] Codex Vaticanus, most likely a mid-fourth-century uncial manuscript produced mostly but not always in three columns per page likely originated in Alexandria, Egypt as its text-type suggests. It is sometimes acknowledged as the oldest codex manuscript containing both the OT and NT books. Its beginning is fragmentary where more than forty chapters of Genesis are missing and the NT part of the volume breaks off in Heb 9:14 in the middle of the word "purify" (Greek, *kathariei*), and the rest of Hebrews and Revelation are supplied by a later hand in a minuscule (lower case cursive) script. Vaticanus

---

[23]   Epp, "Issues in New Testament Textual Criticism," 73–74.

[24]   Westcott and Hort earlier dubbed these few instances as "Western non-interpolations," but they preferred to speak of a "Neutral Text" of the NT manuscripts characterized by the Alexandrian text family. These so-called Western non-interpolations include Matt 27:49; Luke 22:19–20; 24:3, 6, 12, 36, 40, 51, and 52. Other passages may be in this category, but those in Luke and the one in Matthew are the ones most often listed.

[25]   Sinaiticus and Vaticanus occasionally disagree, as in the case of the ending of Mark 1:1 (the last two Greek words). John J. Brogan, following an earlier study by Gordon Fee, observes that Sinaiticus sometimes displays Western text family characteristics in John 1–8. See Brogan, "Another Look at Codex Sinaiticus," in *The Bible as Book: The Transmission of the Greek Text*, ed. S. McKendrick and O. O'Sullivan (London: British Library; New Castle, DE: Oak Knoll, 2003), 18–19. Fee has concluded that "Codex Sinaiticus is a leading Greek representative of the Western Textual tradition in John 1.1–8.38," in his "Codex Sinaiticus in the Gospel of John: A Contribution to Methodology in Establishing Textual Relationships," *NTS* 15 (1968–69): 23–44.

is one of the most important ancient Greek NT texts, but it is also an edited text that is both fragmentary and defective in places. It does not contain all of the letters attributed to Paul, though it may also have included writings of the Apostolic Fathers as did some other uncial or majuscule manuscripts of the fourth and fifth centuries (Codices Sinaiticus includes *Ep. Barn.* and *Shepherd of Hermas* and Alexandrinus includes *1* and *2 Clement*), but its fragmentary state makes that difficult to prove. Its OT portion, however, includes without differentiation several books from the apocryphal collection that are mixed in among the so-called canonical books and not included at the end of the OT portion of the manuscript as we see in the Protestant Bibles that include the Apocryphal or Deuterocanonical books.

Like the Alexandrian text, the Western text manuscripts emerge at roughly the middle to late second century as well, but they were not as carefully produced as the Alexandrian text. According to Metzger, "the chief characteristic of Western readings is fondness of paraphrase. Words, clauses, and even whole sentences are freely changed, omitted, or inserted. Sometimes the motive appears to have been harmonization, while at other times it was the enrichment of the narrative by inclusion of traditional or apocryphal material."[26] As we saw above, there are a few instances when the Western text appears to preserve a more reliable reading than the Alexandrian text, but that is unusual and text critical scholars generally prefer readings from the texts in the Alexandrian text family.

The later Byzantine (Syrian group or Koine) text-type is generally considered a secondary text type, on which the King James Version is based and which is the best-attested text in later manuscripts. It is characterized by inferior and secondary readings and is no longer the preferred text of *most* New Testament scholars.[27] The Alexandrian texts were generally more carefully prepared than the Western texts and more reliable, but no biblical text is completely consistent or without error. The later Byzantine (Syrian or Koine) text-type, sometimes known as the "majority text" or even the "Ecclesiastical" text (roughly middle to late fourth century in its earliest stages), took on many characteristics of the earlier texts, but its copiers did not hesitate to make changes or corrections that they thought were necessary by smoothing out harshness of language and conflating two or more textual traditions, or smoothing out divergent parallel passages. This text became popular in Constantinople (former Byzantium) and in time became the preferred text in the majority of the Greek-speaking churches, but it is not known for its fidelity to the earliest manuscripts and is not as useful in establishing the earliest and most reliable biblical text. The Byzantine text is often characterized by inferior and secondary readings.[28]

---

[26] Metzger, *Textual Commentary*, 6*.
[27] Metzger and Ehrman, *Text of the New Testament*, 218–22.
[28] Ibid., 218–22 and 279–80. For a list of manuscripts that reflect this text type, see 306–7.

Because of the significant expense involved in securing the services of professional scribes, the early Christians often were generally not able to prepare carefully produced professional literary copies of the NT books. Professional scribes in the ancient world were paid well, namely some 750 *denarii* per year plus the scribes' regular maintenance (home, etc.). That amount was more than double and sometimes triple what the average skilled workman received. The early churches were generally not able to employ the best scribes who had the best technical skills to produce careful copies of their sacred scriptures. As a result, they had to make use of what Metzger called "amateur" copiers and this is reflected in many of the earliest manuscripts of the NT. No doubt as a result of this circumstance, many of the errors and changes in the NT writings that emerged early on were passed on in subsequent copies, and later still other changes were introduced.[29]

The care taken in copying NT manuscripts generally improved in the fourth century when it became more common for churches, for a time, to use professional scribes to produce copies of their scriptures. The cost of producing both the OT and NT books by professional scribes in the fourth century was approximately 30,000 *denarii*, or roughly four years' salary for a legionary some 100 years earlier. Kurt and Barbara Aland have noted that by the fourth century those manuscripts prepared on parchment or animal skins, mostly sheep or goatskins, replaced most of the papyrus manuscripts. One sheep or goat normally provided two double folios, namely only four folios of a finished manuscript. Copying the whole of the NT required between 200 and 250 folios to complete the entire project. This means that at least fifty to sixty sheep were needed to produce a volume or codex containing *only* the NT books. The Alands rightly conclude that only the upper classes could afford such an expensive undertaking, but that was not characteristic of typical Christians and their churches.[30]

The commercial centers for literary productions were called *scriptoria*, and greater care was taken in the *scriptoria* to produce copies of the Christian Scriptures. In the later Byzantine era, however, the task of producing copies of the Scriptures was often given to monks in monasteries who produced copies of the Scriptures in their private cells and often with less precision than copies produced in the professional *scriptoria*.

Accidental and even intentional changes continued to appear in biblical manuscripts, until the invention of moveable type and the printing press in the mid-fifteenth century, though with less frequency than was true in the earlier centuries. Difficulties in transcription were compounded by the weariness of posture necessary to make such copies often in less than comfortable places. With the use of an ink pen, such copying required a fresh dip in the ink well after every four to six letters. One can imagine the difficulty involved in producing large

---

[29]   Ibid., 15.
[30]   Aland and Aland, *Text of the New Testament*, 76–77.

manuscripts and the sheer effort in maintaining alert attention to the details of a manuscript while at the same time sitting in cramped positions that strained many of the muscles of the body! As the body wearied and tired, many unintentional errors crept into the copies whether those prepared in the scriptorium or in the cell of a monastery.[31] There is a greater stabilization in the biblical text after around 850 CE and the variants decline, but they were never completely eliminated.[32]

The estimated fluidity of the text in its initial stages makes the task of textual critics formidable. In several cases it is possible to determine that a text was changed for theological reasons,[33] but often it is not. Could a corrector of a text actually have returned or tried to return the text to its original (and better?) state?[34] Epp suggests that rather than seeking an original text, textual scholars are now more likely to be looking for "several layers, levels, or meanings" of the text, though he prefers to call them "dimensions of originality."[35]

When the books of the NT were first written, preserved, reproduced, and circulated in the churches, they were hand copied. Over time and depending on the amount of use of the manuscripts, they wore out and were discarded or stored in a variety of ways, but before they were retired, new copies of earlier copies were made.[36] In the last 120 years or so, thousands of Greek manuscripts and fragments of manuscripts of the NT writings have been discovered and many of them continue to be investigated. In terms of the NT manuscripts, roughly only eight percent of these cover most of the NT writings and the vast majority contain only small portions of the NT writings and most exist only in fragmentary form.

In 1994 the official registry of biblical manuscripts, the Institute for New Testament Textual Research at Münster, Germany, listed over five thousand Greek manuscripts of the NT: 115 papyri, 306 uncial manuscripts, 2,812 minuscule manuscripts, and 2,281 lectionaries.[37] In 2003, the Institute for New Testament Textual Research listed 5,735 Greek manuscripts of the NT, but now it is over 5,740 and more will undoubtedly be added to that number in the future. There are manuscripts or fragments of manuscripts that have yet to be catalogued and

---

[31] Metzger and Ehrman, *Text of the New Testament*, 25–27, provide a useful summary of the processes employed in copying Scripture in antiquity.

[32] Ibid., 275.

[33] For example, a later addition was made for theological reasons to 1 John 5:7–8, and that addition was used by the translators of the King James Bible: "There are three that bear record in heaven, the Father, the Word, and the Holy Ghost: and these three are one."

[34] M. Silva, "Response," in Black, ed., *Rethinking New Testament Textual Criticism*, 147–49, suggests that intentional alterations of the biblical text—whether for theological, historical, stylistic, or other reasons—stand behind Epp's use of the phrase multivalence of the term "original text." See Epp's essay by this title and also idem, "Issues in New Testament Textual Criticism," 74–75.

[35] Epp, "Issues in New Testament Textual Criticism," 75.

[36] See the above comments on the duration of ancient manuscripts in C. A. Evans, "How Long Were Late Antique Books in Use?"

[37] Schnabel, "Textual Criticism," supplies this information.

will soon see the light of day and the number will likely increase even more. The latest published number of NT papyrus manuscripts (the earliest collection of manuscripts dating from the second to the seventh century) now stands at 128, and that number will surely grow. The number of majuscule manuscripts or capital lettered manuscripts without spaces between the words (the next oldest collection dating roughly from the fourth to the tenth century) now stands at 310. There are 2,877 minuscule, or lower case manuscripts with running letters (roughly from the ninth to the fifteenth century), and some 2,432 Greek lectionaries (selected portions of scriptures that were read in churches) that are occasionally listed in the multiple readings in support of a text, but are seldom considered in textual evidence of readings, even though some of them may date earlier than some continuous manuscripts.[38] The numbers will continue to change as more investigations of collections in European museums and libraries are catalogued and examined by competent scholars.[39] According to Epp's analysis of the surviving continuous text manuscripts, there are 2,361 that contain one or more gospels, 792 of Paul's letters, 662 of Acts and the Catholic or General Epistles, and 287 of the book of Revelation.[40]

The major principles of textual criticism are incorporated into the more recent critical editions of the Greek New Testament, but also in newer translations of the Bible such as the recent editions of the *New Revised Standard Version*, *Revised English Bible*, *New International Version*, and the *New Jerusalem Bible*.

Readers generally understand accidental changes to the biblical text because of the difficulties involved in making copies by hand and often in difficult or uncomfortable circumstances accompanied often by dim light and eyestrain, but intentional changes in Christian biblical manuscripts present a greater challenge. As already observed, most of the changes or variants are easily identified by comparison with multiple manuscripts and they are easily corrected. Some scribal corrections were at times simply attempts to harmonize apparently contradictory passages. Most intentional changes were introduced to bring clarity to contemporary theological issues facing the church and to support various orthodox positions of the church. Ehrman cites a number of these deliberate changes in the second to the fourth centuries that reveal the orthodox tendencies to deal with the various heresies that were present in churches. As we briefly noted above,

---

[38]   These numbers are listed in the most recent edition of Metzger and Ehrman, *Text of the New Testament*, 50. The figures change almost annually as more manuscripts are found and placed in the public domain. By the time this book is published, the number of biblical papyri manuscripts and others will likely climb even higher!

[39]   Stanley Porter, a prominent papyrus scholar, recently told told me about containers of manuscripts in European libraries and museums that have not yet been catalogued, examined, and evaluated. Eventually these will doubtless come to light and be published.

[40]   Epp, "Issues in the Interrelation of New Testament Textual Criticism and Canon," 505.

the best known corruption of the biblical text for christological purposes is the *Comma Johanna* (or the "Johannine Comma") in 1 John 5:7–8 where a Trinitarian addition was introduced into the text of 1 John. This change is not found in any known Greek manuscript, but Erasmus likely translated it from the Latin Sistine [SIXT]-Clementine edition of the Latin Vulgate and inserted it under pressure from his contemporaries into the second edition of his Greek New Testament. The *Johannine Comma* includes the words: "For there are three who bear witness in heaven, the Father, the Word, and the Holy Spirit, and these three are one. And there are three who bear witness on earth, the spirit and the water and the blood, and these three are one." This addition, of course, was intended to support the church's understanding of the Trinity, but it has no Greek manuscript textual antecedent. Cyprian in the third century may have known of this addition and it may have originated in North Africa, but all of that is uncertain.[41]

Likewise, there are several additions to the end of Mark's Gospel following 16:8 that indicate that there was widespread belief that the original gospel did not end with the words "for they were afraid" (Greek: *efobounto gar*). As we saw above, a later scribe added 16:9–20, which is largely, though not completely, a summary of the conclusions of the other three canonical gospels. It is likely that a well-intentioned scribe added what was believed to be a more appropriate conclusion to a gospel about good news (compare the beginning of Mark 1:1) instead of ending the story of Jesus on a note of fear. How Mark concluded his Gospel continues to bother many scholars today. Interestingly, Codex Vaticanus ends the gospel in 16:8 in the middle of a column with scribal marks in the margins suggesting some question about the text, but uncharacteristically it also leaves a blank column (the third column, or right hand column of the page) following the ending of that gospel. Leaving a whole column blank in the Vaticanus manuscript is rare. It appears that the copier may have known or believed that something else was needed to complete a book, but was unsure what it was and simply left room for a later hand to complete. Currently a majority of NT scholars, unlike earlier, do not believe that 16:8 is the way the original Gospel ended. It appears to have been lost.

There are also some twenty variations in the NT texts on marriage and divorce in the Synoptic Gospels. The early churches had a considerable stake in this issue and a number of additions or changes were introduced into the NT texts to bring clarity to the matter often for subsequent generations of Christians facing similar circumstances. The variants in the surviving manuscripts were welcomed

---

[41] Ehrman, *Orthodox Corruption of Scripture*, 91–99, describes the history of this passage in the Christian Bible. For a brief discussion of this passage, see R. Schnackenburg, *The Johannine Epistles: A Commentary* (New York: Crossroad, 1992), 44–46. Erasmus added the *Comma* to the second edition of his Greek text.

as Scripture in the communities that received these variant texts.[42] Similarly, the role of women in the church was clearly an issue of contention for some churches as we see in the variants in the texts that mention Priscilla (or Prisca) who is sometimes diminished in stature in the ancient texts. Similarly, the reference to Andronicus and Junia, who were "prominent among the apostles" (Rom 16:7), is challenged in several *later* Greek texts, even though all of the early church fathers agreed that Junia, a female, occupied the role of apostle. One can also see this in the problematic texts of 1 Cor 14:34–35 and 1 Tim 2:8–15 that led some early churches to marginalize the role of women in their ministries.[43]

Many intentional changes were likely introduced throughout the second century before the scriptural status of the NT writings was recognized, but later changes also occurred and are difficult to explain.[44] While all of the various biblical manuscripts functioned authoritatively or canonically in the churches that possessed and read these texts, the NT texts were still fluid and at times varied considerably. Epp aptly concludes: "our multiplicities of texts may all have been canonical (that is, authoritative) at some time and place…."[45] It is likely that many of the textual variants in the NT manuscripts occurred before 200, which may suggest that the later views regarding the inspiration and inviolability of sacred texts were not yet in place with regard to several of the NT writings or with regard to prohibitions

---

[42] Epp, "Issues in the Interrelation of New Testament Criticism and Canon," 514–15, discusses this point and cites the work of David C. Parker, *The Living Text of the Gospels* (Cambridge: Cambridge University Press, 1997), 78–93.

[43] In the case of Priscilla, see Dominika A. Kurek-Chomycz's article, "Is There an 'Anti-Pricscan' Tendency in the Manuscripts? Some Textual Problems with Prisca and Aquila," *JBL* 125, no. 1 (2006): 107–28. In the latter cases, see E. J. Epp, *Junia: The First Woman Apostle* (Minneapolis: Fortress, 2005). In his discussion of 1 Cor 14:34–35, Epp calls to our attention the two dots (now regularly called "*distigme*" = two marks) in the left margin of this text in Codex Vaticanus that point to the doubts the copier had about this text. Epp also notes that the relocation of these verses after 14:40 in several ancient texts adds to their uncertainty (14–20). It is likely that Paul never wrote these verses since it would be rather difficult for women to pray or prophecy, not only with their heads covered (1 Cor 11:5), but also with their mouths shut (14:34–35)! In the case of the 1 Timothy 2:8–15 text, most NT scholars rightly, I think, do not see this as a Pauline text, but that it was written by a later hand written in the name of Paul. This view has been challenged by Philip B. Payne, in his *Man and Woman, One in Christ: An Exegetical and Theological Study of Paul's Letters* (Grand Rapids: Zondervan, 2009), 217–67, who offers one of the best discussions of 14:34–35 available on both the internal and external evidence and concludes with Epp that this passage is clearly an interpolation that interrupts the flow of the argument that Paul is making in the passage. He adds that it is a non-Pauline interpolation. He also notes that 1 Tim 2:12 is the "only verse in the Bible alleged to explicitly prohibit women from teaching or having authority over men" and says it was never intended to be a universal rule in Paul. See his full and helpful discussion of this controversial passage in pp. 337–97.

[44] See the discussion of this in Lee M. McDonald, "The Gospels in Early Christianity: Their Origin, Use, and Authority," in *Reading the Gospels Today*, ed. S. E. Porter (Grand Rapids: Eerdmans, 2004), 150–78.

[45] Epp, "Multivalence," 274–79.

against changing the texts that were simply a common convention that reflected widespread changes in all textual transmissions.[46] The second century has been called the period of most intense changes to the biblical texts,[47] perhaps because at that time their sacred status had not yet been fully established, though, as we saw earlier, several of the NT texts had been treated like scripture before they were called scripture. That factor may have contributed to many changes during the formative period.[48]

Even though some copyists of the NT manuscripts were often careful in their transmission of the biblical text, all of them nevertheless made mistakes, some major, by adding or omitting letters, words, or skipping lines or making corrective or explanatory changes in the texts.[49] Initially the copiers of the church's NT and other Christian writings were probably unaware that they were copying scriptural documents, and, because of insufficient funds to produce quality professional copies, as we saw earlier, churches occasionally used less than qualified copiers to produce copies of their cherished texts. As a result, mistakes or deliberate changes were made in the production of manuscripts of the NT writings.[50] Even when churches were able to pay professional scribes to transcribe their sacred texts, some errors or variants continued. Apparently few attempts were made to stop or correct the variants until the middle to late fourth century and thereafter when professional scribes were employed. Even then, inadvertent and sometimes deliberate changes were made in the manuscripts that were produced and copies of those were passed on in churches often *for centuries.*

The written tradition in some instances may have been circulated quickly and hastily prepared multiple copies of the autographs might not have been uncommon. For example, in the case of Paul's letter to the Romans, presumably delivered by Phoebe (Rom 16:1–2), multiple copies of that letter could have been produced for the various churches in that region and all from the same exemplar.

---

[46] H. Koester, "The Text of the Synoptic Gospels in the Second Century," in *Gospel Traditions in the Second Century: Origins, Recensions, Text, and Transmission,* ed. W. L. Petersen (Notre Dame: University of Notre Dame Press, 1989), 37, makes this suggestion.

[47] For discussion of this, see Koester, *Ancient Christian Gospels,* 275–76 and 295–302. See also his "Text of the Synoptic Gospels," 19–21 and 30–31.

[48] B. D. Ehrman, *Misquoting Jesus: The Story Behind Who Changed the Bible and Why* (San Francisco: HarperSanFrancisco, 2005), 84–89, has understood the seriousness of this problem and observes that the overwhelming number of variations in the surviving NT manuscripts actually outnumbers the words in the NT! While there is considerable agreement on most of the texts, there remain many unsolved issues regarding the original NT texts. See also Epp's "Multivalence of the Term 'Original Text'," published subsequently in Epp, *Perspectives on New Testament Textual Criticism,* 551–81, who discusses the problem of determining an original text of the NT and draws attention to the implications of that inquiry (see 561).

[49] A good discussion of the types of scribal errors may be found in Aland and Aland, *Text of the New Testament,* 282–316; and Metzger, *Text of the New Testament,* 186–206.

[50] See Metzger, *Text of the New Testament,* 15. The lack of good literary skill in the transmission of the NT writings is often seen in the earlier papyrus manuscripts.

There were likely at least five house churches in Rome at that time, but possibly dozens, and it is certainly possible that several churches would have requested copies of that letter for their congregations. Consequently, several "initial" copies could have been circulating in and around Rome in the first century and possibly all made by different copiers.[51] Since no two copies of any surviving ancient document are exactly alike, it is quite possible that while there was considerable overlap in these copies, variants in them would have been passed on in subsequent transmissions of the letter for other churches or even in the same churches. The only question here is whether there were *substantial* changes made in any of these copies, but not whether changes were made. In the early churches some copiers of the text of the NT writings apparently thought it helpful to add clarity to the NT texts they copied to make them more useful to subsequent generations of Christians.

Interestingly, Parker challenges the notion that all copiers were mindful of or even focused on the textual details in their copying of the early Christian manuscripts. With all that they had to do to select, prepare, and use the writing materials and their involvement in the final format of the manuscript, he suggests that the text itself may not have been the highest item on the copiers' agenda.[52] This lack of attention to detail among many copiers may have led to the many ancient warnings against changing the texts being copied. It appears that this warning or strong admonition against changing a sacred text was also a convention that reflected the authoritative nature and importance of a text in question, but also served to discourage a common practice among copiers who not infrequently made changes in the texts they copied.

Since no known autographs of either the OT or NT scriptures have survived antiquity, biblical scholars rely on the work of text-critical scholars and their analysis of multiple textual traditions and individual texts to make informed decisions about the earliest possible and most reliable biblical text. Discerning the earliest possible text through an assessment and comparison of many ancient manuscripts is not an exact science, and is occasionally called an art. What contributes to text-criticism being an inexact discipline is that text-critical scholars do not always agree on the various criteria they employ in the task of discerning the most reliable text of the NT Scriptures.[53] Holmes, for instance, concludes his investigation of several texts and raises questions about the viability of the

---

[51]   This suggestion comes from Eldon J. Epp, "In the Beginning Was the New Testament Text. But Which Text?," in Doble and Kloha, eds., *Texts and Traditions*, 58. He depends here on Robert Jewett, *Romans: A Commentary*, Hermeneia (Minneapolis: Fortress, 2007), 942–48.

[52]   Parker, "Variants and Variance," 29–30.

[53]   See, for instance, Eldon Jay Epp's discussion of these criteria in his "Issues in New Testament Textual Criticism: Moving from the Nineteenth Century to the Twenty-First Century," in *Rethinking New Testament Textual Criticism*, ed. D. A. Black (Grand Rapids: Baker Academic, 2002), 17–76.

traditional established text-critical criteria asking whether: "they 'help only to authenticate decisions made on other grounds, and if so, how do we acknowledge and account for them?"[54]

The more than 200,000 to 400,000 variants in the surviving NT manuscripts[55] pose considerable challenges for those involved in textual criticism. For example, in the well-known Greek Codex Sinaiticus (ca. 350–375 CE), Parker has noted that it alone contains over 27,000 corrections made in its text, "yet in spite of this number it is almost as remarkable to us how many things [in that text] stand uncorrected."[56] For purposes of canonical inquiry, such investigations and knowledge of these variants in the NT writings raise questions about which text of the Bible is authoritative for translators and for the church today. As we observed earlier, the church initially was not focused on the text of their Scriptures so much as the books that comprised their NT Scriptures. The considerable diversity among the ancient texts, though not unlike the diversity in transmission of other ancient documents, is nonetheless evidence that for centuries the church's primary interest in canonization had to do with the *books* that were included in the church's sacred Scriptures and not their *text*, even though, as we will see in the next section, the diversity in the scriptural texts did not go unnoticed in antiquity.

Modern scholars have produced Greek texts that are sometimes referred to as "eclectic" or selective texts that depend on a variety of texts from the traditional text types to construct the best and most reliable NT text. This perspective is now represented in the UBS[5], Nestle-Aland[28] texts, and in Michael W. Holmes, *The Greek New Testament: SBL Edition* (2010).

Despite the diversity in the ancient texts, most if not all of them were considered canonical scripture in the churches that had them and used in worship, instruction, and Christian living. What brought these texts – and their variety of changes and

---

See also his "Traditional 'Canons' of New Testament Textual Criticism: Their Value, Validity, and Viability – or Lack Thereof," in *The Textual History of the Greek New Testament: Changing Views in Contemporary Research*, ed. Klaus Wachtel and Michael W. Holmes, SBLTCS 8 (Atlanta: Society of Biblical Literature, 2011), 79–128.

[54] Michael W. Holmes, "When Criteria Conflict," in Doble and Kloha, eds., *Texts and Traditions*, 11–24, here 24.

[55] Ehrman, *Misquoting Jesus*, 89–90, claims that there are between 200,000 and 400,000 known variants in the more than 5,700 known Greek manuscripts of the NT! He earlier notes that in 1550, John Mill, fellow of Queens College, Oxford, surveyed some one hundred NT manuscripts, as well as patristic citations and versions of the NT, and made the disturbing discovery of some 30,000 variants in them (83–88). Eckhard J. Schnabel, "Textual Criticism: Recent Developments," in *The Face of New Testament Studies: A Survey of Recent Research*, ed. Grant Osborne and Scott McKnight (Grand Rapids: Baker Academic, 2004), 59, suggests that of the more than 5,600 Greek NT manuscripts known at the time of his writing, and the approximately 9,000 versional manuscripts, there are probably some 300,000 variant readings!

[56] David C. Parker, "Variants and Variance," in Doble and Kloha, eds., *Texts and Traditions*, 31.

interpretations – into a manageable collection? The level of diversity in the texts was always held in some check by the church's *regula fidei*. For example, in the details in the story of the Prodigal Son (Luke 15:11–32), the early Christians could allow for some variation in a few minor details of wording, but would never have accepted changes that led the father to reject the returning son or whether the elder brother welcomed him home. There were limitations to the diversity allowable in *most* cases. Also, most of the changes in the texts favored the orthodox traditions circulating in the churches. They did not tend toward the so-called heretical movements in the second and third centuries. There was some acceptable diversity in the churches' Scriptures, but the church's tradition imposed limitations on the amount of diversity that could be tolerated. The church's vigorous defense against heresy in the second through the fourth centuries testifies to the kinds of limits that were acceptable.

Ehrman's conclusion, based on his examination of multiple ancient manuscripts, is that "the texts of these books were by no means inviolable; to the contrary, they were altered with relative ease and alarming frequency," but he acknowledges, as we saw earlier, that "most of the changes were accidental, the result of scribal ineptitude, carelessness, or fatigue. Others were intentional, and reflect the controversial milieu within which they were produced."[57] Evans illustrates from three well-known textual variants that changes were made in the transmission of Christianity's sacred literature. The first of these is the long ending of Mark's Gospel (Mark 16:9–20) that almost all grammarians, textual critics, and commentators agree was not the original ending of Mark's Gospel.[58] It could well be that the original ending that came after 16:8 was lost as the result of damage to the manuscript or for some other reason,[59] but most agree that 16:9–20 was a late intentional insertion into the text of Mark. Evans also discusses John 7:53–8:11, another insertion into a biblical text, adding that if this text was not an original part of John's Gospel, nothing of great significance would be lost. Finally, he observes that Luke 22:43–44 (compare with Matt 26:36–46; Mark 14:32–42; cf. Luke 22:39–46) focuses on the prayer of Jesus with an insertion into the text of an angel appearing from heaven and Jesus sweating as it were drops of blood. These verses are not in the oldest manuscripts but it seems clear that a scribe

---

[57]   Ehrman, *Orthodox Corruption of Scripture*, 275, contends that many of the debates over Christology affected the accuracy of the transcription of the NT manuscripts (274–80). For a helpful discussion of the kinds of variants or changes made in the transmission of the ancient manuscripts, see Metzger and Ehrman, *Text of the New Testament*, 250–71.

[58]   Craig A. Evans, "Textual Criticism and Textual Confidence: How Reliable Is Scripture?" in *The Reliability of the New Testament: Bart D. Ehrman and Daniel B. Wallace in Dialogue*, ed. Robert B. Stewart (Minneapolis: Fortress, 2011), 161–72.

[59]   A majority of biblical scholars today agree that 16:9–20 was not the original ending of Mark's Gospel, but they disagree over whether 16:8 was the actual ending. For a discussion of this, see N. Clayton Croy, *The Mutilation of Mark's Gospel* (Nashville: Abingdon, 2003). He offers a helpful list of scholars who have taken various positions on this matter (174–77).

wanted to insert them into the text early on to enhance the drama and experience of Jesus.[60]

We stated earlier that Helmut Koester claims that the most significant corruptions of the NT Gospel texts came during the first and second centuries.[61] Although, for some textual critics, the evidence for this is not compelling and is mostly inferential based on the lack of a fixed collection of Christian scriptures throughout most of the second century, the variety and number of variants in the third- and fourth-century manuscripts suggests that Koester may be right.[62] This coincides with the fact that while several NT writings were read and cited in the second-century churches, initially they were generally not yet called "scripture" before the middle to end of that century. *Minor* changes in these texts would not likely have caused much concern *at that time*. Radical changes that denied the church's most important sacred traditions about Jesus or the early churches, however, would not have been welcomed or continued in textual transmission. Most would agree here, but we should note that the amount of evidence from this period that can inform us on such textual changes in the second century is meager, namely two small fragments of the Gospel of John (P^{52} and P^{90}) and citations from a few church fathers. Consequently, it is best to be cautious about the amount of changes to the biblical texts in the second and third centuries. Some copies of early manuscripts of NT texts were produced in a responsible and careful manner (e.g., P^{66}, late second century, and P^{75}, early to middle third century), as we will note below.

Some early copiers of the NT texts display skill in their attention to the details of the texts that they copied. Michael Holmes reminds us that "the scribe of P^{75} is one of the best workmen ever to copy a biblical text" and adds that unlike this copier, the later "scribe of Beza – quite apart from the character of the text he was copying – is not a careful workman."[63] Larry Hurtado makes similar qualifications about the quality of transmission of texts in the early churches, adding that while some copiers of early biblical literature may have been "amateurs," it may be

---

[60]   Evans, "Textual Criticism and Textual Confidence." He also cites Raymond E. Brown, "The Lucan Authorship of Luke 22:43–44," in *Society of Biblical Literature 1992 Seminar Papers*, ed. E. H. Lovering Jr. (Atlanta: Scholars Press, 1992), 154–64; and Bart D. Ehrman and M. A. Plunkett, "The Angel and the Agony: The Textual Problem of Luke 22:43–44," *CBQ* 45 (1983): 401–16.

[61]   Koester, "Text of the Synoptic Gospels," 37.

[62]   See Kruger, "Early Christian Attitudes," 63–80. He challenges Helmut Koester and others, including me, who point to the many textual variants, including the intentional variants in the earliest surviving NT manuscripts, as evidence for a fluid period of scriptural identification in the early churches. No one doubts the existence of textual variants, but I contend that they reflect that most (not all) of the copies of the NT manuscripts initially were prepared by amateur copiers whose major concerns did not include textual consistency. That accounts for many of the variants, but not the intentional variants that were either added for clarification or to include current issues facing later churches.

[63]   This quote comes with appreciation from Professor Michael Holmes in personal correspondence, August 16, 2005.

better to say that *some* of the earliest biblical manuscripts produced in the early churches "seem largely to be by skilled scribes, but apparently not of formal book hand quality" which, he says, is "likely a reflection of the socio-economic level of most Christians: able to afford a skilled copyist, but not able to afford the luxury trade."[64]

Most of the variants in the NT manuscripts are obviously unintentional copying errors and are easily understood and corrected. Intentional changes were much fewer in number and often had the aim of either correcting what was believed to be an error in the text, clarifying a text for a particular community of Christians, or promoting a particular bias such as bringing the biblical texts in line with current orthodox beliefs and practices of the communities that received and used these texts. Swanson addresses the many intentional changes in the biblical texts even after their scriptural status had been determined. He claims that these changes in the text demonstrated the

> freedom scribes exercised in the transcription of the text. Evidently there were scribes who did not have a concept of the inviolable nature of the text of scripture. They exercised their freedom to innovate and to express in their own language what a passage of scripture meant to them... The living character of the tradition is perhaps the most possible explanation to account for the marked changes that took place in the sources over the centuries.[65]

Some of the variants in the ancient manuscripts make the work of text critical scholars quite challenging and in several instances their conclusions about the original text are admittedly educated guesses. Metzger and Ehrman offer this sobering conclusion:

> Although in very many cases the textual critic is able to ascertain without residual doubt which reading must have stood in the original, there are not a few other cases where only a tentative decision can be reached, based on an equivocal balancing of probabilities... In textual criticism, as in other areas of historical research, one must seek not only to learn what can be known but also to become aware of what, because of conflicting witnesses, cannot be known.[66]

All ancient biblical manuscripts were copied by hand from earlier copies and the changes in them multiplied in transmission over many centuries. The trained eye readily identifies most of the accidental and even most intentional changes, but what accounts for them is not always clear. Swanson is aware of the daunting challenges before text-critics in establishing the earliest and most reliable NT

---

[64] These comments are from personal correspondence with Professor Hurtado on September 29, 2006.

[65] Some of these intentional changes are discussed in Reuben Swanson, ed., *New Testament Greek Manuscripts: Variant Readings Arranged in Horizontal Lines Against Codex Vaticanus: Romans* (Wheaton, IL: Tyndale House Publications/Pasadena, CA: William Carey International University Press, 2001), xxv.

[66] Metzger and Ehrman, *The Text of the New Testament*, 343.

texts. He also makes the point that despite the many differences in the texts, each manuscript, regardless of the textual changes made by the copiers, was scripture in an early Christian community.[67]

IV. ANCIENT ACKNOWLEDGMENT
OF TEXTUAL VARIANTS

As we saw, until the fourth century, those who copied the church's Scriptures were often less trained than the skilled handbook quality of scribes who were employed to copy formal literature. The rapid spread of the Christian churches in the first few centuries led to the need for many more copies of the church's scriptures, and it appears that those who made the copies sometimes made them in haste. Paleographers, who study ancient handwriting, have identified four basic types of scribes who produced the ancient manuscripts, namely those with the *professional* hand who gave careful attention to detail and excellent craftsmanship (P[46], P[75]), the *documentary* hand who was an experienced literate copier (ca. 200–225), the *reformed documentary* hand that was used in copying literary documents and is called a "book hand" or "literary hand," and finally the *common* hand that was semi-literate and untrained in making documents and is characterized by an inelegant cursive hand. Biblical manuscripts reflect all of these hands including at times the last of these as well.[68] Because some skilled scribes and other lesser skilled literate "amateur" scribes who produced the earliest copies of the NT writings did not generally have the handbook quality skills, it is not surprising to find many errors in the copies they produced.[69]

Metzger and Ehrman acknowledge the different level of skills among copiers and explain why NT manuscripts of the first two centuries were considerably more prone to error:

> The earliest copyists would not have been trained professionals who made copies for a living but simply literate members of a congregation who had the time and ability to do the job. Since most, if not all, of them would have been amateurs in the art of copying, a relatively large number of mistakes no doubt crept into their texts as they reproduced them. It is possible that after the original was placed in circulation it soon became lost or was destroyed, so all surviving copies conceivable have derived from one single, error-prone copy made in the early stages of the book's circulation.[70]

---

[67]   Swanson, *New Testament Greek Manuscripts*, xxv–xxxi.

[68]   See Philip W. Comfort and David P. Barrett, eds., *The Text of the Earliest New Testament Manuscripts*, rev. ed. (Chicago: Tyndale, 2001), 15.

[69]   Metzger and Ehrman, *Text of the New Testament*, 24–25.

[70]   Ibid., 275. Again, the life expectancy of a biblical manuscript that was regularly and frequently used as an exemplar may not have been more than a generation, but it was possible for it to have a much longer shelf life as Evans noted above, perhaps from 100 to 200 years.

Perhaps, we are on more certain ground by suggesting that a large number of the copies and early translations of the biblical literature were made by those with good intentions, but *sometimes* with amateur skills. Metzger and Ehrman cite Augustine who, wistfully reflecting on the frequent mistakes in translating the biblical manuscripts, says: "anyone who happened to gain possession of a Greek manuscript and who imagined that he had some facility in both Latin and Greek, however slight that might be, dared to make a translation" (*De doctrina Christiana* II.xi.16).[71]

Several ancient church fathers commented on the diversity and errors in the NT texts that were circulating in the churches, but overall *little was done* to correct them. Irenaeus (ca. 170), when discussing the number 666 in Rev 13:18, acknowledged the problem of errors among copies of existing manuscripts as well as the lack of original texts to correct them. He concluded that the evidence supports the number 666, but then adds: "I do not know how it is that some have erred following the ordinary mode of speech, and have vitiated the middle number [6] in the name…" He goes on to say that he is "inclined to think that this occurred through the fault of copyists, *as is wont to happen*, since numbers are also expressed by letters; so that the Greek letter which expresses the number of sixty was easily expanded into the letter Iota of the Greeks." After explaining how changes may have happened, Irenaeus warns those who deliberately change the sacred texts, adding that "there shall be no light punishment [inflicted] upon him *who either adds or subtracts anything from the Scripture*" (Irenaeus, *Haer.* 5.30.1, ANF, emphasis added). Eusebius notes that Irenaeus also warned those who would later copy his own work that they take diligent care not to change his treatise. For example, Eusebius reports the conclusion of Irenaeus' closing comment about his text *On the Ogdoad.* It reads:

> I adjure you, who shall copy out this book, by our Lord Jesus Christ, by his glorious advent when he comes to judge the living and the dead, that you compare what you will transcribe and correct it with this copy that you are transcribing, with all care, and you shall likewise transcribe this oath and put it in the copy. (*Hist. eccl.* 5.20.2, LCL, adapted)

This passage shows both Irenaeus' attempt to make sure that copiers of his book make carful use of his exemplar, but it also shows his awareness that editorial changes of texts were quite common in antiquity, hence a warning by the power of a divinity.[72] Not only were those who made copies of the NT writings admonished in the name of God to be careful in making copies of these texts and not to make any changes to them, so also were other writers of antiquity. Changes in the texts that transcribers were copying was not uncommon in antiquity and the vast number of

---

71   Ibid., 24–25.
72   Parker, "Variants and Variance," 25–26.

variants in the NT writings suggest that in several instances those who copied the NT writings may not have been as careful as some have argued. Ancient authors knew that what they wrote could and often would be wrongly copied or intentionally changed.

Origen's knowledge of such errors in the church's scriptural texts is seen in his concern for eliminating them in a comparison of the leading texts of the HB and OT of the Jews and Christians in his *Hexapla* (or Six-Columned Bible) in the third century. He included critical marks in his text to say what he thought should be omitted and what he thought should be included in his attempt to revise and correct the Septuagint (LXX).[73] The notion of an inviolable text, perhaps a convention of the times, still points to the importance of a text in the view of its author (Rev 22:18–19) that the text must go unchanged. Jerome was also aware of the deliberate and accidental changes in the biblical texts and was commissioned by Pope Damasus in 384 to produce a Latin text of the Scriptures that eliminated these errors. His Latin Vulgate was initially challenged, but eventually it was received with wide acclaim in the church. It is apparent that most others did not share Jerome's concern over the errors in the biblical manuscripts and only rarely did the early churches take steps to deal with them. The above not withstanding, until the time of Erasmus in the sixteenth century, it appears that no significant effort was given to stabilizing the NT texts or dealing with the many errors present in them.[74]

The early church fathers were clearly aware of textual variants in the biblical scriptures circulating among churches in the ancient world. Some copyists saw that other antecedent manuscripts differed from the ones they knew, and occasionally some of them made what they thought were corrective changes in order to get back to what they believed was the original text of Scripture – or at least to clarify its meaning. Differences or variants in the manuscripts circulating in churches were well known to several early church fathers. Numerous questions about the original text of the Bible still persist among scholars, but there is no doubt that the variants are plentiful in the surviving manuscripts.

---

[73] See Bruce M. Metzger, "Explicit References in the Works of Origen to Variant Readings in New Testament Manuscripts," in *Biblical and Patristic Studies in Memory of Robert Pierce Casey*, ed. by J. N. Birdsell and R. W. Thomson (Freiberg: Herder, 1963), 78–95, repr. in B. M. Metzger, *Historical and Literary Studies* (Leiden: Brill, 1968), 88–103. I learned these works from Michael Holmes, "Textual Criticism," in *New Testament Criticism & Interpretation*, ed. D. A. Black and D. S. Dockery (Grand Rapids: Zondervan, 1991), 101–34.

[74] For a discussion of this concern, see B. M. Metzger, "St Jerome's Explicit References to Variant Readings in Manuscripts of the New Testament," in *Text and Interpretation: Studies in the New Testament presented to Matthew Black*, ed. E. Best and R. McL. Wilson (Cambridge: Cambridge University Press, 1979), 179–90.

Scholars disagree over whether these variants reflect a different attitude toward the NT texts in their early transmission. Kruger has also listed several of the early church fathers' responses to the willful changes in the churches' NT manuscripts, noting that while the variants were there, there was regularly an attempt to correct them and bring them into line with what was believed to be true and correct or original.[75] He draws attention to the early church fathers' reflections on Deut 4:2 that warned against changing sacred texts (deleting or adding to them), but is aware of the challenge of multiple variants in the NT manuscripts. He acknowledges that "it seems evident that two historical realities *coexisted* within early Christianity: early Christians, as a whole, valued their texts as scripture and did not view unbridled textual changes as acceptable, and at the same time, some Christians changed the New Testament text and altered its wording (and sometimes in substantive ways)."[76] His article challenges my conclusions about the earliest transmissions of the NT texts, namely that they were not initially viewed as sacred Scripture, but he is careful not to deny what is obvious – that the variants in the texts are sometimes significant and occasionally intentional. Whether Deut 4:2 was simply a convention used by ancient authors who wanted to make sure that no one changed what they wrote is not clear, but it is apparent that the admonition was seldom followed.

Many, if not most, of the intentional textual changes were likely made in good conscience with the aim of clarifying or improving the meaning of the biblical text for a subsequent generation of Christians. No doubt all intentional changes have not been clearly identified or explained thereby leaving some questions unanswered about the authenticity of several NT texts. Most of the intentional changes that were made, however, were also favorable to and supportive of orthodox Christianity.[77] The many variants in the NT manuscripts, and the early church fathers' awareness of them and displeasure because of them, suggests that there were efforts to correct them or find ways to eliminate the changes. Kruger correctly draws attention to several examples of the early church fathers' concerns about the variants and changes in the texts of the NT scriptures,[78] but he is aware that those concerns did not eliminate the variants. The sometimes lack of care with which the manuscripts were copied did not go unnoticed, but there were early examples of well-copied manuscripts, as we saw in P[75] and many other manuscripts in the Alexandrian family of biblical manuscripts. Some text traditions, as we saw especially in the Western texts, often show little correlation

---

[75]   Examples of this are in Kruger, "Early Christian Attitudes," 69–80.

[76]   Ibid., 79. Emphasis his.

[77]   Hull, *Story of the New Testament Text*, makes a compelling argument for the proto-orthodox focus of most of the intentional changes to the biblical text. He draws attention to scribal errors that needed correction, but also to necessary changes to clarify the meaning of the text for Christians in a later generation. See my brief review of this volume in *Int* 67 no. 1 (2013): 84–85.

[78]   Kruger, "Early Christian Attitudes," see especially 75–79.

between the recognition of the sacredness of the NT writings and carefulness in their transcriptions. Some Christians were simply not careful in transmitting their sacred scriptures,

Metzger and Ehrman have observed that in producing the early Christian manuscripts, "the speed of production sometimes outran the accuracy of execution."[79] Some copiers, however, were much more careful and quite skillful.[80] That notwithstanding, accidental errors were still present even among the best manuscripts prepared in the fourth century and later well-intentioned and well-trained scribes were also susceptible to a careless moment. The quality of transmission of ancient biblical manuscripts differs from one another in quality in greater or lesser degrees, and the variations in the biblical texts, patristic citations, and lectionaries are considerable. The challenge as a result of this study is to decide which text of the NT scriptures is authoritative for churches today. Although laity dependence on whatever translation they favor will not likely change, a curious pastor and Bible teacher in a local church will occasionally want to know which text is authoritative for the church today. That remains a challenge for text critical scholars.

V. A STABILIZED GREEK TEXT

Erasmus of Rotterdam produced the first published Greek text of the NT in 1516 and it was based primarily on two twelfth-century minuscule manuscripts that he found at the university at Basle, Switzerland. In his subsequent editions, he included five or six additional Greek manuscripts, but none of them dated before the tenth century. His Greek text also included a correction of several Latin translations in Jerome's Vulgate, as well as texts from a late edition of the Vulgate that he translated into Greek when he found the Greek text lacking, as in the final six verses of Revelation and in the Johannine *Comma* (1 John 5:7–8) that was discussed above.

---

[79] Metzger and Ehrman, *Text of the New Testament*, 24.

[80] Ibid., 276–77. They describe the characteristics of the Western text family that was used by Marcion, Irenaeus, and Tertullian. The chief witnesses of the Western text include P^{48}, P^{38}, as well as Codex Bezae (D) and Old Latin versions. For a useful discussion of the variants in these and other NT manuscripts, see Aland and Aland, *Text of the New Testament*, 282–316, and Metzger and Ehrman, *Text of the New Testament*, 186–206. Some of these changes are also summarized with illustrations in Paul D. Wegner, *Journey from Texts to Translations*, 225–26, and in Arthur G. Patzia, *The Making of the New Testament: Origin, Collection, Text and Canon*, 2nd ed. (Downers Grove, IL: InterVarsity, 2011), 230–35, Patzia provides a helpful description of accidental changes (230–35) and intentional changes (235–47) in the NT texts.

Erasmus' first edition of the Greek Text in 1516 was revised four more times in 1519, 1522, 1527, and 1535. The first edition contained hundreds of typographical errors that reveal the haste in which Erasmus prepared his text. Theodore Beza finally revised it again and produced his own Greek text relying heavily on Erasmus' text. This became the textual basis for the NT in the *King James Version* of the Bible.[81] Beza's Greek text was eventually called the *textus receptus* or the "received text" because for generations biblical scholars based their translations and exegesis of the NT on it.[82] While there is little substantial theology lost by using the King James translation, and little of significant theological matter changed by it, it is nonetheless an inferior translation in that it does not generally reflect the earliest and most reliable text tradition of the Greek NT. It includes many additions to the biblical text, most notably John 3:13b; 7:53–8:11; Mark 16:9–20; and 1 John 5:7–8 and others. The more equivocal texts, such as 1 Cor 14:34–35, when seen in the earlier manuscripts such as Codex Vaticanus, have the *distigme* dots in the margin of the text along with the internal flow of the passage, which suggest that the passage has a questionable status in that context. These dots, however, are absent in the later *textual receptus*.

All translators and interpreters of a NT text know the importance of discerning the most reliable biblical text. They are especially concerned with the evidence that supports authenticity and they generally rely heavily on the most recent editions of the Greek NT, namely the Nestle-Aland 28th edition (N/A[28]) of *Novum Testamentum Graece* and the United Bible Society's fifth edition (UBS[5]) of *The Greek New Testament*. I would add that Michael Holmes' *The Greek New Testament* (SBL Edition, 2010) has some 500 differences in his text from the N/A[28] and UBS[5] editions (which essentially have the same text but with different footnotes) and Holmes' text is arguably based on a careful evaluation of the texts in multiple manuscripts, e.g., Mark 1:1; and the later inserted connection of 5:21 with 5:22 that Holmes rightly finds not supported in the best surviving Greek texts. The editors and managers of these major editions know well that many factors are involved in establishing a reliable Greek text, including discerning not only the earliest text, but also the most reliable text. It is also quite possible to produce a very good translation of an inferior early Greek text as well as a poor translation of a very reliable Greek text! Most textual scholars today prefer those texts that have been identified as Alexandrian texts to the Western and Byzantine texts (the so-called *Textus Receptus* or "received text"), with some exceptions as noted above.

---

[81]   See Metzger and Ehrman, *Text of the New Testament*, 142–49, for a more complete discussion of Erasmus' contribution to the stabilization of the Greek text of the NT.

[82]   Ehrman, *Misquoting Jesus*, 78–83, relates that the origins of the term "received text" (*Textus Receptus*) comes from Abraham and Bonaventure Elzevir, who produced an edition of the Greek New Testament in 1633 and told their readers "You now have the text that is *received by all*, in which we have given nothing changed or corrupted" (82, emphasis added).

Again, the diversity in the ancient NT *texts* is evidence that for centuries the church's primary focus in canon formation was on *books* of the Bible and not on the integrity of the biblical text itself. Clarke recognizes this and, in my opinion, correctly observes that there is little ancient concern about a single canonical text of the Bible and the diversity of ancient biblical texts shows that there is no single ecclesiastical form of text.[83] Given the large number of variants and modifications in the ancient NT texts, can all of the diversity be brought into a manageable and reliable biblical text? That, of course, is a significant challenge for scholars today. Undoubtedly the church's traditions, councils, and orthodoxy influenced, and to some extent limited, the scope of the intentional changes in these ancient texts. The church's canon of faith, or the *regula fidei*, was clearly operative during the transmission of these texts and Ehrman is no doubt correct when he observes that loyalty to orthodoxy often affected their transmission. The early church's vigorous defense against what it called heresy in the second through the fourth centuries and even later testifies to the limits of diversity that was acceptable in the ancient churches. This tendency toward orthodoxy in the textual changes is attested in the NT manuscripts.

Ehrman also observes that some of the ancient Christian scribes often "altered the words of the text by putting them 'in other words.' To this extent, they were textual interpreters. At the same time, by *physically* altering the words, they did something quite different from other exegetes, and this difference is by no means to be minimized." He concludes that only from a distance, namely ours, can we evaluate the causes and recognize the effects of these kinds of scribal modifications, and so designate them "the orthodox corruptions of Scripture."[84]

It may be worth noting that throughout the church's history it has carried on its ministries and established its doctrines without the use of the elusive *original* manuscripts of the NT, or even an eclectic text of modern construct. No ancient or modern translation is based on the elusive "original manuscripts" and their absence has not hindered the church from using the only biblical texts that it possesses in its worship, instruction, and mission, namely the eclectic constructs that exist today. Despite the many variants and uncertainties in those manuscripts, all of the NT manuscripts functioned canonically in the communities of faith that received them, and used them in their worship and catechetical training and mission. In other words, while the biblical texts that informed the early Christians contained many transcriptional and intentional alterations, they nevertheless functioned as scripture for those who had them. We do not know of a time when all of the original texts

---

[83] See Kent D. Clarke, "Original Text or Canonical Text? Questioning the Shape of the New Testament Text We Translate," in *Translating the Bible: Problems and Prospects*, ed. S. E. Porter and R. S. Hess, JSNTSup 173 (Sheffield: Sheffield Academic, 1999), 321–22.

[84] Ehrman offers many examples of these kinds of changes in the biblical texts in his *Orthodox Corruption of Scripture*. The quotes above are on p. 280.

of the NT informed the faith of all of the earliest churches. Most early Christians likely never saw an "original," though doubtless some did and others copied them. The loss of the original texts of the biblical literature eventually occurred and all subsequent copies were produced from copies and then copies of copies. Some of those copies were better exemplars than others and some more faithful to the earlier circulated text than others. It is sometimes assumed that the elusive original texts of the Bible were somehow pristine and more pure than the copies that have survived, but the evidence for that assumption is lacking. In the next section I will focus on what we may say about the "original" text of the NT.

VI. THE "ORIGINAL" TEXT

Which text of the NT is the "original" text? Perhaps we should instead ask which text is the "canonical" text, that is, the one that should be read, studied, and followed in the churches? Can such a text be established and how important is the pursuit of it today? Metzger and Ehrman doubt the possibility of ever recovering an original text of the NT and they cite the case of Paul as evidence against the likelihood. Since Paul often used an amanuensis (Rom 16:22; cf. also 1 Pet 5:12), is it likely that we will ever be able to get back to the very words that Paul actually wrote or dictated orally to his writers?[85] They ask even more pointedly, "what does it mean to establish an "original' text?"[86] For example, it is likely that 2 Corinthians initially existed in two or three and possibly even more pieces of correspondence. While it is highly likely that Paul wrote 2 Cor 10–13, it was probably not written at the same time or times when he wrote 2 Cor 1–9. What changes took place that allowed these two writings (or more) to be included in the same letter? The subject matter and tonal change in the letter between these two sections makes it unlikely that both sections were composed on the same occasion. Similarly, 2 Cor 6:14–7:1 is probably an interpolation into the text of 2 Corinthians, *even if Paul wrote it*! The larger passage reads more smoothly and coherently if after 6:13 one goes directly to 7:2. The place of 6:14–7:1 in the text is certainly awkward and probably is a later addition to it. Also, does Phil 3:2 begin a new letter that Paul had written later or earlier and simply was attached to the first half of Philippians? There appears to be a break in the flow and tone of the letter between 3:1 and 3:2. Were there two letters written by Paul to the Philippians and did someone (Paul?) later bring them together in the same letter? If so, what did the "originals" look like?

---

[85]   Metzger and Ehrman, *Text of the New Testament*, 272–74.
[86]   Ibid., 274.

In regard to the Gospels, Koester argues that Matthew and Luke probably used an earlier form of Mark's Gospel (the so-called *Ur*-Mark) than the one in surviving NT manuscripts.[87] Is the text of John 4–7 original or was it added piecemeal to the Gospel? The changes in location between Galilee and Jerusalem are choppy at best and it is unlikely that the stories in these chapters occurred in the sequence that they appear in John's Gospel. It is problematic to say that their sequence was an *original* part of the text of the Gospel. Did John's Gospel end with chs. 20 or 21? As observed above, there is an obvious conclusion in John 20:30–31, but the beginning of ch. 21 seems to ignore the earlier meeting of the risen Christ with the disciples and there is a problem in recognizing him in ch. 21 after they were already commissioned by him in ch. 20. Why, after they were commissioned, were they back fishing in ch. 21 instead of doing their mission? It seems clear that at the least 21:24–25 is not from the writer of chs. 1–20. The purpose of this passage appears to restore Peter back into the good graces of Jesus following his threefold denial of him, but also to explain the death of John that had likely occurred before this addition was penned. Further, was the doxology in Rom 15:33 or 16:25–27 the original ending of that letter? Changes were doubtless made during the earlier stages of the transmission of the NT writings and it is near impossible to establish from what we see in the NT writings an original text or book in several cases.

The traditional goal of textual criticism has been to establish the "original" or earliest and most reliable biblical text, but the overwhelming number of textual variants and the overlapping of several textual traditions make that goal a major challenge. Some scholars continue the hope of recovering the original texts of the Scriptures and eliminating all of the ambiguities in the present texts, but they appear now to be in a minority.[88] Many text-critical scholars conclude that unless some new manuscripts are discovered, we are about as close to the original biblical texts now as we will or can get.[89]

The methodologies employed by textual critics to establish the earliest NT text have limitations and those who investigate the ancient manuscripts are well aware that they are involved in both science and art. Doubts about the methodologies used to establish the earliest texts of Scripture linger among scholars, as we saw above, and few believe that they will ever be able establish an original text through such techniques. Some text-critical scholars are openly skeptical

---

[87] Koester, "Synoptic Gospels in the Second Century," 37.

[88] Philip Wesley Comfort, *The Quest for the Original Text of the New Testament* (Grand Rapids: Baker Book House, 1992), contends that this goal is attainable, but his arguments on pp. 19–40 are not convincing and appear to be more theologically motivated than carefully constructed. He does not adequately deal with the numerous intentional changes that the early copyists made in the biblical texts.

[89] Schnabel, "Textual Criticism: Recent Developments," 75, posits this position.

of those who believe that the establishment of an original text is still possible.[90] Epp, for instance, insists that we must now speak differently about an original text. He explains:

> It is therefore indisputable, in my view, that the often simplistically understood term *original text* has been fragmented by the realities of how our New Testament writings were formed and transmitted, and *original* henceforth must be understood as a term designating several layers, levels, or meanings, though I prefer to call them *dimensions* of originality.[91]

Having himself abandoned the quest for original texts, Epp sees a significant change in the direction of his discipline which includes the "diminution or even the abandonment of the traditional search for the original text in favor of seeing in the living text and its multiplicity of variants the vibrant interactions in the early Christian community." He concludes that the term "original" has "exploded into a complex and highly unmanageable multivalent entity."[92] Some scholars continue their hope of recovering the autographs (originals) and eliminating all of the ambiguities in the present texts, but they appear to be a minority.[93]

Some textual scholars follow now what is called a "reasoned eclectic method" that seeks to employ both the documentary evidence that examines internal criteria as well as the external manuscript traditions in seeking to recover the most reliable biblical text. Epp says this recognizes that "no single criterion or invariable combination of criteria will resolve all cases of textual variation, and it attempts,

---

[90] See Hyeon Woo Shin, *Textual Criticism and the Synoptic Problem in Historical Jesus Research: The Search for Valid Criteria*, CBET (Leuven: Peeters, 2004), 4–9. Throughout this study the usual text critical criteria are challenged and alternate criteria are employed to determine the authentic biblical text and consequently the authentic Jesus in the Synoptic Gospels. Brevard Childs also raises important questions about the criteria employed by text critics. See his Excursus I, "The Hermeneutical Problem of New Testament Criticism," in his *The New Testament as Canon: An Introduction* (Philadelphia: Fortress, 1985), 518–30. He correctly concludes that there is no "neutral text" from which one can draw a "pure textual stream" because "the early period reflects highly complex recensional activity from the outset" (525). He is no doubt correct that the NT text "reflects a pattern of much fluidity with multiple competing traditions at its earliest stage which only slowly over several centuries reached a certain level of textual stability" (526). See also the challenges to the current methodologies by J. K. Elliott, "The Case for Thoroughgoing Eclecticism," in Black, ed., *Rethinking New Testament Textual Criticism*, 139–45; by Stanley E. Porter, "Why So Many Holes in the Papyrological Evidence for the Greek New Testament?," 167–86; and by B. M. Metzger, "The Future of New Testament Textual Studies," 201–8, both in McKendrick and O'Sullivan, eds., *The Bible as Book*.

[91] Epp, "Issues in New Testament Textual Criticism," 75. He also challenges the notion that the original New Testament text can be discovered in his "The Multivalence of the Term 'Original Text'," 264–65. See also Clarke, "Original Text or Canonical Text?," 281–322, especially 285–95, who raises important questions about the ability of scholars to retrieve the original text of the NT.

[92] Epp, "Issues in New Testament Textual Criticism," 76.

[93] Comfort, *The Quest for the Original Text of the New Testament*, does not adequately deal with the numerous intentional changes that the early copyists made in the biblical text.

therefore, to apply evenly and without prejudice any and all criteria – external and internal – appropriate to a given case, arriving at an answer based on the relative probabilities among those applicable criteria."[94] There is instead a call for a greater understanding of the differences between the surviving manuscripts and the social contexts that account for them.[95]

Textual scholars are not ready to ascribe originality to any text of the modern Greek NTs, and the eclectic text that is represented in the modern Greek New Testaments noted above, so far as we can tell, never functioned canonically in any identifiable ancient church nor did it serve to advance any known church's worship, instruction, theology, or mission. There is no single NT manuscript that looks exactly like the current eclectic Greek NT. It is a modern construct but it fills a necessary and useful role today. It may not do so in the future if further discoveries are made since it is still theoretically possible that scholars will be able to get even closer to the elusive original manuscripts.

Through either "reasoned eclecticism" (Michael Holmes) or "thoroughgoing eclecticism" (J. K. Elliott and Bart Ehrman), contemporary NT textual critics now seek to establish the most reliable NT text and make more informed decisions about it.[96] Ehrman, like Epp, is skeptical about any significant changes in what we know about the original text and concludes that the practice of textual criticism today "amounts to little more than tinkering" with the text rather than significantly altering it. He suggests instead that the most important task of textual scholars today is to write a history of the development of the biblical text clarifying how the various social influences impacted its transmission.[97]

We cannot point to any ancient biblical manuscript that looks exactly like the standard eclectic Greek NT texts constructed for scholarly use today, but the present texts of the NT are the best that we now have and we are likely now closer to the originals than what any previous edition of the Greek NT has been able to achieve. What we have is workable and essential for understanding the meaning

---

[94] Eldon Epp, "Decision Points in Past, Present, and Future New Testament Textual Criticism," in *Studies in Theory and Method of New Testament Textual Criticism*, ed. E. Epp and G. Fee (Grand Rapids: Eerdmans), 35. See also Holmes, "When Criteria Conflict."

[95] For a discussion of this, see Epp, "Issues in New Testament Textual Criticism," 71–75; Elliott, "The Case for Thoroughgoing Eclecticism," states: "It may well be that modern textual criticism is less confident about the need to, or its ability to, establish the original text and that its best contribution to biblical studies is to show how variations arose, ideally in what directions, and to explain the significance of all variants," 124.

[96] These scholars' positions are explained in Michael Holmes, "The Case for Reasoned Eclecticism," in Black, ed., *Rethinking New Testament Textual Criticism*, 77–100, and Elliott, "The Case for Thoroughgoing Eclecticism."

[97] B. D. Ehrman, TC [1998]: par 22 = an online journal = *A Journal of Biblical Textual Criticism*. Epp also expresses this same conclusion in his "The Multivalence of the Term 'Original Text'." See also his "Decision Points," 17–44; "Issues in New Testament Textual Criticism," especially 70–76; and Epp, "Issues in the Interrelation of New Testament Textual Criticism and Canon."

of the NT Scriptures today. This discussion, of course, raises again the question of the canonical text of scripture for churches today. All ancient texts have some variance with the biblical texts we use today. Textual critics have solved many of the textual problems for the church today, but some still remain. Whatever an original text looked like in antiquity, we cannot say with certainty that scholars have now recovered it or found it used in any early churches. The churches, however, regularly used whatever texts were available to them to aid in their worship and to clarify their identity and mission. Just as all churches in antiquity read and made use of what they had available to them, that is essentially what churches have always done and that is what they do today.

Thomas Kraus believes that the New Testament critical editions are "on principle reliable" and they reflect a careful analysis of the manuscript tradition, but none of the critical editions considers all of the manuscript evidence that is available, nor could they do so in any reasonable format. Kraus draws attention to the fact that in constructing the best biblical text today, many pieces of information are left out of the reconstruction.[98] For example, while following J. K. Elliott's manuscript evidence from noncanonical sources in the Nestle/Aland edition of the Greek New Testament (the *Fayum-Gospel*) and in the Nestle/Aland 27th Edition (P.Egerton 2) in support of Mark 14:28 and John 5:39 respectively, Kraus acknowledges the difficulty of a stabilized collection of resources for establishing the text of the New Testament. He cites these examples to show that there is no objective selectivity going on, but rather demonstrates "the partially random selection of witnesses for establishing an eclectic text and its critical apparatus."[99] Should text-critical scholars make use of apocryphal Christian writings in establishing the most reliable text of the New Testament? This does not take place often, but it does happen and this underscores the randomness of the selectivity of resources in establishing the eclectic text of the New Testament. I agree with Kraus that while text-critical scholars are doing over-all a commendable job in establishing the earliest and most reliable Greek text, there is still some subjective selectivity involved in that process.[100]

---

[98]   Kraus, *Ad Fontes*, 25. See also the following three helpful articles on this subject that raise the question of what manuscript evidence to include in establishing the text of the New Testament, namely Gordon D. Fee, "The Use of the Greek Fathers for New Testament Textual Criticism," 191–207; J. Lionel North, "The Use of the Latin Fathers for New Testament Textual Criticism," 208–23; and Sebastian P. Brock, "The Use of the Syriac Fathers for New Testament Textual Criticism," 224–36, in Ehrman and Holmes, eds., *The Text of the New Testament in Contemporary Research*. All three of these scholars say that we should make use of these other resources, but they also caution the reader to make a careful analysis and they provide helpful suggestions on how to do this.

[99]   Kraus, *Ad Fontes*, 90–91.

[100] Swanson also makes this point in the introduction to his *New Testament Greek Manuscripts: Romans*, xxv–xxx.

VII. TRANSLATIONS OF THE BIBLE

By the year 2000, there were some 6,809 known living languages and dialects in the world and the whole Bible has been translated into 371 of them, but more have been produced since then. Portions of the Bible have been translated into 1,862 languages and dialects.[101] By the early seventh century, the Scriptures of the church existed in Greek, Old Latin, Gothic, Syriac, Coptic, Armenian, Georgian, Ethiopic, and Sogdian. Generally, the early translations were of poor quality and none of them included all of the books of the NT or in several cases *only* those books. By the time moveable type and the Gutenberg printing press were invented, the Bible had been translated into thirty-three languages and several of those translations contained only portions of the Bible.

The use of translations has been a part of the church almost from its beginning. When Jesus spoke, it is generally agreed that he spoke in Aramaic and probably also Hebrew, but he likely also had some facility in Greek, as some scholars contend. All four of the canonical Gospels were written in Greek and the words of Jesus originally spoken to his disciples were first translated into Greek from Hebrew or Aramaic or both. The Gospels were written in Greek, but many of the traditions in them were likely initially based on Aramaic and Hebrew sources, whether oral or written, and subsequently translated into Greek. This is the first known translation activity in the early churches and that perhaps was the source and motivation for subsequent translations.

One of the oldest traditions about Matthew, according to Papias of Hierapolis (60–130 CE), is that he collected "oracles" of Jesus in the Hebrew language, and "each teacher interpreted [or translated] them as best he could" (Eusebius, *Hist. eccl.* 3.39.16). However, the Gospel of Matthew as we now have it was written in Greek and it is difficult to say what was gained or lost in the initial translation of Jesus' sayings into Greek, but the early Christians took their gospel about Jesus to various places *in Greek*, the most common language in the Greco-Roman world at that time, and there is no indication that they ever thought they were taking something with them that was second rate or inferior because it was a translation. The following discussion focuses on the use, significance, and contents of early translations of the New Testament writings.

A. Early Translations of the Bible

Approximately 9,000 manuscripts of versions or translations of the NT texts have survived antiquity, but as yet their contents, namely the books in them and the reliability of the translations in which they are found, have received little attention from biblical scholars. These and other translations provide an important

---

[101] These figures come from Metzger, *The Bible in Translation*, 8–9.

lesson in the history of the formation of the NT. While some early translations have been lost, the ones that survive are an important source for letting us know what literature the recipients and their translators believed was sacred and they aid textual critics in piecing together the earliest possible text of the NT. The early Christians freely translated their scriptures into several languages including Syriac, especially the Syriac Peshitta, Old Latin, the Armenian translations, and others. Metzger and Ehrman cite Augustine, who was reflecting on the frequent mistakes in translating biblical manuscripts, in the text cited above about the often poor quality of many translations from would-be but inferior translators (see the text of *De doctrina Christiana* II.xi.16 above).[102]

Given the complexity of producing a translation, it can be assumed that when the NT books began to be translated, those writings translated were recognized for their liturgical, catechetical, and missional value for the churches. In other words, we are saying that they were mostly likely recognized as Christian Scripture or that those texts were well on their way toward that recognition. The early Christian translations of both their OT and NT scriptures are a primary resource for what the translators and churches thought was sacred literature. Because of the universal focus of their mission, Christians freely translated their sacred texts into several languages. The earliest translations of the NT were in the Old Latin, Syriac (especially the Peshitta), and Armenian, which date mostly from the third century to the fifth centuries and later. The new translations prepared for various early Christian communities formed a collection of sacred texts (a scriptural canon on a local basis). The following early translations have considerable significance for an understanding of the development of the Christian biblical canon.[103]

1. The *Old Syriac* version. Although only the four canonical Gospels are preserved in two fragmented manuscripts of this translation that dates from the fourth or fifth centuries, the original translation probably dates from the end of the second or beginning of the third century. The Eastern church fathers who used this translation often also refer to Acts and the letters of Paul.

2. The Peshitta (or *Syriac Vulgate*, designated Syr^p) likely comes from the beginning of the fifth century and contains twenty-two NT books (it omits 2 Peter, 2 and 3 John, Jude, and Revelation).

3. The *Philoxenian* version, perhaps produced in the early sixth century; also known as the *Harclean Version* because of a later revision by Thomas of Harkel in the early seventh century. For the first time in this translation the Catholic Epistles and Revelation were added to the Syrian churches' collection of scriptures.

---

[102] Metzger and Ehrman, *Text of the New Testament*, 24–25.

[103] The following list and their contents come from Metzger, *The Bible in Translation*, 25–51.

4. The *Palestinian Syriac* version (ca. fifth century). Only a few fragments of this translation exist and they include the Gospels, Acts and several (not all) of the letters of Paul.

5. The *Old Latin* versions (perhaps late second to early third century). There were a number of Old Latin manuscripts produced during the third century and later that fall generally into two categories: African and European versions. In the surviving fragments, portions of the four canonical Gospels, Acts, and portions of Paul's letters survive, along with a few fragments of Revelation. It may be that Tatian (ca. 170) used an Old Latin Version of the Gospels for his *Diatessaron*, but he may also have used a Greek text that was translated into Syriac.

6. The *Latin Vulgate* version produced by Jerome in the late fourth and likely early fifth centuries in Palestine (Bethlehem). There are a good number of surviving copies of this version containing the whole Bible but, besides the NT writings, there are two codices (Codex Dublinensis, ca. eighth century and Codex Fuldensis, ca. sixth century) that also contain the apocryphal letter of Paul to the Laodiceans.

7. The Coptic Versions (ca. beginning of the third century). Those versions in the Sahidic and Bohairic dialects are the most important among the various manuscripts that have survived, and the contents of these versions include the four Gospels, Acts, and the Pauline letters.

8. The Gothic Version (ca. middle to end of the fourth century). The earliest manuscripts of this version include the four Gospels and some Pauline letters along with a portion of Neh 5–7.

9. The Armenian Versions (late fourth and early fifth centuries). The fifteen hundred or more copies that have survived date from the eighth century and later and some have all of the NT writings, but others are missing various NT books. It is interesting that *3 Corinthians* is also in this version of the NT writings.

10. The Georgian Version. It is possible that the origin of this version goes back to the fourth or fifth century, but the oldest surviving manuscripts of it date from the ninth century. It contains the four Gospels, Acts, and the Catholic Epistles. Near the end of the tenth century, the book of Revelation was translated and added to the collection.

11. The Ethiopic Version (now in the Ge'ez language ca. as early as the fourth or as late as the seventh century). Most of the surviving manuscripts of this version date after the thirteenth century and currently it is not possible to know how much of the NT was initially translated into this language in the earliest stages of the translation since only partial manuscripts have been discovered. This version is the largest known Bible containing more than eighty books and its NT included the twenty-seven books of the NT, but also *Sinodos, 1 Clement*, the *Book of the Covenant*, and *Didascalia*.

Other later and less important translations for our purposes include the Arabic Versions from the eighth century to the nineteenth century, the Sogdian (or Middle Iranian) Version, which dates from the ninth to the eleventh century, and the Old Church Slavonic Version during the ninth century which was important especially for the Bulgarians, the Serbians, Croats, and Eastern Slavs. In the late third to early fourth centuries, some churches were planted in Nubia, but when the Arabs to the north essentially cut them off from the rest of Christendom, they declined numerically and eventually disappeared. There was considerable growth in that church during the sixth century and it is likely that a vernacular Nubian Version was produced between the third to the sixth century, but it is not clear exactly when it was translated or what was included in it at that time.[104]

The obvious point here is that these translations do not contain the same books, though they often overlap considerably in terms of the Gospels and Paul, and they often omit portions of the larger NT canon. Only one of them contains all of the NT books but it contains more besides. With the exception of Jerome's *Latin Vulgate*, none of the translations appear to have been well prepared, and Jerome did not improve on the apocryphal texts that he included in his translation, nor did he think highly of several of the NT writings in his translation of them. His Vulgate is not an even treatment of all of the books in his translation. Some of the difficulties with these early translations had to do with the problem of translating the many nuances of the Greek into other languages. Metzger and Ehrman explain that not only were incompetent translators involved in preparing many of these translations, there were also features of the Greek syntax that are not easily transferred to another language. For example, they explain that: "Latin [unlike the Greek] has no definite article; Syriac cannot distinguish between the Greek Aorist and perfect tenses; Coptic lacks the passive voice and must use a circumlocution. In some cases, therefore, the testimony of these versions is ambiguous."[105]

These various ancient translations tell us which books were received as authoritative scriptures at various times and places as well as something about the beliefs of the churches that used and transmitted them. None of the translations before the fourth century includes all of the NT books and very few after that do. There is much that we do not know about the contents of these translations, since some exist only in fragments and only a few of them have been studied adequately, but the point here is still valid, namely that most of the early versions contain *some* of the books of the NT, especially the Gospels and Paul, but not all of them and some of them contain other books besides the biblical books.

---

[104] For a summary of this version, see ibid., 50–51.
[105] Metzger and Ehrman, *Text of the New Testament*, 95.

In time, *some* of these versions expanded to include more of the canonical books, but the earliest versions often omit several NT books. The same can be said of some of the earliest Greek NT manuscripts. The NT portion of Codex Sinaiticus, for example, contains a complete collection of the NT books, but it also contains some non-canonical books (the *Epistle of Barnabas* and a fragment of the *Shepherd of Hermas*). The various churches that received the early translations generally did not have the whole Bible, but often *only* the NT books that were useful in their worship and instruction.

B. Implications

The greater church in antiquity never claimed that God inspired only one translation of the Scriptures (Greek) and that all others were uninspired. The Syriac Peshitta was surely Scripture to Syrian-speaking Christians who welcomed and used the Peshitta in their worship and instruction in their churches. They did not conclude that their Bible was less inspired than the one used by Greek-speaking Christians. The Ethiopian and Coptic Christians also had their own translations of the NT and they also accepted them as divinely inspired Scripture, not unlike Christians today who welcome as scripture whatever translations are used in their local churches. The variations in the quality of the modern translations are obvious to scholars and clearly not all are created equal.

The Latin Vulgate as a translation eventually, though not initially, came close to being *the* canonical translation for Western churches, but that was not the case in most of the Eastern churches that stayed with the Greek. No early church father made unique claims for the authority of only one translation over the many that were produced. Unlike the later rabbinic Jews, the early Christians were anxious to translate their sacred scriptures into the languages of the people they had evangelized. Some church fathers (Augustine, as we saw above, and also Jerome) noted the poor quality of several translations, but that did not deter the ancient churches from authorizing and accepting translations of their scriptures into the languages of the people.

The vast majority of Christians today cannot read their Bibles in the biblical languages of Hebrew, Aramaic, and Greek, but they nonetheless receive what they have in their native tongues as inspired sacred texts. This is not unlike what occurred in antiquity. Does the authority and inspiration of the biblical text relate only to the original language(s), or does it transcend the Hebrew, Aramaic, and Greek texts in which they were first produced? Is the authority and inspiration of the Scriptures of both Testaments the same in the large number of translations of the biblical text today? The OT Scriptures of most of the early Christians was not the HB, but rather the Greek translation of the Hebrew Scriptures. The notion that the authority of the Scriptures did not transfer to the LXX does not appear in early Christianity – even though there are considerable differences between the Hebrew and the LXX texts as we have seen earlier (and also in later translations).

What bearing does the concept of translation have on inspiration? Does the notion of inspiration apply only to the original manuscripts of the Bible (which we no longer have)? Does inspiration apply to copies of the biblical manuscripts, all of which contain mistakes of one sort or another or at least variants within the manuscripts? And what about our modern translations of the Bible that are based on an eclectic text of the scriptures that does not exist in any of the surviving manuscripts of antiquity and that have numerous variants in them? This is not an argument to abandon any views on the sacredness of the biblical books. On the contrary, I affirm that God continues to speak to the followers of Jesus in a variety of translations, some of which are better than others.

Historically, the church has not spoken with a single voice on the above matters, even though from the beginning of the church portions of the teachings of Jesus that were included in canonical Gospels were translated from Aramaic (probably) into Greek and subsequently into different languages. The church as a whole has never decided on one translation of the Bible, though there were moves in this direction (i.e., Jerome's Latin Vulgate). While many Christians still argue for the sacredness of the King James Bible, which for several centuries was *THE* translation of the Bible in most English-speaking churches, what does that say to those who speak German, Chinese, Arabic, or French or any other languages in which the Bible has been translated? Are those translations any less inspired? Certainly some translations are of better quality than others. Historically, the church has never said that only one translation was acceptable or inspired by God. I am often asked in churches, which translation of the Bible is the best and after an introduction to some of the popular translations circulating in churches, I regularly ask which one they like and read the most and I encourage them to continue reading it.

Although some Christians think that their translation, with which they are most familiar, is an inspired and authoritative translation for the church and the best translation, most thoughtful Christians know that there is more than one translation and no two of them are exactly the same. Also, the best one may not be in English. Given the variety of languages spoken in our world and the hundreds of translations operative in various Christian communities, not to mention the practice of the early churches in copying and translating their sacred scriptures, there should be no question about the status and acceptance of translations in the churches. Theological schools continue to teach seminary students the biblical languages, and I think rightly so since the essence of the message in those languages cannot be precisely translated into another language. That difficulty in translation can be seen in the Prologue to Sirach by the grandson who saw that some things in Hebrew do not translate easily into Greek. That is true in all texts produced in one language and translated into another. Something always gets lost, but more often than not, the core essence of the text in question can be fully understood. No one producing translations today suggests that any one translation of the Bible is solely authoritative for all churches, even though translators appropriately seek to produce translations that they hope will garner widespread approval in many churches, such as the popular *New International Version* and the *New Revised Standard Version*. Those of us who have worked on translations with a committee of scholars know the difficulty of getting complete agreement even in the committee of biblical scholars on the meaning of some biblical terms!

Can there be any one translation of the Bible that alone has final authority in the church today?[106] The answer, of course, is no, but we should observe at the same time that the differences in most of the recent translations of the NT are *generally* minimal with some exceptions, but most of the differences are not considered all that important. Most of the NT translations reliably tell the story of Jesus and clearly present the biblical call to an obedience of faith. Remarkably, the authority of the Bible has not been significantly affected in most churches despite fluidity in the ancient NT texts regarding the challenges associated with translating them.

VIII. CONCLUSION

The New Testament Scriptures of the earliest Christian churches differ in a number of respects from those that most Christians use to today, both in terms of the books contained in them, the texts of those books, and the translations of them. Some early Christian communities produced copies and translations of the NT books from weaker textual traditions circulating among their churches and initially they either did not know or they did not use all of the books that currently make up our NT canon. Some Christians may have adopted something like a "canon within a canon" by teaching and preaching only those books that had more relevance for their communities of faith, but it is more likely that many early churches simply did not have access to all of the books in the current biblical canon whether in the Old or New Testaments. In other cases, some early churches also accepted for centuries other books that are now considered noncanonical writings. Eventually those books, especially *Shepherd of Hermas*, *Epistle of Barnabas*, *1* and *2 Clement*, and *The Didache*, were excluded from various sacred collections and later they did not obtain canonical status. This suggests something akin to "decanonization" in

---

[106] Craig D. Allert, "Is Translation Inspired? The Problems of Verbal Inspiration for a Translation and a Proposed Solution," in *Translating the Bible: Problems and Prospects*, ed. S. E. Porter and R. S. Hess (London: Sheffield Academic), 85–113, discusses this issue and concludes that inspiration is not locked into any one translation. He calls for a redefinition of inspiration that more ably reflects the phenomena of Scripture and contends that inspiration is more appropriately related to the function of Scripture rather than to specific words of its text as we see in 2 Tim 3:16–17. He concludes that translations can in fact be inspired, "because the community views them as accurately reflecting what the community as a whole believes. This reflection is preserved in the canon and is authoritative for the historic orthodox community of faith today" (112). I think he is right!

the early churches. Both inclusion and rejection of some early Christian writings was present in various stages of the ancient churches' development of a biblical canon.

It appears that the churches that had their scriptures in translation (from the Greek) *generally* had fewer books available to them than those who had Greek Bibles, but even those who had their scriptures in Greek likely did not for centuries have all of the twenty-seven books in their collections. In several instances, they also had some extra-canonical books in their collections. As we saw, there are no NT manuscripts that contain all of the books of the NT *and no others* until around the year 1000. In all cases, however, there is no ancient view of inspiration that distinguished the translations of the NT books from those written in the Greek language. Those Christians who received their scriptures in translation also believed that God had inspired their scriptures. Remarkably, the church's oldest theological beliefs were often developed without the aid of a full or complete and carefully translated NT. Their beliefs were largely dependent on the oral and written traditions circulating in churches in the first couple of centuries and the partial collections of the NT Scriptures.

The early churches with translated Scriptures made use of them in their worship, instruction, and mission, even though the translations were not uniform in quality or in the specific books included in them, though most included one or more of the Gospels and several of the letters of Paul. Those translated collections of Scriptures did not have *all* the same books and the quality of the translations was often inferior to other translations. Nevertheless, the churches with their Scriptures in translations accepted what they had as inspired by God and they established their doctrine, worship, and mission on the basis of these translations. How significant is this? Had all of the early Christians owned and used a complete set of the NT books *and no others*, and if their NT books all had the same or a similar biblical text, would that have made any difference in the theology and life of the churches? If so, what would that difference be?

On another note, what might be gained if Christians were informed by the same texts that informed the faith of many ancient Christians, but were not finally included in the current Greek New Testaments? Swanson has raised this question and offers in a highly readable format the various readings of the New Testament books and indicates that ancient manuscripts with those texts were all read as scripture in the communities that had those manuscripts. What difference in the church's theology would some of those readings make today? Swanson suggests that it might well be interesting to pursue that inquiry by comparing the various texts that he cites in his work, both canonical and noncanonical, and what the theological implications that the intentional changes to the biblical text might make.[107] What difference would it make if the sacred books that informed

---

[107] Swanson, *New Testament Greek Manuscripts.*

the early Christians left behind also informed the faith and understanding of Christians today? This is not a call to reform the Christian Bible or its NT, but only that familiarity with the books that informed the early Christians, or some of them, need not be held at arms distance and that we may be able to learn something from them.

We will now look at some of the ancient collections of sacred Christian writings and how various NT books were cited in the early churches.

CHAPTER 20

CODICES, *NOMINA SACRA*, CATALOGUES, AND CITATIONS

I. INTRODUCTION: SOME IMPORTANT ISSUES

Was the Bible of the early churches through the first three centuries the same as the Bible that Christians use today? The short answer, as we saw in the previous chapter, is *no*, but perhaps it would be better to say *not completely*, since there are many similarities! As we saw in the previous chapter, biblical scholars today know that the early churches (roughly before 400 CE) seldom had complete copies of all the books that we now call Scripture and they often had considerably fewer books than what we have in our current NT, even if they recognized a larger collection of Scriptures. It was expensive to have a copy of every book in the OT and NT and most of the early churches would not have had a complete collection of their first Scriptures or all of their Christian Scriptures. As a result of the costs of obtaining their sacred books, they would have been quite selective in what they were able to obtain.

However, most of the churches initially and for some time would have relied on the sacred oral traditions passed on in the churches, along with the early creeds that summarized the essence of their faith and whatever Scriptures they possessed. As we saw in the books in the translations, the most popular Christian writings initially were the Gospels, especially Matthew, and some Pauline letters. However, a few churches, generally the larger and more prosperous churches, had larger collections of sacred texts that eventually made up the church's Bible. The numerous textual variants mentioned in the previous chapters let us know that the early churches were challenged in producing a unified text of their Bible, but, as we saw, it is also probable that most of them were simply not much interested in unified or harmonized texts of the biblical writings. A few notable exceptions have been noted earlier, especially Origen and Augustine, but it does not appear that most of the churches or their leaders were informed about the variants in the texts unless the variants significantly changed the content of the traditions handed on to them. Several changes in the biblical texts circulated in churches well into the second century when the majority of the NT books were not yet widely acknowledged as sacred scripture. However, multiple textual changes continued, as we saw, even long after the fourth through the sixth centuries when orthodoxy had gained almost complete sway in the churches.

By the fourth century, some church fathers showed considerable interest in preserving lists or catalogues of their sacred books that could be read in churches and that interest was coupled with identifying the books that could be or could not be read in churches. This focus seldom discussed the variants in the manuscripts that were read, but, as we saw above, some of church fathers did know that there were variants present in their sacred texts. For the most part, however, churches and their leaders in the first three centuries – the most important formative years of the church – did not focus on many of the canonical questions that trouble Bible scholars today. During that period there was no uniform view in the churches on which books were sacred, though such notions of what was acceptable are clearly detectable in various comments in the second-century church fathers. Fluidity of opinion persisted in such matters even after the emergence of various fixed catalogues of New Testament scriptures well into the fourth century when a broader consensus was emerging. Uncertainty persisted in some churches even following several early church council decisions that deliberated the scope of the church's scriptures (Hippo in 393, Carthage in 397 and 416). Some uncertainty continued whether in regard to the selection of books for the ancient manuscripts, the variants in those manuscripts, or the inferior quality of many of those translations of the NT books. All surviving biblical and non-biblical manuscripts doubtless functioned canonically or authoritatively in the ancient churches that had them. We see in them that there was widespread agreement in the churches on the value of several of NT Scriptures for the church's life and ministry, but there was no uniform agreement in all the churches on which books were sacred and could be read in church worship.

Even after the fourth- and fifth-century canon activity that led to the emergence of a fixed catalogue of NT Scriptures, some churches continued to accept several noncanonical writings as scripture and read them in their worship services. The life, ministry, and theology of all of the ancient churches were built on their use and interpretation of the sacred books in their possession, as well as the traditions and creeds they had received along with those books. Remarkably, the differences in the books included in their Scripture collections, along with the variable texts in those Scriptures, do not appear to have inhibited the church's ministry and growth or its ability to conceptualize its theological positions. In other words, no councils that rejected heretical views circulating in churches did so on the basis of which books those churches read or the variant texts in them, but rather on their acceptance of the sacred traditions that were circulating in the churches from their beginning and whether the books they were reading conformed to those traditions.

The processes that led to the listing of NT writings in a fixed catalogue of sacred scriptures *began* in the first century, but the stabilization or fixing of these catalogues or lists did not come much before the fourth century and then only for some churches. The early churches showed little interest in a fixed collection or uniform text of its sacred texts. Most Christians were familiar with one or more of the canonical Gospels by the end of the first century and some had begun collecting and circulating some of Paul's writings by at least the end of the first century. However, it took much longer for all of the NT writings to gain widespread acceptance as sacred Scripture and even longer to form them into a fixed collection of sacred scriptures.

In what follows, I will focus on the importance and use of the codex in transmitting the NT writings as well as more information on what is actually in many NT manuscripts, but also *nomina sacra* or sacred names in ancient Christian manuscripts and the implications of those for canon formation. I will also include a listing of citations of the NT books in the ancient churches. These all point to *operative* Christian writings in ancient churches, but in several cases also early recognition of their scriptural status in those. The early manuscripts and lists and citations of Christian Scriptures tell us about the status of the canonization of the NT in the emerging churches. These matters clarify some of the many complexities that surround the processes of canon formation and shed light on the development of the NT canon itself.

II. THE USE OF THE CODEX

A. The Birth and Use of the Codex

Soon after the birth of the early church, and probably by the end of the first century, if not sooner, the early churches showed considerable preference for the codex in transmitting their Christian writings, though not an exclusive preference since some biblical manuscripts were also transmitted in rolls.[1] The apostle Paul himself *may* have initiated the church's use of the codex (2 Tim 4:13) which made it easier to transport the early Christian scriptures and sacred texts of sayings of Jesus. By the early second century use of the codex was the most common way of transmitting Christian writings in a majority of the surviving manuscripts.

The Romans are credited with the invention of the codex and were the first to use it for non-literary documents such as one finds in contracts, bills of sale, personal notebooks, school texts, and other such items. Initially, as noted above, these codices were two boards tied together with wax on the inside on which a

---

[1]   See Hurtado, *Earliest Christian Artifacts*, who describes the early Christians' preference for the codex (43–89) and tabulates the frequency of use of the codex in early Christianity (90–93 and 209–26).

stylus could be used to write and the wax could then be erased and used again. In the first century CE, the use of wax was substituted by the use of papyrus sheets.[2] By the end of that century, the use of the codex expanded considerably and larger texts could be incorporated and transmitted in this new book format. The Roman poet Martial (ca. 82–84 CE), for example, encouraged his readers for the sake of convenience to use small codices to transport his epigrams or poems (*Epigrams* 1.2). Later he indicated that other writer's works had also been placed in this format, namely the works of Homer (14.184), Virgil (14.186), Cicero (14.190), Livy (14.190), and Ovid (14.192). At the end of the first century, about twenty percent of the Roman writings were circulated in the codex, but the majority of learned writings continued to be published in the roll or scroll format. The reverse was found in the Christians' transmission of their writings.

B. The Codex in Roman and Christian Use

By the third century CE, the codex was used in approximately fifty percent of Roman literary documents. In the fourth century, the codex had gained parity with the roll or scroll among the Romans for literary documents, primarily with the use of parchment rather than the traditional papyri sheets. According to Gamble, those who produced codices for use in Christian churches were generally aware that they were producing second-class books, or handbooks, and not formal literary writings.[3] This suggests that *initially* the early churches did not receive NT literature as sacred scripture, but rather as informal teaching materials for the church. Gamble concludes that the "fine bookhand" normally seen in literary documents is only rarely seen in Christian texts before the fourth century. They are more typically produced in the less formal round type letters often referred to as a "reformed documentary" type of writing.[4]

This predominant use of the codex in the early Christian communities (ca. 70%) may have its roots in the way that Paul circulated his letters. Early tradition points to Paul's use of the codex for letter writing to churches. For instance, the Latin term *membranai*, transliterated into Greek as μεμβράνας, is sometimes translated

---

[2]   Pliny the Elder gives a description of manufacture of papyrus sheets (*Natural History* 13.74–82), which replaced the wood and wax used in the earlier manufacture of the codex.

[3]   Harry Y. Gamble, *Books and Readers in the Early Church: A History of Early Christian Texts* (New Haven: Yale University Press, 1995), 70. He cites E. G. Turner in this regard noting that "scribes who copied on a codex of papyrus in a single column were aware that they were writing a second-class book." Gamble also discusses the origins of the codex and its widespread use in the early churches, including arguments that suggest that Paul's use of them may be the background for their widespread acceptance by the church and the continuation of their use subsequently. See pp. 49–61.

[4]   Ibid., 66–71. He also discusses the early Christian preference for the informal codices over scrolls.

"parchments" as in 2 Tim 4:13, but the term likely refers to codices.[5] Gamble suggests that the early tradition that Paul wrote to seven churches fits well with the writings regularly attributed to him, namely Romans, 1–2 Corinthians, Galatians, 1–2 Thessalonians, Philippians, Ephesians, Colossians, including Philemon, and that this accounts for ten letters attributed to Paul.[6] Circulation of Paul's writings to these *seven* churches may have inspired a similar pattern of letters to seven churches in the Apocalypse of John (Rev 2–3) and in Ignatius' letters to seven churches in the early second century. The circulation of Paul's writings to *seven* churches may imply their completeness and, despite the many items in them that focused on matters related to local churches, the letters proved quite useful to many churches in subsequent generations.

For our purposes, it is interesting that the ten letters to these seven churches (Romans, 1–2 Corinthians, Galatians, Ephesians, Philippians, Colossians, 1–2 Thessalonians, and Philemon) fit reasonably well on the normal length of a codex of approximately 200–220 pages, but not on a scroll or roll. Gamble notes that these ten letters of Paul would occupy some eighty feet on a roll or scroll manuscript, which is more than double the normal length of most scrolls in antiquity and three times the average size. On the other hand, the usual single codex at the end of the second century CE could accommodate in one volume of 200–220 pages all of the letters of Paul to the seven churches and to Philemon (= ten letters). Because Paul's letters were generally placed in order beginning with the largest (Romans) and descending to the smallest (Philemon), a volume with all of these letters to the seven churches, and in a descending sequence, only made sense if they were placed in one volume rather than in separate rolls or scrolls. The sequence, Gamble claims, would be lost if the letters had circulated in separate rolls and it is unlikely that the tradition of seven churches used in Rev 2–3 and the seven letters of Ignatius to churches would have emerged had Paul's letters not circulated together. The length of a single quire codex at the end of the second century is also the approximate length of the P[46] fragmented codex manuscript that contains the earliest collection of Paul's writings, without the Pastoral Epistles and Philemon, but with the book of Hebrews inserted between Romans and 1 Corinthians (we will discuss this document below).[7]

Before the third century, we know of no papyrus codex exceeding 300 pages; most codices were considerably smaller than that. The oldest papyrus codex containing Paul's writings, P[46] (ca. 200), originally had 208 pages. The last

---

[5] Ibid., 50–55. Hurtado discusses this possibility in *Earliest Christian Artifacts*, 76–79, and while generally sympathetic to Gamble, nevertheless is not convinced that Paul either carried with him a collection of books (codices) or whether early church history supports this interpretation, but he agrees that it is "perfectly possible" that someone in the middle of the first century could have used codices or books.

[6] I am well aware of the doubts of scholars about Paul's authorship of Ephesians, possibly Colossians, 2 Thessalonians, and the Pastorals, but that is not a part of the discussion here.

[7] Gamble, *Books and Readers*, 58–66.

fourteen pages are missing, but the volume was comprised of fifty-two papyrus sheets folded in the middle with writing on both sides to allow for that number of pages. All four Gospels and Acts could be included in a single quire codex of some 200 pages, as we see in P[45] (ca. 250), which is the first known codex to include all four Gospels and in the usual canonical order, but also Acts that is separated from the Gospel of Luke. In the fourth century, and by contrast, the major scriptural majuscule codices increased in size to well over 1,000 pages. For example, the fragmentary Codex Sinaiticus (א 01) containing both OT and NT books has some 1,460 pages and the fragmentary Codex Vaticanus (03) originally had approximately 1,600 pages.[8] The technology necessary for including all of the books of the current Bible into a single codex was not available before the fourth century when multiple quires were sewn together. At that time, the codex became a more significant factor in identifying what literature functioned as Scripture in the churches. Before the time of Constantine, there is no record of a complete NT in one manuscript, let alone a complete Bible with both OT and NT. Codex Sinaiticus is the first to contain all of the books of the NT, but it also includes the *Epistle of Barnabas* and *Shepherd of Hermas*. Some scholars make a distinction between the end of Revelation and the beginning of the *Epistle of Barnabas* and the *Shepherd of Hermas*, but it is difficult to see a significance between them and the other books in that codex.

Before the third century, churches used codices that were more limited in size and there was often only enough room in these small books for one or more gospels and perhaps a few epistles, or some combination of them, but none of them had the capacity to include all of the NT writings, let alone the OT books as well. As we saw, only one papyrus manuscript contains all four Gospels plus Acts (P[45]) by the early to mid-third century and only four papyrus manuscripts have more than one gospel. These include: P[44] (Matthew and John), P[64] + P[67] + P[4] (Matthew and Luke; all three of these papyri are now commonly believed to be part of the same manuscript),[9] P[75] (Luke + John), and P[84] (Mark + John).[10] P[53] has both the Gospel of Matthew and Acts. Only fourteen papyri manuscripts of the existing 128 have more than one book in them.[11] This raises questions about the significance of the

---

8   Epp, "Issues in the Interrelation of New Testament Textual Criticism and Canon," 499 and 510–12, describes this document and others.

9   Metzger and Ehrman, *Text of the New Testament*, 4th ed., 53.

10   A recent update of the Aland lists and categories of Greek NT Papyri is in Wieland Willker online at http://www-uner.uni-bremen.de/~wie/texte/Papyri-list.html.

11   These include: P[30] (1–2 Thessalonians; third century); P[34] (1 Corinthians, 2 Corinthians; seventh century); P[44] (Matthew, John; sixth–seventh century); P[45] (Matthew, Mark, Luke, John; third century); P[46] (Romans, 1 Corinthians, 2 Corinthians, Galatians, Ephesians, Philippians, Colossians, 1 Thessalonians, Hebrews; ca. 200); P[53] (Matthew, Acts; ca. third century); P[61] (Romans, 1 Corinthians, Philippians, Colossians, 1 Thessalonians, Titus, Philemon; ca. 700); P[4] + P[64] + P[67] (Matthew, Luke; ca. 200); P[72] (1 Peter, 2 Peter, Jude [+ *Nativity of Mary*, correspondence of Paul,

codex for canon studies before it was able to contain all of the books of the NT. On the other hand, there are some fifty-two Christian papyrus manuscripts containing apocryphal literature both Jewish and Christian, much of which was discovered near the sites where biblical manuscripts were also discovered. Among this variety of apocryphal religious texts, which is not exhaustive, are the following:

> *Apocalypse of Elijah, Odes of Solomon, Testament of Solomon, Ascension of Isaiah, Apocalypse of Baruch, 4 Esdras, Enoch* (several copies), *Apocryphon of Ezekiel, Sibylline Oracles*, several gospel fragments, sayings or logia of Jesus, *Gospel of Peter, Protevangelium of James, Acts of Peter, Acts of Andrew, Acts of John, Acts of Paul, Acts of Paul and Thecla*, the Corinthian correspondence with Paul, *Letters from Abgar to Jesus and Letters from Jesus to Abgar, Acts of Andrew and Matthew, Apocalypse of Peter*, and *Apocalypse of Paul*.[12]

As a result of these finds, it is all the more important to know what writings were in the earlier codices, as much as what was not in them. The presence or absence of writings in the codices in the second and third centuries reflect what writings functioned as important (sacred?) religious texts in the communities where they were found. Also, accounting for what was *not* in them is a challenge at best during the early centuries when most if not all of the surviving manuscripts are fragmentary. Whatever else was in them is uncertain because of their fragmentary condition, but despite that, what was in the manuscripts that remain has some bearing on what books were viewed as scripture or authoritative literature in the early churches. We can go no further than the evidence allows in surmising what was in and not in these early codex papyrus manuscripts, but what we see in them is suggestive of the literature that had significance in the churches.

In the fourth century when the codex had developed sufficiently to include all of the books of both testaments, it was still unusual to find all of the books that were listed in the various canonical lists or catalogues in a single volume. The earliest manuscripts, as well as those of the fourth century and later, characteristically have a different order or sequence of books than what we are familiar with today. For example, in antiquity and in the manuscripts from the fourth century and following, it is fairly common for the book of Acts to be coupled with the General or Catholic Epistles. The Catholic Epistles in the surviving codices are also generally placed earlier in the Scripture collections than Paul's letters. The usual order of NT collections of books (e.g., Gospels, Acts, letters of Paul, Catholic Epistles), however, are often found grouped together in manuscripts following the fourth century, but the order of these groups varies. Before the fourth century,

---

3 *Corinthians*, letter from 11th *Ode of Solomon*, Melito's *Homily on Passover*, hymn fragment, *Apology of Phileas*, Pss 33 and 34]; third–fourth century); P[74] (Acts, James, 1 Peter, 2 Peter, 1 John, 2 John, 3 John, Jude; seventh century); P[84] (Mark, John; sixth century); P[92] (Ephesians, 2 Thessalonians; third–fourth century).

[12]   These are listed with particular information on their date and provenance in van Haelst, *Catalogue des Papyrus Litteraires*, 199–220.

there were multiple collections of NT books, but the sequence and groupings often varied. Generally speaking, catalogues or listings of biblical books only start to emerge in the first half of the fourth century, beginning with Eusebius, when it was possible to include all of the sacred books in one codex and at that time some stabilization of sequence of books *begins* to take place.

There are no manuscripts dating before or during the fourth century that contain *all* of the books of the NT *and only those books*. Bart Ehrman, owing to an observation by Michael Holmes, notes that of the thousands of the surviving Greek biblical manuscripts fewer than ten contain the entire Bible and only four of them predate the tenth century, and those manuscripts are missing several pages of text![13] Daryl Schmidt contends that those manuscripts purporting to be "complete New Testament manuscripts" are in fact not complete if we ask whether they contain *only* the canonical NT books and nothing else or less! He claims that the two earliest "complete New Testament" codices date from the ninth to the eleventh centuries, namely the minuscule codices 1424 and 175 respectively.[14]

As we saw, the manuscripts sometimes include noncanonical books and more often fewer books than those in the various genres in the NT. Three early majuscule or uncial manuscripts reportedly have the whole NT in them (codices Vaticanus, Sinaiticus, and Alexandrinus), but upon closer examination we see that they either do not include all of the NT books or they add additional books (see Appendix C).

According to Kurt and Barbara Aland, among the most important minuscule manuscripts only those numbered 61, 69, 209, 241, 242, 522, 1424, 1678, 1704, and 2495 are complete.[15] Many of the manuscripts that have survived antiquity are seriously fragmented. Indeed, with the exception of several collections from Egypt that we will focus on below, we are largely missing significant manuscript evidence until the mid-fourth century. Any conclusions drawn about the status of the Christian scriptures before the fourth century CE are, of course, currently tenuous, but it seems reasonable to conclude that in the late second and early third centuries copies of manuscripts of the letters of Paul (P[46]) and Gospels and Acts (P[45]) reflect the recognition of these writings as sacred scripture. There are few manuscripts available from the second and third centuries and those are fragmented. That cannot be inconsequential for our understanding of the beginning stages of early Christianity's adoption of its literature as sacred scripture. Fortunately, we have various testimonies from several church fathers in that period providing information that allows us to draw some tentative conclusions, as we will see.

---

[13]   Ehrman, *Misquoting Jesus*, 222–23 n. 13. See also D. D. Schmidt, "Greek New Testament as a Codex," 469–84, who makes a similar observation.

[14]   Ibid., 470–75.

[15]   Aland and Aland, *Text of the New Testament*, 138–40. See also Schmidt, "Greek New Testament as a Codex," 470–71, who points out the exceptions to this list.

III. THE CHRISTIAN USE OF *NOMINA SACRA*

The non-literary style of Paul's letters to churches characterizes the earliest NT writings as *ad hoc* texts addressing specific situations in churches and this may suggest a reason for their production and transmission in a codex format, namely a non-formal form of communication as in the cases of letters addressing specific situations in his churches. Abbreviations in such communications were not uncommon. In the initial stages of transmission of the Christian writings, possibly even in the late first century, abbreviations for special "holy words" such as God, Lord, Jesus, Christ, and sometimes Spirit were commonly inserted in Christian texts. These abbreviations are regularly called *nomina sacra* or sacred names and the abbreviations normally make use of the first and last letters of a word (or sometimes the first, second, and last letters of a word) with a line over the top of the letters. They are regularly used in the NT manuscripts and in time other terms were added to this collection that eventually included some fifteen such designations.[16] It is quite possible that this practice had its origin in the Jewish use of the Tetragrammaton (יהוה or YHWH) to identify the divine name of God (Yahweh). When the Jewish Scriptures were translated into Greek, it appears that some contractions of "God" (Gk. θεός) and "Lord" (Gk. κύριος) were used to identify the sacred names.

Ludwig Traube apparently was the first to coin the designation *nomina sacra* for the ancient practice of abbreviating terms in documented hand manuscripts.[17] Traube's designation caught on and it has been regularly used ever since to identify the ancient Christian contractions (or "suspensions"[18]). These abbreviations have received considerable attention in text-critical studies as well as among those who examine Christian literary manuscripts. More recently they have been an important focus in the discussions about canon formation.[19] Scholars have debated

---

[16] Hurtado, *Earliest Christian Artifacts*, 134, discusses at length not only the most frequently used abbreviations of *nomina sacra*, but also other Greek words and their abbreviations. These are listed below. Bokedal, *Formation and Significance*, 84–123, also lists these abbreviated words according to frequency, 89–90. Bokedal generally follows Hurtado's conclusions on the *nomina sacra*, and focuses on how these abbreviations functioned in regard to canon formation processes. He also generally agrees with C. H. Roberts, *Manuscript, Society and Belief in Early Christian Egypt* (Oxford: Oxford University Press, 1979).

[17] Ludwig Traube, *Nomina sacra. Versuch einer Geschichte der christlichen Kürzung*, Quellen und Untersuchungen zur lateinischen Philologie des Mittelalters 2 (Munich: Beck, 1907).

[18] A suspended *nomina sacra* example is the first and second letters in a word with a line over the top. For a discussion of these designations, see C. M. Tuckett, "Nomina Sacra: Yes and No?," in Auwers and de Jonge, eds., *The Biblical Canons*, 431–58, here 444–46.

[19] For example, Larry Hurtado, "The Origins of the *Nomina Sacra*: A Proposal," *JBL* 117 (1998): 655–73; idem, *Earliest Christian Artifacts*, 95–134; John Barton, *The Spirit and the Letter: Studies in the Biblical Canon* (London: SPCK, 1997), 121–23; and more recently, in Kruger, *Question of Canon*, 101–2; Bokedal, *Formation and Significance*, 83–123.

their origins (whether Jewish or Christian) and studied their forms (regular and derivate) and their theological implications. Scholars who have written about this practice generally agree that the reverence of the name of God is Jewish, but the debate persists about whether these abbreviations have any explanatory significance. Tuckett summarizes five common agreements among scholarly interpretations of the *nomina sacra* as follows:

> (a) the practice is well-established and consistently applied in the earliest Christian MSS we possess (and hence must go back earlier still), (b) that it is not a simple space-saving device, (c) it is probably a Christian innovation, (d) it represents an attempt to reflect the sacred, religiously "special" nature of the referents of the nouns being abbreviated in this way: hence the description "nomina sacra," (e) such sacredness is probably to be related to the reverence shown in Judaism to the divine name.[20]

The early Christians identified Jesus with κύριος and χριστός, but the distinct designations grew in number and eventually included several terms common in the early church's traditions, some of which were not in themselves sacred terms e.g., *man*, *king*, *mother*, *father*, and also others. The list of the fifteen sacred abbreviations, beginning with the most common, includes the following:[21]

The most cited group includes
Θεος = Θς (God)   Χριστος = Χρ, Χρς, Χς (Christ)
Ιησους = Ιη, Ιης, Ις (Jesus)   Κυριος = Κς (Lord)

The second most cited group includes
σταυρος = στς, στρς (cross)   Πνευμα = Πνα (Spirit)

The third most cited group includes
σταυροω = στω (crucify)   Πατηρ = Πρα (father)
ἀνθρωπος = ανος (man, human being) Ιερουσαλημ = Ιλημ (Jerusalem)
Ὑιος = Υς (son)   Ισραηλ = Ιηλ (Israel)
Πνευματιχος = Πνχς (spiritual)

The fourth most cited group includes
οὐρανος = ουνος (heaven)   μητηρ = μηρ (mother)
Δαυιδ = Δαδ (David)   σωτηρ = σηρ (savior)

It is quite possible that initially several of these so-called *nomina sacra* reflected the non-literary or documentary hand style of writing in early Christian writings since abbreviations were seldom used in literary texts. That changed in the scriptural manuscripts and soon abbreviations were used in all kinds of Christian texts

---

[20] Tuckett, "Nomina Sacra: Yes and No?," 432.
[21] This collection of abbreviated terms is conveniently listed with adaptation in Bokedal, *Formation and Significance*, 89–90. I have not included the genitive forms of the *nomina sacra* that Bokedal includes.

besides the biblical texts. That practice continued not only in sacred texts, but also in literary, and personal correspondence. These abbreviations are in abundance in ancient Christian biblical manuscripts, but also elsewhere in other Christian texts. Their presence in a manuscript identifies the text as Christian, but not necessarily as Scripture in all ancient texts using them.

Hurtado and Bokedal place considerable emphasis on the role of nomina sacra in identifying Christian sacred scripture, but Tuckett challenges whether they were all Christian designations or even whether they were invented by the Christians. He suggests that they may have originated from the church's practice of following the Jewish use of the Tetragrammaton for the name of God (YHWH), but points to several exceptions that Bokedal appears to ignore. He claims that use of the *nomina sacra* is not universal in antiquity. For example, he observes several exceptions to the notion that the *nomina sacra* are reflected in all of the church's biblical books as we see in P.Oxy. 3.407 (P^{52}), a fragment that does not contract χύριε in the *Gospel of Mary*, though ἄνθρωπος is abbreviated. Also a Michigan papyrus manuscript (designated P.Mich. 130) of Shepherd of Hermas does not abbreviate God (θεῷ), and P.Oxy. 4.656 with parts of Genesis does not contract God (θεός). In P^{72} three times χύριος is unabbreviated (1 Pet 3:12; 2 Pet 1:2; 2:9; cf. also 2 Pet 2:20).[22] Perhaps more importantly, Tuckett makes three important claims, arguing that the phenomenon of abbreviations is not confined to Christian texts and observes (1) that some were possibly produced by Jewish scribes and others by non-Christian scribes; (2), this phenomenon is attested across both canonical and noncanonical literature (e.g., *Shepherd of Hermas*, *Gospel of Thomas*, *Gospel of Mary*, and Egerton Papyrus 2), and finally, (3) that the practice of abbreviations in texts is not in itself a Christian phenomenon.[23]

Tuckett questions whether the abbreviations were initially sacred designations, certainly not all of those listed above, and he points out that Moses, Elijah, Isaiah, and other leading prophets were not in themselves given sacred abbreviations, even in biblical texts.[24] He suggests instead that the names were abbreviated to highlight an emphasis for a reader as aids when the lector read the sacred writings to a congregation.[25] Hurtado concedes some of Tuckett's points, especially that some of the *nomina sacra* were not all sacred designations and that others besides the Christians used such designations, but he concludes nevertheless that the four primary designations in question – God, Lord, Jesus, and Christ – do identify Christian manuscripts and these manuscripts are the places of the greatest consistency of use. His summary of these designations is helpful: (1) there is greater consistency in the use of *nomina sacra* than in any of the others and they

---

[22] Tuckett, "Nomina Sacra: Yes and No?," 436–42.
[23] Ibid., 442–43.
[24] Ibid., 445–46.
[25] Ibid., 431–58.

antedate the other such designations; (2) there is greater consistency in use when these four terms are in reference to God and Jesus, showing that these designations emerged as reflections of Christian reverence for Jesus and God; (3) *nomina sacra* forms are characteristic of Christian texts, but less regularly and consistent in private letters, magical texts, and prayer and liturgical texts; (4) in both biblical and nonbiblical texts some Christian scribes are more consistent than others, but the dominant pattern is clear and reflects a practice that was both impressively and quickly appropriated.[26]

AnneMarie Luijendijk has examined the *nomina sacra* in papyrus manuscripts and shows that they were also used in nonliterary texts, such as inscriptions and papyrus letters, as well as in the early Christian New Testament texts, and suggests that this phenomenon of using the *nomina sacra* in nonbiblical texts has not yet received adequate discussion. While acknowledging that scholars still debate the origin of these abbreviations and why they were used, she concludes that they all agree that the *Christian* abbreviations employed by scribes do point to manuscripts produced by Christians. She writes:

> Although the origins of the writing of nomina sacra remain under discussion, no one any longer disputes the Christian character of these contractions. As a matter of fact, scholars always interpret the presence of nomina sacra in literary manuscripts as an indicator that a Christian scribe has copied the manuscript, and apply this principle both for literary manuscripts and for epigraphical and papyrological sources.[27]

Most of the NT and other Christian writings, with the possible exception of the Gospels, were initially produced for small groups of Christians and a formal literary style was not required. The use of *nomina sacra* does not necessarily mean that all texts that included them were viewed *as sacred scripture*, but rather they show that the text was likely produced or copied by a Christian when the four most common *nomina sacra* were used. It is obvious that although the NT manuscripts include them, they are not restricted to the NT manuscripts. Bokedal's arguments for the Christian manuscripts identified as sacred Scripture because of their use of *nomina sacra* appears to ignore or not seriously consider the exceptions presented in Tuckett and Luijendijk. Bokedal claims that the *nomina sacra* "are important for the understanding of the Christian Scripture as Scripture," adding that "ritually as well as textually the *nomina sacra* set the Scriptures apart as Christian Scriptures..."[28] He oddly argues against Ulrich's

---

[26] Hurtado, *Earliest Christian Artifacts*, 125. His extensive response to Tuckett's challenge is on 109–33. This lengthy response reflects the importance of Tuckett's arguments.

[27] AnneMarie Luijendijk, *"Greetings in the Lord": Early Christians and the Oxyrhynchus Papyri*, HTS 59 (Cambridge, MA: Harvard University Press, 2008), Chapter 3: "What's in a *nomen*?" See also her study of the Oxyrhynchus papyri in Luijendijk, "Sacred Scriptures as Trash."

[28] Bokedal, *Formation and Significance*, 241–42.

view that "the books that came to be the Bible did not start off as books of the Bible,"[29] claiming instead, "On the contrary, I would argue, in corporate worship it is precisely, or at least as a rule, the biblical books are read out aloud as part of the common scriptural reading."[30] He concludes from the *nomina sacra* that "the books that came to be the Bible started, at least in part, as books with a unique status." Since the early Christian writings were read in churches, he concludes that they must also have been recognized as Scripture. He seems unconvinced by the fact that the *nomina sacra* were not used exclusively in biblical or scriptural manuscripts, but also in other Christian documents such as Irenaeus and Tertullian, and no one, including Irenaeus and Tertullian themselves, ever suggested that these two church fathers wrote Scripture.

IV. THE BOOKS IN THE EARLY CHRISTIAN MANUSCRIPTS

As we begin this section, it is perhaps wise to remember an important factor that Larry Hurtado brings to this discussion, namely that only about one percent of some 500,000 manuscripts from antiquity have been published and whatever conclusions we draw from the ones that have been published should be tempered with that awareness.[31] He also rightly calls upon biblical scholars to investigate not only the biblical but the other Christian literary texts from antiquity as well in order to see the biblical texts in their broader context. He has put together a helpful listing of these manuscripts together with important data on their origin, contents, form (whether a roll, codex, or *opisthograph*[32]), and identification. His list of manuscripts dates roughly from the second and third centuries, though some of them are from the early part of the fourth century.[33] The majority of the Christian manuscripts (approximately 70%) are in the codex form, but the roll or scroll was also used. In some cases (some 21%) the texts were written in rolls or scroll volumes, and in a few the opisthograph, or backside, of a roll, was used. As noted above, the codex was by far the most common format used for transmitting Christian scriptures, and the roll generally, though not always, for some other writings. There is an overlap in the form of the manuscripts for the same book, as

---

[29]   Ulrich, "Notion and Definition of Canon," 35.
[30]   Bokedal, *Formation and Significance*, 243.
[31]   Hurtado, *Earliest Christian Artifacts*, 24–25.
[32]   An *opisthograph* (Greek = "writings from behind") refers to a roll with writing on the front and back. This practice was unusual in antiquity and sometimes the backside of a roll was used to insert a text for personal use. In a number of cases, the text of the biblical literature was written on the backside of a roll that had other literary texts on the opposite or "recto" (horizontal) side of a papyrus or parchment sheet or roll. See Rev 5:1 where a scroll is written on both sides.
[33]   Hurtado, *Earliest Christian Artifacts*, 209–29.

in the case of the *Shepherd of Hermas*, which appears in all three forms, namely in codex, roll, and opisthograph.[34]

Besides the manuscripts with NT writings in them, occasionally unexpected non-canonical writings were also found in several ancient manuscripts and in the three major forms. None of the ancient papyri manuscripts includes all of the canonical NT books, but some of them also include several non-canonical and canonical writings together (e.g., P[72] cited above). Hurtado concludes that the "physical linkage of texts in one manuscript probably reflects a view of them as sharing some common or related subject matter or significance for readers."[35] I agree and add that this linkage in a number of examples reflects the likelihood that all of the documents in the manuscript are either sacred scripture or important authoritative texts for the community that viewed them bound together.

While most of the early surviving papyrus manuscripts were discovered in Egypt, we must ask how representative Christianity in Egypt was of the rest of the Greco-Roman world. Because of the dry climate in Egypt, more ancient manuscripts survived there than elsewhere, but are the manuscripts discovered there representative of the wider Christian community? Since there were many "translocal" texts in antiquity, that is texts that made their way to other locations in the Greco-Roman world/Mediterranean region in antiquity as in the cases of the writings of Homer, Hesiod, and other classic writers, was this also true in early Christianity? Many of the texts that were deemed relevant or important in Egyptian churches did not have their origin in Egypt, but elsewhere. For example, the Gospel of Mark was written probably in Rome and most of Paul's letters were written in Asia Minor and Greece, but they were all brought to Egypt and to the larger community of Christians throughout the Greco-Roman world likely in a brief period of time (weeks or months, not years). Also, Melito's Paschal sermon was written in Sardis, but it was also quite popular in many other early churches and it was eventually transported to Egypt! To our knowledge, none of the classical or NT texts listed had their origins in Egypt, but rather were brought there likely by Christian missionaries or church participants traveling from one part of the Roman Empire to another. Texts in antiquity were often "translocal," that is, they often were carried to many parts of the Roman Empire shortly after they were written. Several studies have shown how quickly literary texts were transferred from one part of the Roman Empire to another and that appears the case here.[36]

---

[34] Hermas exists in two rolls (P.Oxy. 4706 and BKT 6.2.1), in seven third-century codices (e.g., P.Oxy. 4706, P.Iand. 1.4/LDAB 1094; P.Oxy. 3528/LDAB 1095; P.Oxy. 1828/LDAB 1099; P.Mich. 129/LDAB 1097; P.Oxy. 3527; LDAB 1098; and P.Oxy. 404/LDAB 1101), and in two opisthographs (P.Oxy. 4705; P.Mich. 130/LDAB 1096). These are noted in Hurtado's list cited above in pp. 224–25. He includes a complete collection of these second- and third- (and early fourth-) century Christian literary artifacts in ibid., 209–29.

[35] Ibid., 35.

[36] Hurado (ibid., 25–27) contends that the Christian texts discovered in Egypt were "translocal" and are representative of the wider Christian community. He cites for support Lionel Casson, *Travel in*

Again, however, since we only have access to a small portion of the manuscripts that existed at that time, there is an element of uncertainty here, but from the number of surviving manuscripts from the locations where biblical texts were found among Christians the Psalms, Matthew, John, and the *Shepherd of Hermas* were among the most popular texts. Was that true elsewhere? That, of course, is an important canon question, but because of the translocal character of Christian writings in antiquity it is likely that what was found in Egypt is probably not unique among the early churches there, but Christian texts were likely taken elsewhere in the Greco-Roman world as well.

When non-canonical texts are included in sacred collections, seldom is there anything in them that distinguishes them from the canonical writings, as in the case of P^{72}. Several ancient texts discovered in libraries or collections in Egypt contain fragments of a number of OT and NT books along with several non-canonical writings. These collections have a considerable variety both in the books and texts and date from around the late second through the fourth century. In a brief summary, Hurtado provides the number of Christian manuscripts containing biblical texts in the second and third centuries. Most of these texts as well as other ancient Christian texts were found *in Egypt*. The biblical books and the number of manuscripts for each found there include the following:

Old Testament: Genesis (8), Exodus (8), Leviticus (3), Numbers (1), Deuteronomy (2), Joshua (1), Judges (1), 2 Chronicles (2), Esther (2), Job (1), Psalms (18), Proverbs (2), Ecclesiastes (2), Wisdom of Solomon (1), Sirach (2), Isaiah (6), Jeremiah (2), Ezekiel (2), Daniel (2), Bel and Susanna (1), Minor Prophets (2), Tobit (2), and 2 Maccabees (1).

New Testament: Matthew (12), Mark (1), Luke (7), John (16), Acts (7), Romans (4), 1 Corinthians (2), 2 Corinthians (1), Galatians (1), Ephesians (3), Philippians (2), Colossians (1), 1 Thessalonians (3), 2 Thessalonians (2), Philemon (1), Titus (1), Hebrews (4), James (3), 1 Peter (1), 2 Peter (1), 1 John (1? = P9 or P.Oxy. 402, possibly fourth or fifth century), Jude (2), and Revelation (5).

Christian Apocryphal Writings: *Gospel of Thomas* (3), *Protevangelium of James* (1), *Gospel of Mary* (2), "Egerton" Gospel (1), *Gospel of Peter* (2, possibly P.Oxy. 2949 and P.Oxy. 4009), "Fayum" Gospel (1), *Acts of Paul* (3), *Correspondence of Paul and Corinth* (1), *Apocalypse of Peter* (1), *Apocryphon of Jannes* (1), and *Apocryphon of Moses* (1).

Other Christian Writings, some with an element of doubt about them (?): *Shepherd of Hermas* (11), Irenaeus, *Against Heresies* (2); Melito, *Paschal Homily* (1); Melito, *On Prophecy*? (1); Melito, *Paschal Hymn*? (1), Tatian, *Diatessaron*? (1); *Odes of Solomon* (1); Julius Africanus, *Cesti* (1); Origen, *Gospel Commentary* (1) Origen, *Homily* (1); Origen, *De Principiis* (1); *Sibylline Oracles* (1); Theonas, *Against Manichaeans*? (1); and

---

the Ancient World (London: Allen & Unwin, 1974); and Richard Bauckham's "For Whom Were the Gospels Written?," in *The Gospels for All Christians: Rethinking the Gospel Audiences*, ed. Richard Bauckham (Grand Rapids: Eerdmans), 9–48, especially 32.

some unidentified theological texts (3); unidentified eschatological discourse (1); other unidentified homilies and letters (2); a Jewish and Christian dialogue (1); prayer texts (3); Hymn to the Trinity (1); and exorcistic/apotropaic[37] texts.[38]

Several ancient collections of Christian manuscripts were found in Egypt and they allow us to see that there was no complete agreement on the scope of the Christian Scriptures at that time. These include the Chester Beatty papyri, the Bodmer papyri, and the Oxyrhynchus papyri. While they are sometimes called "libraries" it is probably safer simply to refer to them as collections since the largest number of them was found in a refuse site and we do not know the extent of their relationships with the Christian communities that discarded them or others that were discarded in the same vicinity. We will look briefly at the books in these collections, that may not necessarily be correctly called "libraries,"[39] but Hurtado reminds us that simply finding some of them in the same general locations, including in a city refuse site, does not qualify them as libraries, especially since we know so little about their origin, relationships, and why they were placed in a refuse site at Oxyrhynchus.[40]

Because of these unexplained factors, it is better to call them collections that are not clearly defined. Nevertheless, the discovery of a number of religious texts in a particular location no doubt reflects the presence of a religious community in that vicinity that favored these texts in some way and at a given time. A fourth important collection discovered in the same approximate area in Egypt is the Nag Hammadi papyri that contain no biblical books, but rather a number of gnostic religious texts that have several apostolic names attached to them. These collections are arbitrarily put together and we do not know the original structures in which these books were placed. We can probably say that Christians in the locations where these writings were found did make some use of them, but often it is not clear what that specific use was. For instance, the form of these texts, whether produced in a codex, a roll, or an opisthograph may indicate the way that they were viewed in a community. If a text was written in a codex format, is it more likely that it functioned as scripture in the Christian community that produced it? On the other hand, if it was produced in a used roll or in an opisthograph, did it receive or could it have received a sacred recognition? Approximately one third of the earliest Christian manuscripts contain what we now call "extra-canonical" or "non-canonical" texts that were written on rolls (scrolls). It is difficult to say

---

[37] Apotropaic (Gk. = ἀπότροπος, "turning away") is a reference to exorcisms or the turning away from evil. One who is apotropaic has the power to turn away from evil or misfortune.

[38] Hurtado, *Ancient Christian Artifacts*, 19–24, lists these texts with footnote comments on each one.

[39] Three of these four collections, Bodmer, Chester Beatty, Bodmer, and Nag Hammadi manuscripts, are called libraries by Van Elderen, "Early Christian Libraries."

[40] Hurtado, *The Earliest Christian Artifacts*, 24–26.

what this all means. Did the use of the roll *always* suggest that the writing was not yet viewed as scripture, or just the opposite?[41] Probably not, but in some instances that may have been the case.

Many of these texts are dated from the second through the early fourth century and this suggests the presence of an active Christian community in the region of their location. These ancient Christian papyrus texts were discovered in several locations in Egypt and include the following:

1. *Chester Beatty Papyri*. This collection of NT papyri dates from the early third to the fourth century and was discovered in the Nile Valley in Egypt in the early 1930s. This collection included a large number of papyri containing both OT and NT writings as well as some other writings as well. The OT portion of that collection, as we saw earlier, included Genesis, Numbers, and Deuteronomy, but strangely is lacking Exodus and Leviticus, all of the Former Prophets, the Psalms, and all other wisdom literature. Among the Latter Prophets, it only included Isaiah, Jeremiah, Ezekiel, and Daniel, but the collection includes Ecclesiasticus and *Enoch* as well as a homily by Melito. The fragmentary nature of this collection should give pause before drawing too many conclusions about the Bibles of early Christianity, but again, the presence of these books in one location – or the absence of some books that were popular later among the Christians and added to the biblical canon – should raise some questions about the scope of the sacred collections of Christian scriptures at that time (late second to late third century).

The NT part of that collection has the four canonical Gospels and Acts (P^{45}), the earliest known collection of Paul's letters which omitted 2 Thessalonians, the Pastorals, Philemon (P^{46}), and Revelation (P^{47}). All of these manuscripts are fragmented and we do not know what may have been lost in them (2 Thessalonians and Philemon?) or others. It is an argument from silence to say that we have all that was there or what was intended in those collections. This inference is based only on the texts that survived decomposition and decay, but it is still a wonder why more NT books were not found there. Since P^{46}, a fragmented codex, had room for additional texts, there is still insufficient space for the 2 Thessalonians, Pastorals, and Philemon as we will see below.

2. *The Bodmer Papyri* (third to sixth centuries). This collection was discovered in Upper Egypt in the early 1950s and, besides a large collection of classical and correspondence texts, it contains both OT and NT books dating from the third to the seventh century, including a number of non-canonical religious texts. The OT lacks Leviticus, Judges, Ruth, the Samuels, the Kings, Ezra, Nehemiah, Esther, Ecclesiastes, Ezekiel and the Book of the Twelve Minor Prophets, but also contains Susanna, Tobit, 2 Maccabees, and the *11th Ode of Solomon*.

---

[41] Hurtado, *Earliest Christian Artifacts*, 44–89, has an extended and carefully crafted discussion of this.

The NT collection (P⁶⁶, P⁷², P⁷³, P⁷⁴, P⁷⁵) is missing Mark, all of Paul's writings except Romans and 2 Corinthians, Hebrews, and Revelation. On the other hand, the collection includes the *Protevangelium Jacobi*, *3 Corinthians*, *Acts of Paul*, the *Apology of Phileas*, the *Vision of Dorotheos*, *Shepherd of Hermas*, an apocryphon, and other liturgical hymns including three of Melito's homilies. What can we make of this find of Christian religious manuscripts? What is missing in the collection is as much a puzzle as what it contains!

P⁷² (third to fourth centuries), which is generally identified as the oldest surviving manuscript of Jude and 1–2 Peter (that order) also includes, as we saw briefly earlier, the following writings in this order: the *Nativity of Mary*, correspondence of Paul with the Corinthians and *3 Corinthians*,[42] *Ode* 11 from the *Odes of Solomon*, then Jude, followed by Melito's *Homily on the Passover*, a hymn fragment, the *Apology of Phileas*; Psalms 33 and 34, and finally 1–2 Peter. This manuscript is not uniform, that is, it is unlikely that a single hand produced all of it, and the writings in it are not from the same time.

3. *The Oxyrhynchus Papyri*. This collection dates from the late third to the late sixth century, or even possibly the early seventh centuries, and is catalogued by the siglum P.Oxy., followed by a number. The collection includes many NT writings as well as some non-canonical writings, but without any marks or notations to distinguish them from the canonical writings, however, since they were found in a refuse site, we cannot make a strong case about what distinguishes them. Were they all sacred texts that Christians (or others?) simply discarded after they wore

---

[42]   This work was accepted as scripture in the Syrian as well as Armenian churches from the fourth century and for several centuries later. *3 Corinthians* continued to be included in some Latin sacred manuscripts (some Vulgate revised manuscripts) for almost 1000 years! As recently as 1728, William Whiston of Cambridge accepted the *3 Corinthians* letter as an authentic Pauline correspondence (see his *A Collection of Authentick Records Belonging to the Old and New Testament*, Part II [London: 1728], 585–638, cited in Metzger, *Canon of the New Testament*, 15). It was included in the biblical canon of the Armenian and Syrian Bibles for several centuries. It was rejected by the Syrians probably by the end of the fifth century at the latest, but continued on in the Armenian churches' Bible. *3 Corinthians* still stood at the end of the New Testament in Zoharb's 1805 edition of the Armenian Bible (see Metzger, *Text of the New Testament*, 223). It continues today in Armenian Bibles in an appendix following the New Testament. Both Aphraat (ca. 340 CE) and Ephraem Syrus (ca. 360 CE) commented on it as if it was authentic correspondence of Paul and Aphraat clearly treats it as Scripture. There is a Greek version of it that survives in the Bodmer collection of ancient manuscripts (P.Bod. X/P⁷², third century CE). The five Latin manuscripts that contain *3 Corinthians* are Cod. Ambrose. E53 inf. (tenth century, Milan); Codex Laon 45 (thirteenth century, L); Codex Paris. Lat. 5288 (tenth/eleventh century, P); Codex Zürich Car.C 14 (tenth century, Z); Codex Berlin Ham. 84 (thirteenth century, B). For a discussion of this literature, see Epp, "Issues in the Interrelation of New Testament Textual Criticism and Canon," 603–4. See also Peter S. Cowe, "The Bible in Armenian," in Marsden and Matter. eds., *New Cambridge History of the Bible*, 143–61; and Hovhanessian, "New Testament Apocrypha and the Armenian Version of the Bible." He also lists fifty-four apocryphal writings in Armenian manuscripts on 84–86. See my review of this book for RBL at (http://www.bookreviews.org/bookdetail.asp?TitleId=8951).

out? They are only arbitrarily put together without a usual sequence or groupings and were found without distinguishing features at the same refuse site, hence we cannot be sure that they formed some kind of library. Nor can we say that the rest of that collection is elsewhere, though we can say that the discovery of all of these Christian texts in the same vicinity suggests that these writings were likely sacred texts for the community that at one time held them. The only distinguishing marks among these texts are the forms in which they were produced, namely roll, codex, and *opisthograph*.

This collection has the largest number of NT papyri found in any one location and it warrants a closer look. The collection includes Matthew, Luke, John, Acts, Romans, 1 Corinthians, Galatians, Philippians, 1–2 Thessalonians, Hebrews, James, 1 John, Jude, and Revelation. Missing from the *earlier* Oxyrhynchus papyri are Mark, 2 Corinthians, Ephesians, Colossians, 1–2 Timothy, Titus, Philemon, 1–2 Peter, and 2–3 John. Mark and 1 Peter were included in the later Oxyrhynchus papyri.[43] Given the date and translocal nature of the biblical writings in antiquity, this, of course, raises canonical questions about why some NT books were *not* found there and why some non-canonical books were found among the canonical texts. What did this mean to the community that preserved these writings?

The presence of more than one copy of a manuscript in an ancient collection may be suggestive of a special status in the community that preserved the copies of books. With that in mind, the multiple and the single copies of non-canonical books at Oxyrhynchus include: *Shepherd of Hermas* (7),[44] *Gospel of Thomas* (3), *Gospel of Mary* (2), *Acts of Peter* (1), *Acts of John* (1), *Acts of Paul* (1), *Didache* (1), *Sophia Jesus Christi* (1), *Gospel of Peter* (2), *Apocalypse of Peter* (1?), three unknown Gospels or sayings of Jesus, and *Acts of Paul and Thecla* (1).

Epp notes that all of these books, except perhaps the *Letter of Abgar* (not listed above), were second-century writings and suggests that they all may have been candidates for inclusion in some church's NT. Also important for our purposes, he also observes that nothing found at Oxyrhynchus thus far distinguishes the NT books from the so-called non-canonical Christian books also found there.[45] Even the opisthographs containing a biblical or non-canonical text may have been viewed as Scripture to the communities that had them. Because of the scarcity of writing materials and the considerable expense to produce them, it could be that opisthographs were used to copy Christian sacred texts by the community of Christians in the region where the Oxyrhynchus papyri were found. There are too many variables here to draw any firm conclusions about their format and

---

43   The later Oxyrhynchus source for Mark is 069 and for 1 Peter is 0206.
44   Carolyn Osiek, *The Shepherd of Hermas*, Hermeneia (Minneapolis: Fortress, 1999), 1, observes: "no other non-canonical writing was as popular before the fourth century as the *Shepherd of Hermas*. It is the most frequently attested post-canonical text in the surviving Christian manuscripts of Egypt well into the fifth century."
45   Epp, "Oxyrhynchus New Testament Papyri," especially 10–30.

how they were viewed in that region, but again, it is likely that at the least some if not all of the communities that produced, copied, and received these religious manuscripts received them as sacred literature that informed their faith and religious conduct.

Some other similar examples include P[42] (ca. seventh or eighth century) that contains portions of Luke 1 and 2 in Greek and Coptic, but also an extensive collection of odes or hymns taken from the Jewish Bible and apocryphal literature, and P[apr] (or P[2], a *palimpsest*[46]) that includes Acts, the Catholic Epistles and Revelation, but also fragments of *4 Maccabees*. We pause here to observe that generally speaking the literature that we now describe as non-canonical literature, such as the *Shepherd of Hermas* and a few others, were occasionally included in some ancient manuscripts alongside NT writings with no distinguishing features.[47] When the time came that these additional books were no longer considered sacred Scripture, they were no longer copied or circulated in churches (decanonization). After such decisions in a particular community, there was little motivation to continue copying or preserving those books that were rejected as part of their sacred scriptures. History is replete with copies of the winners, but seldom of the losers!

In his study of Paul, Trobisch claims that less than eight percent of all known manuscripts with collections of Paul's writings contain the whole of the NT.[48] The oldest manuscript containing the letters of Paul, noted above, is the fragmentary P[46] which breaks off at 1 Thess 5:28. It originally had fourteen more pages of space, but that space is not sufficient to include the rest of the writings attributed to Paul, namely, 2 Thessalonians, 1 and 2 Timothy, Titus, and Philemon. That would take another twenty to twenty-three pages. It is likely that the copier included 2 Thessalonians since in all other manuscripts where 1 Thessalonians is included so also is 2 Thessalonians, but including 2 Thessalonians does not account for the rest of the space in the codex. There is simply not enough room in the codex to include the whole Pauline corpus but it is difficult to find any appropriate-size

---

[46] A "palimpsest" manuscript is one that was used earlier and subsequently "re-scraped" or washed and reused for another text. With modern technology, some of the materials originally placed in a material text can be recovered. Sometimes a Christian text was put on a reused palimpsest manuscript. The original text on some palimpsest manuscripts was a biblical text that was subsequently washed and reused for other purposes. Of the 310 uncial NT manuscripts, 68 are palimpsests. See Metzger and Ehrman, *Text of the New Testament*, 21–22.

[47] Besides the Psalms, Matthew, and John, the *Shepherd of Hermas* was the most widely circulating religious text in the early centuries of the church, at least, more manuscript copies of that book have survived than any other Christian writings or OT writings save the ones just mentioned.

[48] See Trobisch website: http://www.bts.edu/faculty/trobisch.htm. According to him, only fifty-nine of 779 manuscripts that contain the letters of Paul also contain the whole NT. This, of course, means portions of the whole New Testament since most of the manuscripts are fragmentary. Trobisch also discusses here Codex Alexandrinus, Codex Ephraemi Rescriptus, Codex Sinaiticus, Codex Vaticanus, Codex Boernerianus, Codex Augiensis, and P[46].

books attributed to Paul that fit into that limited space.[49] Scholars debate whether other letters were known to the scribe or scribes who put this collection together, whether the scribe planned poorly and did not have room for the rest, or whether the scribe knew the rest but chose not to include them and instead chose something else (one or more smaller letters?) in their place.

Further, P[32] contains Titus and P[87] contains Philemon, and both of these manuscripts were produced in the same general area at roughly the same time as P[46] (ca. 200–220 CE). It may be possible that the scribe(s) of P[46] knew of more writings attributed to Paul, but what other text(s) were included in the P[46] codex is perplexing. It is more likely that those who copied writings attributed to Paul were unaware of a *complete* collection of writings later attributed to him. It is also quite possible that a complete collection of Paul's letters was unknown by most churches at the end of the second century, even if several collections of some or many of his writings were circulating in churches earlier. Some NT scholars claim that P[46] was originally a *complete* collection of Paul's writings – including the ending of 1 Thessalonians, 2 Thessalonians, the Pastorals, and Philemon. They argue that the copier simply wrote later in smaller and more crimped letters as well as employed tighter spaces between the lines,[50] but the evidence for this compact conclusion that includes the Pastorals and Philemon is lacking and there is no evidence that there was adequate room for what is missing in the later acknowledged collection of Pauline letters, even if a couple of extra pages were included to accommodate the additional books. That, of course, is an argument from silence that is not justified by any evidence. It also assumes that the copier was woefully off base in his estimates of the purported length necessary to include all of those missing letters that included a complete collection of writings attributed to Paul. No other codex includes the Pastoral letters until the latter part of the fourth century (Codex Sinaiticus). Only eight of the manuscripts dating before the sixth century contain all or most of the letters attributed to Paul. It is highly unlikely that the rest of P[46] could have contained the Pastoral Epistles and Philemon as we have it now. There is simply not enough room in the remaining pages to include the Pastoral Letters, even if the letters were considerably reduced in size and squeezed together to try to accommodate them.[51] While additional pages *could have been attached* to P[46] to include all of the writings attributed to Paul, as some scholars contend, there is no evidence that this took place.

---

[49] Epp, "Issues in Interrelation of New Testament Criticism and Canon," 495–503, discusses this papyri codex at length, and concludes that firm conclusions on its contents are difficult to establish.
[50] S. E. Porter, in *Fundamentals of New Testament Criticism* (Grand Rapids: Eerdmans, 2015), 17–20, makes this argument.
[51] David C. Parker, "The New Testament Text and Versions," in Paget and Schaper, eds., *New Cambridge History of the Bible: Vol. 1, From the Beginnings to 600*, 412–54, has a helpful discussion of the books in the various NT manuscripts and also observes how much this has changed since the earlier 1970 edition of the *Cambridge History of the Bible*.

4. *The Nag Hammadi Library*. The famous Nag Hammadi collection of sacred texts was also found in Egypt, but no NT books are in this collection of Gnostic texts. The collection contains only numerous other religious texts that were a part of the sacred collection belonging to Christians in the Nag Hammadi region. Many of those documents, such as the *Gospel of Thomas*, the *Apocryphon of John*, the *Gospel of Philip*, the *Acts of Peter and the Twelve Apostles*, and others have the names or titles of apostles in their titles. Apostolic names began to be attached to many ancient texts following the emergence of apostolic authority by the middle to late second century. From that time apostolic names emerge as an influential factor in recognizing Christian literature as Scripture. Apostolic names attached to writings at that time suggest that those writings were received and treated as sacred and inspired literature by the gnostic Christian communities that employed those designations and transmitted those writings.[52]

Except for the Nag Hammadi Library, other collections have both canonical and non-canonical books in the papyrus codices, and no collection has the complete collection of OT or NT books that later formed the Christian Bibles in them. The Bodmer and Oxyrhynchus papyri have not only NT writings, but also non-canonical literature. The Chester Beatty papyri include non-canonical writings (*Enoch* and a homily by Melito) in the OT manuscript collection. None of the so-called libraries have a complete collection of the NT writings, but it is likely, as we said above, that all of these religious texts functioned in some sacred or authoritative manner in the churches of that region. It would be difficult to explain their preservation in multiple copies in several instances if that were not the case.

On the basis of the surviving fourth- and fifth-century canonical lists or catalogues, scholars tend to assume that the NT canon was closed no later than the fourth century, but Daryl Schmidt brings to our attention two twelfth-century manuscripts containing not only NT writings, but also non-canonical writings. Specifically, he mentions minuscule 339 (now missing), which according to F. J. A. Hort contained not only the four gospels, but also the *Epistle of Pilate and Reply*, *On the Genealogy of the Virgin*, Revelation and *Synaxarion*, Acts, the Catholic Epistles, the letters of Paul, *Lives of the Apostles*, and a Psalter. Additional material is also found in minuscule 180 from the twelfth century.[53] There is little doubt that many churches had accepted the canonical Gospels, Acts, and several letters of Paul as Christian Scripture by the end of the second century, but additional noncanonical writings in subsequent codices suggest

---

[52] For a description of this collection, see van Elderen, "Early Christian Libraries."
[53] D. D. Schmidt, "The Greek New Testament as a Codex," 474, took this reference from F. H. A. Scrivener, *A Plain Introduction to the Criticism of the New Testament for the Use of Biblical Students*, ed. Edward Miller, 4th ed., 2 vols. (London: George Bell, 1894), 200.

that other literature was also was read in churches long after the fourth and fifth centuries. For example, the late minuscule manuscript Gregory 1505 (ca. twelfth century) discovered at the Laure or Laura monastery on Mt. Athos includes all of the books of the NT except Revelation ending with Hebrews but followed also by psalms and odes. The order is the usual Gospels, Acts, Catholic Epistles, Paul, and Hebrews, but with the two additional collections of psalms and odes.

In the mid-fourth-century Codex Vaticanus (B 03), 1 and 2 Timothy, Titus, and Philemon are missing.[54] What we should make of this is difficult to tell, since the codex is fragmented at the beginning (omitting the first 45 chapters of Genesis) and breaks off in the middle of Heb 9:24. Some scholars continue to argue that the missing books were originally a part of this fragmented manuscript since they are in the other major codices, namely Sinaiticus and Alexandrinus, but the evidence, which includes the absence of the Pastorals before Hebrews in their usual place, nevertheless is insufficient to draw firm conclusions about the contents. Later, the palimpsest codex *Ephraemi Rescriptus* (C 04, ca. fifth century) *reportedly* included all of the NT books, but it is not certain that it includes 2 John and 2 Thessalonians.[55] Codex Sinaiticus (ℵ) (ca. fourth century) contains all of the NT books, but adds *Epistle of Barnabas* and *Shepherd of Hermas*.[56] Codex Alexandrinus (A) (fifth century) includes all of the NT books as well as *1–2 Clement* and the *Psalms of Solomon*. Codex Bezae (D) in the fifth century contains the Gospels and Acts. Codex Claramontanus (D[P], sixth century), in an insertion in this codex between Philemon and Hebrews, has a list of NT books that includes most of the letters attributed to Paul except Philippians, 1–2 Thessalonians, and Hebrews, but adds the *Epistle of Barnabas*, *Shepherd of Hermas*, *Acts of Paul*, and *Apocalypse of Peter*.

Interestingly, there is little evidence before the fourth century that 2 and 3 John were seriously considered sacred scripture by anyone in the church, though there are a few brief and vague allusions to these letters in the second and third centuries.[57] The witness to them is such that there is no clear evidence that they

---

[54]   Epp, "Issues in Interrelation of New Testament Criticism and Canon" 503, has noted that these same books are missing from the earlier P[46].

[55]   The oldest and most complete NT manuscripts (Codex Vaticanus, Codex Sinaiticus, Codex Ephraemi Rescriptus, and Codex Alexandrinus) has Acts followed by the Catholic Epistles come before the letters of Paul, except in the case of Sinaiticus, which has the letters of Paul after the four Gospels and Acts comes after Paul and is followed by the Catholic Epistles.

[56]   Professor James Charlesworth has shared with me that he has seen the missing pages at the beginning of this codex at the St. Catherine's Monastery in the Sinai Peninsula, but is not yet able to publish them due to restrictions from the monastery. See his earlier *BA* 42 (1979): 174–79 and *BA* 43 (1980): 26–34. Awareness of these missing pages has been around for a number of years and the late Raymond E. Brown took note of this unpublished discovery in his *Recent Discoveries and the Biblical World* (Wilmington, DE: Michael Glazier, 1983), 47–48.

[57]   For example, there are some possible parallels in language in the Apostolic Fathers, but they are not conclusive. The earliest and clearest references to 2 and 3 John are in Clement of Alexandria

were accepted as a part of the church's sacred collection until the middle to late fourth century and even then, these letters continued to be rejected by the Syrian church.[58]

The difficulty that some churches had in accepting these small letters may have had to do with their brevity as well as their lack of significant theological content. The same can be said of Jude, but in that case the difficulty of accepting it into the NT canon may have been because it cited *1 En.* 1:9 (v. 14) in a scriptural (authoritative) manner ("Enoch…prophesied"). The absence of the Pastoral Epistles in some early papyri and uncial manuscripts is difficult to explain, unless perhaps they were written after Paul and were not initially acknowledged as Pauline literature. Although if Pauline they would reflect a "later Paul" at the end of his missionary activity, it is difficult to accept them as they are as Pauline texts since they do not reflect his common themes of justification by faith, simple organizational church structure, his eschatology, or his emphasis on the role of the Spirit. It is also possible that because they were sent to individuals and not to churches they were not included in some collections, but the evidence to support these conclusions is not without problems. It may be that some of what is in the Pastorals may reflect authentic Pauline writings (e.g., 2 Tim 1:15–18 and 4:6–22), but the rest may have been written later by some of Paul's disciples or church leaders who followed him.

V. CATALOGUES OF BOOKS AND CANON FORMATION

The production of catalogues or lists of sacred books began for the most part in the fourth and fifth centuries,[59] but one encounters considerable difficulty finding biblical manuscripts that consistently reflect the same books in these lists. The biblical canons reflected in these lists are not always reflected in the manuscripts that survive from the same time and were circulating in churches when the lists were constructed. While there may have been some agreement in principal on what was in the biblical canon, nevertheless in practice there were some obvious

---

(*Strom.* 2.15.66) and Irenaeus who quotes 2 John 11 and 7 (*Haer.* 3.17.8). Neither Irenaeus nor Tertullian refer to 3 John, and none of these early references call 2 and 3 John scripture.

[58] Schnackenburg, *Johannine Epistles*, 42–47.

[59] I am aware of the recent defense of a middle to late third-century dating of the Muratorian Fragment by Armstrong in his "Victorinus of Pettau." His arguments need to be studied in more detail and do show some promise for challenging the usual second-century dating of the Muratorian Fragment. I will examine his arguments more in the next chapter; however, if Victorinus of Pettau was the author of that document, then he is much closer to Eusebius in the fourth century than to Bishop Pius in the second century. Again, Armstrong's work needs both consideration and further study, and he may provide several missing links in this ongoing debate among canon scholars, though Geoffrey Hahneman challenges Armstrong's arguments and conclusions in a forthcoming response.

differences over some books in those lists and over some that are not in them. I have shown below in Appendix C that the various lists or catalogues of sacred books from the fourth to the sixth centuries do not reflect a uniform view of what books comprise the church's NT canon despite considerable overlap.

As we saw earlier, Eusebius (ca. 320–30) offers the first datable catalogue of sacred NT writings that belong to what he called the "Recognized [Gk. = ὁμολογουμένοις] Books."[60] His list includes the four canonical Gospels, Acts, the letters of Paul (14, which includes Hebrews cf. *Hist. eccl.* 3.3.4–5), 1 John, 1 Peter, and possibly Revelation (that order). Among the doubted or disputed books (Gk. = ἀντιλεγομένος) in the churches, he lists James, Jude, 2 Peter, 2 and 3 John, and Revelation (*Hist. eccl.* 3.25.1–3). He himself seems conflicted about the widespread acceptance of Revelation.[61] His analysis of what books were widely acknowledged as sacred or "encovenanted" (Gk. = ἐνδιαθηκης or ἐνδιαθηκους) in his generation reflects one of the earliest moves toward a fixed NT canon. After him, other catalogues and lists of sacred books appear and a comparison of these lists shows that although there was a widely accepted core of NT writings circulating in the early churches of that time, there was also considerable flexibility on the fringes of the NT canon. All of the books that Eusebius identifies as *antilegomenon* (or spoken against or disputed) around 320–30 CE were widely accepted by the end of the fourth century.

The current interest in establishing the time, causes, and boundaries of a fixed Christian biblical canon was of little concern in the early centuries of the church, though by the fourth century such interest *began* to emerge. To gain an appreciation of that interest, it is important to examine the fourth-century social-context when canon formation processes began their final stages. Because of the persecutions the churches endured, accompanied by the burning of its sacred literature, as well as the conversion of Constantine and his subsequent call for religious unity in his new Constantinian Roman Empire, there was a need to determine what literature was viewed as sacred and what literature was not. This process of

---

[60] I will say below that I reject a second-century dating of the Muratorian Fragment since its closest parallels are in the mid-fourth century and later and it does not reflect the sacred collection of any known writer in the second century. Again, the work of Jonathan Armstrong noted above needs more careful scrutiny and that may alter positions on this document, but his views are much closer to the time when these matters of fixed canons were in view in the churches. For further discussion on this, see Chapter 21 below, and for a different perspective carefully argued, see J. Verheyden, "The Canon Muratori: A Matter of Dispute," in Auwers and de Jonge, eds., *The Biblical Canons*, 487–556. Both authors will be considered in the next chapter.

[61] He writes: "In addition to these should be put, if it seem desirable, the Revelation of John" (*Hist. eccl.* 3.25.2), and later adds that Revelation may be among the "not genuine" books (ἐν τοις νοθοις), "if this view prevails" and continues "some reject it, but others count it among the Recognized books" (3.25.4).

stabilizing the books that formed the Christian biblical canon was largely settled for most churches by the late fourth and early fifth centuries.[62]

As we can see in the ancient biblical manuscripts and canon lists, historically the churches seldom agreed on the *full scope* of their OT or NT Scriptures, though most eventually agreed on the scope of the NT canon. However, this was not the case initially. Also, even as late as the Reformation era, Martin Luther challenged the inclusion of Hebrews, James, Jude, and Revelation, and was obviously not pleased with them. In practice, the ancient churches, like many today, tend to have a "canon within the canon," and often in practice adopted a canon different from what church councils accepted. The ancient manuscripts and canon catalogues regularly reflect some diversity as well as overlap in the churches in terms of the books they accepted as scripture. The manuscripts and the canon catalogues reflect some fluidity in the shape of the biblical canons in the times in which they were produced and that fluidity continued for centuries in the churches. In what follows, we will focus on when and where the books in the current NT were cited by the early church fathers.

VI. EARLY CITATIONS, PARALLELS, AND ALLUSIONS

Without question, the canonical Gospels and the Letters of Paul were among the most cited or quoted NT books in the writings of the early church fathers. Occasionally other literature was also cited by the early church fathers and some of those books have survived in some NT manuscripts. The following survey demonstrates the use of the twenty-seven NT books by the church fathers. It is not exhaustive, but reflective of the citations taking place in the first few centuries of the church.

A. Gospels

1. *Matthew*. Matthew was by far the most quoted gospel in the early churches (except in Asia Minor). Apparent similarities between the language in Matthew and other early Christian writings may, however, occasionally reflect a common oral tradition rather than dependence upon Matthew's Gospel itself. The earliest obvious parallels to sayings found in Matthew's Gospel come from Ignatius in the early second century (e.g., compare Ign. *Smyrn.* 1.1 and Matt 3:15; Ign. *Eph.* 19.1–3 and Matt 2:1–12; Ign. *Pol.* 2.2 and Matt 10:16). As noted earlier, however, these sayings are not attributed to Matthew in particular, but rather to the words of Jesus found in Matthew. When the words are precise, they are most likely quotations as well as citations. It is likely that when Ignatius speaks of

---

[62] This is discussed in McDonald, *The Biblical Canon*, 285–322.

"the gospel" (Ign. *Phld.* 5.1–2; 8.2) he has in mind the Gospel of Matthew. The assumption here is that since Ignatius cites the words of Jesus in Matthew, then the Gospel of Matthew was also viewed as a reliable source for Ignatius' teaching about Jesus.

Polycarp also refers to the words of Jesus in Matthew (compare Pol. *Phil.* 2.3 and Matt 7:1–2 and 5:3, 10; Pol. *Phil.* 7.2 and Matt 26:41; Pol. *Phil.* 12.3 and Matt 5.44). Similar or common language and subject matter is found in *1 Clement* (*1 Clem.* 7.7 and Matt 12:41; *1 Clem.* 13.2 and Matt 5:7 and 6:14–15; *1 Clem.* 46.7–9 and Matt 26:24 and 18:6) and *2 Clement* (*2 Clem.* 2.4 and Matt 9:13; *2 Clem.* 3.2 and Matt 10:32; *2 Clem.* 3.5 and Matt 15:8; *2 Clem.* 4.1 and Matt 7:21; *2 Clem.* 6.1 and Matt 6:24 and 16:26).

Papias (ca. 130) refers to Matthew as the author of a collection of "oracles" or sayings of Jesus (Eusebius, *Hist. eccl.* 3.39.16). The *Didache* (late first century) has some language parallels with Matthew (*Did.* 1.2–3 and Matt 7:12 and 5:44–47; *Did.* 3.7 and Matt 5:5; *Did.* 8.1–3 and Matt 6:5–16). The *Epistle of Barnabas* (ca. 130–140) has several parallels in wording with Matthew (e.g., *Barn.* 4.14 and Matt 22:14; *Barn.* 7.3–5 and Matt 27:34, 48).

2. *Mark.* Mark was known by name from the time of Papias (ca. 60–130), but was not used as much in the early churches. Justin Martyr (*Dial.* 106.2–3) points to a passage in Mark and refers to it as "Memoirs" from Peter. Clement of Alexandria has the first clear quotations from Mark in his *Paedagogus* 1.2 and *Strom.* 6.14 (citing Mark 8:36). Irenaeus (*Haer.* 3.14.3) cites Mark by name and quotes Mark 1:1. Papias is the first known person to refer to the Gospel of Mark by name, and he refers to it before he speaks of Matthew, which may indicate Papias' view of which gospel was produced first (Eusebius, *Hist. eccl.* 3.39.14–16). Some Apostolic Fathers also refer to Mark (*1 Clem.* 24.5 and Mark 4:3; *1 Clem.* 46.7–9 and Mark 14:21 and 9:42; *Barn.* 5.9 and Mark 2:17).

3. *Luke.* Marcion (ca. 140) edited the Gospel of Luke for his own purposes, as attested in Irenaeus and Tertullian, as we saw earlier, as well as in the late-second-century *Anti-Marcionite Gospel Prologues.*[63] Language from Luke is often similar to that found in the Apostolic Fathers, though the gospel itself is not cited by name (e.g., *1 Clem.* 46.7–9 and Luke 17:2; *1 Clem.* 48.4 and Luke 1:75; *2 Clem.* 6.1 and Luke 6:24; *2 Clem.* 8.5 and Luke 16:10–12; *2 Clem.* 13.4 and Luke 6:32, 35; *Did.* 1.4 and Luke 6:29; *Barn.* 14.9 and Luke 4:17–19). The evidence of Luke as a separate writing is first discussed by Irenaeus (ca. 170–80, as reported in Eusebius, *Hist. eccl.* 5.8.3).

---

[63] For a brief introduction of these prologues, see McDonald, "Anti-Marcionite (Gospel) Prologues."

4. *John*. As with the other Gospels, there are some parallels between the language of John and the Apostolic Fathers. There are some similarities between John 3:5 and *Herm. Sim.* 9.15.2 and 9.16.2. Both the *Gospel of Philip* and *Testimony of Truth* in the Nag Hammadi gnostic collection make use of John. John was also used by Tatian in producing his harmony of the Gospels, the *Diatessaron* (ca. 170). Irenaeus, originally from Asia, where John was the most popular gospel, argued for a four-gospel canon, possibly to insure the continued acceptance and use of John in the churches (*Haer.* 3.1.1).[64]

B. Acts

References to the book of Acts are rather vague until the time of Justin Martyr (155–60). Some have argued that the Pastoral Epistles made use of Acts, but this is speculative and the evidence supporting that argument is not convincing. The similar topics found in Acts and the Pastorals – ordination, the laying on of hands, the institution of elders by Paul, Timothy's family (Acts 16:1–3; 2 Tim 1:5), and Paul's ministry in Lystra, Iconium, and Derbe (Acts 14:1–20; 16:1; 2 Tim 3:11) – do not require or involve dependence. They could easily be the result of tradition held in common, and since there are no exact word parallels the strength of the case for dependence is not convincing. Parallels in content between Acts and other late-first-century and second-century documents may only demonstrate a common oral or written tradition circulating in the churches. See for example the following:

> *1 Clem.* 2.1 and Acts 20:35
> *1 Clem.* 2.2 and Acts 2:17
> *1 Clem.* 18.1 and Acts 13:22
> *1 Clem.* 59.2 and Acts 26:18
> *2 Clem.* 4.4 and Acts 5:29
> *2 Clem.* 20.5 and Acts 3:15 and 5:31
> Pol. *Phil.* 1.2 and Acts 2:24
> Pol. *Phil.* 2.3 and Acts 20:35
> Pol. *Phil.* 6.3 and Acts 7:52
> Pol. *Phil.* 12.2 and Acts 2:5; 4:12; 8:31; and 20:32
> *Did.* 1.5 and Acts 20:35
> *Did.* 4.8 and Acts 4:32
> *Barn.* 7.2 and Acts 10:42
> *Barn.* 19.8 and Acts 4:32
> *Herm. Sim.* 9.28.2 and Acts 5:41; 9:16; and 15:26

---

[64] See also Eusebius, *Hist. eccl.* 5.8.2–4 and the witness of Clement of Alexandria and Origen preserved in Eusebius, *Hist. eccl.* 6.14.5–7 and 6.25.3–6 respectively.

There are other parallels between Acts 20:17–38 and Ign. *Eph.* 12.1–2, *Diogn.* 3.4, and *Epistula Apostolorum*, but we have no clear evidence of dependence. Justin shows awareness of Luke as a written source (e.g., *1 Apol.* 50.12), but does not refer to Acts as either Scripture or an authoritative source (cf. *1 Apol.* 39.3 and Acts 4:13; *1 Apol.* 49.5 and Acts 13:48; *2 Apol.* 10.6 and Acts 17:23), even though Justin's argument regarding unclean foods (*Dial.* 20.3–4) could have been enhanced by an appeal to Acts 10:14 or 15:29.

While the Martyrs of Lyons and Vienne (preserved in *Hist. eccl.* 5.2.5) has impressive word parallels with Acts that strongly suggests dependence, Irenaeus is the first clear source to appeal to Acts in an authoritative manner (e.g., *Haer.* 1.26.3 and Acts 6:1–6; *Haer.* 3.12.1 and Acts 1:16–17; *Haer.* 4.23.2 and Acts 8). In several cases of parallels between Acts and Irenaeus, Irenaeus views Acts as an authoritative source for substantiating his arguments against heresy in the church. In other words, he uses Acts in a scriptural manner. In the second century, Acts generally is not yet cited as Scripture with the usual scriptural citation formulae, or found in any collections of sacred literature. Appeals to the book, however, continued on in the third century and even increased. Tertullian makes considerable use of Acts in his arguments against Marcionite heresy (*Marc.* 5.1–2 and *Praescr.* 22). The author of the *Acts of Paul* (ca. 197) also refers to Acts, and there are word parallels with Acts in the *Anti-Marcionite Gospel Prologues* (ca. late second century). In the fourth century, Eusebius does not hesitate to place Acts in the collection of "recognized" (ὁμολογουμένα) books (*Hist. eccl.* 3.25.1; cf. 3.4.1, where he also acknowledges that Luke is the author of Acts). Elsewhere Eusebius cites Acts as a historical source (*Hist. eccl.* 2.22.1, 6–7, etc.), and is the earliest known writer to include it in a list of the churches' Scriptures (*Hist. eccl.* 3.4.6).

In several lists of canonical Scriptures, Acts does not serve as a bridge to the Epistles (Mommsen or Cheltenham Catalogue of ca. 360; Clermont ca. 303; in Cyril of Jerusalem (*Catechetical Lectures* 4.33; and Athanasius, *Thirty-Ninth Festal Letter*). In these sources Acts is placed between the Gospels and the Catholic Epistles, which is then followed by the Pauline collection. In Epiphanius (*Pan.* 76.5), Acts comes between the Pauline Epistles and the Catholic Epistles. Pope Innocent placed Acts after all the Epistles and before Revelation. In the Mommsen Catalogue (also known as the Cheltenham List, ca. 360–370, and probably from some Western church),[65] Luke strangely stands last in the Gospels, and Acts follows Paul's letters and comes just before Revelation (Hebrews is omitted). The list concludes with 1, 2, 3 John and 1, 2 Peter (that order). Rather than making use of Acts, Marcion appears to have substituted his own *Antitheses*. At any rate, it is clear that Luke and Acts were separated no later than by the time

---

[65]   This strange list also, identified as Phillipps MS 12266, includes Ps 151, but omits Hebrews, James, and Jude.

of Marcion (ca. 140), and probably earlier. There is apparently no *known* time in the second-century church when the two volumes circulated together, and it is possible that they circulated separately before the end of the first century.

C. Paul's Writings (Genuine and Attributed)

Several of Paul's writings have early attestation in the Christian community and were influential in many churches during the second century. Romans and 1 Corinthians are clearly known to Clement of Rome, who wrote *1 Clement* (ca. 90–95), and, as churches copied and circulated Paul's letters to each other, other letters attributed to Paul became attached to that collection. Initially the Pastorals and Philemon were not included in the collection, but eventually thirteen letters plus Hebrews were all attributed to Paul. The following lists are illustrative of the parallels between Paul's Letters and the writings of the early church fathers.[66] Some of the parallels show obvious dependence, but others may simply be a shared common tradition in the church. The following evidence shows that Romans, 1 Corinthians, and Ephesians are cited more frequently in the early churches than other Pauline letters, and this does not change significantly in the rest of the second century. As we will see from the references below, Paul is not always mentioned by name in these citations, but often only the words in his letters.

1. *Romans*. Origen (185–254) wrote one of the oldest and most influential commentaries on Paul's Letter to the Romans in fifteen volumes. Rufinus (ca. 400) translated Origen's extensive commentary into Latin and subsequently abbreviated it into ten volumes. This reflects the considerable influence that Romans had on developing churches in the first five centuries. Early references to the book of Romans include the following:

> Rom 1:3–4 has parallels in word and thought with Ign. *Smyrn.* 1.1.
> Rom 1:21 has parallels in thought with *1 Clem.* 36.2.
> Rom 1:29–32 has such close parallels with *1 Clem.* 35.5–6 that it is certain that Clement was familiar with Paul's letter.
> Rom 3:21–26 appears to be behind *Diogn.* 9.1.
> Rom 4:3, 10, 17–18 has parallels in *Barn.* 13.7.
> Rom 4:7–9 is similar to *1 Clem.* 50.6–7 in terms of the blessing mentioned at the beginning of the quotation from Ps 32:1–2.
> Rom 6:1 is similar in word and thought to *1 Clem.* 33.1.
> Rom 6:4 is similar to Ign. *Eph.* 19.3.
> Rom 8:5 and 8 are similar to Ign. *Eph.* 8.2.
> Rom 8:32 has parallel language in *Diogn.* 9.2.
> Rom 9:5 is very similar to *1 Clem.* 32.2.

---

[66] Much of what follows was gleaned from *Oxford Society of Historical Theology's New Testament in the Apostolic Fathers*, but also supplemented with more recent materials.

Rom 9:7–13 has parallels in *Barn*. 13.2–3, even if the latter uses it differently than does Paul.
Rom 12:4 has parallel words and thought with *1 Clem*. 38.1.
Rom 12:10 is similar in thought to Pol. *Phil*. 10.1.
Rom 14:10, 12 have several verbal parallels with Pol. *Phil*. 6.2.

2. *1 Corinthians.*

1 Cor 1:11–13 is the same in thought as *1 Clem*. 47.1–3, and dependence seems obvious.
1 Cor 1:18, 20 is similar in word and thought to Ign. *Eph*. 18.1.
1 Cor 2:9 is similar in word and thought to *1 Clem*. 34.8.
1 Cor 2:10 is close to *1 Clem*. 40.1 and Ign. *Phld*. 7.1.
1 Cor 3:1, 16, 18–20 has several parallels in word and notion with *Barn*. 4.11.
1 Cor 4:1 has *some* word parallels with Ign. *Trall*. 2.3, but dependence is difficult to prove.
1 Cor 4:4 has close word and thought parallels with Ign. *Rom*. 5.1.
1 Cor 4:12 may be quoted in *Diogn*. 5.15.
1 Cor 5:7 is close in words to Ign. *Magn*. 10.2.
1 Cor 6:2 has word parallels with Pol. *Phil*. 11.2.
1 Cor 6:9–10 has close word parallels with Pol. *Phil*. 5.3 and Ign. *Eph*. 16.1.
1 Cor 6:15 is similar in thought to *1 Clem*. 46.7.
1 Cor 7:22 is similar in word to Ign. *Rom*. 4.3 (cf. 1 Cor 9:1).
1 Cor 7:39–40 has several close word and thought parallels with *Herm. Mand*. 4.4.1–2.
1 Cor 8:1 is clearly cited in *Diogn*. 12.5.
1 Cor 9:15 is close to Ign. *Rom*. 6.1.
1 Cor 9:17 has word parallels in *Diogn*. 7.1.
1 Cor 9:24 and *1 Clem*. 5.1, 5 may be a parallel.
1 Cor 10:16–17 is similar to Ign. *Phld*. 4.1.
1 Cor 10:24, 33 is similar to *1 Clem*. 48.6.
1 Cor 12:8–9 is similar to *1 Clem*. 48.5, perhaps suggesting dependence.
1 Cor 12:12–26 has clear parallels with *1 Clem*. 37.5 and 38.1, and dependence appears obvious.
1 Cor 12:26 is similar to Pol. *Phil*. 11.4.
1 Cor 13:4–7 has parallels in *1 Clem*. 49.5, and dependence seems clear.
1 Cor 15:20 and *1 Clem*. 24.1 both speak of first fruits.
1 Cor 15:23 has an exact correspondence with *1 Clem*. 37.3.
1 Cor 15:28 is similar to Pol. *Phil*. 2.1.
1 Cor 15:36–37 has several parallels in thought and word with *1 Clem*. 24.4–5.
1 Cor 16:17 is similar in thought to *1 Clem*. 38.2.

3. *2 Corinthians.*

2 Cor 3:18 is similar to *1 Clem*. 36.2.
2 Cor 4:14 has verbal parallels with Pol. *Phil*. 2.2.
2 Cor 5:10 has parallels in word and substance with *Barn*. 4.11–14 and Pol. *Phil*. 6.2.
2 Cor 6:9–10 appears to be cited in *Diogn*. 5.12–16.
2 Cor 6:16 has a close parallel with Ign. *Eph*. 15.3.
2 Cor 10:3 has word parallels in *Diogn*. 5.8.

4. *Galatians*. Galatians is alluded to or cited several times in both the Apostolic Fathers and in several other second- and third-century church fathers.

> Gal 1:1 is very similar to Ign. *Phld.* 1.1.
> Gal 2:9 is also similar to *1 Clem.* 5.2.
> Gal 2:21 has clear word parallels with Ign. *Trall.* 10.1.
> Gal 3:1 is similar to *1 Clem.* 2.1, but the coincidence is not certain.
> Gal 4:26 and Pol. *Phil.* 3.3 share a metaphor.
> Gal 5:11 has clear word parallels with Ign. *Eph.* 18.1.
> Gal 5:17 is similar in wording and thought to Pol. *Phil.* 5.3 and *Diogn.* 6.5.
> Gal 5:21 has clear word parallels with Ign. *Eph.* 16.1.
> Gal 6:2 has a parallel thought in *Diogn.* 10.6.
> Gal 6:7 has verbal and thought parallels with Pol. *Phil.* 5.1.
> Gal 6:14 has clear word parallels with Ign. *Rom.* 7.2.

5. *Ephesians*. Marcion's collection of ten Pauline Letters included a *Letter to the Laodiceans*, which may have been the same as Ephesians. It was widely believed to have been addressed to the Ephesian church. Irenaeus cited it (e.g., *Haer.* 1.3.1, 4; 1.8.4; 5.2.36), as did Clement of Alexandria (*Strom.* 4.65), and Origen (*Cels.* 3.20). It was cited frequently in the Apostolic Fathers and in subsequent church fathers and is not identical with the later pseudonymous Epistle to the Laodiceans. Here are some examples:

> Eph 1:4–6 has parallels with *Barn.* 3.6, especially the notion of what is found and possessed "in the beloved."
> Eph 1:18 has word parallels with *1 Clem.* 59.3 (cf. *1 Clem.* 36.2).
> Eph 2:8–9 has several verbal parallels with Pol. *Phil.* 1.3.
> Eph 2:10 has parallels in *Barn.* 6.11.
> Eph 2:16 has exact word parallels with Ign. *Smyrn.* 1.1.
> Eph 2:20–22 has similar words and thoughts with Ign. *Eph.* 9.1 and *Barn.* 6.11.
> Eph 3:17 has parallels in *Barn.* 6.11.
> Eph 4:3–6 is close in word and thought to *Herm. Sim.* 9.13.5 and *1 Clem.* 46.6–7, but because of the popularity of these words in the first and second centuries, it is not possible to speak of dependence.
> Eph 4:18 is similar to *1 Clem.* 36.2 and 51.5.
> Eph 4:22–24 has parallels in *Barn.* 6.11.
> Eph 4:25–30 has several parallels in word and thought with *Herm. Mand.* 10.2.1–6, although the *Shepherd of Hermas* develops the thought in his own way.
> Eph 4:26 is quite similar to Pol. *Phil.* 12.1.
> Eph 5:1 is similar to Ign. *Eph.* 1.1.
> Eph 5:5 is quite similar to Pol. *Phil.* 11.2.
> Eph 5:16 has word parallels with *Barn.* 2.1 that are close enough to suggest dependence.
> Eph 5:25 has several parallels in word and thought with Ign. *Pol.* 5.1.
> Eph 6:18 is similar in thought to Pol. *Phil.* 12.3.

6. *Philippians*. Philippians was influential in the early church among the orthodox and heterodox (heretics) alike. It was in the collection of Marcion (see Hippolytus, *Ref.* 5.143; 10.318) and among the Sethians, an Orphite sect of the second century that cited Phil 2:6–7. Clement of Rome, Ignatius, and Diognetus refer to Philippians. At the close of the second century, Irenaeus cited Ephesians (*Haer.* 4.18.4), as did Clement of Alexandria (*Christ the Educator* 1.524; *Strom.* 4.12, 19, 94), and Tertullian (*Resurrection of the Flesh* 23; *Marc.* 5.20; *Praescr.* 26). Eusebius says that the Martyrs of Lyons and Vienne also cited Phil 2:6–7 (*Hist. eccl.* 5.2.2). The references or allusions in the Apostolic Fathers do not necessarily show direct dependence, but rather familiarity with the text that may well have had a widespread oral tradition known among some second-century churches. The parallels include the following:

> Phil 1:27 is close in thought and word to *1 Clem.* 3.4, but no clear dependence can be shown.
> Phil 2:10 is similar in both word and thought to Pol. *Phil.* 2.1 (cf. Phil 3:21).
> Phil 2:17 has several verbal parallels with Pol. *Phil.* 1.1, but they are not strong enough to demonstrate dependence.
> Phil 3:15 has several important words and thoughts that are parallel with Ign. *Smyrn.* 11.3.
> Phil 3:18 has similar thoughts as Pol. *Phil.* 12.3.
> Phil 4:13 has close word parallels with Ign. *Smyrn.* 4.2.

7. *Colossians*. Colossians has early attestations among the second-century church fathers, including Justin (*Dial.* 85.2; 138.2), Irenaeus (*Haer.* 3.14.1), Tertullian (*Praescr.* 7), and Clement of Alexandria (*Strom.* 1.1). There was little question about Pauline authorship or about receiving this book in second-century churches. Marcion also accepted it as a part of his collection of writings. References or allusions in the Apostolic Fathers, though few, are as follows:

> Col 1:16–20 is similar to *Barn.* 12.7.
> Col 1:23 has verbal parallels with Pol. *Phil.* 10.1.

There are several other word parallels between Ignatius' writings and Colossians, but while none indicate direct dependence, familiarity with this letter appears obvious:

> Col 1:7 and Ign. *Eph.* 2.1
> Col 1:16 and Ign. *Trall.* 5.2
> Col 1:18 and Ign. *Smyrn.* 1.2
> Col 1:23 and Ign. *Eph.* 10.2
> Col 2:2 and Ign. *Eph.* 17.2
> Col 2:14 and Ign. *Smyrn.* 1.2
> Col 4:7 and Ign. *Eph.* 2.1

8. *1–2 Thessalonians.* There is little solid evidence that Ignatius knew 1 Thessalonians. The parallels may have been simply shared oral tradition circulating in the churches, but that is not the case in all of the parallels. Throughout the rest of the second century there are a few allusions and specific references to these letters. The following are some of the more obvious parallels in the Apostolic Fathers.

> 1 Thess 2:4 has word and thought parallels with Ign. *Rom.* 2.1.
> 1 Thess 5:17 has exact word parallels with Ign. *Eph.* 10.1.
> 2 Thess 1:4 is similar to Pol. *Phil.* 11.3, which mentions Paul by name.
> 2 Thess 3:5 has word parallels with Ign. *Rom.* 10.3.
> 2 Thess 3:15 is quite similar in thought to Pol. *Phil.* 11.4, and dependence is likely.

9. *The Pastoral Epistles.* The Pastoral Epistles (1–2 Timothy and Titus) are not clearly or generally cited in the churches until the late second and early third centuries – and then mostly by Irenaeus.[67] The *Shepherd of Hermas* has some verbal parallels with the Pastorals, but no clear citation of these letters. Some scholars believe that they were written in the mid-second century in response to Marcion or gnostic Christians (cf. 1 Tim 6:20) by someone in the Pauline tradition, that is, in a church founded by Paul that continued as a Christian community largely in ways set out by Paul in his letters. The Pastoral Epistles have some verbal and thought parallels in some of the Apostolic Fathers, but clear dependence on them is difficult to establish. Often some of the same thoughts or words were circulating in the broader church and may simply reflect the use of widely known views and oral traditions in the early church. According to Tertullian, the Pastoral Epistles that he himself accepted as Pauline were not part of Marcion's collection of Paul's Letters. He writes:

> To this epistle [Philemon] alone did its brevity avail to protect it against the falsifying hands of Marcion. I wonder, however, when he received (into his *Apostolicon*) this letter which was written but to one man, that he rejected the two epistles to Timothy and the one to Titus, which all treat of ecclesiastical discipline. His aim, was, I suppose, to carry out his interpolating process even to the number of (St. Paul's) letters. (*Marc.* 3.473–75, ANF; cf. also *Marc.* 5.21).

Marshall claims that there is no doubt that the Pastoral Epistles are cited in the later part of the second century and attributed to Paul and he refers first to Theophilus' *Letter to Autolycum* 3.14,[68] who refers to the "divine word" with parallels with 1 Tim 2:2 (with a parallel to Athenagoras, *Supplicatio* 37.1, ca. 177 CE) and Titus 3:1, 5. He also points to "a clear echo" of Titus 3:4 in Justin, *Dial.* 47.15 (ca. 160–165), and with multiple references in Irenaeus. He also contends

---

[67] For an introduction, see R. W. Wall, "The Function of the Pastoral Epistles Within the Pauline Canon of the New Testament: A Canonical Approach," in Porter, ed., *The Pauline Canon*, 27–44.
[68] Marshall, *Pastoral Epistles*, 5–6.

that this passage makes an allusion to the Pastorals when Theophilus (ca. 170) calls upon his readers to lead a life of submission to leaders and to pray for them so that "we may lead a quiet and peaceable life" (2 Tim 2:2). Marshall also claims that Athenagoras' *Plea for the Christians* 37.2 "echoes" 1 Tim 2:2 and Titus 3:1, but once again these texts may simply reflect what Paul said in Rom 13:1–7 or elsewhere.[69] These parallels may also be the earliest awareness of the Pastoral Epistles among the second-century church fathers and most, if not all, of those references are late, namely from 160–ca. 185 CE. Some of the word or thought parallels may be nothing more than an oral tradition of shared common sayings that have roots in Paul or among Paul's followers. Further, it is not clear that all of the above citations or word parallels reflect an awareness of the scriptural status of the Pastorals in the second century.

Justin (*Dial*. 47.15) uses language similar to Titus 3:4 (namely, "the goodness and loving kindness of God"), but again this may only be an "echo" of something from the *lingua franca* of the day. Marshall also adds a reference to Irenaeus, *Haer*. Preface 1, as evidence for his acceptance of the Pastoral Epistles as Pauline letters.[70] Irenaeus' reference to "vain genealogies," however, is similar to "myths and endless genealogies" in 1 Tim 1:4. On the other hand, a clear case can be made for Irenaeus' citing Titus 3:10 in *Haer*. 1.16.3 where he specifically mentions Paul by name. Other clear examples of Irenaeus' acceptance and citation of the Pastoral Epistles are *Haer*. 2.14.7 citing 1 Tim 6:20; *Haer*. 3.3.3 referring to 2 Tim 4:21; and *Haer*. 3.14.1 citing 2 Tim 4:10–11. The following examples from the Apostolic Fathers are generally parallels that could be attributed to oral tradition from traditions about Paul or possibly citations of the Pastoral Epistles themselves.

a. *1 Timothy.*

> 1 Tim 1:3–5 has strong thought and word parallels with Ign. *Eph*. 14.1 and 20.1 and Ign. *Magn*. 8.1.
>
> 1 Tim 1:15–16 is similar in word and idea to *Barn*. 5.9.
>
> 1 Tim 1:17 has several similar words as *2 Clem*. 20.5, but the words are also common Jewish liturgical expressions.
>
> 1 Tim 3:8 has similar words and thought parallels with Pol. *Phil*. 5.2.
>
> 1 Tim 3:16 has exact wording parallels with *Barn*. 5.6, though the notion may have been a common theme in the oral tradition behind both writings. This same text, which is creedal in formulation, also has a parallel in *Diogn*. 11.3.
>
> 1 Tim 5:5 has several word and thought parallels with Pol. *Phil*. 4.3, and dependence is possible.
>
> 1 Tim 6:7 (see also 6:10) has several word and thought parallels with Pol. *Phil*. 4.1, and dependence is possible.

---

[69]   Ibid., 6.

[70]   Ibid.

b. *2 Timothy.*

2 Tim 1:10 is quite similar to *Barn.* 5.6.
2 Tim 1:16 has several words that overlap with Ign. *Eph.* 2.1 and Ign. *Smyrn.* 10.2.
2 Tim 2:3 is similar to Ign. *Pol.* 6.2.
2 Tim 2:25 has clear word parallels with Pol. *Phil.* 5.2, and dependence is likely, but it is not clear which writer is depending on the other.
2 Tim 4:1 is similar to *Barn.* 7.2 and, again, this may reflect a common Christian perspective of faith that was transmitted orally in the second century or direct dependence.
2 Tim 4:10 is similar in word and thought to Pol. *Phil.* 9.2.

c. *Titus.*

Titus 1:2 is similar to *Barn.* 1.3–4, 6 in both word and thought.
Titus 1:14 (cf. 3:9) has parallel thoughts with Ign. *Magn.* 8.1.
Titus 2:4–5 has several corresponding phrases in *1 Clem.* 1.3.
Titus 3:1 is similar to *1 Clem.* 2.7 and 34.4.
Titus 3:5–8 is similar to *Barn* 1.3–4, 6 in both word and thought.

10. *Philemon.* Philemon 20 has some word parallels with Ign. *Eph.* 2.2, but Ignatius may not have known of Philemon. Again, the parallels may have been simply common knowledge in the churches in the early second century. The Apostolic Church Fathers and the rest of the second-century writers seem to have ignored this little letter.

D. Hebrews

The canonical status of Hebrews was insured when a second-century editor (possibly Pantaenus, the director of a theological school in Alexandria around 170) incorporated this writing into the Pauline corpus of letters. The book's scriptural status was never questioned after that in Alexandria. Eventually the Syrian churches also agreed that Paul wrote Hebrews, and they received it into their Scripture canon. The book was both known and quoted in the East and West, but some Western churches did not accept it as Scripture in the second or third centuries. Clement of Rome, however, made obvious use of Hebrews and incorporated its words into his letter without referring to it as Scripture or making any direct reference to the letter or its author (compare *1 Clem.* 9.3 and Heb 11:5; *1 Clem.* 10.7 and Heb 11:17; *1 Clem.* 17.1 and Heb 11:37; *1 Clem.* 19.2 and Heb 12:1; and especially *1 Clem.* 36.1–5 and Heb 2:18; 3:1; 1:3–4, 7, 13). Other parallels appear in Justin Martyr (ca. 160) who, like Heb 3:1, strangely refers to Christ as an "apostle" (*1 Apol.* 1.12, 63; see also *Dial.* 34 and Heb 8:7; *Dial.* 13 and Heb 9:13–14; and *Dial.* 67 and Heb 12:18–19).

Although Eusebius accepted Hebrews as one of fourteen "obvious and plain" letters by Paul, he nevertheless conceded that others disputed its authorship and that the church in Rome even denied that Paul had written it (*Hist. eccl.* 3.3.4–5). It appears that its authorship was central to the acceptance of Hebrews in the churches. Clement of Alexandria was the first, according to Eusebius, to say that Paul had written Hebrews, but he claimed that it was originally written in Hebrew and that Luke translated it into Greek and omitted Paul's name so as not to offend the Jewish-Christians who were prejudiced against him (*Hist. eccl.* 6.14.2–4). Although Origen acknowledged that some accepted Hebrews as Paul's letter, while others attributed it to Clement of Rome or Luke (*Hist. eccl.* 6.25.11–14), he himself famously held to an agnostic position on the authorship of Hebrews, concluding that "only God knows" who wrote it (6.25.14). Later, Tertullian thought that *Barnabas* wrote it (*Modesty* 20).

Hebrews had a questionable position in the Syriac Peshitta and was placed *after* the Epistles of Paul, not unlike in the current biblical canon, where its position is somewhat equivocal and placed after the smallest Pauline letter instead of in the logical place after Romans or possibly after 1 Corinthians. Augustine and Jerome had doubts about the authorship of Hebrews, but they nevertheless accepted it as Paul's perhaps to insure its inclusion in the biblical canon. Jerome observed that the churches to the West (the "Latins") "do not receive it among the canonical scriptures as St. Paul's" (*Letter to Dardanus* 129), but he included it. The book was eventually included in many of the Scripture canons of the West at the Synod of Hippo in 393 and at the Third and Sixth Synods of Carthage in 397 and 416–419.

E. General (Catholic) Epistles

Except for James, 1 Peter, and 1 John, the General Epistles were not widely known in the churches throughout the second century, and some were variously disputed even in the fourth and fifth centuries.[71]

1. *James*. James had a mixed reception in early Christianity, probably as a result of its apparent contradiction of Paul's teaching on works (cf. Rom 4 and Jas 2). Eusebius classifies the book as one of the disputed (*antilegomena*) writings (*Hist. eccl.* 3.25.1–5), and it is missing from several fourth-century lists of NT works (see Appendix C). While some have suggested that *Didache*, Ignatius, *Ep. Barnabas*, Polycarp, *Shepherd of Hermas*, Diognetus, and Justin may have alluded to James in the second century, it is more likely that only *1 Clement* and *Shepherd*

---

[71]   For a useful introduction to the canonical inclusion of the Catholic Epistles, see R. W. Wall, "A Unifying Theology of the Catholic Epistles: A Canonical Approach," in *The Catholic Epistles and the Tradition*, ed. J. Schlosser, BETL 176 (Leuven: Leuven University Press, Peeters, 2004), 43–71.

of Hermas knew or used James. Origen appears to be the first person to clearly appear to refer to the James Epistle as Scripture and claim that James the brother of Jesus wrote it (see his *Commentary on John* 19.6; compare *Homilies on Exodus* 15.25). The same views emerge later in Dionysius of Alexandria (ca. 250–265) and in Gregory the Thaumaturge (ca. 250–265).

2. *1 Peter*. Although there are several parallel phrases in the *Epistle of Barnabas* and 1 Peter (*Barn.* 5.6 and 1 Pet 1:20), it is only with Polycarp (ca. 69–155) that clear use of 1 Peter is found (e.g., Pol. *Phil.* 1.3 and 1 Pet 1:8; Pol. *Phil.* 10.2 and 1 Pet 2:12). The author of 2 Pet 3:1 (ca. 120–130) refers to the existence of an earlier letter by the Apostle Peter. Eusebius claimed that Papias (ca. 100–150) knew and used 1 Peter (*Hist. eccl.* 3.39.17), and he includes it in his list of the recognized books (3.25.2 and 3.3.1). Irenaeus was the first to use 1 Peter by name (*Haer.* 4.9.2; 4.16.5; 5.7.2), and thereafter many references are made to 1 Peter in the later church fathers. Early witnesses validate the use of the book in the church, and it does not appear to have been seriously questioned in the fourth century, even though it is missing in the Muratorian Fragment.

3. *2 Peter*. Essentially, 2 Peter was under suspicion in the church until the time of Athanasius' *Thirty-Ninth Festal Letter* in 367. Eusebius rejected it (*Hist. eccl.* 3.25.3) and was aware of the widespread doubts about its authenticity (*Hist. eccl.* 3.3.1–4). It was apparently used by the author of the *Apocalypse of Peter* (ca. 110–140) and so might well have been written sometime between 100 and 110. It is one of the several pseudonymous writings in Peter's name (*Preaching of Peter, Gospel of Peter, Acts of Peter, Apocalypse of Peter*, and 2 Peter). All are likely second century. Scholars are divided over the dating of 2 Peter. A few still believe that the Apostle Peter wrote it and they date it between 60 and 65, but since the style is so different from 1 Peter, others think it was written near the end of the first century and still others place it no later than 120–160. George MacRae placed it around 180 at the latest. The problem with dating it early has to do with the few *clear* references to it in the first and second centuries, but also because of the early suspicion of its authorship and its late inclusion in the NT canon.

In my earlier assessment of 2 Peter, I thought that it could have been written as late as 180, but I have now changed that to the early to middle second century. The dependence of the *Apocalypse of Peter* (ca. 110–140) on 2 Peter, or perhaps the other way around, namely 2 Peter depending on the *Apocalypse of Peter*, as well as the fact that it was not in any early manuscripts of the NT, suggests that it was not written in the first century. Recognized books such as 1 Peter, likely dating from the first century and having considerable difference in style and content from 2 Peter, suggests a later date. However, the change in my opinion of the date of 2 Peter does not change anything of significance regarding its initial doubtful place in the NT canon. A date of ca. 120–140 certainly fits within the early church tradition, but it is unlikely a first-century document. It was not included in the earliest catalogues of the NT writings and was rejected by some churches well into the sixth century. Athanasius (367) concluded that the Apostle Peter wrote it and consequently included it in his NT canon. That view eventually carried the day until modern times.

The Syrian churches appear to have held 2 Peter in question until the sixth century. It is absent from the recension of Lucian of Antioch, and the most prominent church father from Antioch, John Chrysostom, never referred to it. The same is true of Theodore of Mopsuestia. Athanasius of Alexandria apparently set the stage for the acceptance of 2 Peter in the churches, but it was still questioned as late as the Reformation, when Martin Luther concluded that the Christian message did not shine well through it.

4. *1 John*. First John was one of the earliest books besides the Gospels and Epistles of Paul to be acknowledged as Scripture and subsequently included in the NT canon. Both Eusebius (*Hist. eccl.* 3.24.17) and Origen (Eusebius, *Hist. eccl.* 6.25.10) accepted it as a part of their sacred collection of Christian Scriptures. It is cited by Irenaeus (*Haer.* 3.17.5, 8), Clement of Alexandria (*Fragmente in Adumbrationes*), and Tertullian (*Prax.* 15; *Marc.* 5.16; *Antidote for the Scorpion's Sting* 12). Apart from the Alogi from Asia Minor in the last third of the second century, who rejected the Gospel of John, Acts, Revelation (see Irenaeus' report in *Haer.* 3.11.12), and probably 1 John as well, few others were opposed to the authenticity of this letter and most writers of antiquity agreed that the Apostle John had written it. Eusebius in the fourth century states that very few leaders of the church ever questioned its authenticity. It was accepted into the Syriac Peshitta no later than the fifth century, but apparently was not included in the early stages of its formation. The earliest obvious citations of the letter appear in Pol. *Phil.* 7; Justin, *Dial.* 123.9; and probably also in Ign. *Eph.* 7.2; see also *Diogn.* 10.3; and the *Gospel of Truth* 27.24 and 31.4–5.

5. *2 and 3 John*. Very little citation of 2–3 John is found prior to the fourth century, and both Eusebius (*Hist. eccl.* 3.25.3) and Origen (Eusebius, *Hist. eccl.* 6.25.10) had doubts about their authenticity. Before then, precious little ancient testimony speaks to their presence, authenticity, or authority. A few possible parallels in the Apostolic Fathers are not conclusive (e.g., Pol. *Phil.* 7.1 and 2 John 7 [cf. also Tertullian, *Flesh of Christ* 24]; Ign. *Smyrn.* 4.1 and 2 John 10–11). Better information is available on the use of these two letters from the time of Clement of Alexandria (*Strom.* 2.15.66). Irenaeus quotes 2 John 11 and 7 in *Haer.* 3.17.8. According to Eusebius, Dionysius of Alexandria knew all three letters of John (*Hist. eccl.* 7.25.11). Eusebius also claims that Papias wrote a commentary on them (*Hist. eccl.* 3.39.1–3). Irenaeus and Tertullian do not mention 3 John, and even the fourth-century Muratorian Fragment (lines 68–69) knew only two letters of John. Elsewhere in the fourth century the three letters are known, but are not

yet generally accepted among the churches as Scripture. They are included in Athanasius's *Thirty-Ninth Festal Letter*, Cyril of Jerusalem (*Catechetical Lectures* 4.36), and the Mommsen or Cheltenham Catalogue (ca. 360 in North Africa), but doubts were still expressed about their inspiration and canonicity by Jerome (ca. 420) in *Illustrious Men* 9.18. Cyprian cites 2 John 10–11 in his *Sententiae episcoporum* 81.

There appears to have been a time when only two letters of John were accepted in the West and in Alexandria. There are no certain references to 3 John until the time of Jerome and Augustine. Although some scholars argue that 2 John and 3 John circulated at first as one letter – hence their common designation under one name and frequent references to only two letters of John – the evidence for this is not convincing. Both 2 John and 3 John have a slim history of use in the church and are seldom referred to until the fourth and fifth centuries, when they both appear in lists of Scriptures and subsequently in theological treatises, where their authority and reception are both questioned and accepted.

6. *Jude*. The Epistle of Jude is used in several early Christian writings: Pol. *Phil.* 3.2 and Jude 3, 20; Pol. *Phil.* 11.4 and Jude 20, 23; *Barn.* 2.10 and Jude 3–4; Athenagoras, *Supplication for Christians* 24–25; Theophilus of Antioch 2.15; Clement of Alexandria, *Christ the Educator* 3.8.44 (quoting Jude 5–6 by name); 3.8.45 (quoting Jude 11); *Strom.* 3.2.11 (quoting Jude 8–16 by name). Eusebius notes Clement's acceptance of Jude (*Hist. eccl.* 6.13.6; 6.14.1). Tertullian implies that Jude was known in Latin translation (*Apparel of Women* 1.3). The book was fully accepted by Athanasius in his *Thirty-Ninth Festal Letter* of 367. The Muratorian Fragment (lines 68–69) mentions Jude in an awkward manner, possibly showing some element of doubt about its acceptance. This is consistent with the questions raised about Jude in the fourth century.

Origen knew of questions about Jude, but this does not deter him from citing the book (e.g., *Commentary on Matthew* 17.30) and Jude 6 (*Commentary on Matthew* 10.17). In the latter text Jude is called a servant of "our Lord Jesus Christ and a brother of James" (see *Commentary on John* 13.37 and Jude 6; *Homily on Ezekiel* 4.1 and Jude 8–9; and *First Principles* 3.2.1, which shows awareness of the book). He was apparently attracted to Jude because of its views on angelology. The widely acknowledged use of Jude in 2 Peter, likely a second-century book, gives further witness to the widespread use of Jude in the second century.

In the fourth and fifth centuries Jude was called into question primarily as a result of its use of *1 En.* 1:9 in Jude 14–15. Throughout the first two centuries of the church, *1 Enoch* was accepted as inspired and sacred in many Christian communities. For example, *1 Enoch* was used by *Assumption of Moses*, *Jubilees*, *Apocalypse of Baruch* (ca. 70 CE), and *Testaments of the Twelve Patriarchs*. In the Christian era, the author of *Epistle of Barnabas* cites *1 Enoch* three times, twice referring to it as Scripture: "It has been written, just as Enoch says" (*Barn.* 4.3, referring to *1 En.* 89:61–64; 90:17) and "For the Scripture says" (*Barn.* 16.5, citing *1 En.* 89:55, 66–67). The appeal of Jude to *1 Enoch*, therefore, was not a problem in the early Christian communities. Only in the third century and later do we find doubts expressed about the canonicity of *1 Enoch*, mostly because of its attributing carnal lust to heavenly beings. Consequently, in the fourth century and later Jude's use of *1 Enoch* led to questions about the place of Jude itself in the Scripture canon.

Eusebius lists Jude among the "doubted" (*antilegomena*) writings in the church (*Hist. eccl.* 3.25.3; cf. 2.23.25), and Jerome (*Illustrious Men* 4) felt obligated to deal with the issue of Jude's use of *1 Enoch*. Didymus of Alexandria (ca. 395) defended Jude against those who attacked its use of *1 Enoch* (see Migne, *Patrologia graeca* 39.1811–18). Jude's offense was not that he made use of *1 Enoch*, as other Christian writers had done, but that he referred to the writing by name. Jude used Jewish apocalypses in much the same manner as did 1–2 Peter. Although Jude cites *1 Enoch* by name, he is nonetheless still within the bounds of what was acceptable in his day.

F. Revelation

There are no certain traces of Revelation in the Apostolic Fathers. The closest parallels, of course, come from the *Visions* section of the *Shepherd of Hermas* and this is to be somewhat expected since both writings are apocalypses:

> *Herm. Vis.* 1.1.3 and Rev 17:3
> *Herm. Vis.* 2.2.7; 4.2.5; 4.3.6 and Rev 3:10 and 7:14
> *Herm. Vis.* 2.4 and Rev 12:1
> *Herm. Vis.* 4.1.6 and Rev 9:3
> *Herm. Sim.* 8.2.1, 3 and Rev 2:10; 3:11; and 6:11
> *Barn.* 7.9 and Rev 1:7, 13
> *Barn.* 21.3 and Rev 22:10–12

Charles claims that Revelation was all but universally accepted (and consequently used in an authoritative manner) in Asia Minor, western Syria, Africa, Rome, and south Gaul in the second century.[72] Justin appears to have been the first to say that John the Apostle wrote the book of Revelation (*Dial.* 81.15; cf. also *1 Apol.* 28, which refers to Rev 12:9). According to Eusebius, Apollonius used Revelation in the second century to write against the Montanists (*Hist. eccl.* 5.18.14). Clement of Alexandria (*Christ the Educator* 2.119) cites Revelation as Scripture and as the work of John the Apostle (*Salvation of the Rich* 42 and *Strom.* 6.106–107). Charles further notes that, according to Tertullian, Marcion rejected the traditional authorship of John and the Alogi of the second century rejected the writing altogether.

---

[72]   R. H. Charles, *A Critical and Exegetical Commentary on the Revelation of St. John*, 2 vols., ICC (Edinburgh: T. & T. Clark, 1920), 1:xcvii–ciii.

As described above, according to Eusebius, Dionysius the Great of Alexandria (ca. 260–64) wrote a critical appraisal of the authorship of the book (*Hist. eccl.* 7.24–25) and he concluded that John the Apostle did not write Revelation. Eusebius placed Revelation among the doubtful books in his collection of Christian writings (*Hist. eccl.* 3.24.18; 3.25.4). Cyril of Jerusalem rejected the book altogether and forbade its use in public or private (*Catechetical Lectures* 4.36). Around 360, Revelation did not get included in the canon list of the Council of Laodicea or in the canon 85 of the *Apostolic Constitutions*. Most scholars contend, as Charles shows,[73] that Revelation was ignored or rejected in many Eastern churches in the fourth century and later, but as we saw earlier, not by all Eastern churches. Some Eastern writers did accept and refer to Revelation: Melito of Sardis, Jerome, Theophilus of Antioch, Apollonius of Hierapolis, Clement of Alexandria, and Origen.

Significant rejection of Revelation in the East did not occur until the end of the fourth century, when Cyril of Jerusalem excluded Revelation without comment (*Catechetical Lectures* 4.36). On the other hand, Epiphanius of Salamis still included it at the end of the fourth century (*Pan.* 76.5), as did Jerome (*Letter to Paul* 53) and Codex Alexandrinus (425).

I should note here once again an earlier word of caution that the above references to or parallels with the books of the NT by individual church fathers do not necessarily mean that all church fathers agreed at the same time that a particular book was Christian Scripture. The opposite is true as we saw in several cases. They do reflect what eventually came to comprise the church's NT canon, and, as we saw, early on other books as well were included.

VII. SUMMARY

The above information may be called the external data that impacts our understanding of the growing citation and recognition of Christian writings that eventually led to the formation of the NT. Each of the above areas enables us to see how the formation of the NT was affected by or reflected in the use of the codex, the books in the manuscripts, sacred lists of Christian Scriptures and in the citations or parallels with the NT books in individual works in the early churches. These factors all shed considerable light on the emerging NT canon, and they let us know that the process of canon recognition was neither immediately settled in all of the churches nor even after several centuries. The processes that led to a final fixation of the NT canon took much longer. The citations of texts show the frequency of use of the NT books in the early churches and also what books had the greatest influence on the ancient churches.

---

[73] Ibid., ci–ciii.

In the next chapter we will examine some of the best known collections of NT books in the early churches, including some of the more controversial ones. Those lists are not exhaustive, but certainly illustrate the development of the church's Scriptures and various attempts to limit the sacred books to a fixed collection.

CHAPTER 21

COLLECTIONS, COUNCILS, AND CANON FORMATION

I. ANCIENT CATALOGUES OF SCRIPTURES AND BIBLICAL CANONS

Most ancient collections or lists of Christian Scriptures date after the first half of the fourth century.[1] The existence of catalogues[2] of sacred writings does not mean that their authors all intended a *fixed* canon collection of Christian Scriptures to which nothing could be added or taken away. Often such collections are simply lists of allusions, citations, or quotations from the NT in other ancient literature used by some of the church fathers. Merely collecting and tabulating these references does not constitute a biblical canon; it says no more than that the theological positions and perspectives of the early church fathers were informed by these earlier writings. Until we come to the third or fourth century, such references often do not prove that the literature was even acknowledged as Scripture.[3] The study of such references can be quite valuable especially as one examines them in the context in which each of these allusions or citations is found, but it is a common error in the study of the biblical canon to view all these references as citations

---

[1]   For the lists, see A. Alexander, *The Canon of the Old and New Testaments Ascertained* (New York: Princeton Press, 1826); F. F. Bruce, *Canon of Scripture*, 205–51; Farmer and Farkasfalvy, *Formation of the New Testament Canon*, 9–22; Grant, *Formation of the New Testament*, 148–80; F. W. Grosheide, *Some Early Lists of the Books of the New Testament*, Textus minores 1 (Leiden: Brill, 1948); Hahneman, *Muratorian Fragment*, 132–82; Koester, *Synoptische Überlieferung*; Kümmel, *Introduction to the New Testament*, 340–55; Metzger, *Canon of the New Testament*, 209–47, 305–15; Souter, *Text and Canon*, 205–37; and M. A. Stuart, *A Critical History and Defense of the Old Testament Canon* (Andover, MA: Allen, Morrill & Wardwell, 1845); and see the updated lists in Appendices A and C.

[2]   "List" is probably not the best term to describe these collections since it suggests that their patristic authors drew up a list of Christian Scriptures. To our knowledge, Irenaeus (except for the four Gospels) and Clement of Alexandria, for example, made no fixed catalogues of Scriptures. For a discussion of this, see A. C. Sundberg, Jr., "The Bible Canon and the Christian Doctrine of Inspiration," *Interpretation* 29 (1975): 364–65.

[3]   Souter, Kümmel, and Farmer and Farkasfalvy all draw this conclusion.

of Scripture. Much of what follows will focus on the most examined catalogue or listing of New Testament books, namely the Muratorian Fragment, but other lists will also be considered as well.

Because scholars often assume that citations and lists of writings are a part of an ancient writer's canon collections, it is important to add a few necessary and partially repeated precautions. First, the presence or absence of citations to the NT literature in the writings of the church fathers does not in itself necessarily imply that the documents referred to were or were not viewed as sacred Scripture *at that time*. Brown contends that patristic citations do, however, give evidence of the acceptance of this literature as authoritative in the life of the church and they likely indicate the beginnings of a Christian canon of Scripture.[4] The specific context of each citation is important before judgments can be made in this regard. Second, the absence of a particular Christian document from the writings of a church father does not necessarily mean he was either unaware of it or did not believe that it was Scripture. Several ancient writings were produced in response to problems facing the church and the ancient writers would seldom have the occasion in such *ad hoc* writings to cite all of the works that they thought were inspired Scriptures. Third, the writings quoted or referred to by one church father in one geographical location are not necessarily representative of all church fathers in the same area and are even less representative of all churches in other areas at the same time.

Finally, as Hurtado reminded us earlier, only a small portion of the total number of ancient written documents is known today, perhaps less than one percent, and perhaps future discoveries will lead to changes in our perspectives about what functioned as sacred writings in antiquity. Some of the early Christian writings were simply lost, e.g., the first letter in Paul's Corinthian correspondence (1 Cor 5:9); or his letter to the Laodiceans (Col 4:16). Some Christian writings were at some point no longer deemed relevant to the present needs of local churches and were either discarded or stored in undiscovered locations, or perhaps turned over to the Diocletian authorities during the fourth-century persecutions, noted earlier. The possibility still exits that additional discoveries, such as those at Qumran and Nag Hammadi, will be found and more documents will emerge that will give us even greater insight into the perplexing questions about the biblical canon. For example, the discoveries of numerous biblical and non-biblical manuscripts in the monasteries on Mount Athos in Greece have already shed considerable light on textual and canonical issues and there is promise for even more to come that will aid biblical, canonical, and textual scholars in their research. Access to those manuscripts has been temporarily halted, but hopefully that situation will change.

No NT writing was consciously written as part of an already existing collection of sacred Scriptures, but many NT writings began to appear in collections in the

---

[4]   See Raymond Brown in Turro and Brown, "Canonicity," 2:530.

early to middle second century. As noted earlier, it is not unreasonable to think that a collection of Paul's Epistles circulated in some churches by the end of the first century,[5] and in the last half of the second century at least three of the canonical Gospels were grouped together by Justin and all four both by Tatian and Irenaeus. Grant suggests that the first collection of Christian Scriptures arose in Alexandria, Egypt, no later than the early second century. His argument is based on examples from Basilides, the Gnostic teacher in Alexandria who wrote during the reign of Hadrian (ca. 117–138) and who cited three of the four canonical Gospels (not Mark) and four letters of Paul *as Scripture*. Grant depends heavily on Hippolytus' attack against Basilides in his *Refutations of All Heresies* (ca. 220–230), a source that not all scholars consider reliable, but more recently Hippolytus' report about Basilides appears more credible. Grant finds it highly instructive that Basilides did an exegesis of John, Luke, and Matthew and introduced each of those books with the same formulas that he used in introducing the recognized scriptural Old Testament texts, namely "this is what the gospels mean when they say" (John 1:9; *Ref.* 7.22.4), or "this is what is meant by" (Luke 1:35; *Ref.* 7.26.9), and "this is proved by the Savior's saying" (John 2:4; *Ref.* 7.27.5). He also shows that according to Hippolytus, Basilides cites Paul's letters with the formula "as it is written" as in his references to Romans (*Ref.* 7.25.1–2), 2 Corinthians and Ephesians (*Ref.* 7.26.7), and 1 Cor 2:13 is introduced with "the scripture says" (*Ref.* 7.25.3).[6] Grant concludes from these examples that "we can, however, definitely infer from Basilides' statements that it was at Alexandria that the idea of treating the New Testament books as scripture first arose," adding that the New Testament books at that time included *at least* three gospels and four letters of Paul.[7] He concludes that Basilides made explicit what other Christians in that region had already believed in Alexandria.[8]

Hippolytus attributes to Basilides no precise collection of NT writings at that time, that is, no closed biblical canon, but only that he considered some NT writings to be sacred Scripture. The clearest example of a limited collection of Paul's writings from the middle second-century comes from Marcion, but his list of Christian writings was far from what came to be known as a canon of NT Scriptures. What becomes obvious in all such collections of NT documents from the time of Marcion until the beginning of the sixth century is the absence of any broad agreement among the churches over what comprised each grouping of Christian texts, how they were ordered, what such a grouping meant, and whether these collections should be considered catalogues of sacred Scriptures.

This does not detract from the fact that Christian writings are not *generally* called Scripture before the middle to end of the second century CE, but that does

---

5   Kümmel, *Introduction to the New Testament*, 338, makes a good case for this.
6   R. M. Grant, *The Formation of the New Testament*, 122–23.
7   Ibid. 124.
8   Ibid. 121–24.

not mean that this practice could not have happened sooner in isolated communities such as Alexandria. With the fourth-century catalogues, we can speak with greater confidence of "canonical lists" of NT Scriptures, but before then the precise boundaries of the Christian Scriptures are not clear. As noted, it is possible and even likely that Origen produced his own list of NT books that he believed were sacred Scripture, but it was not until the end of the fourth century that there was broad agreement on most of the twenty-seven books that make up our present NT. Aland correctly observes that it took centuries longer for a consensus to be reached on our present twenty-seven books.[9]

Exactly when lists of *Christian writings* began to emerge has been a hotly contested issue for years among scholars who debate whether the Muratorian Fragment (MF) should be dated near the end of the second century or in the middle to late third century, or finally from the middle to late fourth century. There was a shift of opinion after several years from broad agreement on the second-century dating of this document with several scholars favoring a fourth-century date. More recently, however, a middle point for dating the MF has been suggested, namely that the author of the MF was dependent on Origen and it was written sometime after him, possibly by Victorinus of Pettau. I will have more to say about this development below.

I will start first with Eusebius who is likely the first of many *in the fourth century* to construct a catalogue of Christian Scriptures and to posit three categories for the surviving Christian writings. For some time several scholars have suggested that Eusebius was the creator of several such lists in the fourth century. Hahneman and Kalin contend that Eusebius created his lists by reading Irenaeus (*Hist. eccl.* 5.8.1), Clement of Alexandria (*Hist. eccl.* 6.14.1–7), and Origen (*Hist. eccl.* 6.25.3–14) and making his own list of what texts they cited in a scriptural manner.[10] If Eusebius tabulated all of the citations of Christian literature in the earlier church fathers and then listed their "canons" or "encovenanted" writings, then he may be the originator of such lists or sacred catalogues. It is difficult to find such lists in the authors themselves, so suggestions from Kalin and Hahneman may be right. Hahneman, for instance, claims that: "Eusebius simply wove together various texts from their [the purported authors'] works in order to create the impression that each of these Church Fathers had a 'canon.' It was Eusebius who created the 'canon' from their comments, not the writers themselves, so that

---

9   Aland, *Problem of the New Testament Canon*, 12.
10   Hahneman, *Muratorian Fragment*, 133, 136; and Kalin, "Re-examining New Testament Canon History." Recently M. J. Kruger, "Origen's List of New Testament Books in *Homiliae in Josuam* 7.1: A Fresh Look," in Keith and Roth, eds., *Mark, Manuscripts, and Monotheism*, 110–11, has challenged Hahneman's assessment of Origen's NT canon claiming that it is consistent with what other books or authors Origen cited or listed in his writings. He also defends Rufinus' translation of Origen stating that it accurately reflects Origen's catalogue of NT writings despite Rufinus' loose translation of it. He also points to Origen's *Comm. Matt.* 10.12 in which Origen believed that the NT canon was complete (116). He may be right and I will return to a discussion of Origen below.

none of these lists are original catalogues."[11] In my earlier assessment of Eusebius' activity, I agreed with Hahneman and Kalin here, but now I see what they say as a possibility and one that does not deny that Origen may have created a list of NT canonical writings.

Hahneman identifies fifteen undisputed catalogues of canonical Scriptures from the fourth and early fifth centuries, to which I have added four manuscripts (listed from #16–#21 with the inclusion of the Muratorian Fragment and the Syriac Peshitta translation):[12]

Source	Date	Provenance
1. Eusebius, *Hist. eccl.* 3.25.1–7	303–325	Palestine/Western Syria
2. Codex Claromontanus, D^P	Sixth century	Alexandria, Egypt
3. Cyril of Jerusalem, *Catechetical Lectures* 4.33	ca. 350	Palestine
4. Athanasius, *Thirty-Ninth Festal Letter*	ca. 367	Alexandria, Egypt
5. Mommsen Catalogue	ca. 365–390	Northern Africa
6. Epiphanius, *Refutation of All Heresies* 76.5	ca. 374–377	Salamis, Cyprus
7. Apostolic Canon 85	ca. 380	Palestine/Western Syria
8. Gregory of Nazianzus, *Carmina* 12.31	ca. 383–390	Asia Minor
9. African Canons	ca. 393–419	Northern Africa
10. Jerome, *Letter* 53	ca. 394	Palestine
11. Augustine, *Christian Doctrine* 2.8.12	ca. 396–397	Northern Africa
12. Amphilochius, *Iambics for Seleucus* 289–319	ca. 396	Asia Minor
13. Rufinus, *Commentary on the Apostles' Creed* 36	ca. 400	Rome
14. Innocent I, *Letter to Exuperius of Toulouse*	ca. 405	Rome
15. Syrian catalogue of St. Catherine's Monastery	ca. 400	Eastern Syria
16. Codex Vaticanus	mid-fourth century	Alexandria, Egypt
17. Codex Sinaiticus	mid-fourth century	Alexandria, Egypt
18. Codex Alexandrinus	fifth century	Asia Minor
19. Syriac Peshitta	ca. 400	Eastern Syria
20. Muratorian Fragment	ca. 350–400	Eastern Mediterranean
21. Codex Hierosolymitanus	ca. 1056	Perhaps Cyprus

There can be no doubt that most of the lists or catalogues of NT writings recovered from antiquity come from the fourth century and later and not before, but does that prove that some church father did not create such a list earlier? It appears likely that Origen had a closed list of NT books, that is, a list of books that *he saw* were widely (never universally) welcomed in the churches and that he himself also acknowledged as Christian Scriptures. It is not clear, however, that other such *closed* lists existed before Origen or that they existed in any other church

---

[11] Hahneman, *Muratorian Fragment*, 136.

[12] Ibid., 133, 171, 172. See Appendix C.2 for the books in each of these canons.

fathers until after Eusebius in the fourth century. As we see in the lists in Appendix C, such lists or catalogues are much more prominent in the fourth century and following. I will conclude below that if the Muratorian Fragment is a second-century document, it had little affect if any on an understanding of the formation of the NT in the second century CE.

The above lists and others reflect the literature that informed the beliefs and thought of the Christian communities at various times and what they considered authoritative in those communities for their beliefs and conduct. There are differences in most of them, but also considerable overlap especially in regard to the canonical Gospels, most of the letters attributed to Paul, Acts, 1 Peter, and 1 John. Although not all of the literature in these lists was specifically called Scripture in the first or early second century, for the most part it seems to function that way in churches that possessed this literature. The above lists indicate to some extent the broad acceptance in the early churches of the majority of the books that now constitute the NT canon – and they also reflect the diversity that existed in churches well into the fifth century and later.

Perhaps we should note here that even in much later catalogues, writings viewed as sacred, doubtful, or rejected were often listed in the same catalogues in separate sections and, as I will observe again later, there would be little need to continue to list rejected books if no one was using them. For example, in the *Stichometry*[13] *of Nicephoris* (ca. 850), its author (not Nicephoris)[14] listed not only the received scriptures, but also some of the rejected books that, although rejected quite early by a majority of churches and in earlier church councils (ca. 393, 397, and 416), continued to be listed as rejected books for more than 100 to almost 500 years later. The NT part of this catalogue has 26 books (without Revelation), but this is followed by books under the title of *antilegomena* ("spoken against" or doubted books) listing the *Apostolic Constitutions*, *1–2 Clement*, Ignatius, Polycarp, and *Shepherd of Hermas* (or *Pastor*).[15]

With regard to the book of Revelation, Euginia Constantinou tells the important story of how Revelation was finally included in the Eastern Orthodox biblical canon, but was not given a place in the lectionaries for reading in their worship services. This anomaly, she argues, is rooted in Eusebius' classifying texts as "universally acknowledged" (ὁμολογουμένοις), "disputed" (ἀντιλεγομένων), and

---

[13]   As noted earlier in Chapter 9 (§V.A), "stichometry" is an ancient method of calculating the number of lines in a manuscript that were used as a basis for payment to copier for the script. The term comes from the Greek στίχος (pl. = στίχοι), referring to a line in a manuscript that normally had 16 syllables or some 36 letters per line.

[14]   The Nicephoris of Constantinople (d. 828) was supposedly the author who constructed this list but someone later (ca. 850) wrongly inserted this list in Nicephorus' *Abridgment of Chronography*, a catalogue of biblical books.

[15]   For these lists and the numbers of lines in each book, see Swete, *Introduction to the Old Testament in Greek*, 346–48. The Old Testament and Apocryphal books in this list are listed in Chapter 9 §V.A.10 and also in Appendix A.

"spurious" (νόθοις) in his *Ecclesiastical History* 3.25.2, 4. Because he accepted Dionysius' earlier doubts about Revelation, she contends that Eusebius' doubts about Revelation largely influenced its rejection by many Eastern churches in the fourth and fifth centuries. Since lectionaries were developed in the fifth century and later, Revelation was not included in the lectionaries despite an earlier acceptance of its retention in the Orthodox biblical canon. Constantiou's arguments are weaker on Revelation's acceptance in the second and third centuries, but better supported for its position in churches in the fourth and fifth centuries. She makes a convincing explanation for Revelation's mixed reception in the East.[16]

Hovhanessian contends that the Armenian Church has not officially accepted a recognized New Testament canon through a church council. He adds that many other non-canonical writings were also included in various Armenian manuscripts and lists throughout Armenian Church history, extending well into the eighteenth and nineteenth centuries. The best-known "additional" books are *3 Corinthians*, *The Repose of the Evangelist John* (or *The Rest of the Blessed John*), and the *Petition of Euthalius*, that were all regularly found in various ancient Armenian scriptural manuscripts, and occasionally also other noncanonical writings. He observes that the Old Syriac, which contained a number of apocryphal books, was the parent translation from which the Armenian translation emerged. He claims that most Armenian translations from the fifth century onward also contained one or more of the three writings listed above, but often even others as well.[17] Pentiuc explains that this "openness" of the canon could happen in the Eastern Orthodox churches precisely because each region is essentially independent of the others ("autocephalous") in such matters as canon and that allows national churches to make different decisions on the scope of their scriptures.[18] He acknowledges that the Eastern Orthodox churches had nothing like a Council of Trent to guide them on such matters and rather offers Theodore Stylianopoulos' view that the phrase "closing of the canon" was not a "rigid principle" in Orthodox churches. Pentiuc challenges Eugene Ulrich's notion of a fixed biblical canon arguing that:

> If one takes into account the clear-cut definition of biblical canon proposed by Ulrich, that the biblical canon is a "closed list" of books tied to the notion of institutional "authority," then strictly speaking only the Roman Catholic Church can claim for herself a biblical canon: a closed list of forty-six books of the Old Testament officially endorsed by the Council of Trent. Ulrich's definition does not apply to the views held by Eastern Orthodox Churches, as there has been no Ecumenical or Pan-Orthodox council (Laodicea in 363 C.E. and Jerusalem in 1672 were but local councils) to decree on a definite number of books considered canonical (that is, a closed list).[19]

---

[16] Euginia Constantinou, "Banned from the Lectionary: Excluding the Apocalypse of John from the Orthodox New Testament Canon," in Hovhanessian, ed., *Canon of the Bible*, 51–61.

[17] Hovhanessian, "New Testament Apocrypha."

[18] Pentiuc, *Old Testament in Eastern Orthodox Tradition*, 129–31.

[19] Ibid., 130–31.

Interestingly, Reuss, after identifying a number of canonical lists, asks whether it is appropriate to speak of a Bible while such variety in the lists persists for centuries. He writes: "In speaking here of Bibles, I am using a term hardly suited to the facts." His observation is based on what can be seen in the catalogues constructed by various church fathers. He adds support for his suggestion by surveying the surviving manuscripts in which he finds the majority of manuscripts contain the Gospels, fewer contain the epistles, and even fewer Revelation. This suggests to him that a firm biblical canon was in a state of flux for much longer than some scholars suggest.[20] His judgment here, I think, is also appropriate for this generation of canon scholars.

II. MARCION

Marcion (died ca. 160) produced the first clearly identifiable collection of *Christian* Scriptures around the mid-second century,[21] but since no independent Marcionite sources or documents have survived, we depend completely on his orthodox critics, especially Irenaeus, Tertullian, Hippolytus, and Eusebius, for our information about him. Fortunately, their reports are extensive and generally considered reliable. As we saw earlier, Marcion reportedly rejected the whole of the OT and accepted only an edited form of the Gospel of Luke and ten of Paul's Epistles. Marcion's collection did not include the Pastoral Epistles, and, according to Koester, there is no evidence that he even knew of them.[22] Tertullian, on the other hand, claims that Marcion both knew and rejected the Pastoral Letters: "I wonder, however, when he received this letter [Philemon] which was written but to one man, that he rejected the two epistles to Timothy and the one to Titus, which all treat of ecclesiastical discipline. His aim, was, I suppose, to carry out his interpolating process even to the number of epistles [of Paul]" (*Marc.* 5.21, ANF).

Marcion may have been aware of the other canonical Gospels (Chapter 18 §II), but it is fairly certain that he initially adopted only Luke and some letters of Paul. Whether he specifically rejected all other Christian writings is not clear, and it is impossible with our limited current knowledge to say that Marcion advocated anything like a closed biblical canon. In any case, as we saw earlier,

---

[20]   Reuss, *History of the Canon*, 253–54.

[21]   To our knowledge, Marcion did not call what he had collected a set of Christian Scriptures. Since the Christian writings of the first and early second centuries are not generally called Scriptures until the end of the second century, it is also unlikely that Marcion used this designation for the writings in his churches for catechetical purposes. He also never called his collection a biblical canon or a New Testament. His collection of Paul's letters, as we observed earlier, was most likely not the first collection of its kind, but it is the only earliest known collection that we can identify.

[22]   Koester, *Introduction to the New Testament*, 2:297–305, suggests that they may have been written after the time of Marcion and in response to him (see 1 Tim 6:20).

the community of churches that followed him demonstrated that their scriptures were not limited to Marcion's collection and their collection of scriptures was not as yet closed for them.

III. VALENTINUS

Valentinus may reflect awareness of a collection of writings earlier than the time of Marcion. Later, Tertullian states that Valentinus (ca. 135–160), in contrast to Marcion, used all the Scriptures and perverted them:

> One man perverts the Scriptures with his hand, another their meaning by his exposition. For although Valentinus seems to use the *entire volume*, he has none the less laid violent hands on the truth only with a more cunning mind and skill than Marcion. Marcion expressly and openly used the knife, not the pen, since he made such an excision of the Scriptures[23] as suited his own subject matter. Valentinus, however, abstained from such excision, because he did not invent Scriptures to square with his own subject-matter, but adapted his matter to the Scriptures; and yet he took away more, and added more, by removing the proper meaning of every particular word, and adding fantastic arrangements of things which had no real existence. (*Praescr.* 38.4–6, ANF, emphasis added)

The phrase "entire volume" (Latin *integro instrumento*) appears to refer to a collection of Scriptures, probably the NT writings, but possibly also the OT Scriptures as well. The context favors the former since Tertullian asks both Marcion and Valentinus what right they have to use the Scripture *received from the Apostles* (*Praescr.* 32), which likely does not refer to the OT writings. While Tertullian uses the term in reference to the OT as one volume (*Praescr.* 36), the context here seems to favor a NT collection. Tertullian evidently believed that Valentinus used a collection of NT writings similar to his own. By ca. 200, the issue of having Christian Scriptures had already been settled for Tertullian and the only question for him was which scriptures Valentinus had in mind, and how he interpreted them, not whether Christian Scriptures existed. Metzger notes that the discovery of the *Gospel of Truth*, believed by some scholars to have been written by Valentinus, shows an acquaintance with the four Gospels, several of Paul's Epistles, Hebrews, and Revelation.[24] If an early dating of this work is accepted, it becomes the earliest and most complete collection of references to the OT and NT writings from a decidedly Western orientation. It is likely that Tertullian's judgment of Valentinus was in part based on his own understanding of NT Scriptures from his own time and not necessarily from Valentinus' time when the status of Christian literature was vague and in an imprecise state of definition.

---

[23] Using the term "Scripture" here for the NT writings *by Tertullian* may be anachronistic and may not have been from Valentinus, but rather from Tertullian at the end of the second century.

[24] Metzger, *Canon of the New Testament*, 124.

IV. THE MURATORIAN FRAGMENT:
A SECOND-, THIRD-, OR FOURTH-CENTURY DOCUMENT?

In 1738–1740 Ludovico Antonio Muratori (1672–1750) discovered a codex manuscript of some 76 leaves in the Ambrosian library in Milan in 1700 (Cod. Ambr. I, 101 sup.), and edited what many canon scholars believe is one of the most important documents for establishing a late second-century date for the formation of a NT canon. His work was published in 1740. Commonly called the Muratorian Canon or Muratorian Fragment (hereafter MF), the complete document that Muratori found is in perhaps a seventh-century or eighth-century document, but the MF fragment in it is a Latin translation of a Greek text that likely dates to the latter part of the fourth century CE. Scholars commonly refer to the Greek original as a late second century-document from around 180–200, or possibly as late as the middle to late fourth century, and thought to have been written in Rome or its vicinity.[25] Scholars are generally less certain about matters of authorship or provenance.

Because of its pivotal place in New Testament canon discussions today, I offer here an extended discussion of the origin of the Muratorian Fragment (hereafter MF). The MF is sometimes hailed as "the oldest extant list of sacred books of the New Testament,"[26] but more regularly the claim is that it is evidence that the formation of a NT canon dates well into the second century CE. This text is critically important to all who argue for an early NT canon (late second century) and I have occasionally dubbed it the "Achilles heel" of NT canon formation. Those who date it early, namely in the late second century CE, use it as a model of canonical consciousness going on in second-century churches at the time of its writing.

The literature on this subject is almost insurmountable and what follows is highly selective of the most recent discussion of this ancient text. Those who date it later, namely the late third century or middle to late fourth century, place it alongside other lists or catalogues of Christian sacred Scriptures that emerged during that period. If the MF comes from the second century, most agree that it is anomalous for that time and has no other known parallels until the fourth and fifth centuries when the churches were more focused on the scope of their Christian Scriptures. Some scholars who date it that early jump to the conclusion that if the MF is second century, then this was a popular view among second-century church fathers who agreed with the notion of a limited collection of NT writings at that time. That, of course, is a jump in logic and beyond the evidence that has survived that transitional period. It goes without saying that someone had to be the first in deciding which NT writings were recognized Christian scriptures, but if

---

[25] Ibid., 193.
[26] Farmer and Farkasfalvy, *Formation of the New Testament Canon*, 161 n. 1.

the author of the MF is that second-century someone, then he/she is clearly ahead of the majority of the church fathers at that time and not at all representative of second-century thinking.

In the following discussion I argue for a fourth-century context in which the MF is more suitably placed, but if it is a second-century text, it had virtually no impact on early Christianity until the middle to late third century, possibly with Victorinus (ca. 260–307) who, like the author of the MF, refers to the parallels between the letters of Paul to seven churches, that is like that of John in Revelation. More likely, it is not clearly used before its appearance in the work of Chromatius of Aquileia in Northern Italy who likely made use of this list in his preface to *Tractatus in Matthaeum* (ca. 398–407). Chromatius may have been the author of the Latin translation of the MF text, but that is not certain. He at least had access to the same Latin text of it that we possess today.[27] Authorship cannot at this time be established and scholars have moved on to the language (Latin or a Greek original), dating, and provenance of the MF. It is not clear that Victorinus wrote the list or whether he made use of the tradition in it that claims that Paul made use of John's words to seven churches when he, Paul, also wrote to seven churches. That placement of Revelation before Paul's writings is both strange and far too early for Revelation.

Guignard, like others in their examinations of the language used, argues against the notion that the MF was originally written in Latin. He dates the Latin of the MF to the second half of the fourth century, but contends that it is based on a Greek original and points to the unusual insertion of the Greek *beta* (β) into the MF Latin text as support of his position. This probably refers either to two letters Paul wrote to the Corinthians or to 2 Corinthians. Strangely this β is inserted before Galatians and is likely a reference to the number two in the Greek, that is, to 2 Corinthians. Since the Latin does not use those alphabetic letters for numbers, it is likely, he claims, that this was an oversight in the Latin translation from Greek.[28] We should note, however, that though some scholars opt for a Latin original text of the MF, there is broad agreement that the MF was originally composed in Greek, but that, if so, does not in itself point to a second-century date of composition.

Guignard's dating of the MF, like most others who appeal to a second-century dating, is based largely on the MF's reference to "bishop Pius" and "very recently in our times" (lines 74–77). Guignard states Sundberg's argument about these words, namely that this refers only to apostolic times versus all other times thereafter, is essentially special pleading.[29] However, the plain reading of the text suggests a time during Pius' bishopric (ca. 140–155) and that is generally

---

[27] Christophe Guignard, "The Original Language of the Muratorian Fragment," *JTS* 66, no. 2 (2015): 597–624, here 601.

[28] Ibid., 615–17. See also Metzger, *Canon of the New Testament*, 194 n. 6.

[29] Ibid., 598–600. For Sundberg's and Hahneman's arguments, see Sundberg, "Canon Muratori," and Hahneman, *Muratorian Fragment*. Their arguments will be discussed below.

considered too early since the "heresies" mentioned at the end of the text, namely the "Cataphrygians" (Montanists), are prominent at the end of the second century (lines 82–85). While it is possible that a lone figure in the second century was interested in the scope of the Christian Scriptures *at that time*, such as we find in Melito's interest in the scope of the church's OT Scriptures (ca. 170), no one else appears interested in that question in the second century. Consequently, even if the MF is a second-century document, it is clearly not representative of the church fathers of that era.[30] The church fathers then were more interested in which Christian writings were divinely written through apostolic figures than in a limited Christian scripture collection.

Perhaps there is yet another option to the impasse among scholars who choose to date the work either at the end of the second century, in the middle to end of the third century, or in the middle to end of the fourth century. Although her full treatment of the Muratorian Fragment is yet to be published, Clare Rothschild offers another intriguing suggestion about the origin and date of the MF, namely that it is a fraudulent document likely penned in the late fourth or early fifth century when an unknown author attempted to root fourth-century notions of canon formation in the second century by references to bishop Pius (ca. 142–157) and with the claim that the *Shepherd of Hermas* was written "very recently in our time."[31] She adds that the MF's aim may have been to anchor fourth-century arguments against the Montanists (Cataphrygians, line 85) in the second century.[32] What commends Rothschild's suggestion is that the Shepherd was widely read in churches well into the fourth century and that the MF itself commends reading the Shepherd, but not in the churches since it was not included among the Apostolic writings. The passage reads: "And therefore it ought indeed to be read; but it cannot be read publicly [or published?] to the people in church either among the Prophets, whose number is complete, or among the Apostles, for it is after [their] time" (lines 77–80). Given its widespread recognition and reading both in the second through the fourth centuries and later, by the fourth century the *Shepherd of Hermas* is generally not placed among the church's Christian Scriptures despite its inclusion in the NT Scriptures in Codex Sinaiticus (ca. 350–375 CE) along with the *Epistle of Barnabas*. Rothschild rightly sees that the MF does not fit easily into the second century and it is more at home in the fourth.

In what follows, I will discuss the arguments for a second-century dating of the MF and offer several of the arguments for dating the MF in the middle to late

---

[30]   Verheyden, "Canon Muratori," 500, concedes this point that the document did not have any obvious influence at that time and that it was not cited by anyone with the possible exception of Victorinus (ca. 260–307) who may have copied a few lines of the text (*De vir.* 3.74).

[31]   Clare Rothschild gave a paper on this topic during the Society of Biblical Literature meetings in 2008 titled "The Muratorian Canon as Fraud," that is more fully developed in her forthcoming work *The Muratorian Fragment*, WUNT (Tübingen: Mohr Siebeck). She has graciously forwarded to me and advance copy of her paper on this topic.

[32]   Ibid.

fourth century when notions of canon formation are more frequently discussed. The MF consists of some eighty-five lines and it is missing both the opening lines and also its conclusion.[33] Because of the significant scholarly attention given to the MF in attempts to establish clarity in NT canon formation, I include its complete text here before discussing its contents.

The Muratorian Fragment[34]

...at which nevertheless he was present, and so he placed [them in his narrative]. (2) The third book of the Gospel is that according to Luke. (3) Luke, the well-known physician, after the ascension of Christ, (4–5) when Paul had taken him with him as one zealous for the law,[35] (6) composed it in his own name, according to [the general] belief. Yet he himself had not (7) seen the Lord in the flesh; and therefore, as he was able to ascertain events, (8) so indeed he begins to tell the story from the birth of John.

(9) The fourth of the Gospels is that of John, [one] of the disciples. (10) To his fellow disciples and bishops, who had been urging him [to write], (11) he said, "Fast with me from today for three days, and what (12) will be revealed to each one (13) let us tell it to one another." In the same night it was revealed (14) to Andrew, [one] of the apostles, (15–16) that John should write down all things in his own name while all of them should review it. And so, though various (17) elements may be taught in the individual books of the Gospels, (18) nevertheless this makes no difference to the faith (19) of believers, since by the one sovereign Spirit all things (20) have been declared in all [the Gospels]: concerning the (21) nativity, concerning the passion, concerning the resurrection, (22) concerning life with his disciples, (23) and concerning his twofold coming; (24) the first in lowliness when he was despised, which has taken place, (25) the second glorious in royal power, (26) which is still in the future. What (27) marvel is it, then if John so consistently (28) mentions these particular points also in his Epistles, (29) saying about himself: "What we have seen with our eyes (30) and heard with our ears and our hands (31) have handled, these things we have written to you"? (32) For in this way he professes [himself] to be not only an eyewitness and hearer, (33) but also a writer of all the marvelous deeds of the Lord, in their order.

(34) Moreover, the acts of all the apostles (35) were written in one book. For "most excellent Theophilus" Luke compiled (36) the individual events that took place in his presence – (37) as he plainly shows by omitting the martyrdom of Peter (38) as well as the departure of Paul from the city [of Rome] (39) when he journeyed to Spain. As for the Epistles of (40–41) Paul, they

---

[33] Hahneman, *Muratorian Fragment*, 5, and most scholars agree that the end of the Muratorian Fragment was truncated and was longer in its original form.

[34] I am using the translation in Metzger, *Canon of the New Testament*, 305–7 and make use of his notes on the MF on pp. 191–201. He adds clarifying material in square brackets and alternative translations in parentheses. The numbers in parentheses identify the number of lines in the text. I added the paragraph breaks and the missing numbers for lines 19, 61, and 69. For the Latin text, both original and restored, see Theron, *Evidence of Tradition*, 106–12.

[35] This suggests, of course, that Luke's authority comes from Paul and his contact with the apostolic community. Such references are found elsewhere at the earliest in the fourth-century Monarchian Prologues and Anti-Marcionite Prologues.

themselves make clear to those desiring to understand, which ones [they are], from what place, or for what reason they were sent. (42) First of all, to the Corinthians, prohibiting their heretical schisms; (43) next, to the Galatians, against circumcision; (44–46) then to the Romans he wrote at length, explaining the order (or, plan) of the Scriptures, and also that Christ is their principle (or, main theme).

It is necessary (47) for us to discuss these one by one, since the blessed (48) apostle Paul himself, following the example of his predecessor (49–50) John, writes by name to only seven churches in the following sequence: to the Corinthians (51) first, to the Ephesians second, to the Philippians third, (52) to the Colossians fourth, to the Galatians fifth, (53) to the Thessalonians sixth, to the Romans (54–55) seventh. It is true that he writes once more to the Corinthians and to the Thessalonians for the sake of admonition, (56–57) yet it is clearly recognizable that there is one Church spread throughout the whole extent of the earth. For John also in the (58) Apocalypse, though he writes to seven churches, (59–60) nevertheless speaks to all.[36] [Paul also wrote] out of affection and love one to Philemon, one to Titus, and two to Timothy; (61) and these are held sacred (62–63) in the esteem of the Church catholic for the regulation of ecclesiastical discipline.

There is current also [an epistle] to (64) the Laodiceans,[37] [and] another to the Alexandrians, [both] forged in Paul's (65) name to [further] the heresy of Marcion, and several others (66) which cannot be received into the catholic church[38] (67) – for it is not fitting that gall be mixed with honey. (68) Moreover, the Epistle of Jude and two of the above-mentioned (or, bearing the name of) (69) John are counted (or, used) in the catholic [Church];[39] and [the book of] Wisdom, (70) written by the friends of Solomon in his honour. (71) We receive only the apocalypses of John and Peter, (72) though some of us are not willing that the latter be read in church. (73) But Hermas wrote the Shepherd (74) very recently, in our times, in the city of Rome, (75) while bishop Pius, his brother, was occupying the [episcopal] chair (76) of the church of the city of Rome. (77) And therefore it ought indeed to be read; but (78) it cannot be read publicly to the people in church either among (79) the prophets, whose number is complete, or among (80) the apostles, for it is after [their] time. (81) But we accept nothing whatever of Arsinous or Valentinus or Miltiades, (82) who also composed (83) a new book of psalms for Marcion, (84–85) together with Basilides, the Asian founder of the Cataphrygians...

There are many questions about this text that have been raised by scholars since the text was first published. Virtually every aspect and every line of the MF has

---

[36]   This explanation appears to come from a later period when the reception of Revelation was more widespread.

[37]   The mention of this letter, if it is *not* the Letter to the Ephesians attributed to Paul, has no clear attestation before the late fourth or early fifth century CE, first attested by Augustine. The fourth- or fifth-century letter is a rambling collection of Paul's words from his epistles, especially Philippians. Reuss, *History of the Canon*, 254, observes that the *Letter to the Laodiceans* circulated in the Latin Vulgate and was passed on and translated into the German and Romance translations from the Middle Ages. It has been found in a version of the Albigenses. The ongoing use of noncanonical writings in churches can also be seen in the continuation of *3 Corinthians* in the Armenian Bibles until the mid-1800s. See Hovhanessian, "New Testament Apocrypha." The Laodicean letter often appears after 2 Corinthians and before Galatians. For a discussion of the Bible in Armenia, see S. Cowe, "Bible in Armenian."

[38]   The references to the "catholic church" or "*catholica*" (lines 62–63, 66, and 68) are more at home in the later fourth-century church than the second century.

[39]   This line makes little sense in the second century since 2 and 3 John were among doubted books (*antilegomena*) as late as the early fourth century (Eusebius, *Hist. eccl.* 3.25).

been studied in considerable detail, including, as Verheyden has noted, in "its content [almost every word] and structure, its author and date, its provenance and sources, its original language, its genre and purpose, its reception and role in the formation of the canon, even its authenticity and textual quality."[40] The authorship is generally considered anonymous or unknown due to its fragmentary condition, but the text has been attributed to several ancient teachers in the church, most commonly Hippolytus of Rome and Victorinus of Pettau, but others as well,[41] and presently there is no agreement among scholars on the authorship of this document.

Regardless of when the MF is dated, there is no evidence that it represented a widely accepted NT canon in the second century, but, if it is a second-century document, it at best only represents the perspective of its unknown author. As noted above, it has no other second-century parallels and its *closest* parallels are in the fourth century. Regardless, there are special challenges in dating the MF due in part to some of the difficulties involved in interpreting several lines in it that I will highlight below. Some of this may be due to the fact that the text was poorly translated. It is widely acknowledged that what has survived is very poor Latin.[42]

Scholars occasionally appear to assume that the presence of a particular theological position or sacred list of sacred NT books in one part of the empire suggests that Christians everywhere at the same time agreed with it. Those familiar with the early churches are well aware of their diversity in a variety of issues, including the recognition of their scriptural texts. As we see in Codex Sinaiticus, the copiers of that manuscript at the end of the fourth century also included the *Epistle of Barnabas* and the *Shepherd of Hermas*, works that were generally not included in fourth-century canonical lists. The point here, of course, is that any suggestion that the MF is reflective of all churches at the end of the second century, goes against the evidence that other writings were recognized as scripture and liturgically used at the end of the second century (e.g., *Gospel of Peter* as we see below). More specifically, if the MF was written in the latter

---

[40] Verheyden, "Canon Muratori," 489.

[41] Ibid., 495–97. Verheyden identifies several possible authors, but observes that Hippolytus has been a favorite for many scholars and presents various arguments in favor of that option, but leaves unanswered the question of authorship, which is a more popular position. J. J. Armstrong has argued at length that Victorinus of Pettau was the author in his "Victorinus of Pettau." I will return to his discussion of authorship below. In an appendix at the end of her chapter on Muratorian Fragment as Fraud, Clare Rothschild lists thirteen options chosen by various scholars since the publication of the MF.

[42] Hahneman, *Muratorian Fragment*, 8, discusses the many "clerical blunders" in the Muratorian Fragment and concludes that the "carelessness of this particular scribe is probably responsible for a significant portion of the barbarous transcription of the Fragment." Metzger, *Canon of the New Testament*, 192, also takes note of "the carelessness of the scribe" of the MF. The same carelessness is recognized by most scholars who examine this text and their comments are summarized in Verheyden, "Canon Muratori"; and more recently also by Eckhard J. Schnabel, "The Muratorian Fragment: The State of Research," *JETS* 57, no. 2 (2014): 231–64, here 233–34.

part of the second century, or even later, there is no evidence that suggests that its perspectives on a NT canon were the same for the majority of other church fathers or the majority of churches at that same time. Irenaeus, for example, is well known for arguing that only the four canonical Gospels were acceptable to the church (see that discussion in Chapter 16 §II.C and D), but Bishop Serapion of Antioch some twenty to thirty years later (ca. 200–211) appears to have been unaware that the Gospels were limited to four and initially, according to Eusebius, he allowed the church at Rhossus to read the *Gospel of Peter* in church worship. He only reversed his decision after returning to Antioch, finding a copy of the book, and reading it. He *then* concluded that it was heretical and contrary to what had been passed on in the churches and consequently ruled that it could not be read in the churches (see Eusebius, *Hist. eccl.* 6.12.1–6). It is likely that the four canonical Gospels were welcomed in most churches by the end of the second century, though priority was often given to Matthew and John over Luke and Mark. Most if not all of the canonical Gospels were welcomed as authoritative documents for the church almost as soon as they were written because they contained the authoritative words and deeds of Jesus that formed the major database for teaching about Jesus in the churches. In most cases, the Gospels functioned like authoritative Scripture before they were actually called Scripture. Besides Irenaeus' fairly detailed arguments for the four canonical gospels, discussed earlier (Chapter 16 §II.D), two other gospel sources were in circulation besides the four canonical Gospels in the late second- and third-century churches. As we saw earlier (Chapter 16 §III), Clement of Alexandria (ca. 180) cited other noncanonical gospel sources in his *Stromata*, such as the *Gospel of the Egyptians* (eight times), the *Gospel of the Hebrews* (three times), and the *Traditions of Matthias* (three times). He even introduced a reference to the *Gospel of the Hebrews* with the formula, "it is written" (*gegraptai*).[43] During a debate with a gnostic Christian, Clement quotes from the *Gospel according to the Egyptians*: "When Salome inquired how long death should have power, the Lord (not meaning that life is evil, and the creation bad) said: 'As long as you women give birth to children'" (*Strom.* 3.6.45). Clement even concedes: "We do not have this saying [of Jesus to Salome] in the four traditional Gospels, but in the *Gospel according to the Egyptians*."[44] The point here, of course, is that Irenaeus' view of "these four and no more" was not universally accepted in his own day or for some time thereafter.

Interestingly, while Clement of Alexandria and others do mention some or all of the four canonical Gospels in the second century, there is no similar defense of

---

[43]   For the origin and use of this gospel in early Christianity, see James R. Edwards, "The Hebrew Gospel in Early Christianity," noted in Chapter 16 §III.

[44]   This reference to the *Gospel of the Egyptians* comes from *Strom.* 3.13.93, but Clement appears to be okay with the fact that his argument is not based "in the four Gospels that have been handed down to us." Several ancient references to these texts and other sources are in Metzger, *Canon of the New Testament*, 132, and 171.

them such as we see in Irenaeus, which obviously presumes that not all second-century church fathers accepted *only* the four canonical Gospels, even if that was the case with Irenaeus. Eusebius acknowledges that some Jewish Christians were especially fond of the *Gospel according to the Hebrews* (*Hist. eccl.* 3.25.5). As we saw above in Serapion's initial willingness to let another gospel be read in his churches, there is no evidence that there was universal recognition of only the canonical Gospels by the end of the second century, which a second-century date for the MF might suggest. In the third century Origen distinguished between what he believed were gospels that were not inspired by the Spirit from the canonical Gospels "Matthew, Mark, John, and Luke" (note that sequence; *Hom. Luc.* 1.1.2). If the matter were firmly established even then, however, why would Origen have felt the need to defend the four (though in a different order)? Both Clement of Alexandria and Origen, as we have seen earlier, also cited as Scripture several other so-called noncanonical works. I agree that the canonical Gospels and most of the letters attributed to Paul were beginning to be called scripture by the end of the second century, but not all of the NT writings were so designated and some not later so designated were welcomed as Scripture as we have seen.

There are many challenges in dating the MF and in what follows I will list some of the arguments scholars offer in favor of a second-century dating, generally around 180–200 CE, though some date it in the early third century, and claim that it was written in the vicinity of Rome on the basis of internal evidence:[45]

(1) The Shepherd of Hermas was counted among the Apostolic Fathers, but was not from the apostolic era so it was rejected because Hermas "wrote the Shepherd *very recently, in our times* [*vero nuperrime temporibus nostris*]" (lines 73–74). Because Hermas, who wrote ca. 140–150 during the time when his brother, Pius, was bishop of Rome (ca. 140–142 to ca. 150–155, d. ca. 155), there are limits on the dating of the *Shepherd of Hermas* (ca. 140–155). This date for the MF is problematic because of the reference to the Cataphrygians (or Montanists, lines 84–85; see Chapter 18 §IV) who emerge around 170 CE (line 84). As a result, those who date the MF in the second century generally do so around 180 or later because of the references to the heresies at the end of the MF. However, the question focuses on whether "our times" should be taken literally as the time of Hermas (ca. 140–150), and few date it that early since it would be problematic because of the reference to the Cataphrygians that is clearly later. The more important question has to do with the reference to the *Shepherd* having been written "very recently in our times" (*nuperrim e/temporibus nostris*). Does this refer to any period after the apostolic period (e.g., 100 to 180 or 400 CE) or

---

[45]   See Grant, *Formation of the New Testament*, 301; Metzger, "Canon of the New Testament," 124; Beare, "Canon of the NT," 527; Goodspeed, *History of Early Christian Literature*, 31; Schneemelcher, "General Introduction," 42; von Campenhausen, *Formation of the Christian Bible*, 242–262; Verheyden, "Canon Muratori"; and Schnabel, "The Muratorian Fragment."

something more specific? Although scholars often conclude that the MF was written at the end of the second century (ca. 180–200), it is difficult to argue this date with any certainty.[46] Does "our times" refer to all times *after* the apostolic times and could it really be as late as the fourth century or even later as Sundberg argued?[47] Is it possible that the problematic interpretation of *"vero nuperrime e/ temporibus nostris"* may be resolved by suggesting that it was a later insertion into the text in an attempt to anachronistically date the MF earlier? Instead of dating the MF either at the end of the second century or at the middle to end of the fourth century, Armstrong contends that it was written by Victorinus of Pettau (Slovenia) in the mid-third century.[48] I will discuss his arguments briefly below.

(2) The arguments for the MF coming from the West are in lines 38–39 and 76, where the author mentions "Paul from the city [of Rome]" (*pauli ab ur be '*; lines 38–39) and the departure of Paul "from the city of Rome" (*urbs Roma*; line 76) which suggests a Western origin of the MF or at least somewhere in the vicinity of Rome.[49]

(3) It is further argued that the absence of James and Hebrews from the list suggests that the document originated in the West and that the absence of four of the Catholic Epistles was an accident.[50]

(4) Von Campenhausen argues for a Western origin of the MF because it lists the Apocalypse of John and the *Apocalypse of Peter* as acceptable books, both of which he claims were routinely rejected in the Eastern churches.[51] He contends that the MF could not have been written later than the end of the second century because:

> At a later period it is hardly conceivable that the Catholic Epistles would be limited to three or four, with no mention of those attributed to Peter, or, on the other hand, that the Apocalypse of Peter and the Wisdom of Solomon would have been acknowledged as part of the NT Canon. Furthermore, the heretics and heresies named by the Muratorianum all still belong to the second century.[52]

On the other hand, Sundberg, who concludes that the fragment was written around 350–400 in the East, proposes several objections to the above arguments

---

[46] Metzger, *Canon of the New Testament*, 193–94

[47] Sundberg, "Canon Muratori," 11.

[48] Armstrong, "Victorinus of Pettau."

[49] Ibid.

[50] See this argument in Schnabel, "Muratorian Fragment," 249.

[51] Von Campenhausen, *Formation of the Christian Bible*, 244–45 n. 192.

[52] Ibid. Given the popularity of 1 Peter in the East and West, Rothschild, *The Muratorian Fragment*, suggests another reason for the omissions, namely, "The Fragmentist's intention to secure early papal authority in a later age is sometimes perceived as contrary to the omission of the Petrine correspondence. Quite the reverse, it could be perceived as precisely the sacrifice necessary to lend credibility to the list. Moreover, the most crucial text in this regard (i.e., papal authority) is neither 1 Peter, nor 2 Peter, but Matthew (e.g., 16:18–19)."

about the date and provenance of the MF.[53] His reasons include: (1) permission was granted to read the *Shepherd of Hermas* in the MF even though it was considered outside the canon. In the time of Irenaeus and Tertullian, the *Shepherd of Hermas* was considered an authoritative scriptural book, not an outside book. Irenaeus, for example, cites *Herm. Mand.* 1 and introduces it saying: "Well did the scripture (γραφὴ) say…" (Irenaeus, *Haer.* 4.20.2). Only later and in the West was the *Shepherd of Hermas* excluded from being read in the churches and some church fathers allowed it to be read in private, but it was not rejected in the second century. Since the MF rejects its reading in the churches ("publicly"), it appears that the MF was written later (fourth century?) when notions of what books were *scriptural* and could be read in churches were more clear.

(2) The Apocalypse of John and *Apocalypse of Peter* are in equivocal positions (lines 71–72), which Sundberg argues is more characteristic of Eastern than Western churches in the third and fourth centuries.

(3) The closest parallels (none are exact) to this list are in Eusebius (ca. 325–330) in the East and in the other lists produced later by other church fathers (see Appendix C for lists).

(4) There are no similar lists in the second century anywhere. Sundberg contends that even if the MF were written in the second century, it has no parallels until the fourth century and could not have played a significant role in the development of the Christian canon of Scriptures that is ascribed to it.[54] This factor is seldom given adequate consideration. While it is possible, according to Armstrong, that the MF was created after Origen in the third century by Victorinus of Pettau, he bases this conclusion in part on Victorinus' well-known poor grasp of the Latin language.[55] However, there is no evidence that Victorinus ever cited or repeated any part of the MF and there are as yet no convincing arguments that he produced the MF. Nevertheless, such a dating does not mean that there was a *widely* accepted NT canon in the second or third centuries. Armstrong's conclusion that Victorinus of Pettau wrote the MF canon has not gone unchallenged. Guignard claims that Armstrong's position is weak because it depends on a Latin rather than a Greek original.[56] He adds that, like the arguments against Hippolytus of Rome as the author of the MF, Victorinus approved of and called

---

[53] Sundberg, "Canon Muratori." Farmer and Farkasfalvy, *Formation of the New Testament Canon,* 161, dismiss Sundberg's article in a footnote without seriously considering his major arguments.

[54] Sundberg, "Bible Canon," 362, suggests that if neither Irenaeus nor Origen had fixed lists of canonical NT Scriptures, then the MF has no parallels until the late fourth century when the ambiguity about accepting several disputed books in Eusebius's three groups disappeared.

[55] J. J. Armstrong appeals to Jerome's remark about Victorinus' poor Latin. It reads: "Victorinus, bishop of Poetovio [Pettau], did not know Latin as well as he did Greek." *Vir. Ill.* 74.1 (*On Illustrious Men,* trans. Thomas P. Halton, FaCh 100 [Washington, DC: The Catholic University of America Press, 1999], 105). Armstrong builds on this as a clue to its authorship. See his arguments in "Victorinus of Pettau." He adds that Victorinus was dependent on Origen.

[56] Guignard, "Original Language of the Muratorian Fragment," 601–9.

the letter to the Hebrews Scripture even if it is not listed among Paul's writings, but Hebrews is strangely absent from the MF. Also, the author of the MF has Paul follow after (his "predecessor") John, who wrote to seven churches (lines 47–50) in the book of Revelation. That would place the dating of Revelation to the 40s or 50s, but Victorinus himself believed that John wrote Revelation during the time of Emperor Domitian (81–96) but did not publish it before the emperor's death (Victorinus, *In Apocalypsin* 10.3).[57]

(5) The argument that the *Shepherd of Hermas* was written "very recently, in our times" is, according to Sundberg, simply a reference to how the ancient churches distinguished the apostolic times from their own; "our times" is a reference to a post-apostolic era as opposed to the times of the apostles. Sundberg gives several examples of this practice, including one from Irenaeus who uses "our times" (*temporibus nostris*) of an event one hundred years before him![58] Verheyden challenges Sundberg's examples and concludes that they are not exact.[59] If the reasons for placing the MF in the late second century are valid – and they are strong though not completely convincing – the date and provenance of the document remain problematic. The authorship is not as important as the date of the list. Further, since in lines 73–80, the author says:

> But Hermas wrote the Shepherd *very recently, in our times*, in the city of Rome, *while bishop Pius, his brother, was occupying the [episcopal] chair* of the church of the city of Rome. And therefore it ought indeed to be read; but *it cannot be read publicly* to the people in church either among the prophets, whose number is complete, or among the apostles, *for it is after [their] time*. (emphasis added)

If taken literally or plainly, the *Shepherd* was written while Hermas' brother, Pope Pius (died ca. 155) *was still living* and serving as Bishop of Rome. This means that the Shepherd was written sometime in the early to middle part of the second century, since "recently in our times" accordingly suggests an earlier date for the MF than the end of the second century. No one today seriously places the MF in the middle of the second century for the reasons noted above, especially because of the reference to the later Cataphrygians,[60] but scholars who prefer an early date prefer the end of the second century or early third century.[61] At least two bishops (Anicetus and Soter) come between Pius and Eleutherius, who was the bishop of

---

[57]   See Metzger, *Canon of the New Testament*, 194; and Guignard, "Original Language of the Muratorian Fragment," 600–602.

[58]   Sundberg, "Canon Muratori," 8–11.

[59]   Verheyden, "Canon Muratori," 501–4.

[60]   As noted earlier, "Cataphrygians" is a *fourth*-century designation for the Montanists. See Rothschild's discussion of this in her forthcoming *Muratorian Fragment*. She claims that the term is a "nickname for the second-century Montanists occurring in neither Greek (Cyril of Jerusalem [ca. 315–387; *Catech.* 16.8]), nor Latin, until the fourth century."

[61]   On the date for the MF, see Verheyden's arguments in "Canon Muratori," 490–91. However there are no parallels to this list in Irenaeus or Hippolytus.

Rome in the time of Irenaeus (*Haer*. 3.3.3). If the MF must be dated in the second century, why not stress the most logical time around 140–150, which would place it in the same time of the *Shepherd of Hermas* or at least the more recent bishop, especially since the comments about the heresiarchs at the end of the MF are both confused and in error? This date is more in keeping with a careful interpretation of the words "*very* recently in our times" than what a late second or early third century time suggests by second century advocates.

Again, while it may well be right that the second-century church fathers distinguished their times from apostolic times, which fits well with the emergence of the priority of apostolic authorship in the middle to late second century, that does not in itself support the notion that the MF is a second-century production. Objections to dating the MF at the end of the second century and in the provenance of Rome generally include the following that are broadly summarized in Verheyden as follows:

(1) As noted earlier, if the Muratorian Fragment is a second-century document and reflects widespread early church notions of a biblical canon, one would expect to see other parallels to it from that general time and location, but none exist. The MF has closer parallels in the middle to late fourth century and the translation of it, if it is a translation from the Greek into Latin, also comes from the late fourth to early fifth century. Ferguson wrote a carefully balanced response to Sundberg's proposal on the date and location for the writing of the Muratorian Fragment and, according to Metzger, he "demolished" Sundberg's thesis.[62] Ferguson grants the possibility that "in our times" could refer to any time after the apostolic times, but holds that it is more compatible with a second-century dating of the document and that Sundberg's suggestion was not the usual way of distinguishing those times.[63] Ferguson, however, is not bothered by the lack of parallels to the MF until the late fourth century and argues that there is no reason that an exception to what was usual couldn't have happened. He contends that "something had to be first, and this may be it."[64] While it is true that someone or something had to be first, it is generally true also that whoever is first is generally alone and not representative of the rest of the contemporary thinkers of that day. Sundberg's observation that there are no clear parallels to the MF until the fourth century is conceded by Ferguson who acknowledges that this is the weakest part of his own argument,

---

[62] Metzger, *Canon of the New Testament*, 193. Rather than dealing with Sundberg's arguments, Metzger appears to have simply dismissed them. At the time he was preparing his volume, however, most biblical scholars accepted the second-century dating and the Western provenance of the Muratorian Fragment. Recently there has been a shift in scholarly opinion on the matter, and now a large number of biblical scholars assign the Muratorian Fragment a later date, with a possible eastern provenance.

[63] E. Ferguson, "Canon Muratori: Date and Provenance," *Studia Patristica* 17, no. 2 (1982): 677–78.

[64] Ibid., 680.

but concludes nevertheless that "we once more confront the matter of a list as the only thing which distinguishes the Canon Muratori from the situation at the beginning of the third century. Each person must decide how much of a novelty a list was and how much weight to put on the absence of lists before the fourth century."[65] He posits that arguments based on parallels are "so tenuous as to fail to carry conviction."[66] However, while it is obvious that somebody had to be first to make a list of authoritative NT books, one can only wonder why the author of the MF produced it more than a 100 or more years before anyone else did and in completely different circumstances facing the churches.

No one else in the second century is discussing a list of books to be read in the churches except Irenaeus in his list of the four Gospels that, as we saw, was not a universal perspective, nor does it include other books of the NT. No one denies that Irenaeus and Melito were among the first to use the terms Old and New Testament in reference to the church's Scriptures, but, as we saw, those terms were not popular in the churches until well into the fourth century. Irenaeus' lengthy and strange way of arguing for the four canonical Gospels – and only these four – as we saw earlier, suggests that not everyone in the second century was as convinced about their canonicity as he was. The preference for the Gospel of John in Asia and Tertullian's preference for Matthew and John over Mark and Luke (see Chapter 16 §IV) suggests that not all of Irenaeus' contemporaries agreed that the Gospels were limited to the four canonical Gospels. Further, Tatian's use of the four canonical Gospels in his *Diatessaron* and his willingness to change their texts to make them more harmonious does not suggest a sanctity that one finds in Rev 22:18–19. Even if some of Tatian's followers later inserted clauses from the *Gospel of Hebrews* and the *Protevangelium of James* into the *Diatessaron*, as seems likely, one still cannot find in Tatian a loyalty to an inspired unchangeable text. He freely adapted the text to eliminate the differences and to make the four Gospels into a unified story. What has survived from the *Diatessaron* clearly shows that the context, especially from the Synoptic Gospels, is often omitted. This is unlike Irenaeus, but interestingly, and also unlike the Fragmentist who rejected *Shepherd of Hermas* as part of the apostolic books but welcomed its private reading, Irenaeus in the last quarter of the second century calls the *Shepherd of Hermas* "scripture" (*Hist. eccl.* 5.8.7). I will say more about the use of *Shepherd of Hermas* below.

What does this say about the inspired status of the Gospels at the end of the second century, and does it indicate that the whole church welcomed only the four canonical Gospels at that time? Since inspiration was attributed to what was believed to be true and all four Gospels were considered true reflections of the story of Jesus it is not a major leap to see that the church eventually welcomed

---

[65]   Ibid., 681.
[66]   Ibid., 680–81.

them all as sacred Scripture. No doubt Tatian and Tertullian saw all four Gospels as responsible and faithful documents, but clearly not as inviolable texts.[67]

Second-century church leaders were not speaking about a well-defined list of books to be read in the churches and, as we observed earlier, Verheyden, a proponent for a second-century dating of the MF, agrees that if the MF was written in the second century it had little influence for decades and even then it only influenced a few.[68]

Admittedly, the arguments for either an earlier or later date have not as yet been completely compelling and that is why scholarly debate continues, and it explains why Verheyden agrees that the reception and influence of MF is not significant. So, why is it regularly assumed by some that the MF had an important impact on canon formation in the second- or third-century churches? If it did not have any influence in the second century, and the evidence does not support any detectable influence of the MF in the second or even third century, should scholars continue to emphasize its importance in the second century? Canon formation becomes a more important factor in the fourth century and in completely different circumstances than what were present earlier (Chapter 16 §§VI–IX).

(2) The MF's listing of the four canonical Gospels without any defense is unlike what we find in the second century with Irenaeus who advocates the use of the Gospel of John and speaks against noncanonical gospels circulating (*Gospel of Judas*). The Fragmentist's order of the Gospels is similar to a *fourth*-century order and its lack of a defense of the four, as we see in Eusebius' reference to them as the well-established "holy tetrad" (*Hist. eccl.* 3.25.1), suggests that the number of Gospels was fixed and that there was no disagreement about the four or their order when the MF list was constructed. The MF listing of the four gospels without argument and without the references like Clement of Alexandria (ca. 170–180) makes to noncanonical gospels noted above suggests, again, a later date. The fixed status of the four Gospels in the churches where this list was produced without reference to others gospels suggests a later period for its formation when the number of Gospels was settled in the majority of churches.

(3) The Muratorian Fragment oddly includes the *Wisdom of Solomon*, an OT apocryphal and pseudonymous writing, in a New Testament list (lines 69–70). This is highly unusual and has its only parallels in the fourth century as we see in Eusebius who lists Irenaeus' Christian scripture collection which also includes Wisdom of Solomon (*Hist. eccl.* 5.8.1–8; ca. 325–330). We see the same later in Epiphanius (*Pan.* 76.5; *fl.* ca. 375–403). Metzger is well aware of this anomaly and after examining all three texts concludes: "why this intertestamental book should

---

[67] Metzger, *Canon of the New Testament*, 115–16.
[68] Verheyden, "Canon Muratori," 547–52.

be included in a list of Christian gospels and epistles is a puzzle that has never been satisfactorily resolved."[69]

Schnabel's understanding of Wisdom of Solomon in a NT catalogue is also not convincing.[70] Eusebius does not list Wisdom of Solomon as an apocryphal or rejected work (*Hist. eccl.* 5.8.7–8, as we see others listed as *antilegomena* or *notha* in 3.25), but rather lists *Shepherd of Hermas* as Scripture and also offers Irenaeus' evidently positive quotations from the Wisdom of Solomon. In the MF, Wisdom of Solomon is placed *after* Jude and two epistles of John, but *before* any reference to the Revelation of John, all of which are welcomed by the Fragmentist (lines 68–71). The context clearly shows an acceptance of the Wisdom of Solomon in the MF and for Eusebius the context is in reference to acceptable texts within a Christian or NT setting.

Interestingly, Eusebius has doubts about the Revelation of John, but the Fragmentist only reflects doubt about the *Apocalypse of Peter*. Later, in his *Panarion*, Epiphanius draws up a list of NT Scriptures and, after naming the Apocalypse of John, includes both the Wisdom of Solomon and Sirach (Ecclesiasticus). Like in Eusebius, this is strange and the only other parallel is in the MF. The other two are in the fourth century. Wisdom is not in a doubtful position in the MF or in the fourth-century texts just cited. The obvious parallels to the MF in this instance come from fourth-century documents.[71] Ferguson acknowledges that the Wisdom of Solomon had more popularity in the East than in the West, but adds that the document was also referred to by Western theologians and cites several texts as evidence (Heb 1:3; *1 Clem.* 3.4; 7.5; 27.5; Tertullian, *Praescr.* 7 and *Against the Valentinians* 2).[72]

This OT "apocryphal" book in a NT list is strange indeed and only has parallels in the later fourth-century lists. Porter and Pitts deny that "Wisdom" is the same as the Wisdom of Solomon, despite the fact that "Wisdom" is a regular reference to the OT apocryphal book welcomed in the early church fathers and with parallels in the NT. Some examples of this are noted above and others are seen in several canon lists in which Proverbs is distinguished from Wisdom (see Appendix A earlier). Porter and Pitts' claim that the reference in the MF to Wisdom is likely Proverbs and not Wisdom of Solomon ignore the majority of early church fathers who regularly referred to Wisdom of Solomon as "Wisdom," and *not* Proverbs which the noted canon scholars Metzger and Ferguson both acknowledge. Although Porter acknowledges the strange location of Wisdom in a collection of Christian Scriptures, he does not acknowledge that the only other

---

[69]   Ibid., 197–98 and 214. Verheyden discusses the anomaly, but his response is not convincing and strangely depends on a possible alternative in the Latin, *ut* instead of *et*.

[70]   Schnabel, "Muratorian Fragment," 242, 249.

[71]   Hahneman, *Muratorian Fragment*, 200–205, also makes this point. F. F. Bruce, *Canon of Scripture*, 81 n. 52, is aware of the parallels to Epiphanius, but does not draw the same inference from it. He appears to have missed the reference in Eusebius.

[72]   Ferguson, "Canon Muratori," 681–83.

parallels are from the fourth century. Some church fathers considered this book a part of the church's OT canon, but in the MF it was placed in a NT list. Porter and Pitts acknowledge this as "an oddity but [it] could easily refer to Proverbs," but that does not solve the problem since you still have an OT book in a NT list and there is nothing to suggest Proverbs. For example, their argument that since "the Wisdom of Solomon is referred to by second-century fathers such as Clement and Tertullian, in any case" apparently resolves the matter for them.[73] They do not appear to get the point that neither Clement nor Tertullian include Wisdom in a collection of *Christian* Scriptures or why Wisdom of Solomon is found among Christian (NT) Scriptures in the MF, but no where else before the fourth century in Eusebius and Epiphanius. Porter and Pitts' brief summation does not show an awareness of the issue in question here.

A more likely explanation for this anomaly *in the fourth century* is that Wisdom of Solomon was a highly prized book, but by that time some church fathers knew that the Jews had excluded it from the HB canon and that some Christians had also excluded it from their OT canon. Consequently some church fathers included it in their NT. Further, since Wisdom of Solomon is missing in the Jewish canon lists, including in those Christian lists that followed the Jewish canon of Scriptures (see Appendix A.1), some church fathers added Wisdom to a NT list. While Porter and Pitts' explanation is not found anywhere in antiquity, it is odd that Wisdom of Solomon begins to reappear in several late fourth- and fifth-century manuscripts (Vaticanus, Sinaiticus, Alexandrinus, and in the stichometry inserted in the OT portion of the insert in the NT section of Codex Claromontanus[74]) and even later (council of Carthage in 416, Augustine, Isidore; see examples in Appendix A).

(4) Most of the other writings in Codex Muratori beside the MF are from the fourth century and Hahneman has argued that the MF likely also is from the fourth century.[75] The others (*De Abraam and Expositio fidei chatolice*) are probably later than the MF, but not by much. Should this be a factor in determining the date of the MF? Not many scholars raise this issue, but Hahneman's point is worth considering.

---

[73] Porter and Pitts, *Fundamentals of New Testament Criticism*, 23–24.

[74] In Codex Claromontanus (D 06; ca. sixth century CE), a stichometric list of OT and NT books is inserted in Paul's Epistles between Philemon and Hebrews. The list is in Latin and Greek and dates from ca. 350–400 CE. While this inserted list lacks Hebrews by that name and perhaps accidentally omits Philippians and 1 and 2 Thessalonians, it includes a strange order of the Gospels (Matthew, John, Mark, Luke) as well as works later rejected, namely, *Barnabas, Shepherd, Acts of Paul*, and *Revelation of Peter*. Wisdom of Solomon is included in the OT portion of that insertion. The reference to *Barnabas* may well be a reference to Hebrews since the line count in Hebrews is the same as here. The author may have been following Tertullian, *De Pudicitia* 20, who lists Hebrews as "Barnabas." See Hahneman, *Muratorian Fragment*, 1992, 140–41.

[75] Hahneman, *Muratorian Fragment*, 20–22.

(5) Hahneman argues that the language of the MF is decidedly fourth-century Latin and widely recognized as a poor translation of a Greek original from the East. While the transition from Greek to Latin in the West began around the middle of the second century, the Latin used in the MF has some peculiarities that Hahneman claims come specifically from the fourth century.[76] For example, the spelling and pronunciation in the text derives from Latin in the third and fourth centuries and several terms that first appear elsewhere appear only at the end of the fourth century,[77] and several confusing passages in the Latin text are probably mistranslations of the Greek.[78] If a Greek original is presumed and an early dating of the Muratorian Fragment is not maintained, then it is possible that the document may have originated in the East rather than the West.

(6) Hahneman claims that the reference to *urbs Roma* in line 76 does not favor a Western (Roman) community, as Ferguson argues, but rather the East. He contends that the more normal phrase employed for Rome in the West was *hic in urbe Roma*, not *urbs Roma*.[79]

(7) The arguments for a Western provenance of the Muratorian Fragment is based largely on the absence of James and Hebrews from the list and the inclusion of the book of Revelation and the *Apocalypse of Peter*, but does this hold up under scrutiny? Revelation, for example, was frequently cited in the East and accepted as Scripture in several churches in the East like in the West in the second, third, and even fourth centuries. Several examples of this include:

    a.   Papias of Hierapolis referred to Revelation.[80]

    b.   Melito of Sardis wrote a book on Revelation (Eusebius, *Hist. eccl.* 4.26.2; Jerome, *Illustrious Men* 24).

    c.   Theophilus of Antioch alluded to Revelation (*Autol.* 2.28) and used its testimonies in a lost work against Hermogenes (Eusebius, *Hist. eccl.* 4.24.1).

    d.   Apollonius of Hierapolis made use of the testimonies in Revelation (Eusebius, *Hist. eccl.* 5.18.13).

    e.   Clement of Alexandria quoted Revelation approvingly (*Christ the Educator* 1.6; 2.11; *Strom.* 6.13, 25).[81]

---

[76] Ibid., 183–214.

[77] Ibid., 12–13. Hahneman cites J. Compos, who shows, for example, that *intimans* (line 45) is first found in *Historica Augusta* (ca. 400), *visor* (line 32) in Augustine's *Against the Academics* 2.7, 19 (ca. 386), and *per ordinem* (lines 33–34) in Jerome's OT Vulgate. In fact, Hahneman claims that in Muratorian Fragment line 13 the Latin text shows enough similarity to the Vulgate to argue that it was not composed in Latin until the fifth century.

[78] Verheyden challenges Hahneman on these points in "Canon Muratori," 503–4.

[79] Hahneman, *Muratorian Fragment*, 22–23.

[80] Ibid., 23. Hahneman cites Andreas Caesariensis, *Revelation* 34, *Sermon* 12; Oecumenius and Arethas, *Commentary on Revelation* 12.7, drawing on A. H. Charteris.

[81] Ibid., 23–25.

f.   Origen frequently cited Revelation (*First Principles* 1.2.10; 4.1.25; *Commentary on John* 1.1, 2, 14, 23, 42). Significant rejection of Revelation in the East apparently did not occur until nearly the end of the fourth century, and Cyril of Jerusalem was the first to exclude Revelation without comment (*Catechetical Lectures* 4.36; see also the later canon 60 appended later to the Council of Laodicea [360] that excludes Revelation). Epiphanius of Salamis, however, still included it as Scripture at the end of the fourth century (*Pan.* 76.5), as did Jerome (*Letter* 53) and it was included in Codex Sinaiticus (ca. 375), Codex Alexandrinus (ca. 425), and possibly also in Codex Vaticanus since it was *restored* (?) to that codex much later.

g.   Athanasius of Alexandria also included it in his 39th *Festal Letter* (367 CE).

(8) The absence of James and Hebrews from the MF is not as surprising as the omission of 1 Peter, since the list included the *Apocalypse of Peter*. Hahneman agrees with Westcott, who earlier concluded that the striking omissions from the Muratorian Fragment make little sense. Westcott claims that 1 Peter, Hebrews, and James "could scarcely have been altogether passed over in an enumeration of books in which the Epistle of St. Jude, and even Apocryphal writings of heretics, found a place."[82] Hahneman follows Tregelles who suggests that the MF may have contained other works that have been lost in the transmission and translation of the text and that as a result the absence of James and Hebrews from the list may not be conclusive evidence for their rejection.[83] Several scholars commonly conclude that these omissions were accidental rather than deliberate.

(9) As noted above, Hahneman and Sundberg state that the plainest meaning of the phrase *nuperrim e(t) temporibus nostris* ("very recently, in our times") (lines 74–75) is that the *Shepherd of Hermas* was written during Pius' episcopacy around 140–154, with the writing of the MF during or shortly after that time, but most scholars know that date is far too early and is even more difficult to fit in with the historical context of the mid-second century.[84]

Verheyden, however, opts for what he calls "circumstantial evidence" to date the Muratorian Fragment in the second century. While he advances a careful understanding of this difficult text, he has yet to resolve some of the pertinent issues related to it, especially why the Wisdom of Solomon shows up in a New Testament catalogue that only has parallels in the fourth century and why the closest parallels to the MF come from the fourth and fifth centuries. His closing

---

[82]   Ibid., 25; B. F. Westcott, *A General Survey of the History of the Canon of the New Testament* (London: Macmillan, 1875; 6th ed., 1889; repr., Grand Rapids: Baker, 1980), 219.

[83]   Hahneman, *Muratorian Fragment*, 25–26; S. P. Tregelles, *Canon Muratorianus: The Earliest Catalogue of the Books of the New Testament* (Oxford: Clarendon, 1867), 98.

[84]   Hahneman, *Muratorian Fragment*, 71–72; and Sundberg, "Canon Muratori." Verheyden, "Canon Muratori," 512–17, rejects Sundberg's and Hahneman's arguments, even though he agrees that there is no foolproof way to date the MF.

salvo after challenging substantially most of the arguments put forth by Sundberg and Hahneman is overstated, namely, he concludes: "I am afraid I have to conclude that the suggestion of a fourth-century, eastern origin for the Fragment should be put to rest not for a thousand years, but for eternity."[85]

I agree with other scholars that Ferguson and Verheyden have put forth commendable and, in several places, very substantial arguments, but I am not convinced that they are compelling for a second-century date. They may be right in regard to the provenance being Rome or its vicinity, since Rome is mentioned in the text and also persons related to Rome (Pius), but doubts still persist as we have seen above. More importantly, can it be insignificant that the names of second-century heretics mentioned in lines 81–85 and the earlier reference to Hermas are all from the second century?[86] That might well be the case if all of those "heresies" were dealt with and were gone before the fourth century, but that is not the case. The Montanist controversies persisted well into the fourth century until at least the council in 381 when it was condemned. Second-century heresies did not disappear at the end of the second century. We may remind ourselves that in the third century Origen continued to mention and argue against Marcion, as did his followers, including Eusebius in the fourth century. Schnabel, Verheyden, Metzger, and others emphasize the second-century dating of these heretics and the *Shepherd*, but they do not mention that these names are also discussed in the third and fourth centuries and that the MF confuses specific information about them such as Basilides who was from Alexandria and Miltiades was not known as a heretic in the second century, but only later in the 381 council. Eusebius also has extended references to Marcion (e.g., *Hist. eccl.* 4.11–14, and 4.28–29) and the Cataphrygians (Montanists) extensively (*Hist. eccl.* 5.3.1–14; and 5.14–19). Again, the reference to the Cataphrygians is a fourth-century designation for the Montanists and is not found in the second century. We should emphasize that references to second-century heresies and heretics in subsequent centuries are not unique. Interestingly, books rejected in the second and third centuries and in fourth- and fifth-century councils continue to be listed in rejected works in the sixth and ninth centuries as we find in Ps.-Athanasius and in the *Stichometry of Nicephorus* (see above discussion). In regard to other so-called rejected books such as the *Epistle of Barnabas* and *Shepherd of Hermas*, *1* and *2 Clement*, and others, they continue to find places in several of the fourth- and fifth-century uncial codices (see Appendix C for examples).

Verheyden's discussion of the use of the *Shepherd of Hermas* is not as convincing since that text and the *Epistle of Barnabas* was included in the late fourth-century Codex Sinaiticus along with the rest of the NT writings. He also does not account for its acceptance as Scripture by Irenaeus or the pre-Montanist Tertullian. The denial of reading the *Shepherd* publicly in churches (or published)

---

[85]   Verheyden, "Canon Muratori," 556.
[86]   Schnabel, "Muratorian Fragment," 240, 243.

since it was not in the apostolic books does not fit well with other texts in the second and third centuries and it continued to be cited positively in later centuries. The popularity of the *Shepherd of Hermas* can be seen in the surviving copies of the NT manuscripts – apart from Gospels of Matthew and John, there are more ancient copies of *Shepherd of Hermas* than any other books of the NT.

Verheyden's arguments related to the *Epistle to the Laodiceans* in the MF are also unconvincing.[87] Tertullian claimed that mention of the *Epistle to the Laodiceans* in Marcion's list is the same as the letter to the Ephesians that was widely accepted and attributed to Paul. It would be difficult to argue that the Pauline Letter to the Ephesians was Marcion's "Letter to the Laodiceans" since that did not have any controversies surrounding it in antiquity and was not doubted by anyone in the second century or later. It is likely that the reference in Col 4:16 is either to a lost Pauline letter or possibly to the letter now called the letter to the Ephesians. However, the loss of that letter led to the production much later of several pseudonymous letters to the Laodiceans that were passed on in the church. Jerome denounced the pseudonymous *Letter to the Laodiceans* (*de Vir. Ill*.5, ca. late fourth century) as did also the author of the MF. While Paul's Letter to the Laodiceans is most likely now lost, the pseudonymous writing denounced in the MF was most likely written in the fourth century and its denunciation by fourth- or fifth-century church fathers suggests that the MF was likely written in the fourth century when such letters were circulating and the church rejected them as pseudonymous texts. Since this *Letter* was rejected and stayed that way, it was likely constructed in the fourth century and likely suggests that the MF that refers to it is also a fourth-century document.

Since Ephesians is already mentioned in the MF (line 51), clearly it was not the same as the epistle or letter to the Laodiceans in lines 63–64, or the *Letter to the Laodiceans* listed by Marcion, which was probably Ephesians, the Fragmentist likely has a different rejected or spurious text in view that was penned much later. If we are talking of a fourth-century pseudonymous document, as seems likely, it follows that the MF is likely also focused on that document. The only letter that has survived by the same name is not heretical but only a collection of sayings of Paul, so it is unlikely that this letter would have been the one rejected by the author of the MF. Ephesians was never rejected by any church father (see Appendix C for examples of listings of Ephesians in various canonical lists). The only known pseudonymous *Letter to the Laodiceans* is found in Latin manuscripts from the sixth to the fifteenth centuries, and Augustine is the first church father to mention such a letter in the late fourth or early fifth centuries. Since the author of the MF rejects this "epistle to the Laodiceans" and places it in the context of advancing the heresy of Marcion, it is strange that no evidence against it appears before the fourth or fifth centuries. While Marcion's reference to a letter to the Laodiceans was later identified by Tertullian as the same as the Epistle to the Ephesians attributed to

---

87   Verheyden, "Canon Muratori," 530–45.

Paul and listed by Marcion among Paul's writings, is this what was in mind by the Fragmentist? If the author of the MF intends a pseudonymous letter after he has already listed a letter to the Ephesians, why is it that no one else mentions such a letter until the fourth or fifth century? It may be that Marcion's mention of a *Letter to the Laodiceans* is the Ephesians epistle since that address is not clear in the surviving manuscripts.[88] Tertullian accepted that this is what Marcion meant and later Jerome also said that what Marcion called Paul's letter to the Ephesian church may be the so-called lost letter of Paul sent to the Laodiceans (Col 4:16), but we simply do not know if the letter in Col 4:16 is the same as the Ephesian letter. However, the letter called "to the Laodiceans" either in Col 4:16 or in Marcion or Tertullian cannot be the same letter as the one rejected later as heresy or rejected in the MF (see the earlier discussion in Chapter 18 §II and Chapter 20 §VI.C.5).[89] Hahneman, in personal correspondence, also notes that the rejection of the *Epistle to the Laodiceans* in the MF is only paralleled at roughly the same time in Jerome. The MF's surprising comment about not reading *Shepherd of Hermas* in church, but that it could be read in private, has its closest parallel in Athanasius' *39th Festal Letter* (367).[90]

Verheyden's earlier observation that the MF was likely received in the churches especially in the third and fourth centuries is helpful. If, according to Armstrong, the MF was known and used by Victorinus of Pettau, which is unlikely, the MF could have been produced at the latest in the last part of the third or early fourth century. The middle to late third century is a possibility if the Fragmentist depended on Origen to produce it, but this is speculation without adequate support presently. Verheyden may be right that Sundberg's arguments that "very recently in our time" is any time after the apostolic period is special pleading,[91] but whether those words in the MF are original to the MF may be debated. Nonetheless, Verheyden puts forth strong challenges to a fourth-century

---

[88] It is well known that the address ἐν Εφέσω was later attached to what we now call Paul's letter to the Ephesians but is absent in the earliest manuscripts.

[89] We noted in Chapter 20 that the earliest Oxyrhynchus papyri do not include Mark, 2 Corinthians, Ephesians, Colossians, 1–2 Timothy, Titus, Philemon, 1–2 Peter, and 2–3 John, but that is not necessarily a rejection of those books, but only of the location in which some books were discarded. That was not the case in the Bodmer and Chester Beatty collections, however, as we saw earlier. There is no clear evidence that the letter to the Ephesians (possibly written initially to the Laodiceans) was specifically rejected by any church fathers. See also Chapter 18 n. 8.

[90] After listing the books that comprise the church's Old and New Testament in Athanasius' 39th *Festal Letter*, he writes the following about reading books that are not canonical, but have value for reading: "There are other books besides these, indeed not received as canonical but having been appointed by our fathers to be read to those just approaching and wishing to be instructed in the word of godliness: Wisdom of Solomon, Wisdom of Sirach, Esther, Judith, Tobit, and that which is called the Teaching of the Apostles, and the Shepherd. But the former, my brethren, are included in the Canon, the latter being merely read; nor is there any place a mention of secret writings." (The English translation comes from *A Select Library of the Nicene and Post-Nicene Fathers of the Christian Church*, Second Series, vol. 4 [New York, 1892], 550–55, slightly revised.)

[91] Verheyden, "Canon Muratori," 504–12.

dating of the MF. There are no other listings of what comprised the church's NT Scriptures until the time of Origen in the early to middle third century. Origen, as most scholars agree, was far ahead of his contemporaries in terms of canon formation consciousness, whether in terms of identifying both the OT and NT canons. The same is true in regard to his interest in the text of the Jewish and Christian Scriptures. It is clear that he heavily influenced Eusebius, as we have seen, and possibly also Victorinus as Armstrong maintains.[92] Origen may even have been the first to use the term χανών in reference to the scope of a collection of scriptures. For example, in Rufinus' translation of Origen's *Commentary on the Song of Songs*, he observes that Origen comments on the extent of the Hebrew Scriptures and that he limits the number of songs that Solomon wrote only to Song of Songs. The text in question reads: "since neither the Church of God has accepted any further songs of Solomon to be read, nor is *anything more contained in the canon* (Lat., *amplius habeatur in canone*) *among the Hebrews* from which the oracles of God were evidently transferred to us, beyond three books of Solomon, which we have."[93]

It may be as Hahneman argues that the best evidence points to the writing of the *Shepherd of Hermas* around 100 CE and not the middle or late second century as some scholars suppose. Part of his argument for the earlier date is the widespread use of and support for the *Shepherd of Hermas* in the second through fourth centuries. As we have already seen, Irenaeus, for example calls it "Scripture" (*Haer.* 4.20.2). Eusebius knew this and acknowledged Irenaeus' reception of the *Shepherd of Hermas* stating: "And he [Irenaeus] not only knew but also received the writing of the Shepherd, saying, 'Well did the Scripture say [καλῶς οὖν ἡ γραφὴ ἡ λέγουσα] "first of all believe that God is one who created and fitted together all things," and so on.' He also made some quotations all but verbally from the Wisdom of Solomon" (*Hist. eccl.* 5.8.7, LCL). What adds to a possible earlier dating of the *Shepherd* is its lack of citations of NT texts in an authoritative manner, something that developed later. He only cites the lost apocryphal *Book of Eldad and Modat* (*Vis.* 7; II.3). Recognition of the *Shepherd of Hermas* also comes from Clement of Alexandria (*Strom.* 1.1.1; 1.85.4; *Ecoligae*

---

[92]   Armstrong, "Victorinus of Pettau."

[93]   Emphasis added. Translation by Gallagher, *Hebrew Scripture in Patristic Biblical Theory*, 38. It may be that in his paraphrasing of Origen, Rufinus incorporated this use of canon (*canone*) from his own later use and understanding of the term, but not necessarily. It is not certain that Athanasius is the first to use that term in reference to a collection of Christian Scriptures, as we saw in Eusebius who used not only ἐνδιάθηκος, but also χανον in several places (e.g., *Hist. eccl.* 6.25.3), which may refer to books that Origen affirmed. Kruger acknowledges the fourth-century use of the term for a list of books, but says that the time when the term was used of a collection of books may not be limited to Athanasius in 363 or 367. He makes a convincing argument on this matter in his "Origen's List of New Testament Books," 105. See also Metzger, *Canon of the New Testament*, 290–93, who summarizes the uses of χανών in the early churches and acknowledges that it was mostly for the rule of faith or church council decisions until the fourth century.

propheticae 45), who frequently quoted the *Shepherd of Hermas* in the same manner that he quoted other Scriptures from both the Old and New Testament writings. It would be strange indeed if Clement and Irenaeus accepted *Shepherd as Scripture*, but the MF at the same time (late second century) rejected it and on the earliest known criterion of that age, namely its lack of apostolic origin and its date (lines 77–80). Tertullian also refers to the work *probably* as Scripture *before* his conversion to Montanism, and as noted above rejected it later. We also saw that the *Shepherd of Hermas* was included in Codex Sinaiticus and in the inserted stichometry in Codex Claromontanus[94] (even though in a secondary position). Eusebius appears to be the first church father to place the *Shepherd of Hermas* in a *disputed* category (*Hist. eccl.* 3.3.6), but the MF, if earlier, strangely rejects it as Scripture (= not "among the apostles") and adds that it is not to be read publicly, but only privately. Eusebius recognizes its acceptance by Irenaeus given its widespread acceptance by well-known church fathers, and that it was still held in high esteem much later (*Hist. eccl.* 5.8.7). Eusebius himself placed it among the "spurious" (νόθος) books (3.25.1–5). Athanasius called the book "most edifying" (ὠφελιμώτατες) in his earlier *De incarnatione verbi dei* (ca. 318), but changed his mind by the time of his famous *Thirty-Ninth Festal Letter* (367).[95] Both Jerome (*Prologue to Kings* [*Prologus Galeatus*]; *Illustrious Men* 10) and Rufinus (*Commentary on the Apostolic Creed* 38) spoke respectfully of the book, even though they placed it in a secondary position, that is, not as a part of their NT canon.[96] The relegation of the *Shepherd of Hermas* to a secondary position and not among the NT Scriptures ("not among the Apostles") is more likely a fourth-century development and not a second-century notion. It appears that Origen, as in the case of *I Enoch*, accepted *Shepherd* as a part of his collection of Christian Scriptures, but later reversed his opinion. The inclusion of the *Shepherd of Hermas* and the *Epistle of Barnabas* in the fourth-century Codex Sinaiticus indicates that these books continued to be read *as Scripture* in some fourth-century churches even after others had excluded them. The fourth century is more likely the context for questioning the status of the *Shepherd* in the churches' Scriptures.

---

94   As noted, this codex includes a strange a stichometric list of OT and NT scriptures between Philemon and Hebrews, including several OT apocryphal books mixed in with the canonical books, but the NT is oddly arranged with the Gospels listed as Matthew, John, Mark and Luke, then its author lists the letters of Paul but not in their typical order (the Pastorals are between Ephesians and Colossians, Philemon, two letters of Peter are listed as two letters presumably from Paul to Peter, then James, 1, 2, 3 John, Jude, *Barnabas*, Revelation, Acts, the *Shepherd of Hermas*, *Acts of Paul*, and *Revelation of Peter*). Hebrews is missing, but it may be what is listed as Ephesians since in Greek they have some similarities at the beginning.

95   Hahneman, *Muratorian Fragment*, 61–69, makes these observations.

96   Ibid., 68–69.

Added to this, Clare Rothschild has noted several factors in the MF that lead her to conclude that it is a fourth-century forgery intended to establish a later view of the church's Christian Scriptures anachronistically in the second century. For example, she observes that the "Fraternity Legend," the reference to Hermas as brother to bishop Pius of Rome (lines 73–76), only has fourth-century parallels, namely, in the *Liberian Catalogue* (*Liber Pontificalis*, ca. 352–366), Pseudo-Tertullian's *Carmen adversus Marcionitas* (ca. 325), and in the *Letter of Pius to Justus of Vienne* (ca. fourth century). Collectively these reflect that the Hermas–Pius legend originated in the fourth century. Added to this, she observes that the reference to the "Cataphrygians" (lines 84–85) is a *fourth-century* designation for the Montanists and not a designation from the second century. She adds that Basilides, the second-century leader of a gnostic sect, is located in Asia in the MF (lines 84–85) rather than Alexandria, a mistake that would not likely be made in the second century nor caught in the fourth century. She also notes that while Miltiades (likely the same as Miltiades, an early leader of the Montanists) in lines 81–82 is rejected as a heretic, he was instead widely welcomed among proto-orthodox teachers in the second century and opposed the Valentinians at Smyrna (ca. 165). Tertullian cited Miltiades positively and placed him in the same camp as Justin and Irenaeus (*Adv. Valent.* 5). Again, this description of Miltiades in the MF is more likely in the fourth century when such particulars were not well remembered than in the second.[97]

Finally, Clare Rothschild lists fourth-century anachronisms that were imposed on the second century for the purpose of establishing a fourth-century perspective on the Christian canon of Scripture in the second century. These include: (1) the order of the four gospels; (2) Luke as a physician and companion of Paul (lines 3–5) is seen in the fourth-century anti-Marcionite Prologues and the Monarchian Prologues; (3) that neither Paul or Luke saw Jesus in the flesh; (4) the authorship of the fourth gospel and John being urged to write by his fellow disciples and bishops (lines 9–16); (5) the *regula fida* (lines 19–26); (6) the "reminiscence of Jerome's fifth-century Latin Vulgate in lines 33–34; (7) reference to Acts as focused on "all" the apostles; (8) reference to the *Epistle to the Laodiceans* (line 64); (9) the "echo of Hermas" (*Mand.* 5.1 in lines 67–68); (10) Jerome's suggestion that Wisdom was produced by Philo or friends of Solomon; (11) the inclusion of the *Apocalypse of Peter*; (12) Eusebius' reference to Miltiades the Montanist; (13) the reference to the "Prophets" and the "Apostles" as "after their time" (lines 79–80); and (14) the omission of texts long approved in the church, especially 1 Peter.[98] She concludes that the MF is "a pseudepigraphon intended to retroject later opinions to an earlier time to enhance their credibility and authority."[99]

---

[97] See her forthcoming, *Muratorian Fragment*.
[98] Ibid. She supplies considerable evidence in her footnotes to support her arguments that these anachronisms reflect the fourth-century period.
[99] Ibid.

On the whole, Sundberg's, Hahneman's, and Rothschild's arguments remain significant for dating the MF well into the fourth century, though not without some qualification as noted above. If we see Origen as having a fixed or limited canon of NT scriptures, *as I now do*, there are no other known parallels to the MF until decades after Eusebius. If the MF is from the second century, it was written at a time when there was no other known focus on a closed collection of Christian Scriptures in the churches and many other Christian texts were circulating in the churches at that time. This circulation of texts includes writings that we now call noncanonical texts, but some of which were cited as Scripture for a long time. There are no other known second-century texts that deny reading the *Shepherd* in churches or that allow it only to be read in private. The MF should probably be dated some time after the mid-fourth century possibly in the East – though we cannot insist on its provenance.[100]

Armstrong's arguments for Victorinus of Pettau as the author of the MF does not seem likely, but since Victorinus died around 305 to 307, and if he constructed this list, it would likely have been just prior to the Diocletian persecution when Christian Scriptures were being collected by authorities and burned and local churches began making decisions over which of their writings could be handed over to the authorities. Victorinus' time of writing would be most likely from 270–305. Was this the time when more decisions on the scope of the Christian Scriptures began to emerge? As we saw earlier, Origen made his decisions earlier in the third century. The arguments against the East, when based solely on Eastern reservations toward the use of the book of Revelation, are not convincing.

Von Campenhausen, Ferguson, Metzger, and Verheyden assume that the Catholic Epistles listed in the Muratorian Fragment (Jude and two epistles of John, see lines 68–69) were all accepted as Scripture by the majority of churches at the end of the second century, and that the church fathers at that time did not include the *Shepherd of Hermas* in that category. However, only 1 John is approved in the early fourth century when 2–3 John are both listed as "disputed books" (Eusebius, *Hist. eccl.* 3.25.2–3). Why two of the epistles of John were welcomed in the second century, but listed as doubtful in the third century (Origen) and early fourth century (Eusebius), is unclear if a second-century date is assumed. In the second century, 2 and 3 John are not listed or identified as Scripture in Irenaeus or Clement of Alexandria, or in the third century in Origen, but they are in the MF (see Appendix C.1). However, they are only widely

---

[100] The discovery of the MF in the West, and its likely translation into Latin, suggests the possibility of a Western origin, but again, the nature of the list itself may be Eastern and has some parallels there in terms of church use of Revelation as we have shown. Also, since translocal texts were quite common in antiquity, it should not be surprising to find an Eastern text in a Western community. See Hahneman, "Muratorian Fragment," 23–25, who shows considerable Eastern use of and favorable references to Revelation during the period in question.

accepted as Scripture after the time of Eusebius who held them in doubt. This is strange indeed if the MF is a second-century canon list and two of John's epistles are accepted.

Conversely, although there are some parallels with the language of the Pastorals in the second century, as we saw earlier, they are not generally called "scripture" or included in lists of Paul's writings until Origen (220–230, see Appendix C.1). This makes the inclusion of them in the MF more at home in the third and fourth centuries than earlier. As we saw earlier, they are not included in P[46] (ca. 200) or Codex Vaticanus (ca. 350–360). Origen includes them and they are included in the MF (lines 59–61) and in all later fourth-century catalogues and manuscripts except in Codex Vaticanus. They are not mentioned in Irenaeus or Clement of Alexandria and it appears that Origen is the first to include them (ca. 220–230). As we saw in Chapter 20, there are some word parallels in some second-century church fathers but it is not clear whether they were common oral traditions circulating in churches at that time. There is no compelling evidence that speaks of their scriptural status until the third or fourth centuries. Scholars have observed that the letters in P[46] gradually decrease in size and that has been argued as evidence that the author wanted to include all of Paul's writings within the scope of that codex. However, as noted earlier, these Pastoral letters attributed to Paul are missing from P[46] namely, the rest of 1 Thessalonians, all of 2 Thessalonians, the Pastorals, and Philemon cannot be fitted within the original contents of P[46] even if all of the pages had been preserved from the fragmented codex. Such arguments to the contrary are from silence and only suppositions. It is not clear what other texts were included in P[46], but there is not enough space in the number of pages in the original codex to include the Pastorals and Philemon without adding additional pages. That, of course has been suggested, but their absence is compatible with what we know about their acceptance in the second and early third centuries. While those supposed additional pages could have been added to the codex, they have not been found and there is no way to show which additional books the copier intended to include in the Pauline collection in this codex. This is often a convenient argument from silence to make sure that P[46] included all of the letters attributed to Paul in antiquity.[101] Although it is likely that by the latter part of the second century the Pastorals were attributed to Paul, perhaps because of their nature as personal letters to specific individuals, some early church fathers did not include them among the church's sacred Scriptures until later. There is considerable speculation here among scholars.

The Muratorian Fragment is an important document for understanding the growth and development of the NT canon of the early Christian church, but it is not as pivotal a document as many scholars have thought. Again, if von Campenhausen and others are correct about the early dating of the MF, it still had

---

[101] Porter and Pitts suggest this in *Fundamentals of NT Textual Criticism*, 15–20.

no known affect on the rest of the church for almost 200 years and it played no known significant role in any canon discussions until the late fourth century. If Armstrong is correct, Origen heavily influenced Victorinus who wrote the MF,[102] but Hahneman, like Guignard, will soon challenge arguments that favor Victorinus as the author. He argues that the Latin in the text cannot be attributed to Victorinus since it has a number of parallels to the Latin language that are 100 years later than Victorinus. He adds: "It is quite possible, of course, that the Fragment was a third century Latin original by a poor Latinist placed among these later translations from Greek, but the oddity would need to be explained by Armstrong, and isn't." Hahneman concludes: "That the Fragment contains parallels of a few earlier traditions (Victorinus) does not preclude a later date, but that the Fragment contains numerous parallels with later traditions does."[103] As a late second-century document, the MF's impact on the churches of that time is completely negligible and cannot be of any consequence in the complicated puzzle of NT canon formation. As a fourth-century document, however, the MF's existence is far more understandable and allows us to view the concerns and criteria of church teachers of a post-Nicene era in establishing its NT canon of Scriptures. While it could have been written in the West or even in the East, the arguments are mixed and are of less consequence than dating the MF.

We have shown several parallels in multiple canon lists in the fourth century, and possibly individually in the case of Origen in the third century, but there are no other parallels to the MF in the second century. Even if the MF influenced Origen (or the other way around, as has been argued recently!) and Victorinus in the late third century and then later fourth-century church fathers, as Verheyden contends,[104] the MF still does not have any clear parallels or influence until the late fourth century. The church was simply not discussing or reflecting on biblical canons in the second century.

My interest in the MF started when I could not find convincing evidence for Harnack's and von Campenhausen's conclusions that the early church responded to Marcion, the gnostics, and the Montanists by creating a more extensive NT canon comprised of books that were already circulating in the churches. They both saw in the MF evidence for their conclusions, but, as we saw earlier (Chapter 18 §§I–V), the second-century church fathers responded to heretical threats not with a biblical canon, but with a canon of faith, *a regula fidei*. Some Christian writings, especially the Gospels, were accepted early on as authoritative voices that proclaimed the church's earliest and most authentic traditions and teachings. Their acceptance as authoritative expressions of the church's faith led some

---

[102] Armstrong, "Victorinus of Pettau."

[103] Geoffrey Hahneman has produced an important forthcoming review of Armstrong's position and recently sent me a copy of his review along with several other objections he has to Armstrong's position.

[104] Verheyden, "Canon Muratori," 552–55.

to acknowledge that literature as Christian Scripture and eventually also other writings that later comprised the church's NT canon. It is problematic, however, to identify an authoritative function (canon as rule or authority) with scripture in all cases, including scripture with a fixed canon, and then conclude that the notions of canon that were present in the fourth century and later were also present in the first and second centuries. If the acceptance of the authority of Christian writings is the same as having a biblical canon, as some scholars say, then confusion arises when scholars impose fourth-century notions of a *closed* biblical canon on the first- or second-century churches, especially in regard to works initially called Scripture, but later rejected. The notion of canon as "rule" is early and the notion of a biblical canon with a fixed collection of NT books is simply not present in the first two centuries. An early expression of this comes likely with Origen, as noted earlier. As we have seen, there were other nonbiblical books in use in churches in the early centuries with no uniform or universal voices against them.

Theodor Zahn strangely argued that most of the NT books were acknowledged as Scripture and therefore canon by the end of the first century,[105] but this assumes that all churches possessed the same NT writings, which is highly unlikely. If most churches affirmed a list of NT books similar to the MF or the present NT canon, why do the earliest translations in the first five centuries not reflect this and what evidence is there that those churches even owned copies of all of the NT books (see Chapter 19 §VII.A–B)?

Unlike earlier, I now acknowledge Origen's interest in what Christian Scriptures should be read in and inform the churches, but he was well ahead of his time. However, the canonical *processes* were on the move from the first century to the formation of the biblical canons in the fourth and later centuries. Until the fourth century, there is little interest in catalogues of Christian Scriptures or fixed biblical canons. While Origen knew that some church fathers disagreed with him on his use of the Deuterocanonical or Apocryphal writings and even Hebrews, that did not deter him from making use of texts later *not included* in the OT or NT. He is not representative of later NT canons. Catholicity, or widespread church use, was important to Origen, but that did not affect his own preference for and use of works that others (Julius Africanus) considered doubtful and rejected. Catholicity, or widespread use, was also important later to Eusebius, who may have inherited this notion from Origen who lived in Caesarea after leaving Alexandria. Origen's books in the library at Caesarea were no doubt a useful resource for Eusebius and his acknowledged admiration of Origen likely also influenced some of his decisions on the scope of the NT canon. For Eusebius, as for Origen, the widespread use or catholicity (ὁμολογουμένα) in churches was an important criterion for canonicity. This notion was not clearly expressed in the second century and neither could it have been.

---

[105] Schnabel, "Muratorian Fragment," 256–57, draws attention to Zahn's position in his *Geschichte des neutestamentlichen Kanon* and with some appreciation of it.

Verheyden observes correctly that: "one cannot speak of a concerted effort all through the second century to establish a formal canon of authoritative books, let alone a firm concern to create one canon for the whole of Christianity."[106] He is also likely correct that by the end of the second century most of the books that were eventually included in the church's NT canon had already obtained a permanent place.[107] But at that time *other* books were still circulating in churches and read as scripture as we have seen. If the MF is a second-century document, Verheyden may be right to acknowledge it not so much as a canon of Scriptures as much as "a kind of introduction to the New Testament."[108] Schnabel also notes that the MF "emphasizes the universal validity of the historical particularity of the authoritative books of the church."[109] I agree, but this is much more reflective of the fourth century than the second. Further, to argue for a "universal" agreement in the second century is strange since we have no evidence that all of the churches or the church fathers possessed copies of all of the books of the NT. In fact, the evidence of the surviving biblical manuscripts and ancient translations reflects the contrary.

For the sake of completeness I refer again to Clare Rothschild's paper, "The Muratorian Canon as Fraud," delivered at the 2008 annual meeting of the Society of Biblical Literature. Her major work on this topic is forthcoming[110] and in it she argues that like other ancient forgeries the MF betrays itself by its use of anachronisms, use of the Vulgate, clichés, plagiarisms, and an array of words and phrases excerpted from other earlier writings. Her major arguments, if sustained, will likely affect current arguments and conclusions about the dating and provenance of the MF. An important reference to such forgeries is below in Athanasius' *Thirty-Ninth Festal Letter.* He writes:

> But the former, my brethren, are included in the Canon, the latter being merely read; nor is there any place a mention of secret writings. But such are the invention of heretics, who indeed write them whenever they wish, bestowing upon them their approval, and assigning to them a date, that so, using them as if they were ancient writings, they find a means by which to lead astray the simple-minded.[111]

---

[106] Verheyden, "New Testament Canon," 399.
[107] Ibid.
[108] Schnabel, "Muratorian Fragment," 238–39, makes this observation and cites as support both Hans Lietzmann and Bruce M. Metzger. Schnabel and several scholars agree on this. Schnabel advances that lists of OT canon books precede the fourth-century canon lists (as in the case of Melito at the end of the second century), but that is not present in what survives in the fragmented MF at its beginning or end as we have it. That suggestion is, of course, an argument from silence, but not necessarily a wrong one. The church at Sardis knew that it had a collection of OT books at the end of the second century, but not one of NT books and Eusebius does not suggest that Melito was interested in the scope of the NT Scriptures at that time.
[109] Ibid., 253.
[110] *The Muratorian Fragment*, WUNT 1 (Tübingen: Mohr Siebeck, forthcoming [scheduled 2018]).
[111] This translation is from *A Select Library of the Nicene and Post-Nicene Fathers*, 550–55, slightly revised.

Again, most of the known translations in the first five centuries do not contain all of the books of the NT. If there was a universal recognition in the second century, and the *Shepherd* was excluded and *Epistle of Barnabas* ignored, why are both documents included in Codex Sinaiticus in the fourth century? And why are producers of later canon lists still condemning the use of some Christian writings in churches well into the sixth to the ninth centuries as we have noted earlier? The use of "universal" is simply not applicable at an early (second-century) stage of the church's development or even in the fourth century since canon issues continued for centuries longer, but a majority of churches appear to have agreed on the scope of their Scriptures in the fourth century. We should also ask what other books were welcomed in some churches that were not later included in the NT canon and how widespread was canon consciousness in churches even after the fourth century. While the collection of canon lists and manuscript evidence reflect considerable overlap in what books were recognized as the church's scriptures, there was not initially or even later a universal recognition of the scope of all of the NT books or even OT books in all churches. There came a time, however, when all Christian churches agreed at least on the twenty-seven books that now comprise the NT canon.

This discussion raises the question of whether the church ever made a decision about the scope of the biblical canon. Schnabel raises the objections of those who focus on the "theology of the Word of God" who claim, "it is not the church who created the canonical Scriptures, but the canonical Scriptures which created the church." He cites among those who make such claims Karl Barth, Gerhard Ebling, Adolf Ritter, Charles Hill, von Campenhausen and others who contend that the Scriptures "imposed" themselves on the church.[112] There may be an element of truth here that I do not contest, but I would say that this element was neither instant, obvious, nor universal, but recognized only after long use and examination in the churches. The NT canon did not create the church as some have argued since the church was born before the NT canon was birthed. The church was born with its faith in Jesus the Christ and with its view that the church's First sacred Scriptures supported their faith in him. None of the NT books had been written when the church was born, but a story of and about Jesus was proclaimed and the church was born. The story itself was born out of an experience with Jesus, the church's Lord, and a later examination of the church's First Scriptures offered clarity to Jesus' followers about his identity, theirs, and their mission in the world. While Protestant scholars generally do not emphasize the role of church councils in the canonization processes, it is only with considerable difficulty that we can ignore the actions of several church councils in 360, 393, 397, 416, and later Trent. All had a say in the Scriptures that could be read in

---

[112] Schnabel, "Muratorian Fragment," 258–60.

the local churches, but mostly their decisions were only about disputed texts and simply recognizing the books that had already obtained widespread approval in the local churches. Not all churches followed the later church council decisions, but the councils did make some decisions generally only on the so-called fringe or disputed books.

Schnabel cites Kruger's conclusion, apparently with approval, that "we might naturally expect that the church would eventually reach a consensus on the boundaries around such [biblical] books..."[113] but this ignores the fact that the whole church has never fully agreed on the scope of the biblical books. Several writings such as *3 Corinthians* circulated in churches for more than 1000 years and in the Armenian churches until the mid-nineteenth century! As we saw earlier, the Ethiopian Christians have long had the largest biblical canon and their canon cannot be easily dismissed. The arguments that Kruger and others have presented leave the impression that only their list of books is inspired by the Spirit and their collection is the correct one that was imposed on the churches by the Spirit and not the institutional church. That is, of course, an over-statement without adequate historical, biblical, or ecclesiastical support.

The very example of the *Shepherd of Hermas* read as Scripture in the early churches, including by Irenaeus who was one of the most prominent second-century church teachers, suggests that there was no universal agreement on all of the books of the NT at an early date. By Kruger's reasoning, we can conclude that the right Scriptures had not yet imposed themselves on all of the church at the end of the second century. While the church today welcomes the canonical Gospels as equally inspired by God, Tertullian gave recognition to Mark and Luke, but not with the same elevated recognition as he had for Matthew and John since the latter were written by Apostles. The notion that all sacred books were early and universally welcomed denies Eusebius' listing of the seven doubted NT books (*Hist. eccl.* 3.25.1–7) and a mixed history in the development of canon formation. There is nothing universal about the MF list in the second century. Whatever happened between the second and fourth centuries that made those books more questionable or acceptable than before is discussed in the various historical circumstances of the developing churches (see Chapter 16 §§VII, VIII, IX). Among the criteria that were finally adopted was whether a book affirmed the historic proclamation and sacred traditions of the church (orthodoxy) that were handed down in the churches from the beginning (e.g., 1 Cor 15:3–8; Phil 2:6–11; 1 Tim 3:16) and were later adapted and interpreted in the churches. Irenaeus, as we saw earlier, could not imagine Christianity without such a tradition (Irenaeus, *Haer.* 1.10.1; 3.3.3; 3.4.1–2; see Chapter 17 §I.C.2–4).

---

[113] Ibid., 261, citing Kruger, *Question of Canon*, 43–44.

V. ATHANASIUS OF ALEXANDRIA (CA. 296–373)

The most famous ancient catalogue of the church's NT Scriptures that eventually carried the day is Athanasius's *Thirty-Ninth Festal Letter* written from Alexandria. It corresponds to the twenty-seven books of the NT acknowledged in churches today, though not in the same order. The Council of Nicea (325) settled the issue of when to celebrate Easter. When Athanasius was appointed Bishop of Alexandria he was invited to write the annual *Festal Letter* to the churches to announce the date of the following Easter so churches would know when to celebrate. He did this from 328 to 373 and in the thirty-ninth such letter (367) he identified the Scriptures of the Old and New Testaments. For our purposes, the pertinent part of that letter is as follows:[114]

> Since, however, I have spoken of the heretics as dead but of ourselves as possessors of the divine writings unto salvation, I am actually afraid lest in any way, as Paul said in writing to the Corinthians, a few of the undefiled may be led astray from the simplicity and purity by the craftiness of certain men and thereafter begin to pay attention *to other books, the so-called sacred (books)*. Therefore, because of fear of you being deceived by these books *possessing the same names as the genuine books*, and because of the present stress of the Church, I exhort you to bear with me for your own benefit as I actually make mention of these heretical writings, which you already know about.

> As I am about to mention these matters, I will back up my venturesomeness by following the example of the evangelist Luke. And I will also say that since *certain men have attempted to arrange for themselves the so-called secret writings and to mingle them with the God-inspired Scripture*, concerning which we have been fully informed even as they were handed down to our fathers by those who were eyewitnesses and servants of the word from the beginning, having been encouraged by true brethren and learning all from the beginning, *I also resolved to set forth in order the writings that are in the list and handed down and believed to be divine*. I have done this so that each person, if he has been deceived, may condemn those who led him astray, and that he who has remained stainless may rejoice, being again reminded of the truth.

> There are then of the Old Testament books…[names of OT books omitted here]

> Those of the New Testament I must not shrink from mentioning in their turn. They are these: Four Gospels, according to Matthew, according to Mark, according to Luke, and according to John.

> Then after these are Acts of the Apostles and the seven letters of the Apostles called the "Catholic" letters, which are as follows: one from James, two from Peter, three from John, and after these one from Jude.

---

[114] This background information comes from F. F. Bruce, *Canon of Scripture*, 77–78.

In addition, there are fourteen letters of Paul the apostle, written in the following order: the first to the Romans, then two to the Corinthians, and thereafter one to the Galatians, one to the Ephesians, one to the Philippians, one to the Colossians, two to the Thessalonians, one to the Hebrews, and, without a break, two letters to Timothy, one to Titus, and one written to Philemon. Last, from John again comes the Revelation.

These are springs of salvation, so that he that is thirsty may be filled with the (divine) responses in them; in these alone is the good news of the teaching of true religion proclaimed; *let no one add to them or take away aught of them.* It was in regard to these that the Lord was ashamed of the Sadducees, saying: "You are being led astray, since you do not know the scripture," and he exhorted the Jews, saying, "Search the scriptures, for they are the very writings that witness concerning me."

But for the sake of being more exact in detail, I also add this admonition, writing out of necessity, that *there are also other books apart from these that are not indeed in the above list, but were produced by our ancestors to be read by those who are just coming forward to receive oral instruction in the word of true religion.* These include the Wisdom of Solomon, the Wisdom of Sirach, Esther, Judith, Tobias, the so-called Teaching of the Apostles, and the Shepherd.

And nevertheless, beloved, though the former writings be in the list [or "are listed," κανονιζο-μένων] and the latter are read, nowhere is there mention of the secret writings (the Apocrypha). They are, rather, a device of heretics, who write them when they will be furnishing them with dates and adding them, *in order that by bringing them forth as ancient books they may thus have an excuse for deceiving the undefiled.*[115]

Athanasius was probably the first to use the term canon (κανών) in reference to a *closed* body of sacred literature, and he also appears to be the first to list the twenty-seven books of our current NT canon, though in a different order (the Catholic Epistles follow Acts and precede Paul).[116] As he indicated in the closing comments, one should not conclude from the use of the verb κανονιζομένων ("canonized" or "listed") in Athanasius's letter that all current and subsequent church leaders agreed fully with his catalogue of sacred texts. He unhesitatingly accepted the book of Revelation as a part of his biblical canon, but several other

---

[115] This more recent and longer translation of Athanasius' 39th *Festal Letter* is adapted from Schneemelcher, "General Introduction," 59–60, and Souter, *Text and Canon*, 196–200. Emphasis also added.

[116] Kümmel, *Introduction to the New Testament*, 350, agrees with this, but this conclusion depends on how early one dates Amphilochius' writing (see below). Some scholars claim that Eusebius was the first to use the term in relation to sacred literature in his discussion of Clement of Alexandria. He writes: "In the first of his [Commentaries] on the Gospel according to Matthew, defending the canon [κανόνα] of the Church, he gives his testimony that he knows only four Gospels" (*Hist. eccl.* 6.25.3, LCL). It is not certain, however, that Eusebius' use of the term κανόνα had to do with a fixed collection of writings; it may refer instead to the faith tradition or *regula fidei* passed on in the churches.

churches in the East did not agree with him. Cyril of Jerusalem and Gregory of Nazianzus, for example, left it out,[117] and even today, as we saw above, the Greek Orthodox lectionary does not include readings from Revelation.[118] While the canon set forth by Athanasius ultimately prevailed in the majority of the churches in succeeding centuries – it was adopted with the help of Augustine at the church councils of Hippo (393) and Carthage (397, 416) – there is no evidence, however, that Athanasius' letter had a determining impact on *all* of the churches of his day whether in the east or even in his own region of Egypt, but it is likely that his list was reflective of the majority of churches with which he was acquainted in his generation. Certainly the list was not something that he himself created, but it reflected the books that most, not all, of the Christians acknowledged as Scripture. The multiple manuscript discoveries in Egypt from this time and later periods do not support the pervasive influence of Athanasius' list even in Egypt, but as in most cases, there was considerable overlap. Not until almost seven hundred years later was the book of Revelation universally accepted into the NT canon of most churches, though many churches appear to have simply ignored it if we consider the content of the surviving manuscripts. We saw above the considerable difference in the number of manuscripts containing the Gospels, Acts, Paul, and the Catholic Epistles compared to Revelation.

VI. CYRIL OF JERUSALEM (CA. 315–386)

Cyril, bishop of Jerusalem, gave a list of Scriptures similar to that of Athanasius except, as noted above, he excluded Revelation. He left behind this statement:

> But the four Gospels alone belong to the New Testament; the rest [of the gospels] happens to be pseudepigrapha and harmful. The Manicheans also wrote [the] Gospel according to Thomas, which indeed, having been camouflaged by the sweetness of its title derived from an evangelist, corrupts the souls of the simpler ones. But accept also the Acts of the twelve Apostles. In addition to these [accept] the seven Catholic Epistles: [the one] of James and [the two] of Peter and [the three] of John and [the one] of Jude; and accept lastly as the seal of all, even of the disciples, the fourteen Epistles of Paul. Let all the rest, however, be placed in secondary [rank]. And those which are not read in the Church, *do not even read them privately as you have heard,* "So much" then about these. (Cyrillus, *Catechetical Lectures* 4.36, Theron, *Evidence of Tradition,* 177, emphasis added)

---

[117] F. F. Bruce, *Canon of Scripture,* 213.
[118] Ibid., 215.

VII. OTHER RELATED CATALOGUES

Bishop Amphilochius of Iconium (after 394) appears to have accepted all of the books in Athanasius' canon except Revelation (which he called spurious), though he also raised doubts about Hebrews and the Catholic Epistles, questioning whether there should be seven or three letters in this grouping.[119] He appears to be the second person to use the term canon (κανών) in reference to a list of Christian Scriptures.[120] Further examples of differences of opinion about what comprised the NT canon are in Chrysostom (407), who never referred to Revelation or to the last four Catholic Epistles, and the *Apostolic Constitutions* (written no earlier than the fourth century), who also added to Athanasius' list *1–2 Clement* and the eight books of the *Constitutions* themselves, but he omitted Revelation.[121] In the late fourth and early fifth centuries, some Eastern churches rejected Revelation, even though they appear to have been in substantial agreement regarding most of the other Christian literature in Athanasius' canon. Dionysius of Alexandria (ca. 230) accepted Revelation as authoritative Scripture, but he did not believe that the Apostle John had written it. He made one of the earliest critical assessments of the book, noting that the vocabulary and style of Revelation were not those of John the Apostle:

> In a word, it is obvious that those who observe their character throughout will see at a glance that the Gospel [John] and Epistle [1 John] have one and the same complexion. But the Apocalypse is utterly different from, and foreign to, these writings; it has no connexion, no affinity, in any way with them; it scarcely, so to speak, has even a syllable in common with them. Nay more, neither does the Epistle (not to speak of the Gospel) contain any mention or thought of the Apocalypse, nor the Apocalypse of the Epistle, whereas Paul in his epistles gave us a little light also on his revelations, which he did not record separately.
>
> And further, by means of the style one can estimate the difference between the Gospel and Epistle and the Apocalypse. For the former are not only written in faultless Greek, but also show the greatest literary skill in their diction, their reasonings, and the constructions in which they are expressed. There is a complete absence of any barbarous word, or solecism, or any vulgarism whatever. For their author had, as it seems, both kinds of word, by the free gift of the Lord, the word of knowledge and the word of speech. But I will not deny that the other writer had seen revelations and received knowledge and prophecy; nevertheless I observe his style and that his use of the Greek language is not accurate, but that he employs barbarous idioms, in some places committing downright solecisms. These there is no necessity to single out now. For I have not said these things in mockery (let no one think it), but merely to establish the dissimilarity of these writings. (Eusebius, *Hist. eccl.* 7.25.22–27, LCL)

---

[119] See Theron, *Evidence of Tradition*, 117.

[120] After listing his books, Amphilochius concludes, "This is perhaps the most faithful [lit. 'unfalsified'] canon [κανών] of the divinely inspired scriptures." The use of the optative with the particle *an* suggests both an element of doubt and a statement of what he hopes will obtain in the churches. See Grosheide, *Some Early Lists*, 20.

[121] Metzger, *Canon of the New Testament*, 214–15.

Koester reminds us that Revelation is absent from many of the surviving NT Greek manuscripts.[122] This may well have had to do as much with the uncertainty over its authorship, as Dionysius shows, as with its actual contents. Well into the sixteenth century, Erasmus of Rotterdam disputed the authorship of the Hebrews, 2 Peter, and Revelation concluding as follows and surprisingly still accepting them as canon in the churches. He explains:

> The arguments of criticism estimated by the rules of logic, lead me to disbelieve that the Epistle to the Hebrews is by Paul or Luke, or that the second of Peter is the work of that apostle, or that the evangelist John wrote the Apocalypse. All the same, I have nothing to say against the contents of these books, which seem to me to be in perfect conformity with the truth. If, however, the Church were to declare the titles they bear to be as canonical as their contents, then I would condemn my doubts, for the opinion formulated by the Church has more value in my eyes than human reasons, whatever they may be." (*Declar.ad censuram facult. theol. paris.*)[123]

Still further, several ancient biblical manuscripts include early noncanonical Christian writings. For example, Codex Claramontanus, a Greek manuscript from the fifth–sixth century, includes a secondarily inserted Latin list of books that includes *Shepherd of Hermas*, *Acts of Paul*, *Revelation of Peter*, and *Epistle of Barnabas*. Codex Alexandrinus (fifth century) contains *1* and *2 Clement*. Codex Hierosolymitanus (eleventh century) includes *1* and *2 Clement*, *Barnabas*, *Didache*, and an interpolated text of the *Letters* of Ignatius. *Barnabas* and *Shepherd of Hermas* are also included in the fourth-century Codex Sinaiticus. As Lake has observed, *Barnabas*, like *1 Clement* and *Hermas*, became canonical literature in some circles, was quoted as Scripture by Clement of Alexandria, and was even called a "Catholic Epistle" by Origen.[124]

VIII. SUMMARY OF LISTS

Other ancient canonical lists could be mentioned, but they are listed in Appendix C and enough has been shown here to argue reasonably that the notion of a closed or fixed NT canon was not a second-century development in the early church and that there were still some differences of opinion about what should comprise the NT canon even in the fourth and fifth centuries. There was never a time in the fourth or fifth centuries when the whole church adopted as Scripture all of the twenty-seven books of the NT – *and those books alone*. While Athanasius and later Augustine and the three late fourth- and early fifth-century councils came to an agreement on the scope of the NT canon, clearly there were other opinions

---

[122] Koester, *Introduction to the New Testament*, 2:256.
[123] I owe this reference to Reuss, *History of the Canon*, 272.
[124] See Lake, *Apostolic Fathers*, LCL, 1:339.

floating around the churches at that time. The four canonical Gospels, for example, were set-aside in the Syrian churches in favor of Tatian's *Diatessaron* until after approximately 400. Many Christians continued to reject in practice parts of the greater church's canon long after there was a general recognition of it.[125]

Only during the Reformation era did the Catholics appear to achieve unity on the NT canon with the decree by the Council of Trent, but by that time Luther had already questioned the full canonical status of James, Hebrews, Jude, and Revelation, not to mention the Deuterocanonical books (the Apocrypha). Protestants have affirmed, with Luther, a shorter OT canon; while the Catholics also include the Deuterocanonical writings and the Eastern Orthodox have an even larger OT canon than the Roman Catholics. As we saw above, Orthodox Christians never had a Council of Trent to determine the scope of their NT Scriptures.[126] They appear to have followed popular tradition in their churches rather than accepting a council decision on the scope of their Scriptures. Quite apart from these traditional church communions, the Ethiopian church, which traces its roots to the fourth-century church, claims a biblical canon of some eighty-one books.[127] At no time in history has the whole church agreed completely on what literature makes up its canon of Scriptures; however, there has been general agreement since the third century regarding the authoritative, or scriptural, status of the four Gospels, Acts, most of the letters attributed to Paul, 1 Peter, and 1 John. The rest of the NT canon appears to have been decided in various councils based perhaps on wide church use, but within individual churches in various regions reservations continued to

---

[125] Aland, *Problem of the New Testament Canon*, 12, gives the example of Cassiodorus (ca. 550), who could not obtain a Western commentary on Hebrews and therefore had the one by Chrysostom translated from Greek. Aland also cites the case of the Spanish synods around 600, which were still fighting against those who rejected Revelation.

[126] For helpful discussion of the biblical canons in the Orthodox Churches, see Hovhanessian, ed., *Canon of the Bible*; and Pentiuc, *Old Testament in Eastern Orthodox Tradition*, 100–135. Georgi R. Parpulov, "The Bibles of the Christian East," in Marsden and Matter, eds., *New Cambridge History of The Bible: From 600–1450*, 309–24.

[127] S. F. Kealy, "The Canon: An African Contribution," *BTB* 9 (1979): 17–19, notes that the Ethiopian Bible contains forty-six OT books and thirty-five NT books and claims that Christian missionaries brought this canon of Scriptures to Ethiopia in 330. Metzger, *Canon of the New Testament*, 227, lists the Ethiopian NT collection as follows: the four Gospels, Acts, the seven Catholic Epistles, fourteen Epistles of Paul (Hebrews included), Revelation, *Sinodos* (four sections), *Ethiopian Clement* (which is different from *1 Clement*), *Book of the Covenant* (two sections), and *Didascalia*. When the canon was subsequently settled in other parts of the church, the Ethiopian community of Christians was isolated from the rest of the Christian world because of the Islamic conquests especially in the seventh century and for nine centuries they did not know of the canonical decisions by the rest of the churches. Hence, they have a larger biblical canon, which may represent an older tradition than does the present biblical canon. See also Cowley, "Biblical Canon" above, and Ephraim Isaac, "The Bible in Ethiopic," in Marsden and Matter, eds., *New Cambridge History of the Bible*, 110–22. He suggests a fourth-century date for the translation of Scriptures into the Ethiopic/Ge'ez language.

linger about the "doubted" books in the NT canon until toward the end of the fourth century for some and later for others.

One result of our examination of lists and their variations is to raise the question of whether the church was correct in perceiving the need for a closed biblical canon since historically churches have never completely agreed on which books should go into it. While most churches today have agreed on the books that comprise the NT, as apparently most of the early churches did, it is not unusual for churches to ignore many of its sacred books, whether Leviticus, Ecclesiastes, or Song of Songs in the OT or Hebrews, 2–3 John, Jude, and Revelation in the NT.

If the earliest Christians intended for the church that followed them to have a closed canon of Scriptures, there is no clear tradition from them that makes this clear. By the end of the second century in the proto-orthodox churches there was a strong tendency to anchor authorship of their sacred traditions in first-century apostolic and eye-witnesses testimony. As a result, many pseudonymous writings emerged in the names of first-century apostles on new texts, but this was not the case initially. In the second century and following, as we will see in the next chapter, apostolic testimony as well as tradition in the churches and consistency with that tradition (orthodoxy) was always a limiting factor in what scriptures were welcomed in most churches. By the third to fourth century, catholicity also became a factor, that is, the writings that were widely read in the majority of churches were more acceptable than those that were not widely read in the majority of churches.

The historical context of the fourth and fifth centuries, however, may also be a key to understanding why the church began to close its canon of Scriptures. The theological controversies of Marcionism, Gnosticism, and Montanism in the second and third centuries no doubt led the church to define more precisely what it believed was Christian tradition and appropriate beliefs, but that began with their *regula fidei* and not by creating a biblical canon. When the churches began to clarify their faith, identity, and mission, the church began to reject writings that were at odds with the churches' traditions, creeds, and earliest writings. At that point, the processes of canonization were well on their way to being settled. That did not happen for all churches at the same time, but over time most churches came to the same conclusions about the broad scope of their biblical canon. The era of conformity that characterized the reign of Constantine and the Roman world contributed to broader agreement in the church and to the unity that it also desired, but also silenced other voices in the churches. The consequent development of a closed biblical canon of authoritative Scriptures and the exclusion (and in some cases destruction) of all other Christian writings surely helped to secure this unity.

IX. CHURCH COUNCILS AND THE BIBLICAL CANON

As we have seen in this study, several individuals played a significant role in the formation of the Christian Bible, especially Justin Martyr, Irenaeus, Tertullian, Origen, Eusebius, Athanasius, Jerome and Augustine. By the end of the fourth century, several prominent church councils also played similar roles: four church councils at Laodicea (360), Hippo (393) and Carthage (397 and subsequently in 416) met to discuss, among other things, what books could be read in the churches and conversely which ones could not. The Council at Laodicea does not say specifically which books could be read except in its canon 59 it denied reading some "private psalms" in church as well as any "uncanonized books (ἀκανόνιστα βιβλία), but only the canonical (κανονικὰ) [books] of the New and Old Testament."[128] After this, perhaps at the end of the fourth century, canon 60 was added to the first 59 canons that identified all of the current NT books except Revelation. The councils above that met and deliberated on the scope of the Christian Bible – that is, what books were to be recognized as authoritative sacred Scriptures and read in the churches – generally reflected what was already in place in their areas, but the Christology that had already been accepted at the earlier Council of Nicea in 318–25 also gave greater clarity to churches when deciding whether to accept some questionable books. However, the Council of Nicea did not discuss or deliberate on the scope of the church's biblical canons. Perhaps the most important question was whether the individual books reflected the perspectives about Jesus in the traditions, creeds, and accepted Scriptures that had been passed on in the churches since apostolic times.

A. Councils on Books Read in Churches and in Private

It has long been thought that the church councils actually determined which books were included in the Bible and which were not, but it is probably more accurate to say that councils generally reflected the decisions and practices of churches represented in their areas, especially the larger and more influential churches. The books that had already obtained prominence and use in the various regions where the councils met are the ones that the church councils affirmed. It appears that only in cases of significant dispute over the so-called fringe books were council decisions made. If church councils made any decisions at all about the scope of the biblical canon, they were only in regard to questionable books that were sometimes in or out of the collections that obtained recognition in some churches. This was not the case in the majority of the New Testament books that had long enjoyed widespread approval and use in the churches probably from the second century. In the middle to late fourth centuries, some books that were disputed early

---

[128]   This translation comes from Theron, *Evidence of Tradition*, 124–25.

on were beginning to be included in the canonical catalogues, namely, Hebrews, James, 2 Peter, 2–3 John, Jude, and Revelation.

The following examples of church council decisions shed light on the views about the church's Scriptures that were held in the communities surrounding those council meetings and how these books and their church constituencies were represented by their respective bishops at the councils. Decisions on the disputed books, and especially those that had been read in many churches for one or two centuries but were no longer read in churches (*Epistle of Barnabas*, *Shepherd*, and others), were more likely to have been made in council decisions. For the most part, however, the churches' Scriptures were *not* determined "from the top," but generally from broad agreement rooted in widespread use in churches. The councils did not so much create biblical canons as they *endorsed* them; their decisions *reflected more the state of affairs at the time that they met*. In regard to the so-called fringe books, church councils generally made decisions that appear to have been based on what the *majority* view was at that time among the churches represented *at each council*. Interestingly, however, centuries after some councils had made such endorsements or prohibitions, Christians were still using books in their worship and instruction that had earlier been rejected by church councils (see Pseudo-Athanasius, ca. 500), and the later *Stichometry of Nicephorus*, ca. 850). Obviously, some churches continued to use books that *they believed* were relevant to their own needs regardless of what church councils decided!

In light of this, it may be useful to reflect on the influence and persuasiveness of councils: why would earlier council decisions about rejected books need to be repeated centuries later if no one was using the so-called non-biblical (rejected) books in their churches? It is safe to assume that what councils decided was not always followed in the churches! This was discussed earlier.

Among the several council decisions regarding its biblical canon, three are probably the most important. Although the Council of Laodicea (360) mentioned reading the books of the New and Old Testaments, as we saw, the specific identity of the books that comprised those books came later in a text that became identified as canon 60. As it happens, these listed books are the same as those that are in Athanasius' canon (367), except that Ruth is combined with Judges, and Esther immediately follows, and Revelation is omitted. The first of the most important council decisions took place in 393 CE, when a church council met at Hippo in North Africa and set forth a biblical canon of both testaments similar to the one produced by Athanasius and affirmed by Augustine. Although the deliberations of this council are now lost, they were summarized in the proceedings of the Council of Carthage in North Africa in 397. This same collection of NT books was repeated in the Council of Carthage that met later in 416. These were apparently the first official church councils to make formal decisions on the scope and contents of the biblical canon, although the later canon 60 attached to the Laodicean Council of 363 may have had some influence on it. Below we will list for easier comparison some of the collections recognized by church fathers of the fourth and fifth centuries, and by some church councils.

As a side note, it is also important to recall that decisions like those made by church councils have continued into the relatively recent past. As late as 1950, the Holy Synod of the Greek Orthodox Church authorized as part of its Old Testament canon the entire Apocrypha, including 2 Ezra, and 3 and 4 Maccabees, which were placed in an appendix. The Old Testament of the Russian Bible of 1956 has the same contents as the Greek Bible, but 3 Ezra and 4 Maccabees are absent.

In the history of Christianity, then, the first Seven Ecumenical Church Councils, from the First Council of Nicea (325) to the Second Council of Nicaea (787), are all collective attempts to reach an orthodox consensus and to unify Christendom under the state church of the Roman Empire. Byzantine Emperors of the Eastern Roman Empire convened all Seven Ecumenical Councils and all were held in that region, yet none of them dealt primarily with the church's Scriptures, that is, with which books formed the church's Bible.

B. The Council of Trent and Afterward

The Eastern churches appear for a while to have been more conservative in their selection of writings for the biblical canon than churches in the West. The most important council at the end of the process (for the Roman Catholic Church) was the Council of Trent. It was the first *ecumenical* church council to deal specifically with the scope of the church's Scriptures and was held at Trent and included twenty-five sessions from 1545–1563. In its fourth session on April 8, 1546, the church set forth its decision regarding the limits of the Old and New Testament canons and included the apocryphal books. This council affirmed the validity of both Scripture and unwritten traditions (church pronouncements) as sources of truth, as well as *the church's sole right to interpret Scripture*, an assertion of pivotal importance during the Reformation. It also affirmed the authority of the text of the Latin Vulgate for its Scripture, though it ordered a revision of it. The main thrust of the council was its repudiation of the spread of Protestantism and some of the books in its Scriptures. The Fourth Session reads in part:

> The holy, ecumenical and general Council…following…the examples of the orthodox Fathers… receives and venerates with a feeling of piety and reverence all the books of the Old and New Testaments, since one God is the author of both; also the traditions, whether relating to faith or to morals, as having been dictated either orally by Christ or by the Holy Ghost, and preserved in the Catholic Church by a continuous succession.

> And it has thought it meet that a list of the sacred books be inserted in this decree, lest a doubt may arise in any one's mind, which are the books that are received by this Synod.[129]

---

[129] Schaff, *Creeds*, 2:80–81.

The books affirmed by decree from the Council of Trent lists the recognized books of the NT[130] as follows:

> Of the New Testament: the four Gospels, according to Matthew, Mark, Luke, and John, the Acts of the Apostles written by Luke the Evangelist; fourteen epistles of Paul the apostle, (one) to the Romans, two to the Corinthians, (one) to the Galatians, to the Ephesians, to the Philippians, to the Colossians, two to the Thessalonians, two to Timothy, (one) to Titus, to Philemon, to the Hebrews; two of Peter the Apostle, three of John the apostle, one of the apostle James, one of Jude the apostle, and the Apocalypse of John the apostle.[131]

After listing the books the document goes on to say,

> But if anyone receive not, as sacred and canonical, the said books entire with all their parts, as they have been used to be read in the Catholic Church, and as they are contained in the old Latin Vulgate edition; and knowingly and deliberately condemn the traditions aforesaid; let him be anathema. Let all, therefore, understand, in what order, and in what manner, the said Synod, after having laid the foundation of the Confession of faith, will proceed, and what testimonies and authorities it will mainly use in confirming dogmas, and restoring morals in the Church.[132]

The First Vatican Council reaffirmed this council decision (1869–70).

In 1559, the Reformed Churches set forth their *Gallican Confession* (*Confessio Gallicana*) and in the *Belgic Confession* (articles IV and V) of 1561 affirmed a biblical canon that excluded the apocryphal books that were included by the Roman Catholic Scriptures. In England in 1562 and 1571, in the Sixth of the *Thirty-Nine Articles*, the Church of England affirmed the use of the apocryphal books, but added that they were not to be used to set forth or establish the church's teaching. After listing the books that belong to the larger Old Testament canon and affirming the current Protestant Old Testament canon, the document concludes: "And the other books (as Hierome [Jerome] saith) the Church doth read for example of life and instruction of manners, but yet doth it not apply to them to establish any doctrine: such are these following…"

After this statement the apocryphal books are listed as follows:

> The Third Book of Esdras, The Fourth Book of Esdras, The Book of Tobias, The Book of Judith, The rest of the Book of Esther, The Book of Wisdom, Jesus the Son of Sirach, Baruch the Prophet, The Song of the Three Children, Of Bel and the Dragon, The Prayer of Manasses, The First Book of Maccabees, The Second book of Maccabees.

The *Thirty-Nine Articles* conclude with a reference to the affirmation of "All the books of the New Testament [27 books], as they are commonly received, we do receive, and account them Canonical."[133]

---

[130] The OT books are listed in Chapter 9 §VII above.
[131] Schaff, *Creeds*, 2:81.
[132] Ibid., 2:82.
[133] American Revision of 1801 in Schaff, *Creeds*, 3:490–91.

C. Councils and Biblical Canons

It may be helpful at this point to integrate our council-oriented history with some of the other significant moments in canon formation that we have noted briefly in previous chapters. In contrast to the ecumenical councils just mentioned, the first council that listed a biblical canon prior to the one established at Trent in 1546 may have been the Synod of Hippo Regius in North Africa (393), but the acts of that council are now lost. As noted earlier, a brief summary of those acts was read and accepted at the later Councils at Carthage in 397 and 419. Augustine significantly influenced these councils and he accepted the earlier NT list of Scriptures set forth by Athanasius in his 367 CE *Festal Letter*. At the Council of Rome initiated by Damasus I in 383, there appears to be an agreement on the biblical canon set forth later at the Council of Hippo, though the list published as we have it may be a sixth-century compilation. Likewise, Damasus I's commissioning of the Latin Vulgate in 383 was likely influential in fixing the biblical canon in the regions of the Western Empire; in 405, Pope Innocent I sent a similar list of sacred books to a Gallic bishop in Toulouse.

It appears that when bishops and councils spoke on the matter of canon formation, they were not defining something *new*, but were rather reflecting and selectively sanctioning that which was already a matter of popular practice and circulation in the churches. We might well recall at this point that the fourth century saw widespread agreement in the West concerning the twenty-seven books that make up the New Testament canon. By the fifth century in the East, and with few exceptions, all of the books of the New Testament, including the long-debated book of Revelation, were accepted as canonical Scripture. In essence, the majority of churches in the East and West agreed on the scope of the New Testament canon by the middle to the end of the fifth century. Again, that does not mean that individual churches had no other notions about which books were their Scriptures; the non-biblical books in the surviving biblical manuscripts imply this.

By way of review, the following is a list of those councils (and in one case, a decision by Innocent I that had an effect comparable to that of these council decisions) that dealt specifically with the scope of the Christian Scriptures.

1. *Council of Laodicea (ca. 360–363)*. Remember that canon 60 that specifically identifies the books is later than the date of the council meeting. This council was a local council of the church, in union with Rome. Canon 60 produced a list of books of the Bible similar to the list of Scriptures affirmed at the much later Council of Trent, though it did not affirm Revelation. This was one of the earliest known council decisions on the scope of the biblical canon. The date for canon 60, as noted above, is uncertain but it largely conforms to the list in Athanasius without Revelation, and likely dates after the council decisions of Hippo and Carthage that reflect the same list but with Revelation.

2. *Council of Rome (382)*. A local church council under the authority of Pope Damasus I (366–384), which gave a list of books of the Old and New Testament that is identical to the list that was later approved at the Council of Trent.

3. *Council of Hippo (393)*. A local North African church council, again operating in union with and under the authority of the Bishop of Rome, approved a list of the books that comprise the Old and New Testament canons. It is the same as that which was later approved at Trent.

4. *Council of Carthage (397)*. Like Hippo above, a local North African church council, in concert with and under the authority of the Bishop of Rome, approved a list of books comprising the church's Old and New Testament canon (again, the list is the same as was later approved by the Council of Trent).

5. Innocent I (Bishop of Rome, 401–417) in 405 responded to a request by Exuperius, Bishop of Toulouse, with a list of canonical books of Scripture. His list was the same as that which was later approved by the Council of Trent. (See the list of Old Testament books in Appendix A and that of the New Testament books listed in Appendix C.)

6. *Council of Carthage (419)*. Like Hippo and the first Carthaginian council above, a local North African church council, again in union with and under the authority of the Bishop of Rome, approved a list comprising the OT and NT canons (the same as that later approved by the Council of Trent).

7. *Council of Florence (1441)*. An ecumenical council that gave a complete list of the Old and New Testament books. This list was later adopted at the Council of Trent. It was also at Florence that the so-called apocryphal books were first identified as "Deuterocanonical" books, that is, as distinct from the "protocanonical" books (the thirty-nine books in the Protestant Old Testament Scriptures that all Christians accept).

8. *Council of Trent (1545–1563)*. This *ecumenical* council was called primarily to respond to the perceived heresy of the Reformers. It is one of the most important councils in Roman Catholic Church history, since it clearly defined church beliefs that are current to this day about the scope of the church's biblical canon. The canon of the Old and New Testaments received final definitions: 46 books in the Old Testament and 27 in the New Testament (see list above). The council concluded that the books of the Old Testament, both "protocanonical" and "deuterocanonical" books, and the books of the New Testament form the church's biblical canon. Both collections were and are held to be of equal authority. The Latin Vulgate edition of the Bible was also accepted as the authoritative version of the Catholic Church's Bible.

D. Deuterocanonical, Protocanonical, and Apocryphal Books

As noted above, the term "deuterocanonical" has been used since the fifteenth and sixteenth centuries in the Catholic Church and subsequently in Eastern Orthodox Christianity to describe certain books and passages of the Christian OT not included in the HB or Protestant OT. The Deuterocanonical books are regularly called the "Apocrypha" in Protestant churches. Although "apocrypha" originally referred to "hidden" books that were often read by new Christians or by those well advanced in their Christian faith, it came to mean for Protestants that which was rejected and not to be read. At least by the late fourth or fifth centuries, individuals and churches began to refer to and even list non-biblical books or *uninspired* books, that is, books whose message was considered false, through which and through whose authors God did *not* speak. They began to call these texts "apocryphal" books. Perhaps because "apocrypha" had taken on such negative connotations, some in the Catholic Church at a council in Florence (see council 7 listed above) began to speak of a "second canon" or "Deuterocanonical" books to identify the Jewish religious writings that were not a part of the "first canon" ("protocanonical") books, but were widely read in churches from the first century. As with the council decisions that we reviewed above, these labels reflect earlier debate among churches and church leaders. Jerome, for one, evidently wanted to recognize only those OT books in the protocanonical collection, the books that were recognized as Scripture by Jews that were also welcomed in a different order by the later Protestant Christians, but Augustine wanted to keep the "second canon" of OT texts and argued persuasively in his day that these books should be read in the churches and therefore classified among the church's sacred Scriptures.

The Roman Catholics regularly include in their Deuterocanonical collection the following books: Tobit, Judith, the Additions to Esther, 1 and 2 Maccabees, the Wisdom of Solomon, the Wisdom of Sirach (= Ecclesiasticus), Baruch (ch. 6 of which is the Epistle of Jeremiah), and the three Additions to the book of Daniel, namely the Prayer of Azariah and the Song of the Three Young Men, Susanna, and Bel and the Dragon. Unlike in some Protestant Bibles that include these books in a separate collection between the OT and NT, in the Roman Catholic OT the deutero-canonical books are included throughout and among the other OT books, not separately. The Eastern Orthodox Churches include not only the Deuterocanonical books in the Roman Catholic biblical canon, but also 3 Maccabees, Ps 151, and 2 Esdras. (1 Esdras in the Catholic Deuterocanonical books is the same as 2 Esdras in the Orthodox Bibles. 2 Esdras in the Catholic Bibles is equivalent to Ezra and also includes Nehemiah.)

The Ethiopian Tewahedo Church Bible has an even broader collection of Old and New Testament Scriptures than the Roman Catholic and Eastern Orthodox churches. Its eighty-one-book biblical canon includes not only those books held by other Christians, but also several others: their Old Testament books include *1 Enoch, Jubilees*, and *1, 2*, and *3 Meqabyan* (not to be confused with 1, 2, and

3 Maccabees); the New Testament also includes beside the usual twenty-seven books, two *Books of the Covenant*, four *Books of Sinodos*, an *Epistle to Clement*, and the *Didascalia* (not exactly the same as an ancient Western book by the same title). The list of books that make up the total of 81 books varies depending on which ancient or modern source one uses.

X. SUMMARY

The recognition of Christian literature as authoritative scripture and useful in the life, worship, and mission of the church came sooner in practice than in formal recognition. As we saw earlier, that is always the case and use came before recognition as Scripture and sub-collections of Scriptures generally circulating in the early churches reflect a scriptural status or at least the value and authority of the writings in such groups (e.g., Gospels, letters of Paul). Christian writings were not *generally* called Scripture until the end of the second century, though they no doubt functioned that way for many Christians even decades before then as we have shown. A few second-century writers make comments about the Gospels and some of Paul's letters and appear to cite them as Scripture. By the end of the second century, the principle of Christian Scriptures had been established in practice in several segments of the Christian community.

This conclusion, however, calls for three important cautions that are reminders of how we began this chapter. First, acknowledgment of the authority of one part of the NT literature at one time does not imply that all parts of it were so recognized everywhere at the same time. Second, because one writer may refer to a Christian book or letter as Scripture, this does not mean that all Christians of the same era came to the same conclusion. Finally, even if *some* of the NT writings were recognized as having the status of Scripture in the second century, this is not the same as a closed canon of Scriptures, even though it is clear that with the recognition of the authority of certain Christian writings the canonical processes were in motion. Further, some of the books that received early recognition as sacred Scripture did not retain that status later.

We will now turn to the question of criteria, namely, why some books were welcomed and others excluded from the church's NT Scriptures.

CHAPTER 22

THE CRITERIA QUESTION

Why did the early churches select the writings that were eventually included in their New Testament? What criteria were employed in the selection and why were some writings that were initially welcomed later rejected for inclusion in the church's second canon of Scriptures? Were there other factors involved in the selection processes that clarify these matters? As we have seen earlier, the relationship between the church's traditions, creeds, and Scriptures is critical for our understanding the final decisions in this matter. Although it appears that churches were in broad agreement on the majority of their NT writings by the end of the second century, they continued to be divided over some books for several centuries. They did not fully agree on the inclusion of the so-called fringe books in the NT canon. They disagreed, however, over some books that were read in some churches initially, but were not finally included in the NT. Why were these "others" eliminated? Our focus in this chapter is on these and several other questions.

I. IDENTIFYING CHRISTIAN SCRIPTURES

Although we are not certain about some of the Jewish Scriptures the early churches initially welcomed as their own sacred Scriptures, we are certain that the majority of them were those that had gained some approval among their fellow Jews before the separation of Jews and Christians that began in 62 CE and continued until 135 CE. The sacred texts that were accepted by some Jews in Palestine before the separation of Jews and Christians were the First Scriptures of the Christians. By the latter part of the second century some Christians were beginning to call them their Old Testament Scriptures. Soon the Christians found that some of their own writings were also quite helpful in their worship and instruction and also in advancing their mission and apologetic. This was especially true with regard to the Gospels and some of the letters attributed to Paul, but eventually other Christian writings were added to a growing collection of texts that informed their faith. These writings were not initially called scripture or seen as equal to their Jewish Scriptures, but by the middle of the second century they were being read alongside of and sometimes instead of the Jewish Scriptures in their worship services (Justin, *1 Apol.* 67). By the late middle to the end of that century some

Christian writings had begun to be called Scripture and placed alongside of their Jewish Scriptures and those two collections of sacred texts began to be called their Old and New Testament Scriptures.

As we saw earlier, the Christian writings were used *as Scripture* before they were called Scripture. Several factors were involved in that process of recognition and this will be the focus of the rest of this chapter. First, of course, is the manner in which the NT writings are cited in their communities of faith. When citations of or allusions to these writings were employed to settle issues of faith, mission, and disciplinary matters, their recognition and authority in the churches was already in place. In this sense, they were used as Scripture before they began to be called Scripture. When they were used in worship in a liturgical setting alongside their First Scriptures, this was another indication that their recognition as Scripture was not far behind. It is quite likely that the Christian writings were read in churches as soon as they were received in the churches. There were no prescriptions about which writings could be read in the earliest churches such as we see later at the end of the second and third centuries. As we will see these first-century Christian writings were read in churches by the middle of the second century, but undoubtedly many of them were also read in churches in the first century. This is assumed or explicitly stated throughout the NT.[1] Occasionally, as in Phil 1:1, the leaders of the churches are included in the address, but that is unusual. Since they were generally addressed to the churches, it is most likely that they were read in the churches. Since it is also probable that most of those in the early churches were unable to read, it may be assumed that the NT writings were read to the congregations to whom the writings were sent.

As we have seen, reading Christian writings in churches alongside of and occasionally instead of the OT writings was happening in some churches no later than the early to middle second century. Doubtless, this also took place in the first century when the letters were sent to the churches and the Gospels were welcomed in the churches. In the second century several Christian writings appear to have had a sacred authority attached to them that was not attached to other Christian writings. For example, around the middle of the second century, in the first known depiction of what happened in Christian worship services, Justin Martyr describes how the prophets and the "memoirs of the apostles," that earlier he identifies as the Gospels (*1 Apol.* 64–66), were read in the worship services on the first day of the week (*1 Apol.* 67). Surprisingly, Justin does not say that the Gospels were read in worship services *alongside* the "Prophets" (a common reference for the OT Scriptures in the churches of his day), but rather that they

---

[1]   See 1 Cor 5:9; Col 4:16, especially in the letters, almost all of which were addressed to congregations. See Rom 1:7; 1 Cor 1:2; 2 Cor 1:1; Gal 1:2; 1 Thess 1:1; 2 Thess 1:1; Heb 13:22; Jas 1:1–2; 1 Pet 1:1–2; 2 Pet 1:1; presumed in 1 John, clearly in 2 John 1 and 3 John 1; Jude 1; but also the book of Revelation (Rev 1:4) and the letters to the churches (chs. 2 and 3) that were all addressed to congregations.

were sometimes read *instead* of the Prophets: "On the day called Sunday there is a meeting in one place of those who live in cities or the country, and *the memoirs of the apostles or the writings of the prophets are read as long as time permits*" (*1 Apol.* 67, ANF; emphasis added). We should also note that Justin lists the Gospels before the "prophets" which illustrates that in the second century it is not unusual for Christian writings to be cited more frequently than the OT Scriptures (see reference to this below). This, of course, points to the stature that these NT writings had attained in the second century and Justin may reflect a long-standing practice in the churches of giving special attention "to the apostles' teaching" (Acts 2:42). It appears likely that in the first century the Gospels (especially Matthew and probably John) were functioning *as Scripture* decades before they were actually called Scripture.

Barton shows several ways in which Scriptures were perceived to be holy by the churches and treated as sacred texts. He identifies: (1) the non-triviality of the text. For instance, in 1 Cor 9:9 Paul quotes Deut 25:4, a relatively unimportant OT text regarding the treatment of an ox treading out grain, as a very important text for the life of the Christian community.[2] The text appears trivial, but because it is Scripture, Paul defends its relevance. Barton goes on to suggest that a text's sacredness can be seen in its (2) non-ephemerality. In other words, a text is sacred if it is relevant to all ages, not merely to a particular time in history. Scripture was always read as relevant to the congregation's own day and situation, but it also transcended that day and place. Early Christian writers, he says, "seem to take it for granted that what Jesus said will always have a bearing on present problems, aspirations, conflicts, and hopes: these sayings are canonical."[3] Barton adds that if a text was believed to be Scripture, it was also believed to be (3) internally self-consistent and not self-contradictory. This perspective can be seen in Justin's famous *Dialogue with Trypho* in which he states that if Trypho had spoken ill of the Scriptures in error or without ill intent, he would be forgiven, but

> if you have done so because you imagined that you could throw doubt on the passage, in order that I might say the scriptures contradicted one another, you have erred. But I shall not venture to suppose or to say such a thing, and if a scripture that appears to be of such a kind be brought forward, and if there be a pretext for saying that it is contrary to some other, *since I am entirely convinced that no scripture contradicts another*, I shall admit rather that I do not understand what is recorded, and shall strive to persuade those who imagine that the scriptures are contradictory to be rather of the same opinion as myself. (*Dial.* 65.2, adapted from ANF; emphasis added)

This concern to maintain the inward consistency of a text is a clear signal of its scriptural status. Speaking about the canonical process of the OT, Ulrich draws attention to the creative work of scribes to harmonize Scriptures. He writes:

---

[2]   Barton, *Holy Writings, Sacred Text*, 129, 134–36.
[3]   Ibid., 137–39.

"Sometimes the presupposition behind harmonization is that this text can be juxtaposed to that text because God is the author of both. That presupposition is clearly behind some of the Qumran, NT, and rabbinic texts."[4] This harmonizing activity of scribes and among later Christian teachers assumes the sacredness of both of the traditions that they are trying to reconcile.

Barton further contends that the early church believed scriptural texts had (4) an excess of meaning. He cites as an example Gal 3:15–18, where Paul emphasizes the special meaning of the singular "seed" of Abraham in Gen 12:7, rather than plural "seeds," indicating that the promises to Abraham would find fulfillment in one man, Jesus. The multilayered meanings of a biblical text, often discovered through allegorical exegesis, emphasized that the text had fluidity and adaptability to ever-changing circumstances. Writings that were searched for deeper meanings by means of the various hermeneutical methodologies, especially allegorical exegesis, were generally acknowledged as sacred texts.[5] Multiple interpretations of texts were often followed by extended interpretations or commentaries, such as those produced by Origen on biblical books. Along with this, and roughly at the same time, many translations of texts were produced. This activity also suggests that what was translated was viewed as sacred. Finally, Barton observes that when (5) *nomina sacra*, the practice of abbreviating sacred names, appear in ancient NT manuscripts, those manuscripts were considered sacred.[6] As we saw earlier, early Christian scribes contracted special words from both the OT and the NT and this, according to Barton, suggests that they viewed both of those collections as sacred in the same sense.[7]

When a text was actually called Scripture is a different matter than whether it functioned that way for a group of churches and later became part of a fixed collection of sacred Scriptures. Scriptural identity could change and in several cases it did before the final fixing of the NT canon. For example, as we saw above, the *Shepherd of Hermas* called the ancient writing *Eldad and Modad* (Modat or Medad) Scripture: "The Lord is near those that turn to him, as it is written [ὡς γέγραπται] in the Book of Eldad and Modat, who prophesied to the people in the wilderness" (*Herm. Vis.* 2.3.4, LCL).[8] That text was somehow lost in antiquity.

---

4   Ulrich, *Dead Sea Scrolls*, 77 n. 75. For example, Isa 2:2–4//Mic 4:1–4; and Obad 1–10// Jer 49:7–22. Interestingly, in a personal communication, J. A. Sanders reminded me that the Masoretes protected the differences and discrepancies in the Masorah; they appear to have abhorred harmonization.

5   Barton, *Holy Writings, Sacred Text*, 142–43, 160.

6   We noted earlier that at a minimum those texts were understood as Christian, but when we see the *nomina sacra* in religious texts, it was most likely viewed as a sacred text, but not completely as we saw earlier in Chapter 20 §III. Other non-scriptural Christian texts also employed the use of the *nomina sacra*.

7   Ibid., 122–23. Barton shows examples of this practice.

8   This apocalypse may be alluded to in *2 Clem.* 11.2. The two names are mentioned in Num 11:26 and at some point a writing appeared in their names.

The *Shepherd* itself was called Scripture for a time and was widely popular in churches in the second through the fourth centuries, as we saw earlier, but it was dropped later from scriptural consideration.

Although we may see specific writings recognized or identified as Scripture by individual churches or ancient writers in antiquity, it does not follow that all churches of the same time, or subsequently, or even in the same location acknowledged the same writings as Scripture. The churches held to a variety of perspectives on the scope of their Scriptures in the second and third centuries, but as we saw earlier, in some cases for a lengthy period of time. Eventually most churches did not accept *Eldad and Modad* as Scripture; *1 Enoch* was recognized as inspired by Jude and by many of the early church fathers until the time of Origen; the Alogi rejected John's Gospel, Revelation, and the book of Hebrews, but all three were finally included in the NT. Other writings that were earlier regarded as sacred Scripture by a large segment of the Christian community were later excluded from that classification. For example, *1 Clement*, the *Letters* of Ignatius, the *Shepherd of Hermas*, and *Epistle of Barnabas* fall into that category. All were called Scripture by some early church writers and even included in some scriptural manuscripts well in the fourth and fifth centuries, but eventually these writings were also dropped from the churches' sacred collections.

After some Christian writings functioned as Scripture alongside the OT Scriptures in Christian worship, and after they were called Scripture in a majority of churches, the final step of canonization was a process of delimitation. In other words, the process was almost complete when a clearly defined collection of Christian Scriptures existed from which some writings were excluded and nothing else could be accepted as Scripture for the churches. After the fourth century, no new documents were considered Scripture by churches or included in their NT Scripture collection. There were exceptions made for accepting some older debated or doubted books (e.g., Revelation, Jude, James, Hebrews), but no new writings were considered. The process at that time involved more exclusion than inclusion of new works or earlier rejected books.

In roughly the fourth and fifth centuries, the recognized adaptability of some Christian writings to multiple contexts further enhanced their selection and placement in the NT canon (see §II.E below). But the recognition of the sacredness of a *book* did not mean that its *text* was automatically fixed. As we saw earlier, *the canonical processes extended only to the books* as such, not to the individual words in them. The individual copiers of Christian Scriptures took considerable liberty with the church's sacred texts for centuries.[9] There was as yet no widely

---

[9]   Ulrich, *Dead Sea Scrolls*, 57–58, and Metzger, *Canon of the New Testament*, 269–70, make this argument for the OT writings and the NT writings, respectively. Metzger illustrates this point with Eusebius and Jerome, both of whom saw textual differences in various manuscripts and wondered which to follow, but neither chose a particular text. Metzger notes that in antiquity "the question of

accepted form of the biblical text, even after a list or catalogue of books emerged that identified the Christian Scriptures (see the discussion of this in Chapter 19 §§III–VI).

Finally, it appears that Christian writers of the second century did not cite the OT books as much as the NT writings. Barton tabulates the frequency of citations of some writings in the late first-century and early second-century church fathers, namely, *Shepherd of Hermas*, *2 Clement*, Ignatius, *Didache*, and Polycarp. He shows that the Christian writings were often cited more frequently in this period than were the OT Scriptures and that this was quite common practice until the third century when the citations began to balance out. He notes that Christians did not cite the OT equally until its scope was becoming finalized for the church in the fourth century and later. He also notes that during the second century "all but a very few OT books (such as Isaiah or the Psalms) already play second fiddle to the Christians' own writings."[10] Barton concludes that this practice may reflect the scarcity of OT texts in the churches but also a relative abundance of Christian texts at the same time. His findings lead him to question the appropriateness of appealing to citations in ancient literature alone to determine what was considered sacred in the early churches.[11] We will now turn to some of the specific criteria involved in the canonical selection processes in the ancient churches.

II. WHAT CRITERIA DID THE CHURCHES EMPLOY?

What criteria were employed by the early church to identify the writings that would eventually make up its biblical canon? It is generally acknowledged that the church used several criteria in order to determine the contents of its NT. We discussed the criteria for the formation of the HB/OT canon earlier (Chapter 13), but those are different from the criteria employed in the selection of the NT writings. No surviving evidence, however, indicates that all churches used the same criteria in selecting their sacred collections. Similarly, no evidence suggests that each criterion listed below weighed equally with all churches in their deliberations about the formation of a NT canon. In fact, the lack of agreement on the so-called fringe books in the NT canon can be seen in the variety of Scripture catalogues and surviving Scripture manuscripts from the fourth to the sixth centuries (see Appendix C). The most common criteria employed in the canonical

---

canonicity pertains to the document *qua* document, and not to one particular form or version of that document" (270).

[10] Barton, *Holy Writings, Sacred Text*, 64.

[11] Ibid., 18–19 and 64–65. He is following here Franz Stuhlhofer, *Der Gebrauch der Bibel von Jesus bis Euseb: Eine statistische Untersuchung zur Kanongeschichte* (Wuppertal: R. Brockhaus, 1988).

process include apostolicity, orthodoxy, antiquity, and use or catholicity. Two other features of ancient Scripture, namely, their adaptability and inspiration, will also be discussed below.[12]

The NT itself contains several exhortations to discern among the prophets who claim to speak in the power of the Spirit (e.g., 1 Cor 12:10; 1 John 4:2; cf. also Matt 7:21–22; 24:24). The author(s) of the *Didache* later gave specific advice concerning both the doctrine and conduct of a prophet or apostle (*Did.* 11.1–13.7). Similarly, there came a time when it was deemed necessary to provide guidelines that determine which books would or would not be included in their Scripture collections, and specifically which could be read as Scripture in the churches. The aim, of course, was to make sure that appropriate (orthodox) teaching, namely the traditions handed down in the churches that gave them their identity, was followed in the churches. When the notion of apostolic authority was emerging in second-century churches, several writings were produced in the name of an apostle in order to secure its wider acceptance in churches than they might have if they had been written in the authors' actual names. Apostolic writings automatically received a more favorable hearing over other documents brought to the churches. In this sense, apostolicity, when determined *then* to be authentic, insured acceptance.

From around the middle of the second century, the inappropriate use of well-known names (pseudonymity) to secure the acceptance of certain Christian writings in the churches emerged with considerable frequency. Initially the churches were confused over the use of pseudonymous names and were reluctant to reject a writing attributed to an apostle, but eventually, as we saw in the example of Serapion, the issue was settled *not* on the basis of attribution to an apostle, but on the basis of the traditions and creeds passed on in the churches from their beginning. These traditions are the basis for what some have called "proto-orthodoxy." Pseudonymity was not started in the second century. Paul himself decided that it was necessary to affix his own peculiar signature to his letters to ensure that other writings circulating in his name would not be taken as genuine (1 Cor 16:21; Gal 6:11; Col 4:18; 2 Thess 3:17; and Phlm 19). The large list of pseudonymous literature in antiquity shows that pseudonymity was a problem that was widespread among Jewish writings, Greco-Roman writings,

---

[12]   To avoid confusion, it is best, I think, to employ the term canon to refer to a delimited collection of Christian literature that makes up our current biblical canon. The term is reserved here only for selected literature in the postbiblical era, when such notions of a closed or fixed biblical canon were discussed. As we saw earlier, there is an important distinction between Scripture and canon in that the latter presumes the former, but not the other way around. Scripture was perceived long before the notion of a fixed collection of Scriptures emerges. I discussed this earlier in Chapters 2 and 3. I distinguished, following Eugene Ulrich, between (1) canon which represents a reflexive judgment on the part of a religious community, (2) canon that denotes a closed list of books, and (3) canon that concerns biblical books rather than the specific text of those books. See his *Dead Sea Scrolls*, 55–61.

and also among Christian writings in the second and following centuries. It became obvious to most church fathers that by the end of the second century and later care was needed in the churches to deal with it. The following criteria are among the various means that some churches employed to identify their sacred Scriptures.

A. Apostolicity

If the early churches from the late second and third centuries and later believed that an apostle had written a particular writing under consideration, that writing was accepted as sacred Scripture and later was included in the church's biblical canon. Eusebius' argument against the supposed apostolic authorship of pseude-pigraphal writings reflects a universally acknowledged authority of apostolic writings and a rejection of most writings not believed to come from an apostle. The primary exceptions, of course, are Mark and Luke. After listing the writings that were widely accepted (ὁμολογουμένα) or "canonical" (ἐνδιαθήκη, lit. "encov-enanted"), Eusebius spoke of disputed writings (ἀντιλεγομένα) which were well known to many if not most churches. It shows that in his time, as well as much earlier, that the question of pseudonymous writings was a controversial issue in the church. While discussing the literature that was considered sacred in the fourth-century church, Eusebius describes those who falsely publish their own writings in the name of an apostle:

> Some have also counted [as canonical or recognized] the Gospel according to the Hebrews in which those of the Hebrews who have accepted Christ take a special pleasure. *These would all belong to the disputed books*, but we have nevertheless been obliged to make a list of them, *distinguishing between those writings which, according to the tradition of the Church, are true, genuine, and recognized, and those which differ from them in that they are not canonical but disputed*, yet nevertheless are known to most of the writers of the Church, in order that we might know them and the writings which are put forward by heretics under the name of the apostles containing gospels such as those of Peter, and Thomas, and Matthias, and some others besides, or Acts such as those of Andrew and John and the other apostles. *To none of these has any who belonged to the succession of the orthodox ever thought it right to refer in his writings.* Moreover, the type and phraseology differs from apostolic style, and the opinion and tendency of their contents is widely dissonant from true orthodoxy and clearly shows that they are the forgeries of heretics. They ought, therefore, to be reckoned not even among spurious books but shunned as altogether wicked and impious. (*Hist. eccl.* 3.25.6–7, LCL, emphasis added)

The church's most important weapon against gnostics and other heretics was its claim to apostolicity, which guaranteed that its oral and written traditions were genuine and accepted in churches. "Apostolic succession" represented the church's claim that the faith received by the apostles from the Lord (Jesus the Christ) was passed on by successive leaders in the church. After listing the succession of leaders in the church, Irenaeus explains the implications of apostolic succession:

The blessed apostles, then, having founded and built up the church committed into the hands of Linus the office of episcopate [he then lists twelve successive leaders]... In this order, and by this succession, *the ecclesiastical tradition from the apostles and the preaching of the truth have come down to us.* And this is the most abundant proof that there is one and the same vivifying faith, which has been preserved in the Church from the apostles until now, and handed down in truth. (*Haer.* 3.3.3, ANF, emphasis added. For the complete quote, see Chapter 16 §II.)

Later Irenaeus writes: "How should it be if the apostles themselves had not left us writings? Would it not be necessary in that case *to follow the course of the tradition which they handed down to those to whom they handed over the leadership* of the churches?" (*Haer.* 3.4.1, adapted from ANF, emphasis added). The NT literature reflected this "apostolic deposit" that was passed on in the churches. The church upheld the apostolic witness in its sacred literature as a way of grounding its faith in Jesus, represented by the apostles' teaching, and insuring that the church's tradition was not severed from its historical roots and proximity to Jesus, the undisputed authority of the church. All of the literature included in the NT was believed to have either apostolic authorship or authorship from those connected to an apostle and apostolic times. Scholars differ, of course, on how successful this belief and aim was.[13]

Tertullian (ca. 200) indicated that the Gospels were written either by the apostles or by "apostolic men" and he gave the former priority over the latter. As we saw earlier, he argued that: "John and Matthew first instill faith in us, but Luke and Mark, who are apostolic men,[14] renew it afterward" (*Marc.* 4.2.2, ANF; cf. also his critique of Marcion in *Marc.* 4.2.5). For Tertullian apostolicity was an essential feature of Christian Scripture. By way of contrast, apostolicity did not seem to be an important factor in the initial production of Christian literature until around the middle to late second century. Apostolic names were not placed on the individual Gospels until toward the last quarter of the second century (Irenaeus especially).

The criterion of apostolicity poses several problems today since some biblical scholars question how much of the NT was actually written by apostles. For example, it is difficult to establish historically that the Apostles John and Matthew wrote the Gospels that bear their names. While some scholars argue strongly for the apostolicity of 1 Peter and 1 John, the arguments are not conclusive. There are also lingering doubts about Paul's authorship of Ephesians, Colossians, 2 Thessalonians, and especially the Pastoral Epistles, even if they may contain

---

[13]   Funk, *Parables and Presence*, 182–86, discusses the success of the church's attempt to ground its faith (traditions) in Jesus through a closed apostolic canon. He acknowledges that the early churches appeal to their apostolic roots aimed at supporting their traditions, but he questions the success of their efforts.

[14]   That is, those connected with the apostolic community or the apostles themselves.

authentic Pauline traditions in them (e.g., 2 Tim 1:15; 4:16–17).[15] Long ago Ernest Best suggested that the ancient church's judgments about the apostolic authorship of the NT writings would likely be evaluated differently today.[16] I have often indicated that some of the disputed books now were rightly accepted (for their contents), but for the wrong reasons (apostolic authorship).

How carefully was the criterion of apostolicity applied in antiquity? Eusebius, for instance, says that there were doubts in the churches about accepting 2 Peter and he focused on the issue of its apostolicity. He accepted 1 Peter because it was widely regarded as genuine, but 2 Peter was not: "Of Peter, one epistle, that which is called his first, is admitted, and the ancient presbyters used this in their own writings as unquestioned, but the so-called second Epistle we have not received as canonical, but nevertheless it has appeared useful to many, and has been studied with other Scriptures" (*Hist. eccl.* 3.3.1, LCL). Eusebius probably accepted as canonical ("recognized") only twenty or twenty-one of the books of our current NT canon. Besides 2 Peter, he questioned the genuineness or authenticity of James, 2 John, 3 John, Jude, Revelation, and recognized that some doubted Hebrew's Pauline authorship, but he included Hebrews among the Letters of Paul (see a more detailed discussion of Eusebius' views on the NT canon in Chapter 16 §VI).

The gnostic Christians of the second century and the Donatists of the fourth century also claimed apostolic support for their teachings.[17] The gnostic *Gospel of Thomas*, for example, may be the first gospel that was specifically attributed to an apostle in its colophon at the end that may not have been placed there by its original author. While scholars today reject apostolic authorship of that gospel, some acknowledge that twenty or more of the sayings of Jesus in it may be authentic.[18]

---

[15] Several important works discuss the challenge of Pauline authorship of the Pastorals: J. D. Quinn and W. Wacker, *The First and Second Letters to Timothy*, Eerdmans Critical Commentary (Grand Rapids: Eerdmans, 2000); I. H. Marshall, *The Pastoral Epistles*, ICC (Edinburgh: T. & T. Clark, 1999); and J. D. Miller, *The Pastoral Letters as Composite Documents*, SNTSM 93 (Cambridge: Cambridge University Press, 1997). See also S. E. Porter's arguments for apostolic authorship of the NT letters in McDonald and Porter, *Early Christianity and Its Sacred Literature*.

[16] E. Best, "Scripture, Tradition, and the Canon of the New Testament," *BJRL* 61 (1978–79): 279.

[17] See the many gnostic documents in Robinson, *Nag Hammadi Library*, that claim either implicitly or explicitly the apostolic tradition, for example, *Acts of Peter* 1 (289) and *Apocryphon of John* 2 and 32 (105–6, 123).

[18] See especially the important collection of noncanonical sayings of Jesus in Crossan, *Sayings Parallels*. Although Crossan has a reputation for finding what he thinks are authentic sayings of Jesus in the most unusual places (e.g., *Gospel of Peter* and *Egerton Papyri*), and probably more than exist, he raises important questions about the application of the apostolic criterion in early Christianity.

After a lengthy debate, the early church concluded that Paul wrote the book of Hebrews, something that modern scholarship, for a variety of reasons (style, theology, vocabulary, etc.), almost universally rejects. Attributing Hebrews to Paul may have come from a desire to get a cherished writing into the biblical canon rather than from the sincere belief that Paul actually wrote it. Origen, like many others in the ancient church, had serious doubts about who wrote the letter, but welcomed it nonetheless. Observing that the thoughts were Paul's but that the style and composition belonged to someone else, he finally concludes: "who wrote the epistle, in truth God knows" (Eusebius, *Hist. eccl.* 6.25.14). Attributing the work to Paul, however, likely secured its place in the NT canon, though doubts about its authorship persisted in antiquity especially in the Eastern churches. This suggests, of course, that other criteria may have been operating perhaps subconsciously. As in the case of Hebrews, for instance, apostolic authorship may have been attributed to a cherished writing that was considered useful in segments of the Christian community in order to justify its continued use in the churches. I will mention this more below. This may also be the case with 2 Peter and Revelation.

In the early churches, the concern for apostolicity may have had as much to do with the authors' historical proximity to Jesus and their presumed firsthand knowledge of him as with apostolic authorship itself. Since Jesus was the supreme authority figure of the church, the opportunity to learn from those who were closest to him was highly valued. This is why Tertullian relegated John and Matthew to higher positions of authority than Mark and Luke. However, it is still the case that whenever apostolic authorship of ancient writings was doubted, typically their canonical status was also questioned.[19]

An important factor that points to the importance of apostolic authorship is the presence of pseudonymous literature circulating in the early churches. Many other writings were attributed to apostles, in fact far more than are in the NT, but they were not included in the canon largely because they were considered pseudonymous. Representatives of all the genres present in the NT (gospel, acts, epistle, and apocalypse), as we saw, are pseudonymously attributed to well-known apostles. This mostly sectarian literature was written in an apostle's name in order to achieve its acceptance in the church.[20] In several instances apostolic authorship of some writings was questioned in antiquity, but some churches nevertheless received them and were apparently reserved in their comments about their origins.

In sum, when discussions of canonicity were being considered, if the majority of churches believed that an apostle wrote a particular book, that writing was accepted and treated as Scripture. When that was determined not to be true, the

---

19   F. F. Bruce, *Canon of Scripture*, 259, makes this point.
20   See above the list in Chapter 18 §V and also in Schneemelcher, *New Testament Apocrypha*, for detailed descriptions and translations.

writing was rejected unless it was believed that someone within the apostolic community produced it (e.g., Mark and Luke–Acts). There is little doubt that the NT books were placed in the NT canon because the majority of leaders in the churches believed that they were written by apostles or members of the apostolic community. It is likely that several books were included in the NT canon because church leaders believed that they were written by an apostle, even though they were not (Hebrews and 2 Peter, Pastoral Epistles, and possibly others).

Perhaps it would be best to bypass issues of authorship, as did most of the first century of Christians, and conclude instead that all of the books of the NT are compatible with the Rule of Faith circulating in the churches from its beginning and are therefore in keeping with the church's sacred traditions about Jesus and the Gospel that is reflected in those writings. This criterion (essentially orthodoxy) was employed when certainty over authorship could not be ascertained. In the final analysis it appears that books deemed to have an important role in the church's life and ministry that cohered with the church's sacred traditions about Jesus were included. I will say more about this below.

Years ago after giving a lecture on this subject in Chicago, I was asked whether I thought that we should continue to accept books that were included in the NT, even if for the wrong reasons, in other words, they were attributed to apostles but probably were not written by them. I said then and still affirm that a book could rightly have been accepted but for the wrong reasons. Although the churches in the mid-second century and later emphasized apostolic authorship, the earliest churches did not and several NT writings were written anonymously, namely the Gospels, Acts, Hebrews and 1 John. While Hebrews was likely and finally welcomed on the basis of its attribution to Paul, its message was nonetheless seen as highly important to Christians facing uncertain times and looking for security and stability. The book of Hebrews told Christians in troubled times where their security is found, namely in the Christ who does not change even amidst the changing and threatening circumstances of life (Heb 13:8, 13–14). While I do not believe that the apostle Peter wrote 2 Peter, its message is consistent with the *Rule of Faith* in the early Christian communities. I am therefore not ready to toss it out of the NT. It has a different emphasis, but it is nonetheless compatible with the early church's broad theological and occasionally apocalyptic perspective.

B. Orthodoxy

Theological issues were a significant concern to the early churches, especially in the second century and afterwards when they had to deal with several heresies that threatened to divide the churches and even destroy the church's traditions that were affirmed by apostolic witness. Those theological traditions played an important role in the development of the church's NT canon. Simonetti offers a fair assessment of the role of the theological interpretations of the church's Scriptures:

We might say that the whole life of the community was conditioned by the interpretation of Scripture. It has been said that the history of doctrine is the history of exegesis, in that the whole development of catholic doctrine is based on the interpretation of a certain number of passages in Scripture in the light of particular needs; but the same could be said of any other aspect of the Church's life: organization, discipline, worship, and so on. For this reason, the study of Holy Scripture was the real foundation of Christian culture in the Church of the earliest centuries.[21]

Because the church's theological truth was rooted in its OT, sacred traditions, and creeds, the traditional theological foundation of the church was central in determining what Christian writings were welcomed into the church's NT canon. The early Christian writings that cohered to those sacred traditions were those that were eventually welcomed into the NT canon. The early churches' employ of the "rule of faith," or the criterion of orthodoxy, was central in determining which Christian writings could be read and taught in the churches as sacred Scripture. As we saw earlier, after initially allowing the church at Rhossus to read the *Gospel of Peter* in the church, Bishop Serapion (ca. 200) reversed his ruling because it did not meet his understanding of the church's criterion of truth. He wrote: "Since I have now learned, from what has been told me, that their mind was lurking in some hole of heresy, I shall give diligence to come again to you; wherefore, brethren expect me quickly" (Eusebius, *Hist. eccl.* 6.12.4, LCL). That text was rejected not because of its questionable authorship, though that may have played some role, but rather according to Eusebius, it was because Serapion believed that the theology of the book was out of step with the "rule of faith" operating in his churches. Serapion's initial willingness to accept the reading of the *Gospel of Peter* in his churches is also instructive. Had there been a widely recognized closed four-gospel canon at that time – and no others – he might well have rejected the *Gospel of Peter* on canonical grounds. In this example, however, perceived apostolic authorship and antiquity evidently took a back seat to the criterion of truth circulating in the churches.

If a writing was out of step with the church's central teaching that had been handed on in the churches, it was rejected (see also Eusebius, *Hist. eccl.* 3.25.7). An important distinguishing mark that led to the formation of the NT literature is its canon of faith.[22] This does not mean that there was unanimous agreement on

---

[21] M. Simonetti, *Biblical Interpretation in the Early Church: An Historical Introduction to Patristic Exegesis*, trans. J. A. Hughes, ed. A. Bergquist and M. Bockmuehl (Edinburgh: T. &. T. Clark, 1994), 1–2.

[22] See, for example, a discussion of this in Ewert, *From Ancient Tablets to Modern Translations*, 131; and also in G. W. Barker, W. L. Lane, and J. R. Michaels, *The New Testament Speaks* (New York: Harper & Row, 1969), 30–31, who ask, "was that which was written a genuine witness to Christ and from Christ?... The church was confident that if a document were genuinely inspired it would conform to the truth which God had revealed through tested witnesses"); and also E. F. Harrison, *Introduction to the New Testament* (Grand Rapids: Eerdmans, 1977), 11–12.

all of the theology of the NT, but only that it was all within the apostolic tradition circulating in the churches. For example, as one examines the NT literature, it is difficult to reconcile some of its theological positions with others including some practical guidelines for living. The Synoptic Gospels declare the imminent arrival of the kingdom of God (Mark 1:15; 13:3–37), but also its presence in the ministry of Jesus (Luke 7:18–23; 11:20; 17:21). On the other hand, John emphasizes the present nature of eternal life (John 3:16; 10:10; 20:30–31) and only once mentions the coming kingdom with an apocalyptic focus (John 5:28–29). Does Paul's view of the death of Jesus "for our sins" (1 Cor 15:3; Rom 3:23–25; Gal 2:21) square with Luke's lack of interest in that matter since he does not include it in the speeches of Acts (Acts 2:14–39; 3:11–26, etc.)? Paul's argument in Rom 13:1–3 that Christians ought to be subject to and not resist the governing authorities because they were appointed by God is difficult to square with Acts 4:19 and 5:28–29, which reject the authority of governing officials in favor of obedience to God. It does not necessarily mean that Paul disagreed with Acts' emphasis on obeying God rather than human institutions or governments, but he emphasized the importance of followers of Jesus to be good citizens. Also, the baptismal formulas in the book of Acts in the name of Jesus (2:38; 10:48; 19:5) are different from the Trinitarian focus in Matt 28:19.[23] There are also differences in the organizational structure of the early church (compare church structure in Acts with that in Paul, John, the Pastorals, and Matt 16:18–19). Käsemann argues that such theological diversity in the early church is "so wide even in the NT that we are compelled to admit the existence not merely of significant tensions, but, not infrequently, of irreconcilable theological contradictions."[24] Stendahl agrees that such differences cannot and should not be resolved through clever exegesis because "when they are overcome by harmonization, the very points intended by the writers are dulled and distorted."[25]

In the midst of the diversity in the NT, is there also a common core of beliefs typical of early Christianity and essential to the church's sacred traditions? Dunn contends that if the NT has a theological core everywhere acknowledged or reasonably assumed it is simply this, "Jesus-the-man-now-exalted."[26] Perhaps others will add to this that Jesus was raised from the dead, he is worthy of faithful obedience, and the promise of the blessing of God awaits all who follow him. This confession, however, is not confined to the NT literature, but is also

---

[23]   See other examples in L. Hartman, *"Into the Name of the Lord Jesus": Baptism in the Early Church* (Edinburgh: T. & T. Clark, 1997).
[24]   Käsemann, "Canon of the New Testament," 100.
[25]   K. Stendahl, *Meanings: The Bible as Document and Guide* (Philadelphia: Fortress, 1984), 63.
[26]   J. D. G. Dunn, *Unity and Diversity in the New Testament*, 2nd ed. (Philadelphia: Westminster, 1992), 377.

affirmed in several noncanonical Christian writings as well.[27] Nevertheless the later churches unquestionably believed that the NT writings reliably conveyed the essential message of and about Jesus the Christ. Apostolicity witnessed to this, but apostolicity was never a substitute for theological content.[28]

Although we often hear claims from those who want to emphasize the differences rather than the common features that unite them, it is nonetheless clear that all of the differences in the theologies of the Bible cannot be negligible or ignored and reconciled through artificial exegesis. The presence of such differences does not mean, however, that there could not have been a common core. George MacRae contends that there were justifiable reasons why the ancient church rejected the gnostic esoteric and ahistorical interpretation of Christian faith. There were boundaries that were common in the earliest churches.[29] Although the Christian proclamation of the first century was broader than the late second-century orthodoxy that eventually obtained prominence in the churches, all ancient theologies were not equally representative of the faith passed on from the first century. There was a typical understanding in the churches of God, Christ, Scripture, Jesus' death for the sins of humanity, and the triumph of Easter faith. Eschatology, as well as the humanity and divinity of Jesus, varied among the Christians in the first and second centuries, but there was little question about the affirmation of Jesus' life after death or forgiveness of sins or that hope was found in him for life beyond death. Although there was never unanimous agreement on many matters, e.g., baptism and church order, it is arguable that the core elements noted above were prominent in most first-century churches, and also in most churches by the end of the second century when affirmations of those perspectives formed early foundational beliefs and were put into creedal formulations that reflected what we now call proto-orthodoxy. Such core beliefs emerged over many other expressions of Christian faith (docetic, gnostic, Marcionite, and Montanist). The specific identity of Jesus was largely resolved for most churches in the fourth-century Council of Nicea, but never completely though there nonetheless was a widely acknowledged core in the Christian faith that is evidenced in the NT writings.

Gerd Theissen contends rightly that most Christian communities shared certain beliefs and that these core beliefs had a role in determining which writings were welcomed into the biblical canon. Other writings and groups that did not measure up to this theological core, such as the *Gospel of Peter* and the other gnostic texts, were excluded. He adds:

---

[27] All of the Apostolic Fathers – Clement of Rome, Ignatius, Polycarp, the Shepherd of Hermas, Barnabas, and the Didachist – could or did agree to this. So perhaps could Marcion also and the Montanists for that matter as we see in the post-Montanist conversion experience of Tertullian.

[28] Von Campenhausen, *Formation of the Christian Bible*, 330, makes this point. See also Bauer, *Orthodoxy and Heresy in Earliest Christianity*.

[29] MacRae, "Why the Church Rejected Gnosticism."

primitive Christianity is governed by two basic axioms, monotheism and belief in the redeemer. In addition there are eleven [*sic*] basic motifs: the motifs of creation, wisdom and miracle; of renewal, representation and indwelling; of faith, *agape* and a change of position; and finally the motif of judgment.[30]

The acceptance in the early churches of a belief in the activity of God in the life, death, and resurrection of the Jesus was central in the majority of the first- and second-century churches.

C. Antiquity

In the ancient world, antiquity appears to have played a significant role in the viability of religious belief. It is similar to apostolicity because it places high value on the writings that were produced close to the time of Jesus by those in the apostolic community. A religion's antiquity enhanced its credibility since what was old with a long history was generally considered more reliable and acceptable than what was new. As we saw earlier (Chapter 18 §II), the church excommunicated Marcion largely over his rejection of the church's OT Scriptures because he robbed the church both of its ability to focus on the prophecy-fulfillment motif from the OT Scriptures that is regularly found in the story of Jesus variously in NT writings, especially the Gospels. The notion of antiquity in canon formation, of course, gave priority to those writings that were closest to the time of Jesus.

The early Christians appear to have believed that with the advent of Jesus something new and important had arrived, surpassing everything that had gone before him.[31] For them the ministry and teaching of Jesus had become the defining moment in history. Consequently, the church's most important authorities were those closest to this defining moment.[32] The early Christians believed that the books and writings that gave them their best access to the story of Jesus, and thus defined their identity and mission, were those that came from the apostolic era. Barton suggests that the books that came from that time, especially the Gospels and Epistles, were so important to the early church that they "were more important than 'Scripture,' [that is, the OT] and to cite them as γραφή [Scripture] might have diminished rather than enhanced them."[33] He claims that with time, as the earlier practice of prophecy declined in the churches, the church appealed more to antiquity and its roots in the OT. We saw earlier that the gift of prophecy

---

[30] Theissen, *A Theory of Primitive Christian Religion* (London: SCM, 1999), 282. Farmer, "Reflections on Jesus and the New Testament Canon," in McDonald and Sanders, eds., *The Canon Debate*, 321–40, emphasizes the importance of the *regula fidei* for the life of the early church and the formation of its canon.

[31] Barton, *Holy Writings, Sacred Text*, 64–65.

[32] Ibid., 64–67.

[33] Ibid., 68.

that was characteristic of the early Christian churches declined considerably by the end of the second century perhaps as a result of abuse and perhaps also because of the Montanist movement that emphasized the role of prophecy in the churches. The church, however, continued to give priority to the period of Jesus' life and ministry as *the* defining moment for the church and to the apostles as those who were closest to him and the best representatives and communicators of this crucial period.

By the fourth century the church excluded from its NT Scriptures writings that it believed were written after the period of apostolic ministry. In this sense, apostolicity and antiquity are two sides of the same issue. This period began to take priority over all other periods in late second-century proto-orthodox teaching. This appears, as we saw, to be one of the reasons that led to the rise of pseudonymous writings in churches. Anchoring the Christian faith in writings that were close to the time of Jesus was certainly the perspective of the author of the Muratorian Fragment who spoke against accepting the *Shepherd of Hermas* as Scripture because it was not written in the apostolic age:[34]

> But Hermas wrote the Shepherd very recently, in our times, in the city of Rome, while bishop Pius, his brother, was occupying the [episcopal] chair of the church of the city of Rome. And therefore it ought indeed to be read; but *it cannot be read publicly to the people in church either among the prophets, whose number is complete, or among the apostles, for it is after [their] time.* (Muratorian Fragment, lines 73–80, Metzger trans., *Canon of the New Testament*, 307, emphasis added)

Antiquity appears to have been an important criterion for canonicity *for some* of the churches, but it is seldom an easy matter to determine. Which Christian writings were among the earliest? Some biblical scholars argue that some of the NT books, especially 2 Peter and the Pastorals, were written later than some noncanonical Christian books such as the *Didache, 1 Clement, Letters* of Ignatius, possibly *Epistle of Barnabas, Shepherd of Hermas*, and even the *Martyrdom of Polycarp*. A few scholars claim that even some of the apocryphal gospels may make similar claims of having been written earlier than some of the NT writings.[35] What this suggests, of course, is that the criterion of antiquity may not have been applied with unfailing success or as carefully in the patristic church as modern scholars would prefer. However, *if* antiquity alone were the chief criterion for canonicity, some rethinking regarding the present biblical canon might well be in order. Some later writings are not less reliable or even less orthodox.

That notwithstanding, the second-century Christians and those later were anxious to read and recognize the earliest and most reliable traditions about Jesus. That cannot have been an uninformed pursuit, regardless of modern conclusions

---

[34] For discussion, see Chapter 21 §I.D and Hahneman, *Muratorian Fragment*, 34–72.
[35] See H. Koester, "Apocryphal and Canonical Gospels," *HTR* 73 (1980): 105–30.

about the dating of individual books. The grounding of Christian faith and doctrine in the life, teachings, death, and resurrection of Jesus and in the witnesses that were believed to come from his closest followers was a regular theme since the first century. Cautious use of this criterion, along with apostolicity, is appropriate and continues to be an appropriate means of getting closer to the defining and fundamental moment of the Christian faith. I have often said that almost all of the writings of the NT are from the first century and almost all of the noncanonical writings are not. It is not unimportant that most of the NT writings arguably are from the first century despite questions about some of them, and those perceived to have been written later were rejected. For the most part, the NT writings are indeed closest to the most important formative time for the church and to those who were closer to the time of Jesus even if that closeness is not always closer than some other traditions (*1 Clement, Didache*, Ignatius, possibly also *Shepherd of Hermas*, and Polycarp). That closer proximity to the time of Jesus does not always equate with reliability, but, in my opinion, it is arguable that the NT writings are more reflective of the story of Jesus in history and faith than any of the gospels, acts, epistles and apocalypses written in the second century and later.

D. Use (Catholicity or the Ecclesiastical Criterion)

Just as the reading of ancient Jewish religious texts in the synagogues was a sign of and criterion for their acceptance as sacred Scripture and canonicity, the same was true in the ancient churches. The widespread use of the NT writings in the ancient churches was apparently an important criterion in their selection for inclusion in the church's NT canon for several important early church fathers. This is likely what Eusebius had in mind when he mentioned that certain writings were "recognized" (ὁμολογουμένα) among the churches and were "encovenanted" (ἐνδιαθήκη, that is, "testamented" or "canonical") writings (see *Hist. eccl.* 3.25.1–7). Eusebius' reference to the use or catholicity of the NT writings most likely came from Origen's influence, although Tertullian (ca. 200) before him also made a similar claim.[36] Similarly, Augustine rejected the "synagogal criterion"[37] for establishing the Christian OT canon, but nevertheless insisted that the widespread use of books in the churches that the Jews had rejected was appropriate as was their including them in the church's OT canon (a reference to the so-called apocryphal or

---

[36] For a careful discussion of this, see Edmon L. Gallagher, *Hebrew Scripture in Patristic Biblical Theory: Canon, Language, Text*, VCSup 114 (Leiden: Brill, 2012), 53–60.

[37] This simply refers to books only accepted by the synagogue or books in the Jewish biblical canon that rejected the apocryphal books that had been welcomed in the churches. Origen, in his correspondence with Julius Africanus, rejected the synagogal criterion saying that it would be wrong to "legislate to the brotherhood [churches] to put away the holy books in circulation among them, and to flatter Jews and persuade them to share with us the copies that are pure and have no fabrication" (*Ep. Afr.* §8). I owe this reference to Gallagher, ibid., 57.

Deuterocanonical writings). Speaking about the books the Jews rejected, he said: "...those books should not be omitted which are agreed to that have been written before the advent of the Savior, because even though they are not accepted by the Jews, yet the Church of that same Savior has accepted them."[38] He emphasizes use or catholicity as a criterion especially in the more influential and presumably larger churches stating that all who are skilled in the scriptures

> will therefore maintain this rule for the canonical scriptures, that he should prefer *those which are accepted by all catholic churches over the others which some do not accept*; but among those which are not accepted by all, he should prefer those which the more numerous and more important churches accept, over those which the churches that are fewer and of less authority maintain. (*De Doctr. Chr.* 2.12, emphasis added)[39]

Bruce says that the criterion of "catholicity" means the unwillingness of a church to be out of step with other churches in regard to which documents were recognized as authoritative.[40] Widespread use of the NT writings by the larger and more influential churches may well have been one of the most determinative factors in the canonical process.[41] For example, the authorship of the book of Hebrews was strongly questioned, yet it was included in the NT canon. This suggests that churches were reluctant to dismiss a useful and cherished document that was widely approved in many churches.

Athanasius and Epiphanius had a greater influence on the church than many lesser-known figures, and also, so did the larger churches in the metropolitan centers such as Antioch, Alexandria, Rome, Ephesus, and Constantinople. They were more likely to have a greater influence on which books were included than the smaller churches in rural areas. While most NT writings were known and used by many if not most of the churches in Eusebius' day, some doubts lingered over others. As noted earlier, these "disputed" (*antilegomenon*) writings included James, 2 Peter, 2 John, 3 John, Jude, probably Revelation, and possibly Hebrews. Eusebius, for example, acknowledges wide acceptance of 1 John, but is reluctant to accept 2 John, 3 John, and Revelation because of the disputes in churches over them. For him, the Gospel of John and 1 John have been "*accepted without controversy by ancients and moderns alike but the other two are disputed*, and

---

[38]   Ibid. This is Gallagher's translation from the preface of *Speculum* 22 when Augustine is discussing the use of the *Book of Wisdom* (cf. also the same argument in favor of Wisdom of Solomon, Sirach, and Judith in *Retract.* 2.20; *Civ.* 17.20; 18.36 respectively).

[39]   Translation by Gallagher, ibid., 56. See also the translation of this same text in Metzger in *Canon of the New Testament*, 237. It is slightly differnt from Gallagher's translation, but still emphasizes the importance of widespread church use.

[40]   F. F. Bruce, "Tradition and the Canon of Scripture," 74.

[41]   Verheyden, "The New Testament Canon," 411, agrees with the other criteria listed above, but concludes that "a criterion far less 'theological' than the others, but certainly not least in importance" was the life and praxis of the church such as usage in church services and liturgy. This, as we will note below, is similar to the arguments of Theodor Zahn.

as to the Revelation there have been many advocates of either opinion up to the present. This, too, shall be similarly illustrated by quotations from the ancients at the proper time" (*Hist. eccl.* 3.24.18, LCL, emphasis added). This shows his considerable interest in what the majority of churches concluded about the matter of the NT Scriptures.

The writings eventually included in the NT canon apparently were welcomed by the majority of churches, and especially by the most influential churches and leaders of those churches. The writings that did not remain in the church's sacred collections were those that did not meet the needs of the greater church and had more difficulty being adapted to the churches' changing needs, but especially because the majority of churches had rejected them.

Speaking in regard to the Jewish scriptures among the Dead Sea Scrolls and acceptance of religious texts recognized as sacred scripture, Ulrich claims that:

> the use of Scripture – whether homiletical or liturgical, whether ancient or contemporary – involves a tripolar dynamic of interaction between the traditional text, the contemporary cultural situation, and the experience of the minister within the community. This tripolar dynamic is a reflection of, and is in faithful continuity with, the process by which the Scriptures were composed.[42]

Not all of the NT writings were used extensively in worship or in church life. For example, Philemon, 2 Peter, Jude, 2 John, and 3 John were not cited or used as often as several writings in the Apostolic Fathers such as *1 Clement*, the *Shepherd of Hermas, Didache, Epistle of Barnabas*, the *Letters* of Ignatius, and *Martyrdom of Polycarp*. If frequency of use or citation is a guide, some doubt remains. Recognizing this, Collins concludes that not all of the NT teachings and writings were of equal value for Christian faith and ministry, nor were they necessarily more important or closer to the canon of truth than certain noncanonical Christian writings. Acknowledging the strong influence of the present NT canon on Christian thought, he nevertheless states that "concern for the truth of history calls for the admission that some books within the canon have had a more influential function in shaping the expression of the church's faith than have others within the canon" and he correctly adds that "some books outside of the canon have had a more striking impact on the formulation of the church's faith than have some individual books among the canonical twenty-seven.[43]

The variety books in the Scripture catalogues of the fourth and fifth centuries shows that the catholicity criterion was broad but far from absolute. That suggests that other historical circumstances besides utilization by large numbers and influential churches also helped determine which books were included in the church's authoritative list. The reaction against Montanism prompted a broad suspicion of prophetic literature, leading to its neglect in succeeding generations

---

42   Ulrich, *Dead Sea Scrolls*, 74.
43   R. Collins, *Introduction to the New Testament*, 39.

of the church, especially in the East. This may have led to the rejection of the *Shepherd of Hermas*. The *Apocalypse of Peter* also was not cited as frequently after the Montanist controversies as it was before, and the book of Revelation itself had a stormy reception in the East, especially through the fourth century.

Verheyden acknowledges that there does not appear to have been a single criterion that was decisive in every case. He correctly concludes: "All these criteria were used in a more or less flexible way, and they all combined a sense of universality and tradition. Taken together, these features apparently made them most useful instruments for the purpose they had to serve."[44]

We may be more explicit about the aspect of catholicity or use as a criterion for canonicity, namely that the books that were welcomed into the Christian canon were those that were read in the liturgy of the churches and not so much in ecclesiastical councils. Long ago Theodor Zahn made this a central component of canon formation and emphasized its ecclesiastical aspect.[45] As Schnabel observes, Zahn "linked the formation of the canon with the worship services in the Christian assemblies."[46] The argument can be made that the councils that met to formalize the books that could be read in churches essentially reflected what was already happening in the churches. It is likely that council decisions were especially helpful in the case of marginal books such as 2 Peter, Jude, and Revelation. For Zahn, the NT canon was those books that were read in the churches and not necessarily those that were approved by a bishop's council and he believed that this recognition took place in the churches at the end of the first century. Perhaps this distinction draws upon the familiar claim in traditional Protestant churches that the church did not *decide* or select which religious texts were Scripture, that is, it did not create the canon, but rather *recognized* those books that were inspired by God. While I am sensitive to that claim, the role of the church in examining the so-called fringe books of the NT canon and also deciding whether they would be read in churches cannot be ignored. I will focus on this issue more below in the discussion of inspiration and canonicity.

E. Adaptability

The Scriptures that were adaptable to the changing circumstances of the church's life are the ones that survived the canonization processes. Some writings that functioned as Scripture earlier in the church's history, such as the *Epistle of Barnabas*, *1 Clement*, the Ignatius' *Letters*, *Shepherd of Hermas*, and *Eldad and Modad*, did not survive the unstated criterion of adaptability. Perhaps for a variety of reasons they fell into disuse and were eventually dropped from the Scripture collections. This happened while the notion of canon was still fluid in the churches,

---

44   Verheyden, "New Testament Canon," 411.
45   *Geschichte des neuestestamentlichen Kanons*, 2 vols. (Erlangen: A Deichert, 1888–92).
46   Schnabel, "Muratorian Fragment," 256–57.

namely, in the second to fourth century. Some noncanonical writings occasionally still appear in NT codices well into the fourth and fifth centuries as we see in the inclusion of *Barnabas* and the *Shepherd of Hermas* that were included in Codex Sinaiticus and the inclusion of *1–2 Clement* in Codex Alexandrinus.

Sanders has long emphasized the importance of the adaptability of the OT and NT Scriptures in the continually changing circumstances of the communities of faith. He makes the case that what was true for ancient Israel in this regard was also true for the church, namely, that the story that had sufficient adaptability to meet the ever-changing needs of the church is what was preserved and canonized. The sacred writings that brought hope into a hopeless situation for the people of Israel told a story that could be applied to new circumstances.[47] The church's story about Jesus was also adaptable to new and changing circumstances facing it and this adaptability was significantly enhanced through the creative hermeneutics that were employed by the church in interpreting their OT and NT Scriptures in order to offer hope and life to the new people of faith. The story of Jesus' life, ministry, death, and resurrection also continued to be adaptable to the changing circumstances of life in the churches in a variety of cultures. Through it, persons of faith perceived that God continued to release from bondage, bring healing, and offer hope to the hopeless. This story and the literature that tells this story continue to be adaptable to new situations and inspire persons in every generation. This is what the church canonized.

F. Inspiration

This is one of the more controversial areas of canon formation, as we saw earlier in Chapter 17 (§IV). Was inspiration a criterion for canonization? The answer appears to be both yes and no. No church father who recognized a NT book as Scripture ever denied its inspiration. On the other hand, it is difficult to make a qualitative difference on this basis between some writings that were accepted as Scripture and others that were not. It is difficult to demonstrate the inspiration of one book over another, for example, Jude over the *Didache* or *1 Clement*. The criterion for making that distinction is missing in antiquity except in so far as inspiration was attributed to the orthodoxy of a writing and was affirmed by the majority of churches, as we saw earlier in Chapter 17.

Theophilus of Antioch (ca. 180) is typical of the belief that Scriptures were inspired when he asserts that "the holy writings teach us, and all the spirit-bearing [inspired] men…that at first God was alone, and the Word in Him" (*Autol.* 2.22, ANF). For him, inspiration involved "men of God carrying in them a holy spirit [πνευματατοφόροι] and becoming prophets, being inspired and made wise by

---

[47]   J. A. Sanders, *From Sacred Story*, 9–39, deals with the adaptability issue in detail.

God, becoming God-taught, and holy and righteous" (*Autol.* 2.9).[48] The author of *2 Clement* believed that *1 Clement* was an inspired document and cites *1 Clem.* 23.3–4 with the words "for the prophetic word also says [λέγει γὰρ καὶ ὁ προγητικὸς λόγος] (*2 Clem.* 11.2), the usual words that designate writings as inspired. *Barnabas* 16.5 introduces a passage from *2 Enoch* with the words "for the Scripture says [λέγει γὰρ ἡ γραφή]." In a somewhat different light, Clement of Rome (ca. 95) told his readers that Paul's letter, 1 Corinthians, was written "with true inspiration [ἐπ' ἀληθείας πνευματικῶς]" (*1 Clem.* 47.3), but he later claimed the same inspiration for himself, saying that his own letter was written "through the Holy Spirit [γεγραμ-μένοις διὰ τοῦ ἁγίου]" (*1 Clem.* 63.2). Ignatius also expressed awareness of his own inspiration: "I spoke with a great voice – with God's own voice... But some suspected me of saying this because I had previous knowledge of the division of some persons: but he in whom I am bound is my witness that I had no knowledge of this from any human being, but the Spirit was preaching and saying this [τὸ δὲ πνεῦμα ἐκήρυσσεν λέγον τάδε]" (Ign. *Phld.* 7.2, LCL).

To what extent did inspiration play a role in the canonization process? Traditionally, many have argued that the biblical canon resulted from the church's recognition of the inspired status of certain writings. As noted earlier, it is more accurate to say that inspiration was a corollary rather than a criterion of canonicity. It is especially difficult to show demonstratively that God inspired a NT writer to write a text, though admittedly, this is what the author of Revelation claims (Rev 22:18–19).

The problem with adding inspiration to the above criteria is twofold. First is the problem of determining what is or is not inspired. This difficulty stems from the term's fluidity of meaning in ancient Christianity. In fact, the church as a whole has never presented a comprehensive and clear definition of inspiration. The resultant ambiguity is seen in the variety of ways the term has been used throughout the ages, including in our own. Second, and more importantly for our purposes, the early church never limited the concept of inspiration to its sacred writings, but rather extended it to everything considered theologically true, whether it was written, taught, or preached.

The ancient church fathers believed that their Scriptures were inspired, but inspiration alone was not the basis for including those works in the NT canon. Several writers of sacred truth believed that they were inspired as they wrote. The author of the book of Revelation, for example, claims prophetic inspiration: "Blessed is the one who reads aloud the words of the prophecy" (Rev 1:3), and "I warn everyone who hears the words of the prophecy of this book: if anyone adds to them, God will add to that person the plagues described in this book; if anyone takes away from the words of the book of this prophecy, God will take away that person's share in the tree of life and in the holy city, which are described in this

---

48   This passage clarifies what Theophilus means by inspiration and perhaps how his and other communities understood it.

book" (Rev 22:18–19). The author of these words believed that he had the voice of prophecy and was inspired by God when he wrote, but this is not as obvious in other NT writings.

The ancient churches assumed the inspiration of their Scriptures, but to what extent did inspiration play a part in the canonizing process? Irenaeus, for example, makes it clear that the Scriptures, even when they are not clearly understood, "were spoken by the Word of God and by His Spirit" (*Haer*. 2.28.2, ANF). This appears on the surface to be more of an *after recognition* based on whether the truth that had been handed down through apostolic succession (the *regula fidei*) was portrayed in the writings in question. Origen maintained that "the Scriptures were written by the Spirit of God, and have a meaning, not such only as is apparent at first sight, but also another which escapes the notice of most" (*First Principles*, Preface 8, ANF).[49] Seeking to discredit the *Doctrine of Peter*, he says that he can show that it was not written by Peter "or by any other person inspired by the Spirit of God" (*First Principles*, Preface 8, ANF). The operating assumption here, of course, is that Scripture is inspired, but heresy and falsehood are not. The criterion for determining a text's inspiration is not easily recognized apart from its affirmation of the church's core tradition passed on in the early churches

As we saw earlier, there are examples of noncanonical authors who claimed, or were acknowledged by others, to have been filled or inspired by the Spirit when they spoke or wrote.[50] The point is that the church's Scriptures were not the only ancient messages or words believed to be inspired by God. Generally speaking, in the early churches the common word for "inspiration" (θεόπνευστος; or "God-breathed"; see 2 Tim 3:16) was used not only in reference to the Scriptures (OT or NT), but also of individuals who spoke or wrote the truth of God. For example, Gregory of Nyssa (ca. 330–95) describes Basil's (330–79) commentary on the creation story and claims that Basil's work was inspired and that his words even surpassed those of Moses in terms of beauty, complexity, and form: it was an "exposition given by inspiration of God...[admired] no less than the words composed by Moses himself."[51] This is quite remarkable since the text in question is compared to the church's OT Scriptures (words of Moses) and believed to be superior to them. This reference does not suggest that there was a qualitative difference in the notion of inspiration in either the biblical or ecclesiastical texts. Similarly, the famous epitaph of Abercius (ca. fourth century) was called an "inspired inscription [θεόπνευστον ἐπίγραμμα]" and a synodical letter of the

---

[49] F. F. Bruce, *Canon of Scripture*, 267–68, notes that Irenaeus was the first Christian writer to allegorize the NT writings because he was among the first to treat NT writings as unreservedly inspired. Thereafter, Origen and others felt free to allegorize the Scriptures because they were considered inspired by God.

[50] Other examples are listed in Sundberg, "Bible Canon," 365–71; and Kalin, "Inspired Community."

[51] Gregory of Nyssa, *Apologia hexaemeron*, quoted by Metzger, *Canon of the New Testament*, 256; see also Kalin, "Argument from Inspiration," 170.

Council of Ephesus (ca. 433) describing the council's condemnation of Nestorius was termed "his [or its] inspired judgment [or decision] [τῆς αὐτοῦ θεοπνεύστου κρίσεως]."[52]

From these and many other examples, we see that the ancient church did not limit inspiration to the Scriptures or even to literature alone. In his *Dialogue with Trypho*, Justin Martyr argues that: "the prophetical gifts remain with us even to the present time. And hence you ought to understand that [the gifts] formerly among your nation [Israel] have been transferred to us" (*Dial.* 82, ANF; see also *Dial.* 87–88). He was speaking of the present and not of the past writing of NT Scriptures. Kalin finds no evidence that the early church confined inspiration to an already past apostolic age or to a collection of sacred writings, even in writings that dealt with the Montanist controversy (see Eusebius, *Hist. eccl.* 5.14–19) in the latter third of the second century.[53] The traditional assumption that the early Christians believed that only the canonical writings were inspired is not demonstrable from the available evidence.

The rabbinic notion that "when the latter prophets died, that is, Haggai, Zechariah, and Malachi, then the Holy Spirit came to an end in Israel" (*t. Sotah* 13:2)[54] was simply not shared by the church.[55] From his investigation of the church fathers up to 400, Kalin failed to turn up one example where an orthodox, but noncanonical, writing was ever called "uninspired"; such a designation appears to have been reserved for heretical authors. He concludes: "If the Scriptures were the only writings the church fathers considered inspired, one would expect them to say so, at least once in a while."[56] He adds that in the early church inspiration applied not only to all Scripture, but also to the Christian community as a whole, as it bore "living witness of Jesus Christ." Only heresy was considered to be uninspired, because it was contrary to this witness.[57] Von Campenhausen agrees here but adds that the presence of prophetic literature among the Montanists – literature believed by the Montanists to be born of or prompted by the Holy Spirit but by others to be misguided – shows that at the end of the second century belief in inspiration was

---

[52] *Vita Abercii* 76. Abercius Marcellus himself, who was bishop of Hieropolis in Phrygia of Asia Minor in the late second century, apparently penned the writing. He died ca. 200 CE. Kalin gives several other examples of the ancient use of the term "inspired" (θεόπνευστος) to show that it was not exclusively used of Scriptures. See Kalin, "Argument from Inspiration," 169–73.

[53] Kalin, "Inspired Community," 543, concludes from his study of Irenaeus, Origen, Eusebius, and other ancient fathers that only the work of the false prophets mentioned in the OT, the heathen oracles, and philosophy were uninspired. See also Kalin, "Argument from Inspiration," 163, 168.

[54] Neusner, *Tosefta*, 885.

[55] See Blenkinsopp, "Formation of the Hebrew Bible Canon," 54 n. 3: "The Holy Spirit (meaning the spirit of prophecy) departed from Israel after the destruction of Solomon's temple (*b. B. Bat.* 12a; *b. Yoma* 21b; *b. Sotah* 48a) or after the death of the last biblical prophets (*b. Yoma* 9b; *b. Sanh.* 11a)." See also idem, "Prophecy and Priesthood in Josephus," *JSS* 101 (1974): 245–55; and J. A. Sanders, "Spinning the Bible," for a similar perspective.

[56] Kalin, "Inspired Community," 544–45.

[57] Ibid., 547.

beginning to be confined to first-century literature.[58] But, if this were the case, we would see more examples of it in the second and later centuries. It would be more accurate to say that inspiration was not limited to the first century, but by the end of the second century the church was beginning to assume that inspired Scripture ceased after the apostolic era.

It is difficult to find any ecclesiastical criteria that clarify inspiration of an ancient document apart from its faithful conveyance of the truth passed on in the churches. As a criterion for canonicity, it played no *discernible* role until a document was later identified as sacred Scripture in the churches. Holladay acknowledges the difficulty that the criterion of inspiration alone brings to the canonization of the Scriptures and how difficult it is to distinguish it from other non-biblical writers who wrote and also claimed to do so by inspiration. He appropriately states:

> Claims of inspiration were and are notoriously difficult to authenticate. If someone claimed to be speaking or writing under the impulse of the Spirit, who could deny it? Since the early church operated with such a strong sense of the Spirit's possession, one of its constant challenges was to distinguish between true and false prophets. Even so, claims of inspiration were commonly made about the NT writings [*1 Clem.* 47.3 and Irenaeus, *Haer.* 2.28.2]. Theophilus of Antioch speaks of the "holy prophets who were possessed by the Holy Spirit of God" [*Autol.* 3.17] and includes the Fourth Evangelist as one of "the spirit-bearing men." [*Autol.* 2.22 citing John 1:1]. He also regards both the OT prophets and the Gospels as "inspired by one Spirit of God" [*Autol.* 3.12]. Origen's exposition of Scripture presupposes as a matter of principle that the same Spirit who inspired the writings of the OT "did the same thing both with the evangelists and the apostles" [*Princ.* 4.16; cf. also *Preface* 8]. In the fourth-century canonical list composed by Amphilochius, bishop of Iconium in Lycaonia, the writings listed are "the most reliable [lit. 'unfalsified'] canon of the divinely inspired scriptures" (Οὗτος ἀψευδέστατος Κανὼν ἂν εἴη τῶν θεοπνεύστων Γραφῶν) [*Iambi ad Seleucum* 318–19]. While this is only a selection of authors who characterized the NT writings as inspired, it represents a widely held view. Inspiration may not have been the only decisive criterion, but it was a prerequisite for canonicity. No writing could have been included in the NT canon had it not been regarded as inspired.[59]

Indeed, but the problem is that throughout early church history other authors of church writings also claimed the inspiration of the Spirit in what they wrote. As we saw earlier, most of the reports from the church councils also indicated

---

58   Von Campenhausen, *Formation of the Christian Bible*, 234–35.

59   Holladay, *Critical Introduction to the New Testament*, in CD-Rom Expanded version, 852–53. Holladay is certainly correct that no NT writing was ever acknowledged as Scripture without also having its inspiration affirmed. The question here is which came first, its inspired status or its affirmation as Scripture? Holladay wisely introduces this section with the following proviso: "While inspiration may not have been the sole differentiating criterion for determining the canonical status of a particular writing, it was a crucial consideration. Numerous early Christian writings, such as the *Shepherd of Hermas* and the *Apocalypse of Peter*, claimed to be divinely inspired. Some NT writings (Revelation) claimed explicit inspiration in a way that other NT writings (Luke–Acts) did not" (852).

that in all of their deliberations the Spirit led them. This continued, as we saw, even in the much later Council of Trent. Barr summarizes the traditional understanding of the role of inspiration and canon formation as follows: "If we take a really strict old-fashioned view of inspiration, all books within the canon are fully inspired by the Holy Spirit, and no books outside it, however good in other respects, are inspired."[60] He later stresses that one of the difficulties in the whole notion of canon in the early church is the difficulty of distinguishing inspired and non-inspired writings.[61] The problem the early church had in deciding what literature was inspired demonstrates a lack of agreement on the meaning of inspiration.[62] The ongoing prophetic ministry of the Spirit, which called individuals through the proclamation of the good news to faith in Jesus the Christ, was believed by the church to be resident in their community of faith and in their ministry, just as it was in the first century. They did not distinguish the filling of the Spirit to proclaim the Christian message from being led by the Spirit or inspired by the Spirit to write. The Christian community believed that God continued to inspire individuals in their proclamation, just as God inspired the writers of the NT literature. They believed that the Spirit was the gift of God to the whole church, not just to writers of sacred literature. There never was any biblical, theological, or ecclesiastical argument in early Christianity that claimed that the Spirit ceased its activity in the church either at the completion of the biblical canon or at any point in its existence.

Does this conclusion pose an affront to the uniqueness and authority of the biblical literature? That would be true if its only unique characteristic is its inspiration. Inspiration was not the distinguishing factor that separated either the apostles from subsequent Christians or the Christian Scriptures from all other Christian literature. Stendahl summarizes the role that inspiration played in early Christianity and biblical tradition thusly: "Inspiration, to be sure, is the divine presupposition for the NT, but the twenty-seven books were never chosen because they, and only they, were recognized as inspired. Strange as it may sound, inspiration was not enough. Other standards had to be applied."[63] Bruce agrees, adding that "inspiration is no longer a criterion of canonicity: it is a corollary of canonicity."[64] Similarly, Metzger notes that the focus of inspiration was on the truth claims of what was written, not inspiration itself. He reasons: "While it is true that the Biblical authors were inspired by God, this does not mean that inspiration is a

---

60   Barr, *Holy Scripture*, 49. Similarly, Achtemeier, *Inspiration of Scripture*, 119, says that the prevailing view is that "God inspired the canonical books with no exception, and no noncanonical books are inspired, with no exception."

61   Barr, *Holy Scripture*, 57.

62   For example, Clement of Alexandria cited the *Didache* as Scripture (*Strom.* 1.100.4) and believed that *1 Clement, Barnabas, Shepherd of Hermas, Preaching of Peter*, and the *Apocalypse of Peter* were inspired literature. See Grant, "New Testament Canon," 302.

63   Stendahl, "Apocalypse of John," 245.

64   F. F. Bruce, *Canon of Scripture*, 268.

criterion of canonicity. A writing is not canonical because the author was inspired, but rather an author is considered to be inspired because what he has written is recognized as canonical, that is, is recognized as authoritative."[65] Inspiration was not a criterion by which a NT book was given the status of Scripture and later placed into a fixed biblical canon, but rather, as Bruce concluded, "a corollary" that follows its recognized status.

III. SUMMARY

The criteria that led to the canonization of the NT literature are not completely clear even today, since no surviving literature identifies the canonical processes or why some books were welcomed but others from the same period and with an equally orthodox position (e.g., *1 Clement*) were not. However, it seems likely that all of the above criteria, with the exception of inspiration, played some role in shaping the NT canon. Ultimately, it appears that the Christian writings that were accorded scriptural status and included in the NT canon were those that best conveyed the earliest Christian proclamation and traditions and also best met the growing needs and interests of local churches in the third and fourth centuries, especially those of the larger and more influential churches. Conversely, the literature that did not reflect the sacred traditions, its *regula fidei*, or those that were no longer deemed relevant to the church's needs, even though it may have been considered pertinent and relevant at an earlier time, was not included in the church's sacred Scriptures and subsequently it was no longer considered inspired by the Holy Spirit.

If this picture is correct, it is not the only time that the church focused on literature that was most relevant to its own historical situation. NT scholars have long recognized that the social circumstances of the life of the church played a significant role in the selection, organization, and editing of the materials that form the NT Gospels. The relevance of NT writings for the churches in subsequent generations must have played some role in their preservation, while other contenders that had ceased being useful to the churches gradually disappeared. In time, after a religious text was acknowledged as scripture and included in a fixed collection, its relevance was made clearer to subsequent generations of Christians through hermeneutics (generally allegory).

This explanation, I believe, best accounts for the variety of books in the surviving NT writings in the ancient church. Although the leaders of the church in the fourth century and later pushed for unity in the recognition of which books were inspired, authoritative, and therefore canonical, unanimity proved unattainable due to diverse circumstances and interests in the churches.

---

[65] Metzger, *Canon of the New Testament*, 257.

Nevertheless, one of the most important factors in understanding the preservation and canonization of the books that make up the current NT is probably usage (catholicity), especially usage in the larger and more influential churches during the third through the fifth centuries.

In summary, it was important to the ancient churches that apostles, or those close to them, produced its sacred NT writings. It was also important to them that these writings affirmed the church's broad core of beliefs and came from the time of the apostles. The continuing relevance and significance of the NT writings for subsequent generations of the church is shown by their widespread use in the life, teachings, and worship of those churches, and this also contributed to their canonization. The end product of the long and complex canonization process was believed to be an authoritative and inspired instrument that continued to be useful in the churches and was adaptable to the ministry and worship of an ever-changing church. That instrument clarified the church's essential identity and mission as a community of Christ.

I will now move to the summation of this volume and highlight some of the more important aspects of canon formation for both the HB/OT and NT.

CHAPTER 23

FINAL REFLECTIONS

We have seen that the formation of the HB and subsequently the Church's OT canon involved long and complex historical processes of development before there was closure, that is, "these books and no more." Although the Jews eventually agreed on the scope of the rabbinic Scriptures that are first identified by name and their tripartite divisions in *b. Baba Batra* 14b (though the context includes 14a and 15a), this was not apparent either to the Jews in the centuries before the time of Jesus or immediately afterwards. It was becoming clearer for some Jews at the end of the first century, but the collections that they describe (Josephus' twenty-two book collection and *4 Ezra*'s twenty-four plus seventy-book collections) are not specific and no one lists or specifically identifies them before the middle to late second century CE in the *b. Baba Batra* text. We have seen that the Jews at Qumran did not subscribe to the notion of a cessation of prophecy (mostly) or accept only the books that finally were included in the rabbinic Tanak or HB.

We have also seen that the early Christians adopted the Scriptures that were circulating among their fellow Jews in the first century before their separation from Judaism, but those books that are identified as Scripture or in a scriptural manner in some NT writings and in some early church fathers are not exactly the same as those in the more limited HB canon. The church has never fully agreed on the books in its OT, but all have agreed *at least* on the books in the HB / Tanak, but not their sequence or order. The Protestants have the same books as in the HB canon, but their order offers a different understanding of those books as Sanders has shown. The order in the Christian OT Scriptures may have been inherited by them, and not necessarily invented by them. By the fourth century, most Christians had agreed on the broad scope of most OT Scriptures, but with differences especially on the acceptance of Esther, Ecclesiastes, and Song of Songs, and with significant differences in the so-called Apocryphal or Deuterocanonical books. The presence and reference to these others books in early Christian writings point to a lack of stabilization in the HB canon well into the first century CE, and in the Christian OT well into the fourth century and later. I have given a summation of the formation of the HB and OT canons at the end of Chapter 13 above and will not repeat that here, though I will focus on that collection of the church's Scriptures below by way of summary of their place in the church's witness of the Christian proclamation. Most of what follows is a summation of the formation of the church's New Testament canon.

The churches also came to a broad agreement on the scope of their NT books by the middle to end of the fourth century, though most of the books in it were at least beginning to recognized as Scripture by the end of the second century. As we have seen, they also called other books Scripture well into the fourth and fifth centuries and in some cases even later, but the majority of churches were in broad agreement on the scope of their NT Scriptures by the end of the fourth century, though that agreement was not universal as we have seen until modern times. Athanasius was the first to identify all of the books in the present NT in his 39th *Festal Letter* in 367. Subsequently Augustine affirmed them and supported their approval at the council in Hippo (393) and later at the councils of Carthage (397 and 416). Other councils after those also affirmed most of the church's NT books. Revelation continued to have some difficulty in recognition for a while longer. Roman Catholics subsequently also affirmed the twenty-seven book collection at the Council of Trent in 1546 and subsequently they were also affirmed by Protestant Christians. Both communities held and today still do affirm the same twenty-seven-book collection of NT Scriptures. The Eastern Orthodox churches, especially the Armenian churches, continued to welcome most of the twenty-seven books, but some of those churches also welcomed other books as sacred texts (e.g., *3 Corinthians*) also until the early to mid-nineteenth century. Eventually, all three major Christian communities affirmed the same twenty-seven-book NT canon.

Biblical scholars generally agree that the writings of the NT addressed the needs of specific communities and that the writers had those needs in mind both when selecting and telling their story (Gospels) or admonishing specific churches (Letters). Since most of the NT writings were *ad hoc* in nature, that is, they were addressed to specific congregations in specific circumstances, it is remarkable that early on these writings were accepted as having significant value for the wider Christian community. They were not all accepted as sacred Scripture at the same time, though the Gospels and most of the letters attributed to Paul were accepted as Scripture in many churches by the end of the second century and earlier for a few church fathers. However, not all churches accepted all of the NT books initially and there were lingering doubts about some of them for centuries. Questions about the authorship of several writings continued in some cases for centuries. These doubted books generally included Hebrews, James, 2 Peter, 2 and 3 John, Jude, and Revelation. Some early manuscripts do not include the Pastoral Epistles, but they were generally well settled in the church's Scriptures by the fourth century.

What is it about these writings that led so many churches to preserve them as their sacred Scriptures? D. Moody-Smith suggests that a distinguishing feature of the NT writings is that they generally continue or presuppose the biblical story of salvation history for the people of God and interpret that history.[1] Those who wrote the gospels, as noted earlier, likely did so with the idea of producing

---

[1]   D. M. Smith, "When Did the Gospels Become Scripture?," 8–9.

an authoritative guide to the Christian faith for the church and with the idea of continuing the biblical story. The NT books were not written *as sacred Scripture*, but rather as documents that told the story of Jesus, and not simply as biographies. They were selected stories about him that were relevant to the communities of faith that followed him and they were intended to lead others to initiate faith in him and follow him. The Evangelists who produced the Gospels might well be offended if they were accused of writing unbiased historical biographies. They were quite biased and each evangelist had a point to make that was relevant to specific communities of faith. The story they told was initially communicated orally, but as time passed and many of Jesus' earlier followers had died, several individuals put parts of his story in writing. Some may have circulated before Jesus was executed, as Dunn, as we saw earlier, suggests. Given Jesus' growing popularity among the people in Galilee and in Judea and the expectations that he was the promised messianic figure who would free the nation from its bondage to Rome, it is quite possible that some parts of the gospel stories were put in writing even before Jesus' death (perhaps the Q document?). The letters and other writings of the NT tell the story of the promotion of the proclamation about Jesus and its implications for faith and mission.

After Jesus' death and following the various reports circulating about his resurrection, several of those committed to proclaim that story put it in writing (Luke 1:1–3) and they combined what had been written about him earlier with what was believed about him after Easter. The aim in those selected biographies was to share reports of Jesus' activities, including his miracles, teachings, and fate along with the implications of that for those who follow him. These selective biographies eventually were called Gospels and were quite useful and helpful to the early churches in their worship, instruction, apologetic, and mission. While those writings were not written as Scripture, in a short period of time they began to function that way in the churches and that was no surprise. Since they focused on Jesus, the Lord of the church, they likely received a significant level of authority early on in what they had to say about him. These and other Christian writings were not initially called Scripture nor were any of the Gospels initially identified by the names of any apostolic figures. The earliest church fathers to cite them cited only the words of Jesus in them, but not the Gospels as individual books written by apostles. In other words, since they told the story of Jesus, they also functioned as Scripture in the churches that had them *before* they were called Scripture. Later they were attributed to apostolic figures and called Scripture in the second century.

Some works were selected for inclusion in the church's new collection of Christian Scriptures called the New Testament and, with their Old Testament writings; these two collections comprised the church's sacred Scriptures. Because the Gospels told the story of Jesus and the implications of his story for those who followed him they were no doubt recognized as authoritative texts early on, but not yet called Scripture until the second century. The letters of Paul were also were recognized in the late first century and throughout the second for their instructional and practical value for the churches' life and ministry and theology. Several of Paul's letters were being circulated in churches by the end of the first century and the early second century. The value of several of these writings was soon recognized (Gospels and Paul). From the early to middle second century, some NT books and some noncanonical books were already functioning *like* Scripture in several churches and possibly earlier. In other words, several NT writings were incorporated into the early church fathers' apologetic for the Christian faith and, as we have shown, they began to be cited *like* Scripture by the middle of the second century at the latest but possibly by around 120–130 in a couple of instances.

The NT canon of Christian Scriptures began with an acknowledgment by the earliest Christians that above all others the authority of Jesus as the living witness in the apostolic community was at the heart of their confessions of faith.[2] The earliest confession of faith in the NT Scriptures is a confession of Jesus as Lord (Rom 10:9). Whatever Jesus said or commanded settled the issue (Matt 28:19). He was the unassailable authority for the church and its Lord. From their beginning, the Christians also accepted the not as yet stabilized Jewish Scriptures that they later called their OT collection of Scriptures and cited them especially in what they believed was their predictive witness to Jesus as the predicted messianic figure who would bring the salvation of God to the people. These First Scriptures of the church were cited as proof of the identity and mission of Jesus and such scriptural proofs were at the heart of early Christian preaching.

The church was born with a collection of sacred scriptures that they believed predicted their Messiah and Lord, Jesus, but its OT was not yet a fixed collection of Jewish Scriptures and the complete scope or extent of that collection is not clear until the middle to end of the second century, but most of it, as we can see from the multiple citations in the NT, included the books in the HB and Christian OT. At first the early followers of Jesus did not see the need for a specifically *Christian* collection of Scriptures and they did not attribute a scriptural status to any Christian writings until at least the end of the first century. The major argument that Porter and Kruger offer in favor of their insistence that the NT writers were consciously aware of writing sacred Scripture is that they believed that they were led the Spirit when they wrote. As observed earlier, Porter concludes "the canon was established *intrinsically* by what the church viewed as *its own internal criteria* as soon as the literature was written, and *the canon was closed as soon as the last of the apostles died*" (emphasis mine).[3] By internal criteria, it appears that the writers were aware

---

[2]   For a helpful discussion of this, see H. Koester, "*Gnomai diaphoroi*: The Origin and Nature of Diversification in the History of Early Christianity," in *Trajectories Through Early Christianity*, ed. James M. Robinson and Helmut Koester (Philadelphia: Fortress, 1971), 117–18.

[3]   Porter and Pitts, *Fundamentals of New Testament Criticism*, 30. Interestingly, Porter's evidence for that conclusion is not compelling and appears to have begun with an a priori assumption rather than from an investigation of the NT itself. If the biblical writers were aware of writing sacred Scripture,

that they were led by the Spirit and were passing on the "truth" of and about Jesus in their proclamations. However, that would imply that others that followed the NT writers who also claimed to be led by the Spirit were also writing Scripture, as in the case of Clement of Rome, Ignatius, Irenaeus, and many others in early church history, including all of the church councils that also made that same claim. How they distinguish their "internal criteria" from later writers led by the Spirit is unclear. While the author of Revelation saw his own writing as inspired by God and having something of a scriptural or prophetic status (Rev 22:18–19), others in the early churches were not so sure and interestingly Revelation was one of the several disputed books in early Christianity for centuries and still it is not read in liturgical worship in Eastern Orthodox churches despite its having been included in their NT canon.

There is nothing in the NT itself that calls for a new or second collection of Christian Scriptures. The writers of the NT do not call their writings something close to "scripture" except possibly in the case of the author of Revelation (1:1–3, 9–11, 17–19; 22:18–19). The earliest followers of Jesus did not see a need for anything more than their Jewish Scriptures and the oral traditions about Jesus circulating among them. When they began to recognize a separate collection of *Christian scriptures*, they also had begun to identify their First Scriptures as "Old Testament" and their new Christian Scriptures as their "New Testament." In the NT, the only Scriptures of the early followers of Jesus were regularly called the Law or Moses and the Prophets, with only one exception (Luke 24:44), in which "psalms" was added to that collection, but the Psalms, as we see in Luke 24:27, was already seen as a part of the "prophets" when Jesus explained his mission to the disciples on the road to Emmaus from "all" of the Scriptures. As long as the memory of the apostolic witness was still fresh in the minds of the Christians and conveyed faithfully by eyewitnesses to the events of Jesus' life and fate, there was little sense of need in the church for written records or reports, let alone a new collection of "scriptures." The Christian writings, especially the Gospels and the letters of Paul, were highly valued as the church continued to grow and apostolic figures were no longer available to teach in person. As a result, what were believed to be apostolic writings were welcomed and read in the church assemblies before they were recognized as sacred scripture.

In the second century, as we saw, Papias was mindful of Mark and Matthew (in that order) but he did not call them "scripture" and preferred instead the oral traditions circulating in the churches over the written traditions. Had Mark and Matthew already been viewed as sacred Scripture at that time (ca. 130), Papias' comments would have made little sense. However, besides the Jewish Scriptures, in the early second century Christian writings were frequently referred to and

---

it seems like they (e.g., Paul) should say so once in a while. Modern preachers often proclaim the "Word of the Lord" but do not suggest to their hearers that their words are Scripture. They only claim that they are proclaiming the truth of the Christian message that is rooted in Scripture.

were cited as evidence for the church's tradition about Jesus. In the early second century and thereafter, the Christian writings were beginning to be more widely recognized as authorities for proclaiming the Christian message and for guidance in the ongoing issues facing the churches.

By the middle to late second century, church leaders were defending the Christian message by appealing to the first-century Christian apostolic tradition circulating in the churches. By the end of the second century this apostolic tradition was seen as an "apostolic deposit" that was believed to have originated with eyewitness authority and passed on in the churches.[4] This was the church's way of dealing with issues facing the churches, including the heretical challenges that they were facing.

The second-century churches taught that this apostolic tradition faithfully conveyed the essence of the Christian faith and it was passed on to succeeding generations through the church's bishops. It affirmed not only that the bishops carefully handed on this canon or confession of faith in the churches, but also that some early Christian literature was believed to have faithfully conveyed that same apostolic message. Throughout the last half of the second century, no closed collection of authoritative Christian writings was widely acknowledged,[5] but that literature was believed to transmit faithfully the message of and about Jesus the Christ and it began to be recognized as Christian Scripture and played an important role in the life of the early churches.

In the last quarter of the second century some core documents (mainly the four Gospels and some Letters of Paul) emerged as authoritative Christian Scriptures that were equal in authority, at least *functionally*, with the OT. At that time, these writings were not a closed biblical canon like those that began to emerge in churches in the fourth and fifth centuries. The regular practice of drawing up closed lists of authoritative NT Scriptures appears to have started with Eusebius, though Origen and Victorinus, as noted earlier, may have provided early antecedents to those catalogues. By the middle fourth century, catalogues of scriptures appeared more frequently in both the East and the West. With the possible exceptions of Melito and Origen, Christian OT canons began to appear more frequently in the fourth century. Prior to these two exceptions, one searches in vain for other Christian canonical catalogues before the fourth century CE.

---

[4]   The importance of the apostolic tradition in the early church, or the apostolic eyewitness account of the words and events of Jesus, was established soon after the death of Jesus (1 Cor 15:3–8; Acts 1:21–22) and after the death of the apostles. It was taken up into the church's witness both for inward community concern (*1 Clem.* 42.1; 2 Pet 3:2) and polemical argument against heresy (Justin, *1 Apol.* 42.4; 50.12; Irenaeus, *Haer.* 3.3.1–3; Tertullian, *Praescr.* 6). In the examples from Irenaeus and Tertullian the guarantee of the accuracy of the church's canon of faith was secured by apostolic succession wherein the truthfulness of their understanding of the Gospel proclamation was passed on from the apostles to the church's bishops and from them to the churches.

[5]   Orthodoxy, or "proto-orthodoxy" was itself only in its early formative stages at this time.

It is likely that Melito's canon is a reflection of a not yet finalized *Jewish* biblical canon in its formative stages.

From the above study of Jewish and Christian biblical canons, several obvious questions emerge and I will only list a few of them here. Were biblical canons the result of conscious decisions at local levels of the churches to identify the books that could be handed over to authorities during the Diocletian persecutions and which could not be turned over? Were the recognized sacred books at that time a natural development in the church in view of, or in response to the Roman cultural influence, that called for conformity and consensus? In what way did contemporary and parallel notions in the ancient world affect the biblical canon? Why was there a felt need for a precisely defined collection of sacred Scriptures in the churches since it did not begin with a fixed collection? In other words, what are the roots of the notion of a *fixed* canon of Scripture? It is not found in the Christian Scriptures themselves. Did the notion come from the influential Hellenistic world where other classics or canons of literature were present? Are fixed scriptural canons actually Christian, as some scholars have questioned? There can be little doubt that scriptural canons had the effect of legitimizing only one branch of early Christianity.

Variations in catalogues of scriptural books continued to circulate in churches well into the modern era, especially in the Eastern Orthodox churches. Verheyden recognizes that there was much less agreement in the East, especially in Syriac Christianity, than in the Western churches and illustrates from the Eastern churches' long preference for Tatian's *Diatessaron* over the four separate canonical Gospels and also for *3 Corinthians* in their sacred Scriptures, especially in the Arminian churches. He also observes that Hebrews and Philemon were only welcomed later in the East, unlike in the West, and that many Eastern churches failed initially to welcome any of the Catholic Epistles or Revelation.[6]

While attempts were made to arrive at a consensus at various council decisions, we know that churches did not always follow those decisions. Also, the precise boundaries of the Christian faith (i.e., beliefs that defined the nature of Christianity) were never *fully* agreed upon either, even though there was considerable agreement by the orthodox churches of a "Roman bent" that the church was broad but not broad enough to allow for the presence of Docetics, gnostics, Marcionites, Ebionites, Montanists, and later others.

As we saw, no set criteria for establishing a Christian biblical canon was present in all council discussions, but the most important criteria included a modified form of apostolicity, orthodoxy, antiquity, and catholicity, as well as the continuing relevance and adaptability of those sacred texts. There are exceptions to all of these criteria and it is clear that they were not all applied appropriately or evenly. Perceived apostolicity and catholicity were among the major factors in later decisions, but not initially.

---

6   Verheyden, "New Testament Canon," 403.

In the Preface, I asked in regard to canon formation whether the church got it right. I said then and now repeat that the answer is: Yes! The Bible as we have it does not answer all of our questions, but it is *sufficient* for faith. The NT canon tells us almost nothing of the childhood of Jesus or what he was like as a young adult prior to the start of his ministry. We also know very little about Paul's post-conversion experience or activity until Barnabas brought him to Antioch to address the issue of Gentiles into a Jewish church.

We can all think of things that we wish had been said or clarified in the church's Scriptures, but, again, what we have is sufficient. All of the current biblical canons are sufficient for Christian faith and all are in agreement on the essential identity of Jesus, faith, the identity and activity of God, as well as the church's identity and mission. They do not tell us everything we want to know, but they all adequately inform Christian faith. This should not imply that I either want to expand the church's Scriptures or eliminate any books currently in them. There are many other questions that I raised in the previous editions of this volume that the inquisitive mind may want to pursue and if so, I refer you to the final chapter there.

Although some have accused me of advocating a change in the present contents of the Bible, that is not my position. I have never advanced adding books to or eliminating books from the Bible, but I do encourage Christians to read the literature that informed many of the early Christians that did not make it into our current Bibles. There are others who do advocate changing the shape of the NT. Hal Taussig, for instance has advanced a new NT canon in his recently published *A New New Testament*.[7] The volume adds ten ancient writings to the NT that include several gnostic texts, namely the *Prayer of Thanksgiving*, the *Gospel of Thomas*, the *Odes of Solomon*, the *Thunder: Perfect Mind*, the *Gospel of Mary*, the *Gospel of Truth*, the *Prayer of the Apostle Paul*, the *Acts of Paul and Thecla*, the *Letter of Peter to Philip*, and the *Secret Revelation of John*. These writings are rare in any other Christian collections of NT Scriptures and all are from the second century or later (in my opinion). Why there is an attempt to add the later writings to the core of the earliest Christian writings, most of which are from the first century, is a puzzle. It is not clear why the authors of the chapters in Taussig's volume include so many of the gnostic texts in their new New Testament. That element rejects generally so much of the earliest traditions of the early churches and does not affirm the church's core teaching that stems from the earliest years of the church.

I do advocate that we study this literature in its own historical context and learn from those writings about the historical context in which early Christianity emerged along with the recognition of its sacred Scriptures. It can be very helpful to be informed by the ancient religious texts not included in our Bibles that also informed the faith of the earliest Christians. I do not see the harm in this and have

---

7   See Hal Taussig, ed., *The New New Testament: A Bible for the Twenty-First Century* (Boston: Houghton Mifflin Harcourt, 2013).

observed over the years that many seminaries, including several conservative seminaries, are essentially saying the same thing and are regularly inviting their students to read the apocryphal and pseudepigraphal writings that informed the thinking of several segments of the early Christian church.

I would also add that there are several benefits, noted below, in reading the so-called noncanonical Christian apocrypha and gnostic writings that informed various segments of early Christianity in the second and third centuries and even later. The context that best reflects late second temple Judaism and early Christianity includes familiarity with several apocryphal and pseudepigraphal Jewish and Christian books. Along with them, there is also considerable value in familiarity with Philo, the Dead Sea Scrolls, Josephus, Rabbinic literature, the early church fathers, and the New Testament Apocrypha books. That literature often provides the context for understanding the formation of the Bible and the emergence of Judaism and Christianity. I also advocate knowing something of the so-called ancient artifacts such as text examinations and awareness of the contents of the surviving biblical manuscripts. All of these sources frequently allow for a better understanding and interpretation of the biblical literature. That context could be expanded to include Egyptian, Mesopotamian, Babylonian, Persian, Hellenistic, and Roman history as well since all of these sources had an influence at various times on the formation and interpretation of the Bible and often bring added clarity to the subject of canon formation.

It is not necessary to change the parameters of the Bible since doing so would only cause more problems in the Jewish and Christian communities than any advantages gained in the process. There are undoubtedly some books in the Bible that do not appear to be as relevant to Jewish or Christian communities today as they were in earlier times since some of them apparently do not now adequately address many of the concerns facing Jews and Christians in the modern world. However, in the past they have done so and in the future may likely do so again. There are many examples in history when different books at various times have affected the faith and actions of the respective communities of faith. The ignored books in the Bible often provide the context for interpreting multiple other biblical texts. There is no need to delete any of them and I do not advocate that.

There remain many areas in canon research that deserve more attention than was possible to explore in these two volumes and so I anticipate that these gaps will be filled by others who are involved in this subject. For example, there is a volume in process that will examine the context and significance of many of the well-known and not so well-known collections and catalogues of the ancient scriptures. Edmon L. Gallagher and John Mead are currently putting this project into its final stages and hopefully it will soon be published. Some other works are also in progress now and more will doubtless emerge in the future as greater clarity on the formation of the church's Bible is established. I hope to contribute to a few of those volumes and examine several areas that need further research in the years ahead. There will doubtless be other literature appear on canon formation because we are continually learning more that broadens our horizons on the subject and we now know much more than was possible to know just a few years ago and that will also be true a few years from now.

My aim in this study has been to shed some light on the dimly lit corridors that led to the formation of our Bible, but also to challenge some earlier notions of canon formation that are, in my opinion, no longer tenable. Because we are still growing in our understanding of this challenging subject it is most likely that other significant contributions will be made in the years ahead. The Bible was formed over a long period of time and in many complex contexts and is invaluable in helping Jews and Christians establish the identity of God and the will of God, and their own identity and mission in the world. Judaism and Christianity would be considerably poorer without all of the advantages that the Scriptures bring to them.

Finally, it may be useful as I complete this study to remind readers what is at the heart of a biblical canon. For the church, the Bible's origin and function are best understood within communities of faith. Those sacred texts function as a guide, model, and authority for Christian faith and the church's mission. Historically the Bible has served a strategically important role in the church's religious experience and witness in the world and I affirm along with many others that its message cannot adequately or fully be understood apart from our faith and submission to its authority. The biblical canon has no important meaning apart from its function as a *rule of faith* and obedience to its precepts. The Bible can be and often is studied historically as a collection of ancient artifacts that occasionally brings satisfaction to those who wish to solve some of its many perplexing puzzles. However, the Bible's *final* meaning *as a biblical canon* can only be understood when it is viewed as a sacred book that functions as an authoritative guide for faith and living. It becomes a sacred canon when we seek to govern our lives accordingly by its admonitions and precepts.[8] It was written from faith to faith and for faith. If the Bible is not canon in the sense of a rule or guide for faith and life, then, of course, it is not a biblical canon at all. It can become simply a book with a lot of interesting ancient religious information, but if that is all that it is, then its role as biblical *canon* is lost. If the Bible, when appropriately interpreted within its own context, is welcomed as sacred Scripture, it will point the church to its final authority, God, and provide guidelines for faith and for living. When its precepts and guidelines are followed as an authoritative guide for faith and action, then it actually becomes a biblical canon.

---

[8]   Bokedal discusses this matter at considerable length in his *Formation and Significance*, 237–78; see also Johnson, *Religious Experience in Earliest Christianity*; and Larry W. Hurtado, "Religious Experience and Religious Innovation in the New Testament," *JR* 80 (2000): 271–88. All three of these scholars recognize the importance of religious experience in early Christianity and in the function of the biblical canon in the church both in antiquity and now. They draw, I think, appropriate conclusions on how Scripture functions in communities of faith.

APPENDICES

APPENDICES

APPENDIX C:
LISTS AND CATALOGUES
OF NEW TESTAMENT SCRIPTURES*

INTRODUCTION

The New Testament Scriptures regularly have the Gospels in first place, but historically have varied on the location of Acts, the Pauline Epistles, the General or Catholic Epistles and even Revelation, though the latter is generally in last place. Revelation is sometimes omitted, suggesting considerable doubt about its scriptural status and perhaps also when it was placed in last place. The significantly fewer surviving manuscripts of Revelation compared to the Gospels, letters of Paul, and the Catholic Epistles similarly reflects the uncertain position of Revelation in early Christianity and in the formation of the Bible. In both the Old and New Testament collections, the major majuscule or uncial manuscripts show greater stability in sequence or order, but never completely. The following collection of lists and catalogues reflect the early fluidity in the formation of the Christian Bible.

In the NT lists below, the most common non-canonical additions include Hermas, Barnabas, Apocalypse of Peter, and Didache. Others include Wisdom of Solomon (in NT lists), *1–2 Clement, Acts of Martyrs*, and *Psalms of Solomon*. Revelation and Hebrews are sometimes omitted and occasionally the Pastorals. While there is obvious and considerable agreement on most of the NT books, there are occasional additions of some so-called noncanonical writings as well as occasional omissions of some canonical writings. In what follows we also see the majority of books that were included in the NT canon, but there are nonetheless exceptions with additions from noncanonical writings and also omissions of canonical writings.

---

* The following lists have been improved and corrected with the kind editing of Edmon Gallagher whose work on the canon catalogues is forthcoming in his Edmon L. Gallagher and John Meade, *The Biblical Canon Lists from Early Christianity: Texts and Analysis* (Oxford: Oxford University Press, 2017). His careful reading and editing of this collection have significantly improved what follows.

1. Three Possible Second- to Third-Century Christian Scripture Lists

Irenaeus (170–80)[1]	Clement of Alexandria (170)[2]	Origen (220–230)[4]
Matt	Jude	Matt
Mark	Barnabas	Mark
Luke	Apocalypse of Peter	Luke and Acts
John	Hebrews	John
Rev	Acts	1 Pet
1 John	Paul (not listed)[3]	2 Pet? (doubtful)
1 Pet		James
Shepherd	Gospels	Jude
Wisdom	Matt	Rev
	Luke	1 John
[Paul mentioned but his epistles	Mark	2–3 John? (doubtful)
are not listed]	John	Hebrews (included but doubts
		Pauline authorship)
(James, 2 Peter, 2–3 John, Jude	[Catholic Epistles and	Paul [14]
are missing)	possibly Revelation included]	

<hr>

[1] Eusebius, *Hist. eccl.* 5.8.2–8 (ca. 320–330, Caesarea, Palestine). While Eusebius attributes this "canon" (ἐνδιαθήκον = "encovenanted," or incorporated) collection to Irenaeus, the list appears to be only Eusebius' listing of Irenaeus' citations of NT texts rather than a specific listing by Irenaeus.

[2] Eusebius, *Hist. eccl.* 6.14.1–7 (ca. 320–330, Caesarea, Palestine). Eusebius claims that Clement of Alexandria included all of the "canonical Scriptures", including the disputed texts, namely Jude, the rest of the Catholic Epistles, the *Epistle of Barnabas*, and the *Apocalypse of Peter*. It is not clear in Eusebius whether this included *all* of the disputed writings he lists in *Hist. eccl.* 3.25 since all are not listed. We have no list from Clement himself, but it is likely that Eusebius composed such a list based on citations of NT texts in Clement. Clement attributes Hebrews to Paul, but says that Paul wrote it to the Hebrews and Luke translated it into Greek, hence the similarities with Acts. It is generally assumed that Clement included all of the writings attributed to Paul, except apparently 1 Timothy. Interestingly, he mentions the Gospels in the order of Matthew, Luke (the two with genealogies), Mark, and John. He may have included Revelation, but that is uncertain

[3] Several of Paul's letters are cited in Clement's *Hypotyposes*, but there is no known listing of all of them.

[4] Eusebius, *Hist. eccl.* 6.25.3–14. This list is consistent with Origen's *Homilies on Joshua* 7.1 translated by Rufinus, though not identical, and is also consistent with his *Homily on Genesis* 13.2. James and Jude are listed only in *Homily* 7, not in Eusebius. Also, *Homily* 7 does not show doubts about 2 Peter or 2–3 John. The order of Paul in last place is unique in Origen and is only identified as 14 that would include Hebrews. This is only in Origen's *Homily* 7.1.

2. Fourth-Century Lists of New Testament Scriptures

Eusebius[5]	Clermont[6]	Cyril of Jerusalem[7]	Athanasius[8]	Cheltenham[9]
Recognized:	*Gospels:*	*New Testament:*	*New Testament:*	*Gospels*
Matt, Mark, Luke,	Matt, John,	Matt, Mark,	*Gospels*	Matt, Mark,
John, Acts, Paul	Mark, Luke	Luke, John	Matt, Mark,	John, Luke
[14],[10] 1 John, 1 Pet,	*Paul:*	Acts	Luke, John	Paul [13 – Heb
[Rev rejected by	Rom, 1–2 Cor,	*Catholic Epistles*[13]	Acts	excluded]
some]	Gal, Eph,	James	*Catholic Epistles:*	Acts
Disputed:	1–2 Tim, Titus,	Peter	James, 1–2 Pet,	Rev
James, Jude,	Col, Phlm	John	1–3, John, Jude	1–3 John
2 Pet, 2–3 John,	To 1–2 Pet[11]	Jude	Paul [14]	1–2 Pet
Rev, *Gos. Heb.*	James	Paul [14]	Rom, 1–2 Cor,	
Spurious:	1–3 John	*Pseudepigrapha*[14]	Gal, Eph, Phil,	(Heb, James
Acts of Paul,	Jude	*Gos. Thom.*	Col, 1–2 Thess,	and Jude
Shepherd,	Heb		Heb, 1–2 Tim,	missing)
Rev. of Peter,	*Ep. Barnabas*[12]		Titus, Phlm	
Barnabas,	Rev		Rev	
Didache	Acts			
Works cited by	*Shepherd*		*Catechetical:*	
heretics:	*Acts of Paul*		*Didache*	
Gospel of Peter	*Rev. of Peter*		*Shepherd*	
Gos. Thom.				
Gospel of Matthias	(Missing:			
Acts of Andrew	Phil, 1–2 Thess)			
Acts of John				

5   Eusebius, *Hist. eccl.* 3.25.1–7 (ca. 320–30, Caesarea, Palestine) lists books welcomed, doubted, and rejected by most. He lists Hebrews as doubted here, but welcomes it himself as Paul's letter (*Hist. eccl.* 3.3.5).

6   This stichometric catalogue is inserted in Codex Claromontanus (D; ca. 350–400, possibly Alexandria, Egypt), written in Latin and inserted between the texts of Philemon and Hebrews in the codex. The inserted text likely is 300–350 CE. Its order of Gospels is different and it adds works later rejected. The omission of Philippians and 1–2 Thessalonians is likely accidental. The order in the catalogue differs from the order of books in the manuscript itself. Stanley E. Porter brought clarity to my earlier confusion about this catalogue in his *How We Got the New Testament*, 129–30 n 185.

7   Cyril of Jerusalem, *Catech.* 4.36 (ca. 350, Jerusalem).

8   Athanasius, *Ep. fest.* 39 (ca. 367, Alexandria, Egypt).

9   The Cheltenham List is also known as the Mommsen Catalogue (identified as Phillipps MS 12266, ca. 360–370, likely from western North Africa). Note the order of the Gospels.

10   The number 14 indicates that Hebrews was included as one of Paul's letters.

11   Interestingly, it appears that the author of this catalogue listed 1 and 2 Peter as having come from Paul to Peter.

12   The reference to *Barnabas* here may be a reference to Hebrews since the line count is the same as Hebrews. The author may have been following Tertullian, *De Pudicitia* 20, who lists Hebrews as "Barnabas." See Hahneman, *Muratorian Fragment*, 140–41.

13   Cyril does not list the specific books here, but only that these four persons produced seven epistles.

14   Cyril rejects *Gospel of Thomas* that was produced by the Manichaeans because "it corrupts the souls of the simple."

3. Lists of Fourth- to Fifth-Century Collections

Epiphanius[15]	Apostolic Canons 85[16]	Gregory of Nazianzus[17]	African Canons[18]	Jerome[19]
Gospels [4]	Gospels [4]	Gospels [4]	Gospels [4]	"Lord's Four"
Matt, Mark,	Matt, Mark,	Matt, Mark,	Matt, Mark,	Matt, Mark,
Luke, John	Luke, John	Luke, John	Luke, John	Luke, John
Paul [14]	Paul [14]	Acts	Acts	Paul [14]
Acts	1–2 Peter	Paul [14]	Paul [14]	Rom, 1–2 Cor,
Catholic Epistles	1–3 John	Catholic Epistles	1–2 Pet	Gal, Eph, Phil,
James, 1 Pet,	James	James, 1–2 Pet,	1, 2, 3 John	1–2 Thess, Col,
1–3 John, Jude	Jude	1–3 John, Jude	Jude	1–2 Tim, Titus,
Rev	*1–2 Clem*		James	Phlm, Heb
Wisdom	*Apos. Con.*		Rev	1–2 Pet
Sir	Acts	(Rev missing)[20]		1–3 John
			Approved to read:	Jude
(Heb missing)	(Rev missing)		*Acts of Martyrs*	James
				Acts
				Rev

15   Epiphanius, *Panarion* 76.5 (ca. 374–377, Salamis, Western Syria). It is strange that he includes Wisdom and Sirach in a NT list.

16   *Apostolic Canons* 85, (ca. 380, Western Syria).

17   Gregory of Nazianzus, *Carm.* 12.31 (ca. 390, Cappadocia, Asia Minor, later ratified by the Trullan Synod in 692).

18   *African Canons* (ca. 393–419, Northern Africa), also known as *Breviarium Hipponense*.

19   Jerome, *Ep.* 53, ca. 394 (Bethlehem, Palestine).

20   Revelation is not listed in this catalogue, but may be presupposed from his description of John as "one who entered heaven."

4. Lists of Fourth- to Fifth-Century Collections (cont.)

Augustine[21]	Amphilochius[22]	Rufinus[23]	Innocent[24]	Syrian Catalog[25]
Gospels [4]	Gospels [4]	*Canonical:*	Gospels [4]	*Gospels [4]*
Matt, Mark,	Matt, Mark,	Gospels [4]	Paul [13][28]	Matt, Mark,
Luke, John	Luke, John	Matt, Mark,	1–3 John	Luke, John
Paul [14]	Acts	Luke, John	1–2 Pet	Acts
Rom, 1–2 Cor,	Paul [14]	Acts	Jude	Gal
Gal, Eph, Phil,	Rom, 1–2 Cor, Gal,	*Paul* [14]	James	1–2 Cor
1–2 Thess, Col,	Eph, Phil, Col, 1–2	1–2 Peter	Acts	Rom
1–2 Tim, Titus,	Thess, 1–2 Tim,	James	Rev	Heb
Phlm, Heb	Titus, Phlm, Heb[26]	Jude		Col
1–2 Pet	*Catholic Epistles* (7?)	1–3 John	(Heb missing)	Eph
1–3 John	James, 1 Pet,	Rev		Phil
Jude	(2 Pet doubted),		*Repudiated:*	1–2 Thess
James	1 John, (2–3 John	*Ecclesiastical:*[27]	[books under the	1–2 Tim
Acts	doubted), Jude	*Shepherd*	names of]	Titus
Rev	(doubted)	*The Two Ways*	Matthias	Phlm
	Rev (doubted)	*Preaching of*	James the less	
		Peter	Peter + John =	(Catholic Epistles,
			Leucian	Rev missing)
			Andrew =	
			Xenocharides	
			and Leonidas	
			Thomas &	
			others	
			Gospel of	
			Thomas?	

[21]   Augustine, *De Doct. chr.* 2.8.12 (ca. 395–400, Hippo Regius, North Africa).

[22]   Amphilochius, *Iambi ad Seleucum* 289–319 (ca. 380, Iconium, Asia Minor). The list concludes by acknowledging that some have questions about 2 Peter, 2 and 3 John, Hebrews, Jude, and Revelation. (?) = doubted by some. The text reads: "one of James, one of Peter, one of John, otherwise three of John, and with them two of Peter, and also Jude's, the seventh." He is unclear whether he prefers 3 or 7 Catholic Epistles. See vol. 37 of Migne's *Patrologia Graeca.*

[23]   Rufinus, *Commentarius in Symbolum Apostolorum* 36 (ca. 394, Rome, Italy).

[24]   Pope Innocent, *Ad Exsuper. Tol.* (ca. 405, Rome, Italy).

[25]   Syrian catalogue of St. Catherine's (ca. 400, Eastern Syria).

[26]   He acknowledges that some dispute or doubt Hebrews, but he does not. "Some call that to the Hebrews spurious, but they say it not well; for the grace is genuine" (vol. 37 of Migne's *Patrologia Graeca*).

[27]   This refers to books that can be read but are not Scripture and are not used to establish doctrine.

[28]   Some add Hebrews to this and make it 14, but this is uncertain.

5. Lists of Fourth- to Fifth-Century Collections (cont.)

Muratorian Fragment[29]	Laodicea Synod Canon 60[30]	Carthage Synod[31]	Eucherius[32]
Gospels	Gospels [4]	Gospels [4]	Matt, Mark, Luke,
...	Matt, Mark, Luke, John	Acts	John, Rom, 1 Cor,
...	Acts	Paul [14]	2 Cor, Eph, 1 Thess,
Luke ["third book"]	Catholic Epistles [7]	Peter [2 books]	Col, 1 Tim, 2 Tim,
John ["fourth Book]	James, 1–2 Pet,	John [3 books]	Heb, Acts, James,
Epistles of John	1–3 John, Jude	Jude	1 John, Rev
Acts	Paul Epistles [14]	James	Missing:
Paul: churches	Rom, 1–2 Cor, Gal, Eph,	Rev	Gal, 2 Thess, Titus,
Cor, Eph, Phil, Col,	Phil, Col, 1–2 Thess, Heb,		Phlm, 2 Pet, 2–3
Gal, Thess, Rom	1–2 Tim, Titus, Phlm		John, Jude
Paul: Individuals			
Phlm, Titus,	(Rev missing)		
1–2 Tim, Jude			
1, 2 or 3 John			
[2 Epistles]			
Wisdom			
Rev			
Apocalypse of Peter			
Forged (and rejected)			
Epistle to the			
Laodiceans			
Epistle to the			
Alexandrians			
Others (?)			
Rejected:			
Shepherd			
Works of Arsinous			
Valentinus			
Miltiades			
Basilides…			
(James, 1–2 Pet			
missing)			

[29] While many scholars contend that this list is a late second-century CE fragment originating in or around Rome, others argue that it was produced around the middle of the fourth century (ca. 350–375). It may well be that it dates after Origen and depends on him, though its order is not Origen's. It reflects the unity but also the diversity in early Christianity and has no parallels in the second century and no influence before the late fourth century.

[30] Council of Laodicea, canon 60 (ca. 367–400, Laodicea, Asia Minor). It was not a part of the original document.

[31] Synod of Carthage, canon 39 (397, North Africa). Observe the difference in order of books. Also he does not always list most of the books, but only indicates the number of books in each category.

[32] Eucherius, Instructiones (ca. 424–55, Lyons).

6. Later New Testament Lists/Catalogues
(Fourth, Fifth, Sixth, and Sixteenth Centuries)

Gelasius[33]	Junilius[34]	Cassiodorus[35]	Isodore[36]	Trent Council[37]
Gospels	Gospels	Gospels	Gospels	Gospels [4]
Matt, Mark,	Matt, Mark,	Matt, Mark,	Matt, Mark, Luke,	Acts
Luke, John	Luke, John	Luke, John	John	Paul [14]
Acts	Acts	Acts		1–2 Pet
Paul [14]	Rev	1 Peter	Paul [14]	1–3 John
Rom, 1–2 Cor,	Paul [14]	James	Rom, 1–2 Cor,	James
Eph, 1–2 Thess,	Rom, 1–2 Cor,	1 John	Gal, Eph, Phil,	Jude
Gal, Phil, Col,	Gal, Eph, Phil,	Paul [13]	1–2 Thess, Col,	Rev
1–2 Tim, Titus,	1–2 Thess, Col,	Rom, 1–2 Cor,	1–2 Tim, Titus,	
Phlm, Heb	1–2 Tim, Col,	Gal, Phil, Col,	Phlm, Heb	
Rev	1–2 Tim, Titus,	Eph, 1–2 Thess,		
1–2 Pet	Phlm, Heb	1–2 Tim, Titus,	1–3 John	
1 John	James	Phlm	1–2 Pet	
2, 3 John	1–2 Pet	Rev	Jude	
Jude	Jude		James	
	1, 2 John	*Missing:*	Acts	
(James missing)		2 Pet, 2–3 John,	Rev	
		Jude, Heb		

---

[33] *Decretum Gelasianum De Libris Recipiendis et non Recipiendis* (ca. sixth century). This canon list is attributed to Pope Gelasius I (492–496), but it is more likely from the sixth century.

[34] Junilius, *Instituta Regularia Divinae Legis*, Book I (ca. 551, North Africa).

[35] Cassiodorus, *Institutiones Divinarum Saecularium Litterarum* (ca. 551–562, Rome).

[36] *Isidore, Bishop of Seville, In Libros Veteris ac Novi Testamenti Prohoemia* (ca. 600).

[37] Council of Trent (Concilium Tridentinum, 1546). Council of Trent (also called the Tridentine Conference because of its three phases). The first period began Feb. 4, 1546, the second began on Oct. 11, 1551; and the third and final began Jan. 18, 1562 and ended Dec. 4, 1563. It met to deal with issues related to the Protestant challenges and though it did not satisfy the Protestants, it was one of the most important steps for the Roman Catholic Church that led to many changes in the church. In the first session, the church listed the Scriptures that comprise their Bible.

7. Uncial Manuscript Collections from the Fourth and Fifth Centuries

Vaticanus (B, Fourth century)[38]	Sinaiticus (א, Fourth century)[39]	Peshitta (Syr^p) (Fifth century)[40]	Alexandrinus (A, Fifth century)[41]
Matt	Matt	Matt	Matt
Mark	Mark	Mark	Mark
Luke	Luke	Luke	Luke
John	John	John	John
Acts	Rom.	Acts	Acts
James	1 Cor	James	James
1 Pet	2 Cor	1 Pet	1 Pet
2 Pet	Gal	1 John	2 Pet
1 John	Eph	Rom	1 John
2 John	Phil	1 Cor	2 John
3 John	Col	2 Cor	3 John
Jude	1 Thess	Gal	Jude
Rom	2 Thess	Eph	Paul [14]
1–2 Cor	Heb	Phil	Rom, 1 Cor, 2 Cor,
Gal	1 Tim	Col	Gal, Eph, Phil, Col,
Eph	2 Tim	1 Thess	1 Thess, 2 Thess,
Phil	Titus	2 Thess	Heb, 1 Tim, 2 Tim,
Col	Phlm	1 Tim	Titus, Phlm
1–2 Thess	Acts	2 Tim	Rev
Heb	James	Titus	1 Clem.
	1 Pet	Philemon	2 Clem.
Missing:	2 Pet	Hebrews	Pss of Solomon
1–2 Tim)	1 John		
Titus	2 John	Missing:	
Phlm	3 John	2 Pet, 2–3 John,	
Rev	Jude	Rev	
	Rev		
	Barnabas		
	Shepherd		
	…		

38   The manuscript breaks off in Heb 9:24 and a later minuscule hand completed the mss and added Revelation, but not the Pastorals and Philemon.

39   This mss has Acts following Letters of Paul and before the Catholic Epistles. It also includes *Epistle of Barnabas* and *Shepherd of Hermas*.

40   Revelation is missing and the Catholic Letters follow Acts and Paul stands at the end.

41   Note that the Catholic Letters follow Acts and Paul comes at the end before Revelation, *1–2 Clement*, and *Psalms of Solomon*.

APPENDIX D:
CURRENT CATALOGUES
OF NEW TESTAMENT SCRIPTURES

1. Modern Scriptures – New Testament Biblical Canons[1]

Protestant	Roman Catholic	Greek Orthodox	Russian Orthodox	Ethiopian
Gospels and Acts Matt, Mark, Luke, John, Acts	*Gospels and Acts* Matt, Mark, Luke, John, Acts	*Gospels and Acts* Matt, Mark, Luke, John, Acts	*Gospels and Acts* Matt, Mark, Luke, John, Acts	*Gospels and Acts* Matt, Mark, Luke, John, Acts
Letters of Paul Rom, 1 Cor, 2 Cor, Gal, Eph, Phil, Col, 1 Thess, 2 Thess, 1 Tim, 2 Tim, Titus, Phlm, Hebr	*Letters of Paul* Rom, 1 Cor, 2 Cor, Gal, Eph, Phil, Col, 1 Thess, 2 Thess, 1 Tim, 2 Tim, Titus, Phlm, Hebr	*Letters of Paul* Rom, 1 Cor, 2 Cor, Gal, Eph, Phil, Col, 1 Thess, 2 Thess, 1 Tim, 2 Tim, Titus, Phlm, Hebr	*Letters of Paul* Rom, 1 Cor, 2 Cor, Gal, Eph, Phil, Col, 1 Thess, 2 Thess, 1 Tim, 2 Tim, Titus, Phlm, Hebr	*Letters of Paul* Rom, 1 Cor, 2 Cor, Gal, Eph, Phil, Col, 1 Thess, 2 Thess, 1 Tim, 2 Tim, Titus, Phlm, Hebr
Catholic Epistles, *Revelation* James, 1 Pet, 2 Pet, 1 John, 2 John, 3 John, Jude, Rev	*Catholic Epistles,* *Revelation* James, 1 Pet, 2 Pet, 1 John, 2 John, 3 John, Jude, Rev	*Catholic Epistles,* *Revelation* James, 1 Pet, 2 Pet, 1 John, 2 John, 3 John, Jude, Rev	*Catholic Epistles,* *Revelation* James, 1 Pet, 2 Pet, 1 John, 2 John, 3 John, Jude, Rev	*Catholic Epistles,* *Revelation* James, 1 Pet, 2 Pet, 1 John, 2 John, 3 John, Jude, Rev
				Syndos Ser'atä Seyon, Te'ezaz, Gessew, Abtlis
				Book of the Covenant Clement Didascalia

---

[1]   The following lists are modified from those provided in Coogan, ed., *The Oxford Encyclopedia of the Books of the Bible*, 1:xv.

SELECT BIBLIOGRAPHY

The following bibliography is not complete, nor does it attempt to list all of the available resources. Instead, it seeks to present the sources that are cited in this volume as well as those that have been consulted or reviewed and each has an important place in understanding the formation of the Bible. There are many other articles and essays that have recently appeared that deserve more attention than was possible to give them in these volumes.

Abegg, M. G. "4QMMT, Paul, and 'Works of the Law'." Pages 203–16 in Flint, ed., *The Bible at Qumran*.

———. "The Hebrew of the Dead Sea Scrolls." Pages 325–58 in vol. 1 of Flint and VanderKam, eds., *The Dead Sea Scrolls After Fifty Years*.

Abegg, M. G., P. Flint, and E. Ulrich. *The Dead Sea Scrolls Bible: The Oldest Known Bible Translated for the First Time into English*. San Francisco: Harper, 1999.

Abraham, W. J. *Canon and Criterion in Christian Theology: From Fathers to Feminism*. Oxford: Clarendon, 1998.

Achtemeier, P. J. *The Inspiration of Scripture: Problems and Proposals*. Philadelphia: Westminster, 1980.

Achtemeier, P. J. et al., eds. *Harper's Bible Dictionary*. San Francisco: Harper & Row, 1985.

Ackroyd, P. R. "The Open Canon." Pages 209–24 in *Studies in the Religious Tradition of the Old Testament*. Edited by P. R. Ackroyd. London: SCM, 1987.

———. "Original Text and Canonical Text." *USQR* 32 (1977): 166–73.

Adler, W. "The Pseudepigrapha in the Early Church." Pages 211–28 in McDonald and Sanders, eds., *The Canon Debate*.

Akenson, D. H. *Surpassing Wonder: The Invention of the Bible and the Talmuds*. New York: Harcourt Brace, 1998.

Aland, K. "Die Entstehung des Corpus Paulinum." Pages 302–50 in *Neutestamentliche Entwurfe*. Edited by Kurt Aland. Theologische Bücherei 63. Munich: Kaiser, 1979.

———. "The Problem of Anonymity and Pseudonymity in Christian Literature of the First Two Centuries." *JTS* 12 (1961): 39–49.

———. *The Problem of the New Testament Canon*. Oxford: Mowbray, 1962.

Aland, K., and B. Aland. *The Text of the New Testament: An Introduction to the Critical Editions and to the Theory and Practice of Modern Textual Criticism*. Rev. and enlarged ed. Translated by E. R. Rhodes. Grand Rapids: Eerdmans, 1989.

Albertz, Rainer, James D. Nogalski, and Jacob Wöhrle, eds. *Perspectives on the Formation of the Book of the Twelve: Methodological Foundations – Redactional Processes – Historical Insights*. BZAW 433. Göttingen: de Gruyter, 2012.

Alexander, A. *The Canon of the Old and New Testaments Ascertained*. New York: Princeton Press, 1826.

———. *The Problem of the New Testament Canon*. Oxford: Mowbray, 1962.

Alexander, L. "The Living Voice: Skepticism Toward the Written Word in Early Christian and in Graeco-Roman Texts." Pages 221–47 in *The Bible in Three Dimensions*. Edited by D. J. A. Clines. Sheffield: JSOT Press, 1990.

Alexander, P. H., et al. *The SBL Handbook of Style for Ancient Near Eastern, Biblical, and Early Christian Studies*. Peabody, MA: Hendrickson, 1999.

Alexander, Philip S. "Criteria for Recognizing Canonical Texts: A Survey and Critique." Paper presented at the Qumran and Canon Seminar of the SNTS, Vienna, August 5, 2009.

———."The Formation of the Biblical Canon in Rabbinic Judaism." Pages 57–80 in Alexander and Kaestli, eds., *The Canon of Scripture*.

Alexander, Philip S., and Jean-Daniel Kaestli, eds. *The Canon of Scripture in Jewish and Christian Tradition*. Lausanne: Zebre, 2007.

Allert, Craig D. *A High View of Scripture? The Authority of the Bible and the Formation of the New Testament Canon*. Evangelical Ressourcement. Grand Rapids: Baker Academic, 2007.

———. "Is Translation Inspired? The Problems of Verbal Inspiration for a Translation and a Proposed Solution." Pages 85–113 in *Translating the Bible: Problems and Prospects*. Edited by S. E. Porter and R. S. Hess. London: Sheffield Academic.

———. *Revelation, Truth, Canon and Interpretation: Studies in Justin Martyr's Dialogue with Trypho*. VCSup 64. Leiden: Brill, 2002.

———. "The State of the New Testament Canon in the Second Century: Putting Tatian's Diatessaron in Perspective." *BBR* 9 (1999): 1–18.

Allison Jr., Dale C. "The Old Testament in the New Testament." Pages 479–504 in Paget and Schaper, eds., *The New Cambridge History of the Bible*. Vol. 1, *From the Beginnings to 600*.

Anderson, G. W. "Canonical and Non-canonical." Pages 113–59 in *The Cambridge History of the Bible*. Vol. 1, *From the Beginnings to Jerome*. Edited by P. R. Ackroyd and C. F. Evans. Cambridge: Cambridge University Press, 1970.

Anderson, Hugh. "*Fourth Maccabees*." *ABD* 4:452–54

———. *The Gospel of Mark*. New Century Bible. London: Oliphant, 1976.

———. *Jesus and Christian Origins*. Oxford: Oxford University Press, 1963.

Anderson, P. N. "Aspects of Historicity in the Gospel of John." Pages 587–618 in *Jesus and Archaeology*. Edited by James H. Charlesworth. Grand Rapids: Eerdmans, 2006.

———. "John and Mark – the Bi-Optic Gospels." Pages 175–88 in *Jesus in Johannine Tradition*. Edited by R. Fortuna and T. Thatcher. Philadelphia: Westminster John Knox, 2001.

Anderson, R. T. "Samaritan Literature." Pages 1052–56 in *Dictionary of New Testament Background*. Edited by C. A. Evans and S. E. Porter. Downers Grove, IL: InterVarsity, 2000.

———. "Samaritans." *ABD* 5:940–47.

Armstrong, J. J. "From the κανὼν τῆς ἀληθείας to the κανὼν τῶν γραφῶν: The Rule of Faith and the New Testament Canon." Pages 30–47 in *Tradition and the Rule of Faith in the Early Church*. Washington, DC: Catholic University Press of America, 2010.

———. "Victorinus of Pettau as the Author of the Canon Muratori." *VC* 62 (2008): 1–35.

Arnold, C. E., ed. *Zondervan Illustrated Bible Background Commentary*. 4 vols. Grand Rapids: Zondervan, 2002.

Attridge, H. W. "Christianity from the Destruction of Jerusalem to Constantine's Adoption of the New Religion: 70–312 C.E." Pages 151–94 in *Christianity and Judaism: A Parallel History of Their Origins and Early Development*. Edited by Hershel Shanks. Washington, DC: Biblical Archaeology Society, 1992.

Audet, J. P. "A Hebrew-Aramaic List of Books of the Old Testament in Greek Transcription." *JTS* 1 (1950): 135–54.

Aune, D. E. "Charismatic Exegesis in Early Judaism and Early Christianity." Pages 125–50 in *The Pseudepigrapha and Early Biblical Interpretation*. Edited by J. H. Charlesworth and C. A. Evans. JSNTSup 119. Sheffield: JSOT Press, 1993.

———. *The New Testament in Its Literary Environment*. Philadelphia: Westminster, 1987.

————. "On the Origins of the 'Council of Javneh' Myth." *JBL* 110 (1991): 491–93.

————. *Prophecy in Early Christianity and the Ancient Mediterranean World*. Grand Rapids: Eerdmans, 1983.

————. "Qumran and the Book of Revelation." Pages 622–48 in vol. 2 of Flint and VanderKam, eds., *The Dead Sea Scrolls After Fifty Years*.

————. *Revelation 1–5*. WBC 52A. Dallas: Word, 1995.

Auwers, J.-M., and H. J. de Jonge., eds. *The Biblical Canons*. BETL 163. Leuven: Louvain University Press, 2003.

Avery-Peck, A. J., Jacob Neusner, and B. Chilton, eds. *Judaism in Late Antiquity*, Part 5, *The Judaism of Qumran: A Systematic Reading of the Dead Sea Scrolls*. Vol. 1, *Theory of Israel*. Leiden: Brill, 2001.

Ayuch, Daniel A. "The Prayer of Manasses." Pages 7–20 in Hovhanessian, ed., *The Canon of the Bible*.

Baaren, T. P. van. "Towards a Definition of Gnosticism." Pages 18–20 in *Le origini dello gnosticismo.* Edited by U. Bianchi. Studies in the History of Religions 12. Leiden: Brill, 1967.

Baehr, P., and M. O'Brien. "Founders, Classics and the Concept of a Canon." *Current Sociology* 42 (1994): 1–149.

Bakke, O. M. (2005), "The Episcopal Ministry and Unity of the Church from the Apostolic Fathers to Cyprian." Pages 379–408 in *The Formation of the Early Church*. Edited by Jostein Adna. WUNT 183. Tübingen: Mohr Siebeck, 2005.

Balás, D. L. "Marcion Revisited: A 'Post-Harnack' Perspective." Pages 95–108 in *Texts and Testaments: Critical Essays on the Bible and Early Church Fathers: A Volume in Honor of Stuart Dickson Currie*. Edited by W. Eugene March. San Antonio: Trinity University Press, 1980.

Balch, D. L. "The Canon: Adaptable and Stable, Oral and Written. Critical Questions for Kelber and Riesner." *Forum* 7 (1991): 183–205.

Baldermann, I. "Didaktischer und 'kanonischer' Zugang: Der Unterricht vor dem Problem des biblischen Kanons." *Jahrbuch für biblische Theologie* 3 (1988): 97–111.

Balla, Peter. *Challenges to New Testament Theology*. WUNT 2/95. Tübingen: J. C. B. Mohr, 1997.

Balz, H. R. "Anonymität und Pseudepigraphie im Urchristentum. Überlengungen zum literarischen und theologischen Problem der urchristlichen und gemeinantiken Pseudepigraphie." *Zeitschrift für Theologie und Kirche* 66 (1969): 403–36.

Bar-Ilan, M. "Writing in Ancient Israel and Early Judaism: Scribes and Books in the Late Second Commonwealth and Rabbinic Period." Pages 21–37 in Mulder, ed., *Mikra*.

Barker, G. W., W. L. Lane, and J. R. Michaels. *The New Testament Speaks*. New York: Harper & Row, 1969.

Barnstone, W., ed. *The Other Bible: Jewish Pseudepigrapha, Christian Apocrypha, Gnostic Scriptures, Kabbalah, Dead Sea Scrolls*. San Francisco: Harper, 1984.

Barr, J. *Fundamentalism*. Philadelphia: Westminster, 1977.

————. *Holy Scripture: Canon, Authority. Criticism*. Philadelphia: Westminster, 1983.

————. Review of K. H. Jobes and M. Silva, *Invitation to the Septuagint. Review of Biblical Literature* (2002). Online: http://www.bookreviews.org/pdf/1341_3027.pdf.

Barrett, Lee C. Review of David Crump, *Encountering Jesus, Encountering Scripture. Int* (2015): 105–6.

Barthélemy, Dominique. "La critique canonique." *Revue de l'Institut Catholique de Paris* 36 (1991): 191–220.

Bartholomew, C. B., Scott Hahn, Robin Parry, Christopher Seitz, and Al Wolters, eds. *Canon and Biblical Interpretation.* Scripture and Hermeneutics 7. Grand Rapids: Zondervan, 2006.

Barton, John. "Canon." Pages 101–5 in *A Dictionary of Biblical Interpretation.* Edited by R. J. Coggins and J. L. Houlden. London: SCM, 1990.

———. *Holy Writings, Sacred Text: The Canon in Early Christianity.* Louisville: Westminster John Knox, 1997.

———. *How the Bible Came to Be.* Louisville: Westminster John Knox, 1997.

———. "'The Law and the Prophets.' Who Are the Prophets?" *Oudtestamentische Studien* 23 (1964): 1–18.

———. "Marcion Revisited." Pages 341–54 in McDonald and Sanders, eds., *The Canon Debate.*

———. "The Old Testament Canon." Pages 105–64 in Paget and Schaper, eds., *The New Cambridge History of the Bible.* Vol. 1, *From the Beginnings to 600.*

———. *Oracles of God: Perceptions of Ancient Prophecy in Israel after the Exile.* Oxford: Oxford University Press, 1986, rev. 2007.

———. *People of the Book? The Authority of the Bible in Christianity.* Louisville: Westminster John Knox, 1988.

———. "Prophecy (Postexilic Hebrew)." *ABD* 5:489–95.

———. "The Significance of a Fixed Canon of the Hebrew Bible." Pages 67–83 in vol. I/1 of *Hebrew Bible / Old Testament: The History of Its Interpretation.* Edited by Magne Magne Sæbø. Göttingen: Vandenhoeck & Ruprecht, 1996.

———. *The Spirit and the Letter: Studies in the Biblical Canon.* London: SPCK, 1997.

———. "Unity and Diversity in the Biblical Canon." Pages 11–26 in *Die Einheit der Schrift und die Vielfalt des Kanons.* Edited by John Barton and Michael Wolter. Berlin: de Gruyter, 2003.

Bauckham, Richard. "Eldad and Modad." Pages 1:255–56 in Bauckham, Davila, and Panayotov, eds., *Old Testament Pseudepigrapha.*

———. "For Whom Were the Gospels Written?" Pages 9–48 in *The Gospels for All Christians: Rethinking the Gospel Audiences.* Edited by Richard Bauckham. Grand Rapids: Eerdmans.

———. *God Crucified.* Grand Rapids: Eerdmans, 1998.

———. *Jesus and the Eyewitnesses: The Gospels as Eyewitness Testimony.* Grand Rapids: Eerdmans, 2006.

———. "Papias and Polycrates on the Origin of the Fourth Gospel." *JTS* 44 (1993): 24–69.

Bauckham, Richard, James R. Davila, and Alexander Panayotov, eds. *Old Testament Pseudepigrapha: More Noncanonical Scriptures.* Vol. 1. Grand Rapids: Eerdmans, 2013.

Bauer, W. *Orthodoxy and Heresy in Earliest Christianity.* Edited by R. Kraft and G. Krodel. Philadelphia: Fortress, 1971.

Baum, Armin D. "Der neutestamentliche Kanon bei Eusebius (*Hist. eccl.* 3.25.1–7) im Kontext seiner literaturgeschichtlichen Arbeit." *Ephemerides theologicae lovanienses* 73 (1997): 307–48.

———. "Papias, der Vorzug der Viva Vox und die Evangelienschriften." *NTS* 44 (1998): 144–51.

Beale, G. K., and D. A. Carson, eds. *Commentary on the New Testament Use of the Old Testament.* Grand Rapids: Eerdmans, 2007.

Beare, G. W. "Canon of the NT." *IDB* 1:520–32.

Beckwith, R. T. "Canon of the Hebrew Bible and the Old Testament." Pages 100–102 in *The Oxford Companion to the Bible.* Edited by B. M. Metzger and M. D. Coogan. New York: Oxford University Press, 1993.

———. "Formation of the Hebrew Bible." Pages 39–86 in Mulder, ed., *Mikra.*

————. *The Old Testament Canon of the New Testament Church and Its Background in Early Judaism*. Grand Rapids: Eerdmans, 1985.

BeDuhn, Jason D. *The First New Testament: Marcion's Scriptural Canon*. Santa Rosa, CA: Polebridge, 2014.

Bellinzoni, A. J. *The Sayings of Jesus in the Writings of Justin Martyr*. Novum Testamentum Supplements 17. Leiden: Brill, 1967.

Berger, K. *Identity and Experience in the New Testament*. Translated by C. Muenchow. Minneapolis: Fortress, 2003.

Bernstein, M. J. "The Employment and Interpretation of Scripture." Pages 29–51 in Kampen and M. J. Bernstein, eds., *Reading 4QMMT*.

Best, E. "Scripture, Tradition, and the Canon of the New Testament." *BJRL* 61 (1978–79): 258–89.

Betz, Otto. "Das Problem des 'Kanons' in den Texten von Qumran." Pages 70–101 in *Der Kanon der Bibel*. Edited by G. Maier. Giessen: Brunnen,1990.

Beyer, Hermann Wolfgang. "κανών." *TDNT* 3:596–602.

Bialik, H. N., and Y. H. Ravnitzky. *The Book of Legends, Sefer Ha-Aggadah: Legends from the Talmud and Midrash*. Translated by W. G. Braude. New York: Schocken, 1992.

Bickerman, Elias J. "Some Notes on the Transmission of the Septuagint." Pages 149–78 in *Alexander Marx: Jubilee Volume on the Occasion of His Seventieth Birthday (English Section)*. New York: The Jewish Theological Seminary of America, 1950.

Bienert, W. A. "The Picture of the Apostle in Early Christian Tradition." Pages 5–27 in vol. 2 of Schneemelcher, ed., *New Testament Apocrypha*.

Birch, B. C. "Tradition, Canon and Biblical Theology." *HBT* 2 (1980): 113–25.

Blackman, E. C. *Marcion and His Influence*. London: SPCK, 1948.

Blenkinsopp, J. "The Formation of the Hebrew Bible Canon: Isaiah as a Test Case." Pages 53–67 in McDonald and Sanders, eds., *The Canon Debate*.

————. *Prophecy and Canon: A Contribution to the Study of Jewish Origins*. Notre Dame: University of Notre Dame Press, 1977.

————. "Prophecy and Priesthood in Josephus." *JJS* 101 (1974): 245–55.

————. " 'We Pay Heed to Heavenly Voices': The 'End of Prophecy' and the Formation of the Canon." Pages 19–31 in *Biblical and Humane: A Festschrift for John F. Priest*. Edited by Linda Bennett Elder, David L. Barr, and Elizabeth Struthers Malbon. Atlanta: Scholars Press, 1996.

Bloch, J. "Outside Books." Pages 202–23 in Leiman, ed., *Canon and Masorah of the Hebrew Bible*.

Blomberg, Craig L. *Can We Still Believe the Bible?* Ada, MI: Brazos, 2014.

Bloom, Harold. *The Western Canon: The Books and Schools of the Age*. New York: Harcourt Brace, 1994.

Blowers, Paul M., ed. and trans. *The Bible in Greek Christian Antiquity*. Notre Dame: University of Notre Dame Press, 1997.

Boccaccini, G., ed. *Enoch and Qumran Origins: New Light on a Forgotten Connection*. Grand Rapids: Eerdmans, 2005.

————. "Finding a Place for the Parables of Enoch within Second Temple Jewish Literature." Pages 263–89 in *Enoch and the Messiah Son of Man: Revisiting the Book of Parables*. Edited by Gabriele Boccaccini. Grand Rapids: Eerdmans, 2005.

Bock, D. L., and J. H. Charlesworth, eds. *Parables of Enoch: A Paradigm Shift*. T & T Clark Jewish and Christian Texts Series 11. London: Bloomsbury, 2013.

Boeft, J. Den, and M. L. Van Poll-van De Lisdonk, eds. *The Impact of Scripture in Early Christianity*. VCSup 44. Leiden: Brill, 1999.

Bogaert, Pierre-Maurice. "The Latin Bible." Pages 505–24 in Paget and Schaper, eds., *The New Cambridge History of the Bible*. Vol. 1, *From the Beginnings to 600*.

———. "The Latin Bible c. 600–900." Pages 69–92 in Marsden and Matter, eds., *The New Cambridge History of the Bible: From 600–1450*.

Bokedal, Tomas. *The Formation and Significance of the Christian Biblical Canon: A Study in Text, Ritual and Interpretation*. London: Bloomsbury T&T Clark, 2014.

———. *The Scriptures and the Lord: Formation and Significance of the Christian Biblical Canon*. Lund: Lund University Press, 2005.

Boring, M. Eugene, Klaus Berger, and Carsten Colpe, eds. *Hellenistic Commentary to the New Testament*. Nashville: Abingdon, 1995.

Bossman, D. M. "Canon and Culture: Realistic Possibilities for the Biblical Canon." *BTB* 23 (1993): 4–13.

Bovon F. "The Canonical Structure of Gospel and Apostle." Pages 516–27 in McDonald and Sanders, eds., *The Canon Debate*.

———. "The Synoptic Gospels and the Non-Canonical Acts of the Apostles." *HTR* 81 (1988): 19–36.

———. "Vers une nouvelle edition de la litterature apocryphe chrétienne." *Augustinianum* 23 (1983): 373–78.

Bovon, F., A. G. Brock, and C. R. Matthews, eds. *The Apocryphal Acts of the Apostles*. Cambridge, MA: Harvard University Press, 1999.

Bowley, James E. "Bible." Pages 73–84 in vol. 1 of Coogan, ed., *The Oxford Encyclopedia of the Books of the Bible*.

———. "Prophets and Prophecy at Qumran." Pages 354–78 in vol. 2 of Flint and VanderKam, eds., *The Dead Sea Scrolls After Fifty Years*.

Bowman, A. K. "The Vindolanda Tablets and the Development of the Book Form." *Zeitschrift für Papyrologie und Epigraphik* 18 (1975): 237–52.

Brakke, David. "Canon Formation and Social Conflict in Fourth-Century Egypt: Athanasius of Alexandria's Thirty-Ninth Festal Letter." *HTR* 87 (1994): 395–419.

Brandt, Peter. *Endgestalten des Kanons: Das Arrangement der Schriften Israels in der jüdischen und christlichen Bibel*. Bonner biblische Beiträge 131. Berlin: Philo, 2001.

———. "Final Forms of the Writings: The Jewish and Christian Traditions." Pages 59–85 in Steinberg and Stone, eds., *The Shape of the Writings*.

Bray, Gerald. "The Bible and Canon Law." Pages 722–34 in Marsden and Matter, eds., *The New Cambridge History of The Bible: From 600–1450*.

Brenton, L. C. L. *The Septuagint Version of the Old Testament*. London: Bagster, 1844.

Brock, Sebastian P. "The Use of the Syriac Fathers for New Testament Textual Criticism." Pages 224–36 in Ehrman and Holmes, eds., *The Text of the New Testament in Contemporary Research*.

Brogan, J. J. "Another Look at Codex Sinaiticus." Pages 17–32 in *The Bible as Book: The Transmission of the Greek Text*. Edited by S. McKendrick and O. O'Sullivan. London: British Library. New Castle, DE: Oak Knoll, 2003.

Brooke, George J. "Between Authority and Canon: The Significance of Reworking the Bible for Understanding the Canonical Process." Pages 85–104 in *Reworking the Bible: Apocryphal and Related Texts at Qumran*. Edited by Esther G. Chazon, Devorah Dimant, and Ruth A. Clements. Leiden: Brill, 2005.

———. *The Dead Sea Scrolls and the New Testament*. Minneapolis: Fortress, 2005.

————. "The Explicit Presentation of Scripture in 4QMMT." Pages 67–88 in *Legal Texts and Legal Issues: Proceedings of the Second Meeting of the International Organization for Qumran Studies, Cambridge 1995: Published in Honour of Joseph M. Baumgarten*. Edited by M. Bernstein, F. García Martínez, and J. Kampen. STDJ 23. Leiden: Brill, 1997.

————. "Rewritten Bible." *EDSS* 2:777–81.

————. "The Rewritten Law Prophets, and Psalms: Issues for Understanding the Text of the Bible." Pages 31–40 in Herbert and Tov, eds., *Bible as Book*.

————. "Was the Teacher of Righteousness Considered to be a Prophet?" Pages 77–97 in De Troyer and Lange, eds., *Prophecy After the Prophets*.

Broshi, M. "What Jesus Learned from the Essenes: The Blessing of Poverty and the Bane of Divorce." *Biblical Archaeology Review* 30 (2004): 32–37, 64.

Brown, Raymond E. "The Lucan Authorship of Luke 22:43–44." Pages 154–64 in *Society of Biblical Literature 1992 Seminar Papers*. Edited by E. H. Lovering Jr. Atlanta: Scholars Press, 1992.

————. *Recent Discoveries and the Biblical World*. Wilmington, DE: Michael Glazier, 1983.

Brown, R. E., and R. F. Collins. "Canonicity." Pages 1034–54 in *The New Jerome Biblical Commentary*. Edited by R. E. Brown, J. A. Fitzmyer, and R. E. Murphy. London: Chapman, 1989.

Broyde, M. J. "Defilement of the Hands, Canonization of the Bible, and the Special Status of Esther, Ecclesiastes, and the Song of Songs." *Judaism* 44 (1995): 65–79.

Bruce, B. J. *Origen: Homilies on Joshua*. Fathers of the Church: A New Translation 105. Washington, DC: Catholic University of America Press, 2002.

Bruce, F. F. *The Books and the Parchments: How We Got Our English Bible*. 5th ed. London: Marshall Pickering, 1991.

————. *The Canon of Scripture*. Downers Grove, IL: InterVarsity, 1988.

————. "Tradition and the Canon of Scripture." Pages 59–84 in *The Authoritative Word: Essays on the Nature of Scripture*. Edited by D. K. McKim. Grand Rapids: Eerdmans, 1993.

Brueggemann, Walter. *An Introduction to the Old Testament: The Canon and Christian Imagination*. Louisville: Westminster John Knox, 2003.

Buchanan, E. S. "The Codex Muratorianus." *JTS* 8 (1907): 537–39.

Budde, Karl. *Der Kanon des Alten Testaments: Ein Abriss*. Giessen: J. Ricker (Alfred Töpelmann), 1900.

Buhl, Frants P. W. *Kanon und Text des alten Testaments*. Leipzig: Academische Buchhandlung, 1891.

Burns, G. L. "Canon and Power in the Hebrew Scriptures." *Critical Inquiry* 10 (1984): 259–89. Repr. pages 65–84 in von Hallberg, ed., *Canons*.

Burridge, R. A. *What Are the Gospels? A Comparison with Graeco-Roman Biography*. SNTSMS 70. Cambridge: Cambridge University Press, 1992.

Buss, Martin J. *Toward Understanding the Hebrew Canon: A Form-Critical Approach*. Hebrew Bible Monographs 61. Sheffield: Sheffield Phoenix, 2013.

Byrne, Brendan. *Romans*. Sacra Pagina 6. Collegeville: Liturgical Press, 1996.

Callaway, Philip R. "The Temple Scroll and the Canonization of the Old Testament." *Revue biblique* 13 (1988): 239–43.

Campbell, Jonathan G. "Scriptural Interpretation at Qumran." Pages 242–66 in Paget and Schaper, eds., *New Cambridge History of the Bible*. Vol. 1, *From the Beginnings to 600*.

Campenhausen, H. von. *Ecclesiastical Authority and Spiritual Power in the Church of the First Three Centuries*. Translated by J. A. Baker. London: A. & C. Black, 1969. German: *Kirchliches Amt und Geistliche Vollmacht*. Tübingen: J. C. B. Mohr, 1953.

———. *The Formation of the Christian Bible*. Translated by J. A. Baker. Philadelphia: Fortress, 1972.

———. *Tradition and Life in the Church: Essays and Lectures in Church History*. Translated by A. V. Littledale. London: Collins, 1968.

Carr, D. M. "Canonization in the Context of Community: An Outline for the Formation of the Tanakh and the Christian Bible." Pages 22–64 in *A Gift of God in Due Season: Essays on Scripture and Community in Honor of James A. Sanders*. Edited by R. Weis and D. Carr. Sheffield: Sheffield Academic, 1996.

———. *The Formation of the Hebrew Bible: A New Reconstruction*. Oxford: Oxford University Press, 2011.

———. "The Song of Songs as a Microcosm of the Canonization and Decanonization Process." Pages 173–89 in van der Kooij and van der Toorn, eds., *Canonization and Decanonization*.

———. *Writing on the Tablet of the Heart: Origins of Scripture and Literature*. Oxford: Oxford University Press, 2005.

Carson, D. A., and John Woodbridge, eds. *Hermeneutics, Authority, and Canon*. Grand Rapids: Zondervan, 1986.

Carson, D. A., and H. G. M. Williamson, eds. *It Is Written: Scripture Citing Scripture: Essays in Honour of Barnabas Lindars*. SSF. Cambridge: Cambridge University Press, 1988.

Casey, R. "The Armenian Marcionites and the Diatessaron." *JBL* 57 (1938): 185–92.

Casson, Lionel. *Travel in the Ancient World*. London: Allen & Unwin, 1974.

Chadwick, H. "The Early Christian Community." Pages 21–61 in *The Oxford Illustrated History of Christianity*. Edited by J. McManners. Oxford: Oxford University Press, 1990.

Chadwick, O. "The Significance of the Deuterocanonical Writings in the Anglican Tradition." Pages 116–28 in Meurer, ed., *The Apocrypha in Ecumenical Perspective*.

Chapman, S. B. "The Canon Debate: What It Is and Why It Matters." *Journal of Theological Interpretation* 4, no. 2 (2010): 273–94.

———. "Canon, Old Testament," Coogan, ed., *The Oxford Encyclopedia of the Books of the Bible* 1:96–109.

———. "How the Biblical Canon Began: Working Models and Open Questions." Pages 29–52 in Finkelberg and Stroumsa, eds., *Homer, the Bible, and Beyond*.

———. *The Law and the Prophets: A Study in Old Testament Canon Formation*. FAT 27. Tübingen: Mohr, 2000.

———. " 'The Law and the Words' as a Canonical Formula within the Old Testament." Pages 26–74 in *The Interpretation of Scripture in Early Judaism and Christianity: Studies in Language and Traditions*. Edited by Craig A. Evans. JSPSup 33. Studies in Scripture in Early Judaism and Christianity 7. Sheffield: Sheffield Academic, 2000.

———. "Modernity's Canonical Crisis: Historiography and Theology in Collision." Pages 651–87 in *Hebrew Bible/Old Testament: The History of Its Interpretation*, 3, Part 1, *The Nineteenth Century – a Century of Modernism and Historicism*. Edited by Magne Magne Sæbø. Göttingen: Vandenhoeck & Ruprecht, 2013.

———. "Reclaiming Inspiration for the Bible." Pages 167–206 in Bartholomew et al., eds., *Canon and Biblical Interpretation*.

———. "Second Temple Jewish Hermeneutics: How Canon Is Not an Anachronism." Pages 281–96 in *Invention, Rewriting, Usurpation: Discursive Fights over Religious Traditions in Antiquity*. Edited by Jörg Ulrich, Anders-Christian Jacobsen, David Brakke. Early Christianity in the Context of Antiquity 11. Frankfurt am Main: Lang, 2011.

———. "What Are We Reading? Canonicity and the Old Testament." *Word and World* 29, no. 4 (2009): 334–47.

Charles, R. H. "An Unknown Dead Sea Scroll and Speculations Focused on the *Vorlage* of Deuteronomy 27:4." Pages 393–415 in *Jesus, Paulus und die Texte von Qumran* [FS H.-W. Kuhn]. Edited by J. Frey and E. E. Popkes. WUNT 2/390. Tübingen: Mohr Siebeck, 2014.

———, ed. *The Apocrypha and Pseudepigrapha of the Old Testament.* 2 vols. Oxford: Clarendon, 1913.

———. *The Book of Enoch.* Oxford: Clarendon, 1912.

———. *The Book of Jubilees or the Little Genesis.* London: Oxford University Press, 1902.

———. *A Critical and Exegetical Commentary on the Revelation of St. John.* 2 vols. ICC. Edinburgh: T. &. T. Clark, 1920.

Charlesworth, J. H. *The Beloved Disciple: Whose Witness Validates the Gospel of John?* Valley Forge: Trinity Press International, 1995.

———, ed. *The Bible and the Dead Sea Scrolls.* The Princeton Symposium on the Dead Sea Scrolls. Waco, TX: Baylor University Press, 2006.

———. *Jesus within Judaism: New Light from Exciting Archaeological Discoveries.* New York: Doubleday, 1988.

———, ed. *The Old Testament Pseudepigrapha.* 2 vols. Garden City, NY: Doubleday, 1983–85.

———. *The Pesharim and Qumran History: Chaos or Consensus?* Grand Rapids: Eerdmans, 2002.

———. "Pseudepigrapha." Pages 836–40 in Achtemeier et al., eds., *Harper's Bible Dictionary.*

———. "Pseudepigraphy." Pages 961–64 in *Encyclopedia of Early Christianity.* Edited by E. Ferguson. New York: Garland, 1990.

———. "What Is a Variant? Announcing a Dead Sea Scrolls Fragment of Deuteronomy." *MAARAV* 16, no. 2 (2009): 201–12.

Charlesworth, J. H., and C. A. Evans. "Jesus in the Agrapha and Apocryphal Gospels." Pages 479–533 in *Studying the Historical Jesus: Evaluations of the State of Current Research.* Edited by B. Chilton and C. A. Evans. NTTS 19. Leiden: Brill, 1994.

Charlesworth, J. H., and L. M. McDonald, eds. *"Non-Canonical" Religious Texts in Early Judaism and Early Christianity.* T&T Clark Jewish and Christian Texts in Contexts and Related Studies 14. London: T&T Clark, 2012.

———. *Sacra Scriptura: How "Non-Canonical" Texts Functioned in Early Judaism and Early Christianity.* T & T Clark Jewish and Christian Texts in Contexts and Related Studies 29. London: Bloomsbury, 2014.

Charteris, A. H. *Canonicity: A Collection of Early Testimonies to the Canonical Books of the New Testament.* Edinburgh: William Blackwood & Sons, 1880.

Chazon, Esther G., Devorah Dimant, and Ruth A. Clements, eds. *Reworking the Bible: Apocryphal and Related Texts at Qumran.* Leiden: Brill, 2005.

Childs, B. S. *Biblical Theology in Crisis.* Philadelphia: Westminster, 1970.

———. *Biblical Theology of the Old and New Testaments: Theological Reflection on the Christian Bible.* Minneapolis: Fortress, 1993.

———. "The Canon in Recent Biblical Studies: Reflections on an Era." Pages 33–57 in Bartholomew et al., eds., *Canon and Biblical Interpretation.*

———. "The Canonical Shape of the Prophetic Literature." *Int* 32 (1978): 46–55.

———. "The Exegetical Significance of Canon for the Study of the Old Testament." Pages 66–80 in VTSup 29. Leiden: Brill, 1978.

———. "Interpretation in Faith: The Theological Responsibility of an Old Testament Commentary." *Int* 18 (1964): 432–39.

———. *Introduction to the Old Testament as Scripture.* Philadelphia: Fortress, 1979.

———. *The New Testament as Canon: An Introduction.* Philadelphia: Fortress, 1985.

———. *Old Testament Theology in a Canonical Context.* Philadelphia: Fortress, 1986.

Christensen, D. L. "The Centre of the First Testament within the Canonical Process." *BTB* 23 (1993): 48–53.

———. *Explosion of the Canon: The Greek New Testament in Early Church History*. North Richland Hills, TX: BIBAL Press, 2004.

———. "Josephus and the Twenty-Two Book Canon of Sacred Scripture." *JETS* 29 (1986): 37–46.

———. "The Lost Books of the Bible." *Bible Review* 14.5 (Oct. 1998): 24–31.

Clabeaux, J. J. *A Lost Edition of the Letters of Paul: A Reassessment of the Text of the Pauline Corpus Attested by Marcion*. Catholic Biblical Quarterly Monograph Series 21. Washington, DC: Catholic University of America Press, 1989.

———. "Marcion." *ABD* 4:514–16.

———. "Marcionite Prologues to Paul." *ABD* 4:520–21.

Clarke, Kent D. "Original Text or Canonical Text? Questioning the Shape of the New Testament We Translate." Pages 281–322 in *Issues in Biblical Translation: Responses to Eugene A. Nida*. Edited by S. E. Porter and R. Hess. JSNTSup 173. Sheffield: Sheffield Academic, 1998.

Clines, David J. A., and J. Cheryl Exum, eds. *The Reception of the Hebrew Bible in the Septuagint and the New Testament: Essays in Memory of Aileen Guilding*. Hebrew Bible Monographs 55. Sheffield: Sheffield Phoenix, 2013.

Coats, George W., and Burke O. Long. *Canon and Authority: Essays in Old Testament Religion and Authority*. Philadelphia: Fortress, 1977.

Cohen, Shaye J. D. *The Significance of Yavneh and Other Essays in Jewish Hellenism*. Texts and Studies in Ancient Judaism 136. Tübingen: Mohr Siebeck, 2010.

Collins, A. Y., ed. *Early Christian Apocalypticism: Genre and Social Setting*. Semeia 36. Decatur, GA: Scholars Press, 1986.

Collins, J. J. "The 'Apocryphal' Old Testament," Pages 165–89 in Paget and Schaper, eds., *The New Cambridge History of the Bible*. Vol. 1, *From the Beginnings to 600*.

———. "Before the Canon: Scriptures in Second Temple Judaism." Pages 225–41 in *Old Testament Interpretation: Past, Present, and Future*. Edited by James Luther Mays, David L. Petersen, and Kent Harold Richards. Nashville: Abingdon, 1995.

———. "Canon, Canonization." Pages 460–63 in Collins and Harlow, eds., *The Eerdmans Dictionary of Early Judaism*.

———, ed. *The Encyclopedia of Apocalypticism*. Vol. 1, *The Origins of Apocalypticism in Judaism and Christianity*. New York: Continuum, 1998.

———. *Introduction to the Hebrew Bible*. Minneapolis: Fortress, 2004.

———. *Introduction to the Hebrew Bible*. 2nd ed. Minneapolis: Fortress, 2013.

———. *Seers, Sybils and Sages in Hellenistic-Roman Judaism*. Boston: Brill, 2001.

Collins, J. J., and Daniel C. Harlow, eds. *Early Judaism: A Comprehensive Overview*. Grand Rapids: Eerdmans, 2012.

———. *The Eerdmans Dictionary of Early Judaism*. Grand Rapids: Eerdmans, 2010.

Collins, N. L. *The Library in Alexandria and the Bible in Greek*. Leiden: Brill, 2000.

Collins, R. F. *First Corinthians*. Sacra Pagina 7. Collegeville, MN: Liturgical Press, 1999.

———. *Introduction to the New Testament*. Garden City, NY: Doubleday, 1983.

Colson, F. H., G. H. Whitaker, and R. Marcus, trans. *Philo*. 12 vols. LCL. Cambridge, MA: Harvard University Press, 1929–62.

Comfort, Philip Wesley, ed. *The Origin of the Bible*. Wheaton, IL: Tyndale, 1992.

———. *The Quest for the Original Text of the New Testament*. Grand Rapids: Baker Book House, 1992.

Comfort, Philip W., and David P. Barrett, eds. *The Text of the Earliest New Testament Manuscripts*. Rev. ed. Chicago: Tyndale, 2001.

Conrad, J. "Zur Frage nach der Rolle des Gesetzes bei der Bildung des alttestamentlichen Kanons." *Theologia viatorum* 11 (1979): 11–19.

Constantinou, Euginia. "Banned from the Lectionary: Excluding the Apocalypse of John from the Orthodox New Testament Canon." Pages 51–61 in Hovhanessian, ed., *The Canon of the Bible*.

Coogan, Michael D. *The Old Testament: A Historical and Literary Introduction to the Hebrew Scriptures*. 3rd ed. Oxford: Oxford University Press, 2014.

Coogan, Michael D., ed. in chief. *The Oxford Encyclopedia of the Books of the Bible*. Oxford: Oxford University Press, 2011.

Cook, J. "Septuagint Proverbs – and Canonization." Pages 79–91 in van der Kooij and van der Toorn, eds., *Canonization and Decanonization*.

Cook, L. Stephen. *On the Question of the "Cessation of Prophecy" in Ancient Judaism*. Texts in Ancient Judaism 145. Tübingen: Mohr Siebeck, 2011.

Cosgrove, Charles H. "Justin Martyr and the Emerging Christian Canon: Observations on the Purpose and Destination of the Dialogue with Trypho." *VC* 36 (1982): 209–32.

Cowe, S. Peter. "The Bible in Armenian," Pages 143–61 in Marsden and Matter, eds., *The New Cambridge History of the Bible: From 600–1450*.

Cowley, R. W. "The Biblical Canon of the Ethiopian Orthodox Church Today." *Ostkirchliche Studien* 23 (1974): 318–24.

Cox, P. *Biography in Late Antiquity: A Quest for the Holy Man*. Berkeley: University of California Press, 1983.

Cranfield, C. E. B. "The Gospel of Mark." *IDB* 3:267–77.

Crawford, Sidnie White. "The 'Rewritten' Bible at Qumran." Pages 1–8 in *Frank Moore Cross Volume*. Eretz-Israel 26. Jerusalem: IES and Hebrew Union College – Jewish Institute of Religion, 1999.

———. *Rewriting Scripture in Second Temple Times*. SDSRL. Grand Rapids: Eerdmans, 2008.

Cribiore, Raffaella. *Writing, Teachers, and Students in Greco-Roman Egypt*. Atlanta: Scholars Press, 1996.

Cross, F. L. "History and Fiction in the African Canons." *JTS* 12 (1961): 227–47.

Cross, F. L., and E. A. Livingstone, eds. *The Oxford Dictionary of the Christian Church*. 4th ed. Oxford: Oxford University Press, 2005.

Cross, F. M. *The Ancient Library at Qumran*. 3rd ed. Minneapolis: Fortress, 1995.

———. "The Evolution of a Theory of Local Texts." Pages 306–20 in *Qumran and the History of the Biblical Text*. Edited by F. M. Cross and S. Talmon. Cambridge, MA: Harvard University Press, 1975.

———. *From Epic to Canon: History and Literature in Ancient Israel*. Baltimore: Johns Hopkins University Press, 1998.

———. "The History of the Biblical Text in the Light of the Discoveries in the Judean Desert." *HTR* 57 (1964): 281–99.

———. "The Text Behind the Text of the Hebrew Bible." Pages 139–55 in *Understanding the Dead Sea Scrolls*. Edited by Hershel Shanks. New York: Vintage, 1992.

Crossan, J. D. *Four Other Gospels*. Minneapolis: Winston, 1985.

———. *Sayings Parallels: A Workbook for the Jesus Tradition*. Philadelphia: Fortress, 1986.

Croy, N. C. *The Mutilation of Mark's Gospel*. Nashville: Abingdon, 2003.

Cruesemann, F. "Das 'portative Vaterland': Struktur und Genese des alttestamentlichen Kanons." Pages 63–79 in vol. 2 of *Kanon und Zensur: Beiträge zur Archäologie der literarischen Kommunikation*. Edited by A. Assmann and J. Assmann. Munich: Wilhelm Fink, 1987.

Cullmann, O. "The Plurality of the Gospels as a Theological Problem in Antiquity." Pages 39–54 in *The Early Church*. Edited by A. J. B. Higgins. Philadelphia: Westminster, 1956.

Cunningham, Philip J. *Exploring Scripture: How the Bible Came to Be*. New York: Paulist, 1992.

Dahl, N. A. "The Origin of the Earliest Prologues to the Pauline Letters." *Semeia* 12 (1978): 233–77.

———. "The Particularity of the Pauline Epistles as a Problem in the Ancient Church." Pages 261–71 in *Neotestamentica et Patristica: Freundesgabe O. Cullmann*. Novum Testamentum Supplement 6. Leiden: Brill, 1962.

Danby, H. *The Mishnah*. Oxford: Oxford University Press, 1933. Repr., 1992.

Danker, F. W. *II Corinthians*. Augsburg Commentaries on the New Testament. Minneapolis: Augsburg, 1989.

Darshan, Guy. "The Twenty-Four Books of the Hebrew Bible and Alexandrian Scribal Methods." Pages 221–44 in Niehoff, ed., *Homer and the Bible*.

Dassmann, E. "Wer schuf den Kanon des Neuen Testaments?: Zum neuesten Buch von Bruce M. Metzger." *Jahrbuch für biblische Theologie* 3 (1988): 275–83.

Daube, David. "Alexandrian Methods of Interpretation and the Rabbis." Pages 27–44 in *Festschrift Hans Lewald*. Basel: Helbing & Lichtenhahn, 1953.

———. "Rabbinic Methods of Interpretation and Hellenistic Rhetoric." *Hebrew Union College Annual* 22 (1949): 239–64.

David, Nora, and Armin Lange, eds. *Qumran and the Bible: Studying the Jewish Scriptures in Light of the Dead Sea Scrolls*. CBET 57. Leuven: Peeters, 2010.

David, Nora, Armin Lange, Kristin De Troyer, and Shani Tzoref, eds. *The Hebrew Bible in Light of the Dead Sea Scrolls*. FRLANT 239. Göttingen: Vandenhoeck & Ruprecht, 2012.

Davidson, S. *The Canon of the Bible: Its Formation, History, and Fluctuations*. London: Henry S. King, 1877.

Davies, W. D., and Dale C. Allison, Jr. *The Gospel According to Saint Matthew*. ICC. Edinburgh: T. & T. Clark, 1997.

Davies, P. R. "The Jewish Scriptural Canon in Cultural Perspective." Pages 36–52 in McDonald and Sanders, eds., *The Canon Debate*.

———. " 'Pen of Iron, Point of Diamond' (Jer 17:1): Prophecy as Writing." Pages 65–81 in *Writings and Speech in Israelite and Ancient Near Eastern Prophecy*. Edited by M. Floyd and E. Ben Zvi. Atlanta: Scholars Press, 2000.

———. "The Prehistory of the Qumran Community." Pages 116–25 in *The Dead Sea Scrolls: Forty Years of Research*. Edited by Devorah Dimant, Uriel Rappaport, and Yad Yitshak Ben-Tsevi. STDJ. Leiden: Brill, 1992.

———. *Scribes and Schools: The Canonization of the Hebrew Scriptures*. Library of Ancient Israel. Louisville: Westminster John Knox, 1988.

Davies, W. D. "Canon and Christology." Pages 19–36 in *The Glory of Christ in the New Testament: Studies in Christology in Memory of George Bradford Caird*. Edited by L. D. Hurst and N. T. Wright. Oxford: Clarendon, 1987.

Davila, James R. "Pseudepigrapha, Old Testament." Pages 1110–14 in Collins and Harlow, eds., *The Eerdmans Dictionary of Early Judaism*.

————. "Quotations from Lost Books in the Hebrew Bible: A New Translation and Introduction, with an Excursus on Quotations from Lost Books in the New Testament." Pages 673–98 in vol. 1 of Bauckham, Davila, and Panayotov, eds., *Old Testament Pseudepigrapha*.

De Boer, E. A. *The Gospel of Mary: Listening to the Beloved Disciple*. London: T&T Clark International, 2004.

De Troyer, Kristin, and Armin Lange, eds. *Prophecy After the Prophets: The Contribution of the Dead Sea Scrolls to the Understanding of Biblical and Extra-Biblical Prophecy*. CBET 52. Leuven: Peeters, 2009.

Deines, Roland. "Pharisees." Pages 1061–63 in Collins and Harlow, eds., *The Eerdmans Dictionary of Early Judaism*.

Delamarter, Steve. *A Scripture Index to Charlesworth's The Old Testament Pseudepigrapha*. Sheffield: Sheffield Academic, 2002.

Dempster, S. "An 'Extraordinary Fact': Torah and Temple and the Contours of the Hebrew Canon." *Tyndale Bulletin* 48 (1997): 23–56, 191–218.

————. "Canons on the Right and Canons on the Left: Finding a Resolution in the Canon Debate," *JETS* 52 (2009): 47–78.

————. *Dominion and Dynasty: A Theology of the Hebrew Bible*. Downers Grove, IL: InterVarsity, 2003.

————. "Torah, Torah, Torah: The Emergence of a Tripartite Canon." Pages 87–127 in *Exploring the Origins of the Bible: Canon Formation in Historical, Literary, and Theological Perspective*. Edited by Craig A. Evans and Emanuel Tov. Grand Rapids: Baker Academic, 2008.

Demsky, A. "Writing in Ancient Israel and Early Judaism: The Biblical Period." Pages 2–20 in Mulder, ed., *Mikra*.

deSilva, David A. *The Jewish Teachers of Jesus, James, and Jude: What Earliest Christianity Learned from the Apocrypha and Pseudepigrapha*. Oxford: Oxford University Press, 2012.

De Troyer, K. *Rewriting the Sacred Text: What the Old Greek Texts Tell Us About the Literary Growth of the Bible*. Text-Critical Studies 4. Atlanta: Society of Biblical Literature, 2003.

Dibelius, M. *From Tradition to Gospel*. Translated by B. L. Woolf. London: Nicholson & Watson, 1934.

Dimant, Devorah, and Reihard G. Kratz, eds. *Rewriting and Interpreting the Hebrew Bible: The Biblical Patriarchs in the Light of the Dead Sea Scrolls*. BZAW 439. Göttingen: de Gruyter, 2013.

Doble, Peter, and Jeffrey Kloha, eds. *Texts and Traditions: Essays in Honour of J. Keith Elliott*. NTTSD 47. Leiden: Brill, 2014.

Dobschütz, E. von. "The Abandonment of the Canonical Ideal." *American Journal of Theology* 19 (1915): 416–29.

Dohmen, C. "Der biblische Kanon in der Diskussion." *Theologische Revue* 91 (1995): 452–60.

Dombrowski, B. W. W. *An Annotated Translation of Miqsat Ma'aseh haTorah (4QMMT)*. Krakow-Weenzen, Poland: Enigma, 1993.

Donelson, L. R. *Pseudepigraphy and Ethical Argument in the Pastoral Epistles*. Hermeneutische Untersuchungen zur Theologie 22. Tübingen: J. C. B. Mohr, 1986.

Dorival, Gilles. "Origen," Pages 605–28 in Paget and Schaper, eds., *The New Cambridge History of the Bible*. Vol. 1, *From the Beginnings to 600*.

DuBois, J.-D. "L'exégese gnostique et l'histoire du canon des écritures." Pages 89–97 in *Les règles de l'inteprétation*. Edited by M. Tardieu. Paris: Cerf, 1987.

Duff, J. "P[46] and the Pastorals: A Misleading Consensus?" *NTS* 44 (1998): 581–82.

Dulles, A. "The Authority of Scripture: A Catholic Perspective." Pages 14–40 in *Scripture in the Jewish and Christian Traditions*. Edited by F. E. Greenspahn. Nashville: Abingdon, 1982.

Duncker, P. G. "The Canon of the Old Testament at the Council of Trent." *CBQ* 15 (1953): 277–99.

Dungan, D. L. *Constantine's Bible: Politics and the Making of the New Testament*. Minneapolis: Fortress, 2007.

———. "The New Testament Canon in Recent Study." *Int* 29 (1975): 339–51.

———. *The Sayings of Jesus in the Churches of Paul: The Use of the Synoptic Tradition in the Regulation of Early Church Life*. Philadelphia: Fortress, 1971.

Dunn, J. D. G. "Has the Canon a Continuing Function?" Pages 558–79 in McDonald and Sanders, eds., *The Canon Debate*.

———. "How the New Testament Canon Began." Pages 122–37 in *From Biblical Criticism to Biblical Faith: Essays in Honor of Lee Martin McDonald*. Edited by Craig A. Evans and W. H. Brackney. Macon, GA: Mercer University Press, 2007.

———. *Jesus Remembered*. Christianity in the Making 1. Grand Rapids: Eerdmans, 2003.

———. "Levels of Canonical Authority." *HBT* 4 (1982): 13–60.

———. *The Living Word*. Philadelphia: Fortress, 1987.

———. *Romans 9–16*. WBC 38B. Dallas: Word, 1988.

———. *Unity and Diversity in the New Testament*. 2nd ed. Philadelphia: Westminster, 1992.

Dunne, John A. *Esther and Her Elusive God: How a Secular Story Functions as Scripture*. Eugene, OR: Wipf & Stock, 2014.

Dyck, E. "What Do We Mean By Canon?" *Crux* 25 (1989): 17–22.

Edrei, Arye, and Doran Mendels. "A Split Jewish Diaspora: Its Dramatic Consequences," *JSP* 16 (2007): 91–137.

Edwards, James R. *The Hebrew Gospel and the Development of the Synoptic Tradition*. Grand Rapids, MI: Eerdmans, 2009.

———. "The Hebrew Gospel in Early Christianity." Pages 116–52 in McDonald and Charlesworth, eds., *"Non-Canonical" Religious Texts*.

Edwards, M. J. "The Epistle to Rheginus: Valentinianism in the Fourth Century." *Novum Testamentum* 37 (1995): 76–91.

Ehrman, B. D. *Forged: Writing in the Name of God—Why the Bible's Authors Are Not Who We Think They Are*. New York: Harper One, 2011.

———. *Lost Christianities: The Battles for Scripture and the Faiths We Never Knew*. New York: Oxford University Press, 2003.

———. *Lost Scriptures: Books That Did Not Make It into the New Testament*. New York: Oxford University Press, 2003.

———. *Misquoting Jesus: The Story Behind Who Changed the Bible and Why*. San Francisco: HarperSanFrancisco, 2005.

———. "The New Testament Canon of Didymus the Blind." *VC* 37 (1983): 1–21.

———. *The Orthodox Corruption of Scripture: The Effect of Early Christological Controversies on the Text of the New Testament*. Oxford: Oxford University Press, 1993.

———. *Studies in the Textual Criticism of the New Testament*. NTTS 33. Leiden: Brill, 2005.

———. "The Text as Window: New Testament Manuscripts and the Social History of Early Christianity." Pages 361–79 in *The Text of the New Testament in Contemporary Research: Essays on the Status Quaestionis*. Edited by B. D. Ehrman and M. W. Holmes. Studies and Documents 46. Grand Rapids: Eerdmans, 1995.

————. "The Text of the Gospels at the End of the Second Century." Pages 95–122 in *Codex Bezae: Studies from the Lunel Colloquium, June 1994*. Edited by D. C. Parker and C.-B. Amphoux. NTTS 22. Leiden: Brill, 1996.

Ehrman, Bart D., and M. W. Holmes, eds. *The Text of the New Testament in Contemporary Research: Essays on the Status Quaestionis*. 2nd ed. Leiden: Brill, 2014.

Ehrman, Bart D., and M. A. Plunkett. "The Angel and the Agony: The Textual Problem of Luke 22:43–44." *CBQ* 45 (1983): 401–16.

Eichhorn, J. G. *Einleitung in das Alte Testament*. Leipzig: Bey Weidmanns Erben & Reich, 1780.

Eisenman, R., and M. Wise. *The Dead Sea Scrolls Uncovered: The First Complete Translation and Interpretation of Fifty Key Documents Withheld for Over Thirty-five Years*. Rockport, MA: Element, 1992.

Elledge, C. D. *The Bible and the Dead Sea Scrolls*. Archaeology and Biblical Studies 14. Atlanta: Society of Biblical Literature, 2005.

————. *The Statutes of the King: The Temple Scroll's Legislation on Kingship (11Q19 LVI 12-LIX 21)*. Cahiers de la Review Biblique 56. Paris: J. Gabalda, 2004.

Ellens, J. H. "The Ancient Library of Alexandria and Early Christian Theological Development." *Occasional Papers of the Institute for Antiquity and Christianity* 27 (1993): 1–51.

Elliott, J. K. "The 'Apocryphal' New Testament," Pages 455–78 in Paget and Schaper, eds., *The New Cambridge History of the Bible*. Vol. 1, *From the Beginnings to 600*.

————, ed. *The Apocryphal New Testament: A Collection of Apocryphal Christian Literature in an English Translation based on M. R. James*. Oxford: Oxford University Press, 1993.

————. "The Case for Thoroughgoing Eclecticism." Pages 139–45 in Black, ed., *Rethinking New Testament Textual Criticism*.

————. "Manuscripts, the Codex, and the Canon." *JSNT* 63 (1996): 105–23.

Ellis, E. E. *The Making of the New Testament Documents*. Leiden: Brill, 2002.

————. *The Old Testament in Early Christianity: Canon and Interpretation in the Light of Modern Research*. Grand Rapids: Baker, 1992.

Emmel, Stephen. "The Christian Book in Egypt: Innovation and the Coptic Tradition." Pages 35–43 in Sharpe and Van Kampen, eds., *The Bible as Book*.

Enns, Peter. "Lives of the Prophets." Pages 892–94 in Collins and Harlow, eds., *The Eerdmans Dictionary of Early Judaism*.

Epp, E. J. "The Codex and Literacy in Early Christianity and at Oxyrhynchus: Issues Raised by Harry Y. Gamble's Books and Readers in the Early Church." *Critical Review of Books in Religion* 10 (1997): 15–37.

————. "Decision Points in Past, Present, and Future New Testament Textual Criticism." Pages 17–44 in *Studies in Theory and Method of New Testament Textual Criticism*. Edited by E. Epp and G. Fee. Grand Rapids: Eerdmans.

————. "In the Beginning Was the New Testament Text, but Which Text? A Consideration of 'Ausgangstext' and 'Initial Text'." Pages 35–70 in Doble and Kloha, eds. *Texts and Traditions*.

————. "Issues in New Testament Textual Criticism." Pages 17–76 in Black ed., *Rethinking New Testament Textual Criticism*.

————. "Issues in the Interrelation of New Testament Textual Criticism and Canon." Pages 485–515 in McDonald and Sanders, eds., *The Canon Debate*.

————. *Junia: The First Woman Apostle*. Minneapolis: Fortress, 2005.

————. "The Multivalence of the Term 'Original Text' in New Testament Textual Criticism." *HTR* 92 (1999): 245–81.

————. "The Oxyrhynchus New Testament Papyri: 'Not without Honor Except in Their Hometown'?" *JBL* 123 (2004): 5–55.

————. "The Papyrus Manuscripts of the New Testament." Pages 1–39 in Ehrman and Holmes, eds., *The Text of the New Testament.*

————. *Perspectives on New Testament Textual Criticism: Collected Essays, 1962–2004.* Supplements to Novum Testamentum 116. Leiden: Brill, 2005.

————. "Textual Clusters: Their Past and Future in New Testament Textual Criticism." Pages 519–79 in Ehrman and Holmes, eds., *The Text of the New Testament.*

————. "Textual Criticism and New Testament Interpretation." Pages 79–105 in *Method and Meaning: Essays on New Testament Interpretation in Honor of Harold W. Attridge.* Edited by Andrew B. McGowan and Kent Harold Richards. Atlanta: Society of Biblical Literature, 2011.

————. "Textual Criticism in the Exegesis of the New Testament, with an Excursus on Canon." Pages 73–91 in *Handbook to Exegesis of the New Testament.* Edited by S. E. Porter. NTTS 25. Leiden: Brill, 1997.

————. "Traditional 'Canons' of New Testament Textual Criticism: Their Value, Validity, and Viability—or Lack Thereof." Pages 79–127 in *The Textual History of the Greek New Testament: Changing Views in Contemporary Research.* Edited by Klaus Wachtel and Michael W. Holmes. SBLTCS 8. Atlanta: Society of Biblical Literature, 2011.

Ernest, J. D. *The Bible in Athanasius of Alexandria.* Leiden: Brill, 2004.

Evans, C. A. *Ancient Texts for NTS: A Guide to the Background Literature.* Peabody, MA: Hendrickson, 2005.

————. *The Bible Knowledge Background Commentary.* 3 vols. Colorado Springs: Victor/ Cook, 2003–2004.

————. "Canon." Pages 85–87 in vol. 1 of Coogan, ed., *The Oxford Encyclopedia of the Books of the Bible.*

————. "The Dead Sea Scrolls and the Canon of Scripture in the Time of Jesus." Pages 67–79 in Flint, ed., *The Bible at Qumran.*

————. *From Biblical Faith to Biblical Criticism: Essays in Honor of Lee Martin McDonald.* Macon, GA: Mercer University Press, 2007.

————. "How Long Were Late Antique Books in Use? Possible Implications for New Testament Textual Criticism." *BBR* 25 (2015): 23–37.

————. "Jesus and the Dead Sea Scrolls." Pages 573–98 in vol. 2 of Flint and VanderKam, eds., *The Dead Sea Scrolls After Fifty Years.*

————. "Luke and the Rewritten Bible: Aspects of Lukan Hagiography." Pages 170–201 in *The Pseudepigrapha and Early Biblical Interpretation.* Edited by J. H. Charlesworth and C. A. Evans. JSNTSup 119. Sheffield: JSOT Press, 1993.

————. *Mark 8:27–16:20.* WBC 34B. Nashville: Thomas Nelson, 2001.

————. "Mishna and Messiah 'in Context': Some Comments on Jacob Neusner's Proposals." *JBL* 112 (1993): 267–89.

————. *Noncanonical Writings and New Testament Interpretation.* Peabody, MA: Hendrickson, 1992.

————. "The Scriptures of Jesus and His Earliest Followers." Pages 185–95 in McDonald and Sanders, eds., *The Canon Debate.*

————. "Textual Criticism and Textual Confidence: How Reliable Is Scripture?" Pages 161–72 in *The Reliability of the New Testament: Bart D. Ehrman and Daniel B. Wallace in Dialogue.* Edited by Robert B. Stewart. Minneapolis: Fortress, 2011.

————. "Why Did the New Testament Writers Appeal to the Old Testament?" *JSNT* 38 (2015): 36–48.

Evans, C. A., R. L. Webb, and R. A. Wiebe, eds. *Nag Hammadi Texts and the Bible*. NTTS 18. Leiden: Brill, 1993.

Evans, C. A., and H. D. Zacharias, eds. *Jewish and Christian Scripture as Artifact and Canon*. LSTS 13. London: T&T Clark, 2009.

Evans, C. F. *Is Holy Scripture Christian?* London: SCM, 1971.

Evans, C. Stephen. "Canonicity, Apostolicity, and Biblical Authority." Pages 146–66 in Bartholomew et al., eds., *Canon and Biblical Interpretation*.

Ewert, D. *From Ancient Tablets to Modern Translations*. Grand Rapids: Zondervan, 1983.

Falk, Daniel K. *The Parabiblical Texts: Strategies for Extending the Scriptures Among the Dead Sea Scrolls*. LSTS 63. London: T&T Clark, 2007.

Fallon, Francis T. "The Prophets of the Old Testament and the Gnostics. A Note on Irenaeus, Adversus Haereses, 1.30.10–11." *VC* 32 (1978): 191–94.

Farkasfalvy, Denis. "The Early Development of the New Testament Canon." Pages 97–160 in *The Formation of the New Testament Canon*. Edited by Harold W. Attridge. New York: Paulist, 1983.

———. "The Ecclesial Setting of Pseudepigraphy in Second Peter and Its Role in the Formation of the Canon." *Second Century* 5 (1985–86): 3–29.

Farley, E. *Ecclesial Reflection*. Philadelphia: Fortress, 1982.

Farmer, W. R. "The Church's Gospel Canon: Why Four and No More." Pages 1246–50 in *The International Bible Commentary*. Edited by W. R. Farmer. Collegeville, MN: Liturgical Press, 1998.

———. "A Dismantling of the Church's Canon." Pages 35–55 in *The Gospel of Jesus: The Pastoral Relevance of the Synoptic Problem*. Edited by W. R. Farmer. Louisville: Westminster John Knox, 1994.

———. "Further Reflections on the Fourfold Gospel Canon." Pages 107–13 in *The Early Church in Its Context: Essays in Honor of Everett Ferguson*. Edited by J. Malherbe, F. W. Norris, and J. W. Thompson. Leiden: Brill, 1998.

———. "Galatians and the Second Century Development of the *Regula Fidei*." *The Second Century: A Journal of Early Christian Studies* 4 (1984): 143–70.

———. *Jesus and the Gospel: Tradition, Scripture and Canon*. Philadelphia: Fortress, 1982.

———. "Matthew and the Bible: An Essay in Canonical Criticism." *Lexington Theological Quarterly* 11 (April 1976): 57–66.

———. "Reflections on Jesus and the New Testament Canon." Pages 321–40 in McDonald and Sanders, eds., *The Canon Debate*.

———. "The Role of Isaiah in the Development of the Christian Canon." Pages 217–22 in *Uncovering Ancient Stones: Festschrift for H. Neil Richardson*. Winona, IN: Eisenbrauns, 1994.

———. "A Study of the Development of the New Testament Canon." Pages 7–86 in *The Formation of the New Testament Canon*. Edited by Harold W. Attridge. New York: Paulist, 1983.

Farmer, W. R., and D. M. Farkasfalvy. *The Formation of the New Testament Canon*. Introduction by A. C. Outler. Edited by H. W. Attridge. New York: Paulist, 1983.

Fee, Gordon D. "Codex Sinaiticus in the Gospel of John: a Contribution to Methodology in Establishing Textual Relationships." *NTS* 15 (1968–69): 23–44

———. *The First Epistle to the Corinthians*. NICNT. Grand Rapids: Eerdmans, 1987.

———. "The Use of the Greek Fathers for New Testament Textual Criticism." Pages 191–207 in Ehrman and Holmes, eds., *The Text of the New Testament in Contemporary Research*.

Feldman, L. H. "Introduction." Pages 17–49 in *Josephus, the Bible, and History*. Edited by L. H. Feldman and G. Hata. Detroit: Wayne State University Press, 1989.

Fenton, J. C. "Pseudonymity and the New Testament." *Theology* 58 (1955): 51–56.

Ferguson, Everett. *Backgrounds of Early Christianity*. 3rd ed. Grand Rapids: Eerdmans, 2003.

———. "Canon Muratori: Date and Provenance." *Studia Patristica* 17, no. 2 (1982): 677–83.

———. "Creeds, Councils, and Canons." Pages 427–45 in *Oxford Handbook of Early Christian Studies*. Edited by S. A. Harvey and D. G. Hunter. Oxford: Oxford University Press, 2008.

———. Review of G. M. Hahneman, *The Muratorian Fragment and the Development of the Canon*. *JTS* 44 (1993): 691–97.

Fernández Marcos, N. *The Septuagint in Context: Introduction to the Greek Versions of the Bible*. Translated by W. G. E. Watson. Leiden: Brill, 2001.

Ferreira, Johan. *Early Chinese Christianity*. Early Christian Studies 17. Strathfield, NSW: St. Paul's, 2014.

Fiedler, L. A., and H. A. Baker Jr., eds. *English Literature: Opening up the Canon*. Baltimore: Johns Hopkins University Press, 1981.

Filoramo, G. *A History of Gnosticism*. Translated by A. Alcock. Oxford: Blackwell, 1990.

Filson, Floyd V. *Which Books Belong in the Bible? A Study of the Canon*. Philadelphia: Westminster, 1957.

Finkelberg, Margalit. "Homer as a Foundation Text." Pages 75–96 in Finkelberg and Stroumsa, eds., *Homer, the Bible, and Beyond*.

———. "Introduction: Before the Western Canon." Pages 1–8 in Finkelberg and Stroumsa, eds., *Homer, the Bible, and Beyond*.

Finkelberg, Margalit, and G. G. Stroumsa, eds. *Homer, the Bible, and Beyond: Literary and Religious Canons in the Ancient World*. Jerusalem Studies in Religion and Culture. Leiden: Brill, 2003.

Finsterbusch, Karin, and Armin Lange, eds. *What Is Bible?* CBET 67. Leuven: Peeters, 2012.

Fitzmyer, Joseph. *Romans*. AB 33. New York: Doubleday, 1993.

Fitzmyer, J. A. *The Dead Sea Scrolls and Christian Origins*. Studies in the Dead Sea Scrolls and Related Literature. Grand Rapids: Eerdmans, 2000.

———. "Paul and the Dead Sea Scrolls." Pages 599–621 in vol. 2 of Flint and VanderKam, eds., *The Dead Sea Scrolls After Fifty Years*.

Flint, P. W. "'Apocrypha,' Other Previously-known Writings, and 'Pseudepigrapha' in the Dead Sea Scrolls." Pages 24–66 in vol. 2 of Flint and VanderKam, eds., *The Dead Sea Scrolls After Fifty Years*.

———. *The Bible at Qumran: Text, Shape, and Interpretation*. Grand Rapids: Eerdmans, 2001.

———. *The Dead Sea Psalms Scrolls and the Book of Psalms*. Leiden: Brill, 1997.

———. "Noncanonical Writings in the Dead Sea Scrolls: Apocrypha, Other Previously Known Writings, Pseudepigrapha." Pages 80–126 in Flint, ed., *The Bible at Qumran*.

Flint, P. W., and J. C. VanderKam, eds. *The Dead Sea Scrolls After Fifty Years: A Comprehensive Assessment*. 2 vols. Leiden: Brill, 1998.

Folkert, K. W. "The 'Canons' of Scripture." Pages 170–79 in *Rethinking Scripture: Essays from a Comparative Perspective*. Edited by M. Levering. Albany: SUNY Press, 1989.

Fowl, S. "The Canonical Approach of Brevard Childs." *Expository Times* 96 (1985): 173–76.

France, R. T. *Jesus and the Old Testament*. London: Tyndale, 1971.

Freedman, D. N. "The Earliest Bible." Pages 29–37 in *Backgrounds for the Bible*. Edited by M. P. O'Connor and D. N. Freedman. Winona Lake, IN: Eisenbrauns, 1987.

———, gen. ed. *The Leningrad Codex: A Facsimile Edition*. Grand Rapids: Eerdmans. Leiden: Brill, 1998.

———. "The Symmetry of the Hebrew Bible." *Studia Theologica* 46 (1992): 83–108.

———. *The Unity of the Hebrew Bible*. Ann Arbor: University of Michigan Press, 1991.

Frend, W. H. C. *The Rise of Christianity*. Philadelphia: Fortress, 1984.

Frerichs, E. S. *The Early Church*. Philadelphia: Fortress, 2008.

———. "The Torah Canon of Judaism and the Interpretation of Hebrew Scriptures." *HBT* 9 (1987): 13–25.

Friedman, S. "The Holy Scriptures Defile the Hands: The Transformation of a Biblical Concept in Rabbinic Theology." Pages 115–32 in *Biblical and Other Studies Presented to Nahum M. Sarna in Honor of His 70th Birthday*. Edited by M. Brettler and M. Fishbane. JSOTSup 154. Sheffield: Sheffield Academic, 1993.

Friedrich, Gerhard. "εὐαγγελίζομαι, *ktl.*" *TDNT* 2:707–37.

Funk, R. W. *Five Gospels: What Did Jesus Really Say? The Search for the Authentic Words of Jesus*. San Francisco: Harper One, 1996.

———. *Honest to Jesus*. San Francisco: HarperSanFrancisco, 1996.

———. "The Incredible Canon." Pages 24–46 in *Christianity in the 21st Century*. Edited by D. A. Brown. New York: Crossroad, 2000.

———. "The New Testament as Tradition and Canon." Pages 151–86 in *Parables and Presence*.

———. "The Once and Future New Testament," Pages 541–57 in McDonald and Sanders, eds., *The Canon Debate*.

———. *Parables and Presence*. Philadelphia: Fortress, 1982.

Fürst, J. *Der Kanon des Alten Testaments nach den Überlieferungen in Talmud und Midrasch*. Leipzig: Dörffling & Franke, 1868.

Gallagher, Edmon L. "The Blood from Abel to Zechariah in the History of Interpretation." *NTS* 60 (2014): 121–38.

———. "The End of the Bible? The Position of Chronicles in the Canon." *Tyndale Bulletin* 65 (2014): 181–99.

———. *Hebrew Scripture in Patristic Biblical Theory: Canon, Language, Text*. VCSup 114. Leiden: Brill, 2012.

———. "Jerome's Prologus Galeatus and the OT Canon of North Africa," *Studia Patristica* 69 (2013): 99–106.

———. "The Old Testament 'Apocrypha' in Jerome's Canonical Theory." *JECS* 20 (2012).

———. "Origen via Rufinus on the New Testament Canon." *NTS* 62, no. 3 (2016): 461–76.

———. "Why Did Jerome Translate Tobit and Judith?" *HTR* 108 (2015): 356–75.

———. "Writings Labeled 'Apocrypha' in Latin Patristic Sources." Pages 1–14 in Charlesworth and McDonald, eds., *Sacra Scriptura*.

Gallagher, Edmon L., and John Meade. *The Biblical Canon Lists from Early Christianity: Texts and Analysis*. Oxford: Oxford University Press, 2017.

Gamble, Harry Y. *Books and Readers in the Early Church: A History of Early Christian Texts*. New Haven: Yale University Press, 1995.

———. "Canon. New Testament." *ABD* 1:852–61.

———. "The Canon of the New Testament." Pages 201–43 in *The New Testament and Its Modern Interpreters*. Edited by E. J. Epp and G. W. MacRae. SBL The Bible and Its Modern Interpreters 3. Philadelphia: Fortress, 1989.

———. "Christianity: Scripture and Canon." Pages 36–62 in *The Holy Book in Comparative Perspective*. Edited by F. M. Denney and R. L. Taylor. Studies in Comparative Religion. Columbia: University of South Carolina Press, 1985.

———. *The New Testament Canon: Its Making and Meaning*. Guides to Biblical Scholarship. Philadelphia: Fortress, 1985.

———. "The New Testament Canon: Recent Research and the Status Quaestionis." Pages 267–94 in McDonald and Sanders, eds., *The Canon Debate*.

—————. "The Pauline Corpus and the Early Christian Book." Pages 265–80 in *Paul and the Legacies of Paul*. Edited by William S. Babcock. Dallas: SMU, 1990.

García Martínez, Florentino. *The Dead Sea Scrolls Translated: The Qumran Texts in English*. Translated by W. G. E. Watson. 2nd ed. Grand Rapids: Eerdmans, 1996.

García Martínez, Florentino, and E. J. C. Tigchelaar. *The Dead Sea Scrolls: Study Edition*. 2 vols. Leiden: Brill, 1997–98.

Geer Jr., Thomas C., rev. by Jean-François Racine. "Analyzing and Categorizing New Testament Greek Manuscripts." Pages 497–518 in Ehrman and Holmes, eds., *The Text of the New Testament*.

Gerhardsson, B. *Memory and Manuscript*. Grand Rapids: Eerdmans, 1998.

—————. *The Reliability of the Gospel Tradition*. Peabody, MA: Hendrickson, 2001.

Gerstenberger, Erhard S. "Canon Criticism and the Meaning of Sitz im Leben." Pages 20–31 in *Canon, Theology, and Old Testament Interpretation: Essays in Honor of Brevard S. Childs*. Edited by Gene M. Tucker, David L. Peterson, and Robert R. Wilson. Philadelphia: Fortress, 1988.

—————. *Israel in the Persian Period: The Fifth and Fourth Centuries BCE*. Atlanta: Society of Biblical Literature, 2011.

Gese, H. "Die dreifache Gestaltwerdung des Alten Testaments." Pages 299–328 in *Mitte der Schrift? Ein jüdisch-christliches Gespräch: Texte des Berner Symposions vom 6.–12. Januar 1985*. Edited by M. A. Klopfenstein et al. Judiaca et Christiana 11. Bern: Lang, 1987.

Gheorghita, R. *The Role of the Septuagint in Hebrews*. Tübingen: Mohr, 2003.

Georgi, Dieter. *The Opponents of Paul in Second Corinthians*. Philadelphia: Fortress, 1986.

Gilbert, M. "The Book of Ben Sira: Implications for Jewish and Christian Traditions." Pages 81–91 in *Jewish Civilization in the Hellenistic-Roman Period*. Edited by S. Talmon. Philadelphia: Trinity, 1991.

Gnuse, R. *The Authority of the Bible: Theories of Inspiration, Revelation, and the Canon of Scripture*. New York: Paulist, 1985.

Goehring, J. E., C. W. Hedrick, J. T. Sanders, and H. D. Betz, eds. *Gnosticism and the Early Christian World*. Sonoma, CA: Polebridge, 1990.

Golb, Norman. *Who Wrote the Dead Sea Scrolls?* New York: Scribners, 1995.

Gooding, David W. "Aristeas and Septuagint Origins: A Review of Recent Studies." *VT* 13 (1963): 357–78.

Goodspeed, E. J. "The Canon of the New Testament." *IDB* 1:63–71.

—————. *The Formation of the New Testament*. Chicago: University of Chicago Press, 1926.

—————. *A History of Early Christian Literature*. Chicago: University of Chicago Press, 1983.

—————. *An Introduction to the New Testament*. Chicago: University of Chicago Press, 1937.

—————. *The Key to Ephesians*. Chicago: University of Chicago Press, 1956.

—————. *The Meaning of Ephesians*. Chicago: University of Chicago Press, 1933.

Gorak, J. *The Making of the Modern Canon: Genesis and Crisis of a Literary Idea*. London: Athlone, 1991.

Goshen-Gottstein, Moshe H., ed. *The Hebrew University Bible: The Book of Isaiah*. Jerusalem: Magnes, 1995.

Gould, E. P. *A Critical and Exegetical Commentary on the Gospel According to St. Mark*. ICC. Edinburgh: T. &. T. Clark, 1896.

Grabbe, Lester L. *A History of the Jews and Judaism in the Second Temple Period*. London: T&T Clark, 2004.

—————. "Law of Moses in Ezra Tradition: More Virtual Than Real?" Pages 91–114 in *Persia and Torah: The Theory of Imperial Authorization of the Pentateuch*. Edited by J. W. Watts. Atlanta: SBL, 2001.

Graetz, Heinrich H. Kohelet. *Der alttestamantliche Kanon und sein Abschluss*. Anhang 1. Leipzig: Winter, 1871.

Graham, W. A. *Beyond the Written Word: Oral Aspects of Scripture in the History of Religion*. Cambridge: Cambridge University Press, 1987.

———. "Scripture." Pages 133–45 in vol. 13 of *Encyclopaedia of Religion*. Edited by Mircea Eliade. New York: Macmillan, 1987.

Grant, R. M. *The Apostolic Fathers: A New Translation and Commentary*. 6 vols. New York: Nelson, 1964–68.

———. "The Creation of the Christian Tradition: From Tradition to Scripture and Back." Pages 18–36 in *Perspectives on Scripture and Tradition*. Edited by J. F. Kelly. Notre Dame: Fides, 1976.

———. "From Tradition to Scripture and Back." Pages 18–36 in *Scripture and Tradition*. Edited by Joseph F. Kelley. Notre Dame: Fides, 1976.

———. *The Formation of the New Testament*. New York: Harper & Row, 1965.

———, ed. *Gnosticism: A Source Book of Heretical Writings from the Early Christian Period*. New York: Harper, 1961.

———. *Heresy and Criticism: The Search for Authenticity in Early Christian Literature*. Louisville: Westminster John Knox, 1993.

———. "The New Testament Canon." Pages 284–307 in *The Cambridge History of the Bible*. Vol. 1, *From the Beginnings to Jerome*. Edited by P. R. Ackroyd and C. F. Evans. Cambridge: Cambridge University Press, 1970.

———. "The Oldest Gospel Prologues." *Anglican Theological Review* 23 (1941): 231–45.

———. Review of Geoffrey Mark Hahneman, *The Muratorian Fragment and the Development of the Canon*. *Church History* 64 (1995): 639.

Green, J. B., and L. M. McDonald, eds. *The World of the New Testament: Cultural, Social, and Historical Contexts*. Grand Rapids: Baker Academic, 2013.

Green, R. P. H., trans. *Saint Augustine: On Christian Teaching*. Oxford World's Classics. Oxford: Oxford University Press, 1997.

Greenspoon, L. "The Dead Sea Scrolls and the Greek Bible." Pages 101–27 in vol. 1 of Flint and VanderKam, eds., *The Dead Sea Scrolls After Fifty Years*.

Gregory, Andrew, and Christopher Tuckett, eds. *The Reception of the New Testament in the Apostolic Fathers*. New Testament and the Apostolic Fathers 1. Oxford: Oxford University Press, 2006.

———. *Trajectories Through the New Testament and Apostolic Fathers*. New Testament and the Apostolic Fathers 2. Oxford: Oxford University Press, 2006.

Gregory, C. R. *Canon and Text of the New Testament*. International Theological Library. Edinburgh: T. & T. Clark, 1907.

Groh, Dennis E. "Hans von Campenhausen on Canon: Positions and Problems." *Interpretation* 28 (1974): 331–43.

Grosheide, F. W. *Some Early Lists of the Books of the New Testament*. Textus minores 1. Leiden: Brill, 1948.

Gross, Andrew. "Temple Scroll (11QTemple)." Pages 1291–94 in Collins and Harlow, eds., *The Eerdmans Dictionary of Early Judaism*.

Guignard, Christophe. 2015. "The Original Language of the Muratorian Fragment." *JTS* 66, no. 2: 596–624.

Guillory, J. "Canon." Pages 233–49 in *Critical Terms for Literary Study*. Edited by F. Lentricchia and T. McLaughlin. Chicago: University of Chicago Press, 1990.

———. *Cultural Capital: The Problem of Literary Canon Formation*. Chicago: University of Chicago Press, 1993.

Gundry, Robert H. *Matthew: A Commentary on His Handbook for a Mixed Church Under Persecution*. 2nd ed. Grand Rapids: Eerdmans, 1994.

Gutwenger, Engelbert. "The Anti-Marcionite Prologues." *Theological Studies* 7 (1946): 393–408.

Haelst, Joseph van. *Catalogue des Papyrus Litteraires Juifs et Chretiens*. Paris: Publications de la Sorbonne, 1976.

Hahn, Ferdinand. "Die Heilige Schrift als älteste christliche Tradition und als Kanon." *Evangelische Theologie* 40 (1980): 456–66.

Hahneman, G. M. "More on Redating the Muratorian Fragment." Pages 359–65 in *Studia Patristica* 19. Edited by E. A. Livingstone. Leuven: Peeters, 1988.

———. *The Muratorian Fragment and the Development of the Canon*. Oxford Theological Monographs. Oxford: Clarendon, 1992.

———. "The Muratorian Fragment and the Origins of the New Testament Canon." Pages 405–15 in McDonald and Sanders, eds., *The Canon Debate*.

Halivni, David Weiss. *The Formation of the Babylonian Talmud*. Translated by Jeffrey L. Rubenstein. New York: Oxford University Press, 2013.

———. *Peshat and Derash: Plain and Applied Meaning in Rabbinic Exegesis*. New York: Oxford University Press, 1991.

Hallberg, R. von, ed. *Canons*. Chicago: University of Chicago Press, 1984.

Hancock, Rebecca S. "Canon, Hebrew Bible." Pages 87–96 in vol. 1 of Coogan, ed., *The Oxford Encyclopedia of the Books of the Bible*.

Hanson, R. P. C. *Origen's Doctrine of Tradition*. London: SPCK, 1954.

Harnack, A. von. *Marcion: Das Evangelium vom fremden Gott*. 2nd ed. Leipzig: Hinrichs, 1924.

———. *The Origin of the New Testament and the Most Important Consequences of the New Creation*. Translated by J. R. Wilkinson. New York: Macmillan, 1925.

Harrington, D. J. "Introduction to the Canon." Pages 7–21 in vol. 1 of *The New Interpreter's Bible*. 12 vols. Nashville: Abingdon, 1994.

———. "The Old Testament Apocrypha in the Early Church and Today." Pages 196–210 in McDonald and Sanders, eds., *The Canon Debate*.

Harrington, D. J., and J. Strugnell. "Qumran Cave 4 Texts: A New Publication." *JBL* 112 (1993): 491–99.

Harris, J. Rendel. "Marcion and the Canon." *Expository Times* 18 (1906–1907): 392–94.

Harris, R. Laird. *Inspiration and Canonicity of the Bible: An Historical and Exegetical Study*. Grand Rapids: Zondervan, 1969.

Harris, William. "Why Did the Codex Supplant the Book-Roll?" Pages 71–85 in *Renaissance Society and Culture: Essays in Honor of Eugene F. Rice, Jr.* Edited by John Monfasani and Ronald G. Musto. New York: Italica, 1991.

Harrison, Carol. "Augustine." Pages 676–97 in Paget and Schaper, eds., *The New Cambridge History of the Bible*. Vol. 1, *From the Beginnings to 600*.

Harrison, E. F. *Introduction to the New Testament*. Grand Rapids: Eerdmans, 1977.

Hartman, L. *"Into the Name of the Lord Jesus": Baptism in the Early Church*. Edinburgh: T. &. T. Clark, 1997.

Hatch, W. H. P. "The Position of Hebrews in the Canon of the New Testament." *HTR* 29 (1936): 133–51.

Hayward, C. T. R. "Scripture in the Jewish Temple," Pages 321–44 in Paget and Schaper, eds., *The New Cambridge History of the Bible*. Vol. 1, *From the Beginnings to 600*.

Head, Peter M. Review of *The Biblical Canon*. *JSNT* 30 (2008): 114–15.

Heckel, Th. *Vom Evangelium des Markus zum viergestaltigen Evangelium.* WUNT 120. Tübingen: J. C. B. Mohr (Paul Siebeck), 1999.

Hedrick, Charles W. "Kingdom Sayings and Parables of Jesus in *The Apocryphon of James*: Tradition and Redaction." *NTS* 29 (1983): 1–24.

———. "Thomas and the Synoptics: Aiming at a Consensus," *Second Century* 7 (1989– 90): 39–56.

Hedrick, C. W., and R. Hodgson Jr., eds. *Nag Hammadi, Gnosticism, and Early Christianity.* Peabody, MA: Hendrickson, 1986.

Heine, R. E. "The Role of the Gospel of John in the Montanist Controversy." *Second Century* 6 (1987): 1–19.

Helmer, C., and C. Lanmesser, eds. *One Scripture or Many? Canon from Biblical, Theological and Philosophical Perspectives.* New York: Oxford University Press, 2004.

Helyer, Larry R. "The Hasmoneans and the Hasmonean Era." Pages 38–53 in Green and McDonald, eds., *The World of the New Testament.*

Hendel, Ronald. "The Oxford Hebrew Bible: Prologue to a New Critical Edition." *VT* 58 (2008): 324–51.

Hengel, M. *The Four Gospels and the One Gospel of Jesus Christ.* Harrisburg, PA: Trinity, 2000.

———. *Judaism and Hellenism: Studies in Their Encounter in Palestine During the Early Hellenistic Period.* Philadelphia: Fortress, 1974.

———. *The Septuagint as Christian Scripture: Its Prehistory and the Problem of Its Canon.* Translated by M. E. Biddle. Edinburgh: T. &. T. Clark, 2002.

———. "The Titles of the Gospels and the Gospel of Mark." Pages 64–84 in *Studies in the Gospel of Mark.* Edited by M. Hengel. Translated by J. Bowden. London: SCM, 1985.

Henne, P. "La datation du Canon de Muratori." *Revue biblique* 100 (1993): 54–75.

Hennecke, E., ed. *New Testament Apocrypha.* Edited by W. Schneemelcher. English translation edited by R. M. Wilson. 2 vols. Philadelphia: Westminster, 1963.

Herbert, E. D., and E. Tov, eds. *The Bible as Book: The Hebrew Bible and the Judaean Desert Discoveries.* London: The British Library. New Castle, DE: Oak Knoll, 2002.

Herklots, H. G. G. *How Our Bible Came to Us.* London: Ernest Benn, 1957.

Heron, A. I. C. "Doctrine of the Canon." Pages 344–45 in vol. 1 of *The Encyclopedia of Christianity.* Edited by E. Fahlbusch et al. Grand Rapids: Eerdmans. Leiden: Brill, 1999.

Higgins, A. J. B. *The Historicity of the Fourth Gospel.* London: Lutterworth, 1960.

Hill, A. E. *Baker's Handbook of Bible Lists.* Grand Rapids: Baker, 1981.

Hill, Charles E. "The Debate Over the Muratorian Fragment and the Development of the Canon." *WTJ* 57 (1995): 437–52.

———. "Justin and the New Testament Writings." Pages 42–48 in *Studia Patristica* 30. Edited by E. A. Livingstone. Leuven: Peeters, 1997.

———. "Papias of Hierapolis." *Expository Times* 117 (2006): 309–15

———. "What Papias Said About John (and Luke): A 'New' Papian Fragment." *JTS* 49 (1998): 582–629.

Hill, C. E., and Michael J. Kruger, eds. *The Early Text of the New Testament.* Oxford: Oxford University Press, 2014.

Hillmer, M. R. "The Gospel of John in the Second Century." PhD diss., Harvard University, 1966.

Hock, R. F. "The Favored One: How Mary Became the Mother of God." *Bible Review* 17, no. 3 (2001): 13–25.

Hoffman, Thomas A. "Inspiration, Normativeness, Canonicity, and the Unique Sacred Character of the Bible." *CBQ* 44 (1982): 447–69.

Hoffmann, R. Joseph. *Marcion, On the Restitution of Christianity: An Essay on the Development of Radical Paulinist Theology in the Second Century*. Chico, CA: Scholars Press, 1984.

Hofius, O. "Isolated Sayings of Jesus." Pages 88–91 in vol. 1 of Schneemelcher, ed., *New Testament Apocrypha*.

———. "Unknown Sayings of Jesus." Pages 336–60 in *The Gospel and the Gospels*. Edited by P. Stuhlmacher. Grand Rapids: Eerdmans, 1991.

Holladay, Carl A. *A Critical Introduction to the New Testament: Interpreting the Message and Meaning of Jesus Christ*. Expanded CD-Rom Version. Nashville: Abingdon, 2005.

Hollerich, Michael J. "Eusebius." Pages 629–52 in Paget and Schaper, eds., *The New Cambridge History of the Bible*. Vol. 1, *From the Beginnings to 600*.

Holmes, Michael W. *Apostolic Fathers: Greek Texts and English Translations*. 3rd ed. Grand Rapids: Baker Academic, 2007.

———. "The Biblical Canon." Pages 406–26 in *The Oxford Handbook of Early Christian Studies*. Edited by Susan Ashbrook Harvey and David G. Hunter. Oxford: Oxford University Press, 2008.

———. "The Case for Reasoned Eclecticism." Pages 77–100 in Black, ed., *Rethinking New Testament Textual Criticism*.

———. "The Martyrdom of Polycarp and the New Testament Passion Narrative." Pages 407–32 in vol. 2 of *Trajectories Through the New Testament and the Apostolic Fathers*. Edited by Andrew Gregory and Christopher Tuckett. The New Testament and the Apostolic Fathers. Oxford: Oxford University Press, 2005.

———. "Textual Criticism." Pages 101–34 in *New Testament Criticism and Interpretation*. Edited by D. A. Black and D. S. Dockery. Grand Rapids: Zondervan, 1991.

———. "When Criteria Conflict." Pages 11–24 in Doble and Kloha, eds., *Texts and Traditions*.

Hoover, R. W. "How the Books of the New Testament Were Chosen." *Bible Review* 9 (1993): 44–47.

Horbury, W. "The Wisdom of Solomon in the Muratorian Fragment." *JTS* 45 (1994): 149–59.

Horsley, R. A., and J. S. Hanson. *Bandits, Prophets, and Messiahs: Popular Movements in the Time of Jesus*. San Francisco: Harper, 1985.

Houston, G. W. *Inside Roman Libraries: Book Collections and Their Management in Antiquity*. Studies in the History of Greece and Rome. Chapel Hill, NC: The University of North Carolina Press.

Hovhanessian, Vahan S., ed. *The Canon of the Bible and the Apocrypha in the Churches of the East*. Bible in the Christian Orthodox Tradition 2. New York: Lang, 2012.

———. "New Testament Apocrypha and the Armenian Version of the Bible." Pages 63–87 in Hovhanessian, ed., *The Canon of the Bible*.

Howorth, H. H. "The Origin and Authority of the Biblical Canon in the Anglican Church." *JTS* 8 (1906–1907): 1–40.

Hübner, H. "Vetus Testamentum und Vetus Testamentum in Novo receptum: Die Frage nach dem Kanon des Alten Testaments aus neutestamentlicher Sicht." *Jahrbuch für biblische Theologie* 3 (1988): 147–62.

Hughes, J. *Secrets of the Times: Myth and History in Biblical Chronology*. JSOTSup 66. Sheffield: JSOT Press, 1990.

Hull, Robert F. Jr. *The Story of the New Testament Text: Movers, Materials, Motives, Methods, and Models*. SBLRBS 58. Atlanta: Society of Biblical Literature, 2010.

Hultgren, A. J., and S. A. Haggmark, eds. *The Earliest Christian Heretics: Readings from Their Opponents*. Minneapolis: Fortress, 1996.

Hunt, Alice W. "Zadok, Zadokites." *NIDB* 5:952–54.

Hunt, H. "An Examination of the Current Emphasis on the Canon in Old Testament Studies." *Southwestern Journal of Theology* 23 (1980): 55–70.

Hurtado, L. W. *The Earliest Christian Artifacts: Manuscripts and Christian Origins.* Grand Rapids, MI: Eerdmans, 2006.

———. "The New Testament in the Second Century: Texts, Collections, and Canon." Pages 3–17 in *Transmission and Reception: New Testament Text-Critical and Exegetical Studies.* Edited by J. W. Childers and D. C. Parker. Piscataway, NJ: Gorgias, 2006.

———. "The Origins of the *Nomina Sacra*: A Proposal." *JBL* 117 (1998): 655–73.

———. "Religious Experience and Religious Innovation in the New Testament," *JR* 80 (2000): 271–88.

Hurtado, Larry W., and Chris Keith. "Writing and Book Production in the Hellenistic and Roman Periods," Pages 63–80 in Paget and Schaper, eds., *The New Cambridge History of the Bible*. Vol. 1, *From the Beginnings to 600.*

Hutchinson, Robert J. "What the Rabbi Taught Me About Jesus," *Christianity Today* (September 1993): 28.

Isaac, Ephraim. "The Bible in Ethiopic." Pages 110–22 Marsden and Matter, eds., *The New Cambridge History of The Bible: From 600–1450.*

Jacob, E. "Principe canonique et formation de l'Ancien Testament." Pages 101–22 of *Congress Volume: Edinburgh 1974.* Vetus Testamentum Supplement 28. Leiden: Brill, 1975.

Jacobs, Mignon R., and Raymond F. Person, Jr., eds. *Israelite Prophecy and the Deuteronomistic History: Portrait, Reality, and the Formation of a History.* Ancient Israel and Its Literature 14. Atlanta: Society of Biblical Literature, 2013.

Jeffery, A. "The Canon of the Old Testament." *IDB* 1:32–45.

Jenkins, P. *Hidden Gospels: How the Search for Jesus Lost Its Way.* Oxford: Oxford University Press, 2001.

Jenson, R. W. *Canon and Creed Interpretation.* Louisville: Westminster John Knox, 2010.

Jepsen, A. "Kanon und Text des Alten Testaments." *Theologische Literaturzeitung* 74 (1949): 65–74.

———. "Zur Kanongeschichte des Alten Testaments." *ZAW* 71 (1959): 114–36.

Jeremias, J. *The Unknown Sayings of Jesus.* 2nd ed. London: SPCK, 1964.

Jewett, Robert. *Romans: A Commentary.* Hermeneia. Minneapolis: Fortress, 2007.

Jobes, K. H., and M. Silva. *Invitation to the Septuagint.* Grand Rapids: Baker, 2000.

———. "Response to J. Barr's Review of Invitation to the Septuagint." *Review of Biblical Literature* (2002). Online: http://www.bookreviews.org/pdf/1341_3027.pdf. Reprinted in *Bulletin of the International Organization for Septuagint and Cognate Studies* 35 (2002): 43–46.

Johnson, L. T. "The New Testament's Anti-Jewish Slander and Conventions of Ancient Polemic." *JBL* 108 (1989): 419–41.

———. *Religious Experience in Earliest Christianity.* Minneapolis: Fortress, 1998.

———. *The Writings of the New Testament: An Interpretation.* Rev. ed. Philadelphia: Fortress, 1999.

Jonas, H. *The Gnostic Religion.* Boston: Beacon, 1963.

Jones, B. A. *The Formation of the Book of the Twelve: A Study in Text and Canon.* SBLDS 149. Atlanta: Scholars Press, 1995.

Jonge, M. de. "The Old Testament in the Pseudepigrapha." Pages 459–86 in Auwers and de Jonge, eds., *The Biblical Canons.*

Jurgens, W. A. *The Faith of the Early Fathers: A Source-book of Theological and Historical Passages from the Christian Writings of the Pre-Nicene and Nicene Eras.* Collegeville, MN: Liturgical Press, 1979.

Kaestli, J.-D. "La place du Fragment de Muratori dans l'histoire du canon." *Cristianesimo nella storia* 15 (1995): 609–34.

Kaestli, J.-D., and Otto Wermelinger, eds. *Canon de l'Ancien Testament: Sa formation et son histoire*. Geneva: Labor et Fides, 1984.

Kahle, P. E. *The Cairo Geniza*. 2nd ed. Oxford: Blackwell, 1959.

Kalin, E. R. "Argument from Inspiration in the Canonization of the New Testament." ThD diss., Harvard University, 1967.

———. "A Book Worth Discussing: Canon and Community: A Guide to Canonical Criticism." *Concordia Theological Monthly* 12 (1985): 310–12.

———. "Early Traditions About Mark's Gospel: Canonical Status Emerges, the Story Grows." *Concordia Theological Monthly* 2 (1975): 332–41.

———. "The Inspired Community: A Glance at Canon History." *Concordia Theological Monthly* 42 (1971): 541–49.

———. "The New Testament Canon of Eusebius." Pages 386–404 in McDonald and Sanders, eds., *The Canon Debate*.

———. "Re-examining New Testament Canon History, 1: The Canon of Origen." *Currents in Theology and Mission* 17 (1990): 274–82.

Kamesar, Adam. "Jerome," Pages 653–75 in *The New Cambridge History of the Bible*. Vol. 1, *From the Beginnings to 600*.

Käsemann, E. "The Canon of the New Testament and the Unity of the Church." Pages 95–107 in *Essays on New Testament Themes*. London: SCM, 1968.

———. *Das Neue Testament als Kanon: Dokumentation und kritische Analyse zur gegenwärtgen Discussion*. Göttingen: Vandenhoeck & Ruprecht, 1970.

Katz, Peter. "Justin's Old Testament Quotations and the Greek Dodekapropheten Scroll." Pages 343–53 in *Studia Patristica 1*. Edited by K. Aland and F. L. Cross. Berlin: Akademie-Verlag, 1957.

———. "The Old Testament Canon in Palestine and Alexandria." *ZNW* 47 (1956): 191–217.

———. *Philo's Bible: The Aberrant Text of Bible Quotations in Some Philonic Writings and Its Place in the Textual History of the Greek Bible*. Cambridge: Cambridge University Press, 1950.

Kealy, S. F. "The Canon: An African Contribution." *BTB* 9 (1979): 13–26.

Keck, L. E. "Scripture and Canon." *Quarterly Review* 3 (1983): 8–26.

Kee, H. C., ed. *Cambridge Annotated Study Apocrypha: New Revised Standard Version*. Cambridge: Cambridge University Press, 1994.

Keener, C. S. *Acts: An Exegetical Commentary*, 4 vols. Grand Rapids: Baker Academic, 2012–14.

———. *The IVP Bible Background Commentary: New Testament*. Downers Grove, IL: InterVarsity, 1993.

Keith, Chris, and Dieter T. Roth, eds. *Mark, Manuscripts, and Monotheism: Essays in Honor of Larry W. Hurtado*. LNTS 528. London: Bloomsbury T&T Clark, 2014.

Kelly, J. F. *Why Is There a New Testament?* Background Books 5. Wilmington, DE: Michael Glazier, 1986.

Kelly, J. N. D. *Early Christian Doctrines*. New York: Harper & Row, 1978.

Kelsey, D. H. *The Uses of Scripture in Recent Theology*. Philadelphia: Fortress, 1975.

Kenyon, F. G. *Our Bible and the Ancient Manuscripts*. Rev. A. V. Adams. New York: Harper & Brothers, 1958.

Kermode, F. "The Argument About Canons." Pages 78–96 in *The Bible and the Narrative Tradition*. Edited by F. McConnell. Oxford: Oxford University Press, 1986.

King, K. *The Gospel of Mary*. Santa Rosa, CA: Polebridge, 2003.

————. *Revelation of the Unknowable God with Text, Translation, and Notes to NHC IX,3 Allogenes.* Santa Rosa, CA: Polebridge, 1995.

Kinzig, W. "*Kaine diatheke*: The Title of the New Testament in the Second and Third Centuries." *JTS* 45 (1994): 519–44.

Klein, W. W., C. L. Blomberg, and R. L. Hubbard. *Introduction to Biblical Interpretation.* Dallas: Word, 1993.

Klijn, A. J. N. "Die Entstehungsgeschichte des Neuen Testaments." Pages 64–97 in *Aufstieg und Niedergang der römischen Welt: Geschichte und Kultur Roms im Spiegel der neueren Forschung 2.26.1.* Edited by H. Temporini and W. Hasse. Berlin: de Gruyter, 1992.

Knight, D. A. "Canon and the History of Tradition: A Critique of Brevard Childs' Introduction to the Old Testament as Scripture." *HBT* 2 (1980): 127–49.

Knoppers, Gary N. *1 Chronicles 1–9: A New Translation with Introduction and Commentary.* AB 12. New York: Doubleday, 2003.

Knox, John. *Marcion and the New Testament.* Chicago: University of Chicago Press, 1942.

Koch, K. "Pseudonymous Writing." Pages 712–14 in *Interpreter's Dictionary of the Bible: Supplementary Volume.* Edited by K. Crim. Nashville: Abingdon, 1976.

Koester, H. *Ancient Christian Gospels: Their History and Development.* Philadelphia: Trinity, 1990.

————. "Apocryphal and Canonical Gospels." *HTR* 73 (1980): 105–30.

————. "*Gnomai diaphoroi*: The Origin and Nature of Diversification in the History of Early Christianity." Pages 114–57 in Robinson and Koester, eds., *Trajectories Through Early Christianity.*

————. "The Intention and Scope of Trajectories." Pages 269–79 in Robinson and Koester, eds., *Trajectories Through Early Christianity.*

————. *Introduction to the New Testament.* 2 vols. 2nd ed. New York: de Gruyter, 1995–2000.

—— "Revelation 12:1–12: A Meditation." Pages 138–44 in *From Biblical Criticism to Biblical Faith: Essays in Honor of Lee Martin McDonald.* Edited by Craig A. Evans and W. H. Brackney. Macon, GA: Mercer University Press, 2007.

————. *Synoptische Überlieferung bei den apostolischen Vätern.* Texte und Untersuchungen 65. Berlin: Akademie-Verlag, 1957.

————. "The Text of the Synoptic Gospels in the Second Century." Pages 19–37 in *Gospel Traditions in the Second Century: Origins, Recensions, Text, and Transmission.* Edited by W. L. Petersen. Notre Dame: University of Notre Dame Press, 1989.

————. "Writings and the Spirit: Authority and Politics in Ancient Christianity." *HTR* 84 (1991): 353–72.

Kofoed, J. B. *Text History: Historiography and the Study of the Biblical Text.* Winona Lake, IN: Eisenbrauns, 2005.

Kohler, W.-D. *Die Rezeption des Matthäusevangeliums in der Zeit vor Irenaeus.* WUNT 2/24. Tübingen: Mohr Siebeck, 1987.

Köstenberger, Andreas. "Hearing the Old Testament in the New: A Response." Pages 255–94 in *Hearing the Old Testament in the New Testament.* Edited by S. E. Porter. Grand Rapids: Eerdmans, 2006.

Kooij, A. van der. "The Canonization of Ancient Books Kept in the Temple of Jerusalem." Pages 17–40 in *Canonization and Decanonization.* Edited by A. Van Der Kooij and L. Van Der Toorn. Studies in the History of Religions 82. Leiden: Brill, 1998.

Kooij, A. van der, and K. van der Toorn, eds. *Canonization and Decanonization.* Studies in the History of Religion 82. Leiden: Brill, 1998.

Koorevaar, Hendrik J. "Die Kronik als intendierter Abschuß des altestamentlischen Kanons." *JETh* 11 (1997): 42–76.

———. "The Torah Model as Original Macrostructure of the Hebrew Canon: A Critical Evaluation." *ZAW* 122 (2010): 64–80.

Kortner, U. H. J. *Papias von Hierapolis: Ein Beitrag zur Geschichte des frühen Christentums*. FRLANT 133. Göttingen: Vandenhoeck & Ruprecht, 1983.

Kraemer, D. "The Formation of Rabbinic Canon: Authority and Boundaries." *JBL* 110 (1991): 613–30.

———. "The Reception of the Bible in Rabbinic Judaism: A Study in Complexity." *Journal of the Bible and Its Reception* 1, no. 1 (2014): 29–46.

Kraus, Thomas J. *Ad Fontes: Original Manuscripts and Their Significance for Studying Early Christianity: Selected Essays*. TENT 3. Leiden: Brill, 2007.

Kraus, Thomas J., Michael J. Kruger, and Tobias Nicklas, eds. *Gospel Fragments: The "Unknown Gospel" on Papyrus Egerton 2, Papyrus Oxyrhynchus 840, Other Gospel Fragments*. Oxford Early Christian Gospel Texts. Oxford: Oxford University Press, 2009.

Kraus, Thomas J., and Tobias Nicklas. "The World of New Testament Manuscripts." Pages 1–11 in *New Testament Manuscripts: Their Texts and Their World*. Edited by T. J. Kraus and T. Nicklas. TENT 2. Leiden: Brill, 2006.

Kraus, W., and R. G. Wooden, eds. *Septuagint Research: Issues and Challenges in the Study of the Greek Jewish Scriptures*. SBLSCS 53. Edited by Melvin Peters. Atlanta: Society of Biblical Literature, 2006.

Kruger, M. J. *Canon Revisited: Establishing the Origins and Authority of the New Testament Books*. Wheaton, IL: Crossway, 2012.

———. "Early Christian Attitudes Toward the Reproduction of Texts." Pages 63–80 in Hill and Kruger, eds., *The Early Text of the New Testament*.

———. "Origen's List of New Testament Books in *Homiliae in Josuam* 7.1: A Fresh Look." Pages 99–117 in Keith and Roth, eds., *Mark, Manuscripts, and Monotheism*.

———. *The Question of Canon: Challenging the Status Quo in the New Testament Debate*. Downers Grove, IL: InterVarsity, 2013.

Kruger, Michael, and Tomas Bokedal. *The Formation and Significance of the Christian Biblical Canon: A Study in Text, Ritual and Interpretation*. London: Bloomsbury T&T Clark, 2014.

Kuck, D. W. "The Use and Canonization of Acts in the Early Church." PhD diss., Yale University, 1975.

Kugel, J. L., and R. A. Greer. *Early Biblical Interpretation*. Library of Early Christianity 3. Philadelphia: Westminster, 1986.

Kümmel, Werner G. "The Formation of the Canon of the New Testament." Pages 475–510 in *Introduction to the New Testament*. Translated by H. C. Kee. London: SCM, 1975.

———. *Introduction to the New Testament*. Translated by H. C. Kee. London: SCM, 1975.

Kurek-Chomycz, Dominika A. "Is There an 'Anti-Pricscan' Tendency in the Manuscripts? Some Textual Problems with Prisca and Aquila." *JBL* 125 (2006): 107–28.

Kurtzinger, J. *Papias von Hierapolis und die Evangelien des Neuen Testaments*. Regensberg: Pustet, 1983.

Ladd, G. E. *A Theology of the New Testament*. Grand Rapids: Eerdmans, 1974.

Lake, K., trans. *The Apostolic Fathers*. 2 vols. LCL. Cambridge, MA: Harvard University Press, 1912–13.

———. "The Sinaitic and Vatican Manuscripts and the Copies Sent by Eusebius to Constantine." *HTR* 11 (1918): 32–35.

Lampe, G. W. H. "The Early Church." In *Scripture and Tradition*. Edited by F. W. Dillistone. London: Lutterworth, 1995.

Lange, Armin. "Oral Collection and Canon: A Comparison Between Judah and Greece in Persian Times." Pages 9–47 in Evans and D. Zacharias, eds., *Jewish and Christian Scripture*.

————. "The Status of the Biblical Texts in the Qumran Corpus and the Canonical Process." Pages 20–30 in Herbert and Tov, eds., *Bible as Book*.

LaSor, W. S., D. A. Hubbard, and F. W. Bush. *Old Testament Survey: The Message, Form, and Background of the Old Testament*. Grand Rapids: Eerdmans, 1982.

Law, Timothy M. *When God Spoke Greek: The Septuagint and the Making of the Christian Bible*. Oxford: Oxford University Press, 2013.

Law, Timothy M., and Alison Salvesen. *Greek Scripture and the Rabbis*. BET 66. Leuven: Peeters, 2012.

Lawlor, H. J. "Early Citations from the Book of Enoch." *Journal of Philology* 25 (1897): 164–225.

Lawson, R. P. *The Song of Songs: Commentaries and Homilies*. Westminster, MD: Newman, 1957.

Layton, B. *The Gnostic Scriptures*. Garden City, NY: Doubleday 1987.

Le Boulluec, Alain. "The Bible in Use Among the Marginally Orthodox in the Second and Third Centuries." Pages 197–216 in *The Bible in Greek Christian Antiquity*. Edited by P. M. Blowers. Notre Dame: University of Notre Dame Press, 1997.

Lea, T. D. "The Early Christian View of Pseudepigraphic Writings." *JETS* 27 (1984): 65–75.

Leaney, A. R. C. *The Jewish and Christian World*. Cambridge: Cambridge University Press, 1984.

————. "Theophany, Resurrection, and History." *StEv* 103, no. 5 (1968): 101–13.

Lee, Kyong-Jin. *The Authority and Authorization of the Torah in the Persian Period*. CBET 64. Leuven: Peeters, 2011.

————. *The Jewish and Christian World, 200 B.C. to A.D. 200*. Cambridge Commentaries 7. Cambridge: Cambridge University Press, 1984.

Leiman, S. Z., ed. *The Canon and Masorah of the Hebrew Bible: An Introductory Reader*. New York: Ktav, 1974.

————. *The Canonization of the Hebrew Scripture: The Talmudic and Midrashic Evidence*. Hamden, CT: Archon, 1976.

————. "Inspiration and Canonicity: Reflections on the Formation of the Biblical Canon." Pages 56–63 and 315–18 in *Jewish and Christian Self-Definition*. Vol. 2, *Aspects of Judaism in the Graeco-Roman Period*. Edited by E. P. Sanders, A. I. Baumgarten, and A. Mendelson. Philadelphia: Fortress, 1981.

————. "Josephus and the Canon of the Bible." Pages 50–58 in *Josephus, the Bible, and History*. Edited by L. H. Feldman and G. Hata. Detroit: Wayne State University Press, 1989.

Lemcio, Eugene. "The Gospels and Canonical Criticism." *BTB* 11 (1981): 114–22.

Lesky, A. A *History of Greek Literature*. New York: Crowell, 1966.

Levine, L. I. *The Ancient Synagogue*. New Haven: Yale University Press, 2000.

Levison, John R. "Spirit, Holy." Pages 1252–55 in Collins and Harlow, eds., *The Eerdmans Dictionary of Early Judaism*.

Levy, B. B. *Fixing God's Torah: The Accuracy of the Hebrew Bible Text in Jewish Law*. Oxford: Oxford University Press, 2001.

Lewis, J. P. "Jamnia (Jabneh), Council of." *ABD* 3:634–37.

————. "Jamnia Revisited." Pages 146–62 in McDonald and Sanders, eds., *The Canon Debate*.

————. "Some Aspects of the Problems of Inclusion of the Apocrypha." Pages 161–207 in Meurer, ed., *The Apocrypha in Ecumenical Perspective*.

————. "What Do We Mean by Jabneh?" *Journal of Bible and Religion* 32 (1964): 125–32.

Lieberman, S. *Hellenism in Jewish Palestine*. New York: Jewish Theological Seminary, 1950, 1962.

Lienhard, Joseph T. *The Bible, the Church, and Authority: The Canon of the Christian Bible in History and Theology.* Collegeville, MN: Liturgical Press/Michael Glazier, 1995.

Lietzmann, H. "Wie wurden die Bucher des Neuen Testaments Heilige Schrift?" Pages 15–98 in *Kleine Schriften*, vol. 2. Edited by K. Aland. Texte und Untersuchungen 68. Berlin: Akademie, 1907.

Light, Laura. "The Thirteenth Century and the Paris Bible." Pages 380–91 in Marsden and Matter, eds., *The New Cambridge History of The Bible: From 600–1450.*

Lightfoot, John. *A Commentary on the New Testament from the Talmud and Hebraica.* Oxford: Oxford University Press, 1859. Repr. in Grand Rapids: Baker, 1979.

Lightstone, J. N. "The Formation of the Biblical Canon in Judaism of Late Antiquity: Prolegomenon to a General Reassessment." *Studies in Religion* 8 (1979): 135–42.

———. "Mishnah's Rhetoric, Other Material Artifacts of Late-Roman Galilee, and the Social Formation of the Early Rabbinic Guild." Pages 474–504 in *Text and Artifact in the Religions of Mediterranean Antiquity: Essays in Honour of Peter Richardson.* Edited by S. Wilson and M. Desjardins. Studies in Christianity and Judaism. Waterloo: WLU, 2000.

———. *Society, the Sacred, and Scripture in Ancient Judaism: A Sociology of Knowledge.* Studies in Christianity and Judaism 3. Waterloo, ON: Wilfrid Laurier University Press, 1988.

Lim, Johnson T. K., ed. *The Holy Spirit: Unfinished Agenda.* Singapore: Genesis–Word N Works, 2014.

Lim, Timothy H. " 'All These He Composed Through Prophecy'." Pages 61–73 in De Troyer and Lange, eds., *Prophecy after the Prophets.*

———. "The Alleged Reference to the Tripartite Division of the Hebrew Bible." *Revue de Qumran* 77 (2001): 23–37.

———. "Authoritative Scriptures and the Dead Sea Scrolls." Pages 303–22 in Lim and Collins, eds., *The Oxford Handbook of The Dead Sea Scrolls.*

———. "The Defilement of the Hands as a Principle Determining the Holiness of Scriptures," *JTS* 61, no. 2 (2010): 501–15.

———. *The Formation of the Jewish Canon.* AYBRL. New Haven: Yale University Press, 2013.

———. *Holy Scripture in the Qumran Commentaries and Pauline Letters.* Oxford: Clarendon, 1997.

———. "A Theory of the Majority Canon," *Expository Times* 124, no. 7 (2012): 1–9.

Lim, Timothy H., and John J. Collins. *The Oxford Handbook of The Dead Sea Scrolls.* Oxford: Oxford University Press, 2010.

Lim, Timothy H., Hector L MacQueen, and Calum M. Carmichael, eds. *On Scrolls, Artefacts and Intellectual Property.* JSPSup 38. Sheffield: Sheffield Academic, 2001.

Limberis, V. "The Battle Over Mary." *Bible Review* 17, no. 3 (2001): 22–23.

Lindemann, A. *Paulus im ältesten Christentum: Das Bild des Apostels und die Rezeption der paulinischen Theologie in der frühchristlichen Literatur bis Markion.* Beiträge zur historischen Theologie 58. Tübingen: Mohr Siebeck, 1979.

Link, H.-G. "Der Kanon in ökumenischer Sicht." *Jahrbuch für biblische Theologie* 3 (1988): 83–96.

Logan, A. H. B. *Gnostic Truth and Christian Heresy: A Study in the History of Gnosticism.* Peabody, MA: Hendrickson, 1996.

Lohr, W. A. "Kanonsgeschichtliche Beobachtungen zum Verhältnis von mundlicher und schriftlicher Tradition im zweiten Jahrhundert." *ZNW* 85 (1994): 234–58.

Lohse, E. *The New Testament Environment.* Translated by J. E. Steely. Nashville: Abingdon, 1976.

Lovering, E. H. "The Collection, Redaction, and Early Circulation of the Corpus Paulinum." PhD diss., Southern Methodist University, 1988.

Luhrmann, D. "Gal. 2.9 und die katholischen Briefe." *ZNW* 72 (1981): 65–87.

Luijendijk, AnneMarie. *"Greetings in the Lord": Early Christians and the Oxyrhynchus Papyri*. HTS 59. Cambridge, MA: Harvard University Press, 2008.

———. "Sacred Scriptures as Trash: Biblical Papyri from Oxyrhynchus." *VC* 64 (2010): 217–54.

Lupieri, E. *The Mandaeans: The Last Gnostics*. Translated by C. Hindley, Grand Rapids: Eerdmans, 2002.

Luttikhuizen, Gerard P. "The Thought Patterns of Gnostic Mythologizers and Their Use of Biblical Traditions." Pages 89–101 in *The Nag Hammadi Library After Fifty Years: Proceedings of the 1995 Society of Biblical Literature Commemoration*. Edited by J. D. Turner and A. McGuire. Leiden: Brill, 1997.

Luz, U. *Matthew 21–28: A Commentary*. Translated by J. E. Crouch. Hermeneia. Minneapolis: Fortress, 2005.

Maccoby, Hyam. *Early Rabbinic Writings*. Cambridge Commentaries on Writings of the Jewish & Christian World, 200 BC to AD 200. Cambridge: Cambridge University Press, 1988.

MacDonald, D. R. "Apocryphal New Testament." Pages 38–39 in Achtemeier et al., eds., *Harper's Bible Dictionary*.

———. *Christianizing Homer: "The Odyssey," Plato, and "The Acts of Andrew"*. New York: Oxford University Press, 1994.

———. *Does the New Testament Imitate Homer? Four Cases from the Acts of the Apostles*. New York: Yale University Press, 2003.

———. *The Homeric Epics and the Gospel of Mark*. New Haven: Yale University Press, 2000.

MacGregor, Geddes. *The Bible in the Making*. London: John Murray, 1961.

MacMullen, R. *Christianizing the Roman Empire (A.D. 100–400)*. New Haven: Yale University Press, 1984.

MacRae, G. W. "Why the Church Rejected Gnosticism." Pages 126–33 and 236–38 in *Jewish and Christian Self-Definition*. Vol. 1, *The Shaping of Christianity in the Second and Third Centuries*. Edited by E. P. Sanders. Philadelphia: Fortress, 1980.

Magness, J. *The Archaeology of Qumran and the Dead Sea Scrolls*. Grand Rapids: Eerdmans, 2002.

———. *Debating Qumran: Collected Essays on Its Archaeology*. Interdisciplinary Students in Ancient Culture and Religion 4. Leuven: Peeters, 2004.

Maier, J. "Zur Frage des biblischen Kanons im Frühjudentum im Licht der Qumranfunde." *Jahrbuch für biblische Theologie* 3 (1988): 135–46.

Malamat, A. "A Forerunner of Biblical Prophecy: The Mari Documents." Pages 33–52 in *Ancient Israelite Religion: Essays in Honor of Frank Moore Cross*. Edited by P. D. Miller, P. D. Hanson, and S. D. McBride. Philadelphia: Westminster, 1987.

Margolis, M. L. *The Hebrew Scriptures in the Making*. Philadelphia: Jewish Publication Society, 1922.

Marsden, Richard, and E. Ann Matter, eds. *The New Cambridge History of the Bible: From 600–1450*. Cambridge: Cambridge University Press, 2012.

Marshall, I. H. *The Pastoral Epistles*. ICC. Edinburgh: T. & T. Clark, 1999.

Martinez, Florentino Garcia, and Eibert J. C. Tigchelaar. *The Dead Sea Scrolls: Study Edition*. Leiden: Brill. Grand Rapids: Eerdmans, 1998.

Marxsen, Willi. *The New Testament as the Church's Book*. Translated by James E. Mignard. Philadelphia: Fortress, 1972.

Mason, S. "Josephus and His Twenty-two Book Canon." Pages 110–27 in McDonald and Sanders, eds., *The Canon Debate*.

———. *Life of Josephus: Translation and Commentary*. Flavius Josephus Translation and Commentary 9. Leiden: Brill, 2000.

Massaux, E. *The Influence of the Gospel of Saint Matthew on Christian Literature Before Saint Irenaeus*. Translated by N. J. Belval and S. Hecht. Edited by A. J. Bellinzoni. New Gospel Studies 5/1–3. Macon, GA: Mercer University Press, 1990–93.

McArthur, H. K. "The Eusebian Sections and Canons." *CBQ* 27 (1965): 250–56.

McDonald, Lee Martin. "Ancient Biblical Manuscripts and the Biblical Canon." Pages 255–81 in *Pseudepigrapha and Christian Origins: Essays from the Studiorum Novi Testamenti Societas*. T&T Clark Jewish and Christian Texts Series 4. New York: T&T Clark, 2008.

———. "Anti-Judaism in the Early Church Fathers." Pages 215–52 in *Anti-Semitism and Early Christianity: Issues of Polemic and Faith*. Edited by C. A. Evans and D. A. Hagner. Minneapolis: Fortress, 1993.

———. "Bible: Christian Scripture and Other Writings." Pages 381–90 in vol. 1 of *The Oxford Encyclopedia of Ancient Greece and Rome*. Edited by Michael Gargarin. Oxford: Oxford University Press, 2010.

———. *The Biblical Canon: Its Origin, Transmission, and Authority*. Grand Rapids: Baker Academic, 2007, 2011.

———. "Canon." Pages 777–809 in *The Oxford Handbook of Biblical Studies*. Edited by J. W. Rogerson and J. M. Lieu. Oxford: Oxford University Press, 2006.

———. "Canon (of Scripture)." Pages 205–10 in *Encyclopedia of Early Christianity*. Edited by E. Ferguson. 2nd ed. New York: Garland, 1997.

———. "Canon of the New Testament." Pages 536–47 in vol. 1 of *The New Interpreter's Dictionary of the Bible*. Edited by Katherine D. Sakenfeld. Nashville: Abingdon, 2006.

———. "Canons and Rules of Faith." In *The Oxford Handbook of Early Christian Biblical Interpretation*. Edited by Paul M. Blowers and Peter W. Martens. Oxford: Oxford University Press, Forthcoming.

———. "The First Testament: Its Origin, Adaptability, and Stability." Pages 287–326 in *From Tradition to Interpretation: Studies in Biblical Intertextuality in Honor of James A. Sanders*. Edited by C. A. Evans and S. Talmon. Biblical Interpretation Series 18. Leiden: Brill, 1997.

———. *Forgotten Scriptures: The Selection and Rejection of Early Religious Writings*. Louisville, KY: Westminster John Knox, 2009.

———. *Formation of the Bible: The Story of the Church's Canon*. Peabody, MA: Hendrickson, 2012.

———. *The Formation of the Christian Biblical Canon*. 2nd ed. Peabody, MA: Hendrickson, 1995.

———. "(Gospel) Prologues." *ABD* 1:262–63.

———. "The Gospels in Early Christianity: Their Origin, Use, and Authority." Pages 150–78 in *Reading the Gospels Today*. Edited by S. E. Porter. Grand Rapids: Eerdmans, 2004.

———. "Hellenism and the Biblical Canons: Is There a Connection?" Pages 13–49 in *Christian Origins and Hellenistic Judaism: Social and Literary Contexts for the New Testament*. Edited by S. E. Porter and A. W. Pitts. Early Christianity in Its Hellenistic Context 2. Leiden: Brill, 2013.

———. "The Holy Spirit and Scriptural Canons." Pages 107–11 in Lim, ed., *The Holy Spirit*.

———. "Identifying Scripture and Canon in the Early Church: The Criteria Question." Pages 416–39 in McDonald and Sanders, eds., *The Canon Debate*.

———. "Lost Books." Pages 581–87 in vol. 1 of Coogan, ed., *The Oxford Encyclopedia of the Books of the Bible*.

———. "Non-canonical: Religious Texts in Early Judaism and Early Christianity." Pages 1–8 in McDonald and Charlesworth, eds. *"Non-Canonical" Religious Texts*.

———. "The *Odes of Solomon* in Ancient Christianity: Reflections on Scripture and Canon." Pages 108–36 in Charlesworth and McDonald, eds., *Sacra Scriptura*.

———. *The Origin of the Bible: A Guide for the Perplexed*. London: T&T Clark, 2011.

———. "The Parables of Enoch in Early Christianity." Pages 329–63 in Bock and Charlesworth, eds., *Parables of Enoch*.

———. "Pseudonymous Writings and the New Testament." Pages 367–78 in Green and McDonald, eds., *The World of the New Testament*.

———. "The Reception of the Writings and Their Place in the Biblical Canon," In *The Oxford Handbook of the Writings of the Hebrew Bible*. Edited by Donn F. Morgan. Oxford: Oxford University Press, forthcoming 2017.

———. Review of Vahan S. Hovhanessian, ed., *The Canon of the Bible and the Apocrypha in the Churches of the East. RBL*, September 27, 2013. Online: http://www.bookreviews.org/bookdetail.asp?TitleId=8951.

———. "The Scriptures of Jesus: Did He Have a Biblical Canon?" Pages 827–62 in *Jesus Research: New Methodologies and Perceptions*. Edited by James H. Charlesworth, with Brian Rhea and Petr Pokorny. Second Princeton-Prague Symposium on Jesus Research. Grand Rapids, MI: Eerdmans, 2014.

———. *The Story of Jesus in History and Faith: An Introduction*. Grand Rapids: Baker Academic, 2013.

———. "What Do We Mean By Canon? Ancient and Modern Questions." Pages 8–40 in McDonald and Charlesworth, eds., *"Non-Canonical" Religious Texts*.

McDonald, Lee Martin, and James H. Charlesworth, eds. *"Non-canonical" Religious Texts in Early Judaism and Early Christianity*. T&T Clark Jewish and Christian Texts Series 14. London: Bloomsbury, 2012.

McDonald, L. M., and S. E. Porter. *Early Christianity and Its Sacred Literature*. Peabody, MA: Hendrickson, 2000.

McDonald, Lee Martin, and J. A. Sanders, eds. *The Canon Debate*. Peabody, MA: Hendrickson, 2002.

McGrath, A. *In the Beginning: The Story of the King James Bible and How It Changed a Nation, a Language, and a Culture*. New York: Random House, 2001.

McLay, R. T. "Biblical Texts and the Scriptures for the New Testament Church." In *Hearing the Old Testament Through the New: The Use of the Old Testament in the New Testament*. Edited by S. E. Porter. McMaster New Testament Studies. Grand Rapids: Eerdmans, Forthcoming.

———. Review of M. Hengel, *The Septuagint as Christian Scripture. Bulletin of the International Organization for Septuagint and Cognate Studies* 36 (2003): 139–43.

———. *The Use of the Septuagint in New Testament Research*. Grand Rapids: Eerdmans, 2003.

Meade, D. G. *Pseudonymity and Canon: An Investigation into the Relationship of Authorship and Authority in Jewish and Earliest Christian Tradition*. Grand Rapids: Eerdmans, 1986.

Meecham, Henry G. *The Letter of Aristeas*. Manchester: Manchester University Press, 1935.

———. *The Oldest Version of the Bible*. London: Holborn, 1932.

Metzger, B. M. *The Bible in Translation: Ancient and English Versions*. Grand Rapids: Baker, 2001.

———. "Canon of the New Testament." Pages 123–27 in *Dictionary of the Bible*. Edited by J. Hastings. Edinburgh: T. & T. Clark, 1963.

———. *The Canon of the New Testament: Its Origin, Development, and Significance*. Oxford: Clarendon, 1987.

———. "Explicit References in the Works of Origen to Variant Readings in New Testament Manuscripts." Pages 78–95 in *Biblical and Patristic Studies in Memory of Robert Pierce Casey*. Edited by J. N. Birdsell and R. W. Thomson. Freiberg: Herder, 1963.

———. "The Formulas Introducing Quotations of Scripture in the New Testament and in the Mishnah." Pages 52–63 in *Historical and Literary Studies: Pagan, Jewish, and Christian*. Edited by B. M. Metzger. NTTS 8. Leiden: Brill, 1968.

———. "The Future of New Testament Textual Studies." Pages 201–8 in McKendrick and O'Sullivan, eds., *The Bible as Book*, 203

———. "Introduction to Apocryphal/Deuterocanonical Books." Pages iii–xv in *The New Oxford Annotated Bible with the Apocryphal/Deuterocanonical Books*. Edited by B. M. Metzger and R. E. Murphy. New York: Oxford University Press, 1991.

———. *An Introduction to the Apocrypha*. New York: Oxford University Press, 1957.

———. "Literary Forgeries and Canonical Pseudepigrapha." *JBL* 91 (1972): 3–24.

———. "St Jerome's Explicit References to Variant Readings in Manuscripts of the New Testament." Pages 179–90 in *Text and Interpretation. Studies in the New Testament Presented to Matthew Black*. Edited by E. Best and R. McL. Wilson. Cambridge: Cambridge University Press, 1979.

Metzger, B. M., and B. D. Ehrman. *The Text of the New Testament: Its Transmission, Corruption, and Restoration*. 3rd ed. New York: Oxford University Press, 1992.

Meurer, S., ed. *The Apocrypha in Ecumenical Perspective: The Place of the Late Writings of the Old Testament Among the Biblical Writings and Their Significance in the Eastern and Western Church Traditions*. Edited by Translated by P. Ellingworth. United Bible Societies Monograph Series 6. New York: United Bible Societies, 1991.

Meyer, Eric M. "Khirbet Qumran and Its Environs." Pages 21–45 in Lim and Collins, eds., *The Oxford Handbook of the Dead Sea Scrolls*.

Meyer, R. "προφήτης, *ktl.* " *TDNT* 6:812–28.

———. "Bemerkungen zum literargeschichtlichen Hintergrund der Kanontheorie des Josephus." Pages 285–99 in *Josephus-Studien: Untersuchungen zu Josephus, d. antiken Judentum u. d. Neuen Testament: Otto Michel z. 70. Geburtstag gewidmet*. Edited by Otto Betz, Klaus Haacker and Martin Hengel. Göttingen: Vandenhoeck & Ruprecht, 1974.

———. "Supplement on the Canon and the Apocrypha." *TDNT* 3:978–87.

Michaels, J. R. "Inerrancy or Verbal Inspiration? An Evangelical Dilemma." Pages 49–70 in *Inerrancy and Common Sense*. Edited by R. R. Nicole and J. R. Michaels. Grand Rapids: Baker, 1980.

Milavec, A. *The Didache: Faith, Hope, and Life of the Earliest Christian Communities, 50–70 C.E.* New York: Newman, 2003.

Milgrom, J. "An Amputated Bible, Peradventure." *Bible Review* 39 (1994): 17, 55.

Milik, J. T. *Ten Years of Discovery in the Wilderness of Judaea*. Translated by J. Strugnell. Studies in Biblical Theology 26. London: SCM, 1959.

Miller, J. D. *The Pastoral Letters as Composite Documents*. SNTSMS 93. Cambridge: Cambridge University Press, 1997.

Miller, J. W. *How the Bible Came to Be: Exploring the Narrative and Message*. Mahwah, NJ: Paulist, 2004.

———. *The Origins of the Bible: Rethinking Canon History*. Theological Inquiries. New York: Paulist, 1994.

Miller, P. D. "Der Kanon in der gegenwärtigen amerikanischen Diskussion." *Jahrbuch für biblische Theologie* 3 (1988): 217–39.

Mitchell, Margaret M. "The Emergence of the Written Record." Pages 177–94 in *The Cambridge History of Christianity*. Vol. 1, *Origins to Constantine*. Edited by M. Mitchell and F. M. Young. Cambridge: Cambridge University Press, 2006.

Montague Rhodes James. *The Lost Apocrypha of the Old Testament: Their Titles and Fragments*. London: Society for Promoting Christian Knowledge. New York: Macmillan, 1920.

Moo, Douglas J. *Romans*. NICNT. Grand Rapids: Eerdmans, 1996.

Morgan, Donn F. *Between Text and Community: The "Writings" in Canonical Interpretation*. Minneapolis: Fortress, 1990.

Moore, C. A. *Daniel, Esther, and Jeremiah: The Additions*. AB 44. Garden City, NY: Doubleday, 1977.

Moore, C. F., trans. *Tacitus: The Histories*. 2 vols. LCL. Cambridge. MA: Harvard University Press, 1931–37.

Moore, G. F. "*Conjectanea Talmudica*: Notes on Rev 13:18; Matt 23:35f.; 28:1; 2 Cor 2:14–16; Jubilees 34:4, 7; 7:4." *JAOS* (1905): 315–33

———. "The Definition of the Jewish Canon and the Repudiation of Christian Scriptures." Pages 99–125 in Leiman, ed., *Canon and Masorah of the Hebrew Bible*.

Morgan, Donn F. *Between Text and Community: The "Writings" in Canonical Interpretation*. Minneapolis: Fortress, 1990.

———. "Canon and Criticism: Method or Madness?" *Australasian Theological Review* 68 (1986): 83–94.

Morgan, R. L. "Let's Be Honest About the Canon: A Plea to Reconsider a Question the Reformers Failed to Answer." *Christian Century* 84 (1967): 717–19.

Morrice, W. *Hidden Sayings of Jesus: Words Attributed to Jesus Outside the Four Gospels*. Peabody, MA: Hendrickson, 1997.

Mulder, M. J., ed. *Mikra: Text, Translation, Reading, and Interpretation of the Hebrew Bible in Ancient Judaism and Early Christianity*. Compendia rerum iudaicarum ad Novum Testamentum 2/1. Minneapolis: Fortress, 1990.

Müller, M. *The First Bible of the Church*. Sheffield: JSOT Press, 1996.

Müller, Mogens, and Henrik Tronier, eds. *The New Testament as Reception*. Copenhagen International Seminar 11. JSNTSup 230. London: Sheffield Academic, 2002.

Müller, Reinhard, Juha Pakkala, and Bas ter Haar Romeny, eds. *Evidence of Editing: Growth and Change of Texts in the Hebrew Bible*. Atlanta: Society of Biblical Literature, 2014.

Munier, Ch. "Canonical Collections." Pages 141–43 in vol. 1 of *Encyclopedia of the Early Church*. Edited by Angelo Di Berardino. New York: Oxford University Press, 1992.

Murphy, R. E. "A Symposium on the Canon of Scripture: 1. The Old Testament Canon in the Catholic Church." *CBQ* 28 (1966): 189–93.

Murray, Robert. "How Did the Church Determine the Canon of the New Testament?" *HeyJ* 11 (1970): 115–26.

Müssner, Franz *The Historical Jesus in the Gospel of John*. Translated by W. J. O'Harah. New York: Herder & Herder, 1966.

Nagy, Gregory. *The Best of the Achaeans: Concepts of the Hero in Archaic Greek Poetry*. Baltimore: Johns Hopkins University Press, 1979.

———. "The Library of Pergamon as a Classical Model." Pages 185–232 in *Pergamon: Citadel of the Gods*. Edited by H. Koester. HTS 46. Harrisburg, PA: Trinity Press International.

———. *Pindar's Homer: The Lyric Possession of an Epic Past*. Baltimore: Johns Hopkins University Press, 1990.

Nelson, R. S. "Canons." Page 374 in vol. 1 of *Oxford Dictionary of Byzantium*. Edited by P. Kazhdan. New York: Oxford University Press, 1991.

Neusner, J. "The Formation of Rabbinic Judaism: Yavneh (Jamnia) from A.D. 70–100." Pages 3–42 in vol. 2 of *Aufsteig und Niedergang der römischen Welt: Geschichte und Kultur Roms im Spiegel der Neueren Forschung, Principat*. Edited by W. Haase. Berlin: de Gruyter, 1979.

———. *Judaism and Christianity in the Age of Constantine: History, Messiah, Israel, and the Initial Confrontation*. Chicago: University of Chicago Press, 1987.

———, "Masorah." Page 415 in vol. 2 of *Dictionary of Judaism in the Biblical Period: 450 BCE to 600 CE*. Edited by Jacob Neusner and W. S. Green. New York: Macmillan, 1996.

———. *Messiah in Context: Israel's History and Destiny in Formative Judaism*. Philadelphia: Fortress, 1984.

———. *Midrash in Context: Exegesis in Formative Judaism*. Philadelphia: Fortress, 1983.

———. "The Mishna in Philosophical Context and out of Canonical Bounds." *JBL* 112 (1993): 291–304.

———. "Rabbinic Judaism in Late Antiquity." Pages 72–84 in *Judaism: A People and Its History*. Edited by R. M. Seltzer. New York: Macmillan, 1989.

———. *Rabbinic Literature and the New Testament: What We Cannot Show, We Do Not Know*. Valley Forge, PA: Trinity, 1994.

———. *The Rabbinic Tradition About the Pharisees Before 70*. 3 vols. Leiden: Brill, 1971.

———. *The Talmud: A Close Encounter*. Minneapolis: Fortress, 1991.

———. "Targums in the New Testament." Pages 616–617 in vol. 2 of *Dictionary of Judaism in the Biblical Period: 450 B.C.E.–600 C.E.* Edited by J. Neusner. New York: Simon & Schuster, 1996.

———. *The Tosefta*. 2 vols. Peabody, MA: Hendrickson, 2002.

Neusner, J., and W. S. Green. *Writing with Scripture: The Authority and Uses of the Hebrew Bible in the Torah of Formative Judaism*. Minneapolis: Fortress, 1989.

Nicholson, Ernest W. *Deuteronomy and the Judaean Diaspora*. Oxford: Oxford University Press, 2014.

Nickelsburg, George. "Enoch." *ABD* 2:516.

Niditch, Susan. *Oral Word and Written Word*. Library of Ancient Israel. Nashville: Westminster John Knox, 1996.

Niederwimmer, K. *The Didache: A Commentary*. Edited by H. W. Attridge. Translated by L. M. Maloney. Hermeneia. Minneapolis: Fortress, 1998.

Niehoff, Maren R., ed. *Homer and the Bible in the Eyes of Ancient Interpreters*. JSRC 16. Leiden: Brill, 2012.

Nienhuis, David R., and Robert W. Wall. *Reading The Epistles of James, Peter, John and Jude: The Shaping and Shape of a Canonical Collection*. Grand Rapids: Eerdmans, 2013.

Nigosian, S. A. *From Ancient Writings to Sacred Texts: The Old Testament and Apocrypha*. Baltimore: The Johns Hopkins University Press, 2004.

Nissinen, Martti. "Pesharim as Divination. Qumran Exegesis, Omen Interpretation and Literary Prophecy." Pages 43–60 in De Troyer and Lange, eds., *Prophecy After the Prophets*.

Nissinen, Martti, C. L. Seow, and Robert L. Ritner. *Prophets and Prophecy in the Ancient Near East*. SBL Writings from the Ancient World 12. Atlanta: Society of Biblical Literature, 2003.

Nordenfalk, Carl. "The Apostolic Canon Tables." *Gazette des beaux–arts* 62 (1963): 17–34.

North, J. Lionel. "The Use of the Latin Fathers for New Testament Textual Criticism." Pages 208–23 in Ehrman and Holmes, eds., *The Text of the New Testament in Contemporary Research*.

Oepke, Alrecht. "κρύπτω, ktl." *TDNT* 3:957–1000.

Ofer, Yosef. "The Shattered Crown: The Aleppo Codex 60 Years After the Riots." *BAR* 34, no. 5 (2008): 39–49.

Ohlig, K.-H. *Die theologische Begründung des neutestamentlichen Kanons in der alten Kirche.* Düsseldorf: Patmos, 1972.

———. *Woher nimmt die Bibel ihre Autorität? Zum Verhältnis von Schriftkanon, Kirche und Jesus.* Düsseldorf: Patmos, 1970.

Oikonomos, E. "The Significance of the Deuterocanonical Writings in the Orthodox Church." Pages 16–32 in Meurer, ed., *The Apocrypha in Ecumenical Perspective.*

Oliver, William G. "Origen and the New Testament Canon." *Restoration Quarterly* 31 (1989): 13–26.

O'Neill, J. C. "The Lost Written Records of Jesus' Words and Deeds Behind Our Records." *JTS* 42 (1991): 483–503.

Orlinsky, Harry M. "Some Terms in the Prologue to Ben Sira and the Hebrew Canon." *JBL* 110 (1991): 483–90.

Osiek, C. "The Shepherd of Hermas: An Early Tale That Almost Made It into the New Testament." *Bible Review* 10 (1994): 48–54.

———. *The Shepherd of Hermas.* Hermeneia. Minneapolis: Fortress, 1999.

Ossandón, Juan Carlos, "On The Formation of the Biblical Canon: An Extended Review of L. M. McDonald's Book." *Annales Theologici* 24 (2010): 437–52.

Oulton, J. E. L., and H. Chadwick, eds. *Alexandrian Christianity: Selected Translations of Clement and Origen.* Library of Christian Classics 2. Philadelphia: Westminster, 1954.

Outler, A. C. "The 'Logic' of Canon Making and the Tasks of Canon-Criticism." Pages 263–76 in *Texts and Testaments: Critical Essays on the Bible and the Early Church Fathers.* Edited by W. E. March. San Antonio: Trinity University Press, 1980.

Oxford Society of Historical Theology: The New Testament in the Apostolic Fathers. Oxford: Clarendon, 1905. [No author listed.]

Paap, A. H. R. E. *Nomina Sacra in the Greek Papyri of the First Five Centuries AD: The Sources and Some Deductions.* Leiden: Brill, 1959.

Pagels, E. "Visions, Appearances and Apostolic Authority: Gnostic and Orthodox Traditions." Pages 415–30 in *Gnosis: Festschrift für Hans Jonas.* Edited by B. Aland. Göttingen: Vandenhoeck & Ruprecht, 1978.

Paget, J. C., and J. Schaper, eds. *The New Cambridge History of the Bible.* Vol. 1, *From the Beginnings to 600.* Cambridge: Cambridge University Press, 2013.

Pakkala, Juha. *Ezra the Scribe: The Development of Ezra 7–10 and Nehemiah 8.* BZAW 347. Berlin: de Gruyter, 2004.

———. *God's Word Omitted: Omissions in the Transmission of the Hebrew Bible.* FRLANT 251. Göttingen: Vandenhoeck & Ruprecht, 2013.

Painchaud, Louis. "The Use of Scripture in Gnostic Literature." *JECS* 4 (1996): 129–47.

Parker, David C. *The Living Text of the Gospels.* Cambridge: Cambridge University Press, 1997.

———. "The New Testament Text and Versions," Pages 412–54 in Paget and Schaper, eds., *The New Cambridge History of the Bible.* Vol. 1, *From the Beginnings to 600.*

———. "Variants and Variance." Pages 25–34 in Doble and Kloha, eds., *Texts and Traditions.*

Parmenter, Dorina Miller. "The Bible as Icon: Myths of the Divine Origins of Scripture." Pages 298–309 in Evans and Zacharias, eds., *Jewish and Christian Scripture.*

Parpulov, Georgi R. "The Bibles of the Christian East." Pages 309–24 in Marsden and Matter, eds., *The New Cambridge History of The Bible: From 600–1450.*

Patte, C. M. *Communities of the Last Days: The Dead Sea Scrolls, the New Testament, and the Story of Israel.* Downers Grove, IL: InterVarsity, 2000.

Patterson, L. G. "Irenaeus and the Valentinians: The Emergence of the Christian Scriptures." Pages 189–220 in *Studia Patristica 18.3*. Edited by E. A. Livingstone. Leuven: Peeters, 1989.

Pattie, T. S. "The Creation of the Great Codices." Pages 61–72 in Sharpe and Van Kampen, eds., *The Bible as Book*.

Patzia, A. G. "Canon." Pages 85–92 in *Dictionary of Paul and His Letters*. Edited by G. F. Hawthorne and R. P. Martin. Downers Grove, IL: InterVarsity, 1993.

———. *The Making of the New Testament: Origin, Collection, Text and Canon*. Downers Grove, IL: InterVarsity, 1995, 2nd ed. 2011.

Paulsen, Henning. "Die Bedeutung des Montanismus für die Herausbildung des Kanons." *VC* 32 (1978): 19–52.

Payne, Philip B. *Man and Woman, One in Christ: An Exegetical and Theological Study of Paul's Letters*. Grand Rapids: Zondervan, 2009.

Paz, Yakir. "Re-Scripturalizing Traditions: Designating Dependence in Rabbinic Halakhic and Homeric Scholarship." Pages 269–98 in *Homer and the Bible in the Eyes of Ancient Interpreters*. Edited by Maren R. Niehoff. Leiden: Brill, 2012.

Pearson, Birger A. *Gnosticism, Judaism, and Egyptian Christianity*. Minneapolis: Fortress, 1990.

———. "Gnostic Interpretation of the Old Testament in the Testimony of Truth (NHC IX.3)." *HTR* 73 (1980): 311–19.

———. "James, 1–2 Peter, Jude." Pages 371–406 in *The New Testament and Its Modern Interpreters*. Edited by E. J. Epp and G. W. MacRae. Society of Biblical Literature: The Bible and Its Modern Interpreters 3. Philadelphia: Fortress. Atlanta: Scholars Press, 1989.

———. "Use, Authority and Exegesis of Miqra in Gnostic Literature." Pages 635–52 in Mulder, ed., *Mikra*.

Peels, H. G. L. "The Blood 'from Abel to Zechariah' (Matthew 23,35; Luke 11,50f). and the Canon of the Old Testament." *ZAW* 113 (2001): 583–601.

Pelikan, J. *Whose Bible Is It? A History of the Scriptures Through the Ages*. New York: Viking Penguin, 2005.

Penner, Kenneth M. "Citation Formulae as Indices to Canonicity in Early Jewish and Early Christian Literature." Pages 62–84 in McDonald and Charlesworth, eds., *"Non-Canonical" Religious Texts*.

———. "Dead Sea Scrolls." Pages 173–92 in vol. 1 of Coogan, ed., *The Oxford Encyclopedia of the Books of the Bible*.

Pentiuc, Eugen J. *The Old Testament in Eastern Orthodox Tradition*. Oxford: Oxford University Press, 2014.

Perkes, K. S. L. "Scripture Revision Won't Be a Bible." *Arizona Republic*, October 24, 1993, B1, B4.

Perkins, P. *The Gnostic Dialogue*. New York: Paulist, 1980.

———. "Gnosticism and the Christian Bible." Pages 355–71 in McDonald and Sanders, eds., *The Canon Debate*.

———. *Gnosticism and the New Testament*. Minneapolis: Fortress, 1993.

———. "Spirit and Letter: Poking Holes in the Canon." *Journal of Religion* 76 (1996): 307–27.

Perrin, N. *Thomas and Tatian: The Relationship Between The Gospel of Thomas and the Diatessaron*. Academia Biblica 5. Leiden: Brill, 2002.

Petersen, W. L. "The Diatessaron of Tatian." Pages 77–96 in *The Text of the New Testament in Contemporary Research: Essays on the Status Quaestionis: A Volume in Honor of Bruce M. Metzger*. Edited by B. D. Ehrman and M. W. Holmes. Studies and Documents 46. Grand Rapids: Eerdmans, 1995.

―――. "Tatian's Diatessaron." Pages 403–30 in *Ancient Christian Gospels: Their History and Development*. Edited by Helmut Koester. Philadelphia: Trinity, 1990.

―――. *Tatian's Diatessaron: Its Creation, Dissemination, Significance, and History in Scholarship*. VCSup 25. Leiden: Brill, 1994.

―――. "Textual Evidence of Tatian's Dependence Upon Justin's 'APOMNEMONEUMATA.'" *NTS* 36 (1990): 512–34.

Pfeiffer, R. H. "Canon of the OT." *IDB* 1:498–520.

―――. *History of Classical Scholarship: From the Beginnings to the End of the Hellenistic Age*. Oxford: Clarendon, 1968.

Pietersma, Albert, and Benjamin G. Wright, eds. *A New English Translation of the Septuagint*. New York: Oxford University Press, 2007.

Pilhofer, P. "Justin und das Petrusevangelium." *ZNW* 81 (1990): 60–78.

Pirie, P. W. "Callimachus." Pages 276–78 in *The Oxford Classical Dictionary*. Edited by Simon Hornblower and Antony Spawforth. 3rd ed. Oxford: Oxford University Press, 1996.

Plaks, Andrew. "Afterword: Canonization in the Ancient World: The View from Farther East." Pages 267–76 in Finkelberg and Stroumsa, eds., *Homer, the Bible, and Beyond*.

Plisch, Uwe-Karsten. *The Gospel of Thomas: Original Text with Commentary*. Translated from German by Gesine S. Robinson. Stuttgart: Germany: Deutsche Bibelgesellschaft, 2008.

Porter, S. E. "Canon, New Testament," Coogan, ed., *The Oxford Encyclopedia of the Books of the Bible* 1:109–120.

―――. *How We Got the New Testament: Text, Transmission, Translation*. ASBT. Grand Rapids: Baker Academic, 2013.

―――, ed. *The Language of the New Testament: Classic Essays*. Sheffield: JSOT Press, 1991.

―――. "Pauline Authorship and the Pastoral Epistles: Implications for Canon." *BBR* 5 (1995): 105–23.

―――. ed. *The Pauline Canon*. Leiden: Brill, 2004.

―――. "When and How Was the Pauline Canon Compiled? An Assessment of Theories." Pages 95–128 in Porter, ed., *The Pauline Canon*.

―――. "Why So Many Holes in the Papyrological Evidence for the Greek New Testament?" Pages 167–86 in McKendrick and O'Sullivan, eds., *The Bible as Book*.

Porter, Stanley E., and Gregory P. Fewster, eds. *Paul and Pseudepigraphy*. PAST 8. Leiden: Brill, 2013.

Porter, S. E., and Andrew W. Pitts. *Fundamentals of New Testament Textual Criticism*. Grand Rapids: Eerdmans, 2015.

―――. "Paul's Bible, His Education and His Access to the Scriptures of Israel." *JGRChJ* 5 (2008): 9–41.

Porton, G. G. "Sadducees." *ABD* 5:892–95.

Powrey, Emerson B. *Jesus Reads Scripture: The Function of Jesus' Use of Scripture in the Synoptic Gospels*. BINS. Leiden: Brill, 2003.

Pretty, Robert A., *Adamantius: Dialogue on the True Faith in God: De Recta in Deum Fide*. Edited by Garry W. Trompf. Leuven: Peeters, 1997.

Price, R. M. "The Evolution of the Pauline Canon." *Hervormde teologiese studies* 53 (1997): 36–67.

Prinsloo, Willem S. "The Psalms." Pages 364–436 in *Eerdmans Commentary on the Bible*. Edited by James D. G. Dunn and John W. Rogerson. Grand Rapids: Eerdmans, 2003.

Purvis, J. D. *The Samaritan Pentateuch and the Origin of the Samaritan Sect*. Harvard Semitic Monographs 2. Cambridge, MA: Harvard University Press, 1968.

―――. "The Samaritans and Judaism." Pages 81–98 in *Early Judaism and Its Modern Interpreters*. Edited by R. A. Kraft and G. W. E. Nickelsburg. Atlanta: Scholars Press, 1986.

Pury, Albert de. "The Ketubim, a Canon within the Canon." Pages 41–56 in Alexander and Kaestli, eds., *The Canon of Scripture*.

Qimron, E., and J. Strugnell. *Qumran Cave 4.V: Miqsat Ma'ase ha-Torah*. DJD 10. Oxford: Clarendon, 1994.

Quasten, J. *Patrology*. Vol. 2, *The Ante-Nicene Literature After Irenaeus*. Utrecht-Antwerp: Spectrum, 1950, 1975.

Quinn, J. D., and W. Wacker. *The First and Second Letters to Timothy*. Eerdmans Critical Commentary. Grand Rapids: Eerdmans, 2000.

Quispel, G. "Marcion and the Text of the New Testament." *VC* 52 (1998): 349–60.

Rabin, C., and E. Tov, eds. *The Hebrew University Bible: The Book of Jeremiah*. Jerusalem: Magnes.

Rahlfs, Alfred, and Robert Hanhart, eds. *Septuaginta*. Rev. ed. Stuttgart: Deutsche Bibelgesellschaft, 2006.

Rajak, Tessa. *Translation and Survival: The Greek Bible of the Ancient Jewish Diaspora*. Oxford: Oxford University Press, 2009.

Reed, S. A., et al., eds. *The Dead Sea Scrolls Catalogue: Documents, Photographs, and Museum Inventory Numbers*. Atlanta: Scholars Press, 1994.

Regev, Eyal. "Sadducees." *NIDB* 5:32–36

Rendtorff, R. *Canon and Theology: Overtures to an Old Testament Theology*. Overtures to Biblical Theology. Minneapolis: Fortress, 1993.

Resnick, Irven M. "The Codex in Early Jewish and Christian Communities." *Journal of Religious History* 17 (1992): 1–17.

Reuss, E. W. *History of the Canon of the Holy Scriptures in the Christian Church*. Translated by D. Hunter. Edinburgh: Hunter, 1891.

Richards, E. Randolph. "The Codex and the Early Collection of Paul's Letters." *BBR* 8 (1998): 151–66.

———. "Reading, Writing, and Manuscripts," in Green and McDonald, eds., *The World of the New Testament.*, 345–66.

———. *The Secretary in the Letters of Paul*. WUNT, 2nd Series 42. Tübingen: Mohr/Siebeck, 1991.

Richardson, C. C., ed. *Early Christian Fathers*. New York: Macmillan, 1970.

Rist, M. "Pseudepigraphy and the Early Christians." Pages 75–91 in *Studies in New Testament and Early Christian Literature: Essays in Honor of Allen P. Wikgren*. Edited by D. E. Aune. Novum Testamentum Supplements 33. Leiden: Brill, 1972.

Ritter, A. M. "Die Entstehung des neutestamentlichen Kanons: Selbstdurchsetzung oder autoritative Entscheidung?" Pages 93–99 in vol. 2 of *Kanon und Zensur: Beiträge zur Archäologie der literarischen Kommunikation*. Edited by A. Assman and J. Assmann. Munich: Fink, 1987.

Robbins, G. A. "Eusebius' Lexicon of 'Canonicity.' " *Studia Patristica* 25 (1993): 134–41.

———. " 'Fifty Copies of Sacred Writings' (*VC* 4.36): Entire Bibles or Gospel Books?" *Studia patristica* 19 (1989): 91–98.

———. "Muratorian Fragment." *ABD* 4:928–29.

———. "ΠΕΡΙ ΤΩΝ ΕΝΔΙΑΘΗΚΩΝ ΓΡΑΦΩΝ: Eusebius and the Formation of the Christian Bible." PhD diss., Duke University, 1986.

Roberts, B. J. "The Old Testament Canon: A Suggestion." *BJRL* 46 (1963–64): 164–78.

Roberts, C. H. "Books in the Greco-Roman World and in the New Testament." Pages 48–66 in vol. 1 of *Cambridge History of the Bible*. Edited by P. R. Ackroyd and C. F. Evans. Cambridge: Cambridge University Press, 1970.

———. "The Christian Book and the Greek Papyri." *JTS* 50 (1949): 155–68.

————. *Manuscript, Society, and Belief in Early Christian Egypt*. London: Oxford University Press, 1979.

Roberts, C. H., and T. C. Skeat. *The Birth of the Codex*. London: Oxford University Press for the British Academy, 1987.

————. *Manuscript, Society and Belief in Early Christian Egypt*. Oxford: Oxford University Press, 1979.

Robinson, J. A. T. *The Priority of John*. Edited by J. F. Coakley. London: SCM, 1985.

Robinson, J. M., ed. *The Nag Hammadi Library in English*. 3rd ed. San Francisco: Harper, 1988.

Robinson, J. M., and H. Koester, eds. *Trajectories Through Early Christianity*. Philadelphia: Fortress, 1971.

Rothschild, Clare. *The Muratorian Fragment*. WUNT. Tübingen: Mohr Siebeck, forthcoming.

Rudolph, K. " 'Gnosis' and 'Gnosticism'—The Problems of Their Definition and Their Relation to the Writings of the New Testament." Pages 21–37 in *The New Testament and Gnosis: Essays in Honour of Robert McL. Wilson*. Edited by A. H. B. Logan and A. J. M. Wedderburn. Edinburgh: T. & T. Clark, 1983.

————. *Gnosis: The Nature and History of Gnosticism*. Translated and edited by R. M. Wilson. San Francisco: Harper & Row, 1987.

Rüger, H. P. "The Extent of the Old Testament Canon." *Bible Translator* 40 (1989): 301–8.

Rutgers, L. V. "The Importance of Scripture in the Conflict between Jews and Christians: The Example of Antioch." Pages 293–98 in Rutgers et al., eds., *The Use of Sacred Books*.

Rutgers, L. V., P. W. van der Horst, H. W. Havelaar, and L. Teugels, eds. *The Use of Sacred Books in the Ancient World*. CBET 22. Leuven: Peeters, 1998.

Ruwet, J. "Clement d'Alexandrie: Canon des écritures et apocryphes." *Biblica* 29 (1948): 77–99, 240–68, 391–408.

Ryle, H. E. *The Canon of the Old Testament: An Essay on the Gradual Growth and Formation of the Hebrew Canon of Scripture*. 2nd ed. London: Macmillan, 1909.

Sæbø, Magne. *On the Way to Canon: Creative Tradition History in the OT*. JSOTSup 191. Sheffield: Sheffield Academic, 1998.

Saldarini, A. J. "Pharisees." *ABD* 5:289–303.

————. *Pharisees, Scribes, and Sadducees in Palestinian Society: A Sociological Approach*. Wilmington, DE: Glazier, 1988.

————. "Within Context: The Judaism Contemporary with Jesus." Pages 21–40 in *Within Context: Essays on Jews and Judaism in the New Testament*. Edited by D. P. Efroymson, E. J. Fisher, and L. Klenicki. Collegeville, MN: Liturgical Press, 1993.

Sand, A. "κανών." Page 249 in vol. 2 of *Exegetical Dictionary of the New Testament*. Edited by H. Balz and G. Schneider. Grand Rapids: Eerdmans, 1990–93.

Sanders, E. P. "The Dead Sea Sect and Other Jews: Commonalities, Overlaps, and Differences." Pages 7–44 in *The Dead Sea Scrolls in Their Historical Context*. Edited by T. Lim. Edinburgh: T. & T. Clark, 2000.

Sanders, J. A. "Adaptable for Life: The Nature and Function of Canon." Pages 531–60 in *Magnalia Dei: The Mighty Acts of God: Essays on the Bible and Archaeology in Memory of G. Ernest Wright*. Edited by F. M. Cross, W. E. Lemke, and P. D. Miller Jr. New York: Doubleday, 1976.

————. "The Book of Job and the Origins of Judaism." *BTB* 39, no. 2 (2009): 60–70.

————. "Canon: Hebrew Bible." *ABD* 1:837–52.

————. *Canon and Community: A Guide to Canonical Criticism*. Guides to Biblical Studies. Philadelphia: Fortress, 1984.

————. "Canon as Shape and Function." Pages 87–97 in *The Promise and Practice of Biblical Theology*. Edited by J. Reumann. Minneapolis: Fortress, 1991.

————. "Canonical Context and Canonical Criticism." *HBT* 2 (1980): 173–97.

————. "Cave 11 Surprises and the Question of Canon." *McCormick Quarterly* 21 (1968) 284-317.

————. "Deuteronomy." Pages 89–102 in *The Books of the Bible*. Vol. 1 of *The Old Testament/ The Hebrew Bible*. Edited by B. W. Anderson. New York: Scribner's, 1989.

————. "Early Judaism: 580 BCE to 70 CE." *Judaism*. Forthcoming 2017.

————. "From Prophecy to Testament: An Epilogue." Pages 252–58 in *From Prophecy to Testament: The Function of the Old Testament in the New*. Edited by C. A. Evans. Peabody, MA: Hendrickson, 2004.

————. *From Sacred Story to Sacred Text*. Philadelphia: Fortress, 1987.

————. "Hermeneutics of Text Criticism." *Textus: Studies of the Hebrew University Bible Project* 18 (1995): 1–26.

————. "Intertextuality and Canon." Pages 316–33 in *On the Way to Nineveh: Studies in Honor of George M. Landes*. Edited by S. Cook and S. Winter. Atlanta: Scholars Press, 1999.

————. "The Issue of Closure in the Canonical Process." Pages 252–63 in McDonald and Sanders, eds., *The Canon Debate*.

————. *The Monotheizing Process: Its Origins and Development*. Eugene, OR: Cascade, 2014.

————. "Origen and the First Christian Testament." Pages 134–42 in Peter W. Flint, Emanuel Rob, and James C. VanderKam, eds. *Studies in the Hebrew Bible, Qumran, and the Septuagint Presented to Eugene Ulrich*. Leiden: Brill, 2006.

————. "Palestinian Manuscripts 1947–72." *JJS* 24 (1973): 74–83.

————. *The Psalms Scroll of Qumran Cave 11*. DJD IV. Oxford: Clarendon, 1965.

————. "Scripture as Canon for Post-Modern Times." *BTB* 25 (1995): 56–63.

————. "Scripture as Canon in the Church." Pages 121–43 in *L'interpretazione della Bibbia nella chiesa: Atti del Simposio promosso dalla Congregazione per la dottrina della fede, Roma, Settembre 1999*. Città del Vaticano: Libreria editrice vaticana, 2001.

————. "The Scrolls and the Canonical Process." Pages 1–23 in vol. 2 of Flint and VanderKam, eds., *The Dead Sea Scrolls After Fifty Years*.

————. "Spinning' the Bible." *Bible Review* 14, no. 3 (1998): 22–29, 44–45.

————. "Stability and Fluidity in Text and Canon." Pages 203–17 in *Traditions of the Text: Studies Offered to Dominique Barthélemy in Celebration of His 70th Birthday*. Edited by G. Norton and S. Pisano. Göttingen: Vandenhoeck & Ruprecht, 1991.

————. "The Stabilization of the Tanak." Pages 225–53 in *A History of Biblical Interpretation: The Ancient Period*. Edited by A. J. Hauser and D. F. Watson. Grand Rapids: Eerdmans, 2003.

————. "The Task of Text Criticism." Pages 315–27 in *Problems in Biblical Theology: Essays in Honor of Rolf Knierim*. Edited by Henry T. C. Sun et al. Grand Rapids: Eerdmans, 1997.

————. "Text and Canon: Old Testament and New." Pages 373–94 in *Mélanges Dominique Barthélemy: Études bibliques*. Edited by P. Casetti, O. Keel, and A. Schenker. Orbis biblicus et orientalis 38. Göttingen: Vandenhoeck & Ruprecht, 1981.

————. *Torah and Canon*. Philadelphia: Fortress, 1972.

————. "*Variorum* in the Psalms Scroll." *HTR* 59 (1966): 83–94.

Sanders, E. P., ed. *Jewish and Christian Self-Definition*. Vol. 1, *The Shaping of Christianity in the Second and Third Centuries*. Philadelphia: Fortress, 1980.

Sanders, J. E. "Jesus in Historical Context." *Theology Today* 3 (1993): 429–48.

Sanders, J. N. "The Literature and Canon of the New Testament." Pages 676–82 in *Peake's Commentary of the Bible*. Edited by M. Black and H. H. Rowley. London: Thomas Nelson & Sons, 1962.

Sandmel, S. *Judaism and Christian Beginnings*. New York: Oxford University Press, 1959.

———. "On Canon." *CBQ* 28 (1966): 189–207.

———. "A Symposium on the Canon of Scripture: 3. On Canon." *CBQ* 28 (1966): 203–7.

Sandt, H. van de, and D. Flusser. *The Didache: Its Jewish Sources and Its Place in Early Judaism and Christianity.* Compendia rerum iudaicarum ad Novum Testamentum 3/5. Minneapolis: Fortress, 2002.

Sarna, Nahum M. "Ancient Libraries and the Ordering of Biblical Books." Pages 53–66 in *Studies in Biblical Interpretation*. Philadelphia: JPS, 2000.

———. "Canon, Text, and Editions." Pages 816–36 in vol. 1 of *Encyclopaedia Judaica*. Jerusalem: Keter, 1971.

Sawyer, John F. A. *Sacred Languages and Sacred Texts.* Religion in the First Christian Centuries. London: Routledge, 1999.

Satlow, Michael L. *How the Bible Became Holy.* New Haven: Yale University Press, 2014.

Scanlin, Harold P. "Text, Truth and Tradition: The Public's View of the Bible in Light of the Dead Sea Scrolls." Pages 295–96 in Herbert and Tov, ed., *The Bible as Book*.

———. "What Is the Canonical Shape of the Old Testament Text We Translate?" Pages 207–20 in *Issues in Bible Translation*. Edited by Philip C. Stine. UBS Monograph Series 3. London: United Bible Societies, 1988.

Schaff, P. *The Creeds of Christendom With a History and Critical Notes*. 3 vols. 6th ed. Revised by D. S. Schaff. Grand Rapids: Baker, reprinted from Harper & Row, 1931, 1983, 1998.

———. *History of the Christian Church*. Vol. 2, *Ante-Nicene Christianity A.D. 100–325*. Grand Rapids: Eerdmans, reprinted from Charles Scribner's Sons, 1910, 1980.

Schaper, Joachim, "The Literary History of the Hebrew Bible," Pages 105–44 *The New Cambridge History of the Bible*. Vol. 1, *From the Beginnings to 600*.

Schiffman, L. *The Halachah at Qumran*. Leiden: Brill, 1975.

———. "The Place of 4QMMT in the Corpus of Qumran MSS." Pages 81–98 in *Reading 4QMMT: New Perspectives on Qumran Law and History*. Edited by J. Kampen and M. J. Bernstein. Atlanta: Scholars Press, 1996.

———. *Reclaiming the Dead Sea Scrolls: Their True Meaning for Judaism and Christianity*. New York: Doubleday, 1995.

———. "The Term and Concept of Torah." Pages 173–91 in Finsterbusch and Lange, *What Is Bible?*

Schlossnikel, R. F. *Bedeutung im Rahmen von Textund Kanongeschichte*. Vetus Latina: Die Reste der altlateinischen Bibel 20. Edited by E. Beuron. Freiburg: Herder, 1991.

———. *Der Brief an die Hebräer und das Corpus Paulinum: Eine linguistische "Bruchstelle" im Codex Claromontanus*. Paris: Bibliothèque Nationale grec 107 + 107A + 107B, 1991.

Schmidt, D. D. "The Greek New Testament as a Codex." Pages 469–84 in McDonald and Sanders, eds., *The Canon Debate*.

Schmidt, H.-C. "Das Spätdeuteronomistische Geschichtswerk Genesis I–2. Regum XXV und seine theologische Intention." Pages 261–79 in *Congress Volume: Cambridge 1995*. Edited by J. A. Emerton. VTSup 66. Leiden: Brill, 1997.

Schminck, A. "Canon Law." Pages 372–74 in vol. 1 of *Oxford Dictionary of Byzantium*. Edited by P. Kazhdan. New York: Oxford University Press, 1991.

Schnabel, Eckhard J. "History, Theology, and the Biblical Canon: An Introduction to Basic Issues." *Themelios* 20 (1995): 16–24.

———. "The Muratorian Fragment: The State of Research." *JETS* 57, no. 2 (2014): 231–64.

————. "Textual Criticism: Recent Developments." Pages 59–75 in *The Face of NTS: A Survey of Recent Research*. Edited by S. McKnight and G. R. Osborne. Grand Rapids: Baker, 2004.

Schnackenburg, R. *The Johannine Epistles: A Commentary*. New York: Crossroad, 1992.

Schneemelcher, W. "General Introduction." Translated by G. Ogg. Pages 19–68 in vol. 1 of E. Hennecke, ed., *New Testament Apocrypha*.

————, ed. *New Testament Apocrypha*. Translated by R. M. Wilson. 2nd ed. 2 vols. Louisville: Westminster John Knox, 1991–92.

Schniedewind, William M. *How the Bible Became a Book*. Cambridge: Cambridge University Press, 2004.

————. "Writing and Book Production in the Ancient Near East." Pages 46–62 in *The New Cambridge History of the Bible*. Vol. 1, *From the Beginnings to 600*.

Schoedel, William R. "Papias." Pages 235–70 in *Aufstieg und Niedergang der römischen Welt: Geschichte und Kultur Roms im Spiegel der neueren Forschung* 2.27.1. Edited by H. Temporini and W. Haase. Berlin: de Gruyter, 1998.

————. "Scripture and the Seventy-two Heavens of the First Apocalypse of James." *Novum Testamentum* 12 (1970): 118–29.

Schrenk, Gottlob. "γραφή, ktl." *TDNT* 1:742–73.

Schrodel, Wm. R. "Papias." *ABD* 5:140.

Schröter, Jens. *From Jesus to the New Testament: Early Christian Theology and the Origin of the New Testament Canon*. Translated by Wayne Coppins. Waco, TX: Baylor University Press. Tübingen: Mohr Siebeck, 2007, 2013.

Schürer, Emil. *History of the Jewish People in the Age of Jesus Christ*. Rev. ed. Edinburgh: T. & T. Clark. 1986.

Schwartz, B. J. "Bible." Pages 121–25 in *The Oxford Dictionary of the Jewish Religion*. Edited by R. J. Z. Werblowsky and G. Wigoder. New York: Oxford University Press, 1997.

Schwartz, Daniel R. "Special People or Special Books? On Qumran and New Testament Notions of Canon." Pages 49–62 in Ruth A. Clements and Daniel R. Schwartz, *Text, Thought, and Practice in Qumran and Early Christianity*. Leiden: Brill, 2009.

Schweizer, Eduard. "Kanon?" *Evangelische Theologie* 31 (1971): 339–57.

Scrivener, F. H. A. *A Plain Introduction to the Criticism of the New Testament for the Use of Biblical Students*. Edited by Edward Miller. 4th ed. 2 vols. London: George Bell, 1894.

Segal, M. H. "The Promulgation of the Authoritative Text of the Hebrew Bible." *JBL* 72 (1953): 35–47.

————. *Sefer Ben-Sirah ha-Shalem*. Jerusalem: Bialik, 1953.

Seitz, Christopher R. *The Goodly Fellowship of the Prophets: The Achievement of Association in Canon Formation*. Acadia Studies in Bible and Theology. Grand Rapids: Baker Academic, 2009.

————. *Prophecy and Hermeneutics: Toward a New Introduction to the Prophets*. Studies in Theological Interpretation. Grand Rapids: Baker Academic, 2007.

Shanks, H. "Contrasting Insights of Biblical Giants." *Biblical Archaeology Review* 30, no. 4 (2004): 32–33.

Shanks, Monte A. *Papias and the New Testament*. Eugene, OR: Pickwick, 2013.

Sharpe, John L., III, and Kimberly Van Kampen, eds. *The Bible as Book: The Manuscript Tradition*. London: The British Library. New Castle, DE: Oak Knoll, 1998

Sheler, J. L. "Cutting Loose the Holy Canon: A Controversial Re-examination of the Bible." *U.S. News and World Report* (November 8, 1993): 75.

Shelley, B. L. *By What Authority? The Standards of Truth in the Early Church*. Grand Rapids: Eerdmans, 1965.

Sheppard, G. T. "Canon." Pages 62–69 in vol. 3 of *The Encyclopedia of Religion*. Edited by M. Eliade. New York: Macmillan, 1987.

———. "Canonical Criticism." *ABD* 1:861–66.

———. "Canonization: Hearing the Voice of the Same God Through Historically Dissimilar Traditions." *Int* 37 (1982): 21–33.

Shinn, H. W. *Textual Criticism and the Synoptic Problem in Historical Jesus Research: The Search for Valid Criteria*. CBET 36. Leuven: Peeters, 2004.

Shires, H. M. *Finding the Old Testament in the New*. Philadelphia: Westminster, 1974.

Shuler, P. L. *A Genre for the Gospels: The Biographical Character of Matthew*. Philadelphia: Fortress, 1982.

Silberman, Lou H. "The Making of the Old Testament Canon." Pages 1209–15 in *The Interpreter's One-Volume Commentary on the Bible*. Edited by Charles M. Laymon. New York: Abingdon, 1971.

Silva, M. "Old Testament in Paul." Pages 630–42 in *Dictionary of Paul and His Letters*. Edited G. F. Hawthorne and R. P. Martin. Downers Grove, IL: InterVarsity, 1993.

———. "Response." Pages 141–50 in *Rethinking New Testament Textual Criticism*. Edited by D. A. Black. Grand Rapids: Baker, 2002.

Silver, D. J. *The Story of Scripture: From Oral Tradition to the Written Word*. New York: Basic, 1990.

Simon, Richard. *Critical History of the Text of the New Testament: Wherein Is Established the Truth of the Acts on Which the Christian Religion Is Based*. Translated by Andrew Hunwick. NTTSD 43. Leiden: Brill, 2013.

Simonetti, M. *Biblical Interpretation in the Early Church: An Historical Introduction to Patristic Exegesis*. Translated by J. A. Hughes. Edited by A. Bergquist and M. Bockmuehl. Edinburgh: T. & T. Clark, 1994.

Skarsaune, O. *The Proof from Prophecy: A Study in Justin Martyr's Proof-Text Tradition: Text-Type, Provenance, Theological Profile*. Novum Testamentum Supplement 56. Leiden: Brill, 1987.

Skeat, T. C. "The Codex Sinaiticus, The Codex Vaticanus, and Constantine." *JTS* 50 (1999): 583–625.

———. "A Codicological Analysis of the Chester Beatty Papyrus Codex of Gospels and Acts (P[45])." *Hermathena* 155 (1993): 27–43.

———. "Irenaeus and the Four-Gospel Canon." *Novum Testamentum* 34 (1992): 194–99.

———. "The Oldest Manuscript of the Four Gospels." *NTS* 43 (1997): 1–34.

———. "The Origin of the Christian Codex." *Zeitschrift für Papyrologie und Epigraphik* 102 (1994): 263–68.

———. "The Use of Dictation in Ancient Book-Production." *Proceedings of the British Academy* 42 (1956): 195–97.

Smart, J. D. *The Strange Silence of the Bible in the Church: A Study in Hermeneutics*. Philadelphia: Westminster, 1970.

Smend, Rudolf. "Questions About the Importance of Canon in the Old Testament Introduction." *JSOT* 16 (1980): 45–51.

Smith, C. M., and J. W. Bennett. *How the Bible Was Built*. Grand Rapids: Eerdmans, 2005.

Smith, D. M. "John, the Synoptics, and the Canonical Approach to Exegesis." Pages 166–80 in *Tradition and Interpretation in the New Testament: Essays in Honor of E. Earle Ellis*. Edited by G. F. Hawthorne and O. Betz. Grand Rapids: Eerdmans, 1987.

———. "The Pauline Literature." Pages 265–81 in *It Is Written: Scripture Citing Scripture: Essays in Honour of Barnabas Lindars*. Edited by D. A. Carson and H. G. M. Williamson. Cambridge: Cambridge University Press, 1988.

———. "When Did the Gospels Become Scripture?" *JBL* 119 (2000): 3–20.

———. "Why Approaching the New Testament as Canon Matters." *Int* 40 (1986): 407–11.

Smith, J. Z. "Canons, Catalogues, and Classics." Pages 300–307 in van der Kooij and van der Toorn, eds., *Canonization and Decanonization*.

Smith, Lesley. "The Glossed Bible." Pages 363–79 in Marsden and Matter, eds., *The New Cambridge History of The Bible: From 600–1450*.

Smith, M. *Palestinian Parties and Politics That Shaped the Old Testament*. New York: Columbia University Press, 1971.

Snyder, H. Gregory. *Teachers and Texts in the Ancient World: Philosophers, Jews and Christians*. Religion in the First Christian Centuries. London: Routledge, 2000.

Souter, A. *The Text and Canon of the New Testament*. New York: Scribner, 1917.

Sparks, H. F. D. "Canon of the Old Testament." Pages 121–23 in *Hastings Dictionary of the Bible*. Edited by F. C. Grant and H. H. Rowley. 2nd ed. Edinburgh: T. & T. Clark, 1963.

———. *The Formation of the New Testament*. London: SCM, 1952.

Sperber, Daniel. "Targum." Pages 675–76 in *Oxford Dictionary of the Jewish Religion*. Edited by R. J. Zwi Werblowsky and Geoffrey Wigoder. New York: Oxford University Press, 1997.

Spina, Frank A. "Canonical Criticism: Childs Versus Sanders." Pages 165–94 in *Interpreting God's Word for Today: An Inquiry into Hermeneutics from a Biblical Theological Perspective*. Edited by W. McCown and J. E. Massey. Anderson, IN: Warner, 1982.

Stackert, Jeffrey. *Prophet Like Moses: Prophecy, Law, and Israelite Religion*. Oxford: Oxford University Press, 2014.

Stanton, G. N. *Gospel Truth? New Light on Jesus and the Gospels*. London: HarperCollins, 1995.

———. *The Gospels and Jesus*. Oxford: Oxford University Press, 1989.

Steck, O. H. *Der Abschluss der Prophetie im Alten Testament: Ein Versuch zur Frage der Vorgeschichte des Kanons*. Biblisch-theologische Studien 17. Neukirchen-Vluyn: Neukirchener, 1991.

———. "Der Kanon des hebräischen Alten Testaments." Pages 231–52 in *Vernunft des Glaubens: Wissenschaftliche Theologie und kirchliche Lehre*. Edited by J. Rohls and G. Wenz. Göttingen: Vandenhoeck & Ruprecht, 1988.

Steinberg, Julius. *Die Ketuvim: ihr Aufbau und ihre Botschaft*. Bonner Biblische Beiträge 152. Hamburg: Philo, 2006.

Steinberg, Julius, and Timothy J. Stone. "The Historical Formation of the Writings in Antiquity." Pages 1–58 in Steinberg and Stone, eds., *The Shape of the Writings*.

———, eds. *The Shape of the Writings*. Siphrut 16. Winona Lake, IN: Eisenbrauns, 2015.

Stemberger, Günter. "Sadducees." Pages 1179–81 in Collins and Harlow, eds., *The Eerdmans Dictionary of Early Judaism*.

Stendahl, K. "Ancient Scripture in the Modern World." Pages 201–14 in *Scripture in the Jewish and Christian Traditions*. Edited by F. E. Greenspahn. Nashville: Abingdon, 1982.

———. "The Apocalypse of John and the Epistles of Paul in the Muratorian Fragment." Pages 239–45 in *Current Issues in New Testament Interpretation: Essays in Honor of Otto A. Piper*. Edited by W. Klassen and G. F. Snyder. London: SCM, 1962.

———. "The Formation of the Canon: The Apocalypse of John and the Epistles of Paul in the Muratorian Fragment." Pages 239–45 in *Current Issues in New Testament Interpretation: Essays in Honor of Otto A. Piper*. Edited by W. Klassen and G. F. Snyder. London: SCM, 1962.

———. *Meanings: The Bible as Document and Guide*. Philadelphia: Fortress, 1984.

Stendebach, F. J. "The Old Testament Canon in the Roman Catholic Church." Pages 33–45 in Meurer, ed., *The Apocrypha in Ecumenical Perspective*.

Stern, David. "On Canonization in Rabbinic Judaism." Pages 227–52 in Finkelberg and Stroumsa, eds., *Homer, the Bible, and Beyond*.

Steyn, G. F. *Septuagint Quotations in the Context of the Petrine and Pauline Speeches of the Acta Apostolorum*. Kampen: Pharos, 1995.

Stone, Michael E. *4 Ezra*. Hermeneia. Minneapolis: Fortress, 1990.

———. "Esdras, Second Book of." *ABD* 2:611–14.

Stone, Timothy J. "The Biblical Canon According to Lee McDonald." *EuroJTh* 18, no. 1 (2009): 55–64.

———. *Compilational History of the Megilloth: Canon, Contoured Intertextuality and Meaning in the Writings*. FAT 2/59. Tübingen: Mohr Siebeck, 2013.

Streeter, B. H. *The Four Gospels: A Study of Origins Treating of the Manuscript Tradition, Sources, Authorship and Date*. London: MacMillan, 1924.

Stroker, W. D. *Extracanonical Sayings of Jesus*. Society of Biblical Literature Resources for Biblical Study 18. Atlanta: Scholars Press, 1989.

Stuart, M. *A Critical History and Defense of the Old Testament Canon*. Andover, MA: Allen, Morrill & Wardwell, 1845.

Stuhlhofer, Franz. *Der Gebrauch der Bibel von Jesus bis Euseb: Eine statistische Untersuchung zur Kanongeschichte*. Wuppertal: Brockhaus, 1988.

Stuhlmacher, P. "The Significance of the Old Testament Apocrypha and Pseudepigrapha for the Understanding of Jesus and Christology." Pages 1–15 in Meurer, ed., *The Apocrypha in Ecumenical Perspective*.

Sundberg, A. C., Jr. "The Bible Canon and the Christian Doctrine of Inspiration." *Int* 29 (1975): 352–71.

———. "Canon Muratori: A Fourth-Century List." *HTR* 66 (1973): 1–41.

———. "Canon of the NT." Pages 136–40 in *Interpreter's Dictionary of the Bible: Supplementary Volume*. Edited by Keith Crim. Nashville: Abingdon, 1976.

———. "Dependent Canonicity in Irenaeus and Tertullian." Pages 403–9 in *Studia evangelica III*. Texte und Untersuchungen 88. Berlin: Akademie, 1964.

———. "The Making of the New Testament Canon." Pages 1216–24 in *The Interpreter's One-Volume Commentary on the Bible*. Edited by Charles M. Laymon. New York: Abingdon, 1971.

———. "The Old Testament: A Christian Canon." *CBQ* 30 (1968): 403–9.

———. "The Old Testament of the Early Church." *HTR* 51 (1958): 205–26.

———. *The Old Testament of the Early Church*. Cambridge, MA: Harvard University Press, 1964.

———. " 'The Old Testament of the Early Church' Revisited." *Festschrift in Honor of Charles Speel*. Edited by T. J. Seinkewicz and J. E. Betts. Monmouth, IL: Monmouth College Press, 1996.

———. "The Septuagint: The Bible in Hellenistic Judaism." Pages 68–90 in McDonald and Sanders, eds., *The Canon Debate*.

———. "A Symposium on the Canon of Scripture: 2. The Protestant Old Testament Canon: Should It Be Re-examined?" *CBQ* 28 (1966): 194–203.

———. "Toward a Revised History of the New Testament Canon." Pages 452–61 in *Studia evangelica IV*. Texte und Untersuchungen 89. Berlin: Akademie, 1964.

Suter, D. W. "Apocrypha, Old Testament." Pages 36–38 in *Harper's Bible Dictionary*. Edited by P. J. Achtemeier et al. San Francisco: Harper & Row, 1985.

Swanson, Reuben, ed. *New Testament Greek Manuscripts: Variant Readings Arranged in Horizontal Lines Against Codex Vaticanus: Romans*. Wheaton, IL: Tyndale. Pasadena, CA: William Carey International University Press, 2001.

Swanson, T. N. "The Closing of the Collection of Holy Scripture: A Study in the History of the Canonization of the Old Testament." PhD diss., Vanderbilt University, 1970.

Swarat, U. *Alte Kirche und Neues Testament: Theodor Zahn als Patristiker*. Wuppertal: Brockhaus, 1991.

Sweeney, Marvin A. *Tanak: A Theological and Critical Introduction to the Jewish Bible*. Minneapolis: Fortress, 2011.

———. "Tanak Versus Old Testament: Concerning the Foundation for a Jewish Theology of the Bible." Pages 353–72 in *Problems in Biblical Theology: Essays in Honor of Rolf Knierim*. Edited by H. T. C. Sun and K. L. Eades. Grand Rapids: Eerdmans, 1997.

Swete, H. B. *An Introduction to the Old Testament in Greek*. Rev. R. R. Ottley. 2nd ed. Cambridge: Cambridge University Press, 1914. Repr., Peabody, MA: Hendrickson, 1989.

Talbert, C. H. *What Is a Gospel? The Genre of the Canonical Gospels*. Philadelphia: Fortress, 1977.

Talmon, Shemaryahu. "The Crystallization of the 'Canon of Hebrew Scriptures' in Light of Biblical Scrolls from Qumran." Pages 5–20 in Herbert and Tov, eds., *The Bible as Book*.

———. "Heiliges Schrifttum und kanonische Bücher aus jüdischer Sicht: Überlegungen zur Ausbildung der Grösse 'Die Schrift' im Judentum." Pages 45–79 in *Mitte der Schrift? Ein jüdisch-christliches Gespräch: Texte des Berner Symposions vom 6.–12 January 1985*. Edited by M. Klopfenstein et al. Judaica et christiana 11. Bern: Lang, 1987.

———. *Text and Canon of the Hebrew Bible: Collected Essays*. Winona Lake, IN: Eisenbrauns, 2010.

Talshir, Zipora. "Several Canon-Related Concepts Originating in Chronicles." *ZAW* 113 (2001): 386–403.

Taussig, Hal, ed. *The New New Testament: A Bible for the Twenty-First Century*. Boston: Houghton Mifflin Harcourt, 2013.

Taylor, Joan. *Jewish Women Philosophers of First-Century Alexandria: Philo's "Therapeutae" Reconsidered*. Oxford: Oxford University Press, 2003.

Taylor, Joan, and Philip R. Davies. "The So-Called Therapeutae of *De Vita Contemplativa*: Identity and Character." *HTR* 91 (1998): 3–24.

Thackeray, H. St. J. *The Septuagint and Jewish Worship*. 2nd ed. London: Oxford University Press, 1923.

Theissen, G. *A Theory of Primitive Christian Religion*. London: SCM, 1999.

Theobald, C., ed. *Le canon des Ecritures: Etudes historiques, exégétiques et systématiques*. Lectio Divina 140. Paris: Cerf, 1990.

Theron, Daniel J. *Evidence of Tradition*. Grand Rapids: Baker Book House, 1980.

Tobias, Thomas J., Michael J. Kruger, and Tobias Nicklas, eds. *Gospel Fragments: The "Unknown Gospel" on Papyrus Egerton 2, Papyrus Oxyrhynchus 840, Other Gospel Fragments*. Oxford Early Christian Gospel Texts. Oxford: Oxford University Press, 2009.

Toit, Andrie B. du. "Canon: New Testament." Pages 102–4 in *The Oxford Companion to the Bible*. Edited by Bruce M. Metzger and M. D. Coogan. New York: Oxford University Press, 1993.

Toit, Jaqueline S. du. *Textual Memory: Ancient Archives, Libraries and the Hebrew Bible*. Sheffield: Sheffield Phoenix, 2010.

Thiselton, Anthony C. *The Holy Spirit – In Biblical Teaching, Through the Centuries and Today*. Grand Rapids: Eerdmans, 2013.

Topping, R. R. "The Canon and the Truth: Brevard Childs and James Barr on the Canon and the Historical Critical Method." *Toronto Journal of Theology* 8 (1992): 239–60.

Tov, E. "The Biblical Texts from the Judaean Desert: An Overview and Analysis of the Published Texts." Pages 139–66 in Herbert and Tov, eds., *Bible as Book*.

————. *The Greek and Hebrew Bible: Collected Essays on the Septuagint.* VTSup 72. Leiden: Brill, 1999.

————. *The Greek Minor Prophets Scroll from Naḥal Ḥever (8ḤevXIIgr).* DJD 8. Oxford: Clarendon, 1990.

————. "Groups of Biblical Texts Found at Qumran." Pages 85–102 in *Time to Prepare the Way in the Wilderness: Papers on the Qumran Scrolls by Fellows of the Institute for Advanced Studies of the Hebrew University.* Edited by D. Dimant and L. H. Schiffman. Jerusalem: Jerusalem University, 1989–90.

————. "Hebrew Biblical Manuscripts from the Judaean Desert: Their Contribution to Textual Criticism." *JJS* 39 (1988): 5–37.

————. "The History and Significance of a Standard Text of the Hebrew Bible." Pages 49–66 in *Hebrew Bible/Old Testament: The History of Its Interpretation.* Vol. 1, *From the Beginnings to the Middle Ages (Until 1300).* Göttingen: Vandenhoeck & Ruprecht, 1996.

————. "Modern Editions of the Hebrew Bible," Pages 389–411 in Paget and Schaper, eds., *The New Cambridge History of the Bible.* Vol. 1, *From the Beginnings to 600.*

————. "The Nature of the Large-Scale Differences Between the LXX and MT STV, Compared with Similar Evidence in Other Sources." Pages 121–44 in *The Earliest Text of the Hebrew Bible: The Relationship Between the Masoretic Text and the Hebrew Base of the Septuagint Reconsidered.* Edited by Adrian Schenker. SBLSCS 52. Atlanta: Society of Biblical Literature, 2003.

————. "Recensional Differences Between the Masoretic Text and the Septuagint of Proverbs." Pages 43–56 in *Of Scribes and Scrolls: Studies on the Hebrew Bible, Intertestamental Judaism, and Christian Origins Presented to John Strugnell.* Edited by H. W. Attridge, J. J. Collins, and T. H. Tobin. Lanham, MD: University Press of America, 1990.

————. "Scribal Practices and Physical Aspects of the Dead Sea Scrolls." Pages 45–60 in *The Bible as a Book.* Edited by J. L. Sharpe and K. Van Kampen. London: Oak Knoll, 1998.

————. "Scribal Practices Reflected in the Paleo-Hebrew Texts from the Judean Desert." *Scripta Classica Israelica* 15 (1996): 268–73.

————. "Scribal Practices Reflected in the Texts from the Judean Desert." Pages 403–29 in vol. 1 of Flint and VanderKam, eds., *The Dead Sea Scrolls After Fifty Years.*

————. "The Status of the Masoretic Text in Modern Text Editions of the Hebrew Bible: The Relevance of Canon." Pages 234–51 in McDonald and Sanders, eds., *The Canon Debate.*

————. *The Text-Critical Use of the Septuagint in Biblical Research.* 2nd ed. Jerusalem: Simor, 1997.

————. *Textual Criticism of the Hebrew Bible.* Minneapolis: Fortress, 1992.

————. *Textual Criticism of the Hebrew Bible.* 3rd ed. rev. and expanded. Minneapolis: Fortress, 2012.

Tov, E., and S. A. Pfann, eds. *Companion Volume to the Dead Sea Scrolls Microfiche Edition.* Leiden: Brill, 1995.

Towner, W. Sibley. "Daniel 1 in the Context of Canon." Pages 285–98 in *Canon, Theology, and Old Testament Interpretation: Essays in Honor of Brevard S. Childs.* Edited by Gene M. Tucker, David L. Peterson, and Robert R. Wilson. Philadelphia: Fortress, 1988.

Traube, L. *Nomina Sacra: Versuch einer Geschichte der christlichen Kürzung.* Munich: Beck, 1907.

Trebolle Barrera, J. "Canon, Old Testament." Pages 548–63 in vol. 1 of *New Interpreter's Dictionary of the Bible.* Edited by Katherine D. Sakenfeld. Nashville: Abingdon, 2006.

————. *The Jewish Bible and the Christian Bible: An Introduction to the History of the Bible.* Translated by W. G. E. Watson. Grand Rapids: Eerdmans, 1998.

———. "Origins of a Tripartite Old Testament Canon." Pages 128–45 in McDonald and Sanders, eds., *The Canon Debate*.

Tregelles, S. P. *Canon Muratorianus: The Earliest Catalogue of the Books of the New Testament.* Oxford: Clarendon, 1867.

Trobisch, D. *The* First Edition *of the New Testament.* Oxford: Oxford University Press, 2000.

———. *Paul's Letter Collection: Tracing the Origins.* Philadelphia: Fortress, 1994.

Tucker, Gene M. "Prophetic Superscriptions and the Growth of a Canon." Pages 56–70 in *Canon and Authority: Essays in Old Testament Religion and Theology.* Edited by G. W. Coats and B. O. Long. Philadelphia: Fortress, 1977.

Tuckett, C. M. "Nomina Sacra: Yes or No?" Pages 431–58 in Auwers and de Jonge, eds., *The Biblical Canons*.

———. Review of *The Biblical Canon, JTS* 60 (2009): 594–96.

Turner, C. H. "Appendix to W. Sanday's Article: 'The Cheltenham List of the Canonical Books, and the Writings of Cyprian'." *Studia Biblica* 3 (1891): 304–25.

———. "Latin Lists of the Canonical Books: 3. From Pope Innocent's Epistle to Exsuperius of Toulouse (A.D. 405)." *JTS* 13 (1911–12): 77–82.

Turro, J. C., and R. E. Brown. "Canonicity." Pages 515–34 in vol. 2 of *The Jerome Biblical Commentary.* Edited by R. E. Brown, J. A. Fitzmyer, and R. E. Murphy. Englewood Cliffs, NJ: Prentice-Hall, 1968.

Ulrich, Eugene. "The Bible in the Making: The Scriptures at Qumran." Pages 77–93 in *The Community of the Renewed Covenant.* Edited by E. Ulrich and J. VanderKam. Christianity and Judaism in Antiquity 10. Notre Dame: University of Notre Dame Press, 1994.

———. "The Bible in the Making: The Scriptures at Qumran." [Updated]. Pages 51–66 in Flint, ed., *The Bible at Qumran*.

———. "Canon." Pages 117–20 in vol. 1 of *Encyclopedia of the Dead Sea Scrolls.* Edited by L. H. Schiffman and J. C. VanderKam. Oxford: Oxford University Press, 2000.

———. "The Canonical Process, Textual Criticism, and Latter Stages in the Composition of the Bible." Pages 267–91 in *Sha'arei Talmon: Studies in the Bible, Qumran, and the Ancient Near East Presented to Shemaryahu Talmon.* Edited by M. Fishbane and E. Tov. Winona Lake, IN: Eisenbrauns, 1992.

———. "The Community of Israel and the Composition of Scriptures." Pages 327–42 in *Studies in Biblical Intertextuality in Honor of James A. Sanders.* Edited by C. A. Evans and S. Talmon. Biblical Interpretation Series 18. Leiden: Brill, 1997.

———. "The Dead Sea Scrolls and the Biblical Text." Pages 79–100 in vol. 1 of Flint and VanderKam, eds., *The Dead Sea Scrolls After Fifty Years*.

———. *The Dead Sea Scrolls and the Origins of the Bible.* Studies in the Dead Sea Scrolls and Related Literature. Grand Rapids: Eerdmans, 1999.

———. "The Jewish Scriptures: Texts, Versions, Canons." Pages 97–119 in Collins and Harlow, eds., *The Eerdmans Dictionary of Early Judaism*.

———. "The Non-attestation of a Tripartite Canon in 4QMMT." *CBQ* 65 (2003): 202–14.

———. "The Notion and Definition of Canon." Pages 21–35 in McDonald and Sanders, eds., *The Canon Debate*.

———. "The Old Testament Text and Its Transmission." Pages 83–104 in Paget and Schaper, eds., *The New Cambridge History of the Bible*. Vol. 1, *From the Beginnings to 600*.

———. "Pluriformity in the Biblical Text, Text Groups, and Questions of Canon." Pages 23–41 in *The Madrid Qumran Congress: Proceedings of the International Congress on the Dead Sea Scrolls Madrid, 18–21 March, 1991.* Edited by J. Trebolle Barrera and L. Vegas Montaner. 2 vols. STDJ 11. Leiden: Brill, 1992.

———. "Qumran and the Canon of the Old Testament." Pages 66–75 in Auwers and de Jonge, eds., *The Biblical Canons*.

———. "The Qumran Biblical Scrolls: The Scriptures of Late Second Temple Judaism." Pages 67–87 in *The Dead Sea Scrolls in Their Historical Context*. Edited by T. Lim. Edinburgh: T. & T. Clark, 2000.

Unnick, W. C. van. "ἡ καινὴ διαθήκη: A Problem in the Early History of the Canon." *Studia patavina* 4 (1961): 212–27.

Urbach, E. E. "Torah." Pages 85–100 in Judaism: A People and Its History. Edited by Robert M. Seltzer. New York: Macmillan, 1989.

Valantasis, R. *The Beliefnet Guide to Gnosticism and Other Vanished Christianities*. New York: Doubleday, 2006.

Van Der Horst, Pieter W. *Jews and Christians in Their Greco-Roman Context*. WUNT 196. Tübingen: Mohr Siebeck, 2006.

Van Elderen, Bastiaan. "Early Christian Libraries." Pages 45–59 in Van Kampen and Sharpe, eds., *The Bible as Book*.

VanderKam, J. C. "1 Enoch, Enochic Motifs, and Enoch in Early Christian Literature." Pages 33–101 in *The Jewish Apocalyptic Heritage in Early Christianity*. Edited by James C. VanderKam and William Adler. Assen: Van Gorcum. Minneapolis: Fortress, 1996.

———. "Authoritative Literature in the Dead Sea Scrolls." *Dead Sea Discoveries* 5 (1998): 382–402.

———. *The Dead Sea Scrolls Today*. Grand Rapids: Eerdmans, 1994.

———. "Ezra–Nehemiah or Ezra and Nehemiah." Pages 55–75 in *Priests, Prophets, and Scribes: Essays on the Formation and Heritage of Second Temple Judaism in Honour of Joseph Blenkinsopp*. Edited by E. Ulrich, J. Wright, R. P. Carroll, and P. R. Davies. JSOTSup 149. Sheffield: JSOT Press, 1992.

———. *From Revelation to Canon: Studies in the Hebrew Bible and Second Temple Literature*. Journal for the Study of Judaism Supplement 62. Leiden: Brill, 2000.

———. "The Interpretation of Genesis in 1 Enoch." Pages 129–48 in Flint, ed., *The Bible at Qumran*.

———. "Questions of Canon Viewed Through the Dead Sea Scrolls." *BBR* 11 (2001): 269–92.

———. "Questions of Canon Viewed Through the Dead Sea Scrolls." Pages 91–109 in McDonald and Sanders, eds., *The Canon Debate*.

VanderKam, J. C., and W. Adler, eds. *The Jewish Apocalyptic Heritage in Early Christianity*. Compendia rerum iudaicarum ad Novum Testamentum 3/4. Minneapolis: Fortress, 1966.

VanderKam, J. C., and P. Flint. *The Meaning of the Dead Sea Scrolls: Their Significance for Understanding the Bible, Judaism, Jesus, and Christianity*. San Francisco: Harper, 2002.

Van Seters, John. *The Edited Bible: The Curious History of the "Editor" in Biblical Criticism*. Winona Lake, IN: Eisenbrauns, 2006.

Veldhuis, Niek. "Mesopotamian Canons." Pages 9–28 in Finkelberg and Stroumsa, eds., *Homer, the Bible, and Beyond*.

Veltri, Giuseppe. *Libraries, Translations, and "Canonic" Texts: The Septuagint, Aquila and Ben Sira in the Jewish and Christian Traditions*. JSJSup 109. Leiden: Brill, 2006.

Verheyden, J. "The Canon Muratori: A Matter of Dispute." Pages 487–556 in Auwers and de Jonge, eds., *The Biblical Canons*.

———. "The New Testament Canon," Pages 389–411 in Paget and Schaper, eds., *The New Cambridge History of the Bible*. Vol. 1, *From the Beginnings to 600*.

Vermes, G. "Bible Interpretation at Qumran." *Eretz Israel* 20 (1989): 184–91.

———. *The Complete Dead Sea Scrolls in English*. London: Penguin, 1995.

———. *The Dead Sea Scrolls: Qumran in Perspective*. Philadelphia: Fortress, 1977.

Vokes, F. E. "The Didache and the Canon of the New Testament." Pages 427–36 of *Studia evangelica III*. Texte und Untersuchungen 88. Berlin: Akademie, 1964.

Von Wahlde, Urban C. "Archaeology and John's Gospel." Pages 523–86 in *Jesus and Archaeology*. Edited by James H. Charlesworth. Grand Rapids: Eerdmans, 2006.

Wagner, J. R. *Heralds of the Good News: Isaiah and Paul in Concert in the Letter to the Romans*. Leiden: Brill, 2003.

Wainwright, Geoffrey. "The New Testament as Canon." *Scottish Journal of Theology* 28 (1975): 551–71.

Walker, B. *Gnosticism: Its History and Influence*. Wellingborough, UK: Aquarian, 1989.

Wall, R. W. "The Acts of the Apostles in Canonical Context." *BTB* 18 (1986): 1–31.

———. "The Canon and Christian Preaching." *The Christian Ministry* 17, no. 5 (1986): 13–17.

———. "The Canon of the NT." In *New Testament Interpretation Today*. Edited by Joel B. Green. Grand Rapids: Eerdmans, forthcoming.

———. "The Function of the Pastoral Epistles within the Pauline Canon of the New Testament: A Canonical Approach." Pages 27–44 in Porter, ed., *The Pauline Canon*.

———. "Reading the New Testament in Canonical Context." Pages 370–93 in *Hearing the New Testament: Strategies for Interpretation*. Edited by J. B. Green. Grand Rapids: Eerdmans, 1995.

———. "A Unifying Theology of the Catholic Epistles: A Canonical Approach." Pages 43–71 in *The Catholic Epistles and the Tradition*. Edited by J. Schlosser. BETL 176. Leuven: Leuven University Press/Peeters, 2004.

Wall, R. W., and E. Lemcio. *The New Testament as Canon: A Reader in Canonical Criticism*. Sheffield: Sheffield Academic, 1992.

Wallace, Daniel B. "The Majority Text Theory: History, Methods, and Critique." Pages 711–44 in Ehrnan and Holmes, eds., *The Text of the New Testament*.

Waltke, B. K. "Samaritan Pentateuch." *ABD* 5:932–40.

Wasserstein, Abraham, and David J. Wasserstein. *The Legend of the Septuagint: From Classical Antiquity to Today*. Cambridge: Cambridge University Press, 2006.

Wegner, Paul D. *The Journey from Texts to Translations: The Origin and Development of the Bible*. Grand Rapids: Baker Academic, 1999.

Weitzman, M. P. *The Syriac Version of the Old Testament: An Introduction*. Cambridge: Cambridge University Press, 1999.

Westcott, B. F. *A General Survey of the History of the Canon of the New Testament*. London: Macmillan, 1875. 6th ed. 1889. Repr., Grand Rapids: Baker, 1980.

Wevers, J. W. *Notes on the Greek Text of Exodus*. SBLSCS 30. Atlanta: Scholars Press, 1990.

———. "Septuagint." *IBD* 4:273–78.

———. "A Study in the Narrative Portions of the Greek Exodus." Pages 295–303 in *Scripta, Signa, Vocis*. Edited by H. L. J. Vanstiphout et al. Groningen: Egbert Forsten, 1986.

Widengren, Geo. *The Ascension of the Apostle and the Heavenly Book*. Uppsala: Uppsala University Press, 1950.

Wildeboer, G. *The Origin of the Canon of the Old Testament: An Historico-Critical Enquiry*. Translated by B. W. Bacon. London: Luzac & Co., 1895. Republished by the Cornell University Library Digital Collections, Lexington, KY, 2010.

Williams, P. J. "The Syriac Versions of the Bible." Pages 527–35 in Paget and Schaper, eds., *The New Cambridge History of the Bible*. Vol. 1, *From the Beginnings to 600*.

Williams, R. R. *Authority in the Apostolic Age*. London: SCM, 1950.

Wilson, N. G., trans. *Photius: The Bibliotheca*. London: Duckworth, 1994.

Wink, W. *Cracking the Gnostic Code: The Powers in Gnosticism*. Society of Biblical Literature Monograph Series 46. Atlanta: Scholars Press, 1993.

Wise, M. O., M. G. Abegg, and E. M. Cook. *The Dead Sea Scrolls: A New Translation*. San Francisco: HarperCollins, 1996.

Wright III, Benjamin G. "Translation as Scripture: The Septuagint in Aristeas and Philo." Pages 47–61 in *Septuagint Research: Issues and Challenges in the Study of the Greek Jewish Scriptures*. Edited by Wolfgang Kraus and R. Glenn Wooden. Septuagint Research 53. Atlanta: Society of Biblical Research, 2006.

Würthwein, E. *The Text of the Old Testament: An Introduction to Kittel-Kahle's Biblia Hebraica*. Oxford: Oxford University Press, 1957.

———. *Text of the Old Testament*. Translated by E. F. Rhodes. 2nd ed. Grand Rapids: Eerdmans, 1995.

Wyrick, Jed. *The Ascension of Authorship: Attribution and Canon Formation in Jewish, Hellenistic, and Christian Traditions*. Cambridge, MA: Harvard University Press, 2004.

Yadin, Y. *The Temple Scroll*. 3 vols. Jerusalem: Israel Exploration Society, 1983.

———. "The Temple Scroll, the Longest and Most Recently Discovered Dead Sea Scroll." Pages 161–77 in vol. 2 of *Archaeology and the Bible: The Best of BAR: Archaeology in the World of Herod, Jesus, and Paul*. Edited by H. Shanks and D. P. Cole. Washington, DC: Biblical Archaeology Society, 1990.

Yarbro Collins, Adela. *Mark*. Hermeneia. Minneapolis: Fortress, 2007.

Yee, Gale A., Hugh R. Page Jr., and Matthew J. M. Coomber, eds. *Fortress Commentary on the Bible: The Old Testament and Apocrypha*. Minneapolis: Augsburg Fortress, 2014.

Yoder, J. H. "The Authority of the Canon." Pages 265–90 in *Essays on Biblical Interpretation: Anabaptist-Mennonite Perspectives*. Edited by Willard Swartley. Text-Reader Series 1. Elkhart, IN: Institute of Mennonite Studies, 1984.

Young, F., L. Ayres, and A. Louth, eds. *The Cambridge History of Early Christian Literature*. New York: Cambridge University Press, 2004.

Zahn, Molly M. "Rewritten Scripture." Pages 323–36 in Lim and Collins, eds., *The Oxford Handbook of the Dead Sea Scrolls*.

Zahn, Theodore. *Forschungen zur Geschichte des neutestamentlichen Kanons und der altkirchlichen Literatur*. 10 vols. Leipzig: A. Deichert, 1881–1929.

———. *Geschichte des neutestamentlichen Kanons*. 2 vols. Erlangen: A. Deichert, 1888–92.

Zeitlin, Solomon. "An Historical Study of the Canonization of Hebrew Scriptures." *Proceedings of the American Academy for Jewish Research* 3 (1931–32): 164–201. Repr. in *The Canon and Masorah of the Hebrew Bible*. Edited by Sid Z. Leiman. New York: KTAV, 1974.

Zenger, E., ed. *Die Tora als Kanon für Juden und Christen*. Herders biblische Studien 10. Freiburg: Herder, 1996.

Zetzel, J. E. G. "Re-creating the Canon: Augustan Poetry and the Alexandrian Past." Pages 107–29 in von Hallberg, ed., *Canons*.

Zevit, Z. "The Second–Third Century Canonization of the Hebrew Bible and Its Influence on Christian Canonizing." Pages 133–60 in van der Kooij and van der Toorn, eds., *Canonization and Decanonization*.

Zsengeller, Jozsef, ed. *Rewritten Bible After Fifty Years: Texts, Terms, or Techniques? A Last Dialogue with Geza Vermes*. Leiden: Brill, 2014.

Zuntz, G. "Aristeas." *IDB* 1:219–21.

———. *The Text of the Epistles: A Disquisition upon the Corpus Paulinum*. Schweich Lectures, 1946. London: British Academy Press, 1953.

INDEX OF REFERENCES

(for Volume II)

INDEX OF AUTHORS

(for Volume II)

INDEX OF SUBJECTS

(Spanning Volumes I and II)